20th -Century American Composers

by

Harold Gleason and Warren Becker

2nd Edition

Frangipani Press

181622   FRANGIPANI PRESS - TIS PUBLICATIONS
P.O. Box 669
Bloomington, Indiana 47402
ISBN 0-89917-266-0
LC 80-53732

PREFACE TO THE SECOND EDITION

This Series of *Outlines* of "20th-Century American Composers" is an outgrowth of a study of compositions heard at the programs of the Festival of American Music, Eastman School of Music, Rochester, New York. The Festival was first organized in 1925 by the director of the Eastman School of Music, Dr. Howard Hanson, and continued annually to 1971. The list of composers and compositions form an imposing roster; however, only seventeen representative composers have been chosen for inclusion in these *Outlines*.

The *Outlines* are designed as an efficient resource in the study of the music of these composers. Each *Outline* includes a brief biography, a list of compositions with the date of composition or publication and the publisher, when possible. A discussion of the style includes a summary of the compositional techniques, devices and forms used by the composer. Presented also is a quotation by the composer which gives some insight into his attitudes toward music, concepts of composing or association with other musicians.

The extensive bibliographies for each *Outline* include a list of books and articles written by the composer and a list of books and articles about the composer. References to each composer found in the books of the General Bibliography are listed in code form. In addition, in each *Outline* there are references to individual compositions numbered according to the original "Compositions" list. Each *Outline* concludes with a list of doctoral dissertations about the composer and his works.

In the second edition it has been the intention of the authors to make the bibliographies exhaustive, as far as possible, thus giving a complete overview of the composers' works and the extent of their influence. The inclusion of some entries in foreign publications reveals a certain breadth of interest and significance of the composers' works beyond the boundaries of the United States.

There has been no attempt to evaluate the music of the composers or the references in the bibliographies. The latter may be a complete book, an extended article or only a brief mention.

The authors are particularly grateful to the librarians and staffs of the Central Library, University of California, San Diego, and the James White Library, Andrews University, Michigan, for their assistance in making materials available.

August 1, 1980
San Diego, California

Harold Gleason
Warren Becker

CONTENTS

20th-Century American Composers

A CHRONOLOGICAL LIST OF COMPOSERS

ABBREVIATIONS

A (A.) – Alto voice (Solo alto)
ACA – American Composers Alliance
ACA-Bul – American Composers Alliance Bulletin
Alpha – Alpha Music Co.
Am (Amer) – American
Am Choral R – American Choral Review
AME – American Music Edition
Amer Merc – American Mercury
Amer-Scand Rev – American-Scandinavian Review
Am Mus Dgt – American Music Digest
Am Mus Tcr – American Music Teacher
Am Org – The American Organist
AMP – Associated Music Pub.
Am Rec G – The American Record Guide
AMS Papers – American Musicological Society Papers
arr. – arranged, arranger
ARSC – Association for Recorded Sound Collections, Inc.
Arte Mus – Arte Musical: revista de doutrina noticiario e critica
ASCAP – ASCAP Today (American Society of Composers, Authors and Publishers)
ASOL – American Symphony Orchestra League Newsletter
ASPN – Annapolis Symphony Orchestra Program Notes
Assn Am Col B – Association of American Colleges Bulletin
ASUC – Proceedings of the American Society of University Composers

B (B.) – Bass voice (Solo bass)
Bar. – Solo baritone voice
bar – baritone horn
BB – Billboard
B-B – Boelke-Bomart, Inc. (AMP)
Bel-Mills – Belwin-Mills Publishing Corp.
BH – Boosey & Hawkes, Inc.
BMC – Boston Music Co.,
BMI – Broadcast Music, Inc.
Bom – Bomart Publications, Inc.
Boonin – Joseph Boonin, Inc.
Brass Q – Brass Quarterly
Brit J Aesthetics – British Journal of Aesthetics
BSCBul – Boston Symphony Orchestra Concert Bulletin
bsn – bassoon

BSPN (Bost Sym) – Boston Symphony Orchestra Program Notes
BufPPN – Buffalo Philharmonic Orchestra Program Notes
Bul AMS – Bulletin of the American Musicological Society
Bul – Bulletin

Can Composer – The Canadian Composer
Can Mus J – Canadian Music Journal
Carmelite – (Carmel-by-the-Sea, California)
c-b – contrabass
CCB – C. C. Birchard (Summy-Birchard Publishing Co.)
Century – Century Music Publishing Co.
CF – Carl Fischer, Inc.
CFP – C. F. Peters Corp.
cham – chamber
Chap – Chappel & Co., Inc.
ChiSPN (ChSPN, Chi Sym) – Chicago Symphony Orchestra Program Notes
Choir G – Choir Guide
Choral G – Choral and Organ Guide
Chr Sc Mon Mag – Christian Science Monitor Magazine
CinSPN (CiSPN) – Cincinnati Symphony Orchestra Program Notes
clar – clarinet
Clave – Clave, Vox de la Juventud Musical Uruguaya
ClSPN (Clev Orch) – Cleveland Symphony Program Notes
College Mus – College Music Symposium
Cont Keybd – Contemporary Keyboard
Contrepoints – Contrepoints, une Revue de musique
CRME – Council for Research in Music Education Bulletin
Cur – J. Curwen & Sons
Current Mus – Current Musicology

Dallas SPN (Dallas Sym) – Dallas Symphony Program Notes
d-b – double bass
Decision – Decision, a Review of Free Culture
Deiro – Pietro Deiro Publications
Delk – Delkas Music Publishers
Diap – The Diapason

Down Bt – Down Beat
Duch – Duchess Music Co.

EBM – Edward B. Marks Music Corporation
ECS – E. C. Schirmer Music Co.
ed. – edition, editor
Ed Mus Mag – Educational Music Magazine
E-hn – English horn
Encounter – Encounter, Literature, Arts, Politics
EM – Edition Musicus
E-V – Elkan-Vogel Co., Inc.

FC – Franco Colombo Publications
fl – flute
FFLP (FLP) – Fleischer Free Library of Philadelphia
Flam – Harold Flammer, Inc.
FoF – Facts on File

Gal – Galaxy Music Corporation
Golden – Golden Press
GS – G. Schirmer, Inc.

Harms – T. B. Harms Co.
Heterofonia – Heterofonia: revista musical bimestral
HiFi – High Fidelity
HiFi/MA – High Fidelity/Musical America
HiFi R – HiFi/Stereo Review
hn – horn
hp – harp
Hrsbg Sym – Harrisburg Symphony Orchestra Program Notes
Hud Roz – Hudebni Rozhledy
HWG – H. W. Gray (Belwin-Mills)

Intam Inst Mus Res (Intam Mus Res Yrbk) – Inter-American Institute for Musical Research Yearbook
Intam Mus B – Inter-American Music Bulletin
Int Mus – International Musician
Int R Aesthetics & Soc Mus – International Review of the Aesthetics and Sociology of Music
Instrument – The Instrumentalist
ISPN – Indianapolis Symphony Orchestra Program Notes

J – Journal
J Aesthetics – The Journal of Aesthetics and Art Criticism
JAMS – Journal of the American Musicological Society

JF – J. Fischer and Bro.
J Mus Theory – Journal of Music Theory
J Res Mus Ed – Journal of Research in Music Education

KC Phil – Kansas City Philharmonic Program Notes
Ken Rev – Kenyon Review

LAPPN – Los Angeles Philharmonic Symphony Program Notes
LAPS Mag – Los Angeles Philharmonic Symphony Magazine
Leeds – Leeds Music Corp.
Lit Dgt – Literary Digest
London Mus – London Musical Events
LOSPN – Little Orchestra Society Program Notes
LSVL Orch – Louisville Orchestra Program Notes

MA – Musical America
Mag – Magazine
Magyar Zene – Magyar Zene, zenetudomanyi folyoirat
mar – marimba
MC – Musical Courier
meas. – measure
MENC – Music Educators' National Conference
Mens en Mel – Mens en Melodie
Merc – Mercury Music Corp.
Meri – Merion Music, Inc.
Metro – Metronome
MH – Musikhandel
MJQ – MJQ Music (AMP)
ML – Music and Letters
Mm – Merrymount Music, Inc.
MM – Modern Music
MOMAC – Momac Music Co.
Mo Mus Rec – Monthly Musical Record
MP – Music Press
MQ – The Musical Quarterly
MR – The Music Review
Ms – mansucript
m-S. – solo mezzo-soprano
MSPN – Minneapolis Symphony Program Notes
MT – The Musical Times
MTNAPro – Proceedings of the Music Teachers National Association
Mus Anal – Musical Analysis
Mus Artists – Music and Artists
Mus & Mus – Music and Musicians
Mus Club Mag – Music Clubs Magazine
Mus Denmark – Musical Denmark
Mus Dgt – Music Digest

Mus d'Oggi – Musica d'Oggi; rassegna di vita e di cultura musicale
Mus Ed J – Music Education Journal
Mus e Radio – Musique et Radio
Mus Events – Musical Events
Mus Guide – Music Guide
Musica – Musica; Zweimonatsschrift für alle Gebiete des Musiklebens
MusicAGO – Music: The AGO and RCCO Magazine
Musicology – Journal of the Musicological Society of Australia
Musikleben – Musikleben (Mainz)
Mus J – Music Journal
Mus Leader – Musical Leader
Mus News – Music News
Mus Opin – Musical Opinion
Mus Pub J – Music Publishers' Journal
Mus Rec – Music Record and Opera News
Mus Scene – Music Scene
Mus (SMA) – Music; the Official Journal of the Schools Music Association
Mus Tcr – Music Teacher and Piano Student
Mus Trades – The Music Trades
Mus u Ges – Musik und Gesellschaft
Mus u Kir – Musik und Kirche
Mus West – Music in the West
Mus y Artes – Boletin de Musica y Artes Visuales
mvt – movement

Narr. – narrator
NatlSPN (Natl Sym) – National Symphony Program Notes
NATS – National Association of Teachers of Singing Bulletin
Nat Ed Assn Pro – National Education Association Proceedings
Neue ZFM – Neue Zeitschrift für Musik
News Letter – Newsletter of the American Symphony Orchestra League
Nine Cen Mus – Nineteenth Century Music
NMC – National Music Council Bulletin
NME – New Music Edition (Pres)
NOPPN – New Orleans Philharmonic Program Notes
Norsk Mus – Norsk Musikerblad
NW – Newsweek
NYHT – New York Herald Tribune
NYPPN (NY Phil) – New York

Philharmonic Program Notes
NYT – New York Times
NZ – Neue Zeitschrift für Musik

ob – oboe
OeMZ – Oesterreichische Musikzeitschrift
Okla Sym – Oklahoma Symphony Program Notes
Op. – Opus
Opera Can – Opera Canada
Opera N – Opera News
Oper u Konzert – Oper und Konzert
orch – orchestra
Orchester – Das Orchester; Organ der Deutschen Orchester Vereinigung
org – organ

p. (pp.) – page (pages)
Peer – Peer International Corp.
perc – percussion
Perf Arts Can – Performing Arts in Canada
Piano Q – Piano Quarterly
PitSPN (Pitt Sym) – Pittsburgh Symphony Program Notes
PNM – Perspectives of New Music
pno – piano
POPN – Philadelphia Orchestra Program Notes
PP – published privately
Pres – Theodore Presser Co.
Pro-Musica – Pro-Musica Quarterly

Q Jl Library Congress – United States, Library of Congress, Quarterly Journal
Q Jl of Current Acq – United States, Library of Congress, Quarterly Journal of Current Acquisitions
qtr – quartet

R (Rev) – Review
Rass Mus – La Rassegna Musicale
RCM – Royal College of Music Magazine
Rec Coll – The Record Collector; A Magazine for Collectors of Recorded Vocal Art
Rev Mus – La Revue Musicale
RMA – Royal Musical Association Proceedings
R Mus Chile – Revista Musical Chilena
R Mus Ital – Nuova Rivista Musicale Italiana
RPPN (Roch Phil) – Rochester Philharmonic Orchestra Program Notes

Ruch Muz – Ruch Muzyczny

S (S.) – Soprano voice (Solo Soprano)
Sal – Éditions Salabert
SA Sym – San Antonio Symphony Program Notes
SATB – mixed chorus (soprano, alto, tenor, bass)
sax – saxophone
S-B – Summy-Birchard Publishing Co.
Schallplatte u Kir – Schallplatte und Kirche
School Mus – The School Musician
Schott – B. Schott's Söhne
Schweiz Mus – Schweizerische Musikzeitung
Seattle Sym – Seattle Symphony Orchestra Program Notes
sec. – section
SFSPN (SF Sym) – San Francisco Symphony Program Notes
Shaw – Shawnee Press
SLSPN (SL Sym) – St. Louis Symphony Program Notes
SMPC – Southern Music Publishing Co.
Son Spec – Sonorum Speculum
Sovet Muz – Sovetskaya Muzyka

Sp. – Speaker
Spec – Spectator: Arts, Letters, Science
SR – The Saturday Review
SR/World – Saturday Review/World Magazine
SSA – women's chorus (first and second sopranos, alto)
Stereo R – Stereo Review
Strad – The Strad
SWMusician – The Southwestern Musician
sym – symphony
Sym News – Symphony News: Newsletter of the American Symphony Orchestra League

T (T.) – Tenor (Solo Tenor)
tba – tuba
timp – timpani
Today's Ed – Today's Education (formerly NEA Journal)
tr. – translation, translator
transc. – transcription
trb – trombone
Triangle – The Triangle of Mu Phi Epsilon
trpt – trumpet
TTBB – men's chorus (first and second tenor, first and second bass)

UChiP – University of Chicago Press
UNESCO – United Nations' Educational, Scientific, and Cultural Organization
US News – U. S. News and World Report

Vic Rec Rev – Victor Record Review
Vie Music – La Vie Musicale
Violin – Violins and Violinists
Vital Speeches – Vital Speeches of the Day
vla – viola
vlc – violoncello
vln – violin
VMP – Valley Music Press

Wall St J – Wall Street Journal
Wein – Weintraub Music Co.
Woodwind – Woodwind Magazine
Wood World Brass – Woodwind World–Brass and Percussion
World Mus – The World of Music
ww (wdwd) – woodwinds

ZVUK – Zvuk: Jugoslovenska musicka revija

OUTLINE I

SAMUEL BARBER (b. 1910)

I. Life

1910   Born in West Chester, Pennsylvania, March 9. His mother, a sister of Louise Homer, was a singer and pianist. He began the study of piano at the age of six. Composed his first piece (*Sadness*, 1917).

1924   Entered the Curtis Institute of Music the year that it opened, October, 1924. Studied piano (George Boyle, Isabelle Vengerova), voice (Emilio de Gorgoza), composition (Rosario Scalero), conducting (Fritz Reiner). Graduated from high school, 1926. Traveled in Italy (summers, 1931, 1932) with Gian-Carlo Menotti, also a student at Curtis. Works composed at Curtis include *Serenade for String Quartet* (1929), *Dover Beach* (1931), *Overture to The School for Scandal* (1931), *Sonata for Violoncello and Piano* (1932).

1933   Completed work at Curtis with a Bachelor of Music degree. Spent the summer (1933) in Italy with Menotti and winter (1934) in Vienna. Studied singing and conducting and appeared in concerts. Returned to New York (1934) and attempted to earn money by singing German lieder on the radio.

1935   Awarded the American Prix de Rome (1935). Settled at the American Academy, and spent the next two years composing and traveling. His successful career as a composer began in 1935 with the award of a Pulitzer Traveling Scholarship (1935-1936) and many performances of his music from that time on.

1937   *Symphony in One Movement* was the first American composition to be given a performance at the Salzburg Festival.

1939   Taught orchestration and conducted a small chorus at Curtis Institute (1939-1942). After 1942 he devoted himself to composition and accepted no more teaching appointments.

1942   Inducted into the army. Assigned to special services and later transferred to the Army Air Forces. Commissioned to write a work for the A. A. F (*Symphony No. 2*, Op. 19, 1944).

1945   After the war he was awarded a Guggenheim Fellowship and went to Europe. He returned to "Capricorn," his home near Mt. Kisco, New York, which he and Menotti had purchased. Since then most of his music has been composed there.

1947   Received the Music Critics Circle Award (*Concerto for Violoncello*).

1952   Elected a vice-president of the Executive Board of the International Music Council of UNESCO.

1958   Awarded the Pulitzer Prize for music (*Vanessa*). Received the Henry Hadley medal from the National Association for American Composers and Conductors for "exceptional services to American music."

1959   Awarded an honorary Doctor of Music degree from Harvard University.

1963   Awarded a second Pultizer Prize (*Concerto for Piano*).

1964   Commissioned to write an opera for the opening of the Metropolitan Opera House, Lincoln Center, 1966 (*Antony and Cleopatra*).

Samuel Barber has been the recipient of many honors, awards and commissions in addition to those listed above.

Note: Biographies of varying lengths and importance will be found in many of the books listed in the Bibliography at the end of this *Outline* under "References to Samuel Barber."

II.   Compositions (all published by G. Schirmer)

A.   Orchestra

		Date
1.	Serenade, Op. 1 (strings; also str qrt)	1929
2.	Overture to The School for Scandal, Op. 5	1931
3.	Music for a Scene from Shelley, Op. 7	1933
4.	Symphony No. 1, Op. 9 (Symphony in One Movement)	1936; revised 1942
5.	Adagio for Strings, Op. 11 (arr. from String Quartet No. 1)	1936
6.	Essay for Orchestra No. 1, Op. 12	1937
7.	Essay for Orchestra No. 2, Op. 17	1942
8.	Symphony No. 2, Op. 19	1944; revised 1947
9.	Capricorn Concerto, Op. 21 (fl, ob, trpt, str)	1944
10.	Night Flight, Op. 19A (rev. version of 2nd mvt, Sym 2)	1947
11.	Medea: Ballet Suite, Op. 23	1947
12.	Medea's Meditation and Dance of Vengeance, Op. 23A	1947
13.	Knoxville: Summer of 1915, Op. 24 (S., fl, ob, clar, bsn, 2 hn, trpt, hp, str) (on text of James Agee)	1947
14.	Souvenirs: Ballet Suite, Op. 28 (also pno solo; 2 pno 4 hands)	1952
15.	Introduction to Act II (Vanessa)	1958
16.	Intermezzo from Act IV (Vanessa)	1958
17.	Die Natali, Op. 37	1960
18.	Chorale Prelude on Silent Night (from Die Natali) (also org)	1961
19.	Fadograph from a Yestern Scene (after James Joyce's Finnegans Wake)	1971

B.   Concerto

20.	Concerto for Violin, Op. 14	1939
21.	Concerto for Violoncello, Op. 22	1945
22.	Toccata Festiva for Organ and Orchestra, Op. 36 (also org and str orch)	1960
23.	Concerto for Piano, Op. 38	1962

C.   Band

24.	Commando March	1943

D.   Chamber

25.	Serenade for String Quartet, Op. 1 (also str orch)	1929
26.	Sonata for Violoncello and Piano, Op. 6	1932
27.	String Quartet, No. 1, Op. 11	1936
28.	Summer Music for Woodwind Quintet, Op. 31 (fl, ob, clar, bsn, hn)	1956
29.	Canzone (vln, pno) (transc. from 2nd mvt of Concerto for Piano) (also fl, pno)	1962
30.	Mutations from Bach (4 hns, 3 trpt, 3 trb, tba, timp)	1967

E.   Piano

31.	Four Excursions, Op. 20	1944
32.	Sonata for Piano, Op. 26	1949
33.	Souvenirs, Op. 28 (arr. from the ballet suite) (also for pno 4 hands; orch)	1952
34.	Nocturne (Homage to John Field), Op. 33	1957
35.	Under the Willow Tree (arr. Vanessa)	1958

F.   Organ

36.	Adagio for Strings, Op. 11 (arr. from str orch)	1936
37.	Wondrous Love, Op. 34	1958

G.   Choral (a cappella unless otherwise indicated)

38.	The Virgin Martyrs. Op. 8, No. 1 (Helen Waddell) (SSAA)	1935
39.	Let Down the Bars, O Death, Op. 8, No. 2 (Emily Dickinson) (SATB)	1936
40.	Three Reincarnations, Op. 16 (James Stephens) (SATB) 1. Mary Hynes; 2. Anthony O'Daly; 3. The Coolin'	1936-1940

G.   Choral (cont.)

41.   A Nun Takes the Veil (Heaven-Haven), Op. 13, No. 1 (G. M. Hopkins)   1937
    (SSAA; TTBB; SATB; also voice, pno)

42.   Sure on This Shining Night, Op. 13, No. 3 (James Agee)   1938
    (SATB; also voice, pno)

43.   A Stopwatch and an Ordnance Map, Op. 15 (Stephen Spender)   1940
    (TTBB, 4 hn, 3 trb, tba, timp)

44.   Prayers of Kierkegaard, Op. 30 (Soren Kierkegaard) (S., SATB, orch)   1954

45.   Under the Willow Tree (from *Vanessa*) (SATB)   1958

46.   Easter Chorale, Op. 40 (SATB, brass, timp, org)   1965

47.   The Lovers, Op. 43 (Pablo Neruda) (Bar., SATB, orch)   1971

H.   **Solo Vocal** (with piano unless otherwise indicated)

48.   Collected Songs (includes all songs up to 1955)   1955

49.   Three Songs, Op. 2   1927-1934
    a.   The Daisies (James Stephens) 1927
    b.   With Rue My Heart is Laden (A. E. Housman) 1928
    c.   Bessie Bobtail (James Stephens) 1934

50.   Dover Beach, Op. 3 (Matthew Arnold) (with str qrt; also pno)   1931

51.   Three Songs, Op. 10 (James Joyce) (also with cham orch)   1936
    a.   Rain has Fallen   c. I Hear an Army
    b.   Sleep Now

52.   Four Songs, Op. 13   1937-1940
    a.   A Nun Takes the Veil (G. M. Hopkins)
    b.   The Secrets of the Old (W. B. Yeats)
    c.   Sure on This Shining Night (James Agee) (also with cham orch)
    d.   Nocturne (Frederic Prokosh) (also with cham orch)

53.   Two Songs, Op. 18   1942-1943
    a.   The Queen's Face on a Summery Coin (Robert Horan)
    b.   Monks and Raisins (José Garcia Villa) (also with cham orch)

54.   Knoxville: Summer of 1915, Op. 24 (James Agee)   1947
    (S. with cham orch; also with pno)

55.   Nuvoletta, Op. 25 (James Joyce)   1947

56.   Mélodies passagères, Op. 27 (Rainer Maria Rilke)   1951
    a.   Puisque tout passe   d.   Le Clocher chante
    b.   Un Cygne   e.   Départ
    c.   Tombeau dans un Parc

57.   Hermit Songs, Op. 29 (anonymous Irish Texts, 8th to the 13th centuries)   1953
    a.   At Saint Patrick's Purgatory   f.   Sea-Snatch
    b.   Church Bell at Night   g.   Promiscuity
    c.   St. Ita's Vision   h.   The Monk and His Cat
    d.   The Heavenly Banquet   i.   The Praises of God
    e.   The Crucifixion   j.   The Desire for Hermitage

58.   Must the Winter Come so Soon (from *Vanessa*)   1958

59.   Under the Willow Tree (from *Vanessa*) (also vocal duet)   1958

60.   A Hand of Bridge, Op. 35 (Gian-Carlo Menotti) (four solo voices, cham)   1960

61.   Andromache's Farewell, Op. 39 (J. P. Creagh, after Euripedes,   1963
    The Trojan Women) (S. and orch; also with pno)

62.   Five Songs   1969
    a.   Despite and Still (Robert Graves)   d.   My Lizard (Theodor Roethke)
    b.   In the Wilderness (Robert Graves)   e.   Solitary Hotel (James Joyce)
    c.   A Last Song (Robert Graves)

63.   Three Songs, Op. 45   1974
    a.   Now Have I Fed and Eaten up the Rose (James Joyce)
    b.   A Green Lowland of Pianos (Czeslaw Milosz)
    c.   O Boundless, Boundless Evening (Christopher Middleton)

I.   Opera

64.	Vanessa, Op. 32 (Gian-Carlo Menotti)	1958
65.	A Hand of Bridge, Op. 35 (Gian-Carlo Menotti)	1959
	(a short chamber opera for 4 solo voices and cham orch)	
66.	Antony and Cleopatra, Op. 40 (William Shakespeare, adapted by Franco Zeffirelli) (new revised version, 1973)	1966

J.   Ballet

67.	The Serpent Heart, Op. 23 (revised to Cave of the Heart, 1947)	1946
68.	Souvenirs, Op. 38	1952

Note: The following abbreviations are used in Section III of this *Outline*.

 5. *Adagio*: Adagio for Strings
 9. *Capricorn*: Capricorn Concerto
23. *Concerto Pno*: Concerto for Piano
21. *Concerto Vlc*: Concerto for Violoncello
20. *Concerto Vln*: Concerto for Violin
 7. *Essay 2*: Essay for Orchestra No. 2
13. *Knoxville*: Knoxville: Summer of 1915

 2. *School*:   Overture to The School for Scandal
25. *Serenade*: Serenade for String Quartet
32. *Son Pno*: Sonata for Piano
43. *Stopwatch*: A Stopwatch and an Ordnance Map
27. *Str Qrt 1*: String Quartet No. 1
 4. *Sym 1*: Symphony No. 1

III.   Style (techniques and devices)

"If more governments loved music we should have no need of ambassadors at all." "Believe me, I admire your musicianship and vast experience, but your statement that 'dance music cannot be of longer duration than 14 1/2 minutes in a symphony concert' seems arbitrary and untenable. What if Maestro Eugene should say that 15 1/2 minutes were the maximum duration, or Maestro Wilhelm 22 minutes, or Maestro Arturo 3 minutes? The thought is too terrifying to pursue. . . If you do not have my complete blessing, you do have my very best wishes."

From a letter to a famous conductor. Samuel Barber

A.   General characteristics
　　1.　1929-1939: Traditional, generally conservative. Highly developed lyricism, logical construction, economy of means.
　　2.　1940-1947: Transitional period, fusion of basic lyricism with increased dissonance and complexity. Texture becomes increasingly contrapuntal. Gradual growth toward contemporary techniques.
　　3.　1947-on: Increasing tonal freedom (some atonality); harmony and counterpoint become more dissonant; some use of twelve-tone techniques.
B.   Melodic line
　　1.　Lyric: *School* (letter C); *Sym 1* (Nos. 2-3, second theme); *Adagio*; *Concerto Vln* (first two movements).
　　2.　Wide leaps: *Sym 1* (p. 1); *Essay 2* (p. 3); *Son Pno* (first movement, p. 5, second theme; fourth movement, fugue theme).
　　3.　Angular, jagged (including wide leaps): *Sym 2*; *Capricorn* (p. 15, meas. 5); *Essay 1* (pp. 21-23, pic, fl); *Concerto Vlc* (first and last movements, beginning).
　　4.　Chromatic: *Stopwatch*; *Son Pno* (first movement, meas. 1-4).
　　5.　Melodic intervals as a unifying device: *Anthony O'Daly* (melody above and below note E); *Sym 2* (seconds); *Capricorn* (p. 2, meas. 1-3, seconds); *Medea Suite* (seconds, sevenths, ninths); *Knoxville* (seconds, ninths).
C.   Harmony
　　1.　Strong tonality (used as a means of unification). *School* (pp. 1-19).
　　2.　Full sonorities: *Sym 1* (before Nos. 34, 36).

3. Chromatic: *Medea Suite*; *Son Pno* (p. 42, diatonic melody).
4. Chords built on fourths: *The Desire for Hermitage (Hermit Songs)*.
5. Third relationships: *Adagio* (p. 3).
6. Dissonance: *Sym 1* (Nos. 41-42; 47-50); *Son Pno*; *Knoxville* (alternating F-sharp minor and A major).
7. Polyharmony: *Essay 2* (Fugue); *Excursions No. 1* (p. 7, meas. 4-10); *Medea Suite*; *Sym 2* (Andante; Presto).
8. Twelve-tone techniques: *Son Pno* (first movement, pp. 3, 5, 9; third movement, pp. 25-26). Rows used principally as accompaniments to thematic material. Notes sometimes added to chords based on rows.

D. Counterpoint
1. An essential part of his style, although used moderately.
2. Fugal style: *Essay 2* (p. 21, polytonal); *Capricorn* (pp. 2-3); *Son Pno* (last movement); *School* (Coda).
3. Canon: *Sure on This Shining Night* (canon at the third); *Capricorn* (pp. 2-3); *Sym 2* (finale); *Concerto Vlc* (slow movement).

E. Rhythm
1. Rhythms in general are energetic and varied. Changing time signatures and unusual time signatures are infrequent.
2. Regular: *Overture*; *Adagio*; *Essay 2* (before No. 11).
3. Superimposed: *Sym 1* (No. 14, brass); *Excursions* (p. 3).
4. Syncopated: *Sym 1* (Nos. 29-31); *Capricorn* (letters M-P).
5. Polyrhythm: *Vanessa* (p. 72).
6. Isorhythm: *Son Pno* (p. 38).
7. Changing time signatures: *Capricorn* (pp. 2-5; 16-20); *The Secrets of Old*.
8. Unusual time signatures: *Monks and Raisins* (7/8).

F. Form
1. Strong feeling for form; free use of classic forms.
2. Sonata-allegro: *School* (Exposition, p. 2; Development, p. 14; Recapitulation, p. 21); *Str Qrt 1* (first movement); *Son Pno* (first movement).
3. Chaconne (Passacaglia): *Sym 1* (No. 42).
4. Variations: *Sym 2* (finale).
5. Ostinato: *Excursions* (I, III); *Sym 2* (first movement; finale); *Concerto Vlc* (second theme); *Medea* (*Dance of Vengeance*).
6. Concerto Grosso: *Capricorn*.
7. Rondo idea: *Capricorn* (finale, A - B - A^1 - C - A^2 - B^1 - A^3); *Knoxville* (A section includes melody first sung); *Stopwatch* (double refrain).
8. Movements built out of material stated at the beginning: *Serenade* (first movement); *Sym 1* (first movement, four sections: I. Exposition of three themes and development; II. Scherzo, first theme transformed; III. Andante, based on the second theme; *Passacaglia* (first theme in bass, third theme above); *Capricorn* (first movement); *Son Pno* (first movement).
9. Cyclic idea: *Str Qrt 1* (two movements; conclusion based on the first movement); *Essay 1* (A - B form; conclusion based on principal theme of A section); *Essay 2* (fugue subject, before No. 11, is derived from p. 3 and timpani at No. 2).

G. Orchestration
1. Based on traditional principles and the normal orchestra. Idiomatic use of instruments coupled with restraint and variety. Solo instruments require virtuoso performance.

H. Unusual features
1. Glissando pizzicati: *Knoxville* ("the bleak spark crackling").
2. Musical realism: *Nuvoletta*.
3. No time signatures: *Hermit Songs*.
4. Jazz style, folk material: *Excursions*.

5. Use of radio beam (in original version): *Sym 2* (second movement).
6. Dance movements: *Souvenirs*.

BIBLIOGRAPHY

Books about Samuel Barber

1. Broder, Nathan. *Samuel Barber*. New York: G. Schirmer, 1954. Reviews in *Notes* 11 (1953-1954), 559; *MC* 150 (Nov 1, 1954), 43; *Mus Clubs Mag* 34 (Jan 1955), 39; *Pan Pipes* 47 (Jan 1955), 80; *Mus Opinion* 78 (Feb 1955), 283; *ML* 36 (Apr 1955), 174-175; *MQ* 41 (1955), 105; *Jl of Research* 3 (Spring 1955), 64-65; *HiFi* 5 (Sept 1955), 13; *MA* 76 (Jan 1, 1956), 46; *MR* 17 (May 1956), 164; *Bost Sym* (Sep 28, 1962), 78.

Articles by Samuel Barber

1. "Birth Pangs of a First Opera," *NYT* 107 (Jan 12, 1958), sec. 2, p. 9.
2. "On Waiting for a Libretto," *Opera News* 22 (Jan 27, 1958), 4-6.
3. "Make Mingle with Our Tambourines," *Opera News* 31 (Sep 17, 1966), 32.

References to Samuel Barber

Books
(See the General Bibliography)

AbrHY; AbrMM; ASC-BD; ASC-SC; AusMT; Baker; BakSL; BauTC; BloYA; BluPC; BMI-OP; Bull; CatPC; ChaAC; ChaAM; CobCS; CohCT; ComA; CurB (1944, 1963); DalTT; DemMT; DerETM; DowO; DukLH; Edm-II; EdMUS; EweAC; EweCB; EweCS; EweCT; EweDB; EweNB; EweYA; GolMM; GosMM; Grove; HanIT; HitMA; HodSD; HowMM; How-OA; HowOC; HowSH; JohSH; KinAI; KolMA; LeiMW; LeiSK; MacAC; MacIC; MelMN; MelRT; MueAS; MyeTC; ParMH; PersTH; PeyNM; PleSM; PorM3S; ReiAC; ReiCC; RobCM; RowFC; SalTM; SanWM; SchCC; StevHS; ThoAM; ThompIC; ThoRL; ThomsMS; UlrCM; WWA; WWM; YouCD; YouCT.   Annual Report of the Academy of Rome, 1936, 1937.

Articles

1. Brief mention: *Etude* 61 (Jan 1943), 13; 64 (Dec 1946), 167; 69 (Jan 1951), 13; *MA* 72 (Dec 15, 1952), 26; *NYT Mag* (Jan 12, 1958), 34.
2. "Wins J. H. Bearns music prize for composers," *NYT* (Apr 12, 1933), 24:4.
3. "Gets Prix de Rome," *NYT* (May 10, 1935), 24:6.
4. *NYT* (Jun 26, 1935), 19:3; *MC* 3 (Dec 7, 1935), 23.
5. "Samuel Barber's Music given at a Special Concert," *MA* 57 (Mar 25, 1937), 34.
6. "Radzioski's Audience Acclaims Barber's Latest Work," *NW* 9 (Apr 3, 1937), 28.
7. Lieberson, Goddard. "Over the Air." *MM* 16, No. 1 (1938), 65.
8. *NW* 11 (Apr 11, 1938), 24; 12 (Nov 14, 1938), 30.
9. *NYT* 9 (Feb 9, 1941), 7:2; 9 (Aug 10, 1941), 6:1.
10. Horan, Robert. "Samuel Barber," *MM* 20, No. 3 (1942-1943), 161.
11. Copland, Aaron. "From the '20's to the '40's and Beyond," *MM* 20, No. 2 (1942-1943), 80.
12. *NYT* (Mar 4, 1944), 11:3; (Mar 10, 1944), 21:3.
13. "Case of Samuel Barber," *NW* 23 (Mar 13, 1944), 94.
14. Sabin, Robert. "Samuel Barber," *MA* 64 (Apr 10, 1944), 7, 25.
15. "Big Names in Chicago," *MM* 22, No. 3 (1944-1945), 121.
16. *Current Biography* (Sep 1944); *Current Biography Yearbook* (1944), 30-32.

17. *New York Post* (May 9, 1946).
18. Horan, Robert. "And Three Modern Young Men Lead a Modern Life in This Swiss Chalet: Capricorn, Mt. Kisco, N. Y.," *American Home* 36 (July 1946), 36-38.
19. "Wins New York Music Critics Circle Award," *NYT* (Jun 28, 1946), 16:5.
20. "Gets Koussevitzky Music Foundation — Write Opera," *NYT* (Dec 29, 1946), sec. 2, p. 7:2.
21. "Commission to Write Piano Sonata for 25th Anniversary of Composers' League," *NYT* (Sep 24, 1947), 20:4.
22. "Summer 1945; Knoxville: Summer of 1915," *NW* 31 (Apr 19, 1948), 84.
23. Broder, Nathan. "The Music of Samuel Barber with List of Works," *MQ* 34 (1948), 325.
24. "Samuel Barber," *POPN* (Feb 21, 1949), 493.
25. Dexter, Harry. "Samuel Barber and His Music," *Mus Opin* 5 (Mar 1949), 285; 5 (Apr 1949), 343.
26. "Returns to U S from Rome," *NYT* (Dec 15, 1949), 46:7.
27. "House in Mt. Kisco," *Time* 55 (Feb 6, 1950), 34.
28. Berger, Arthur. "Spotlight on the Moderns," *SR* 34 (May 26, 1951), 62; 35 (Jan 26, 1952), 54.
29. "A Barber Festival," *Am Rec G* 17 (May 1951), 297-298.
30. Quillian, James. "The Songs of Samuel Barber," *Repertoire* 1 (Oct 1951), 17.
31. Porter, Andrew. "Music of Today," *London Mus* 7 (Aug 1952), 28-29.
32. Repass, R. "American Composers of Today," *London Mus* 8 (Dec 1953), 28-29.
33. Heinsheimer, Hans W. "Bugles and Bells (Generation of American Composers of Importance Without Interest in Musical Theatre)," *MC* 149 (Mar 1, 1954), 6.
34. Keats, Sheila. "Reference Articles on American Composers; an Index," *Juilliard Rev* 1 (Fall 1954), 22.
35. Gräter, M. "Der Sänger von Capricorn," *Melos* 21 (Sep 1954), 247-250.
36. Sargeant, Winthrop. "Musical Events; Presentation of New Cantata, Prayers of Kierkegaard," *New Yorker* 30 (Dec 18, 1954), 141.
37. Kolodin, Irving. "Barber on Kierkegaard," *SR* 37 (Dec 25, 1954), 23.
38. "Samuel Barber," *Pan Pipes* 47 (Jan 1955), 30.
39. "A Stopwatch and an Ordnance," *Mus Opin* 78 (Feb 1955), 285.
40. Evett, Robert. "How Right is Right? " *Score* No. 12 (June 1955), 37.
41. Stambler, Bernard. "Four American Composers," *Juilliard Rev* 2 (Winter 1955), 7-16.
42. Kolodin, Irving. "Music to My Ears; First Performance of Medea's Meditation and Dance of Vengeance," *SR* 39 (Feb 18, 1956), 27.
43. "U. S. Composers in a Bright Era," *Life* 40 (May 21, 1956), 142.
44. Ellsworth, Ray. "Americans on Microgroove," *HiFi* 6 (Aug 1956), 61.
45. "We Salute Samuel Barber," *Mus Club Mag* 37 (Nov 1957), 8.
46. *NYT* (Jan 5, 1958), sec. 6, p. 24:3; (Jan 12, 1958), sec. 6, p. 34:1; (Jan 16, 1958), 33:3.
47. Coleman, Emily. "Samuel Barber and Vanessa," *Theatre Arts* 42, No. 1 (Jan 1958), 68, 86.
48. " Vanessa premièred," *FoF* 18 (Jan 15, 1958), 42G2.
49. Turner, Charles. "The Music of Samuel Barber," *Opera News* 22 (Jan 27, 1958), 7.
50. "Dear Mother, I was Meant to be a Composer," *NW* 51 (Jan 27, 1958), 62-63.
51. "Wins Pulitzer," *FoF* 18 (May 5, 1958), 152G2.
52. "Wins Pulitzer Prize for 'Vanessa'," *NYT* (May 6, 1958), 39:1, 34:3.
53. "Award for Composition Played by Philadelphia Orchestra," *NYT* (May 18, 1958), 23:5.
54. "American Composers and Conductors Association Hadley Medal," *NYT* (May 21, 1958), 40: 3.
55. "Elected to American Academy of Arts and Letters," *NYT* (Dec 6, 1958), 18:4.
56. "To American Academy," *FoF* 18 (Dec 5, 1958), 434D1.
57. "American Composers—Samuel Barber," *MC* 159 (Feb 1959), 41.
58. "Samuel Barber," *Composer of the Americas* 5 (1959), 14-21.
59. "Award from National Institute of Arts and Letters," *NYT* (May 21, 1959), 28:2.
60. "Harvard University Honorary Degree," *NYT* (Jun 12, 1959), 3:1.

61. "Classified Chronological Catalog of Works by the United States Composer Samuel Barber," *Intam Mus B* No. 13 (Sep 1959), 22-28.
62. "One of Most Admired Contemporary American Composers," *NYT* (Oct 25, 1959), 13:1.
63. Ardoin, John. "Samuel Barber at Capricorn," *MA* 80 (Mar 1960), 4.
64. "Honored by Curtis Music Institute," *NYT* (Mar 10, 1960), 37:1.
65. Waters, Edward N. "Annual Report on Acquisitions: Music," *Q Jl of Current Acq* 18 (Nov 1960), 15.
66. *NYT* (Nov 17, 1960), 45:4.
67. "American Premières," *Time* 77 (Jan 13, 1961), 42.
68. Rands, Bernard. "Samuel Barber—A Belief in Tradition," *Mus Opin* 84 (Mar 1961), 353.
69. Briggs, John. "Samuel Barber," *Int Mus* 60 (Dec 1961), 20.
70. *NYT* (Jan 25, 1962), 24:4.
71. "To be Official US Guest to 3rd Soviet Composers Congress," *NYT* (Mar 25, 1962), sec. 2, p. 13:2; (Mar 30, 1962), 27:2; (Apr 14, 1962), 14:3.
72. Parmenter, Ross. "Barber Sitting in (American is Observer at Soviet Composers Congress)," *NYT* 111 (Mar 25, 1962), sec. 2, p. 13.
73. Yarustovsky, Boris. "Journey to America," *J Res Mus Ed* 10, No. 2 (1962), 124.
74. Sargeant, Winthrop. "Musical Events," *New Yorker* 39 (Apr 13, 1963), 153.
75. Kolodin, Irving. "The Trojan Woman," *SR* 46 (Apr 20, 1963), 28.
76. "Wins Pultizer," *FoF* 23 (May 6, 1963), 180E2.
77. "Wins Pulitzer Prize for Piano Concerto No. 1," *NYT* (May 7, 1963), 35:1, 4; 42:1.
78. *NYT* (May 16, 1963), 41:1.
79. *Current Biography* (Sep 1963); *Current Biography Yearbook* (1963), 17-19.
80. Sargeant, Winthrop. "Musical Events," *New Yorker* 39 (Nov 16, 1963), 127-128.
81. Kolodin, Irving. "Barber Concerto Performed by the New York Philharmonic Orchestra," *SR* 46 (Nov 23, 1963), 33.
82. "Trustee of J. F. Kennedy Memorial Library," *NYT* (Jan 14, 1964), 17:1.
83. "New York Music Critics Circle Award," *NYT* (May 20, 1964), 37:1.
84. *PNM* 4, No. 1 (1965), 179.
85. Heinsheimer, Hans W. "Birth of an Opera," *SR* 49 (Sep 17, 1966), 49-50.
86. *NYT* (Sep 17, 1966), 18:2.
87. Freeman, John W. "In the Grand Tradition," *Opera News* 31 (Sep 17, 1966), 40-41.
88. Freeman, John W., and W. Mayer. "Met's Double Christening; Two New Works by Americans," *Mus J* 24 (Oct 1966), 23-25.
89. Salzman, Eric. "Samuel Barber," *HiFi Rev* 17 (Oct 1966), 77-89.
90. Salzman, Eric, and J. Goodfriend. "Samuel Barber: a Selective Discography," *HiFi Rev* 17 (Oct 1966), 88.
91. Waters, Edward N. "Harvest of the Year; Selected Acquisitions of the Music Division," *Q Jl Library of Congress* 24, No. 1 (1967), 54.
92. Butterworth, Niel. "American Composers," *Music SMA* 2, No. 1 (1967), 39.
93. Heinsheimer, Hans W. "The Composing Composer," *ASCAP* 2, No. 3 (1968), 4-7.
94. Fairleigh, James P. "Serialism in Barber's Solo Piano Works," *Piano Q* 18, No. 72 (1970), 13-17.
95. "New York Philharmonic Honors 60th Birthday," *NYT* (Dec 19, 1970), 18:2.
96. *NYT* (Sep 12, 1971), 82:1; (Oct 3, 1971), sec. 2, p. 15:5; (Nov 14, 1971), sec. 2, p. 16:8.
97. Soria, Dorle J. "Artist Life; Production of Antony and Cleopatra," *HiFi/MA* 24 (Sep 1974), 5-6.
98. Kolodin, Irving. "Evening with Carter, Rubinstein, and Barber," *SR* 2 (Mar 22, 1975), 34.
99. "Gets Arts and Letters Award," *FoF* 36 (May 19, 1976), 504C3.
100. "Samuel Barber Work Commissioned (for Van Cliburn International Piano Competition)," *Mus Club Mag* 55, No. 3 (1976), 15.
101. Smith, Rollin. "American Organ Composers," *MusicAGO* 10 (1976), 18.
102. Elson, James. "The Songs of Samuel Barber," *NATS* 34, No. 1 (1977), 18.

References to Works by Samuel Barber

5. Adagio for Strings: *NYT* (Oct 27, 1938), 26:3; (Nov 6, 1938), 48:5; (Nov 13, 1938), sec. 9, p. 8:2; (Nov 20, 1938), sec. 9, p. 8:4; (Nov 27, 1938), sec. 9, p. 6:3; (Dec 25, 1938), sec. 9, p. 8:4; *POPN* 44 (1943-1944), 213; *MQ* 33 (1947), 186; *POPN* (Mar 18, 1949), 711; *Diap* 40 (Nov 1, 1949), 28; *Strad* 60 (Apr 1950), 372; *MC* 142 (Nov 1, 1950), 29; *CiSPN* (Oct 9, 1953), 17-21; *SF Sym* (Feb 16, 1966), 19; *EweCB*, 9; *HitMU*, 211.

61. Andromache's Farewell: *NY Phil* (Apr 4, 1963), D-K; *NYT* (Apr 5, 1963), 30:1; *New Yorker* 39 (Apr 13, 1963), 153; *SR* 46 (Apr 20, 1963), 28; *Mus J* 21 (May 1963), 68; *MA* 83 (Jun 1963), 22; *Notes* 21 (1963-1964), 458; *MA* 83 (Jan 1964), 70; *HiFi/MA* 18 (Feb 1968), MA8.

66. Antony and Cleopatra: *NYT* (May 7, 1964), 39:1; *MA* 84 (Jul 1964), 18; *NYT Mag* (Aug 28, 1966), 32; *Opera N* 31 (Sep 17, 1966), 28-35, 36-38, 40-41; *SR* 49 (Sep 17, 1966), 49; *Variety* 244 (Sep 21, 1966), 66; *New Yorker* 42 (Sep 24, 1966), 114; *NW* 68 (Sep 26, 1966), 98; *Life* 61 (Sep 30, 1966), 30 B; *Atlantic* 218 (Sep 1966), 126; *SR* 49 (Oct 1, 1966), 35; *New Republic* 155 (Oct 22, 1966), 23; *Melos* 33 (Oct 1966), 333-335; *Mus J* 24 (Oct 1966), 23-25; *Reporter* 35 (Nov 17, 1966), 57; *HiFi Rev* 17 (Nov 1966), 4; *Neue ZFM* 127 (Nov 1966), 447; *Opera* 17 (Nov 1966), 843-845; *HiFi/MA* 16 (Nov 1966), MA8-10; *MM* 15 (Nov 1966), 20; *BB* 78 (Nov 26, 1966), 64; *Mus Leader* 98 (Dec 1966), 3; *Dance Mag* 40 (Dec 1966), 29; *Ruch Muz* 11, No. 1 (1967), 15; *Musica* 21, No. 4 (1967), 176; *Am Rec G* 33 (May 1967), 871-872; *Natl Sym* (Feb 24, 1968), 27; *Intam Mus B* No. 66 (Jul 1968), 3; *SR* 52 (Mar 29, 1969), 52; *NYT* (Dec 11, 1971), 22:1; *New Yorker* 47 (Dec 18, 1971), 116; *SR/World* 1 (Jun 1, 1974), 44; *HiFi/MA* 24 (Sep 1974), MA5-6; *NYT* (Feb 7, 1975), 13:2; *Variety* 278 (Feb 12, 1975), 81; *New Yorker* 51 (Feb 24, 1975), 123-124; *SR* 2 (Mar 22, 1975), 34; *Mus J* 33 (Apr 1975), 38; *Opera N* 39 (Apr 5, 1975), 36; *HiFi/MA* 25 (May 1975), MA25; *Opernwelt* 5 (May 1975), 49-51; *Opera N* 40 (Aug 1975), 16-21.

29. Canzone for Violin and Piano: *Notes* 22 (1965-1966), 813.

9. Capricorn Concerto: *MM* 22, No. 1 (1944-1945), 30; *Notes* 4 (1946-1947), 99; *HitMU*, 211.

23. Concerto for Piano: *NYT* (Feb 20, 1962), 31:3; *NYPPN* (Sep 24, 1962); *NYHT* (Sep 25, 1962); *NYT* (Sep 25, 1962), 32:4; *Bost Sym* (Sep 28, 1962), 78; *MA* 82 (Nov 1962), 18; *Show* 2 (Dec 1962), 39; *MQ* 49 (1963), 94-97; *Pan Pipes* 55, No. 2 (1963), 7; *MM* 11 (Feb 1963), 45; *Mus Opin* 86 (Feb 1963), 285; *MT* 104 (Mar 1963), 192; *Mus d'Oggi* 6, No. 4 (1963), 171; *SR* 46 (Nov 23, 1963), 33; *MA* 83 (Dec 1963), 178; *SF Sym* (Mar 18, 1964), 13; *Am Rec G* 31 (Jan 1965), 392; *Sovet Muz* 29 (Jan 1965), 94; *(Jun 1965), 93;* *MM* 13 (Aug 1965), 41; *Chi Sym* (Oct 7, 1965), 11; *Phila Orch* (Oct 22, 1965-1966), 19; *LSVL Orch* (Apr 12, 1966); *OeMZ* 33 (Jan 1978), 45.

20. Concerto for Violin: *NYT* (Dec 29, 1940), sec. 9, p. 7:5; *NYHT* (Feb 12, 1941); *BSPN* (1941-1942), 831; *MA* 62 (Mar 25, 1942), 36; *BSCBul* 12 (Jan 7, 1949), 594; *Strad* 60 (Oct 1949), 186; *Mus Rev* 11 (Nov 1950), 327; *Strad* 61 (Jan 1951), 338; *MC* 162 (Dec 1960), 16; *Sovet Muz* 31 (Feb 1967), 83; *Mus & Mus* 25 (Nov 1976), 58; *Mus J* 35 (Dec 1977), 36.

21. Concerto for Violoncello: *BSPN* (Apr 5, 1946); *ChSPN* (Apr 14, 1949), 29; *MQ* 35 (1949), 286; *Notes* 8 (1950-1951), 392; *MA* 71 (Aug 1951), 30; *Notes* 11 (1953-1954), 146; *Strad* 84 (Jan 1974), 529; *EweCB*, 10.

50. Dover Beach: *HiFi Rev* 21 (Oct 1968), 109; *HitMU*, 211.

6. Essay, No. 1: *NYT* (Oct 27, 1938), 26:3; (Nov 6, 1938), 48:5; (Nov 13, 1938), sec. 9, p. 8:2; (Nov 20, 1938), sec. 9, p. 8:4; (Nov 27, 1938), sec. 9, p. 6:3; (Dec 25, 1938), sec. 9, p. 8:4; *MQ* 33 (1947), 196; *NYPPN* (Dec 7, 1950); *CiSPN* (Oct 9, 1953), 21; *Natl Sym* (Apr 11, 1967), 20; *EweCB*, 9; *MacIC*, 551; *HitMU*, 211.

7. Essay No. 2: *BSPN* (Apr 25, 1941); *NYT* (Jul 26, 1943), 14:8; *Notes* 2 (1944-1945), 175;

CiSPN (Dec 28, 1951), 274-277; *POPN* (Oct 17, 1952), 80; *Pitt Sym* (Feb 25, 1966), 19; *SF Sym* (Mar 1967), 26; *EweCB*, 10.

31. Excursions: *MM* 22, No. 4 (1944-1945), 267; *NYT* (Oct 20, 1975), 45:1.

19. Fadograph from a Yestern Scene: *NYT* (Sep 12, 1971), 94:5; *Sym News* 22, No. 6 (1971), 24; *NYT* (Nov 7, 1971), 83:3; *Mus J* 30 (Jan 1972), 74; *HiFi/MA* 22 (Jan 1972), MA25-26; *ASCAP* 5, No. 3 (1972), 30.

65. A Hand of Bridge: *NYT* (Apr 7, 1960), 45:1; *MA* 80 (May 1960), 39-40; *Notes* 18 (1960-1961), 641.

57. Hermit Songs: *MQ* 40 (1954), 589; *MA* 74 (Dec 15, 1954), 30; *Mus Opin* 78 (Jan 1955), 225; *MQ* 41 (1955), 551, 553; *Notes* 12 (1955), 333; *NATS* 23, No. 2 (1966), 8; *MelMS*, 198.

13. Knoxville: Summer of 1915: *NW* 31 (Apr 19, 1948), 84; *MQ* 34 (1948), 328; 35 (1949), 387; *Mus Club Mag* 29 (Dec 1949), 16; *Notes* 7 (1949-1950), 309; *MA* 70 (Jan 15, 1950), 89; *MC* 141 (Feb 15, 1950), 54; *Mus Club Mag* 29 (Feb 1950), 20; *Notes* 7 (Mar 1950), 309-310; *CiSPN* (Oct 21, 1950), 53-57; *Time* 74 (Nov 23, 1959), 72; *SR* 45 (Sep 29, 1962), 47; *Mus J* 25 (Dec 1967), 89; *Stereo Rev* 22 (Jun 1969), 75-76; 23 (Aug 1969), 8; *MelMN*, 202; *HitMU*, 211.

47. The Lovers: *NYT* (Jan 24, 1971), sec. 3, p. 15:5; (Sep 24, 1971), 36:6; (Oct 3, 1971), sec. 2, p. 15:5; (Oct 7, 1971), 56:1; *SR* 54 (Oct 23, 1971), 14-15; *Mus Ed J* 58 (Nov 1971), 16; *Sym News* 22, No. 6 (1971), 24; *Int Mus* 70 (Dec 1971), 11; *HiFi/MA* 22 (Jan 1972), MA23; *Mus J* 30 (Jan 1972), 75; *ASCAP* 5, No. 3 (1972), 30; *Pan Pipes* 64, No. 2 (1972), 28.

11. Medea: Ballet Suite: *Theatre Arts Mag* 31 (May 1947), 31; *POPN* 1947-1948), 311; *MQ* 34 (1948), 328; *Notes* 7 (1949-1950), 431; *MC* 141 (Feb 15, 1950), 54; *Musikleben* 6 (May 1953), 173; *SL Sym* (Jan 12, 1962), 317; *SF Sym* (Feb 28, 1962), 29; *Seattle Sym* (Oct 29, 1962), 9; *Clev Orch* (Nov 29, 1962), 284; *EweCB*, 11.

12. Medea's Meditation and Dance: *Time* 67 (Feb 13, 1956), 42; *MA* 76 (Feb 15, 1956), 223; *SR* 39 (Feb 18, 1956), 27; *MC* 153 (Mar 1, 1956), 14; *Notes* 14 (1956-1957), 449; *Mus Opin* 80 (Jan 1957), 221; (Apr 1957), 393; *Notes* 14 (Jun 1957), 449; *Dallas Sym* (Mar 31, 1969), 23-25; *NYT* (Jun 6, 1975), 3:1; *MacIC*, 552.

56. Mélodies passagères: *MQ* 38 (1952), 435; *Mus Opin* 76 (Oct 1952), 33; *MC* 146 (Nov 1, 1952), 29; *MA* 72 (Dec 1952), 26; *Notes* 10 (1952-1953), 497.

 3. Music for a Scene from Shelley: *NYT* (Apr 16, 1939), sec. 10, p. 7:8; *Detroit Sym* (Feb 23, 1967), 436.

30. Mutations from Bach: *NYT* (Oct 8, 1968), 42:2; *Am Mus Dgt* 1 (Dec 1969), 45.

17. Die Natali: *New Yorker* 36 (Jan 14, 1961), 106; *MA* 81 (Feb 1961), 16; *MC* 163 (Feb 1961), 13; *Okla Sym* (Dec 4, 1962), 122-124; *CiSPN* (Dec 14, 1962), 314-316; *Notes* 20 (1962-1963), 317; *Chi Sym* (Dec 19, 1968), 13-15.

55. Nuvoletta: *MC* 147 (Feb 15, 1953), 39; *MA* 74 (Feb 15, 1954), 224.

 2. Overture to The School for Scandal: *BSCBul* No. 15 (Feb 10, 1950), 793-794; *LAPS Mag* (Mar 30, 1950), 657; *ChiSPN* (Mar 1, 1951), 9; *NYPPN* (Mar 18, 1951); *BSCBul* No. 24 (Apr 25, 1952), 1137; *CiSPN* (Nov 7, 1952), 135.

44. Prayers of Kierkegaard: *NYT* (Dec 9, 1954), 40:3; *MC* 150 (Dec 15, 1954), 30; *New Yorker* 30 (Dec 18, 1954), 141; *Time* 64 (Dec 20, 1954), 57; *MC* 151 (Jan 1, 1955), 13; *MA* 75 (Jan 1, 1955), 14, 17; *Choral G* 7 (Jan 1955), 29; *London Mus* 10 (Jul 1955), 31-32; *Strad* 66 (Jul 1955), 85; *MQ* 41 (1955), 227; *MT* 86 (Aug 1955), 433-434; *Mus Opin* 79 (Dec 1955), 157; *MR* 19 (Aug 1957), 247; *CiSPN*, (Nov 1968), 128-140; *Am Mus Dgt* 1 (Oct 1969), 7; *Mus J* 34 (Jul 1976), 70; 35 (Dec 1977), 36; *MelMN*, 200.

32. Sonata for Piano: *MA* 70 (Feb 1950), 332; *MC* 141 (Feb 1, 1950), 29; (Feb 15, 1950), 42; *MQ* 36 (1950), 276-279; *Notes* 7 (Jun 1950), 448; *MR* 11 (Nov 1950), 329; *ML* 33 (Oct 1952), 352; *JAMS* 5 (1953), 145-146; *MR* 31 (1970) 123-135; *HiFi/MA* 22 (Jan 1972), 83; *Am Rec G* 38 (Apr 1972), 355; *EweCB*, 11; *HitMU*, 211.

26. Sonata for Violoncello and Piano: *Repertoire* 1 (Oct 1951), 50-51.

48. Songs: *MT* 91 (Jan 1950), 31; *Repertoire* 1 (Aug 1951), 17-22; *Mus Opin* 79 (Dec 1955), 157; *MR* 19 (Aug 1958), 247; *Opera News* 33 (Apr 19, 1969), 34; *HiFi/MA* 19 (Jul 1969), MA22-23; *Mus Ed J* 59 (May 1973), 14; *NYT* (May 2, 1974), 64:5; *World Mus* 16, No. 3 (1974), 77; *Melos* 4, No. 4 (1974), 238.

68. Souvenirs: *MC* 147 (Mar 15, 1953), 30; *Int Musician* 52 (Dec 1953), 11; *Mus Opin* 77 (Aug 1954), 651; *CiSPN* (Oct 22, 1954), 87-88; *Notes* 12 (Jun 1955), 483-484; *Center* 2 (Nov 1955), 2-5; *MA* 75 (Dec 1, 1955), 5.

43. A Stopwatch and an Ordnance Map: *MQ* 33 (1947), 136; *Mus Opin* 78 (Feb 1955), 285; *MR* 16 (Nov 1955), 341.

28. Summer Music for Woodwind Quintet: *NYT* (Nov 17, 1956), 17:8; *Notes* 15 (1957-1958), 148; *Mus Opin* 80 (Jul 1957), 599.

4. Symphony No. 1 (Symphony in One Movement): *NYT* (Dec 14, 1936), 28:8; *MA* 57 (Feb 10, 1937), 30; *NYT* (Mar 25, 1937), 29:3; (Mar 26, 1937), 24:1; *MA* 57 (Apr 10, 1937), 20; *NYT* (May 2, 1937), sec. 2, p. 10:6; *POPN* (1943-1944), 361; *Mus Opin* 74 (Jul 1951), 533; *MR* 13 (Aug 1952), 246; *POPN* (Jan 13, 1956), 367; *Pitt Sym* (Mar 23, 1962), 25; *SF Sym* (Jan 9, 1963), 15; *Pitt Sym* (Dec 30, 1965), 23; *Dallas Sym* (Oct 24, 1966), 13; *CiSPN* (Apr 3, 1969), 719-722; *Detroit Sym* (Nov 16-18, 1972), 155; *EweCB*, 9.

8. Symphony No. 2: *BSPN* (Mar 3, 1944); *MA* 64 (Mar 25, 1944), 21; *MQ* 35 (1949), 296; *POPN* (Jan 21, 1949), 491; *MC* 139 (Feb 15, 1949), 24; *Mus Opin* 73 (Jul 1950), 583; *MC* 142 (Dec 1, 1950), 42; *BSCBul* 21 (Apr 6, 1951), 1052; *MA* 71 (Apr 15, 1951), 6; *Mus Opin* 74 (Aug 1951), 589; *ML* 33 (Jan 1952), 89; *MR* 16 (May 1955), 161, 164; 17 (May 1956), 164; *SF Sym* (Mar 14, 1957), 583; *(EweCB*, 10.

22. Toccata Festiva: *NYT* (Oct 1, 1960), 10:3; *Diap* 51 (Nov 1, 1960), 3; *MA* 80 (Nov 1960), 23; *MC* 162 (Nov 1960), 20; *Am Org* 43 (Dec 1960), 19; *Pan Pipes* 54, No. 2 (1962), 2; *Phila Orch* (Oct 5, 1962), 15; *Hud Ruz* 21, No. 2-3 (1968), 62.

35. Under the Willow Tree (Vanessa, arr. for pno): *Notes* 21 (1963-1964), 249.

64. Vanessa: *NYT* (Jan 7, 1956), 21:3; (Nov 6, 1956), 31:6; (Mar 23, 1957); *MC* 156 (Oct 1957), 12; *NYT* (Jan 12, 1958), sec. 2, p. 9:3; (Jan 16, 1958), 33:1, 3; *Variety* 209 (Jan 22, 1958), 2; *SR* 41 (Jan 25, 1958), 41; *New Yorker* 33 (Jan 25, 1958), 108; *NYT* (Jan 26, 1958), sec. 2, p. 9:1; *NW* 51 (Jan 27, 1958), 62-63; *Time* 71 (Jan 27, 1958), 59-60; *Opera N* 5 (Jan 27, 1958), 22; *New Republic* 138 (Jan 27, 1958), 18; *Nation* 186 (Feb 1, 1958), 106; *NYT* (Feb 17, 22, 1958); *MA* 78 (Feb 1958), 5; *OeMZ* 13 (Feb 1958), 70-72; *MC* 157 (Feb 1958), 10; *BB* 70 (Mar 3, 1958), 9; *NYT* (Mar 17, 1958), 21:6; *Int Musician* 56 (Mar 1958), 36; *Neue ZFM* 119 (Mar 1958), 151-152; *Opera* 9 (Mar 1958), 165; *Schweiz Mus* 98 (Mar 1958), 133; *HiFi Mus* 5 (Mar 1958), 33; *Mus d'Oggi* 1 (Mar 1958), 197; *Theatre Arts* 42 (Mar 1958), 66-68; *Canon* 11 (Mar-Apr 1958), 284; *MQ* 44 (1958), 235; *NYT* (Apr 26, 1958), 14:4; *Musica* 12 (Apr 1958), 218-219; *NYT* (May 6, 1958), 34:3; (May 21, 1958), 32:4; *Art and Architecture* 75, No. 7 (Jul 1958), 4; *NYT* (Aug 13, 1958), 24:4; (Aug 17, 1958), 71:5; (Aug 19, 1958), 23:2; *SR* 41 (Sep 13, 1958), 65; *America* 99 (Sep 13, 1958), 629; *MA* 78 (Sep 1958), 6; *SR* 41 (Sep 27, 1958), 53; *Chesterian* 33 (Autumn 1958), 52; *MT* 99 (Oct 1958), 546; *Opera* 9 (Oct 1958), 621-623; *Musica* 12 (Oct 1958), 598; *MC* 158 (Oct 1958), 33; *Neue ZFM* 119 (Oct 1958), 590; *Mens En Mel* 13 (Oct 1958), 310; *Mus d'Oggi* 1 (Oct 1958), 505-506; *MR* 19 (Nov 1958), 325-327; *Am Rec G* 25 (Nov 1958), 178; *Mus Opin* 82 (Nov 1958), 103; *HiFi Mag* 8 (Nov 1958), 55-56; *NYT* (Jan 8, 1959), 26:1; *Variety* 213 (Jan 14, 1959), 2; *MA* 79 (Jan 15, 1959), 22; *NYT* (Jan 18, 1959), sec. 2, p. 9:1; (Feb 15, 1959), sec. 2, p. 9:7; *MC* 159 (Feb 1959), 41; *Opera* 10 (Apr 1959), 214; *Notes* 17 (1959-1960), 139; *Can Mus J* 4, No. 2 (1960), 44; *St. Cecilia* 10, No. 4 (1961), 36; *Mus d'Oggi* 4 (Jul-Aug 1961), 177; *Opera* 12 (Autumn 1961), 43; *Rass Mus* 31, No. 2 (1961), 131; *Opera N* 26 (Sep 30, 1961), 29; 28 (Dec 18, 1963), 34; *MA* 83 (Dec 1963), 268-270; *New Yorker* 41 (Mar 20, 1965), 174; *SR* 48 (Mar 27, 1965), 22; *Opera N* 29 (Apr 3, 1965) (whole issue); *Opera* 16 (May 1965), 334; *HiFi/MA* 15 (Jun

1965), 114; *SR/World* 1 (Jun 1, 1974), 44; *Wall St J* (May 31, 1978), 18; *Opera N* 42 (May 1978), 22-25; *Variety* 291 (Jun 21, 1978), 90; *Opera N* 43 (Aug 1978), 44; *Opera Can* 19, No. 3 (1978), 28; *HiFi/MA* 28 (Oct 1978), MA43; *Mus & Mus* 27 (Oct 1978), 39; *KolMO*, 591.

37. Wondrous Love: *Notes* 17 (1960), 479.

Dissertations about Samuel Barber and His Works

1. Albertson, John E. *A Study of Stylistic Elements of Samuel Barber's "Hermit Songs" and Franz Schubert's "Die Winterreise."* University of Missouri–Kansas City, 1969.

2. Arlton, Dean L. *American Piano Sonatas of the Twentieth Century: Selective Analyses and Annotated Index.* Columbia University, 1968. (Sonatas by Barber, Carter, Dello Joio, Griffes, Ives, Persichetti and Thomson)

3. Dailey, William A. *Techniques of Composition Used in Contemporary Works for Chorus and Orchestra on Religious Texts—as Important Representative Works of the Period from 1952 through 1962. The Following Works will be Considered: "Canticum Sacrum"–Stravinsky, "Prayers of Kierkegaard"–Barber, "Magnificat"–Hovhaness.* Catholic University of America, 1965.

4. Friedewald, Russell E. *A Formal and Stylistic Analysis of the Published Music of Samuel Barber.* State University of Iowa, 1957.

5. Hanson, John R. *Macroform in Selected Twentieth-Century Piano Concertos.* University of Rochester, Eastman School of Music, 1969.

6. James, Woodrow C. *The Use of Harmonic Tritone in Selected Passages from the Music of Representative Contemporary Composers.* Michigan State University, 1966.

7. Lickey, E. Harold. *An Analysis of Samuel Barber's "Knoxville: Summer of 1915."* Indiana University, 1970.

8. Pisciotta, Louis V. *Texture in the Choral Works of Selected Contemporary American Composers.* Indiana University, 1967. (Refers to music by Barber, Berger, Carter, Copland, Della Joio, Foss, Harris, Hovhaness, Schuman and Thompson)

9. Rhoades, Larry L. *Theme and Variation in Twentieth-Century Organ Literature: Analyses of Variations by Alain, Barber, Distler, Dupré, Duruflé and Sowerby.* Ohio State University, 1973.

10. Rickert, Lawrence G. *Selected American Song Cycles for Baritone Composed since 1945.* University of Illinois, 1965.

11. Robinson, Richard W. *Reading Contemporary Choral Literature: An Analytical Study of Selected Contemporary Choral Compositions with Recommendations for the Improvement of Choral Reading Skills.* Brigham Young University, 1969. (Analyzes compositions by Barber, Copland, Dello Joio, Foss, Ives, Persichetti, Pinkham and Schuman)

12. Service, Alfred R., Jr. *A Study of the Cadence as a Factor in Musical Intelligibility in Selected Piano Sonatas by American Composers.* State University of Iowa, 1958.

13. Walters, Willard G. *Technical Problems in Modern Violin Music as Found in Selected Concertos, with Related Original Exercises and Etudes.* State University of Iowa, 1958.

14. Wathen, Lawrence S. *Dissonance Treatment in the Instrumental Music of Samuel Barber.* Northwestern University, 1960.

15. Wolf, Henry S. *The Twentieth Century Piano Sonata.* Boston University, 1957. (Sonatas by Barber, Carter, Copland, Griffes, Harris, Ives, MacDowell and Shepherd)

OUTLINE II

JOHN ALDEN CARPENTER (1876 - 1951)

I. Life

1876   Born in Park Ridge, near Chicago, Illinois, February 28. A lineal descendant and namesake of the Pilgrim, John Alden. Studied piano with his mother and Amy Fay (1887-1891).

1893   Entered Harvard University; studied composition with John Knowles Paine.

1897   Graduated from Harvard with a Bachelor of Arts degree and entered his father's business in Chicago (mill, railway, shipping supplies). In 1909 he became vice-president and retired from the business in 1936. Lived in Chicago with frequent trips to Europe, and followed a successful career in music and business.

1900   Married Rue Winterbotham.

1906   Studied composition with Edward Elgar (Rome, summer 1906) and Bernhard Ziehn (Chicago, 1908-1912).

1915   First orchestral work, *Adventures in a Perambulator*, performed by the Chicago Symphony Orchestra.

1918   Elected a member of the National Institute of Arts and Letters.

1921   Made a Knight of the French Legion of Honor. Honorary Master of Arts degree from Harvard (1922); honorary Doctor of Music degrees from the University of Wisconsin (1933) and Northwestern University (1941).

1931   Married Ellen Waller Borden after the death of Rue Winterbotham Carpenter in 1929.

1936   Retired from business. A skilled composer, he continued to make music his avocation.

1947   Awarded the Gold Medal of the National Institute of Arts and Letters.

1951   Died, April 26, in Chicago.

John Alden Carpenter has been the recipient of many honors and commissions in addition to those listed above.

Note: Biographies of varying lengths and importance will be found in many of the books listed in the Bibliography at the end of this *Outline* under "References to John Alden Carpenter."

II. Compositions (published by G. Schirmer)

A. Orchestra

		Date
1.	Adventures in a Perambulator	1914
2.	Symphony No. 1 ("Sermons in Stone," from Shakespeare)	1917; revised 1940
3.	Birthday of the Infanta (ballet-pantomime)	1918; revised 1940
4.	A Pilgrim Vision	1920
5.	Krazy Kat (jazz-pantomime)	1921; revised 1948
6.	Skyscrapers (ballet suite)	1924
7.	Patterns (piano obbligato)	1932
8.	Sea Drift (tone poem, after Walt Whitman)	1933; revised 1944
9.	Danza	1935
10.	Symphony in One Movement (based on Symphony No. 1)	1940
11.	Symphony No. 2	1941; revised 1947
12.	Dance Suite (based on Polonaise, Tango, Danza, for piano)	1942

13.	The Anxious Bugler (symphonic poem)	1943
14.	The Seven Ages (symphonic poem, after Shakespeare)	1945
15.	Concerto for Orchestra (Carmel)	1948

B.   Concerto

16.	Concertino for Piano and Orchestra	1915; revised 1947
17.	Concerto for Violin and Orchestra	1936

C.   Chamber

18.	Sonata for Piano and Violin	1913
19.	String Quartet	1927
20.	Piano Quintet (pno, str qrt)	1934

D.   Piano

21.	Polonaise Américaine	1912
22.	Impromptu	1915
23.	Little Indian	1917
24.	Little Dancer	1918
25.	Tango Américaine	1920
26.	Diversions (5 pieces)	1923
27.	Danza	1947

E.   Choral (a cappella unless otherwise indicated)

28.	A Cradle Song (arr. SSAA; TTBB)	1911
29.	When I Bring You Colour'd Toys (arr. SATB; SSA)	1913
30.	The Sleep That Flits on Baby's Eyes (arr. SSA)	1913
31.	The Home Road (John Alden Carpenter) (arr. SATB; SAB; SSA)	1916
32.	Song of Faith (Carpenter, based on Walt Whitman and George Washington) (SATB, orch, pno or org, narrator)	1931
33.	Song of Freedom (Morris H. Martin) (unison chorus, pno or org)	1941

F.   Solo Vocal (with piano unless otherwise indicated)

34.	Improving Songs for Anxious Children (Rue Winterbotham Carpenter)	1902

a.	Scout	g.	Spring	m.	A Plan
b.	Practicing	h.	Varia Glutton	n.	Brother
c.	For Careless Children	i.	Good Ellen	o.	Making Calls
d.	Red Hair	j.	War	p.	Contemplation
e.	The Liar	k.	Vanity	q.	When the Night Comes
f.	A Wicked Child	l.	Humility		

35.	Go, Lovely Rose (Edmund Waller)	1908
36.	May the Maiden (Sidney Lanier)	1908
37.	Looking-Glass River (Robert Louis Stevenson)	1909
38.	The Green River (Douglas)	1909
39.	The Little Fly (William Blake)	1909
40.	Chanson d'Automne (Paul Verlaine)	1910
41.	Le Ciel (Paul Verlaine)	1910
42.	Il pleure dans mon coeur (Paul Verlaine)	1910
43.	Dansons la Gigue (Paul Verlaine)	1910
44.	Where the Misty Shadows (Paul Verlaine)	1911
45.	Don't Care (Barnes)	1911
46.	A Cradle Song (William Blake) (also SSAA; TTBB)	1911
47.	To One Unknown (Robert Dudley)	1912
48.	Les Silhouettes (Oscar Wilde)	1912
49.	Fog Wraiths (M. Howells)	1912
50.	Her Voice (Oscar Wilde)	1912
51.	Gitanjali ("Song-Offerings") (song cycle) (Rabindranath Tagore) (also with orch)	1913

    a.   When I Bring to You Colour'd Toys (also SATB; SSA)
    b.   On the Day When Death Will Knock at the Door

F.   Solo Vocal (cont.)
    c.   The Sleep That Flits on Baby's Eyes (also SSA)
    d.   I Am Like a Remnant of a Cloud
    e.   On the Seashore of Endless Worlds
    f.   Light, My Light

52. The Player-Queen (William Butler Yeats)	1914
53. The Day is No More (Rabindranath Tagore)	1915
54. Water-Colors (four Chinese tone-poems, translated by H. A. Giles) (with cham orch)	1915

    a.   On a Screen   c.   The Highwaymen
    b.   The Odalisque   d.   To a Young Gentleman

55. The Home Road (J. A. Carpenter) (also SATB; SAB; SSA)	1917
56. Berceuse de la Guerre (Émile Cammaerts)	1918
57. Serenade: Slumber Song (Siegfried Sassoon)	1920
58. Four Negro Songs (Langston Hughes)	1926

    a.   Shake Your Brown Feet, Honey   c.   Jazz Boys
    b.   The Cryin' Blues   d.   That Soothin' Song

G.   **Ballet**

59. The Birthday of the Infanta (after Oscar Wilde)	1918
60. Krazy Kat (after George Herriman cartoons)	1921
61. Skyscrapers (a ballet of modern American life)	1924

III.   Style (techniques and devices)

"All music that lives is based on a mood, whether directly or indirectly." "Cut yourself off from all tradition. Get loose! I'm from New England and I know what a Puritanical influence can do." "With only a few exceptions everything that I have written has started from a non-musical basis."

John Alden Carpenter

A.   General characteristics
1.   A conservative-modernist; a careful workman with facile melodic invention. A large part of his music is based on literary sources. Humor and fantasy are an important part of his style (*Adventures in a Perambulator*).
2.   Early works, mainly songs, show the influence of French impressionism. Some use of classical form (*Sonata for Piano and Violin*, 1911).
3.   Program music with extensive use of descriptive ideas adapted to American subjects (*Skyscrapers*, 1924). One of the first American composers to use the jazz idiom in serious music (*Krazy Kat*, 1921).
4.   Trend toward absolute music (*String Quartet*, 1927) with some French impressionism (*Sea Drift*, 1933); use of the complex rhythms and devices formerly used in program music. After his retirement in 1936, he wrote several non-programmatic orchestral works.

B.   Melodic line
1.   Generally flowing and graceful with small intervals, particularly in the songs.
2.   Blues melody: *Skyscrapers* (p. 89, meas. 1; p. 93, meas. 7; p. 97, meas. 7).
3.   Whole-tone scale: *Concertino* (p. 59, meas. 4).
4.   Chromatic line: *Sea Drift* (p. 25, meas. 2).
5.   Recurring themes: *Adventures* (My Nurse; The Perambulator; Myself).
6.   Flatted sevenths and mediants: *Skyscrapers* (p. 90).
7.   Popular melodies: *Skyscrapers* (pp. 65, 112); *Concertino* (closing pages); *Adventures* (p. 29).

C.   Harmony
1.   Extensive use of triads and sevenths diatonically, ninths, elevenths, added tones;

parallel chords, chromaticism, whole-tone chords, particularly in impressionistic works.
2.   Chromatic: *Sonata Pno Vln* (p. 19); *Piano Quintet* (p. 1); *Green River*.
3.   Whole-tone progressions: *Green River*.
4.   Parallel sevenths: *Krazy Kat* (p. 4); *Sea Drift* (p. 18).
5.   Parallel augmented triads: *Birthday* (p. 103).
6.   Added sixths (jazz influence): *Skyscrapers* (p. 90).
7.   Chords built on fourths: *String Quartet* (p. 3, meas. 4).
8.   Chords built on fifths: *Piano Quintet* (pp. 38-40).
9.   Cacophony: *Skyscrapers* (p. 6).

D.   Counterpoint
1.   Style basically homophonic, with almost no use of melodic counterpoint.
2.   Free canonic imitation: *Sonata Pno Vln* (p. 12, meas. 9).
3.   Use of jazz ostinato: *Skyscrapers* (p. 32).

E.   Rhythm
1.   Jazz influence and rhythms: *Krazy Kat* (p. 28, meas. 8); *Skyscrapers* (p. 32, meas. 2-6; pp. 50, 69, 74, 90, 103); *Patterns*; *Four Negro Songs*.
2.   Spanish influence: *Birthday* (pp. 42, 48); *Concertino* (pp. 10, 45); *Danza*; *String Quartet* (last section).
3.   Quintuple meter: *Skyscrapers* (p. 7); *Concertino* (third movement).
4.   Cross accents: *Skyscrapers* (pp. 36, 42); *Quartet* (p. 3).
5.   Irregular rhythmic division of the measure (4/4 = 3 + 2 + 3): *Skyscrapers* (p. 50).
6.   Quadruple and triple patterns together: *Concertino*.
7.   Changing time signatures: *Skyscrapers* (throughout); *Birthday* (p. 107).
8.   Percussive rhythmic effects: *Piano Quintet* (piano, p. 50, meas. 2).
9.   Polymeter: *Serenade* (p. 116).

F.   Form
1.   Sonata-allegro: *Sonata Pno Vln* (Theme I, p. 3, meas. 5; Theme II, meas. 15; Development, meas. 49; Recapitulation, p. 8).
2.   Cyclic: *Sonata Pno Vln*; *String Quartet*.
3.   Rondo: *Sonata Pno Vln* (second movement: A - B - A - C - A - D - B).
4.   A - B - A: *Sonata Pno Vln* (third movement); *Concertino* (second movement).

G.   Orchestration (*Skyscrapers*)
1.   Colorful, descriptive, sometimes overly elaborate. Frequent use of harp, celesta, piano, glockenspiel.
2.   Three saxophones (p. 114); banjo (p. 121).
3.   Traffic lights (p. 3), three anvils (p. 18); whistle, thunder machine, two pianos.
4.   Percussive use of piano: *Piano Quintet*.

BIBLIOGRAPHY

Articles by John Alden Carpenter

1.   "New Spirit in American Musical Composition," *Current Opinion* 54 (Jan 1913), 32-33.
2.   "Gallery of Musical Celebrities," *Etude* 48 (Feb 1930), 101-102.
3.   "A Letter from the Choral and Instrumental Association of Chicago," *Recreation* (Oct 1947).
4.   "A Letter about Bernhard Ziehn," *MQ* 37 (1951), 435.

References to John Alden Carpenter

Books
(See the General Bibliography)

ASC-BD; ASC-SC; AusMT; Baker; BakSL; BauTC; BIM; Bull; CatPC; ChaAC; ChaAM; CopCM; CopON; CurB (1947, 1951); DowO; DukLH; EdMUS; EweAC; EweCB; EweCS; EweDE; EweMC; GosMM; Grove; HitMU; HodSD; HowMM; HowOA; HowOC; HowSH; JohSH; KinAI; KolMA; LeiMW; LeiSK; MacIC; MelMS; MorrCA; MueAS; PanMC; PavMH; PersTH; ReiAC; ReiCC; SalMO; SanWM; SloMS; SpaMH; StevHS; ThoAM; ThompIC; ThoMR; UptAS; WWA (1946-1947); YatTC; YouCD; YouCT; International Who's Who, 1947.

Rosenfeld, Paul. *Musical Chronicle.* New York: Harcourt Brace, 1923.

Articles

1. Brief mention: *MQ* 7 (1921), 305; 8 (1922), 612; 9 (1923), 123, 148; 11 (1925), 376, 392; 15 (1929), 292; 18 (1932), 11, 100; 19 (1933), 47, 169, 356, 357; *Time* 31 (Jun 27, 1938), 36; *MQ* 25 (1939), 266; *MM* 17 (1939-1940), 256; *PNM* 2, No. 2 (1963), 17.
2. Gunn, G. D. "The Present State of American Music," *MTNAPro* 13 (1918), 34.
3. Maxwell, Leon R. "America's Contribution to Song Literature," *MTNAPro* 14 (1919), 154.
4. Mason, Daniel Gregory. "Music as Decoration; Mr. J. A. Carpenter Uses It in His New Pantomime, Birthday of the Infanta," *Arts and Decoration* 12 (Mar 1920), 322.
5. Gilman, Lawrence. "Monsieur Satie and Mr. Carpenter," *North American Rev* 215 (May 1922), 692-697.
6. Strickland-Anderson, Lily. "Rabindranath Tagore, Poet-Composer, an Appreciation," *MQ* 10 (1924), 463.
7. Upton, William Treat. "Some Recent Representative American Song Composers," *MQ* 11 (1925), 392.
8. Hanson, Howard. "A Forward Look in American Composition," *MTNAPro* 20 (1925), 119.
9. Jones, Robert Edmond. "Two Settings for *Skyscrapers,*" *MM* 3, No. 2 (1925-1926), 21.
10. Sanborn, Pitts. "Making the Grand Tour," *MM* 6, No. 3 (1928-1929), 35.
11. Thorpe, H. C. "Interpretative Studies in American Song," *MQ* 15 (1929), 88.
12. Downes, Olin. "John Alden Carpenter, American Craftsman," *MQ* 16 (1930), 442.
13. Borowski, Felix. "John Alden Carpenter: with List of Compositions," *MQ* 16 (1930), 449.
14. Rosenfeld, Paul. "Taylor, Carpenter and Loeffler," *New Republic* 66 (Mar 18, 1931), 128.
15. Howard, John Tasker. "John Alden Carpenter," *MM* 9, No. 1 (1931-1932), 8.
16. Thompson, Randall. "The Contemporary Scene in American Music," *MQ* 18 (1932), 9.
17. "Engaged to E. W. Borden," *NYT* (Jan 11, 1933), 16:7; (Jan 25, 1933), 12:7.
18. "Marriage," *NYT* (Jan 31, 1933), 21:5.
19. Sargeant, Winthrop. "Bernhard Ziehn, Precursor," *MQ* 19 (1933), 169, 441.
20. "Returns to U. S. from Sweden," *NYT* (Oct 2, 1937), 18:5.
21. "Carpenter Returns from Sweden," *MA* 57 (Oct 1937), 32.
22. "Boston Men Play Carpenter Music," *MA* 59 (Mar 1939), 11.
23. "Orchestras," *MA* 59 (Dec 1939), 12.
24. "Peaceful Music," *Time* 36 (Nov 4, 1940), 58.
25. "Music in Recreation," *Recreation* 40 (Oct 1946), 352-353.
26. "Wins Gold Medal, from National Institute of Arts and Letters," *NYT* (Feb 14, 1947), 19: 6; (May 23, 1947), 18:5.
27. "Biography," *Current Biography* (May 1947); *Current Biography Yearbook* (1947), 94-96.

28. "John Alden Carpenter," *Pan Pipes* 43 (Dec 1950), 114.
29. Hanson, Howard. "John Alden Carpenter," *SR* 34 (Feb 24, 1951), 50.
30. "Receives National Arts Foundation Award," *NYT* (Feb 28, 1951), 31:2.
31. "75th Birthday," *NYT* (Mar 1, 1951), 32:5.
32. Leonard, W. "Carpenter Birthday Observed in Chicago Symphony Season," *MA* 71 (Apr 1, 1951), 21.
33. "Obituary," *NYT* (Apr 27, 1951), 23:4; *Am Org* 34 (Apr 1951), 130; *Variety* 182 (May 2, 1951), 75; *BB* 63 (May 5, 1951), 48; *MA* 71 (May 7, 1951), 24; *NW* 37 (May 7, 1951), 58; *Time* 57 (May 7, 1951), 86; *MT* 92 (Jun 1951), 280; *Violins* 12 (Jun-Jul 1951), 180; *Current Biography* (May 1951); *Current Biography Yearbook* (1951), 99.
34. "John Alden Carpenter: a Musical Humanist," *MA* 71 (May 1951), 12.
35. "John Alden Carpenter Dies," *Symphony* 5 (May 1951), 3.
36. "Carpenter Among Notables Lost by Music," *MC* 143 (May 15, 1951), 7.
37. "Opera has Lost," *Opera News* 16 (Dec 17, 1951), 31.
38. Mitchell, William J. "Review of Bernhard Ziehn by H. J. Moser," *MQ* 37 (1951), 435.
39. "AmerAllegro," *Pan Pipes* 44 (Jan 1952), 23.
40. *NYT* (Jul 28, 1952), 12:4.
41. "Stage Honors Memory of John Alden Carpenter," *MA* 72 (Sep 1952), 24.
42. Cook, J. Douglas. "Composer tells how," *SR* 37 (June 26, 1954), 41.
43. Keats, Sheila. "Reference Articles on American Composers: an Index," *Juilliard Rev* 1 (Fall 1954), 24.
44. Waters, Edward N. "Annual Report on Acquisitions: Music," *Q Jl of Current Acq* 18 (Nov 1960), 17.
45. Hager, Mina. "Speak for Yourself, John Alden Carpenter," *Mus J* 28 (Mar 1970), 66-67.
46. "100th Anniversary of John Alden Carpenter," *Pan Pipes* 68, No. 20 (1976), 26.

References to Works by John Alden Carpenter

1. Adventures in a Perambulator: *ChiSPN* (Mar 19, 1915); *NYT* (Nov 8, 1915); *North American Rev* 202 (Dec 1915), 912-914; *BSPN* (Dec 24, 1915); *MQ* 16 (1930), 452; 23 (1937), 41; 38 (1952), 482; *EweCB*, 55.
3. Birthday of the Infanta: *BSPN* (Feb 25, 1921); *MQ* 9 (1923), 125; 16 (1930), 462; *ChiSPN* (Feb 27, 1951), 9; *GosMM*, 37.
16. Concertino for Piano: *BSPN* (Feb 13, 1920); *ChiSPN* (Mar 18, 1967), 33.
15. Concerto for Orchestra (Carmel): *NYPPN* (Nov 20, 1949); *Opera* 14 (Dec 1949), 38; *MA* 69 (Dec 15, 1949), 8.
17. Concerto for Violin: *MA* 57 (Nov 25, 1937), 26; *BSPN* (Mar 3, 1939); *MA* 59 (Mar 25, 1939), 11.
9. Danza: *BSPN* (Jan 17, 1936).
51. Gitanjali: *MQ* 16 (1930), 451.
5. Krazy Kat: *ChiSPN* (Dec 23, 1921); *Vanity Fair* (Apr 1922); *Lit Dgt* 73 (Apr 15, 1922), 33; *New Republic* 32 (Oct 11, 1922), 175-176; *MQ* 9 (1923), 148, 474; 16 (1930), 452; 21 (1935), 53; *NYT* (Jul 30, 1975), 15:1; *HitMU*, 178.
7. Patterns: *BSPN* (Oct 21, 1932).
26. Piano Pieces: *MQ* 16 (1930), 458.
8. Sea Drift: *ChiSPN* (Nov 30, 1933); *NYHT* (Nov 4, 1934); *MC* 143 (Jun 1951), 16-17; *EweCB*, 57.
14. The Seven Ages: *NYT* (Nov 25, 1945), sec. 2, p. 4:6; *GosMM*, 43.
6. Skyscrapers: *Metropolitan Opera Program* (Feb 19, 1926); *Outlook* 142 (Mar 3, 1926), 314-315; *Lit Dgt* 88 (Mar 13, 1926), 24-25; *Survey* 56 (Apr 1, 1926), 35-37; *BSPN* (Dec 9, 1927); *Christian Science Monitor* (Dec 10, 1927); *MQ* 15 (1929), 621; 16 (1930), 464; 19 (1933), 356; *MA* (Dec 10, 1939), 27; *ChiSPN* (Feb 27, 1951), 13; *EweCB*, 56; *GosMM*, 39; *MacIC*, 155; *HitMU*, 178.

32. Song of Faith: *BSPN* (Feb 23, 1932); *NYHT* (May 1, 1932); *GosMM*, 40.
     Songs: *MQ* 11 (1925), 392; 15 (1929), 126; 16 (1930), 451.
19. String Quartet: *MQ* 16 (1930), 45; *NYT* (Feb 12, 1931), 21:2.
10. Symphony in One Movement: *NYHT* (Nov 23, 1940).
 2. Symphony No. 1: *BSPN* (Apr 19, 1918).
11. Symphony No. 2: *NYPPN* (Oct 22, 1942); *NYHT* (Oct 23, 1942).

Dissertation about John Alden Carpenter and His Works

Pierson, Thomas C. *The Life and Music of John Alden Carpenter.* Rochester, NY: University of
     Rochester, Eastman School of Music, 1952.

OUTLINE III

ELLIOTT (COOK) CARTER, Jr. (b. 1908)

I. Life

1908   Born in New York City, December 11, of well-to-do parents.

1922   Attended the Horace Mann High School (1922-1926); developed an interest in music and received the encouragement of Charles Ives who lived near by (1924-1925).

1926   Entered Harvard University; majored in English literature. Studied music privately with Newton Swift (piano) and Hans Ebell (solfeggio) at the Longy School of Music, Cambridge. Continued the study of music with Walter Piston (harmony and counterpoint) and visiting professor Gustav Holst (composition).

1930   Graduated from Harvard (Bachelor of Arts degree). Continued studies as a graduate student with Walter Piston, Archibald T. Davison (choral composition), Gustav Holst, Edward Burlingame Hill (music history) (Master of Arts degree, 1932).

1932   Studied in Paris with Nadia Boulanger (1932-1935). Graduated from the *École Normale de Musique* with a *Licence de contrepoint* (1935). Also learned mathematics, Latin and Greek. First compositions for Harvard productions (1933-1936).

1935   Returned to the United States; came to New York to live in 1936.

1936   Music Director of the Ballet Caravan (1937-1939). Began to write articles for *Modern Music* (1937).

1939   Married Helen Frost-Jones, a sculptor and art critic. First performance of the short ballet, *Pocahontas*. Head of music department at St. John's College, Annapolis, MD. Also taught mathematics, physics, philosophy and Greek (1939-1941).

1942   Completed *Symphony No. 1*. Served as music consultant with the Office of War Information (1943).

1945   Awarded first Guggenheim Fellowship (*Sonata for Piano*).

1946   Professor of composition, Peabody Conservatory of Music, Baltimore (1946-1948). Composed mostly chamber music (1947-1954).

1948   Professor of composition, Columbia University (1948-1950).

1950   Awarded second Guggenheim Fellowship (*String Quartet No. 1*).

1953   Awarded American Prix de Rome. Won first prize in the *Concours International de Composition pour Quatuor à Cordes* in Liège (*String Quartet No. 1*).

1956   Elected a member of the National Institute of Arts and Letters.

1958   Taught at the Salzburg Seminars in Austria.

1960   Awarded the Pulitzer Prize for Music; New York Music Critics Circle Award; in 1961, UNESCO Citation (*String Quartet No. 2*). Professor of composition, Yale University (1960-1962).

1961   Awarded the honorary Doctor of Music degree, New England Conservatory of Music.

1962   Composer-in-residence, American Academy, Rome. Also held a similar position in West Berlin (1964). Was the American delegate to the East-West Encounter in Tokyo.

1964   Elected a member of the American Academy of Arts and Sciences.

1965   Received the Creative Arts Award from Brandeis University.

1968   Professor-at-large, Cornell University.

1973   Received his third Pulitzer Prize (*String Quartet No. 3*).

Elliott Carter has been the recipient of many honors, awards and commissions in addition to those listed above.

Note: Biographies of varying lengths and importance will be found in many of the books listed in the Bibliography at the end of this *Outline* under "References to Elliott Carter."

II. Compositions

A. Orchestra

		Date	Publisher
1.	Prelude, Fanfare and Polka (cham orch)	1938	AMP
2.	Pocahontas (ballet suite)	1941	AMP
3.	Symphony No. 1	1942	AMP
4.	Holiday Overture	1944; revised 1961	AMP
5.	Elegy for Strings (arr. from vla, pno)	1946	Peer
6.	The Minotaur (ballet suite)	1947	AMP
7.	Variations for Orchestra	1955	AMP
8.	Symphony for Three Orchestras	1976	

B. Concerto

9.	Concerto for English Horn	1937	
10.	Double Concerto for Harpsichord, Piano, with two cham orch	1961	AMP
11.	Concerto for Piano	1965	
12.	Concerto for Orchestra	1969	AMP

C. Chamber

13.	Sonata for Flute	1934	
14.	Canonic Suite for Quartet of Alto Saxophones	1939	AMP
	Fanfare; Nocturne; Tarantella		
15.	Pastoral for Viola (or E-hn or clar), Piano	1943	NME
16.	Adagio for Viola and Piano	1943	
17.	Elegy for Viola (or vlc) and Piano	1943	Peer
18.	Elegy for String Quartet (arr. from No. 17)	1946	Peer
19.	Sonata for Violoncello and Piano	1948	AMP
20.	Woodwind Quintet (fl, ob, clar, bsn, hn)	1948	AMP
21.	Eight Etudes and a Fantasy (fl, ob, clar, bsn)	1950	AMP
22.	Eight Pieces for Four Timpani (one player)	1950-1966	AMP

  a. Saëta (1950-1966) e. Improvisation (1950-1966)
  b. Moto perpetuo (1950-1966) f. Canto (1966)
  c. Adagio (1966) g. Canaries (1950-1966)
  d. Recitative (1950-1966) h. March (1950-1966)

23.	String Quartet No. 1	1951	AMP
24.	Sonata for Flute, Oboe, Violoncello and Harpsichord	1952	AMP
25.	Canonic Suite for Four Clarinets (from No. 14)	1945	AMP
26.	String Quartet No. 2	1959	
27.	String Quartet No. 3	1971	
28.	Canon for 3 (3 equal instruments: 3 trpt or trpt, clar, ob)	1972	AMP
29.	Brass Quintet (2 trpt, hn, 2 trb)	1974	AMP
30.	Duo for Violin and Piano	1974	AMP

D. Piano

31.	Sonata for Piano	1946	MP

E. Choral (a cappella unless otherwise indicated)

32.	Tarantella (Ovid) (TTBB, orch)	1936	
33.	To Music (Robert Herrick) (SATB)	1937	Peer
34.	The Bridge (oratorio)	1937	
35.	Madrigal Book for mixed voices	1937	
36.	Heart Not so Heavy as Mine (Emily Dickinson) (SATB)	1938	
37.	The Defense of Corinth (François Rabelais) (Sp., TTBB, pno 4 hands or 2 pno)	1941	Mm
38.	The Harmony of Morning (Mark van Doren) (SSAA, cham orch or pno)	1944	AMP

E.	Choral (cont.)		
39.	Musicians Wrestle Everywhere (Emily Dickinson) (SSATB, a cappella or with str orch)	1945	Merc
40.	Emblems (Allen Tate) (TTBB, pno)	1947	Merc
F.	**Solo Vocal** (with piano unless otherwise indicated)		
41.	Tell Me Where is Fancy Bred (William Shakespeare) (voice, guitar)	1938	AMP
42.	Dust of Snow (Robert Frost)	1942	AMP
43.	The Line Gang (Robert Frost)	1943	AMP
44.	The Rose Family (Robert Frost)	1943	AMP
45.	Voyage (Hart Crane)	1943	VMP
46.	Warble for Lilac Time (Walt Whitman) (pno or cham orch)	1943	Peer
47.	A Mirror on Which to Dwell (Elizabeth Bishop) (S., nine players) cycle of six poems	1975	
G.	**Opera**		
48.	Tom and Lily (three-act comic)	1934	
H.	**Ballet**		
49.	The Ball Room Guide	1937	
50.	Pocahontas	1939	AMP
51.	The Minotaur	1947	AMP
I.	**Incidental Music**		
52.	The Merchant of Venice (alto voice, guitar)	1938	AMP

Note: The following abbreviations are used in Section III of this *Outline*. The number indicates the number of the composition as listed in Section II.

37.	*Defense*: The Defense of Corinth	19.	*Son Vlc*: Sonata for Violoncello and Piano	
18.	*Elegy*: Elegy for String Quartet			
21.	*Etudes*: Eight Etudes and a Fantasy	31.	*Son Pno*: Sonata for Piano	
38.	*Harmony*: The Harmony of Morning	23.	*Str Qrt 1*: String Quartet No. 1	
39.	*Musicians*: Musicians Wrestle Everywhere	3.	*Sym 1*: Symphony No. 1	
		7.	*Variations*: Variations for Orchestra	

III.   Style (techniques and devices)

"I have tried to give musical expression to experiences anyone living today must have when confronted with so many remarkable examples of unexpected types of changes and relationships of character uncovered . . . in every domain of science and art." "I like music to be beautiful, ordered and expressive of the more important aspects of life."   Elliott Carter

A.   General characteristics
1.   Continuous development of a new and highly original style through the assimilation and synthesis of modern techniques of Stravinsky, Bartók, Schoenberg, Hindemith, Berg and Ives.
2.   Complete mastery of techniques, expressiveness and outstanding developments, particularly in rhythm and tempo, are found in the *Sonata for Piano* (1946), *Sonata for Violoncello and Piano* (1948), *Variations for Orchestra* (1955), *String Quartet No. 2* (1959).
3.   Precise directions for performance.
B.   Melodic line
1.   Independence of each part achieved by use of characteristic intervals and rhythms and placing players apart: *Str Qtr 2*.
2.   Irregular: *Musicians*.

3.   Dominating interval of a second: *Etudes*.
4.   Lyrical: *Str Qrt 1* (vla, meas. 200-290).
C.   Harmony
"The tendency to fad has been greatly encouraged by the promulgation of systems, particularly harmonic systems."   Elliott Carter
1.   Simple harmonic material: *Elegy*.
2.   Chromatic (non-twelve-tone): *Variations*.
3.   Parallel (tonal): *Variations* (p. 52).
4.   Combination of mixed intervals: *Str Qrt 1* (p. 29).
5.   Influence of twelve-tone techniques: *Variations*.
6.   Overtones from depressed keys: *Son Pno* (p. 27).
7.   Polychordal: *Sym 1*.
8.   Dominating chord (E, F, A-flat, B-flat) and its intervals used thematically: *Str Qtr 1*.
D.   Counterpoint
1.   Basic style is contrapuntal.
2.   Very dissonant: *Woodwind Quintet*; *Holiday*.
3.   Long contrapuntal lines: *Str Qtr 1*.
4.   Fugal techniques: *Defense*.
5.   Canonic writing: *Defense*; *Harmony*.
6.   Cross accents: *Musicians*; *Son Pno*; *Str Qrt 1*.
7.   Invertible: *Str Qrt 1*.
E.   Rhythm
1.   Developed extraordinary rhythmic complexities leading to "metrical modulation" ("passing from one metronomic speed to another by lengthening or shortening the value of the basic note unit").
2.   Metrical modulation: *Son Vlc*; *Etudes* (*Fantasy*); *Str Qrt 1*; *Variations*.
3.   Polyrhythm: *Str Qrt 1*.
4.   Changing time signatures: *Str Qrt 1* (p. 5).
5.   Syncopated: *Emblems* (last movement).
6.   Simultaneous accelerandos and ritards: *Double Concerto*.
7.   Shifted accents: *Musicians*; *Son Pno*.
8.   Changing speeds at different times in all four instruments: *Str Qrt 1* (first and last movements).
9.   Quick changing metronome markings in the same meter: *Variations* (Nos. 4, 6).
10.   Different meters in all four parts of one measure: *Str Qrt 1* (No. 290); *Str Qrt 2* (Tempo giusto).
11.   Characteristic rhythms for each instrument: *Str Qrt 2*.
12.   Unusual time signatures (10/16, 21/8): *Str Qrt 1*; *Son Vlc*.
F.   Form
1.   Variation as a basic principle: *Str Qrt 1* (last movement); *Variations*.
2.   Meter used as a basis of form: *Son Pno*.
3.   Tempo used as a structural element: *Str Qrt 1, 2*.
4.   Unique: *Str Qrt 2*.
5.   Cyclic devices: *Son Pno* (slow sections, movements 1, 2); *Son Vlc* (first subject reappears at end).
6.   Cantus firmus variations: *Harmony*.
7.   Ostinato: *Minotaur*.
G.   Orchestration
1.   A master of orchestration. Frequent use of unusual groups of instruments.
2.   Very large percussion section: *Double Concerto*.

BIBLIOGRAPHY

Books about Elliott Carter

1. Edwards, Allen F. and E. C. Edwards. *Flawed Words and Stubborn Sounds: A Conversation with Elliott Carter.* New York: W. W. Norton, 1971. Reviews in *Mus & Mus* No. 1 (Jan 1972), 3-6; *Instrument* 26 (Feb 1972), 13; *Mus J* 30 (Feb 1972), 13; *Tempo* No. 99 (1972), 22-24; *Notes* 29, No. 2 (1972), 249-251; *Mus Ed J* 59 (May 1973), 82-83; *PNM* 11, No. 2 (1973), 146-155.
2. Jackson, Richard. *Elliott Carter: Sketches and Scores in Manuscript.* New York: New York Public Library, 1973. Review in *Notes* 31, No. 3 (1975), 568.
3. Stone, Else, and Kurt Stone, eds. *The Writings of Elliott Carter—An American Composer Looks at Modern Music.* Bloomington: Indiana University Press, 1977.

Articles by Elliott Carter

1. "New York Season, 1937," *MM* 14, No. 2 (1936-1937), 90.
2. "Late Winter, New York," *MM* 14, No. 3 (1936-1937), 147.
3. "The Sleeping Beauty," *MM* 14, No. 3 (1936-1937), 173.
4. "Season's End in New York," *MM* 14, No. 4 (1936-1937), 237.
5. "With the Dancers," *MM* 14, No. 4 (1936-1937), 55.
6. "Opening Notes, New York," *MM* 15, No. 1 (1937-1938), 36.
7. "In the Theatre," *MM* 15, No. 1 (1937-1938), 45.
8. "With the Dancers." *MM* 15, No. 1 (1937-1938), 55.
9. "Homage to Ravel," *MM* 15, No. 2 (1937-1938), 96.
10. "Vacation Novelties, New York," *MM* 15, No. 2 (1937-1938), 96.
11. "With the Dancers," *MM* 15, No. 2 (1937-1938), 118.
12. "Orchestras and Audiences, Winter, 1938," *MM* 15, No. 3 (1937-1938), 167.
13. "Musical Reactions," *MM* 15, No. 3 (1937-1938), 199.
14. "Season's End, New York, Spring, 1938," *MM* 15, No. 4 (1937-1938), 228.
15. "Recent Festival in Rochester," *MM* 15, No. 4 (1937-1938), 243.
16. "Coolidge Crusade; WPA; New York Season," *MM* 16, No. 1 (1938-1939), 33.
17. "Once Again Swing; Also 'American Music'," *MM* 16, No. 2 (1938-1939), 99.
18. "The Case of Mr. Ives: Winter Notes," *MM* 16, No. 3 (1938-1939), 172.
19. "O Fair World of Music!" *MM* 16, No. 4 (1938-1939), 238.
20. "Season of Hindemith and Americans," *MM* 16, No. 4 (1938-1939), 249.
21. "New York Season Opens," *MM* 17, No. 1 (1939-1940), 34.
22. "American Music on the New York Scene," *MM* 17, No. 2 (1939-1940), 93.
23. "Stravinsky and Other Moderns in 1940," *MM* 17, No. 3 (1939-1940), 164.
24. "The Changing Scene, New York," *MM* 17, No. 4 (1939-1940), 237.
25. "Composers by the Alphabet,"*MM* 19, No. 1 (1941-1942), 70.
26. "Films and Theatre," *MM* 20, No. 2 (1942-1943), 205.
27. "Theatre and Films," *MM* 20, No. 4 (1942-1943), 282.
28. "American Figure, with Landscape," (Henry Franklin Gilbert) *MM* 20, No. 4 (1942-1943), 219.
29. "Theatre and Films," *MM* 21, No. 1 (1943-1944), 50.
30. "New Compositions," *SR* 27 (Jan 22, 1944), 32.
31. "Charles Ives: His Vision and Challenge," *MM* 21, No. 4 (1943-1944), 199.
32. "Music as a Liberal Art," *MM* 22, No. 1 (1944-1945), 12.
33. "What's New in Music," *SR* 28 (Jan 20, 1945), 13.
34. "Gabriel Fauré," *Listen* 6, No. 1 (May 1945), 8.
35. "New Publications of Music," *SR* 29 (Jan 26, 1946), 34.
36. "Walter Piston," *MQ* 32 (1946), 354-373.

37. "The Composer's Viewpoint [The League of Composers]," *National Music Council Bulletin* 7, No. 1 (Sep 1946), 10.
38. "An American Destiny," [Ives] *Listen* 9, No. 1 (Nov 1946), 4.
39. "Scores for Graham: Festival at Columbia," *MM* 23, No. 1 (1946), 53-55.
40. "Fallacy of the Mechanistic Approach [The Schillinger System]," *MM* 23, No. 3 (1946), 228.
41. "Wallingford Riegger," *ACA-Bul* 2, No. 1 (1952).
42. "Function of the Composer in Teaching the General College Student," *Bulletin of the Society of Music in the Liberal Arts College* 3, No. 1 (1952), Supplement, p. 3.
43. "The Rhythmic Basis of American Music," *Score* 12 (Jun 1955), 27.
44. "Autobiographical Sketch" in *The 25th Anniversary Report of the Harvard Class of 1930*. Cambridge: Harvard University Press, 1955, p. 165.
45. "Music in the Twentieth Century." in the *Encyclopedia Britannica*, v. 16 (1957) under "Music," p. 16.
46. "Roger Sessions' Music," *MQ* 45 (1959), 375-381.
47. "Current Chronicle: Italy," *MQ* 45 (1959), 530-541.
48. "Sixty Staves to Read," *NYT* (Jan 24, 1960), sec. 2, p. 9:7.
49. "Shop Talk by an American Composer," *MQ* 46 (1960), 189-201; also in *LanPM,* 51; *HayTV,* 411.
50. "Current Chronicle: Germany," *MQ* 46 (1960), 367-371.
51. Elliott Carter and Vladimir Ussachevsky, "Reel vs. Real," *ASOL* 11, Nos. 5-6 (1960), 8-10.
52. "The Milieu of the American Composer," *PNM* 1, No. 1 (1962), 149.
53. "An American Destiny," *BSPN* (Nov 2, 1962), 355.
54. "Letters to the Editor ('Artificial Divisions' in our Present System of Notation)," *J Mus Theory* 7, No. 2 (1963), 270-273.
55. "Letter from Europe," *PNM* 1, No. 2 (1963), 195-205.
56. "The Case of Mr. Ives," *PNM* 2, No. 2 (1964), 125-128.
57. "Expressionism and American Music," *PNM* 4, No. 1 (1965), 1-13.
58. "The Time Dimension in Music," *Mus J* 23 (Nov 1965), 29.
59. "Current Chronicle: New York," *MQ* 52 (1966), 93-101.
60. "In Memoriam: Edgar Varèse," *PNM* 4, No. 2 (1966), 7.
61. "The Composer in Academia; Reflections on a Theme of Stravinsky," *College Mus* 10 (1970), 68-70.
62. "Igor Stravinsky, 1882-1971," *PNM* 9, No. 2 (1971).
63. "In Memoriam: Stefan Wolpe, 1902-1972," *PNM* 11, No. 1 (1972), 3-11; *Tempo* No. 102 (1972), 17-18; 103 (1972), 63-64.
64. "To Think of Milton Babbitt," *PNM* 14, No. 1 (1976), 29-31.
65. "Documents of a Friendship with Ives," *Tempo* 117 (Jun 1976), 2-10.
66. "Was ist amerikanische Musik?" *OeMZ* 31 (Oct 1976), 468-470.
67. "Music and the Time Screen," *Current Thought in Musicology*, ed. John W. Grubbs. Austin: University of Texas Press, 1976.
68. "The Milieu of the American Composer," *HiFi/MA* 27 (Sep 1977), MA16.

References to Elliott Carter

Books
(See the General Bibliography)

ACA-Bul III/2; AusMT; Baker; BIM; BloYA; BMI-C; BMI-MW; BMI-OP; BMI-P; BMI-SC; CatPC; ChaAC; ChaAM; ClaEA; CobCS; CohCT; ColHM; ComA 5; CopNM; CopON; CopTN; CurB(1960); DalTT; DavPM; DerETM; DukLH; Edm-I; EdMUS; EweAC; EweNB; EweCS; Grove; HanTC; HayTV; HinOC; HitMU; HowOA; JabCAC; KinAI; LanPM; MacIC; MelMN; MelRT; MitLM; MyeTC; PAC; PavMH; PersTH; PeyNM; PorM3S; ReiCC; SalzTM;

SanWM; SchCC; SpaMH; StevHS; ThoAJ; ThoAM; ThompIC; ThoMR; ThoRL; WhiWW; WilTM; WooWM; YatTC.

Articles

1. Brief mention: *MQ* 26 (1940), 107; *SR* 36 (Mar 14, 1953), 17; *MQ* 40 (1954), 589; 41 (1955), 93, 521; 42 (1956), 245; *PNM* 1, No. 1 (1962), 126; No. 2 (1963), 14, 50, 58, 98, 148, 183, 190, 194; 2, No. 2 (1964), 14, 17, 75.
2. Rosenfeld, Paul. "The Newest American Composers," *MM* 15, No. 3 (1937-1938), 157.
3. "Wins Juilliard School of Music Publishing Contest," *NYT* (Jun 4, 1940), 19:3.
4. "Appointed St. John's College Musical Activities Tutor and Director," *NYT* (Aug 16, 1940), 16:5.
5. "Musicians Wrestle Everywhere," *MR* 10 (Feb 1949), 75.
6. Goldman, Richard F. "Current Chronicle," *MQ* 37 (1951), 83-89.
7. "Elliott Cook Carter," *Pan Pipes* 44 (Jan 1952), 26-27.
8. Harmon, Carter. "Elliott Carter," *NYT* (Mar 30, 1952).
9. "Elliott Cook Carter," *Pan Pipes* 45 (Jan 1953), 44.
10. Shulsky, Abraham. "Elliott Carter (Study of His Works)," *ACA-Bul* 3, No. 2 (1953), 2-11.
11. "Chronological List of Carter Works with Reviews," *ACA-Bul* 3, No. 2 (1953), 12-16.
12. *NYT* (May 27, 1953).
13. Kyle, Marguerite K. "AmerAllegro," *Pan Pipes* 46 (Jan 1954), 33-34.
14. "Belgium (Concours International de Composition pour Quatuor à Cordes)," *Violins* 15 (Jan-Feb 1954), 9.
15. Keats, Sheila. "Reference Articles on American Composers: An Index," *Juilliard Rev* 1 (Fall 1954), 21.
16. "Elliott Carter," *Pan Pipes* 47 (Jan 1955), 35.
17. Glock, William. "A Note on Elliott Carter (Rhythmic Innovations)," *Score* 12 (Jun 1955), 47-52.
18. Daniel, Oliver. "The New Festival: Elliott Carter," *ACA-Bul* 5, No. 1 (1955), 5.
19. "Contributors to This Issue," *Score* 12 (Jun 1955), 94.
20. Kyle, Marguerite K. "AmerAllegro," *Pan Pipes* 48 (Jan 1956), 40.
21. "Became Member of the National Institute of Arts and Letters," *NYT* (Feb 7, 1956), 38:4.
22. "Elected to the American Academy of Arts and Letters," *NYT* (May 24, 1956), 25:1.
23. "Elite Composer," *Time* 67 (May 28, 1956), 48.
24. Kyle, Marguerite K. "AmerAllegro," *Pan Pipes* 49 (Jan 1957), 41.
25. Goldman, Richard F. "The Music of Elliott Carter [with List of His Works]," *MQ* 43 (1957), 151-170.
26. Ellsworth, Ray E. "Classic Modern," *Down Beat* 24 (Sept 19, 1957), 36.
27. Koegler, Horst. "Salzburg (Seminar in American Studies)," *MC* 157 (Jan 1958), 14.
28. Kyle, Marguerite K. "AmerAllegro," *Pan Pipes* 51 (Jan 1959), 55.
29. "The High Cost of Creativity," *HiFi Rev* (May 1959), 34.
30. "Elliott Carter," *Composers of the Americas* 5 (1959), 29-35.
31. Koegler, Horst. "Begegnungen mit Elliott Carter," *Melos* 26 (Sep 1959), 356-358.
32. Salzman, Eric. "Unity in Variety," *NYT* (Mar 20, 1960), sec. 2, p. 9.
33. "Wins Pulitzer," *FoF* 20 (May 2, 1960), 154D1.
34. "Wins Pulitzer Prize (String Quartet No. 2)," *NYT* (May 3, 1960), 1:3.
35. "Biographical Sketch," *NYT* (May 3, 1960), 34: 3, 5; 38:2.
36. *NYT* (Jun 18, 1960), 12:4.
37. "Biography," *Current Biography* (Nov 1960); *Current Biography Yearbook* (1960), 79-80.
38. Daniel, Oliver. "Carter and Shapero," *SR* 43 (Dec 17, 1960), 43.
39. Copland, Aaron. "America's Young Men of Music," *Mus & Mus* 9 (Dec 1960), 11.
40. "Became Treasurer of National Institute of Arts and Letters," *NYT* (Feb 15, 1961), 26:6.

41. Boretz, Benjamin. "Sessions Festival," *MA* 81 (Mar 1961), 26.
42. "New York Music Critics Circle Award," *NYT* (Apr 19, 1961), 34:1.
43. "'UNESCO Composition Prize," *NYT* (May 20, 1961), 13:4.
44. "Composer for Professionals," *Time* 77 (May 26, 1961), 80.
45. Kyle, Marguerite K. "AmerAllegro," *Pan Pipes* 53, No. 2 (1961), 46.
46. *NYT* (Sep 7, 1961), 41:4.
47. "Became Member of National Institute of Arts and Letters," *NYT* (Feb 13, 1962), 40:2.
48. "Elliott Carter," *St. Cecilia* 11 (Apr 1962), 40.
49. Kyle, Marguerite K. "AmerAllegro," *Pan Pipes* 54, No. 2 (1962), 41.
50. "New York Music Critics Circle Citation (for Double Concerto)," *NYT* (May 23, 1962), 37:2.
51. "Appointed to Music Advisory Commission, Hopkins Center, Dartmouth College," *NYT* (May 27, 1962), 96:2.
52. Günther, Siegfried. "USA-Sinfoniker des 20. Jahrhunderts," *Orchester* 10 (Dec 1962), 395.
53. Boretz, Benjamin. "Music," *Nation* 196 (Apr 6, 1963), 294-296.
54. Kyle, Marguerite K. "AmerAllegro," *Pan Pipes* 55, No. 2, (1963), 42.
55. Watts, D. "Musical Events," *New Yorker* 39 (Jun 8, 1963), 163-165.
56. Wuorinen, Charles. "The Outlook of Young Composers," *PNM* 1, No. 2 (1963), 58.
57. "Letters: Brickbats and a Bouquet for Sir John," *MA* 84 (Sep 1964), 4.
58. "Elected a Director of Walter W. Naumburg Foundation," *NYT* (Mar 3, 1965), 34:3.
59. "Honored at Brandeis University," *NYT* (Mar 29, 1965), 43:1.
60. *NYT* (May 13, 1965), 39:5.
61. Kyle, Marguerite K. "AmerAllegro," *Pan Pipes* 57, No. 2 (1965), 50.
62. Henderson, Robert. "Elliott Carter," *MM* 14 (Jan 1966), 20-23.
63. "Elliott Carter," *SFSPN* (Mar 1, 1966), 30.
64. Kyle, Marguerite K. "AmerAllegro," *Pan Pipes* 58, No. 2 (1966), 56.
65. *NYT* (Jul 16, 1966), 15:2.
66. "Aspen Report: Mozart and Elliott Carter in Colorado," *HiFi/MA* 16 (Oct 1966), MA20.
67. "Treat Worth the Travail," *Time* 89 (Jan 13, 1967), 44.
68. Saal, Hubert. "Piano vs. Orchestra," *NW* 69 (Jan 16, 1967), 94.
69. "Honorary Degree from Princeton University," *NYT* (Jun 14, 1967), 36:6.
70. Potvin, Gilles. "Seven Leading Composers Look at the Music of To-day and Its Public," *Mus Scene* 237 (Sep-Oct 1967), 5.
71. "In the News," *BMI* (Mar 1968), 7.
72. Kostelanetz, Richard. "The Astounding Success of Elliott Carter," *HiFi/MA* 18 (May 1968), 41-45.
73. Hamilton, David. "New Craft of the Contemporary Concerto: Carter and Sessions," *HiFi* 18 (May 1968), 67-68.
74. Kastendieck, Miles. "Elliott Carter," *BMI-MW* (Jun 1968), 5.
75. Kondracki, Michal. "List z USA," *Ruch Muz* 12, No. 15 (1968), 17.
76. Hamilton, David. "American Pioneers of the New Music," *HiFi/MA* 18 (Sep 1968), 30.
77. *NYT* (Sep 22, 1968), sec. 2, p. 25:1; (Oct 20, 1968), sec. 2, p. 20:5; (Mar 2, 1969), sec. 2, p. 21:1.
78. "Elliott Carter" (Biography Portrait), *Mus Club Mag* 49, No. 1 (1969), 10.
79. "International Music Congress: Forum (The Sounds of Things to Come)," *Mus & Artists* 2, No. 1 (1969), 29.
80. "60th Birthday," *NYT* (Feb 17, 1969), 31:1.
81. "Carter Anniversary Concert," *HiFi/MA* 19 (May 1969), MA18-19.
82. Stone, Kurt. "Current Chronicle," *MQ* 55 (1969), 559-572.
83. Northcott, Bayan. "Composers of the Sixties," *Mus & Mus* 18 (Jan 1970), 36.
84. *NYT* (Feb 1, 1970), sec. 2, p. 23:1.
85. Morgan, Robert Porter. "Early Carter Expertly Performed," *HiFi* 20 (Feb 1970), sec. 1, p. 84.

86. Waters, Edward N. "Variations on a Theme: Recent Acquisitions of the Music Division," *Q Jl Library Congress* 27, No. 1 (1970), 57-58.

87. Morgan, Robert Porter. "Records: Carter," *Am Mus Dgt* 1, No. 5 (1970), 45.

88. "Concerto premiered in New York," *FoF* 30 (Feb 5, 1970), 213A2.

89. Kolodin, Irving. "Music to My Ears," *SR* 53 (May 2, 1970), 28.

90. Hamilton, David. "Carter's Virtuoso Concerto," *HiFi* 20 (May 1970), sec. 1, p. 22.

91. Wimbush, Roger. "Here and There," *Gramophone* 47 (May 1970), 1752.

92. "Honorary Degree from Harvard University," *NYT* (Jun 12, 1970), 24:3.

93. Boretz, Benjamin. "Conversation with Elliott Carter," *PNM* 8, No. 2 (1970), 1-22.

94. "Wins Gold Medal Award from National Institute of Arts and Letters," *NYT* (Jan 24, 1971), 66:4.

95. "Carter's 'Musical Problems'," *BMI* (May 1971), 23.

96. Kolodin, Irving. "Music to My Ears: Concert at McMillin Theatre of Columbia University," *SR* 54 (May 8, 1971), 33.

97. *NYT* (May 27, 1971), 34:1.

98. DeRhen, Andrew. "Elliott Carter," *HiFi/MA* 21 (July 1971), MA18-19.

99. Cohn, Arthur. "His Own Man, the Music of Elliott Carter," *Am Rec G* 37 (Jul 1971), 756-759.

100. Haieff, Alexei, and others. "Stravinsky: A Composers' Memorial," *PNM* No. 2 (1971), 1-6.

101. "Music Journal's 1972 Gallery of Living Composers," *Mus J* 30, Annual (1972), 37.

102. Rorem, Ned. "Elliott Carter," *New Republic* 166 (Feb 26, 1972), 22.

103. Northcott, Bayan. "Elliott Carter—Continuity and Coherence," *Mus & Mus* 20 (Aug 1972), 28-32.

104. "Chamber Music," *New Yorker* 48 (Feb 3, 1973), 82.

105. Porter, Andrew. "Musical Events," *New Yorker* 43 (Feb 3, 1973), 82.

106. *NYT* (Feb 4, 1973), sec. 2, p. 15:1.

107. Bender, William. "Atonal Prism," *Time* 101 (Feb 5, 1973), 59-60.

108. Hamilton, David. "Music," *Nation* 216 (Feb 19, 1973), 250-252.

109. "Spotlight," *Mus J* 31 (Mar 1973), 24.

110. Kolodin, Irving. "New Quartet by Elliot[t] Carter," *SR Educ* 1 (Mar 1973), 80.

111. "Wins Pulitzer," *FoF* 33 (May 7, 1973), 387G2.

112. "Wins Pulitzer Prize for String Quartet No. 3," *NYT* (May 8, 1973), 32:1.

113. "Biographical Sketch," *NYT* (May 8, 1973), 32:1.

114. "Music Awards," *MQ* 96 (1973), 509.

115. Kastendieck, Miles. "Elliott Carter," *BMI* 3 (1973), 36-37.

116. Smith Patrick J. "Elliott Carter—Musician of the Month," *HiFi/MA* 23 (Aug 1973), MA4-5.

117. Hamilton, David. "Aspen: Amidst the Mountains, Contemporary Music," *HiFi/MA* 23 (Dec 1973), MA20-21.

118. ———"Music: Performance of the Double Concerto by Group for Contemporary Music," *Nation* 218 (Jan 19, 1974), 93.

119. Shawe-Taylor, Desmond. "Musical Events: Performance of Concerto for Orchestra by the New York Philharmonic," *New Yorker* 49 (Feb 18, 1974), 104-106.

120. Griffiths, Paul. "20th-Century," *MT* 115 (Feb 1974), 153-155.

121. "The Pulitzer Prizes (Some Winners in Music)," *BMI* 2 (1974), 23.

122. Brandt, William E. "The Music of Elliott Carter: Simultaneity and Complexity," *Mus Ed J* 60 (May 1974), 24-32.

123. "Overtones," *Mus Ed J* 60 (May 1974), 5.

124. Hamilton, David. "Unique Imagination of Elliott Carter," *HiFi* 24 (Jul 1974), 73-75.

125. Fleming, Shirley. "The Composer's String Quartet Conducts a Competition," *HiFi/MA* 24 (Aug 1974), MA19.

126. Mayer, Martin. "Recordings," *Esquire* 82 (Aug 1974), 30.

127. Morgan, Robert P.   "Elliott Carter's String Quartets (Analysis)," *Mus News* 4, No. 3 (1974), 3-11.
128. Porter, Andrew.   "Music Events: Composers' Showcase Concert at the Whitney Museum," *New Yorker* 50 (Nov 11, 1974), 199-200.
129. *NYT* (Nov 1, 1974), 26:1; (Nov 17, 1974), sec. 2, p. 19:1; (Dec 18, 1974), 57:1.
130. Griffiths, Paul. "Radio," *MT* 115 (Dec 1974), 1069.
131. *NYT* (Jan 15, 1975), 52:1 (Transcription of Purcell's "Fantasy on One Note" for Strings).
132. Kolodin, Irving.   "The all-Moussoursky 'Boris'—Ligeti, Carter," *SR/World* 2 (Jan 25, 1975), 50-52.
133. "Carter Vogue," *Time* 105 (Feb 10, 1975), 65.
134. *NYT* (Feb 23, 1975), sec. 2, p. 21:7; (Mar 9, 1975), sec, 2, p. 21:1.
135. Kolodin, Irving.   "Evenings with Carter, Rubinstein, and Barber," *SR* 2 (Mar 23, 1975), 33.
136. Saylor, Bruce.   "American Brass Quintet: Carter," *HiFi/MA* 25 (Apr 1975), MA29-30.
137. "People are Talking About . . . ," *Vogue* 165 (Apr 1975), 152-153.
138. "Elliott Carter and the Composer's Quartet," *Mus & Mus* 24 (Nov 1975), 12.
139. "Composers in Focus," *BMI* (Winter 1975), 18.
140. Porter, Andrew.   "Musical Events: Performance of 'A Mirror on Which to Dwell'," *New Yorker* 52 (Mar 8, 1976), 122.
141. Weber, J. F.   "An Elliott Carter Discography," *ARSC* 8, No. 1 (1976), 33-39.
142. "Boston," *Mus J* 36 (Jan 1978), 39.

References to Works by Elliott Carter

29. Brass Quintet: *NYT* (Dec 17, 1974), 32:1; *New Yorker* 50 (Dec 30, 1974), 54-56; *HiFi/MA* 25 (Apr 1975), MA29; *Mus Ed J* 61 (Apr 1975), 92.
22. Caneries [Canaries] for Timpani: *HiFi/MA* 22 (Dec 1972), MA23.
28. Canon for Three: *NYT* (Jan 24, 1972), 22:1; *BMI* 2 (Apr 1972), 11; *Tempo* No. 98 (1972), 22.
12. Concerto for Orchestra: *ClSPN* (Dec 18, 1969), 435-445; *NYPPN* (Feb 5, 1970), F-H; *NYT* (Feb 6, 1970), 27:1; *SR* 53 (Feb 21, 1970), 50; *NZ* 131 (Mar 1970), 126; *BMI* (Apr 1970), 8; *Int Mus* 68 (Apr 1970), 32; *HiFi/MA* 20, sec. 1, p. 22; sec. 2, p. 21; *Intam Mus B* No. 78-98 (July-Oct 1970); *World Mus* 12, No. 1 (1970), 73; *Am Mus Dgt* 1, No. 5 (1970), 20; *ClSPN* (Jan 21, 1971), 486-493; *HiFi/MA* 21 (Mar 1971), 82; *NZ* 133 (Jan 1972), 31; *Mus & Mus* 21 (Nov 1972), 70; *MT* 116 (Oct 1975), 894; *Mus & Mus* 24 (Oct 1975), 50.
11. Concerto for Piano: *BSPN* (Jan 6, 1967), 792; *NYT* (Jan 7, 1967), 21:1; *Boston Globe* (Jan 7, 1967); *SR* 50 (Feb 11, 1967), 85; *BMI* (Mar 1967), 7; *HiFi/MA* 17 (Mar 1967), MA16; *Nation* 204 (Apr 3, 1967), 445; *Musica* 21, No. 4 (1967), 176; *HiFi/MA* 18 (May 1968), 67; *Am Rec G* 34 (Jun 1968), 936; *BufPPN* (Oct 10, 1968), 9-15; *Melos* 36 (Mar 1969), 122; *NZ* 130 (Apr 1969), 167; *Orchester* 17 (May 1969), 211; *MQ* 55 (1969), 559-572; *MT* 111 (May 1970), 520; *Mus & Mus* 18 (May 1970), 60; *Am Mus Dgt* 1, No. 6 (1970), 14; *Mus & Mus* 26 (Aug 1978), 32.
37. The Defense of Corinth: *Notes* 7 (Jun 1950), 442; *MA* 70 (Aug 1950), 29; *Mus News* 42 (Sep 1950), 19; *MQ* 43 (1957), 154.
10. Double Concerto: *NYT* (Sep 7, 1961), 41:4; *Juilliard Rev* 8, No. 3 (1961), 15; *MA* 81 (Oct 1961), 29; *Mus Mag* 163 (Oct 1961), 26; *Neue ZFM* 122 (Nov 1961), 469; *MQ* 48 (1962), 96-99; *PNM* 1, No. 1 (1962), 195; *NYT* (May 23, 1962), 37:2; *MA* 82 (Jun 1962), 6; *MM* 10 (Jul 1962), 25; *Strad* 73 (Jul 1962), 111; *Mus Mag* 164 (Jul 1962), 43; *MT* 103 (Jul 1962), 466; *Mus Opin* 85 (Aug 1962), 648; *PNM* 1, No. 2 (1963), 23, 25, 174, 177, 192; *Notes* 22, No. 1 (1965), 819; *RMA* 94 (1967-1968), 12-16; *HiFi/MA* 19 (Feb 1969), 85; (Aug 1969), MA12; *MT* 111 (Oct 1970), 101-107; *Am Rec G* 37 (Jul 1971), 756-759.

30. Duo for Violin and Piano: *NYT* (Mar 23, 1975), 48:6; *New Yorker* 51 (Apr 7, 1975), 129; *Mus J* 33 (Apr 1975), 34; *Sym News* 26, No. 2 (1975), 27.

21. Eight Etudes and a Fantasy: *MQ* 37 (1951), 85; *MA* 72 (Nov 15, 1952), 8; *HiFi* 8 (May 1958), 54; *Notes* 18 (1960-1961), 318; *NYHT* (Mar 28, 1961); *MQ* 47 (1961), 398; *PNM* 1, No. 2 (1963), 203.

22. Eight Pieces for Four Timpani: *MQ* 38 (1952), 59; *Notes* 18 (1960-1961), 653; *Percussionist* 12, No. 1 (1974), 7-15; *Harmonie* 138 (Jun-Aug 1978), 61.

5. Elegy for String Orchestra: *Notes* 17 (1959-1960), 149.

18. Elegy for String Quartet: *Notes* 16 (1958-1959), 314.

40. Emblems: *MQ* 43 (1957), 159.

38. The Harmony of Morning: *NYHT* (Feb 27, 1945); *Notes* 12 (1954-1955), 496; *MA* 75 (Jun 1955), 28; *MQ* 43 (1957), 154.

36. Heart not so Heavy: *Mus News* 41 (Jul 1949), 17.

4. Holiday Overture: *MQ* 36 (1950), 446-447; *MA* 81 (Jan 1961), 240; *Notes* 20 (1962-1963), 407; *Natl Sym* (Feb 21, 1967), 23; *POPN* (Oct 27, 1967), 15-17; *MM* 16 (Dec 1967), 46.

6. The Minotaur: *Theatre Arts* 31 (Jul 1947), 9; *New Yorker* 32 (May 26, 1956), 120.

47. A Mirror on Which to Dwell: *New Yorker* 52 (Mar 8, 1976), 122; *BMI* (Spring 1976), 32-35; *HiFi/MA* 26 (Jun 1976), MA27; *Mus & Mus* 25 (Dec 1976), 4; *Schweiz Mus* 117, No. 1 (1977), 36; *NMC* 27, No. 2 (1978), 21.

39. Musicians Wrestle Everywhere: *NYHT* (Jan 16, 1951); *MQ* 43 (1957), 154.

11. Piano Concerto (see Concerto for Piano)

31. Piano Sonata (see Sonata for Piano)

2. Pocahontas: *MQ* 34 (1948), 8.

24. Sonata for Flute, Oboe, Violoncello, Harpsichord: *NYT* (Nov 11, 1953), 35:6; *Notes* 13 (1955-1956), 525; *SR* 43 (Dec 17, 1960), 43; *Metro* 78 (May 1961), 38; *PNM* 1, No. 2 (1963), 23; *HiFi/MA* 20 (Feb 1970), 84; *Stereo R* 24 (Mar 1970), 86; *MT* 114 (Jul 1973), 726; *HitMU*, 228.

31. Sonata for Piano: *NYHT* (Mar 13, 1948); *ML* 30 (Jan 1949), 89; *MR* 10 (Feb 1949), 45; *MQ* 37 (1951), 85; 41 (1955), 521; *Juilliard Rev* 3 (Fall 1956), 10; *MM* 11 (Jan 1963), 46; *PNM* 2, No. 2 (1964), 127; *MR* 34, Nos. 3-4 (1973), 282-293; *MelMN*, 103; *HitMU* 227.

19. Sonata for Violoncello and Piano: *MC* 141 (Mar 15, 1950), 23; *Mus News* 42 (Jul 1950), 2; *NYHT* (Nov 20, 1950); *MQ* 37 (1951), 83; *SR* 35 (Mar 29, 1952), 48; *Notes* 11 (1953-1954), 434; *MA* 75 (Feb 18, 1955), 188; *PNM* 2, No. 2 (1964), 127; *MT* 111 (Feb 1970), 184; *HiFi/MA* 20 (Feb 1970), 84; *Stereo R* 24 (Mar 1970), 86; *MelMN*, 106; *HitMU*, 228.

23. String Quartet No. 1: *NYT* (Feb 27, 1953), 17:2; *NYHT* (May 5, 1953); *MA* 73 (Nov 1, 1953), 27; *ACA-Bul* 3, No. 1 (1953), 13, 23; 4, No. 1 (1954), 20; *MT* 97 (Jan 1956), 36; *NYT* (Dec 9, 1956), sec. 2, p. 19; *MQ* 43 (1957), 130-132; *Notes* 14 (May 1957), 198; *MA* 78 (Nov 15, 1958), 24; *MQ* 46 (1960), 193; *PNM* 1, No. 2 (1963), 23; 2, No. 2, (1964), 125-128; *Sovet Muz* 36 (Oct 1972), 84-87; *HanTC*, 347; *MelMN*, 113; *ThoRL*, 35.

26. String Quartet No. 2: *MQ* 46 (1960), 361-364; *NYT* (Mar 20, 1960), sec. 2, p. 9:6; (Mar 26, 1960), 14:1; (Mar 27, 1960), sec. 1, p. 14; (Apr 3, 1960), sec, 2. p. 9:1; *MC* 161 (Apr 1960), 36; *Nation* 190 (Apr 16, 1960), 344; *MT* 101 (Jun 1960), 373, 377; *MQ* 46 (1960), 361-364; *Score* 27 (Jul 1960), 22-26; *Melos* 28 (Feb 1961), 35-37; *NYT* (May 7, 1961), sec. 2, p. 19; *MC* 163 (May 1961), 6; *PNM* 1, No. 2 (1963), 18; *Notes* 21 (1963-1964), 261; *MT* 110 (Jun 1969), 52; *HiFi/MA* 24 (Jul 1974), 73-75; *MQ* 61 (1975), 165-168; *Mus & Mus* 25 (Dec 1976), 51; *MacIC*, 507; *MelMN*, 115.

27. String Quartet No. 3: *SR* 1 (Feb 10, 1973), 80; *NYT* (Jan 25, 1973), 54:3; *Mus Ed J* 59 (Mar 1973), 16; *Mus & Mus* 21 (Mar 1973), 58; *NYT* (May 8, 1973), 32:1; *World Mus* 15, No. 1 (1973), 91; *HiFi/MA* 23 (May 1973), MA16; *R Mus Ital* 7, No. 2 (1973), 266-

270; *Mus & Mus* 22 (Sep 1973), 22; *Pan Pipes* 66, No. 2 (1974), 25-27; *HiFi/MA* 24 (Jul 1974), 73-75; *MQ* 61 (1975), 157-165; *Mus & Mus* 24 (Oct 1975), 50; (Nov 1975), 12; *Current Mus* 20 (1975), 9.

String Quartets: *SR* 53 (May 2, 1970), 28; *HiFi/MA* 20, (Jul 1970), sec. 2, p. 19; *Stereo R* 26 (Feb 1971), 89; *Amer Rec G* 37 (Jul 1971), 756-759; *SR* 2 (Mar 22, 1975), 33.

8. Symphony for Three Orchestras: *New Yorker* 53 (Mar 7, 1977), 101-104; *R Mus Ital* 11, No. 2 (1977), 251-253; *SR* 4 (Apr 2, 1977), 37; *MT* 118 (Apr 1977), 329; *Mus Ed J* 63 (May 1977), 66; *OeMZ* 32 (May-Jun 1977), 277; *HiFi/MA* 27 (Jun 1977), MA32; *BMI* No. 1 (1977), 2; *Sym News* 28, No. 3 (1977), 47; *Mus & Mus* 26 (Feb 1978), 53.

3. Symphony No. 1: *ACA-Bul* 3, No. 2 (1953); *MA* 81 (Jan 1961), 250; *Notes* 22 (1964-1965), 820.

33. To Music: *Notes* 13 (1955-1956), 348.

7. Variations for Orchestra: *Louisville Courier J* (Apr 23, 1956); *MQ* 43 (1957), 164; *San Francisco Chronicle* (June 19, 1961); *MC* 163 (Jul 1961), 61; *POPN* (Dec 6, 1962), 25-27; *MA* 83 (Feb 1963), 27; *PNM* 1, No. 2 (1963), 15; *MT* 107 (Oct 1966), 884; *MR* 27, No. 4 (1968), 331; *HiFi/MA* 19 (Feb 1969), 85; *KCPhil* (Apr 26, 1969), 23; *Am Mus Dgt* 1, No. 4 (1970), 24; *Am Rec G* 37 (Jul 1971), 756-759; *MR* 34, No. 1 (1973), 62-65; *MacIC* , 508; *HitMU*, 228.

45. Voyage: *PNM* 2, No. 2 (1964), 127.

Vocal Works: *SR* 54 (May 8, 1971), 33.

20. Woodwind Quintet: *ACA-Bul* 4, No. 2 (1954), 21; *NYHT* (Feb 28, 1959).

Dissertations about Elliott Carter and His Works

1. Arlton, Dean L. *American Piano Sonatas of the Twentieth Century: Selective Analyses and Annotated Index.* Columbia University, 1968.
2. Armstrong, Donald J. *A Study of Some Important Twentieth Century Secular Compositions for Women's Chorus with a Preliminary Discussion of Secular Choral Music from a Historical and Philosophical Viewpoint.* University of Texas, 1968.
3. Breedon, Daniel F. *An Investigation of the Influence of the Metaphysics of Alfred North Whitehead upon the Formal-dramatic Compositional Procedures of Elliott Carter.* University of Washington, 1975.
4. Geissler, Fredrick D. *Variations on a Modern American Trumpet Tune for Solo Trumpet and Concert Band.* Cornell University, 1974.
5. Grau, Irene Rosenburg. *Compositional Techniques Employed in the First Movement of Elliott Carter's Piano Concerto.* Boston University, 1973.
6. Johnson, Lilla Joyce. *Rhythmic Techniques in Twentieth Century Music Including Those Employed in the Piano Sonatas of Elliott Carter and Leon Kirchner.* Northwestern University, 1972.
7. Marcus, Genevieve. *New Concepts in Music from 1950 to 1970: A Critical Investigation of Contemporary Aesthetic Philosophy and Its Translation into Musical Structures.* University of California, Los Angeles, 1973.
8. Pisciotta, Louis V. *Texture in the Choral Works of Selected Contemporary American Composers.* Indiana University, 1967.
9. Schweitzer, Eugene W. *Generation in String Quartets of Carter, Sessions, Kirchner, and Schuller: A Concept of Forward Thrust and Its Relationship to Structure in Aurally Complex Styles.* University of Rochester, Eastman School of Music, 1966.
10. Service, Alfred R., Jr. *A Study of the Cadence as a Factor in Music Intelligibility in Selected Piano Sonatas by American Composers.* State University of Iowa, 1958.
11. Shin, Randall Alan. *An Analysis of Elliott Carter's Sonata for Flute, Oboe, Cello, and Harpsichord (1952).* University of Illinois, 1975.

12. Wennerstrom, Mary Hannah. *Parametric Analysis of Contemporary Musical Form*. Indiana University, 1967.
13. Wilhite, Carmen Irene. *Piano Sonatas by Elliott Carter: A Foreshadowing of His Later Style; A Lecture Recital, Together with Three Recitals of Selected Works*. North Texas State University, 1977.
14. Wolf, Henry S. *The Twentieth Century Piano Sonata*. Boston University, 1957.

OUTLINE IV

AARON COPLAND (b. 1900)

I. **Life**

1900 Born in Brooklyn, New York, November 14, of Russian-born parents. Educated in Brooklyn public schools.

1913 Studied piano with Leopold Wolfson, Victor Wittgenstein, Clarence Adler. Decided to become a composer about 1916.

1917 Studied theory with Rubin Goldmark (1917-1921). Graduated from Brooklyn Boys' High School (1918).

1921 Studied composition with Nadia Boulanger at Fontainebleau (summer, 1921), her first American student; continued study in Paris (1921-1924).

1924 Returned to the United States. First American performance of his music (League of Composers concert), *Cat and the Mouse*, *Passacaglia* for piano.

1925 First orchestral performance, *Symphony for Organ and Orchestra* (New York Symphony with Nadia Boulanger, organist). Awarded two Guggenheim Fellowships (1925, 1926). Worked at the MacDowell Colony intermittently.

1927 Lecturer on music at the New School for Social Research, New York (1927-1937). Soloist with Boston Symphony Orchestra (Serge Koussevitsky) in his *Concerto for Piano and Orchestra*.

1928 Organized, with Roger Sessions, the Copland-Sessions Concerts in New York: performed mostly American music (1928-1931). Concerts of American music in Paris (1929). Interest in *Gebrauchsmusik* in Germany (Weill, Hindemith).

1932 Organized the American Festivals of Contemporary Music at Yaddo, Saratoga Springs, New York. First visit to Mexico.

1933 Became a director of the League of Composers. Wrote many articles for *Modern Music* (1926-1946).

1934 Began to write in a more popular style for a larger audience (*El Salón México*).

1935 Guest lecturer at Harvard University (1935-1937). Founder and president of the American Composers Alliance (1937-1945).

1939 Began the composition of film scores in Hollywood.

1940 Associated with the Berkshire Music Center, Tanglewood, MA, as composer and administrator (1940-1965).

1941 Toured Latin America as lecturer, conductor, pianist under the program of Inter-American Relations.

1942 Elected a member of the National Institute of Arts and Letters.

1945 Awarded the Pulitzer Prize for Music (*Appalachian Spring*); New York Music Critics Circle Award (Ballet: *Appalachian Spring*).

1947 New York Music Critics Circle Award (*Symphony No. 3*).

1950 Oscar award from the Academy of Motion Picture Arts for film score *The Heiress*.

1951 Appointed to the Charles Eliot Norton chair of poetry at Harvard University (*Music and Imagination*).

1953 Artist-in-residence at the American Academy in Rome (1953-1954).

1956 Received Gold Medal award from the American Academy of Arts and Letters.

1960 Guest conductor of the Yomiuri Nippon Symphony Orchestra in three concerts of his own music.

1964 Received Presidential Medal of Freedom.

1970 Received the Howland Memorial Prize from Yale University. Decorated with the

Commander's Cross of the Order of Merit in West Germany. Elected honorary member of the *Accademia Santa Cecilia*, Rome.

Numerous honorary degrees: Princeton University, 1956; Brandeis University, 1957; Wesleyan College, 1958; Temple University, 1959; Howard University, 1961; Rutgers University, 1967; Ohio State University, 1970; New York University, 1970; Columbia University, 1971; York University, England, 1971.

Aaron Copland has been the recipient of many honors, awards and commissions in addition to those listed above.

Note: Biographies of varying lengths and importance will be found in many of the books listed in the Bibliography at the end of this *Outline* under "References to Aaron Copland."

II.   Compositions

	Date	Publisher
A. Orchestra		
1. Cortège Macabre (from the ballet, Grogh)	1923	BH
2. Symphony No. 1 for Organ and Orchestra	1924	BH
3. Music for the Theatre (cham orch)	1925	BH

a. Prologue	d. Burlesque	
b. Dance	e. Epilogue	
c. Interlude		

	Date	Publisher
4. Dance Symphony (from the ballet, Grohg)	1925	BH
5. Nocturne	1926	AMP
6. Two Pieces (str orch)	1928	BH

a. Lento Molto	b. Rondino (1923)

	Date	Publisher
7. Symphony No. 1 (version, without organ, of the Symphony for Organ and Orchestra)	1928	
8. Symphonic Ode	1929; revised 1955	BH
9. Short Symphony (Symphony No. 2)	1933	BH
10. Statements	1934	BH

a. Militant	d. Subjective
b. Cryptic	e. Jingo
c. Dogmatic	f. Prophetic

	Date	Publisher
11. El Salón México	1936	BH
12. Fantasia Mexicana (arr. from El Salón México)	1936	BH
13. Music for Radio (Saga of the Prairie)	1937	BH
14. Billy the Kid: Suite (from the Ballet)	1938	BH

a. The Open Prairie	e. Celebration Dance
b. Street in a Frontier Town	f. Billy's Death
c. Card Game at Night	g. Open Prairie Again
d. Gun Battle	

	Date	Publisher
15. Billy the Kid: Waltz (cham orch)	1938	BH
16. An Outdoor Overture	1938	BH
17. Quiet City (cham orch)	1940	BH
18. Our Town: Suite (from the Film)	1940	BH
19. John Henry: Railroad Ballad (cham orch)	1940; revised 1952	BH
20. Lincoln Portrait (Narr. and orch)	1942	BH
21. Rodeo: Suite (from the Ballet)	1942	BH

a. Buckaroo Holiday	c. Saturday Night Waltz
b. Corral Nocturne	d. Hoe-Down (str orch)

	Date	Publisher
22. Music for the Movies (from The City, 1939; Of Mice and Men, 1939; Our Town, 1940)	1942	BH

a. New England Countryside	d. Story of Grovers Corners
b. Barley Wagons	e. Threshing Machines
c. Sunday Traffic	

23.	Fanfare for the Common Man (brass, timp, perc)	1942	BH
24.	Appalachian Spring: Suite (from the Ballet)	1944	BH
25.	Variations on a Theme by Eugene Goosens	1944	
26.	Letter from Home	1944; revised 1962	BH
27.	Danzón Cubano (arr. for orch)	1942-1944	BH
28.	Symphony No. 3 (No. 23 incorporated *in toto*)	1946	BH
29.	The Red Pony: Suite (from the Film)	1948	BH

     a. Morning on the Ranch   d. Walk to the Bunkhouse
     b. The Gift   e. Grandfather's Story
     c. Dream March and Circus Music f. Happy Ending

30.	Preamble for a Solemn Occasion (Narr. optional)	1949	BH
31.	The Tender Land: Suite (from the Opera)	1957	BH

     a. Introduction and Love Music   c. The Promise of Living
     b. Party Scene

32.	Variations for Orchestra (orchestral version of Piano Variations	1957	BH
33.	Dance Panels (from the Ballet)	1959; revised 1962	BH
34.	Two Mexican Pieces (cham orch)	1959	BH

     a. Mexican Landscape   b. Danza de Jalisco

35.	Nonet (arr. for str orch)	1961	BH
36.	Connotations	1962	BH
37.	Down a Country Lane (arr. from pno)	1962	BH
38.	Music for a Great City: Suite (from the Film, Something Wild)	1964	BH
39.	Inscape	1967	BH
40.	Three Latin-American Sketches (cham orch)	1967	BH

     a. Estribillo   c. Danza de Jalisco
     b. Paisaje mexicano

| 41. | Music for Movies | 1973 | |

B. Concerto

42.	Concerto for Piano and Orchestra (Jazz Concerto)	1926	BH
43.	Concerto for Clarinet (hp, pno, str)	1948	BH

C. Band

44.	An Outdoor Overture (arr. from orch)	1938	BH
45.	Billy the Kid: Celebration Dance and Waltz (arr. from orch)	1938	BH
46.	Lincoln Portrait (arr. from Narr. and orch)	1942	BH
47.	Variations on a Shaker Melody: Simple Gifts (arr. from Appalachian Spring)	1956	BH
48.	Emblems	1964	BH
49.	Inaugural Fanfare (wind ensemble)	1969	BH

D. Chamber

50.	Two Pieces (vln, pno)	1926	Schott

     a. Nocturne   b. Ukelele Serenade

51.	Two Pieces (str qrt or str orch)	1928	BH

     a. Lento Molto   b. Rondino (1923)

52.	Vitebsk (Study on a Jewish Theme) (vln, vlc, pno)	1929	BH
53.	Sextet (str qrt, clar, pno) (arr. from Short Symphony)	1937	BH
54.	Billy the Kid: Celebration Dance (arr. for vln, pno; vlc, pno)	1938	BH
55.	Billy the Kid: Waltz (arr. for vln, pno; vlc, pno)	1938	BH
56.	Rodeo: Hoe-Down (arr. for vln, pno)	1942	BH
57.	Sonata for Violin and Piano	1943	BH
58.	Concerto for Clarinet (arr. for clar, pno)	1948	BH
59.	Quartet for Piano and Strings (vln, vla, vlc, pno)	1950	BH
60.	Nonet (3 vln, 3 vla, 3 vlc)	1960	BH
61.	Duo for Flute and Piano	1970	BH
62.	Threnody, Igor Stravinsky in Memoriam (fl, vln, vla, vlc)	1972	

E.   **Piano** (solo piano unless otherwise indicated)

63. The Cat and the Mouse (Scherzo Humoristique)	1919	BH
64. Passacaglia	1922	Sal
65. Dance of the Adolescent (arr. for 2 pno from the ballet, Grohg)	1925	BH
66. Sentimental Melody	1926	Schott
67. Concerto for Piano (arr. for 2 pno)	1926	BH
68. Piano Variations	1930	BH
69. El Salón México (arr. for 2 pno)	1936	BH
70. Fantasia Mexicana (arr. for pno)	1936	BH
71. Two Children's Pieces	1936	CF

    a.   Sunday Afternoon Music   b.   The Young Pioneers

72. Billy the Kid (arr. for pno; 2 pno)	1938	BH

    a.   Card Game   b.   Celebration Dance
    b.   The Open Prairie

73 Billy the Kid: Waltz (arr. for pno; 2 pno)	1938	BH
74. Our Town (arr. for pno)	1940	BH

    a.   Story of Our Town   c.   The Resting-Place on the Hill
    b.   Conversation at the Soda Fountain

75. Sonata for Piano	1941	BH
76. Rodeo (arr. for 2 pno)	1942	BH

    a.   Saturday Night Waltz   b.   Hoe-Down

77. Danzón Cubano (2 pno; arr. for pno)	1942	BH
78. Four Piano Blues	1948	BH

    a.   Freely Poetic (1947)   c.   Muted and Sensuous (1948)
    b.   Soft and Languid (1934)   d.   With Bounce (1926)

79. Piano Fantasy	1957	BH
80. Dance Panels (arr. for pno)	1959; rev. 1962	BH
81. Down a Country Lane	1962	BH
82. Danza de Jalisco (arr. 2 pno)	1963	BH
83. Night Thought (Homage to Ives)	1972	BH

F.   **Organ**

84. Symphony for Organ and Orchestra (arr. for org, pno)	1924	BH
85. Episode	1941	HWG
86. Preamble for a Solemn Occasion (arr. for org)	1953	BH

G.   **Choral** (a cappella unless otherwise indicated)

87. The House on a Hill (E. A. Robinson) (SSAA, pno)	1925	ECS
88. An Immortality (Ezra Pound) (S. SSA, pno)	1925	ECS
89. What do We Plant? (Henry Abbey) (SA, pno)	1935	BH
90. That's the Idea (from The Second Hurricane) (Edwin Denby) (S. B. SATB)	1937	BH
91. Lark (Genevieve Taggard) (Bar. SATB)	1938	ECS
92. Las Agachadas: The Shakedown Song (SSAATTBB)	1942	BH
93. North Star (from the Film)	1943	BH

    a.   Song of the Guerrillas (Ira Gershwin) (Bar. TTBB, pno or orch)
    b.   The Younger Generation (Ira Gershwin) (SA; SSA; SATB, pno)

94. In the beginning (Genesis) (m-S. SSAATTBB)	1947	BH
95. Old American Songs, Set I	1950	BH

    a.   The Boatmen's Dance (arr. for Bar. SATB or TTBB, pno or orch)
    b.   The Dodger (arr. for Bar. TTBB, pno or orch)
    c.   Long Time Ago (arr. for SATB; SSA, pno or orch)
    d.   Simple Gifts (arr. for SA or TB, pno or orch)
    e.   I Bought Me a Cat (arr. for S. T. SATB; T. Bar. B. TTB; SSA, pno or orch)

96. Old American Songs, Set II	1952	BH

    a.   The Little Horses (arr. for SA; SSA; SATB; TTBB, pno or orch)
    b.   At the River (arr. for SA; SSA; SATB; TTBB, pno or orch)
    c.   Ching-a-ring Chaw (arr. for SSAA; SATB, pno or orch)

G. Choral (cont.)

   97. The Tender Land (from the Opera)   1954   BH
      a. Stomp Your Foot (SATB or TTBB, pno 4 hands or orch)
      b. The Promise of Living (SATBB, pno 4 hands or orch)
   98. Canticle of Freedom (John Barbour)   1955; revised 1965   BH
      (SATB, orch) (Finale arr. for SATB, pno)

H. **Solo Vocal** (with piano unless otherwise indicated)

   99. Old Poem (Chinese, tr. Arthur Waley)   1920   Sal
  100. As it Fell Upon a Day (Richard Barnefield) (S. fl, clar)   1923   BH
  101. Poet's Song (e. e. cummings)   1927   BH
  102. Vocalise   1928   BH
  103. Twelve Poems of Emily Dickinson   1950   BH
      a. Nature, The Gentlest Mother   g. Sleep is Supposed to Be
      b. There Came a Wind   h. When They Come Back
      c. Why Do They Shut Me Out?   i. I Felt a Funeral
      d. The World Feels Dusty   j. I've Heard an Organ Talk
      e. Heart, We Will Forget Him   k. Going to Heaven
      f. Dear March, Come In!   l. The Chariot
  104. Old American Songs, Set I (pno or orch)   1950   BH
      a. The Boatmen's Dance   d. Simple Gifts
      b. The Dodger   e. I Bought Me a Cat
      c. Long Time Ago
  105. Old American Songs, Set II (pno or orch)   1952   BH
      a. The Little Horses   d. At the River
      b. Zion's Walls   e. Ching-a-Ring Chaw
      c. The Golden Willow Tree
  106. Dirge in Woods (George Meredith)   1954   BH
  107. The Tender Land   1954   BH
      a. Laurie's Song (Horace Everett) (pno or orch)

I. **Opera**

  108. The Second Hurricane (Edwin Denby)   1937   BH
      A play-opera for high school students (7 children's voices,
      SATB, Sp, orch)
  109. The Tender Land (Horace Everett)   1954   BH
      (soloists, SATB, Sp, orch)

J. **Ballet**

  110. Grohg (Harold Clurman)   1925   Ms
      (see Cortége Macabre, 1923; Dance Symphony, 1925)
  111. Hear Ye! Hear Ye! (Ruth Page)   1934   Ms
  112. Billy the Kid (Eugene Loring)   1938   Ms
  113. Rodeo (Agnes de Mille)   1942   Ms
  114. Appalachian Spring (Martha Graham)   1944   BH
  115. Dance Panels (Heinz Rosen) (also for pno)   1959; revised 1962   BH

K. **Incidental Music** (film scores)

  116. The City (Pare Lorenz, Henwar Rodakiewicz, Oscar Serlin)   1939   Ms
  117. Of Mice and Men (John Steinbeck)   1939   Ms
  118. Our Town (Thornton Wilder)   1940   Ms
  119. North Star (Lillian Hellman)   1943   Ms
  120. The Cummington Story (documentary film)   1945   Ms
  121. The Red Pony (based on a story by John Steinbeck)   1948   Ms
  122. The Heiress (based on Washington Square by Henry James)   1949   Ms
  123. Something Wild   1964   Ms

L. **Incidental Music** (stage, television)

  124. Miracle at Verdun (play by Hans Chlumberg) (cham orch)   1931   Ms
  125. The Five Kings (play by Orson Welles from Shakespeare)   1939   Ms
      (five instruments)

L.   Incidental Music (stage, television) (cont.)

126. From Sorcery to Science (puppet show) (orch)	1939	Ms
127. Quiet City (play by Irwin Shaw) (clar, sax, trpt, pno)	1939	Ms
128. The World of Nick Adams (television drama based on Ernest Hemingway)	1957	Ms

Note: The following abbreviations are used in Section III of this *Outline*. The number indicates the number of the composition as listed in Section II.

94. *Beginning*: In the Beginning
14. *Billy*: Billy the Kid: Suite
42. *Concerto Pno*: Concerto for Piano
79. *Fantasy*: Piano Fantasy
20. *Lincoln*: Lincoln Portrait
11. *México*: El Salón México
59. *Qrt Pno Str*: Quartet for Piano and Strings

75. *Son Pno*: Sonata for Piano
57. *Son Vln Pno*: Sonata for Violin and Piano
24. *Spring*: Appalachian Spring: Suite
28. *Sym 3*: Symphony No. 3
18. *Town*: Our Town: Suite
68. *Variations*: Piano Variations

III. Style (techniques and devices)

"The fact is that the whole history of music is a history of continuous change. There never was a great composer who left music exactly as he found it." "Music that is born complex is not inherently better or worse than music that is born simple."   Aaron Copland

A.   General characteristics
1.   1924-1929: French influence of Boulanger; strong influence of American jazz; some influence of Stravinsky (*Music for the Theatre*). *Concerto for Piano* (1926) his last "experiment" with symphonic jazz. Interest in the "new" ideas of the 1920's and early 1930's.
2.   1929-1935: abstract style; complex, thin texture; sharp dissonance; exploration of serial techniques; *Variations for Piano* (1930); *Statements* (1935); influence of "neoclassicism;" *Short Symphony* (1933).
3.   1935-1941: simplification; interest in music of more popular appeal (*El Salón México*); folk music and folk-like tunes; *Gebrauchsmusik*; music for radio; ballet (*Billy the Kid*); young people (*The Second Hurricane*); incidental music (*Quiet City*).
4.   1942-1968: return to a more austere, abstract, non-programmatic style integrated with some popular elements. Development of serial techniques after 1950.
B.   Melodic line
1.   Smooth: *Son Pno* (end); *Billy* (Nos. 29-32).
2.   Jagged: *Statements* (beginning); *Connotations*.
3.   Short motives (also harmonic and rhythmic) with wide skips: *Sym 3* (pp. 1, 26).
4.   Declamatory; repeated notes: *Theatre* (beginning); *Beginning* (No. 40).
5.   "Blues" thirds (alternating major and minor): *Theatre* (*Dance*, bsn solo); *Variations* (beginning).
6.   Folk melodies: *México* (No. 7); *Lincoln* (No. 40); *Billy* (before shooting scene); *Spring* (No. 55); *John Henry*.
7.   Folk-like motives: *Sym 3* (p. 51, meas. 4; p. 96, meas. 3).
8.   Borrowed theme: *Vitebsk*.
9.   Quarter tones: *Ukelele Serenade*; *Vitebsk*.
C.   Harmony
1.   Triads are often step-wise and generally non-functional. Chords of the seventh and ninth are often unresolved. Chords built on fourths and fifths and open fourths and fifths are characteristic.
2.   Open fourths and fifths: *Billy*; *Spring*.
3.   Parallel triads: *Sym 3* (p. 52, meas. 19).

4. Thirds and perfect fourths: *Sym 3* (p. 9, meas. 3).
5. Triads moving by second relationship: *Concerto* (clar, pno; p. 2).
6. Triads: *Lincoln* (Nos. 40-50); *Spring* (Nos. 18, 19); *Variations* (No. 7); *México* (Nos. 8, 27).
7. Major and minor triads together: *Variations*.
8. Melodic triads: *Spring* (beginning; Nos. 15-19).
9. Secundal harmony: *Son Pno* (p. 14).
10. Quartal harmony: *Fantasy* (p. 2).
11. Added-note chords: *Billy* (p. 85).
12. Polychords: *Fantasy* (p. 5).
13. Polytonality: *Variations* (No. 5); *Theatre* (*Prologue*; second theme); *Concerto Pno* (No. 19); *Vitebsk*.
14. Free serial techniques: *Qtr Pno Str* (1950); *Fantasy*; *Poet's Song*; *Variations* (No. 7).
15. First completely twelve-tone work: *Connotations* (1962).
16. "Pointillistic" technique: *Sextet* (first movement, recapitulation); *Variations* (No. 3).
17. Chords with all intervals inverted (mirror): *Vitebsk* (p. 2).

D. Counterpoint
1. Moderate use of polyphonic devices and forms. Canon or imitation in two or more parts (often in inversion and with short motives) is characteristic: *Sym 1* (*Finale*, E-hn, ob).
2. Dissonant two- and three-part: *Sonata* (vln, pno) (pp. 3, 31); *Statements* (*Subjective*).
3. Counterpoint between outer voices: *Sym 3* (p. 4, meas. 7; p. 27, meas. 5).
4. Fugato: *Sym 3* (p. 136).
5. Canonic: *Statements* (*Jingo*, No. 12); *Son Vln Pno* (pp. 3, 31); *Variations* (No. 1); *Rodeo* (*Buckaroo Holiday*); *Two Pieces for String Orchestra* (second piece, recapitulation).
6. Mirror canon: *Spring* (No. 63); *Beginning* (No. 200).

E. Rhythm
1. Strong rhythms (simple, complex, jazz, Latin American), polyrhythms, and irregular meters are characteristic.
2. Rapid changes of meter: *Sym 3* (p. 121); *Vocalize*; *Theatre* (No. 5); *Spring* (Nos. 35, 49); *México* (No. 33).
3. Syncopation (usually in melody, sometimes in ostinati): *Billy* (No. 15); *México* (No. 4); *Spring* (No. 37); *Theatre* (No. 5); *Rodeo* (*Waltz*).
4. Polyrhythm: *Billy* (No. 16); *Theatre* (No. 9); *Sextet* (Finale); *Danzón Cubano*; *Rodeo* (*Buckaroo Holiday*).
5. Jazz rhythm: *Theatre* (*Dance*, Nos. 15, 19); *México* (Nos. 15, 31); *Concerto Pno* (second movement).
6. Complex rhythm: *Variations* (No. 16); *Son Pno*.
7. Simple rhythm: *Spring* (Nos 6, 55); *Lincoln* (No. 55); *Statements* (*Jingo*).

F. Form
1. Classical forms (sonata, symphony, variations) comparatively rare. Jazz elements often introduced. Ballets and incidental music, arranged in Suites, are among his best known works.
2. *Passacaglia* (pno) in 4/4 time.
3. Symphonic: *Sym 3* (first movement, three themes, arch form; second movement, scherzo - trio; third movement, free; fourth movement, sonata-allegro).
4. Return in last movement of themes from first movement suggests over-all A - B - A form: *Theatre*; *Sym 3*; *Spring*.

G. Orchestration
1. Brilliant, varied and usually in solid colors; clean, careful scoring; no unnecessary doublings; particularly skillful in small combinations. Exceptionally large orchestra and unusual instruments avoided. Scoring generally idiomatic.

2. Special coloring: *México* (E-flat clar in clarion register); *Spring* (B-flat clar, p. 1, meas. 2); *Quiet City* (trumpet used melodically).
3. Piano: *Theatre*; *Spring*.
4. Speaker: *Lincoln*; *Preamble*.
5. Saxophone: *Theatre*.

BIBLIOGRAPHY

Books by Aaron Copland

1. *What to Listen for in Music.* New York: McGraw Hill, 1939, revised 1957; Mentor, 1964. (tr. German, Italian, Spanish, Dutch, Arabic, Chinese) *MM* 16 (1938-1939), 135; *MQ* 31 (1945), 424; *Mus Tcr* 36 (May 1957), 243; *HiFi* 7 (Jul 1957), 75; *MT* 98 (Dec 1957), 667; *Notes* 15 (Dec 1957), 116; *Neue ZFM* 119 (Jun-Jul 1958), 392; *Mo Mus Rec* 88 (Jul-Aug 1958), 149.
2. *Our New Music.* New York: McGraw Hill, 1941. *NYT* (Oct 19, 1941), sec. 9, p. 7:1; (Oct 26, 1941), sec. 9, p. 8:5; (Nov 2, 1941), sec. 9, p. 6:5; (Nov 30, 1941), sec. 9, p. 7:1; *MQ* 31 (1945), 420.
3. *Music and Imagination.* Cambridge: Harvard University Press, 1952; Mentor, 1959. *NYT* (Oct 12, 1952), sec. 7, p. 7:1; *SR* 35 (Oct 25, 1952), 34; *MA* 72 (Nov 1, 1952), 34; *Notes* 10 (Dec 1952-1953), 95; *Symphony* 6 (Dec 1952), 15; *HiFi* 2 (Nov-Dec 1952), 23; *Crescendo* 3 (Jan-Mar 1953), 16; *Etude* 71 (Feb 1953), 6; *SWMusician* 20 (Nov 1953), 4; *Mo Mus Rec* 83 (Dec 1953), 253-255; *MQ* 39 (1953), 107-109; *ML* 35 (Jan 1954), 50-52; *MT* 95 (Jan 1954), 21; *Mus Opin* 77 (Jan 1954), 221; *Tempo* 31 (Spring 1954), 35; *MT* 101 (Mar 1960), 160; *Mus Opin* 97 (Nov 1973), 73.
4. *Copland on Music.* New York: Doubleday, 1960; W. W. Norton, 1963. (reprint, 1976) *NYT* (Nov 13, 1960), sec. 7, p. 7; *Variety* 221 (Nov 30, 1960), 50; *Instrument* 15 (Dec 1960), 20; *Notes* 18 (1960-1961), 412; *Mus Leader* 95 (Aug 1963), 17; *Mus J* 21 (Oct 1963), 76; 35 (Apr 1977), 36.
5. *The New Music: 1900-1960.* New York: W. W. Norton, 1968. (revised and enlarged edition of *Our New Music*). *Mus J* 26 (Mar 1968), 101; *Tempo* 88 (Spring 1969), 63; *Pan Pipes* 61, No. 2 (1969), 31; *MT* 110 (Aug 1969), 840; *Am Mus Tcr* 18, No. 3 (1969), 44; *Piano Q* 18, No. 70 (1969-1970), 21; *Mus Ed J* 56 (Jan 1970), 11; *Am Rec G* 36 (Jun 1970), 846; *Am Mus Tcr* 20, No. 3 (1971), 33.

Books about Aaron Copland

1. Berger, Arthur. *Aaron Copland.* New York: Oxford University Press, 1953; Westport, CT: Greenwood Press, 1971. *NYT* (Nov 8, 1953), sec. 7, p. 3:3; *SR* 36 (Nov 28, 1953), 36; *MC* 148 (Dec 15, 1953), 10; *MA* 74 (Jan 1, 1954), 28; *Mus Club Mag* 33 (Jan 1954), 18; *MQ* 40 (1954), 93; *JAMS* 7 (1954), 157; *Notes* 11 (Mar 1954), 306; *Tempo* 13 (Spring 1954), 34; *Pan Pipes* 46 (May 1954), 13; *ML* 35 (Jul 1954), 245-247; *Mo Mus Rec* 84 (Nov 1954), 243; *Mus e radio* 52 (Dec 1962), 403.
2. Smith, Julia. *Aaron Copland: His Work and Contribution to American Music.* New York: Dutton, 1955. *MC* 153 (Jan 15, 1956), 30; *Mus Club Mag* 35 (Mar 1956), 13; *MT* 97 (Mar 1956), 135; *Pan Pipes* 48 (Mar 1956), 11; *SR* 39 (Apr 7, 1956), 17; *MA* 76 (May 1956), 29; *School Mus* 27 (Jun 1956), 23; *Jl Research* 4 (Fall 1956), 139; *Etude* 74 (Nov 1956), 8; *Notes* 14 (Mar 1957), 256.
3. *Aaron Copland: A Complete Catalogue of His Works.* New York: Boosey & Hawkes, 1960.
4. Dobrin, Arnold. *Aaron Copland: His Life and Times.* New York: Thomas Y. Crowell, 1967. *CRME* 13 (Spring 1968), 39; *Clavier* 7, No. 5 (1968), 6; *Notes* 24, No. 3 (1968), 500.

5.   Peare, Catherine Owens. *Aaron Copland, His Life*. New York: Holt, Rinehart and Winston, 1969.

Articles by Aaron Copland

1.   "Gabriel Fauré: A Neglected Master," *MQ* 10 (1924), 573.
2.   "George Antheil," *MM* 2, No. 1 (1925-1926), 26.
3.   "Letter on Gustav Mahler," *NYT* (Apr 5, 1925), sec. 9, p. 6:1.
4.   "America's Young Man of Promise," *MM* 3, No. 3 (1925-1926), 13-20.
5.   "Playing Safe at Zürich," *MM* 4, No. 1 (1926-1927), 28.
6.   "Jazz Structure and Influence," *MM* 4, No. 2 (1926-1927), 9.
7.   "Forecast and Review," *MM* 5, No. 1 (1927-1928), 31.
8.   "Stravinsky's 'Oedipus Rex'," *New Republic* 54, No. 691 (Feb 29, 1928), 68.
9.   "Music Since 1920," *MM* 5, No. 3 (1927-1928), 16.
10.   "Carlos Chávez—Mexican Composer," *New Republic* 54, No. 700 (May 2, 1928), 322.
11.   "The Lyricism of Milhaud," *MM* 6, No. 2 (1928-1929), 14.
12.   "From a Composer's Notebook," *MM* 6, No. 4 (1928-1929), 115.
13.   "Modern Orchestration Surveyed by Wellesz," *MM* 8, No. 1 (1930-1931), 41.
14.   "A Note on Nadia Boulanger," *Fontainebleau Alumni Bul* (May 1930).
15.   "Contemporaries at Oxford, 1931," *MM* 9, No. 1 (1931-1932), 17.
16.   "Stravinsky and Hindemith Premières," *MM* 9, No. 2 (1931-1932), 85.
17.   "The Composer and His Critic," *MM* 9, No. 4 (1931-1932), 143.
18.   "One Hundred and Fourteen Songs," *MM* 11, No. 2 (1933-1934), 59.
19.   "Scherchen on Conducting and Ewen on Composers," *MM* 12, No. 2 (1934-1935), 94.
20.   "The American Composer Gets a Break," *The American Mercury* 34 (Apr 1935), 490.
21.   "Active Market in New Music Records," *MM* 13, No. 2 (1935-1936), 45.
22.   "Pioneer Listener," *New Republic* (Apr 15, 1936), 291 (review of *Discoveries of a Music Critic* by Paul Rosenfeld).
23.   "Our Younger Generation—Ten Years Later," *MM* 13, No. 4 (1935-1936), 3.
24.   "Mexican Composer—Silvestre Revueltas," *NYT* (May 9, 1937), sec. 11, p. 5:2.
25.   "World of the Phonograph," *American Scholar* 6, No. 1 (1937), 27-37.
26.   "Scores and Records," *MM* 14, No. 1 (Nov 1936), 39; No. 2 (Jan 1937), 98; No. 3 (Mar 1937), 167; No. 4 (May 1937), 230; 15, No. 1 (Nov 1937), 45; No. 2 (Jan 1938), 109; No. 3 (Mar 1938), 179; No. 4 (May 1938), 244; 16, No. 1 (Nov 1938), 50; No. 2 (Jan 1939), 122; No. 3 (Mar 1939), 185.
27.   "Thomson's Musical State," *MM* 17, No. 1 (1939-1940), 63.
28.   "Second Thoughts on Hollywood," *MM* 17, No. 3 (1939-1940), 260.
29.   "Composer from Brooklyn; Autobiography," *Magazine of Art* 32 (Sept 1939), 522.
30.   "The Aims of Music for Films," *NYT* (Mar 10, 1940), sec. 11, p. 7:4.
31.   "On Composing Music Scores for Films," *NYT* (Jun 23, 1940), sec. 9, p. 3:3.
32.   "The Composer Gets Wise," *MM* 18, No. 1 (1940-1941), 18.
33.   "The Musical Scene Changes," *Twice a Year* 5, 6 (1940-1941), 340.
34.   "Some Notes on My 'Music for the Theatre'," *Vic Rec Rev* (Mar 1941), 6.
35.   "Five Post-Romantics," *MM* 18, No. 4 (1940-1941), 218 (from *Our New Music*).
36.   "The Composers of South America," *MM* 19, No. 2 (1941-1942), 75.
37.   "Latin-Americans in Music," *WQXR Program Book* (Jun 1942).
38.   "From the '20's to the '40's and Beyond," *MM* 21, No. 2 (1943-1944), 78.
39.   "Serge Koussevitsky and the American Composer," *MQ* 30 (1944), 255-261.
40.   "The American Composer Today," *U. S. A.* (Government Publication) vol. 2, No. 10, p. 23.
41.   "On the Notation of Rhythm," *MM* 21, No. 4 (1943-1944), 217.
42.   "Fauré Festival at Harvard," *NYHT* (Nov 25, 1945).
43.   "Neglected Works: A Symposium," *MM* 23, No. 1 (1946), 3.
44.   "Memorial to Paul Rosenfeld," *Notes* 4 (1946-1947), 147.

45. "South American Report," *NYT* (Dec 21, 1947), sec. 2, p. 9:3.
46. "The New 'School' of American Composers," *NYT Magazine* (Mar 14, 1948), 18.
47. "Review of Benjamin Britten's 'The Rape of Lucretia'," *Notes* 4 1946-1947), 190.
48. "Influence, Problem, Tone," *Dance Index* 6, Nos. 10, 11, 12 (1947), 249.
49. "The Art of Darius Milhaud," *SR* 31 (Jun 26, 1948), 43.
50. "Review of Stefan Wolfe's 'Two Songs for Alto and Piano'," *Notes* 6 (1948-1949), 172.
51. "Review of Darius Milhaud's 'First Symphony'," *SR* 31 (Jun 26, 1948), 43.
52. "The Personality of Stravinsky," in *Igor Stravinsky*, ed. Edwin Corle. New York, 1949, p. 121.
53. "On the Composer's Craft," *International Musician* (May 1949).
54. "Review of Peter Gradenwitz's 'The Music of Israel'," *NYHT* (Oct 2, 1949).
55. "Tips to Moviegoers: Take Off Their Ear-Muffs," *NYT* (Nov 6, 1949), sec. 6, p. 28.
56. "Review of René Leibowitz's 'Schoenberg and His School'," *NYHT* (Nov 27, 1949).
57. "A Modernist Defends Modern Music," *NYT* (Dec 25, 1949), sec. 6, p. 11.
58. "Review of Leon Kirchner's 'Duo for Violin and Piano'," *Notes* 7 (1949-1950), 434.
59. "The American Musical Scene," *Musik Olympiad* (Salzburg) 1, No. 1 (1950).
60. "A Modernist Defends Modern Music," *BSCBul* No. 14 (Feb 3, 1950), 760; also No. 56.
61. "Review of William Schuman's 'Fourth String Quartet'," *MQ* 37 (1951), 394.
62. "Problems de la Musique de Film," *Vie Music* 1 (Mar 1951), 5.
63. "An Indictment of the Fourth B," *NYT Magazine* (Sep 21, 1952), 18; *Mus J* 10 (Nov 1952), 13.
64. "The Gifted Listener," *SR* 35 (Sep 27, 1952), 41.
65. "Creativity in America," *Proceedings, National Institute of Arts and Letters* (1953), 33.
66. "Review of Darius Milhaud's 'Notes Without Music'," *NYHT* (Feb 22, 1953).
67. "Review of Halsey Steven's 'The Life and Music of Béla Bartók'," *NYHT* (May 3, 1953).
68. "The measure of Kapell," *SR* 36 (Nov 28, 1953), 67.
69. "Festival in Caracas," *NYT* (Dec 26, 1954), sec. 2, p. 9:6.
70. "Music: As an Aspect of the Human Spirit," *MC* 151 (Feb 1, 1955), 54.
71. "Modern Music: Reply to Henry Pleasants," *NYT* (Mar 13, 1955), sec. 6, p. 15.
72. "At the Thought of Mozart," *HiFi* 6 (Jan 1956), 53.
73. "Rubin Goldmark: A Tribute," *Juilliard Rev* 3, No. 3 (Fall 1956), 15.
74. "The Dilemma of Our Symphony Orchestras," *MC* 154, No. 5 (Nov 1956), 6.
75. "Fantasy for Piano: Composer Explains its Particular Problems," *Tempo* 46 (1958), 13.
76. "The Twentieth Century: Reorientation and Experiment," in *Music and Western Man*, ed. Peter Garvie. New York: Philosophical Library, 1958, p. 281.
77. *The Pleasures of Music* (Monograph). Durham: University of New Hampshire, 1959.
78. "Pleasures of Music," *Sat Evening Post* 232 (Jul 4, 1959), 18.
79. "Making Music in the Star-Spangled Manner," *MM* 8 (Aug 1960), 8.
80. "Composer and Composing," *SR* 43 (Aug 27, 1960), 33-35.
81. "A Tribute to Franz Liszt," *HiFi* 5 (Oct 1960), 46-49.
82. "Nadia Boulanger: An Affectionate Portrait," *Harpers* 221 (Oct 1960), 49-51.
83. "A Businessman Who Wrote Music on Sundays," *MM* 9 (Nov 1960), 18.
84. "America's Young Men of Music," *MM* 9 (Dec 1960), 11.
85. "A Quarter-Century Reflection," *ACA* 11, No. 2-4 (1963), 1.
86. "An Indictment of the Fourth B," *Mus J* 22 (Mar 1964), 29; also No. 62.
87. "In Memory of Marc Blitzstein," *PNM* 2, No. 2 (1964), 6.
88. "The Composer and His Critic," *PNM* 2, No. 2 (1964), 22; also No. 17.
89. "Neglected Works: A Symposium," *PNM* 2, No. 2 (1964), 31; also No. 43.
90. "The Contemporary Scene: Excerpt from Address, May 1966," *SR* 49 (Jun 25, 1966), 49.
91. "Are My Ears on Wrong?" *SFSPN* (Feb 1967), 6.
92. "Vom richtigen Anhören der Musik," *Orchester* 16 (Mar 1968), 141.
93. "Composers Conducting Their Own Works," *NYT* (Jun 9, 1968), sec. 2, p. 17:1.
94. "Copyright Revision and the U. S. Symphonic Composer (testimony before House sub-com-

mittee on 1909 Copyright Act revision),'' *ASCAP* 7, No. 2 (1975), 9.
95. "Music is the Message," *Chris Sc Mon* 68 (Jul 22, 1976), 24 (reprint from *Music and Imagination*).

References to Aaron Copland

Books
(See the General Bibliography)

AbrHY; AbrMM; AntBB; ASC-BD; ASC-SC; AusMT; BacMM; Baker; BakSL; BauTC; BIM; BloYA; BluPC; BMI-OP; BroOH; BrooCG; Bull; CatPC; ChaAC; ChaAM; ClaEA; CobCS; CohTC; ColHM; ComA-1; CopON; CopTN; CowAC; CurB (1940, 1951); DalTT; DavPM; DemMT; DerETM; DowO; DukLH; EdmI; EscCF; EweAC; EweCB; EweCS; EweDE; EweNB; EweYA; GolMM; GolTP; GosMM; GraMM; GrosSH; Grove; HanIT; HitMU; HodSD; HowMM; HowOA; HowOC; HowSH; JohOA; JohSH; KinAI; KolMO; LeiMW; LeiSK; MacAC; MacIC; MelMN; MelMS; MelRT; MorgCM; MorrCA; MueAS; MyeTC; NorLC; OveFA; PanMC; PAC; PavMH; PersTH; PeyNM; PleSM; PorM3S; ReiCA; RosAH; RosDM; RosMI; RowFC; SalMO; SalzTM; SamLM; SanWM; SchCC; SesRM; SloMS; StevHS; StevePC; ThoAJ; ThoAM; ThompGM; ThompIC; ThoMR; ThoMS; ThoRL; WhiWW; WooWM; WWA; WWM; YatTC; YouCD; YouCT.

Rosenfeld, Paul. "Copland Without Jazz," in *By Way of Art*. New York: Doward-McCann, 1928, p. 266.
Clurman, Harold. *The Fervent Years*. New York: A. A. Knopf, 1950.
Mille, Agnes de. *Dance to the Piper* (*Rodeo*). New York: Little, Brown, 1952.

Articles about Aaron Copland

Brief mention: *MQ* 15 (1929), 292, 607, 615; 16 (1930), 24; 18 (1932), 11; 20 (1934), 214; 21 (1935), 54; *Etude* 59 (Mar 1941), 152; *MQ* 28 (1942), 140; *MM* 20, No. 2 (1942-1943), 99; *Life* 16 (Apr 24, 1944), 58; *MQ* 43 (1946), 362; 370; *SR* 32 (Aug 6, 1949), 160; 33 (Jun 3, 1950), 27; *Etude* 69 (Jan 1951); *SR* 35 (Oct 25, 1952), 33; *MQ* 40 (1954), 591; 41 (1955), 421; *SR* 39 (Apr 7, 1955), 17; *MA* 75 (Jul 1955), 13; *MQ* 42 (1956), 35, 245; *PNM* 1, No. 1 (1962), 2; 1, No. 2 (1963), 151, 211; 2, No. 2 (1964), 14, 16, 126, 176; 4, No. 1 (1966), 158, 172; 4, No. 2 (1966), 26, 35.
1. Goldberg, Isaac. "Aaron Copland and His Jazz," *The American Mercury* 26 (1927), 63.
2. Rosenfeld, Paul. "Copland Without Jazz," in *By Way of Art*. New York: Doward-McCann (1928), 266.
3. *NYT* (Feb 10, 1930), 21:1; (Mar 17, 1930), 20:4; (Apr 14, 1930), 24:7.
4. *NYT* (Mar 16, 1931), 24:3.
5. Rosenfeld, Paul. "Aaron Copland's Growth," *New Republic* 76 (May 27, 1931), 46-47.
6. ————"New American Music," *Scribner's Magazine* 89 (Jun 1931), 624-632.
7. Thomson, Virgil. "Aaron Copland," *MM* 9, No. 2 (1931-1932), 67.
8. Goldberg, Isaac. "Aaron Copland," *Disques* 3 (1932), 285.
9. *NYT* (May 8, 1932), sec. 8, p. 6:1; (Dec 22, 1932), 20:6.
10. "Elected to Executive Board of League of Composers," *NYT* (Mar 5, 1933), sec. 9, p. 6.
11. "Composers get a Chance to Exhibit in One-man Shows," *NW* 6 (Nov 2, 1935), 41.
12. *NYT* (Oct 12, 1935), 13:3.
13. Slonimsky, Nicolas. "The Six of American Music," *Chris Sc Mon Mag* (Mar 17, 1937), 8.
14. *NYT* (May 9, 1937), sec. 11, p. 5:2.
15. *NYT* (Aug 8, 1938), 9:1; (Nov 27, 1938), sec. 9, p. 8:5.
16. Rosenfeld, Paul. "The Advance of American Music," *Ken Rev* (Spring 1939), 185.
17. *NYT* (May 8, 1939), 20:4.
18. "For the People," *Time* 33 (Jun 5, 1939), 60.

19. Rosenfeld, Paul. "Copland, Harris, Schuman," *MQ* 25 (1939), 372-376.
20. *NYT* (Mar 10, 1940), sec. 11, p. 7:4.
21. "Elected President of the American Composers Alliance," *NYT* (May 24, 1940), 23:3.
22. "Biography," *Current Biography* (Sep 1940); *Current Biography Yearbook* (1940), 190.
23. "Honored by Town Hall Club," *NYT* (Feb 17, 1941), 11:1.
24. Diamond, David. "The Composer and Film Music," *Decision* 1 (Mar 1941), 57.
25. *NYT* (May 30, 1941), 17:3.
26. "Portrait of a Composer," *NYT* (Aug 24, 1941), sec. 9, p. 6:6.
27. *NYT* (Dec 21, 1941), sec. 9, p. 7:6; (Jun 18, 1942), 24:2.
28. Mellers, Wilfrid H. "Language and Function in American Music," *Scrutiny* 10 (1942), 346.
29. *NYT* (Nov 4, 1942), 26:4; (Dec 20, 1942), sec. 8, p. 6:3.
30. Kochnitzky, Leon. "Musical Portraits," *MM* 20, No. 1 (1942-1943), 27.
31. Morton, Lawrence. "Music Notes," *Script* (Mar 20, 1943), 24.
32. Mellers, Wilfrid H. "American Music," *Ken Rev* 5, No. 3 (Summer 1943), 370.
33. Eyer, Ronald F. "Meet the Composer: Aaron Copland," *MA* 63, No. 16 (Dec 10, 1943), 7.
34. *NYT* (Jan 10, 1944), 15:5; (Jan 22, 1944), 9:1; (Mar 1, 1945), 23:4.
35. Berger, Arthur. "Aspects of Aaron Copland's Music," *Tempo* 10 (Mar 1945), 2.
36. ————"The Music of Aaron Copland, with List of Works," *MQ* 31 (1945), 420-447.
37. "Wins Pulitzer Prize (Appalachian Spring: Ballet)," *NYT* (May 8, 1945), 16:1, 3.
38. *NYT* (Feb 17, 1946), 36:6; (Oct 15, 1946), 27:6; (Oct 20, 1946), sec. 2, p. 7:1.
39. Sargeant, Winthrop. "The Case of Aaron Copland," *Tomorrow* 5, No. 10 (Jun 1946), 54.
40. Canby, Edward T. "Music and Electricity," *SR* 29 (Aug 17, 1946), 31.
41. "Gets Boston Symphony Orchestra Merit Award," *NYT* (Jan 10, 1947), 16:1.
42. Lederman, Minna. "Some American Composers," *Vogue* 137 (Feb 1, 1947), 184.
43. "Commissioned by Kostelanetz to Compose UN Symphony," *NYT* (Feb 16, 1947), sec. 2, p. 9:2.
44. "Re-elected Composers League National Chairman," *NYT* (May 8, 1947), 30:2.
45. *NYT* (Jun 1, 1947), sec. 2, p. 7:7.
46. "Wins New York Music Critics Circle Award," *NYT* (Jun 6, 1947), 26:2.
47. Heinsheimer, Hans W. "Aaron Copland," *Tomorrow* 7, No. 3 (Nov 1947), 17.
48. *NYT* (Nov 17, 1947), 25:4; (Dec 21, 1947), sec. 2, p. 9:3.
49. Fuller, Donald. "A Symphonist Goes to Folk Sources," *MA* 63, No. 3 (Feb 1948), 29.
50. "New School of American Composers," *NYT* (Mar 14, 1948), sec. 6, p. 18.
51. Kubly, Herbert. "America's No. 1 Composer," *Esquire* 28, No. 4 (Apr 1948), 57.
52. "Aaron Copland in Brazil," *Bulletin Pan Amer Union* 82 (May 1948), 293.
53. Heylbut, Rose. "America Goes to the Ballet," *Etude* 66 (Jul 1948), 401.
54. Salas, J. Orrego, Wilfrid Mellers, Arthur Berger. *Tempo* 9 (Autumn 1948). Entire issue devoted to Aaron Copland.
55. Anthiel, George. "American Music Must Grow Up," *Tomorrow* 8, No. 16 (Feb 1949), 35.
56. "Aaron Copland on the Composer's Craft," *Int Musician* 47 (May 1949), 34.
57. Hanson, Howard. "The Flowering of American Music," *SR* 32 (Aug 6, 1949), 160.
58. *NYT* (Nov 6, 1949), sec. 6, p. 28; (Dec 25, 1949), sec. 6, p. 11; (Jan 8, 1950), sec. 6, p. 6:5; (Jan 15, (1950), sec. 6, p. 2:5; sec. 6, p. 4:3, 4; (Apr 21, 1950), 25:6.
59. "Cincuentenario de dos musica," *Rev Mus Chilena* 6 (Spring 1950), 115.
60. Behrens, E. "Says Aaron Copland–'Take off the Ear Muffs'," *Mus Club Mag* 29 (Apr 1950), 10.
61. "Retired as Board Chairman, League of Composers," *NYT* (May 22, 1950), 16:2.
62. Cowell, Henry. "Twelve Poems of Emily Dickinson; Song Cycle," *MQ* 36 (1950), 453.
63. "Copland to be Feted," *MC* 142 (Oct 15, 1950), 12.
64. *NYT* (Oct 8, 1950), 95:1; (Oct 29, 1950), sec. 2, p. 7:1; (Nov 5, 1950), sec. 2, p. 9:2; (Nov 6, 1950), 32:7.
65. "Aaron Copland Reaches the Half-Century Mark," *MA* 70, No. 13 (Nov 15, 1950), 14.

66. "Trail Blazer from Brooklyn," *Time* 56 (Nov 20, 1950), 50-52.
67. Berger, Arthur. "The Home-Grown Copland," *SR* 33 (Nov 25, 1950), 72.
68. Smith, Cecil. "League of Composers Program Celebrates Copland Birthday," *MA* 70 (Dec 1, 1950), 18.
69. "Copland Feted by Composers' League," *MC* 142 (Dec 1, 1950), 40.
70. Hopkins, Anthony. "The Music of Copland," *Sight and Sound* 19, No. 8 (Dec 1950), 336.
71. Kyle, Marguerite K. "AmerAllegro," *Pan Pipes* 43 (Dec 1950), 111-113.
72. Moor, Paul. "Aaron Copland," *Theatre Arts* 35, No. 1 (Jan 1951), 40.
73. Rosenwald, Hans. "Contemporary Music," *Mus News* 43 (Jan 1951), 7.
74. Goldman, Richard F. "Current Chronicle," *MQ* 37 (1951), 89.
75. Downes, Olin. "Le 50^e Anniversaire de Aaron Copland," *Vie Music* 1 (Mar 1951), 4.
76. "Appointed Norton Professor of Poetry, Harvard University," *NYT* (Mar 11, 1951), 78:5.
77. "Copland in Harvard Poetry Post," *MC* 143 (Mar 15, 1951), 19.
78. "Biography," *Current Biography* (Mar 1951); *Current Biography Yearbook* (1951), 136-139.
79. Sternfeld, Frederick. "Copland as a Film Composer," *MQ* 37 (1951), 161-175.
80. *NYT* (May 13, 1951), sec. 2, p. 7:8.
81. Finkelstein, Sidney. "The Music of Aaron Copland," *Amer Rec G* 17 (May 1951), 290-294.
82. *NYT* (Jun 1, 1951), 20:6; (Jun 10, 1951), sec. 2, p. 5:7.
83. Frankenstein, Alfred. "Art and Music," *Magazine of Art* 44, No. 8 (Dec 1951), 303.
84. "Aaron Copland," *Film Mus Notes* 10 (Mar-Apr 1951), 3; *Tempo* 21 (Autumn 1951), 1; *Pan Pipes* 44 (Jan 1952), 27.
85. Finkelstein, Sidney. "The Music of Aaron Copland," *Mus Parade* 17 (Jun 1951), 329-333.
86. Flanagan, William. "American Songs, A Thin Crop," *MA* 72, No. 3 (Feb 1952), 23.
87. *NYT* (Feb 24, 1952), sec. 2, p. 7:7; (May 29, 1952), 24:1; (Jun 8, 1952), sec. 2, p. 7:8; (Sep 21, 1952), sec. 6, p. 18; (Sep 28, 1952), sec. 6, p. 2:3; (Oct 5, 1952), sec. 6, p. 4:5; (Oct 12, 1952), sec. 6, p. 6:3.
88. Berger, Arthur. "The Music of Aaron Copland," *Perspectives* (London) 1 (Autumn 1952), 105-130.
89. "Modern Music," *Int Mus News* 1 (Nov 1952), 5.
90. *NYT* (Jan 17, 1953), 12:4.
91. "A. Copland," *Pan Pipes* 45 (Jan 1953), 45.
92. "Wicked Music," *New Republic* 128 (Jan 26, 1953), 7.
93. *NYT* (May 27, 1953), 18:2.
94. Brant, LeRoy V. "America, Involved in Music, is Becoming Great in Music," *Etude* 71 (Apr 1953), 9.
95. "A. Copland, Assistant Director, Berkshire Music Center," *NYT* (May 15, 1953), 91:5.
96. "An Editorial ('Blackballing of Certain American Composers Caused by Bending to Warped Notions of Americanism')," *Down Beat* 20 (Jun 3, 1953), 125.
97. Haggin, Bernard H. "Music; Music for Listeners of Today," *Nation* 177 (Jul 25, 1953), 79.
98. Citkowitz, Israel. "Aaron Copland: Personal Note," *BSCBul* 2 (Oct 17, 1953), 68.
99. Berger, Arthur. "Copland Landmark," *SR* 36 (Oct 31, 1953), 74.
100. RePass, R. "American Composers of Today," *London Mus* 8 (Dec 1953), 25.
101. "Notes of the Day," *Mo Mus Rec* 84 (Jan 1954), 1-3.
102. Heinsheimer, Hans W. "Bugles and Bells (Generation of American Composers of Importance Without Interest in Musical Theatre)," *MC* 149 (Mar 1, 1954), 5.
103. Finkelstein, Sidney. "Aaron Copland and American Music," *Masses and Mainstream* 7 (Mar 1954) 50-56.
104. Berger, Arthur. "Hindemith, Copland; Recordings," *SR* 37 (Mar 27, 1954), 63.
105. Morton, Lawrence. "Copland (Review of Recordings)," *MQ* (1954), 294-296.
106. *NYT* (Mar 28, 1954), sec. 2, p. 7:7; (Apr 6, 1954), 35:2.

107. McCarty, C. "Book of Copland Misses Target of His Filmusic," *Down Beat* 21 (Jun 16, 1954), 5.

108. *NYT* (Aug 15, 1954), 77:1.

109. Blitzstein, Marc. "Music for the Theatre," *MQ* 40 (1954), 454-456.

110. Keats. Sheila. "Reference Articles on American Composers; An Index," *Juilliard Rev* 1 (Fall 1954), 24.

111. Yates, Peter. "Dylan Thomas, Aaron Copland and Emery on Ornaments," *Arts and Architecture* 71, No. 9 (Sep 1954), 6.

112. *NYT* (Oct 10, 1954), sec. 2, p. 9:1.

113. Berger, Arthur. "Spotlight on the Moderns," *SR* 37 (Oct 30, 1954), 78.

114. "Aaron Copland; Chronological Catalog of the Works of the American Composer," *Musica Y Artes* 57-58 (Nov-Dec 1954), 33-38.

115. "Elected to American Academy of Arts and Letters," *NYT* (Dec 17, 1954), 28:3.

116. "Composer-Chairman—League of Composers International Society of Contemporary Music," *NYT* (Dec 2, 1954), 38:1.

117. Porter, Andrew. "Aaron Copland," *London Musical Events* 9 (Dec 1954), 33; (Jan 1955), 31.

118. "Aaron Copland Elected to American Academy," *MC* 151 (Jan 1, 1955), 28.

119. Porter, Andrew. "Aaron Copland's Theatre and Film Music (includes List of Ballet Music on Records)," *London Musical Events* 10 (Jan 1955), 31.

120. "Aaron Copland," *Pan Pipes* 47 (Jan 1955), 37.

121. *NYT* (Mar 13, 1955), sec. 6, p. 15; (Mar 27, 1955), sec. 6, p. 4:4; (Apr 3, 1955), sec. 6, p. 4:4.

122. "Aaron Copland," *Composers of the Americas* 1 (1955), 26-35.

123. "Inducted into American Academy of Arts and Letters," *NYT* (May 26, 1955), 62:1.

124. Carter, Elliott. "The Rhythmic Basis of American Music," *Score* 12 (Jun 1955), 28.

125. Berger, Arthur. "Stravinsky and the Younger American Composers," *Score* 12 (Jun 1955), 38-46.

126. Salas, J. Orrego. "Aaron Copland's Vision of America," *Américas* 7 (Jun 1955), 17-21.

127. Berger, Arthur. "An Aaron Copland Discography," *HiFi* 5 (Jul 1955), 64-69.

128. Stambler, Bernard. "Four American Composers (Copland, Schuman, Barber, Ives)," *Juilliard Rev* 2 (Winter 1955), 7-16.

129. Häusler, Josef. "Aaron Copland in Deutschland," *Musica* 9 (Nov 1955), 559.

130. *NYT* (Jan 1, 1956), sec. 7, p. 5:1.

131. "National Institute of Arts and Letters Election," *NYT* (Jan 20, 1956), 7:2.

132. "Named Honorary Member of St. Cecilia Academy of Rome," *NYT* (Mar 6, 1956), 27:1.

133. Haggin, Bernard H. "Music," *Nation* 182 (Mar 24, 1956), 247.

134. *NYT* (Mar 29, 1956), 24:3.

135. "Thumb Nail Notes on American Composers," *Mus Tcr* 35 (Mar 1956), 159.

136. "U. S. Composers in a Bright Era," *Life* 40 (May 21, 1956), 145.

137. "Wins Gold Medal," *NYT* (May 24, 1956), 25:1.

138. "Honorary Degree, Princeton University," *NYT* (Jun 13, 1956), 41:3.

139. *NYT* (Jun 16, 1956), 12:1.

140. Ellsworth, Ray. "Americans on Microgroove," *HiFi* 6 (Aug 1956), 64.

141. "World of Music," *Etude* 74 (Oct 1956), 5.

142. Overton, Hal. "Copland's Jazz Roots," *Jazz Today* 1 (Nov 1956), 40.

143. "Second in Our Poll of America's Most Distinguished Composers We Salute—Aaron Copland," *Mus Club Mag* 36 (Jan 1957), 7.

144. "Appointed Visiting Slee Professor, Buffalo University," *NYT* (Jan 25, 1957), 16:3.

145. Thomson, Virgil. "Presentation Speech," *Proceedings, American Academy of Arts and Letters*, Series 2, No. 7 (1957).

146. "Guide to Record Collection; Aaron Copland Suggests A Basic Mahler Library," *HiFi* 4 (Mar-Apr 1957), 26.

147. Gräter, Manfred. "Aaron Copland besucht Europa," *Melos* 27 (Apr 1957), 108-110.
148. "Honorary Degree, Brandeis University," *NYT* (Jun 10, 1957), 18:5.
149. Arlen, Walter, and Albert Goldberg. "Ojai Festival Revolves Around Works of Copland," *MA* 77 (Jul 1957), 10.
150. *NYT* (Aug 9, 1957), 11:2.
151. Taubman, Howard. "A Week for Youth; Plan for Orchestras to Give Some Time Each Season to Young Composers," *NYT* (Aug 11, 1957), sec. 2, p. 7:1.
152. *NYT* (Jan 31, 1958), 24:6; (Feb 2, 1958), 78:4.
153. Sargeant, Winthrop. "Musical Events," *New Yorker* 33 (Feb 8, 1958), 115.
154. Kolodin, Irving. "Mödl as Isolde, Copland as Conductor," *SR* 41 (Feb 15, 1958), 31.
155. "New York Philharmonic," *MC* 157 (Mar 1958), 15.
156. Crankshaw, Geoffrey. "Aaron Copland," *Chesterian* 32 (Spring 1958), 97-101.
157. Gold, Don. "Aaron Copland; the Well-Known American Composer Finds Virtues and Flaws in Jazz," *Down Beat* 25 (May 1, 1958), 16.
158. *NYT* (May 12, 1958), 25:1.
159. Eble, Charles. "Iowa University Honors Copland," *MA* 78 (Jul 1958), 33.
160. *NYT* (Aug 8, 1958), 9:1.
161. Blanks, Fred R. "Aaron Copland, a Vital Force in American Music," *Canon* 12 (Aug 1958), 413-415.
162. Keller, Hans. "Dartington Summer School," *Mus Opin* 82 (Oct 1958), 15.
163. Ottaway, Hugh. "Radio Notes," *Mus Opin* 82 (Oct 1958), 35.
164. *NYT* (Dec 5, 1958), 39:7.
165. "Copland Conducts Little Orchestra," *MA* 79 (Jan 15, 1959), 16.
166. "Receives Philadelphia Music Academy Award," *NYT* (Jan 25, 1959), 70:7.
167. Newman, Brian. "Aaron Copland," *Gramophone* 36 (Feb 1959), 396.
168. "American Composers—Aaron Copland," *MC* 159 (Mar 1959), 39.
169. Singer, Samuel L. "Philadelphia (Philadelphia Academy of Music Award for Distinguished Service of Music)," *MC* 159 (Mar 1959), 28.
170. Evans, Peter. "The Thematic Technique of Copland's Recent Works," *Tempo* 51 (Spring-Summer 1959), 2-13.
171. *NYT* (Jul 27, 1959), 21:2; (Nov 20, 1959), 36:1; (Nov 22, 1959), 83:4.
172. Goldman, Richard F. "The Copland Festival," *Juilliard Rev* 8, No. 1 (1960-1961), 14.
173. Schuman, William. "A Birthday Salute to Aaron Copland," *Juilliard Rev* 8, No. 1 (1960-1961), 6.
174. "Program (Juilliard Concert in Celebration of 60th Birthday)," *Juilliard Rev* 8, No. 1 (1960-1961), 8-13.
175. Dumm, Robert W. "Boston," *MC* 161 (Feb 1960), 41.
176. "Brandeis University Creative Arts Award," *NYT* (Mar 5, 1960), 17:6.
177. *NYT* (Mar 8, 1960), 38:4; (Mar 17, 1960), 29:4.
178. "This Month's Personality," *MM* 8 (Apr 1960), 5.
179. "Copland Conducts His Own Compositions," *Mus Events* 15 (Apr 1960), 11.
180. Drew, David. "Aaron Copland Returns," *New Statesman* 59 (Apr 30, 1960), 620.
181. Shneerson, Grigori. "Amerikanskie Kompozitory v Moskve," *Sovet Muz* 24 (May 1960), 135-137.
182. "Aaron Copland," *Canon* 13 (May-Jun 1960), 239.
183. Scott-Maddocks, D. "Aaron Copland," *MM* 8 (Jun 1960), 25.
184. Lade, John. "Aaron Copland Concert," *MT* 101 (Jun 1960), 372.
185. "Aaron Copland Tours the USSR, Japan and the UK," *World Mus* 3 (Jun 1960), 56.
186. "Editorial Notes," *Strad* 71 (Jun 1960), 53.
187. Goodwin, Noel. "England," *MC* 161 (Jun 1960), 13.
188. Noble, Jeremy. "Music Survey," *Mus Events* 15 (Jun 1960), 14.
189. *NYT* (Jun 12, 1960), 46:4; (Aug 15, 1960), 18:1.
190. Kyle, Marguerite K. "AmerAllegro," *Pan Pipes* 52, No. 2 (1960), 43.

191. Grigoriev, L., and Y. Platek. "Two American Composers in Moscow," *Mus J* 18 (Jun-Jul 1960), 60.
192. *NYT* (Nov 12, 1960), 15:3; (Nov 13, 1960), 87:3.
193. Salzman, Eric. "Dean of Our Composers at Sixty," *NYT* (Nov 13, 1960), sec. 6, p. 51.
194. "Visit to Peekskill," *NW* 56 (Nov 14, 1960), 98.
195. *NYT* (Nov 15, 1960), 47:4. 5; (Nov 17, 1960), 45:4.
196. Sargeant, Winthrop. "Copland as Conductor," *New Yorker* 36 (Nov 19, 1960), 150.
197. "Copland at Sixty," *Time* 76 (Nov 21, 1960), 93.
198. Trimble, Lester. "Profile at Sixty," *MA* 80 (Nov 1960), 13.
199. Foldes, Andor. "Porträts," *Musica* 14 (Nov 1960), 749.
200. Swickard, Ralph. "All-Copland Concert Honors 60th Birthday," *Mus West* 16 (Dec 1960), 10.
201. Sabin, Robert. "Philharmonic Marks Copland's Birthday," *MA* 80 (Dec 1960), 37.
202. Trimble, Lester. "Copland Guest with Philharmonic," *MA* 80 (Dec 1960), 37.
203. "Copland Conducts Concert with the Philharmonic," *MC* 162 (Dec 1960), 18.
204. Trimble, Lester. "Copland Birthday Concerts," *MA* 80 (Dec 1960), 84.
205. Skovran, Dusan. "Beograd," *ZVUK* 49-50 (1961), 551.
206. Goldman, Richard F. "Aaron Copland," *MQ* 47 (1961), 1-3.
207. "Headlines of 1960," *MA* 81 (Jan 1961), 20.
208. "Copland Poetic and Copland Extroverted," *HiFi* 6 (Feb 1961), 72.
209. Trimble, Lester. "Music; Concert Version of Second Hurricane by Students from High School of Music and Art, N. Y.," *Nation* 192 (Feb 11, 1961), 127.
210. *NYT* (Mar 15, 1961), 44:1.
211. Rich, Alan. "Composer's Showcase," *MA* 81 (Mar 1961), 47.
212. Kyle, Marguerite K. "AmerAllegro," *Pan Pipes* 53, No. 2 (1961), 47.
213. "Copland at Sixty," *Tempo* 57 (Spring 1961), 1.
214. "Aaron Copland's Anniversary Year," *Mus & Dance* 51 (Apr 1961), 13.
215. Marsh, Robert C. "As High Fidelity Sees It," *HiFi* 11 (May 1961), 29.
216. "TV show gets Emmy award," *FoF* 21 (May 16, 1961), 180D2.
217. Blake, A. "American Classical Releases," *Metro* 78 (Jun 1961), 27.
218. "Honorary Degree from Harvard University," *NYT* (Jun 16, 1961), 3:2.
219. Naylor, P. "Aaron Copland at College," *RCM* 57, No. 3 (1961), 72.
220. Ottaway, Hugh. "Radio Notes," *Mus Opin* 84 (Jul 1961), 621.
221. "Gets MacDowell Award," *FoF* (Aug 19, 1961), 368B1.
222. "Edward MacDowell Medal," *NYT* (Aug 20, 1961), 80:4.
223. "Six on the State of Music (Future of Symphony Orchestra and Musicians)," *Mus Mag* 163 (Oct 1961), 23.
224. *NYT* (Nov 15, 1961), 51:7.
225. Kerman. J. "American Music: The Columbia Series," *Hudson Rev* 14 (Fall 1961), 408-418.
226. "Brooklyn Academy Honor," *NYT* (Nov 18, 1961), 7:3.
227. "President of Edward MacDowell Association," *NYT* (Jan 25, 1962), 24:4; 25:1.
228. *NYT* (Feb 4, 1962), sec. 4, pp. 24, 25; (Feb 15, 1962), 23:6; (Feb 20, 1962), 31:1, 2.
229. Taylor, M. "Aaron Copland," *MM* 10 (Mar 1962), 41.
230. Garvie, Peter. "Aaron Copland," *Can Mus J* 6, No. 2 (1962), 3-12.
231. Chapman, Ernest. "I S. O.–L. P. O.–B. B. C.," *Mus Events* 17 (Apr 1962), 12.
232. "Editorial Notes," *Strad* 72 (Apr 1962), 437.
233. Tircuit, Heuwell. "Tokyo," *Mus Mag* 164 (Apr 1962), 41.
234. Beale, Jane G. "Seattle," *Mus Mag* 164 (Apr 1962), 64.
235. "Music in London," *MT* 103 (Apr 1962), 242.
236. "Appointed to Music Advisory Commission, Hopkins Center, Dartmouth College," *NYT* (May 27, 1962), 96:2.
237. Yarustovsky, Boris. "Journey to America," *J Res Mus Ed* 10, No. 2 (1962), 124.

238. Kyle, Marguerite K. "AmerAllegro," *Pan Pipes* 54, No. 2 (1962), 42.
239. Chávez, Carlos. "Ives y Copland," *Clave* 49 (Aug-Sep 1962), 19-23.
240. *NYT* (Sep 24, 1962), 34:4, 6-8.
241. Günther, Siegfried. "USA-Sinfoniker des 20. Jahrhunderts," *Orchester* 10 (Dec 1962), 395.
242. Freeman, John W. "The Reluctant Composer," (an interview) *Opera N* 27 (Jan 26, 1963), 8-12.
243. Goodwin, Noel. "The Quiet American," *MM* 11 (Feb 1963), 16.
244. "Previously Unpublished Composers' Letters as Written to Clair R. Reis," *MA* 83 (Jan 1963), 14.
245. Kyle, Marguerite K. "AmerAllegro," *Pan Pipes* 55, No. 2 (1963), 43.
246. Kammerer, Rafael. "Three by Copland from CRI," *Am Rec G* 30 (Sep 1963), 43.
247. Voss, R. H. "Industrialist Serves Music: Cincinnati's Mr. Corbett," *Mus J* 22 (Mar 1964), 78.
248. "Aaron Copland," *MM* 12 (May 1964), 11; *Mus Events* 19 (May 1964), 24.
249. Schmidt-Garre, Helmut. "Vier Komponisten in eigener Sache," *Neue ZFM* 125, No. 2 (1964), 69.
250. Thomson, Virgil. "Aaron Copland," *PNM* 2, No. 2 (1964), 21.
251. Evans, Peter. "Copland on the Serial Road," *PNM* 2, No. 2 (1964), 141.
252. "American in London," *NW* 63 (Jan 8, 1964), 88.
253. "Music from Manhattan; Copland's Music for a Great City, Played by London Symphony Orchestra at Royal Festival Hall, London," *Time* 83 (Jun 9, 1964), 60.
254. "Receives U S Medal of Freedom," *NYT* (Jul 4, 1964), 1:7.
255. Diether, Jack. "1947-48 Copland, and Previn's Conducting Debut," *Am Rec G* 30 (Aug 1964), 1096-1098.
256. "Copland Night," *MA* 84 (Sep 1964), 36.
257. "Wins Freedom Medal," *FoF* 24 (Sep 14, 1964), 335A5.
258. *NYT* (Sep 15, 1964), 15:3.
259. "Aaron Copland—Amerikas førende Komponist," *Norsk Mus* 53 (Nov 1964), 5.
260. Kyle, Marguerite K. "AmerAllegro," *Pan Pipes* 56, No. 2 (1964), 49.
261. *NYT* (May 17, 1965), 43:5; (Jul 29, 1965), 19:3.
262. Conly, J. M. "Aaron Copland Looks Ahead," *Reporter* 33 (Aug 12, 1965), 54.
263. "Retires from Berkshire Music Center," *NYT* (Aug 18, 1965), 39:1.
264. Kyle, Marguerite K. "AmerAllegro," *Pan Pipes* 57, No. 2 (1965), 51.
265. *NYT* (Aug 25, 1965), 29:1.
266. Kay, Norman. "Copland, All-American Composer," *MM* 14 (Sep 1965), 21-24.
267. *NYT* (Nov 19, 1965), 45:2.
268. "Thank You, Aaron Copland; Messages from His Colleagues, Former Students and Friends on His 65th Birthday," *Am Rec G* 32 (Nov 1965), 196-205.
269. "Aaron Copland—Articulate Composer," *Mus Events* 20 (Nov 1965), 26.
270. Soria, Dorle J. "A Tree of Many Branches," *HiFi/MA* 15 (Nov 1965), 196.
271. Chapman, Eric. "Copland and the L. S. O.," *Mus Events* 20 (Dec 1965), 33.
272. Dickinson, Peter. "Music in London: Copland," *MT* 106 (Dec 1965), 954.
273. Mason, Eric. "The Composer Speaks," *Mus & Mus* 14 (Jan 1966), 36.
274. Goodwin, Noel. "Copland Conducts," *Mus & Mus* (Jan 1966), 42.
275. Kyle, Marguerite K. "AmerAllegro," *Pan Pipes* 58, No. 2 (1966), 57.
276. "Aaron Copland," *SFSPN* (Mar 1, 1966), 23.
277. "Wins Pulitzer Prize," *NYT* (Apr 24, 1966), 76:7; (May 11, 1966), 33:2.
278. *NYT* (Jul 16, 1966), 15:2; (Aug 28, 1966), sec. 2, p. 19:2; (Sept 4, 1966), sec. 7, p. 18.
279. Flanagan, William. "Aaron Copland," *HiFi R* 16 (Jun 1966), 43-54.
280. Cole, Hugo. "Aaron Copland," *Tempo* 76 (Spring 1966), 2-6; 77 (Summer 1966), 9-15.
281. "Aaron Copland w Warszawie," *Ruch Muz* 10, No. 5 (1966), 8.

282. Soria, Dorle J. "The Devil and Aaron Copland," *HiFi/MA* 16 (Nov 1966), MA14.
283. Butterworth, Neil. "American Composers," *Music SMA* 2, No. 1 (1967), 39.
284. Kyle, Marguerite K. "AmerAllegro," *Pan Pipes* 59, No. 2 (1967), 68.
285. "February's Guest Artists," *SFSPN* (Feb 1967), 9.
286. *NYT* (Mar 13, 1967), 47:2.
287. Baker, Doy. "Aaron Copland: Close Up," *School Mus* 39 (Aug 1967), 36-38.
288. Kolodin, Irving. "Music to My Ears," *SR* 50 (Sep 9, 1967), 45.
289. ———"Copland at the Bowl, Samuel at Cabrillo," *SR* 50 (Sep 9, 1967), 45.
290. Szmolyan, Walter. "Gespräch mit Aaron Copland," *OeMZ* 22 (Oct 1967), 612.
291. Picoto, José Carlos. "Aaron Copland e o Jazz," *Arte Mus* 33, No. 25-26 (1967), 37-39.
292. Cone, Edward T. "Conversation with Aaron Copland," *PNM* 6, No. 2 (1968), 57-72.
293. Kyle, Marguerite K. "AmerAllegro," *Pan Pipes* 60, No. 2 (1968), 66.
294. *NYT* (Jan 22, 1968), 24:2.
295. "Honors for Members," *ASCAP* 2, No. 3 (1968), 34.
296. Frymire, Jack. "Copland 68," *Mus & Artists* 1, No. 5 (1968), 18 (an interview).
297. Wimbush, Roger. "Here and There," *Gramophone* 46 (Dec 1968), 823.
298. "International Music Congress: Forum (The Sound of Things to Come)," *Mus and Artists* 2, No. 1 (1969), 23.
299. "Retires as President, MacDowell Colony," *NYT* (Jan 30, 1969), 39:1.
300. Mayer, William R. "The Composer in the U. S. and Russia: A Frank Talk between Copland and Khachaturian," *ASCAP* 3, No. 1 (1969), 22-25.
301. Kyle, Marguerite K. "AmerAllegro," *Pan Pipes* 61, No. 2 (1969), 48.
302. *NYT* (Feb 5, 1969), 38:1.
303. Mayer, William R. "Copland and Khachaturian—Historic Meeting," *Mus J* 27 (Mar 1969), 25-27.
304. Greenfield, Edward. "Abe Lincoln in Britain," *HiFi* 19 (Mar 1969), 28.
305. Alsina, Carlos Roque, and others. "Kann ein Komponist vom Komponieren Leben?" *Melos* 36 (Apr 1969), 156.
306. Evett, Robert. "Brooklyn Eagle," *Atlantic* 224 (Oct 1969), 135.
307. Tippett, Sir Michael Kemp. "The American Tradition," *Am Mus Dgt* 1 (Oct 1969), 21.
308. Northcott, Bayan. "Copland in England," *Mus & Mus* 18 (Nov 1969), 34-36.
309. Varga, Balint Andras. "Ketten Aaron Copland-rol," *Muzsika* 13 (Jan 1970), 34-36.
310. Moor, Paul. "Festival de Berlin 1970," *Buenos Aires Mus* 25, No. 422 (1970), 5.
311. Greenhalgh, John. "Copland's Mixed Bag," *Mus & Mus* 18 (Jan 1970), 36.
312. "Concert Notes," *Strad* 80 (Jan 1970), 435.
313. Simmons, David. "London Music," *Mus Opin* 93 (Jan 1970), 182.
314. Waters, Edward N. "Variations on a Theme—Recent Acquisitions of the Music Division," *Q Jl Library Congress* 27, No. 1 (1970), 58.
315. Hamilton, David. "Aaron Copland: A Discography of the Composer's Performances," *PNM* 9, No. 1 (1970), 149-154.
316. Dower, Catherine. "Aaron Copland—Giant on the Contemporary Music Scene," *Musart* 23, No. 2 (1970), 10.
317. Greenfield, Edward. "Lobster Quadrille in London," *Am Mus Dgt* 1, No. 4 (1970), 31-42.
318. Mayer, William R. "Interview with Aaron Copland and Aram Khachaturian," *Composer* (U. S.) 2, No. 2 (1970), 44-47.
319. "Awards and Grants," *Mus J* 28 (Jun 1970), 14.
320. "Article on Role of U. S. Universities in New Music Movement," *NYT* (Jul 26, 1970), sec. 2, p. 13:7; (Jul 26, 1970), 49:4; (Aug 30, 1970), sec. 2, p. 30:4.
321. Menuhin, Yehudi, and others. "In Memoriam 1945, Szeptember 26," *Muzsika* 13 (Sep 1970), 7.
322. "Copland Wins Awards (Receives Commander's Cross of the Order of Merit of the Federal Republic of Germany)," *Variety* 260 (Sep 23, 1970), 68.
323. "Concert and Gets Award," *NYT* (Oct 31, 1970), 35:1.

324. Kastendieck, Miles. "Copland Honored by N. Y. Philharmonic," *Chr Sc Mon* 62 (Nov 4, 1970), 4.
325. "Interview on 70th Birthday," *NYT* (Nov 8, 1970), sec. 2, p. 17:3.
326. Kolodin, Irving. "Music to My Ears," *SR* 53 (Nov 14, 1970), 48.
327. "Kid from Brooklyn," *NW* 76 (Nov 23, 1970), 139.
328. *NYT* (Nov 19, 1970), 42:6; (Nov 26, 1970), 60:2.
329. "An Aaron Copland Photo Album (Aaron Copland Commentary)," *HiFi/MA* 20 (Nov 1970), 56-63.
330. "Goldovsky–Copland–Schneider–Wilson Make Great NMC 1970 Team," *School Mus* 42 (Nov 1970), 66.
331. Soria, Dorle J. "Artist Life," *HiFi/MA* 20 (Nov 1970), MA4.
332. Marcus, Leonard. "Some Copland Incidentals," *HiFi/MA* 20 (Nov 1970), 4.
333. Bernstein, Leonard. "Aaron Copland, an Intimate Sketch," *HiFi* 20 (Nov 1970), 53-55.
334. Hamilton, David. "Recordings of Copland's Music," *HiFi* 20 (Nov 1970), 64-66.
335. Soria, Dorle J. "Copland, P. S.," *HiFi* 20 (Dec 1970), MA32.
336. Mellers, Wilfrid H. "Homage to Aaron Copland," *Tempo* 95 (Winter 1970-1971), 2-4.
337. Cole, Hugo. "Popular Elements in Copland's Music," *Tempo* 95 (Winter 1970-1971), 4-10.
338. "Copland at 70," *Tempo* 95 (Winter 1970-1971), 1.
339. Matthews, David. "Copland and Stravinsky," *Tempo* 95 (Winter 1970-1971), 10-14.
340. Young, Douglas. "The Piano Music," *Tempo* 95 (Winter 1970-1971), 15-22.
341. Kay, Norman. "Aspects of Copland's Development," *Tempo* 95 (Winter 1970-1971), 23-29.
342. "Aaron Copland is Now Seventy Years Young," *School Mus* 42 (Jan 1971), 59.
343. "Aaron Copland–His 70th Birthday," *Mus J* 29 (Jan 1971), 10.
344. *NYT* (Feb 21, 1971), 75:6, 8.
345. Greenfield, Edward. "Project Copland Nears Completion," *HiFi/MA* 21 (Feb 1971), 13.
346. Cox, Ainslee. "Copland on the Podium," *Mus J* 29 (Feb 1971), 27.
347. *NYT* (Feb 28, 1971), sec. 2, p. 15:1.
348. Orga, Ates. "Copland," *Mus & Mus* 19 (Feb 1971), 68.
349. Smith, Patrick J. "N. Y. Philharmonic: Copland Tribute," *HiFi/MA* 21 (Feb 1971), MA26.
350. "Copland Featured at DePauw University Festival," *Diap* 62 (Mar 1971), 1.
351. *NYT* (Apr 25, 1971), sec. 2, p. 15:1; (Jun 19, 1971), 18:1.
352. "The Role of the Composer," *Can Composer* 63 (Oct 1971), 24-35.
353. *NYT* (Nov 14, 1971), 79:4; (Dec 18, 1971), 36:1.
354. "Elected President, American Academy of Arts and Letters," *NYT* (Dec 9, 1971), 59:3.
355. Kyle, Marguerite K. "AmerAllegro," *Pan Pipes* 64, No. 2 (1972), 49.
356. Simmons, David. "London Music," *Mus Opin* 95 (July 1972), 510.
357. *NYT* (Apr 10, 1972), 11:1; (Aug 13, 1972), sec. 7, p. 24.
358. Greenfield, Edward. "Copland Premiere on Disc," *HiFi* 22 (Sep 1972), 14.
359. East, Leslie. "Copland (Albert Hall)," *Mus & Mus* 21 (Oct 1972), 62.
360. *NYT* (Oct 29, 1972), 69:6.
361. Valencia, Ernesto. "Aaron Copland, el Hombre el Musico, la Leyenda," *Heterofonia* 4, No. 24 (1972), 9-11 (English summary, pp. 47-48).
362. Reyer, Carolyn, and Robert Fullerton. "Copland Conducts in Appalachia," *Mus J* 30 (Annual 1972), 4.
363. "Conversation with Copland," *Mus Ed J* 59 (Mar 1973), 40-49.
364. Kyle, Marguerite K. "AmerAllegro," *Pan Pipes* 65, No. 2 (1973), 47.
365. "Sounds of America; a Bicentennial Series (an interview)," *Mus Ed J* (Mar 1973), 38-49.
366. Stevenson, Joe. "A Conversation with Aaron Copland," *Your Mus Cue* 1, No. 2 (1973), 21.
367. "New Composition Composed for Van Cliburn International Piano Competition," *NYT*

(Jun 6, 1973), 54:2.

368. *NYT* (Sep 23, 1973), 118:3; (Nov 14, 1973), 60:1; (Dec 5, 1973), 1:2.

369. "Composer Aaron Copland Named to Serve on ASCAP Board of Directors," *School Mus* 45 (Dec 1973), 53; *ASCAP* 6, No. 2 (1974), 5.

370. Shawe-Taylor, Desmond. "Music Events: Connotations for Orchestra Performed by the New York Philharmonic," *New Yorker* 49 (Jan 7, 1974), 63.

371. Hamilton, David. "Music: The New York Philharmonic's Retrospective Performance of Copland's Connotations," *Nation* 218 (Jan 19, 1974), 93.

372. Furie, Kenneth. "Familiar Copland with a Surprise; Recording of Appalachian Spring," *HiFi* 24 (Feb 1974), 14.

373. Kyle, Marguerite K. "AmerAllegro," *Pan Pipes* 66, No. 2 (1974), 46.

374. *NYT* (Feb 12, 1975), 50:4.

375. Kyle, Marguerite K. "AmerAllegro," *Pan Pipes* 67, No. 2 (1975), 50.

376. Fisher, Fred. "Contemporary American Style: How Three Representative Composers Use the Row," *Clavier* 14, No. 4 (1975), 34-37.

377. "Dello Joio Replaces Copland for Bicentennial," *Variety* 278 (Apr 2, 1975), 79.

378. Coolidge, R. "Aaron Copland's 'Passacaglia:' an Analysis," *Mus Anal* 2, No. 2 (1975), 33-36.

379. "Honorary Degree," *NYT* (Jun 6, 1975), 12:1.

380. Burns, Mary T. "Analysis of Selected Folk-Style Themes in the Music of Bedřich Smetana and Aaron Copland," *Am Mus Tcr* 25 (Nov 1975), 8-10.

381. Jones, Robert. "Musician of the Month; an Interview," *HiFi/MA* 25 (Nov 1975), MA6.

382. *NYT* (Oct 5, 1975), 103:1; (Nov 2, 1975), sec. 2, p. 29:7; (Nov 9, 1975), sec. 2, p. 21:1; (Nov 12, 1975), 48:1; (Nov 13, 1975), 51:1; (Nov 16, 1975), 72:4; (Nov 23, 1975), 58:1, 4.

383. "Concert Review (Aaron Copland Salute)," *Variety* 281 (Nov 19, 1975), 55.

384. Dickinson, Peter. "Copland at 75," *MT* 116 (Nov 1975), 967.

385. Jacobson, Robert. "Viewpoint," *Opera N* 40 (Nov 1975), 5.

386. "Tribute to Aaron Copland," *Pan Pipes* 68, No. 1 (1975), 20.

387. Smit, Leo. "For and About Aaron on His 75th," *SR* 3 (Nov 29, 1975), 49.

388. "Aaron Copland 75," *Mus U Ges* 25 (Nov 1975), 700.

389. Kenyon, Nicholas. "The Scene Surveyed: Aaron Copland, Who is 75 This Month, Talks about Music in America," *Mus & Mus* 24 (Nov 1975), 22.

390. "Copland's Sheepskin," *Variety* 281 (Jan 28, 1976), 62.

391. "Copland–Coast to Coast," *Newsletter Boosey & Hawkes* 9, No. 2 (Spring 1976), 7.

392. Kolodin, Irving. "Copland (and Others) on Copland," *Stereo R* 36 (Mar 1976), 106.

393. "$250,000 Fellowship Fund Honoring Aaron Copland set up for MacDowell Colony," *Mus Club Mag* 55, No. 3 (1976), 22.

394. Kern, Fred. "Ragtime Wins Respectability," *Clavier* 15, No. 4 (1976), 24-30.

395. Lipman, Samuel. "Copland as American Composer," *Commentary* 61 (Apr 1976), 70-74.

396. Palmer, Christopher. "Aaron Copland as Film Composer," *Crescendo Int* 14 (May 1976), 24.

397. Brown, Alan M. "El Salón México (analysis)," *Mus Tcr* 55 (Jun 1976), 17.

398. Smith, Rollin. "American Organ Composers," *MusicAGO* 10, (Aug 1976), 18.

399. Ashwell, Keith. "Copland Gives Banff a Bicentennial Focus," *Perf Arts Can* 13, No. 3 (1976), 18.

400. Johnson, Harriet. "Aaron Copland, Dean of American Composers," *Int Mus* 75 (Jul 1976), 6.

401. "Leading Composer Looks at American Music Today," *US News* 81 (Oct 4, 1976), 68.

402. Freedman, Guy. "A Copland Portrait (an interview)," *Mus J* 35 (Jan 1977), 6-8.

403. "Aaron Copland Honored at University of Bridgeport," *School Mus* 48 (Feb 1977), 16.

404. Kyle, Marguerite K. "AmerAllegro," *Pan Pipes* 70, No. 2 (1978), 36.

405. "Golden Baton Awards," *Variety* 291 (May 31, 1978), 2. *Wood World Brass* 17, No. 5 (1978), 25.

406. "Highest National Awards in Arts Presented to Aaron Copland and Exxon Corporation by the American Symphony Orchestra League," *Sym News* 29, No. 3 (1978), 12.

407. "Names, Dates and Places," *Opera N* 42 (Jun 1978), 7.

References to Works by Aaron Copland

92. Las Agachadas: *ML* 34 (1953), 269.

95. American Folk Songs (arr. for chorus): *Notes* 9 (1951-1952), 649.

114. Appalachian Spring: *NW* 25 (May 28, 1945), 106; *BSPN* (Oct 5, 1945); *MQ* 35 (1949), 286; *Etude* 69 (May 1951), 57; *NYPPN* (Feb 4, 1954); *POPN* (Dec 16, 1955), 267; *MA* 79 (Mar 1959), 37; *Okla Sym* (Jan 30, 1962), 174; *PNM* 4, No. 1 (1965), 173; *Mus J* 25 (Dec 1967), 89; *HiFi/MA* 24 (Feb 1974), 14; *NYT* (Feb 9, 1974), 34:1; *Stereo R* 32 (Apr 1974), 108; *NYT* (Dec 17, 1975), 41:1; *Hrsbg Sym* (Nov 18, 1975), 19; *EweCB*, 68; *MacIC*, 389.

100. As It Fell Upon a Day: *MQ* 24 (1938), 30; 37 (1951), 89.

112. Billy the Kid: *MQ* 25 (1939), 372; *BSPN* (Jan 30, 1942); *MQ* 34 (1948), 8; 40 (1954), 622; *POPN* (Dec 16, 1955), 267; *EweCB*, 66; *MacIC*, 394-397; *HitMU*, 200.

98. Canticle of Freedom: *NYT* (May 15, 1955), sec. 2, p. 7:7; *MA* 75 (Jun 1955), 20; 75 (Dec 1, 1955), 17; *MQ* 42 (Jan 1956), 90-92; *Notes* 13 (1955-1956), 529; *Am Choral R* 10, No. 3 (1968), 135.

63. The Cat and the Mouse: *MQ* 34 (1948), 2; *Clavier* 7, No. 9 (1968), 16-18.

105. Ching-a-Ring Chaw: *Notes* 13 (1955-1956), 529.

116. The City: *MQ* 25 (1939), 372; 27 (1941), 163; 31 (1945), 424; 35 (1949), 116; *HitMU*, 200.

43. Concerto for Clarinet: *Woodwind* 3 (Nov 1950), 14; *Clarinet* 1 (Fall 1950), 24; *POPN* (Nov 24, 1950), 160-163; *SR* 33 (Dec 9, 1950), 31; *New Yorker* 26 (Dec 9, 1950), 141; *Int Musician* 49 (Dec 1950), 21; *MA* 70 (Dec 15, 1950), 27; *MC* 142 (Dec 15, 1950), 12; *MQ* 37 (1951), 260-262; *New Statesman and Nation* 41 (Jun 9, 1951), 648; *MT* 92 (Aug 1951), 372; *LAPS Mag* (Nov 15, 1951), 17; *MR* 12 (Nov 1951), 309; *Time* 58 (Dec 17, 1951), 68; *ML* 33 (Oct 1952), 366; *London Mus* 7 (Nov 1952), 32; *MQ* 38 (1952), 655-659; *London Mus* 9 (Aug 1954), 32; *SA Sym* (Nov 17, 1962), 17; *Houston Sym* (Mar 3, 1969), 19.

67. Concerto for Piano: *BSPN* (Jan 28 1927); *NYHT* (Feb 4, 1927); *MQ* 31 (1945), 437; *BSCBul* 2 (Oct 17, 1953), 64; *MQ* 42 (1956), 556; *NYT* (Jan 5, 1964), sec. 2, p. 9:5; (Jan 10, 1964), 19:2; *MA* 84 (Feb 1964), 22.

36. Connotation: *NYPPN* (Sep 23, 1962), 44; *NYT* (Sep 24, 1962), 34:4; *Mus Leader* 94 (Oct 1962), 6; *MA* 82 (Nov 1962), 18; *Nation* 195 (Nov 10, 1962), 314; *Neue ZFM* 123 (Dec 1962), 564; *Show* 2 (Dec 1962), 39; *Am Rec G* 29 (Jan 1963), 332-334; *NYPPN* (Jan 31, 1963), C-D; *Mus Events* 18 (Feb 1963), 13; *HiFi* 13 (Feb 1963), 73; *Pan Pipes* 55, No. 2 (1963), 6; *MQ* 49 (1963), 91-93; *MT* 104 (Apr 1963), 265; *MM* 11 (Apr 1963), 42; *Tempo* 64 (Spring 1963), 30-33; *MA* 83 (Apr 1963), 33; *PNM* 2, No. 2 (1964), 141-149; *Natl Sym* (Feb 21, 1967), 28; *HitMU*, 224.

120. The Cummington Story: *MQ* 31 (1945), 426.

115. Dance Panels: *Mus J* 22 (Jan 1964), 112; *Musica* 18, No. 1 (1964), 16.

77. Danzón Cubano: *NYT* (Sep 22, 1945), 14:6; *Mus Survey* 2 (Autumn 1949), 110; *MQ* 35 (1949), 286; *ML* 31 (1950), 92; *MR* 13 (May 1952), 158.

4. Dance Symphony: *NYPPN* (Jun 20, 1966); *Stereo R* 22 (Jun 1969), 76; *Hrsbg Sym* (Nov 18, 1975), 18; *HitMU*, 180.

81. Down a Country Lane: *Notes* 18 (1960-1961), 245; *Life* 52 (Jun 29, 1962), 44.

106. Dirge in Woods: *NYT* (Mar 29, 1955), 34:2.

61. Duo for Flute and Piano: *HiFi/MA* 22 (Jan 1972), MA24; *Mus J* 29 (Dec 1971), 79.

11. El Salón México: (see under "S")

103. Emily Dickinson Songs: (see "Twelve Poems by Emily Dickinson")

23. Fanfare for the Common Man: *Brass Q* 1 (Mar 1958), 187; *Cont Keybd* 3 (Oct 1977), 30; *HitMU*, 200.

79. Fantasy for Piano: (see "Piano Fantasy")

 2. First Symphony: (see "Symphony No. 1")

78. Four Piano Blues: *Notes* 6 (1948-1949), 492; *Music Survey* 3 (Summer 1950), 50; *Pan Pipes* 43 (Dec 1950), 111; *ML* 33 (1952), 266; *Mus & Mus* 2 (Apr 1971), 13.

122. The Heiress: *Film Mus Notes* 9 (Nov-Dec 1949), 17; *MQ* 37 (1951), 161.

21. Hoe-Down, from *Rodeo*: *Mo Mus Rec* 79 (Jan 1949), 22.

39. Inscape: *SR* 50 (Sep 9, 1967), 45; *NYPPN* (Sep 13, 1967); *Mus J* 25 (Oct 1967), 54; *NYT* (Oct 20, 1967), 53:1; *SR* 50 (Nov 4, 1967), 50; *Mus J* (Dec 1967), 73; *HiFi/MA* 18 (Jan 1968), MA14; *Mus Opin* 92 (Dec 1968), 119; *MT* 109 (Dec 1968), 1131; *Mus & Mus* 17 (Dec 1968), 49; *Tempo* 87 (Winter 1968-1969), 29.

94. In the Beginning: *ML* 35 (1954), 77; *MR* 16 (1955), 161, 164, 264; *Am Rec G* 30 (Aug 1964), 1098; *Tempo*, 101 (1972), 56.

19. John Henry: *Notes* 11 (1953-1954), 277; *MR* 16 (May 1955), 161, 164.

20. A Lincoln Portrait: *BSPN* (Mar 26, 1943); *NYT* (Jan 16, 1946), 18:7; *BSCBul* 12 (Jan 7, 1949), 623; *SWMusician* 18 (Jul 1952), 3; *NYT* (Jan 17, 1953), 12:4; (Feb 1, 1953), sec. 2, 7:7; *CiSPN* (Feb 20, 1953), 472-477; *SFSPN* (Feb 14, 1959), 15; *NYT* (Feb 20, 1962), 31:1; (Jul 17, 1964), 16:1; (Feb 17, 1969), 30:1; *Stereo R* 30 (Feb 1973), 55; *EweCB*, 67; *HitMU*, 200.

38. Music for a Great City: *NYT* (May 27, 1964), 47:1; *MT* 105 (1964), 520; *Mus Events* 19 (Jul 1964), 17; *NYT* (Jul 17, 1964); *Strad* 75 (Jul 1964), 85; *MM* 12 (Jul 1964), 27; *POPN* (Apr 22, 1965), 15; *NYT* (May 13, 1965), 39:5; (May 17, 1965), 43:5; *Notes* 23 (1966-1967), 833; *PitSPN* (May 10, 1968), 853-857.

13. Music for Radio: *MA* 58 (Oct 25, 1938), 8; *HitMU*, 200.

 3. Music for the Theatre: *BSPN* (Nov 20, 1925); *NY Sun* (Jan 8, 1926); *MQ* 16 (1930), 26; 31 (1945), 421; 34 (1948), 4; 40 (1954), 454; *HitMU*, 179.

83. Night Thoughts (Hommage to Ives): *Pan Pipes* 66, No. 2 (1974), 29.

60. Nonet: *MC* 163 (Apr 1961), 30; *Intam Mus B* 23 (May 1961), 8; *MC* 163 (Jun 1961), 24, 60; *MA* 81 (Jun 1961), 21; (Jul 1961), 37; *MQ* 47 (1961), 533; *PNM* 1, No. 1 (1962), 172-179; *ML* 43 (1962), 378; *MM* 11 (Nov 1962), 65; *Tempo* 64 (Spring 1963), 6-11.

117. Of Mice and Men: *MQ* 27 (1941), 163; 35 (1949), 116; 37 (1951), 169; *EweCB*, 65; *HitMU*, 200.

104. Old American Songs: *Repertoire* 1 (Oct 1951), 37; *ML* 33 (1952), 94; *MQ* 38 (1952), 655-659; *London Mus* 9 (Nov 1954), 42; *MR* 16 (Aug 1955), 268; *MA* 75 (Nov 15, 1955), 20.

118. Our Town: *MQ* 27 (1941), 164; 31 (1945), 435; *Notes* 3 (1945-1946), 307; *MQ* 35 (1949), 116; 39 (1953), 307.

16. An Outdoor Overture: *NYT* (Dec 4, 1938), sec. 10, p. 11:8; *MQ* 25 (1939), 372; *ML* 33 (1952), 266; *HitMU*, 200.

64. Passacaglia: *MQ* 34 (1948), 2; 40 (1954), 294.

42. Piano Concerto: (see "Concerto for Piano")

79. Piano Fantasy: *NYT* (Oct 20, 1957), 9:8; (Oct 26, 1957), 18:3; *MC* 156 (Nov 1, 1957), 5; (Nov 15, 1957), 29; *MA* 77 (Nov 15, 1957), 24, 28; *Nation* 185 (Nov 16, 1957), 375; *Juilliard Rev* 5 (Winter 1957-1958), 13-27; *Notes* 15 (1957-1958), 660; *MQ* 44 (1958), 90-92; *Rev Mus Chilena* 12 (Jan-Feb 1958), 82; *Tempo* 46 (Winter 1958), 13; 51 (1959), 2; *Mus Opin* 83 (Mar 1960), 385; *Am Rec G* 27 (Dec 1960), 315; *MT* 110 (Mar 1969), 289; *HiFi/MA* 22 (Feb 1972), MA19; *HitMU*, 224.

75. Piano Sonata: (see "Sonata for Piano")

68. Piano Variations: *Musical Mercury* 1, No. 3 (Aug-Sep 1934), 85; *MQ* 31 (1945), 428; 40 (1954), 294; *HanIT*, 308; *HitMU*, 180, 199.

51. Pieces for String Quartet: *PNM* 4, No. 2 (1966), 36.

30. Preamble for a Solemn Occasion: *MA* 70 (Jan 1, 1950), 10; *POPN* (Apr 10, 1953), 674;

Mus Opin 76 (Jun 1953), 543; *Notes* 11 (1953-1954), 276; *MR* 16 (1955), 161, 164; *BSPN* (Nov 2, 1962), 331.

59. Quartet for Piano and Strings: *MA* 70 (Nov 15, 1950), 6; *MC* 142 (Nov 15, 1950), 3; *Symphony* 5 (Jul-Aug 1951), 4; *Strad* 62 (Feb 1952), 293; *MQ* 38 (1952), 655; *Strad* 63 (Feb 1953), 330; *Tempo* 51 (1959), 2; *HitMU*, 224; *RobCM*, 324.

127. Quiet City: *BSPN* (Apr 18, 1941); *BSCBul* 21 (Apr 6, 1951), 1049; *POPN* (Apr 19, 1953), 674.

121. The Red Pony: *Film Music Notes* (Feb 1949); *NYPPN* (Oct 16, 1949); *MQ* 35 (1949), 116; *Mus Opin* 74 (Sep 1951), 651; *MR* 13 (Aug 1952), 238; *Am Rec G* 30 (Aug 1964), 1096.

113. Rodeo: *MQ* 31 (1945), 434; *Notes* 4 (1946-1947), 191; *Repertoire* 1 (Jan 1952), 141; *ML* 36 (1955), 98; *SFSPN* (Mar 31, 1955), 647; *MA* 75 (Apr 1955), 8; *HiFi/MA* 22 (Apr 1972), MA10; *Hrsbg Sym* (Nov 18, 1975), 20.

11. El Salón México: *BSPN* (Oct 14, 1938); *MQ* 31 (1945), 423; 33 (1947), 186; *NYPPN* (Feb 22, 1951); *Tempo* 95 (Winter 1970-1971), 15-22; *EweCB*, 65.

108. The Second Hurricane: *NYT* (Jul 26, 1936), sec. 9, p. 5:1; (Mar 14, 1937), sec. 2, p. 6:5; sec. 6, p. 5:5; (Apr 1, 1937), 19:5; (Apr 8, 1937), 20:4; (Apr 22, 1937), 18:4; *New Republic* 91 (May 19, 1937), 48; *MM* 16, No. 2 (1938-1939), 136; *MA* 79 (Dec 1, 1959), 40; 80 (May 1960), 35; *MC* 161 (May 1960), 19; *MT* 105 (Jul 1964), 502; *HiFi/MA* 27 (Sep 1977), MA17-19.

53. Sextet (str qrt, clar, pno): *MQ* 34 (1948), 3; *Notes* 6 (1948-1949), 634; *ML* 33 (1952), 371; *MQ* 40 (1954), 473.

9. Short Symphony (Symphony No. 2): *MQ* 31 (1945), 423; *Mus Opin* 78 (Jun 1955), 545; *New Yorker* 32 (Feb 2, 1957), 72, 90; *MA* 77 (Feb 1957), 232; *NYT* (Feb 10, 1957), 9; *MR* 19 (Aug 1958), 247; *PitSPN* (Oct 7, 1966), 97; *NYPPN* (Dec 15, 1966), B; *Stereo R* 22 (Jan 1969), 76.

103. Sleep Is Supposed To Be: *Mus & Mus* 18 (Nov 1969), 34-36.

123. Something Wild: *NYT* (Oct 1, 1961), sec. 6, p. 78; (Dec 21, 1961), 30:6.

75. Sonata for Piano: *MM* 19 (1941-1942), 246; *Partisan R* 10 (1943), 187; *MQ* 40 (1954), 294; 59 (1973), 462-466.

57. Sonata for Violin and Piano: *Arts and Architecture* 61, No. 7 (1944), 15; *MQ* 31 (1945), 436.

103. Song Cycle: (see "Twelve Poems of Emily Dickinson")

10. Statements: *MQ* 34 (1948), 10; *BSCBul* No. 5 (Nov 18, 1949), 270; *ML* 36 (Jan 1955), 98; *Mus Opin* 84 (Sep 1961), 729; *PitSPN* (May 16, 1969), 857-861; *MacIC*, 391-394.

8. Symphonic Ode: *BSPN* (Feb 19, 1932); *NYHT* (Mar 4, 1932); *New Republic* 70 (Apr 20, 1932), 274; *MQ* 31 (1945), 422; *MA* 76 (Feb 15, 1956), 225; *MC* 153 (Mar 1, 1956), 17, 25; *PNM* 2, No. 2 (1964), 141; *Mus Opin* 91 (Nov 1967), 71; *MM* 16 (Dec 1967), 46; *HiFi/MA* 18 (Jan 1968), 14; *HitMU*, 180.

2. Symphony No. 1: *MA* 84 (May 1964), 30.

9. Symphony No. 2: (see "Short Symphony")

28. Symphony No. 3: *BSPN* (Oct 18, 1946); *Time* 38 (Oct 28, 1946), 55; *Notes* 5 (1947-1948), 254; *Tempo* 74 (Autumn 1948), 20; *MQ* 35 (1949), 287; *ChiSPN* (Nov 14, 1950), 13; *SR* 36 (Oct 31, 1953), 74; *MQ* 40 (1954), 294; *NYT* (Feb 9, 1956), 37:2; *MT* 97 (Sep 1956), 483; *MT* 99 (Jan 1958), 29; *NYPPN* (Jan 30, 1958); *Am Rec G* 26 (Oct 1959), 98; *Seattle Sym* (Jan 15, 1962), 9; *Detroit Sym* (Feb 24, 1966), 412; *Am Rec G* 33 (Jun 1967), 933; *HiFi/MA* 18 (Sep 1968), MA19; *Mus Opin* 94 (Jan 1971), 176; *BloYA*, 63; *EweCB*, 69; *HanIT*, 311.

109. The Tender Land: *Center* 1 (Mar 1954), 14-16; *NYT* (Mar 28, 1954), sec. 2, p. 7:7; *MA* 74 (Apr 1954), 5; *NYT* (Apr 2, 1954), 24:1; *Opera N* 18 (Apr 5, 1954), 15; *Variety* 194 (Apr 7, 1954), 57; *New Yorker* 30 (Apr 10, 1954), 74; *Time* 63 (Apr 12, 1954), 65; *NW* 43 (Apr 12, 1954), 68; *MC* 149 (Apr 15, 1954), 21; *SR* 37 (Apr 17, 1954),

109. The Tender Land (cont.): 25; *NYT* (Apr 23, 1954), 23:4; *Nation* (Apr 24, 1954); *MQ* 40 (1954), 394-397; *Tempo* 31 (Spring 1954), 10-16; *Center* 1 (May 1954), 6-8; *Melos* 21 (Jul-Aug 1954), 223-233; *NYT* (Aug 3, 1954), 15:1; (Aug 8, 1954), sec. 2, p. 7:8; *Opera* 5 (Aug 1954), 495-499; *Opera N* 19 (Nov 1, 1954), 16; *MT* 95 (Oct 1954), 558; *Notes* 13 (1955-1956), 529; *MA* 76 (Nov 1, 1956), 24; *Notes* 14 (1956-1957), 56; *NYT* (Nov 22, 1959), 83:4; *New Statesman* 63 (Mar 9, 1962), 348; *MM* 10 (Apr 1962), 40; *MT* 103 (Apr 1962), 245; *Opera* 13 (May 1962), 345; *Mus Opin* 85 (May 1962), 461; *NYT* (Jul 29, 1965), 19:2; *Opera* 17 (Feb 1966), 165; *SR* 49 (Mar 26, 1966), 60; *HiFi R* 16 (Jun 1966), 64; *Opera N* 31 (Sep 10, 1966), 34; *Opera* 19 (Aug 1968), 685; *PitSPN* (May 16, 1969), 875-885; *New Yorker* 51 (Feb 2, 1976), 75-78; *Opera N* 40 (Feb 28, 1976), 46; *Opernwelt* 3 (Mar 1976), 37-39; *HiFi/MA* 26 (May 1976), MA30; *Opera Can* 17, No. 2 (1976), 38; *Opera N* 41 (Oct 1976), 65; 43 (Aug 1978), 45; *Opera Can* 19, No. 3 (1978), 29.

 28. Third Symphony: (see "Symphony No. 3")

 40. Three Latin-American Sketches: *Sym News* 23, No. 3 (1972), 31; *World Mus* 14, No. 4 (1972), 86.

 62. Threnody I, Igor Stravinsky in Memoriam: *Tempo* 98 (1972), 22; *HiFi/MA* 23 (Sep 1973), MA21.

103. Twelve Poems of Emily Dickinson: *MQ* 36 (1950), 453; *Mus News* 42 (Aug 1950), 15; *Pan Pipes* 43 (Dec 1950), 111; *ML* 33 (Jul 1952), 274, 371; *MR* 14 (Aug 1953), 249; *Notes* 11 (1953-1954), 156-160; *Tempo* 103 (1972), 33-37; *MelMN*, 95.

 50. Ukelele Serenade: *MQ* 38 (1952), 483.

 32. Variations for Orchestra: *MC* 157 (Apr 1958), 37; *Mus Opin* 92 (Dec 1968), 119; *ClSPN* (Apr 9, 1970), 974-977; *Hrsbg Sym* (Nov 18, 1975), 19.

 68. Variations for Piano: (see "Piano Variations")

 52. Vitebsk: *MQ* 31 (1945), 432; *MA* 81 (Jan 1961), 158; *Am Rec G* 33 (Oct 1966), 142; *HitMU*, 180, 199.

Dissertations about Aaron Copland and His Works

 1. Baskerville, David R. *Jazz Influence on Art Music to Mid-Century*. University of California, Los Angeles, 1965.

 2. Brookhart, Charles Edward. *The Choral Music of Aaron Copland, Roy Harris, and Randall Thompson*. George Peabody College for Teachers, 1960.

 3. Bullock, Bruce L. *Aaron Copland's Concerto for Clarinet*. North Texas State University, 1971.

 4. Cavendish, Thomas H. *Folk Music in Selected Twentieth Century American Opera*. Florida State University, 1966.

 5. Coleman, Jack. *The Trumpet: Its Use in Selected Works of Stravinsky, Hindemith, Shostakovitch, and Copland*. University of Southern California, 1965.

 6. Del Rosso, Charles F. *A Study of Selected Solo Clarinet Literature of Four American Composers as a Basis for Performance and Teaching*. Columbia University, 1969.

 7. Easter, Stanley E. *A Study Guide for the Performance of Twentieth Century Music from Selected Ballet Repertoires for Trombones and Tuba*. Columbia University, 1969.

 8. Hanson, John R. *Macroform in Selected Twentieth-Century Piano Concertos*. University of Rochester, Eastman School of Music, 1969.

 9. James, Woodrow C. *The Use of Harmonic Tritone in Selected Passages from the Music of Representative Contemporary Composers*. Michigan State University, 1966.

10. Jennings, Vance S. *Selected Twentieth Century Clarinet Solo Literature: A Study in Interpretation and Performance*. University of Oklahoma, 1972.

11. Mabry, Sharon Cody. *Monograph I: Twelve Poems of Emily Dickinson by Aaron Copland: A Stylistic Analysis*. George Peabody College for Teachers, 1977.

12. McCandless, William E. *Cantus Firmus Techniques in Selected Instrumental Compositions,*

1910-1960. Indiana University, 1974.

13. Mills, Ralph Lee. *Technical and Fundamental Problems in the Performance of Clarinet Solo Literature.* University of Southern California, 1965.

14. Pisciotta, Louis Vincent. *Texture in the Choral Works of Selected Contemporary American Composers.* Indiana University, 1967.

15. Plinkiewisch, Helen E. *A Contribution to the Understanding of the Music of Charles Ives, Roy Harris, and Aaron Copland.* Columbia University, 1955.

16. Robison, Richard W. *Reading Contemporary Choral Literature: An Analytical Study of Selected Contemporary Choral Compositions with Recommendations for the Improvement of Choral Reading Skills.* Brigham Young University, 1969.

17. Sahr, Hadassah Gallup. *Performance and Analytic Study of Selected Piano Music by American Composers.* Columbia University, 1969.

18. Service, Alfred R., Jr. *A Study of the Cadence as a Factor in Music Intelligibility in Selected Piano Sonatas by American Composers.* State University of Iowa, 1958.

19. Smith, Julia F. *Aaron Copland, His Work and Contribution to American Music: A Study of the Development of His Musical Style and an Analysis of the Various Techniques of Writing He Has Employed in His Works.* New York University, School of Education, 1952.

20. Spicknall, Joan Singer. *The Piano Music of Aaron Copland: A Performance-Tape and Study of His Original Works for Piano Solo.* University of Maryland, 1974.

21. Stevens, Elizabeth Mruk. *The Influence of Nadia Boulanger on Compositions in the United States: A Study of Piano Solo Works by Her American Students.* Boston University, 1975.

22. Walters, Michael J. *Aspects of Applied Instrumental Conducting: 1969-1971.* University of Miami, 1971.

23. Wolf, Henry S. *The Twentieth Century Piano Sonata.* Boston University, 1957.

OUTLINE V

HENRY (DIXON) COWELL (1897-1965)

I. Life

1897 Born in Menlo Park, near San Francisco, California, March 11. Earliest musical experiences were Chinese opera and folk tunes and dances of his Irish father and his Iowa-born English-Irish mother.

1902 Studied violin (1902-1905), received little formal education.

1908 Began to compose in his own way, experimenting with new techniques in the use of the "string and percussion" piano.

1912 Gave the first public performance (San Francisco Musical Club) of his piano music using "tone-clusters" (*The Tides of Manaunaun*).

1913 First formal musical training at the University of California, Berkeley (1913-1917), under the direction of Charles Seeger (composition), E. G. Strickland (theory), Wallace Sabin (counterpoint).

1917 Bandmaster in the Army, World War I.

1918 Studied at the Institute of Applied Music, New York (1918-1920), with R. Huntington Woodman, Percy Goetchius (theory, composition), Richard Buhlig (piano).

1919 Wrote his book *New Musical Resources* (published 1930).

1923 Toured Europe five times playing his own music (1923-1933); encouraged by Arnold Schoenberg, Béla Bartók, Artur Schnabel, the painter Wassily Kandinsky. Made twelve annual tours of the United States. Developed extensive use of piano strings by plucking and striking and in other ways varying the tone quality. Devised new techniques of notation.

1927 Founder and editor (1927-1936) of *New Music*, a periodical publication of modern compositions; first work published was by Carl Ruggles (*Men and Mountains*). President of the American Composer's Alliance (1927-1931).

1931 Awarded Guggenheim Fellowships (1931-1932); studied primitive and oriental music with Erich von Hornbostel at the University of Berlin. Collaborated with Leon Theremin in producing the Rhythmicon, an electrical instrument capable of producing complex combinations of rhythms. Invited by Schoenberg to play for his master classes and attend his lectures.

1940 Appointed Consultant for the Music Division of the Pan American Union.

1941 Married Sidney Hawkins Robertson, an ethnomusicologist. Began his lengthy series of Hymns and Fuguing Tunes.

1951 Elected a member of the National Institute of Arts and Letters. Professor of Composition, Columbia University (1951-1956).

1953 Awarded an Honorary Doctor of Music degree from Quaker College, Wilmington, Ohio.

1956 Lecture trip around the world, with his wife, under the auspices of the Rockefeller Foundation and United States Information Agency.

1961 Returned to Japan and Iran to take part in East-West Music Encounter.

1965 Died December 10, in Shady, New York.

Henry Cowell taught at Stanford University; New School for Social Research, New York; University of Southern California; Mills College; Peabody Conservatory of Music; Columbia University. Among his pupils were John Cage and George Gershwin.

Henry Cowell has been the recipient of many honors, awards, and commissions in addition to those listed above.

Note: Biographies of varying lengths and importance will be found in many of the books listed in the Bibliography at the end of this *Outline* under "References to Henry Cowell."

II. Compositions (selected)

Henry Cowell wrote a very large number of compositions, variously estimated at 500 or more. Many of his works in manuscript (Ms) are in the process of publication.

A. Orchestra

		Date	Publisher
1.	Vestiges	1914-1920	FFLP
2.	Some Music; Some More Music	1915-1916	AMP
3.	Symphony No. 1	1916-1917	FFLP
4.	Ensemble (cham orch) (arr. from Ensemble for String Quintet, 1924)	1925	AMP
5.	Irish Suite (pno, cham orch)	1925	FFLP

      a. Fairy Bells   b. Leprechaun   c. Banshee

		Date	Publisher
6.	Sinfonietta (cham orch) (based on Ensemble, 1924 and 1925)	1928	AMP
7.	Steel and Stone (cham orch)	1929	ACA
8.	Synchrony	1930	CFP
9.	Reel No. 1	1930	Ms
10.	Reel No. 2	1930	Ms
11.	Polyphonica (for 12 instruments)	1930	AMP
12.	Exultation (for 10 instruments)	1930	
13.	Heroic Dance (cham orch)	1931	ACA
14.	Competitive Sports (cham orch)	1931	
15.	Rhythmicana (for Rhythmicon and orch)	1931	FFLP
16.	Hornpipe	1933	FFLP
17.	Four Continuations (cham orch)	1933	
18.	Vox Humana	1936	FFLP
19.	Old American Country Set	1937	AMP

      a. Blarneying Lilt   d. Sunday Meeting House
      b. Comallye   e. Cornhuskers' Hornpipe
      c. Charivari (Shivaree)

		Date	Publisher
20.	Symphony No. 2 (Anthropos: "Mankind")	1938	CFP
21.	Celtic Set (arr. for orch)	1939	GS
22.	Symphonic Set, Op. 17 (arr. from Toccanta)	1939	BH
23.	American Melting Pot	1939	ACA
24.	Pastorale and Fiddler's Delight	1939	AMP
25.	Shoonthree ("Music of Sleep") (arr. from band)	1939	Merc
26.	Shipshape Overture (also for band)	1939	
27.	Ancient Desert Drone	1940	AMP
28.	Tales of Our Countryside (pno, orch)	1941	AMP

      a. Deep Tides   c. The Harp of Life
      b. Exultation   d. Lilt of the Reel

		Date	Publisher
29.	Symphony No. 3 (Gaelic)	1942	AMP
30.	Suite 1943 (pno, str orch)	1943	AMP
31.	American Pipers	1943	AMP
32.	Hymn and Fuguing Tune No. 2 (str orch)	1944	AMP
33.	United Music	1944	AMP
34.	Big Sing (cham orch)	1945	ACA
35.	Hymn and Fuguing Tune No. 3	1945	AMP
36.	Hymn and Fuguing Tune No. 5 (arr. str orch)	1945	AMP
37.	Festival Overture for Two Orchestras	1946	AMP
38.	Symphony No. 4 (Short Symphony)	1946	AMP

39.	Hymn, Chorale and Fuguing Tune No. 8 (str orch)	1947	AMP
40.	Symphony No. 5	1948	AMP
41.	Overture	1949	Peer
42.	Saturday Night at the Fire House (cham orch)	1949	AMP
43.	Symphony No. 6	1950-1955	CFP
44.	Symphony No. 7 (cham orch)	1952	AMP
45.	Symphony No. 8 (choral - SATB)	1952	ACA
46.	Fiddler's Jig (vln, str orch)	1952	AMP
47.	Symphony No. 9 (cham orch)	1953	AMP
48.	Symphony No. 10 (cham orch)	1953	AMP
49.	Rondo for Orchestra	1953	AMP
50.	Symphony No. 11 (Seven Rituals of Music)	1953	AMP
51.	Ballad (str orch)	1954	AMP
52.	Hymn and Fuguing Tune No. 10 (ob, str orch)	1955	AMP
53.	Variations for Orchestra	1956	AMP
54.	Ensemble for String Orchestra (arr. from String Quintet, 1924)	1956	AMP
55.	Symphony No. 12	1956	AMP
56.	Persian Set (cham orch)	1957	CFP
57.	Music for Orchestra, 1957	1957	AMP
58.	Ongaku ("Music" or "The Art & Science of Sound")	1957	AMP
59.	Symphony No. 13 (Madras) (cham orch)	1958	CFP
60.	Antiphony (divided orch)	1959	CFP
61.	Ensemble (str orch; arr. from Ensemble, 1924)	1959	AMP
62.	Symphony No. 14	1960	AMP
63.	Variations on Thirds (2 solo vla, str orch)	1960	CFP
64.	Symphony No. 15 (Thesis)	1960	AMP
65.	Duo Concertante (fl, hp, orch)	1961	AMP
66.	Chiaroscuro	1961	AMP
67.	Symphony No. 16 (Icelandic)	1962	AMP
68.	Hymn and Fuguing Tune No. 16 (vln, orch)	1963	CFP
69.	Symphony No. 17 (Lancaster)	1963	Ms
70.	Symphony No. 18	1963	Ms
71.	Symphony No. 19	1964	AMP
72.	Symphony No. 20	1964	CFP
73.	Air (vln, str orch		ACA
74.	Air and Scherzo (alto sax, cham orch)		AMP
75.	Characters (cham orch)		Alpha
76.	Havana Hornpipe		ACA
77.	Hymn (str orch)		ACA
78.	Jig (cham orch)		ACA

B.   Concerto (with orchestra unless otherwise indicated)

79.	Concerto for Piano	1928	E-V
80.	Concerto Piccolo (Little Concerto) (pno, orch or band)	1942	AMP
81.	Concerto for Percussion	1959	CFP
82.	Concerto for Accordion	1960	Deiro
83.	Concerto for Harmonica	1962	CFP
84.	Concerto for Koto	1964	AMP
85.	Concerto for Harp	1965	
86.	Concerto No. 2 for Koto	1965	

C.   Band

87.	Celtic Set (also for orch)	1939	GS
	a. Reel b. Casine c. Hornpipe		
88.	Shoonthree	1939	Merc

89. Shipshape Overture	1939	GS
90. A Curse and a Blessing (full band or symphonic band)	1939	Peer
a. The Curse of Balor of the Evil Eye		
b. The Blessing of Lugh of the Shining Face		
91. Symphony No. 3 (Gaelic) (band with str)	1942	AMP
92. Hymn and Fuguing Tune No. 1	1943	Leeds
93. Animal Magic	1944	Leeds
94. Grandma's Rhumba	1945	
95. A Solemn Musick	1949	GS
96. Fantaisie	1952	
97. The Exuberant Mexican	1959	ACA
98. Festive Occasion		ACA
99. Singing Band		AMP

D.   Chamber

100. Quartet Romantic (fl/vln, vln, vla, vlc)	1914-1915	Mm
101. Quartet Euphometric (str qrt)	1916-1919	Mm
102. String Quartet No. 1	1916	AMP
103. Ensemble for String Quintet (2 vln, vla, 2 vlc; thunder sticks ad lib)	1924	AMP
104. Seven Paragraphs (vln, vla, vlc)	1925	CFP
105. Suite for Violin and Piano	1927	AMP
106. Quartet	1927	
107. Suite for Woodwind Quintet (fl, ob, clar, bsn, hn)	1931	Mm
108. String Quartet No. 2 (Movement for String Quartet)	1934	AMP
109. Ostinato Pianissimo (pno, perc)	1934	NME
110. String Quartet No. 3 (Mosaic)	1935	AMP
111. Six Casual Developments for five instruments	1935	Pres
112. String Quartet No. 4 (United)	1936	CFP
113. Sarabande (ob, clar, perc)	1937	
114. Three Ostinati with Chorales (ob/clar, pno)	1938	Merc
115. Pulse (percussion)	1939	FFLP
116. Two-Bits (fl, pno)	1941	CF
a. A Tuneful Bit b. A Blarneying Bit		
117. Trickster Coyote (fl, perc)	1942	
118. Action in Brass (2 trpt, hn, 2 trb/2 bar)	1943	EM
119. How Old is Song (arr. for vln, pno)	1944	Peer
120. Hymn and Fuguing Tune No. 4 (3 recorders)	1945	CFP
121. Sonata No. 1 for Violin and Piano	1945	AMP
122. Hymn and Fuguing Tune No. 7 (vla, pno)	1946	Peer
123. Hymn, Chorale and Fuguing Tune No. 8 (str qrt; also str orch)	1947	AMP
124. Tom Binkley's Tune (euphonium/baritone, pno)	1947	Mm
125. Tall Tale (2 trpt, hn, 2 trb/bar, tba)	1947	Mm
126. Hymn and Fuguing Tune No. 9 (vlc, pno)	1950	AMP
127. Set of Five (vln, pno, perc)	1952	CF
128. Sailor's Hornpipe (4 sax)	1952	Peer
129. Triad for Trumpet and Piano	1953	Peer
130. Ballad (woodwind or string quintet)	1954	AMP
131. Prelude and Allegro for Violin and Harpsichord	1955	AMP
132. String Quartet No. 5	1956	CFP
133. Hymn and Fuguing Tune No. 12 (3 hn)	1957	AMP
134. Hymn and Fuguing Tune No. 13 (trb, pno)	1958	AMP
135. Homage to Iran (vln, pno)	1959	CFP
136. Rondo (3 trpt, 2 hn, 2 trb)	1959	CFP

137.	Twenty-six Simultaneous Mosaics (clar, vln, vlc, pno, perc)	1963	CFP
138.	Hymn and Fuguing Tune No. 15 (vln, vlc)	1963	Ms
139.	Hymn and Fuguing Tune No. 16 (arr. for vln, pno)	1963	CFP
140.	Hymn and Fuguing Tune No. 17 (2 sax)	1964	Ms
141.	Trio in Nine Short Movements for Violin, Cello and Piano	1964	AMP
142.	Air and Scherzo (alto sax, pno)		AMP
143.	Fanfare for the Forces of the South American Allies (3 trpt, 2 hn, 2 trb)		BH
144.	Four Declamations With Returns (vlc, pno)		AMP
145.	Gravely and Vigorously (vlc)		AMP
146.	Invention (hp)		AMP
147.	Perpetual Rhythm (accordion)		AMP
148.	Quartet (fl, ob, vlc, harpsichord)		AMP
149.	Saxophone Quartet		Peer
150.	Suite (fl, vln, vlc, hp)		AMP
151.	Three Pieces for Three Recorders		AMP
152.	Trio (9 movements) (vln, vlc, pno)	1965	CFP
153.	Tune Takes a Trip (5 B-flat clar)		EBM
154.	Six Casual Developments (clar, pno)	1971	Meri

E.   Piano

155.	Tides of Manaunaun	1912	AMP
156.	Dynamic Motion	1913	AMP
157.	What's This?	1913	AMP
158.	Piano Works, Vol. 1	1912-1959	AMP

    a.   Tides of Manaunaun (1912)   f.   Episode (1916)
    b.   Exultation (1919)   g.   Two Part Invention (1950)
    c.   The Banshee (1925)   h.   Tiger (1928)
    d.   Aeolian Harp (1923)   i.   Advertisement (1914;
    e.   Fabric (1917)   revised 1959)

159.	Anger Dance	1917	AMP
160.	Six Ings	1920	AMP

    a.   Floating   c.   Fleeting   e.   Wafting
    b.   Frisking   d.   Scooting   f.   Seething

161.	Three Irish Legends	1912-1920	AMP

    a.   Tides of Manaunaun b.   The Hero Sun   c.   The Voice of Lir

162.	Antinomy	1921	AMP
163.	Amiable Conversation	1922	AMP
164.	The Snows of Fugi-Yama	1922	AMP
165.	The Harp of Life	1925	AMP
166.	The Lilt of the Reel	1925	AMP
167.	Morceau pour piano avec cordes (pno & pno strings)	1926	
168.	Fairy Answer	1929	AMP
169.	Sinister Resonance	1930	AMP
170.	The Irishman Dances	1934	CF
171.	The Irish Minstrel Sings	1934	CF
172.	Celtic Set (arr. for pno; pno 4 hands)	1939	GS

    a.   Reel   b.   Casine   c.   Hornpipe

173.	Hilarious Curtain Opener and Ritournelle	1939	NME
174.	Maestoso	1940	NME
175.	Hymn and Fuguing Piece	1942	Duch
176.	Hymn and Fuguing Tune No. 6 (incorporated into the last movement of Symphony No. 4)	1946	CFP
177.	A Group (five teaching pieces)	1949	Century

178. Two Woofs   NME
179. Amerind Suite   1938   Shaw
    a.   The Power of the Snake   c.   Deer Dance
    b.   The Lover Plays His Flute
180. The Trumpet of Angus Og
181. Jig
182. Danza Heroica
183. Two Ritournelles   NME
    a.   Recorded Collection: 20 Piano Pieces   AMP
    b.   Recorded Collection: The Piano Music of Henry Cowell   AMP
184. Bounce Dance   1956
185. Sway Dance   1958   Meri

F. Harpsichord
186. Set of Four for Harpsichord   1960   AMP

G. Organ
187. A Processional   1942   HWG
188. Prelude   1958   AMP
189. Hymn and Fuguing Tune No. 14   1962   AMP

H. Accordion
190. Iridescent Rondo in Old Modes   1959   MOMAC

I. Chorus (a cappella unless otherwise indicated)
191. The Thistle Flower (SSAA)   1928
192. The Coming Light   1939
193. Fire and Ice (Robert Frost) (TTBB, pno, or band, or orch)   1942   BMC
194. American Muse (Stephen Vincent Benét)   1943   Merc
195. The Irishman Lilts (SATB vocalise, pno; also SSA)   1944   AMP
196. Hymn and Fuguing Tune No. 5 (SSATB vocalise)   1945   AMP
197. To America (SSAATB, 2 orch)   1946   AMP
198. The Road Leads Into Tomorrow (Dora Hagemeyer) (SSATBB)   1947   AMP
199. Ballad of the Two Mothers (Elizabeth Harold) (SSATBB)   1950   Peer
200. Evensong at Brookside (Henry Cowell) (TTBBB)   1950   Peer
201. Day, Evening, Night, Morning (P. L. Dunbar)   1950   Peer
    (TTBBB; falsetto or boy's voice ad lib)
202. Song for a Tree (SSA; pno ad lib)   1951   S-B
203. Spring at Summer's End (SSA)   1951   Peer
204. Symphony No. 8 (Choral) (SSATBB, orch)   1952   ACA
205. Psalm 121 (SSAATTBB)   1953   AMP
206. Sweet Christmas Song (SATB)   1954   EBM
207. ". . . if He please" (Edward Taylor)   1954   CFP
    (SATB, boy's chorus or SA, orch)
208. A Thanksgiving Psalm (Dead Sea Scrolls) (TTBB, orch)   1956   AMP
209. Hymn and Fuguing Tune No. 11 (TTBB, orch)   1956   AMP
210. Septet (SSATB vocalise, clar, pno)   1956   CFP
211. Edson Hymns and Fuguing Tunes (SATB, orch)   1960   AMP
212. The Creator (SSAATTBB, orch)   1963   CFP
213. Ultima Actio (José de Diego) (SSATB)   1964   AMP
214. Choral Suite (SSAATB, orch)   AMP
215. Garden Hymn for Easter (SATB, pno)   Merc
216. Lilting Fancy (SATB vocalise)   Merc
217. The Lily's Lament (Elizabeth Lomax) (SSA, pno)   EBM
218. The Morning Cometh (T. C. Furnes) (S., SATB)   Merc
219. Supplication (Henry Cowell) (Unison SATB,   CFP
    2 trpt, 2 trb, org; timp ad lib)

220. Sweet was the Song the Virgin Sang (SATB, pno or org)		AMP
221. Do You Doodle as You Dawdle? (SATB)		CFP
J. Solo Vocal (with piano unless otherwise indicated)		
222. Where She Lies (Edna St. Vincent Millay)	1924	Cur
223. Rest (Catherine Riegger)	1930	NME
224. Sunset (Catherine Riegger)	1930	NME
225. Chrysanthemums (S., 2 sax, 4 str)	1937	
226. Vocalise (S., fl, pno)	1937	CFP
227. Toccanta (Toccata-Cantata) (S., fl, vlc, pno)	1938	BH
228. How Old is Song? (Henry Cowell) (S., pno strings)	1942	Peer
229. The Donkey (G. K. Chesterson)	1946	Merc
230. St. Agnes Morning (Maxwell Anderson)	1947	Merc
231. Daybreak (William Blake)	1950	Peer
232. Spring Comes Singing (Dora Hagemeyer)	1954	AMP
233. The Little Black Boy (William Blake)	1963	CFP
234. Firelight and Lamp (Gene Baro)	1964	CFP
235. High Let the Song Ascend (S., fl, pno)		AMP
236. The Pasture (Robert Frost)		EBM
237. The Birthing of Manaunaun		
K. Opera		
238. O'Higgins of Chili	1949	Ms
L. Ballet		
239. The Building of Banba (voices, cham orch)	1922	Ms
240. Atlantis (cham orch)	1926	Ms

Note: The following abbreviations are used in Section III of this *Outline*. The number indicates the number of the composition as listed in Section II.

118.	*Action*: Action in Brass	114.	*Ostinati*: Three Ostinati with Chorales
163.	*Amiable*: Amiable Conversation	230.	*St. Agnes*: St. Agnes Morning
93.	*Animal*: Animal Magic	22.	*Set*: Symphonic Set, Op. 17
79.	*Concerto*: Concerto for Piano	121.	*Sonata*: Sonata for Violin and Piano
27.	*Drone*: Ancient Desert Drone	38.	*Sym 4*: Symphony No. 4
127.	*Five*: Set of Five	40.	*Sym 5*: Symphony No. 5
92.	*H & F 1*: Hymn and Fuguing Tune No. 1	155.	*Tides*: The Tides of Manaunaun
166.	*Lilt*: Lilt of the Reel		

III.   Style (techniques and devices)

"Today every composer is faced with the problem I embraced for myself in my youth: How may one learn to live in the whole world of music—to live, and to create? No single technique, no single tradition is any longer enough." "Western and Eastern arts must come together on an equal basis."
Henry Cowell

A.   General characteristics
1.   First use of tone-clusters (piano, 1911-1912; orchestra, 1915-1916). First piece for piano strings (*Aeolian Harp*, 1923).
2.   Development of dissonant chromaticism and rhythmic forms (1919-1932). Strong influence of American and Irish-American traditions.
3.   Interest in the Southern folk hymn (from 1941) led to many Hymn and Fuguing Tune pieces. These were used in all types of music—piano, organ, chamber music, orchestra—and several were incorporated into his symphonies.
4.   Oriental influence seen in "exotic" scales, forms and instruments (mainly after 1956).

B. Melodic line
  1. Unusual melodic gifts; used all types of melody, often folk-like. Borrowed tunes rare.
  2. Smooth and lyrical: *Five* (vln); *Sym 9*; *Ostinati* (*Choral 2*, ob).
  3. Scalewise: *Sym 4* (first movement, trpt 1, meas. 2-6, 8-12 and vln 1, meas. 14-19, 22-28).
  4. Arpeggiated: *Tall Tale* (trpt, meas. 1-8).
  5. Disjunct: *Tiger* (meas. 16-18).
  6. Modal: *Sym 4* (first movement, fl 1, 3, from letter D, meas. 1-6; *Tides.*
  7. Folk tune style: *Sym 4* (p. 24, meas. 3; p. 33, meas. 1).
  8. With tonal harmony: *Action* (second movement, trpt 1, meas. 1-8). Without tonal harmony: *Woof* 1 (left hand).
  9. Borrowed: *Animal* (Eskimo tune).
 10. Chromatic: *What's This?* (meas. 1-6).
 11. Thirds: *Action* (first movement, trpt meas. 1-7).
 12. Folk hymn and folk tune influence: *Sonata* (first movement, pno, upper part, meas. 1-10). *Sym 4* (p. 24, p. 33).
 13. Ballad style: *Sonata* (third movement, vln, meas. 1-9).
 14. Early use of twelve-tone row: *Sym 6* (1950).
 15. Traditional style and twelve-tone techniques: *Sym 6.*
C. Harmony
  1. Generally dissonant, except in pieces in folk style and Hymns and Fuguing Tunes which often used a free diatonic modality. Tone-clusters considered secundal chords (based on the interval of a second).
  2. Quintal: *Sym 4* (second movement, meas. 11-23).
  3. Pandiatonic: *Set* (fourth movement).
  4. Modal: *Ostinati* (*Choral 2*, Dorian; *Choral 3*, Mixolydian); *Spring Comes Singing.*
  5. Tonal: *Action* (second movement, meas. 1-8); *Sym 12.*
  6. Pedal point: *Drone*; *St. Agnes* (last measures).
  7. Twelve-tone techniques: *Sym 6* (first use, 1950); *Sym 16.*
  8. Polyharmony: *Concerto* (first movement, orch parts); *Sym 4* (second movement, meas. 1-8).
  9. Tone-clusters
    a. Pentatonic: *Tiger* (right arm, meas. 43-45); *Exultation*; *Amiable.*
    b. Diatonic: *Tiger* (left arm, meas. 33-36); *Reel* (meas. 17-24); *Tides.*
    c. Chromatic: *Tiger* (right hand, meas. 4; both forearms, meas. 5); *Antinomy.*
    d. *Concerto* (second movement, vln, meas. 7-11).
    e. Tone-clusters and triads: *Concerto* (first movement, after letter E, meas. 5-11; first movement, near end).
    f. Early orchestral use: *Some More Music* (1916); *Concerto* (1929); used homophonically: *Reel*; *Harp.*
 10. Non-chromatic harmony with chromatic line: *Sym 11* (p. 15).
 11. Parallel triads, separately and combined: *Sym 12* (tonal and polytonal).
 12. Folk style: *Tall Tale.*
D. Counterpoint
  1. Chromatic dissonant counterpoint: *Dynamic Motion*; *What's This?*; *Some More Music*; *Sinfonietta*; *Concerto*; *Sym 4.*
  2. Conservative "fuguing-tune" style: *Sym 4* (fourth movement, letters D-P); Hymn and Fuguing Tunes; Symphonies Nos. 6, 7, 9, 10.
  3. Dissonant combinations: *Concerto.*
    a. Melody in tone-clusters against melody in triads (first movement, cadenza, meas. 10-16).
    b. Melody in small tone-clusters against melody in large tone-clusters (first movement, cadenza, meas. 22-31).

      c.   Four melodies (first movement, 3/2 measure after F: unison; thirds; octaves; major 6/4 triads).

      d.   Five melodies (second movement, meas. 19-22: octaves [low strings]; tone-clusters [upper strings]; 3 ob; fl and clar; pno).

      e.   Florid diatonic counterpoint against pentatonic melody with pentatonic tone-clusters.

   4.   Canon: *Seven Paragraphs* (No. 6).

E.   Rhythm

   1.   "Musical rhythm is made up of three elements—time, metre, and tempo." Cowell

      a.   Experiments with complex rhythmic patterns of various kinds including polyrhythms. Cowell believed in the "possibilities for orderly development of rhythmic structures in relation to melodic and harmonic ones."

   2.   Rhythm dictated by vibration ratios of the harmony: *Quartets* (1915-1916).

   3.   Complex: *Concerto* (Finale); *Sym 5* (beginning, 11/8); *Fabric* (pno).

   4.   Regular: *Set* (third movement); *Sinfonietta* (first and third movements).

   5.   Repeated notes or chords: *Drone* (vlc, meas. 19-22); *Homage to Iran* (p. 4).

   6.   Repeated rhythm pattern: *Ostinati* (I, meas. 2).

   7.   Changing time signatures: *Concerto* (second movement, meas. 37); *Sym 4* (pp. 8, 10).

   8.   Syncopation: *Concerto* (first movement, meas. 4-11 after G); *Set* (fifth movement, meas. 1-12); *Animal* (C-D).

   9.   Recitative: *Set* (meas. 55, fl).

  10.   Dance rhythms: *Sonata* (*Jig*); *Lilt* (*Reel*); *Ostinati* (III. *Reel*); *Action* (Two-step).

  11.   Polyrhythms: *Sonata* (second movement, meas. 42-49); *Concerto* (third movement, fifth meas. before L); *Fabric*.

  12.   Polymeter: *Woof II*.

F.   Form

   1.   Considered an extension of rhythm. Wide variety of forms with the incorporation of many American and Oriental traditions. Hymns and Fuguing Tunes used in many extended works for first and/or last movements, often with slow movements in ballad style and jigs in place of scherzos (*Sonata*; *Sym 4, 6, 7, 9, 10*).

   2.   Song form: *Sym 4* (second movement).

   3.   A - B - C - A' - B' - C' - A': *Sym 4*.

   4.   Aleatory: *Quartet No. 3* (Mosaic) (five short movements to be played in any order).

   5.   Fugal: *Sym 11* (last movement).

   6.   Scherzo (rare, usually a jig): *Sinfonietta* (second movement).

   7.   Cyclic: *Sym 15*.

   8.   Sonata-form fuguing movement: *Sonata* (second movement).

G.   Orchestration

   1.   Scores for a wide variety of instruments, including a few oriental instruments, and makes unusual use of conventional instruments.

   2.   Unusual use of instruments in *Concerto*, third movement.

      a.   String harmonics (after I, meas. 5-9).

      b.   Glissando tremolo (after I, meas. 4).

      c.   Glissando trill (two measures before L).

      d.   Glissando tone-cluster (one measure before M).

      e.   Trombone trill (five measures before L).

   3.   Superior scoring for full orchestra: *Synchrony*.

   4.   Oriental instruments: *Persian Set* (tar, Persian drum); *Sym 13* (tabla-tarang; jala-tarang).

   5.   Saxophone: *Sym 3*; *Set*; *Air and Scherzo*; *Saxophone Quartet*.

   6.   Wind chimes: *Ensemble*.

   7.   Large number of percussion instruments: *Concerto for Percussion*.

H. Unusual use of the piano
  1. Tone-clusters in *Tiger*.
    a. With palm (meas. 3); both forearms (meas. 5); fist (meas. 37); finger tips (meas. 67).
    b. White notes (meas. 33-36); black notes (meas. 43-45); chromatic (meas. 4, 5).
    c. Silent, for resonance (meas. 41-47).
  2. Glissando: *Concerto* (third movement, five measures ending at G; after I, meas. 34).
  3. Arpeggio: *Concerto* (third movement, after M, meas. 5).
  4. Plucked and muted strings: *Sinister Resonance*; *Dynamic Motion*; *Aeolian Harp*; *Sonata* (fifth movement, before last "a tempo"); *Banshee* (two players, one holds down the damper pedal, the other plays on the strings).
  5. Descriptive realism: *Tides* (low tone-clusters); *The Donkey*.
  6. Sweeping the strings after the keys of the chord have been depressed: *How Old Is Song?*
  7. Lowest strings played with a padded gong stick: *Synchrony*.

BIBLIOGRAPHY

Books by Henry Cowell

1. *New Musical Resources*. New York: Alfred A. Knopf, 1930; Something Else Press, 1969. *Intam Inst Mus Res* 5 (1969), 101-104; *Mus Anal* 1, No. 1 (1972), 21.
2. *American Composers on American Music; A Symposium*, ed. Henry Cowell. Stanford: Stanford University Press, 1933; reprint: New York: Frederick Ungar, 1962. (Chapters by Cowell, Varèse, Harris, Becker, Brant, Salzedo, Slonimsky, Seeger, Ives). *J Mus Theory* 6, No. 2 (1962), 304; *MA* 82 (May 1962), 44; *Mus J* 20 (May 1962), 59; *Notes* 19, No. 3 (1962), 438.
3. *Charles Ives, the Man and His Music* (with Sidney Cowell). New York: Oxford University Press, 1955; reprint (paperback), 1969. Spanish edition: tr. Floreal Mazía. *Charles Ives y su Musica*. Buenos Aires: Rudolfo Alonz Editor, 1971. *Notes* 12 (1954-1955), 217; *Perspectives USA* No. 13 (1955), 38-56; *Instrument* 24 (Aug 1969), 16; *MT* 110 (Nov 1969), 1144; *SR* 52 (Jun 21, 1969), 62; *Mus Opin* 93 (Apr 1970), 369; *NATS* 26, No. 3 (1970), 41-42.

Articles by Henry Cowell

1. "Modernism Needs No Excuses, Says Cowell," *MA* 45 (Jan 27, 1925), 9.
2. "America Takes A Front Rank in Year's Modernist Output," *MA* 45 (Mar 28, 1925), 5, 35.
3. "The Value of Eclecticism," *Sackbut* 5 (Apr 1925), 264.
4. "The Process of Musical Creation," *Amer J of Psychology* 37 (Apr 1926), 233-236.
5. "Experiments with Ultra-Modern Songs," *Singing* 1 (Jun 1926), 17.
6. "Our Inadequate Notation," *MM* 4, No. 3 (1926-1927), 29-33.
7. "Moravian Music," *Pro Musica* 5 (Jun 1927), 25-29.
8. "How Young Hungary Expresses Individuality," *MA* 46 (Jun 4, 1927), 11.
9. "Impasse of Modern Music," *Century* 114 (Oct 1927), 671-677.
10. "Unlocking the Secrets of 'Modern' Scores," *Singing and Playing* 2 (Dec 1927), 18.
11. "The Music of Edgard Varèse," *MM* 5, No. 2 (1927-1928), 9-19.
12. "New Terms for New Music," *MM* 5, No. 4 (1927-1928), 21-27.
13. "Carlos Chávez," *Pro Musica* 7 (Jun 1928), 19-23.
14. "Analysis of an Unfamiliar American Composer [Slonimsky]," *Singing* 3 (Aug 1928), 26.
15. "Four Little-Known Modern Composers," *Aesthete* 1, No. 3 (Aug 1928), 1, 19-20 [Chávez, Ives, Slonimsky, Weiss].

16. "Music," *American Annual: An Encyclopedia of Current Events* (1928), 542-546.
17. "Music of the Hemispheres," *MM* 6, No. 3 (1928-1929), 12-18.
18. "Hidden Irish Treasure," *MM* 6, No. 4 (1928-1929), 31-33.
19. "Why the Ultra-Modernists Frown on Krenek's Opera," *Singing and Playing* 4 (Feb 1929), 15, 39.
20. "Joys of Noise," *New Republic* 59 (Jul 31, 1929), 287.
21. "Conservative Music in Radical Russia," *New Republic* 59 (Aug 14, 1929), 339-341.
22. "Abstract versus Programmatic Music," *Carmelite* 2 (Oct 16, 1929), 6.
23. "Music," *American Annual: An Encyclopedia of Current Events* (1929), 500-503.
24. "Vocal Innovators of Central Europe," *MM* 7, No. 2 (1929-1930), 34-38.
25. "A Musician's Experiences in Russia," *Churchman* 141 (Apr 26, 1930), 10.
26. "Three Native Composers: Ives, Ruggles, Harris," *The New Freeman* 1 (May 3, 1930), 184-186.
27. "Batons are Scepters," *New Freeman* 1 (Jul 2, 1930), 374-376.
28. "Carl Ruggles," *Carmelite* 3 (Aug 1930).
29. "Bericht aus Amerika: Amerikanische Musik? " *Melos* 9 (Aug 1930), 362-365.
30. "Bericht aus Amerika: Die beiden wirklichen Amerikaner: Ives und Ruggles," *Melos* 9 (Oct 1930), 417-420.
31. "The New Music Society," *Argonaut* (Oct 18, 1930), 6.
32. "Adventures in Soviet Russia," *San Franciscan* 5 (Dec 1930), 16.
33. "Bericht aus Amerika: Die kleineren Komponisten," *Melos* 9 (Dec 1930), 526-529.
34. "Music," *American Annual: An Encyclopedia of Current Events* (1930), 536-539.
35. "The 'Sones' of Cuba," *MM* 8, No. 2 (1930-1931), 45-47.
36. "Music of and for the Records," *MM* 8, No. 3 (1930-1931), 32-34.
37. "Harmonic Development in Music," *New Freeman* (Mar 30, 1931), 63; (Apr 6, 1931), 111.
38. "Playing Concerts in Moscow," *MC* 102 (May 23, 1931), 6, 30.
39. "What Constitutes Modern Music? " *Carmelite* 4, (Jul 28, 1931).
40. "Bericht aus Amerika: Die Eingewanderten," *Melos* 10 (Aug 1931), 275-277.
41. "The Development of Modern Music," *Ohio State U. Bulletin* 36, No. 3 (Sep 15, 1931), 375-379.
42. "Basis of Musical Pleasure," *American Mercury* 24 (Nov 1931), 372-376.
43. "Creation and Imitation," *Fortnightly* 1 (Nov 20, 1931), 5.
44. "Why Modern Music," *Women's City Club Magazine* 5 (Dec 1931), 16.
45. "Music," *American Annual: An Encyclopedia of Current Events* (1931), 513-515.
46. "Charles Louis Seeger, Jr.," *Fortnightly* 1 (Jan 15, 1932), 5-7.
47. "Roy Harris, an American Composer," *Sackbut* 12 (Apr 1932), 133-135.
48. "Elbow Music!" *Emanu-El and the Jewish J* 72 (Jul 8, 1932), 1, 5.
49. "Charles Ives," *MM* 10, No. 1 (1932-1933), 24-33.
50. "Charles E. Ives," *Disques* 3, No. 9 (Nov 1932), 374-377.
51. "Music," *American Annual: An Encyclopedia of Current Events* (1932), 485-488.
52. "Towards Neo-Primitivism," *MM* 10, No. 3 (1932-1933), 12.
53. "Music," *American Annual: An Encyclopedia of Current Events* (1933), 514-517.
54. "Who is the Greatest Living Composer? " *Northwest Musical Herald* 7 (Jan 1933), 7.
55. "Double Counterpoint," *Dune Forum* 1 (Mar 15, 1934), 78.
56. "Irish Traditional Music," *Irish Review* 1, No. 2 (May 1934), 21, 30.
57. "Recent Creative Tendencies in American Music," *Sovet Muz* 7 (Jun 1934), 3-19.
58. "How Relate Music and Dance? " *Dance Observer* 1, No. 5 (Jun 1934), 52.
59. "Jazz Today," *Trend* 2 (Oct 1934), 162-164.
60. "Kept Music," *Panorama* 2 (Dec 1934), 6.
61. "Music," *American Annual: An Encyclopedia of Current Events* (1934), 390-394.
62. "The Scientific Approach to Non-European Music," *Music Vanguard* 1 (Summer 1935), 62-67.
63. "An American Composer on Yugoslav Folk Music," *Balkan Herald* 1 (Aug 1935), 4.

64. " 'Useful' Music," *New Masses* 17 (Oct 29, 1935), 26.
65. "Music," *American Annual: An Encyclopedia of Current Events* (1935), 473-476.
66. "The Music of Iceland," *Musical Mercury*, 3 (Sep 1936), 48-50.
67. "Music," *American Annual: An Encyclopedia of Current Events* (1936), 472-475.
68. "Yugoslav Folk-Music," *Living Age* 35 (Dec 1936), 351.
69. "Relating Music and Concert Dance," *Dance Observer* 4 (Jan 1937), 1, 7-9.
70. "Creative Music in the South Today," *Southern Literary Messenger* 1 (Oct 1939), 657-659.
71. "John J. Becker: A Crusader from Kentucky," *Southern Literary Messenger* 1 (Oct 1939), 657-659.
72. "Charles Seeger: A Portrait," *Magazine of Art* 33 (May 1940), 288.
73. "Teaching Children to Create Music," *New Era* 21 (Jul 1940), 180-183.
74. "Wallingford Riegger Leaves the South," *Southern Literary Messenger* 2 (Sep 1940), 510-512.
75. "Music in Films: A Symposium of Composers," *Films* 1 (Winter 1940), 5-20.
76. "Drums Along the Pacific," *MM* 18, No. 1 (1940-1941), 46-49.
77. "Creating a Dance: Form and Composition," *Educational Dance* 3 (Jan 1941), 2.
78. "Roldán and Caturla of Cuba," *MM* 18, No. 2 (1940-1941), 98.
79. "The League's Evening of Films," *MM* 18, No. 3 (1940-1941), 176-178.
80. "New Sounds in Music for the Dance," *Dance Observer* 8 (May 1941), 64, 70.
81. "Community Festival," *NYHT* (Jun 8, 1941), sec. 6, p. 2.
82. "Summer Festivals in the U. S. A.," *MM* 19, No. 1 (1941-1942), 42-44.
83. "In Time of Bitter War," *MM* 19, No. 2 (1941-1942), 83-87.
84. "Improving Pan-American Music Relations," *MM* 19, No. 4 (1941-1942), 263-265.
85. "Music in Soviet Russia," *Russian Review* 1 (Apr 1942), 74-79.
86. "A New Opera on an American Theme," *NYT* (May 24, 1942), sec. 10, p. 7.
87. "Our Country Music," *MM* 20, No. 4 (1942-1943), 243-247.
88. "A Conservative Interprets the Modern," *SR* 26 (Jan 30, 1943), 25.
89. "Eastman School Festival Presents Works of North and South America in Programs Featuring Premieres," *MC* 127 (May 5, 1943), 3, 5.
90. "Whither Music in America? Barriers Down!" *Front Democracy* 10 (Oct 1943), 29-31.
91. "Folk Music in a Democracy," *MTNAPro* 38 (1944), 172-174.
92. "Bartók and His Violin Concerto," *Tempo* 8 (Sep 1944), 4-6.
93. "Shaping Music for Total War," *MM* 22, No. 4 (1944-1945), 223-226.
94. "The Contemporary Composer and His Attitude Toward Band Music," *Mus Publishers J* 3 (Jan 1945), 17, 46.
95. "Cuban Art Music," *NYHT* (Apr 22, 1945), sec. 4, p. 5.
96. "Serious Composers of Cuba," *NYT* (Apr 29, 1945), sec. 2, p. 4.
97. "Concert Music: Critic-Composer, Orchestras Cross-Country, Earl Robinson Records," *Swank* (Sep 1945), 26, 30.
98. "The Use of Music by the OWI," *MTNAPro* 40 (1946), 61-65.
99. "The American Scene, Part 3: Folk Music," *Listen* 8 (May 1946), 8, 11.
100. "The Schillinger Case," *MM* 23, No. 3 (Summer 1946), 226-228.
101. " 'Cuauhnahuac' by Silvestre Revueltas," *Notes* 4 (1946-1947), 107.
102. "Composers in the Business World," *MTNAPro* 41 (1947), 48.
103. "Music Around the World," *Listen* 9, No. 4 (Feb 1947), 4-7.
104. "Joseph Schillinger as Composer," *Music News* 39 (Mar 1947), 5.
105. "Wallingford Riegger, 'Quartet No. 1'," *Notes* 4 (1946-1947), 358.
106. "Goldman's Influence," *NYHT* (Dec 28, 1947), sec. 5, p. 7.
107. "Review (Thomson)," *Notes* 5 (Mar 1948), 260-262.
108. "Review (Ives)," *Notes* 5 (Jun 1948), 412.
109. "Music as Propaganda," *BulAMS* (Sep 1948), 9.
110. "Wallingford Riegger," *MA* 68 (Dec 1, 1948), 9, 29.

111. "Current Chronicle (McPhee, Moore, Thomson)," *MQ* 34 (1948), 410-415.
112. "Paul Creston," *MQ* 34 (1948), 533-543.
113. "Current Chronicle (Luening)," *MQ* 34 (1948), 599-603.
114. "Current Chronicle (Schoenberg)," *MQ* 35 (1949), 106-111.
115. "Review (Mennin)," *Notes* 6 (Mar 1949), 328.
116. "Current Chronicle (Ornstein, Varèse, Blitzstein, Harrison)," *MQ* 35 (1949), 292-296.
117. "Current Chronicle (Moore)," *MQ* 35 (1949), 448-451; 458-465.
118. "Current Chronicle (Ives, Riegger, Thomson, Hindemith)," *MQ* 35 (1949), 458.
119. "Current Chronicle (Thomson)," *MQ* 35 (1949), 619-622.
120. "Teaching as a Composer's Craft," *Composer's News-Record* 9 (Spring 1949), 1, 8.
121. "43-Tone Minstrelsy," *SR* 32 (Nov 26, 1949), 65.
122. "Current Chronicle (Sessions)," *MQ* 36 (1950), 94-98.
123. "Current Chronicle (Sessions, Roldán, Prokofieff, Ruggles)," *MQ* 36 (1950), 268-274.
124. "Music," *Collier's Encyclopedia*, vol. 13 (1950), 310-315.
125. "Rhythm," *Collier's Encyclopedia*, vol. 16 (1950), 19-20.
126. "Song," *Collier's Encyclopedia*, vol. 17 (1950), 36-37.
127. "Current Chronicle (Menotti, Schoenberg, Harrison, Edmunds)," *MQ* 36 (1950), 447-453.
128. "Current Chronicle (Strang, Sessions, Kirchner, Antheil, Weiss)," *MQ* 36 (1950), 587-592.
129. "Review (Sessions)," *Notes* 8 (Dec 1950), 168-170.
130. "Current Chronicle (Wigglesworth, Creston, Diamond)," *MQ* 37 (1951), 76-83.
131. "Current Chronicle (Mennin, Lee, Swanson)," *MQ* 37 (1951), 248-253.
132. "Be Familiar with American Music," *Mus Club Mag* 31 (Nov 1951), 17.
133. "Current Chronicle (Hovhaness, Ives)," *MQ* 37 (1951), 396-402.
134. "Current Chronicle (Cage, Feldman, Boulez, Wolff, Busoni)," *MQ* 38 (1952), 123-126.
135. "Current Chronicle (Weisgall)," *MQ* 38 (1952), 285-287.
136. "On Programming American Music," *Mus Club Mag* 31 (May 1952), 23.
137. "Current Chronicle (Menotti)," *MQ* 38 (1952), 291-298.
138. "More on Programming American Music," *Mus Club Mag* 32 (Sep 1952), 34.
139. "Current Chronicle (Goeb, Haieff, Tippett)," *MQ* 38 (1952), 440-445.
140. "Current Chronicle (Percussion Music, Ussachevsky)," *MQ* 38 (1952), 595.
141. "What Should Composers Study? " *Peabody News* 6 (Fall 1952).
142. "Concert and Recital: Byron and Schumann," *NYHT* (Jan 23, 1953).
143. "Current Chronicle (Balinese Music, Milhaud)," *MQ* 39 (1953), 98-103.
144. "Current Chronicle (Stravinsky, Musique Concrète)," *MQ* 39 (1953), 251-255.
145. "Current Chronicle (Becker, Berger)," *MQ* 39 (1953), 426-432.
146. "Current Chronicle (Antheil)," *MQ* 39 (1953), 600-604.
147. "Pioneer at Fifty-Six," *Time* 62 (Nov 30, 1953), 71.
148. "Current Chronicle (Canadian Music)," *MQ* 40 (1954), 58-62.
149. "Current Chronicle (Bloch, Antheil)," *MQ* 40 (1954), 235-243.
150. "Current Chronicle (Brant, Kabuki)," *MQ* 40 (1954), 397-403.
151. "Contemporary Musical Creation in Education," *Etude* 72 (Sep 1954), 11, 49.
152. "This I Believe," *Mus Club Mag* 34 (Sep 1954), 25.
153. "The Music and Motives of Charles Ives," *Center* 1, No. 5 (Sep 1954), 2-5.
154. "If You Like to Play: A Musical Instrument Is A Good Companion," *House & Garden* 106 (Dec 1954), 115, 169.
155. "Current Chronicle (Ives)," *MQ* 41 (1955), 85-89.
156. "Current Chronicle (Surinach, Villa-Lobos)," *MQ* 41 (1955), 223-227.
157. "Behind the Scenes in Music," *Mus Club Mag* 34 (1955), 25.
158. "Current Chronicle (Meyrowitz, Varèse)," *MQ* 41 (1955), 368-373.
159. "Current Chronicle (Martinů)," *MQ* 41 (1955), 514-517.
160. "The Flavour of American Music," *Score* 12 (Jun 1955), 5-8.

161. "A Note on Wallingford Riegger," *Juilliard Review* 2 (Spring 1955), 53-55.
162. "Composing with Tape," *HiFi Music at Home* 2 (Jan 1956), 23, 57-59.
163. "Current Chronicle (Madrigals, Copland)," *MQ* 41 (1956), 86-92.
164. "Current Chronicle (Chávez, Lees)," *MQ* 42 (1956), 240-244.
165. "The Program of Creative Music," *Recreation* 49 (May 1956), 212.
166. "Current Chronicle (Schuman, Thomson)," *MQ* 42 (1956), 386-390.
167. "From Tone Clusters to Contemporary Listeners," *Mus J* 14 (Jan 1956), 5.
168. "A Word on Adolph Weiss," *ACABul* 7, No. 3 (1958), 2.
169. "Notes from the East," *NYT Book Review* (Dec 27, 1959), 7, 17.
170. "A Note on Wallingford Riegger," *ACABul* 9, No. 3 (1960), 14.
171. "The Composer's World," *Music in Ghana* 2 (May 1961), 36-49.
172. "Freedom for Young Composers," *Mus J* 20 (Mar 1962), 29, 70.
173. "The Traveling Ear," *House Beautiful* 104 (May 1962), 34-36.
174. "Homage to Charles Ives," *Pro Amer Acad Arts and Letters & Nat Inst Arts and Letters* Series II (1963), 263-272.
175. "Music of the Orient," *Mus J* 21 (Sep 1963), 24-26.
176. "International Music," *World Union-Goodwill* 3 (Feb 1964), 22-25.
177. "Mein Weg zu den Clusters," *Melos* 40, No. 5 (1973), 288-296.

Book Reviews by Henry Cowell

1. McPhee, Colin. *A House in Bali. Notes* 4 (1946-1947), 84.
2. Newlin, Dika. *Bruckner, Mahler, Schoenberg. MQ* 33 (1947), 409.
3. Salazar, Adolf. *Music in Our Time. MQ* 33 (1947), 126.
4. Seeger, Peeter. *How to Play the 5-String Banjo. Notes* 11 (1953-1954), 598.
5. Slonimsky, Nicolas. *Music of Latin America. Notes* 2 (1944-1945), 171.
6. ———————*Thesaurus. Notes* 4 (1946-1947), 171.

Record Reviews by Henry Cowell

1. "Review of Records (Ives, Villa-Lobos)," *MQ* 39 (1953), 323-325.
2. "Review of Records (Bartók)," *MQ* 39 (1953), 641-645.
3. "Review of Records (Seeger)," *Notes* 11 (Sep 1954), 598.
4. "Review of Records (Creston)," *MQ* 40 (1954), 624.
5. "Review of Records (Bartók)," *MQ* 41 (1955), 261.
6. "Review of Records (Caturla, Roldán, Porter, Ives, Donovan)," *MQ* 42 (1956), 118.
7. "Review of Records (Porter, Donovan, Hively)," *MQ* 42 (1956), 419.
8. "Review of Records (Ives, Wolpe)," *MQ* 43 (1957), 136, 142.
9. "Review of Records (Bartók, Ives, Porter)," *MQ* 43 (1957), 165.
10. "Review of Records (Band Masterpieces)," *MQ* 44 (1958), 402.

References to Henry Cowell

Books
(See the General Bibliography)

AbrMM; ACA-Bul; ACA-SC; AusMT; Baker; BarMA; BasSM; BauTC; BIM; BloYA; BluPC; BMI-C; BMI-MW; BMI-OP; BMI-P; BMI-SC; Bull; CatPC; ChaAC; ChaAM; ClaEA; CobCS; CohCT; ComA (2); CopCM; CopTN; CowAC; DalTT; DavPM; DemMT; DerETM; Edm-I; EdMUS; EscCF; EweAC; EweCB; EweCS; EweDE; EweNB; EweWT; EweYA; GolTP; GonSS; GosMM; Grove; HitMU; HowMM; HowOA; HowOC; HowSH; JohSH; KinAI; LanOH; LeiMW; LeiSK; MacIC; MasDA; MasTA; MelMN; MelMS; MorrCA; MueAS; MyeTC; NorLC; NymEM; PavMH; PersTH; PeyNM; PorM3S; ReiCA; ReiCC; RosAH;

RosDM; SalMO; SalzTM; SamLM; SamMO; SanWM; SchCC; SchWC; SloMS; SmiWM; SteiAS; StevePC; ThoAJ; ThoAM; ThompIC; ThoMR; ThoMS; ThoRL; UptAS; WhiWW; WWM; YatTC; YouCD.

Genetic Studies of Genius, ed. Lewis Terman. Stanford: Stanford University Press, 1930, vol. 3, p. 322.

"Sixty-fifth Birthday—50th Anniversary of His Debut," *BMI Brochure*, 1962.

Saylor, Bruce. *The Writings of Henry Cowell*. Brooklyn: Institute for Studies in American Music, 1977.

Articles

Brief mention: *MQ* 10 (1924), 623; 18 (1932), 15; 19 (1933), 57, 357, 416; 20 (1934), 218; 24 (1938), 13, 17, 30; *MM* 20, No. 2 (1942-1943), 101; *MQ* 33 (1947), 19, 105, 321; 34 (1948), 12; 36 (1950), 39, 55, 593; 39 (1953), 30; 42 (1956), 142; *PNM* 1, No. 1 (1962), 180; 1, No. 2 (1963), 28, 190, 203; 2, No. 1 (1963), 95; 2, No. 2 (1964), 14, 16, 19; 4, No. 1 (1965), 3, 4, 7, 9, 23.

1. Perkins, Francis. "Cowell Displays New Methods of Attack," *NYHT* (Feb 5, 1924), 6.
2. Slonimsky, Nicolas. "By Innovation Shall Hearers Recognize Him," *Boston Evening Transcript* (Mar 9, 1929), sec. 3, p. 8.
3. Bauer, Marion. "New Musical Resources," *MM* 7, No. 3 (1929-1930), 43.
4. *NYT* (Apr 1, 1931), 37:3.
5. Goldberg, Isaac. "Henry Cowell," *Mus Record* 1 (1933), 97.
6. Kolodin, Irving. "Composers on Composers," *MM* 10, No. 4 (1932-1933), 226.
7. Copland, Aaron. "Our Young Generation," *MM* 13, No. 4 (1935-1936), 6.
8. *NYT* (Dec 12, 1935), 32:6.
9. Slonimsky, Nicolas. "The Six of American Music," *Chr Sc Mon Mag* (Mar 17, 1937), 8-9.
10. *NYT* (Feb 12, 1940), 15:2.
11. Seeger, Charles. "Henry Cowell," *Magazine of Art* 33 (May 1940), 288, 322.
12. Kerr, Harrison. "The American Music Center," *Notes* 1 (1943-1944), 35.
13. *NYT* (Feb 17, 1946), 36:6.
14. Gerschefski, Edwin. "Henry Cowell, with List of Works," *MM* 23, No. 4 (1946), 254-260.
15. Yates, Peter. "Parsley for Henry," *Arts and Architecture* 67, No. 10 (Oct 1950), 45.
16. Thomson, Virgil. "Cowell's Magazine," *NYHT* (Nov 2, 1947), sec. 5, p. 6.
17. *NYT* (Mar 7, 1949).
18. "Henry Cowell," *Pan Pipes* 43 (Dec 1950), 115.
19. "New Member of National Institute of Arts and Letters," *NYT* (Feb 1, 1951), 23:1.
20. Rosenwald, Hans. "Contemporary Music," *Mus News* 43 (Feb 1951), 10.
21. "Henry Cowell at Peabody," *Opera* 16 (Nov 1951), 6.
22. Berger, Arthur. "Spotlight on the Moderns," *SR* 35 (Jan 26, 1952), 42.
23. "Henry Cowell," *Pan Pipes* 44 (Jan 1952), 27; 45 (Jan 1953), 45.
24. "Cowell, the Pioneer," *NW* 41 (Mar 9, 1953), 84.
25. *NYT* (Nov 17, 1953), 36:8.
26. "Pioneer at 56," *Time* 62 (Nov 30, 1953), 71.
27. "Henry Cowell Concert," *MA* 73 (Dec 1, 1953), 25.
28. RePass, R. "American Composers of Today," *London Mus* 8 (Dec 1953), 28.
29. "Concert Hall," *ACABul* 3, No. 4 (1953-1954), 12-13.
30. Gerschefski, Edwin. "Henry Cowell," *ACABul* 3, No. 4 (1953-1954), 3.
31. Harrison, Jay. "Cowell—Peck's Bad Boy of Music," *ACABul* 3, No. 4 (1953-1954), 5.
32. "Catalog of Henry Cowell's Compositions," *ACABul* 3, No. 4 (1953-1954), 6.
33. Kyle, Marguerite K. "AmerAllegro," *Pan Pipes* 46 (Jan 1954), 34.
34. "Chronological Catalog of the Works . . . of Henry Cowell," *Musica y Artes* 51-52 (May-Jun, 1954), 15-21.
35. Keats, Sheila. "Reference Articles on American Composers," *Juilliard Rev* 1 (Fall 1954), 25.

36. "Henry Cowell," *Pan Pipes* 47 (Jan 1955), 37.
37. Daniel, Oliver. "The New Festival," *ACABul* 5, No. 1 (1955), 6.
38. "Behind the Scenes in Music," *Mus Club Mag* 34 (Jun 1955), 25.
39. Kyle, Marguerite K. "AmerAllegro," *Pan Pipes* 48 (Jan 1956), 40.
40. "Henry Cowell," *Composers of the Americas* 2 (1956), 25-35.
41. Ellsworth, Ray. "Americans on Microgroove," *HiFi* 6 (Aug 1956), 63.
42. Brant, Henry. "Henry Cowell—Musician and Citizen," *Etude* 75 (Feb 1957), 15; (Mar 1957), 20; (Apr 1957), 22.
43. Downes, Edward. "American Composer Encircles the Globe," *NYT* (Aug 25, 1957), sec. 2, p. 7:2.
44. "Astonished Athenians," *NW* 50 (Sep 23, 1957), 96.
45. "Bad Boy at 60," *Time* 70 (Sep 23, 1957), 44.
46. Daniel, Oliver. "Collection by Cowell," *SR* 40 (Sep 28, 1957), 92.
47. Kyle, Marguerite K. "AmerAllegro," *Pan Pipes* 50 (Jan 1958), 47.
48. Ringo, James. "The Lure of the Orient," *ACABul* 7, No. 2 (1958), 10.
49. Kyle, Marguerite K. "AmerAllegro," *Pan Pipes* 51 (Jan 1959), 56.
50. "Gift to the Orient," *Time* 73 (Apr 20, 1959), 62.
51. Schonberg, Howard C. "Henry Cowell: Champion of the Avant-Garde," *HiFi Systems* 1, No. 4 (Spring 1959), 6.
52. Weisgall, Hugo. "The Music of Henry Cowell," *MQ* 45 (1959), 484-507.
53. Kyle, Marguerite K. "AmerAllegro," *Pan Pipes* 52, No. 2 (1960), 44.
54. "Mela and Fair," *MA* 80 (Jan 1, 1960), 42.
55. "Composer's Showcase," *MC* 161 (May 1960), 36.
56. Stuckenschmidt, Hans H. "Die Dadaisten von Greenwich Village," *Melos* 27 (Sep 1960), 276.
57. French, Richard F. "Music 1957," *MQ* 46 (1960), 551.
58. "American Premières," *Time* 77 (Jan 13, 1961), 42.
59. Kyle, Marguerite K. "AmerAllegro," *Pan Pipes* 53, No. 2 (1961), 47.
60. "Honoring the American Composer," *Int Mus* 59 (May 1961), 37.
61. *NYT* (Jan 10, 1962), 29:5.
62. "Became Member of National Institute of Arts and Letters," *NYT* (Feb 13, 1962), 40:2; *FoF* 22 (1962, Annual Appendix), 496F1.
63. *NYT* (Mar 3, 1962), 13:2; (Mar 11, 1962), sec. 2, p. 11:1; (Mar 13, 1962), 28:1.
64. "Concert Honors Henry Cowell (Sixty-Fifth Birthday and Fiftieth Anniversary of His First Concert Appearance)," *Juillard Rev* 9, No. 2 (1962), 20.
65. Herst, E. "World Premières Add Interest to Varied Events in New York," *Mus West* 17 (Apr 1962), 19.
66. Helm, Everett. "Henry Cowell—American Pioneer," *MA* 82 (Apr 1962), 32.
67. "Henry Cowell is Sixty-Five," *ACABul* 10, No. 2 (May 1962), 13.
68. Kerr, Russell. "50 Years of Cowell . . . at 65," *Mus Mag* 164 (May 1962), 10-12.
69. "Slonimsky on Cowell," (reprint from Cowell's book *American Composers on American Music*), *Mus Mag* 164 (May 1962), 12.
70. Helm, Everett. "Henry Cowell Concert," *MA* 82 (May 1962), 38.
71. "Received American Composers and Conductors Hadley Medal," *NYT* (May 28, 1962), 25:4.
72. Yurchenco, Henrietta. "Cowell on the Middle East," *MA* 82 (Jun 1962), 45.
73. Daniel, Oliver. "Jubilee Fare," *SR* 46 (Mar 30, 1963), 71.
74. Kyle, Marguerite K. "AmerAllegro," *Pan Pipes* 54, No. 2 (1962), 42; 55, No. 2 (1963), 43; 56, No. 2 (1964), 49.
75. Mellers, Wilfrid. "The Avant-Garde in America," *RMA* 90 (1963-1964), 1-13.
76. "Three for CRI," *MA* 84 (Feb 1964), 51.
77. "Letters: Brickbats and a Bouquet for Sir John (Sir John Barbirolli and Contemporary Music)," *MA* 84 (Sep 1964), 4.

78. "The Cowell Papers (Presented to New York Public Library)," *MA* 84 (Sep 1964), 17.
79. Daniel, Oliver. "Henry Cowell," *BMI* (Mar 1965), 15.
80. "American Composers Alliance Laurel Leaf Award," *NYT* (May 21, 1965), 22:2.
81. "Retires from Columbia University Faculty," *NYT* (Jun 30, 1965), 43:3.
82. Soria, Dorle J. "From the Groves of Academe," *HiFi/MA* 15 (Oct 1965), 146.
83. "Dies," *FoF* 25 (Dec 10, 1965), 505B1; *NYT* (Dec 11, 1965), 33:1; (Dec 20, 1965), 50:1.
84. "Obituary," *NYHT* (Dec 11, 1965); *Variety* 241 (Dec 22, 1965), 71.
85. Kyle, Marguerite K. "AmerAllegro," *Pan Pipes* 57, No. 2 (1965), 51.
86. "$1,000. P. K. Thorne Grant," *NYT* (Jan 18, 1966), 33:2.
87. Newman, Joel. "Henry Cowell, December 10, 1965," *Am Recorder* 7, No. 1 (1966), 11.
88. Lyons, James. "Obituary," *Am Rec G* 32 (Jan 1966), 434.
89. Mitchell, William J. "Henry Dixon Cowell—March 11th, 1897-December 10th, 1965," *IFMC* 18 (1966), 77.
90. Dickinson, Peter. "Henry Dixon Cowell (1897-1965)—A Tribute," *Composer* 18 (Jan 1966), 28.
91. "From the Editor," *Am Rec G* 32 (Jan 1966), 434.
92. Asch, Moses. "Henry Cowell (1897-1965)," *Sing Out* 16, No. 1 (1966), 96.
93. "Obituary," *Melos* 33 (Jan 1966), 35; *MT* 107 (Feb 1966), 145; *Clavier* 5, No. 1 (1966), 82; *Int Mus* 64 (Mar 1966), 22.
94. *NYT* (Mar 5, 1966), 18:1.
95. Chase, Gilbert. "Henry Cowell," *Intam Inst Mus Res* 2 (1966), 98-100.
96. Newlin, Dika. "Cowell on Discs—And Otherwise," *Pan Pipes* 58, No. 2 (1966), 28.
97. "In the News," *BMI* (Feb 1966), 5.
98. Albrecht, Otto E. "Henry Cowell (1897-1965)," *JAMS* 19, No. 3 (1966), 432.
99. "Henry Cowell 1897-1965," *Mus Ed J* 52, No. 4 (1966), 205.
100. Goldman, Richard F. "Henry Cowell (1897-1965): A Memoir and An Appreciation," *PNM* 4, No. 2 (1966), 23-28.
101. Kyle, Margueriet K. "AmerAllegro," *Pan Pipes* 59, No. 2 (1967), 68.
102. "The Many Worlds of Music," *BMI* (Feb 1967), 4.
103. Dickinson, Peter. "Extreme Experimenter and Naïve Nationalist—Henry Cowell (1897-1965)," *Composer* 23 (Spring 1967), 10-13.
104. Romano, Jacobo. "Retratos de musicos americanos: Henry Cowell," *Buenos Aires Mus* 24, No. 399 (1969), 3.
105. *NYT* (Mar 20, 1970).
106. Stedron, Milos. "Janáček a modernismus tricatych let," *Hud Roz* 23, No. 2 (1970), 74.
107. Waters, Edward N. "Variations on a Theme; Recent Acquisitions of the Music Division," *Q J Library Congress* 27, No. 1 (1970), 52-53.
108. Wen-Chung, Chou. "Asian Concepts and Twentieth-Century Western Composers," *MQ* 57 (1971), 220-221.
109. Oesch, Hans. "Henry Cowell, Pionier und Aussenseiter der Neuen Musik," *Melos* 40, No. 5 (1973), 287-288.
110. Daniel, Oliver. "Henry Cowell," *Stereo R* 33 (Dec 1974), 72-82.
111. Gilbert, Steven E. " 'The Ultramodern Idiom': A Survey of New Music," *PNM* 12, Nos. 1-2 (1973-1974), 282-284.
112. Myers, Theldon. "Henry Cowell," *Composer (U. S.)* 6, No. 15 (1974-1975), 19-27.
113. Saylor, Bruce. "Looking Backwards; Reflections on Nostalgia in the Musical Avant-Garde," *Centerpoint* 1, No. 3 (1975), 4.
114. Gillespie, Don C. "John Becker, Musical Crusader of Saint Paul," *MQ* 62 (1976), 195-217.
115. Vermeulen, Ernest. "Holland Festival presenteert Amerikaanse muziek," *Mens En Mel* 31 (Jun 1976), 161-167.
116. Smith, Rollin. "American Organ Composers," *MusicAGO* 10 (Aug 1976), 18.
117. Hays, Doris. "Noise Poise," *Mus J* 35 (Feb 1977), 14-17.

118. "Committee for 20th Century Music: Henry Cowell Retrospective," *HiFi/MA* 27 (Aug 1977), MA25.
119. "The Northwestern University School of Music Library (Cowell Repository)," *NATS* 35, No. 1 (1978), 38.
120. "Northwestern Music Library Now Henry Cowell Repository," *School Mus* 49 (Apr 1978), 38.
121. "Three Libraries to House Cowell Music and Recordings," *Clavier* 17, No. 5 (1978), 56.

References to Works by Henry Cowell

The number preceding the title refers to the number of the composition as listed in Section II.

158. Advertisement: *HitMU*, 186.
 31. American Pipers: *NYPPN* (Jan 23, 1949); *MA* 69 (Feb 1949), 264-265; *Mus News* 41 (Apr 1949), 28.
199. Ballad of the Two Mothers: *Notes* 8 (Mar 1951), 404.
158. Banshee: *HitMU*, 186.
 34. Big Sing: *ISPN* (Feb 28, 1948); *EweYA*, 159.
184. Bounce Dance: *Etude* 75 (Feb 1957), 26.
     Carol for Orchestra: *NMC* 28, No. 2 (1968), 20; *BMI* (Feb 1968), 18.
 87. Celtic Set (band): *MQ* 36 (1950), 593.
 66. Chiaroscuro: *Mus Mag* 163 (Dec 1961), 54.
212. The Creator: *Mus J* 24 (May 1966), 82.
 84. Concerto for Koto: *NYT* (Dec 27, 1964), sec. 2, p. 13:1; (Dec 30, 1964), 14:1; *MM* 13 (Feb 1965), 41; *BMI* (Mar 1965), 8, 9.
 81. Concerto for Percussion: *Time* (Jan 13, 1961); *MA* 81 (Mar 1961), 24; *PitSPN* (Jan 4, 1963).
 79. Concerto for Piano: *PNM* 4, No. 2 (1966), 28.
 90. A Curse and A Blessing: *MC* 143 (Jan 1, 1951), 30; *Notes* 8 (1950-1951), 565.
201. Day, Evening, Night, Morning: *Notes* 8 (Jun 1951), 571-572.
231. Daybreak: *MC* 143 (Mar 1, 1951), 27; *MA* 71 (Jul 1951), 30; *Notes* 8 (Sep 1951), 753; *Repertoire* 1 (Jan 1952), 158.
 65. Duo Concertante: *ACABul* 10, No. 3 (1962), 17.
211. Edson Hymns and Fuguing Tunes: *Washington Evening Star* (Feb 24, 1964).
 54. Ensemble for String Orchestra: *Notes* 21 (1963-1964), 250; Adagio: *NYHT* (Jan 29, 1965); *NYT* (Jan 29, 1965).
200. Evensong at Brookside: *Notes* 8 (1951), 404.
158. Fabric: *PNM* 1, No. 2 (1963), 17; *HitMU*, 187.
     "Feast of Fascination by Henry Cowell," *Am Rec G* 30 (Feb 1964), 476-477.
     Ground and Fuguing Tune: *Diap* 47 (Sep 1, 1956), 18.
135. Homage to Iran: *ACABul* 10, No. 1 (1961), 26; *Notes* 19, No. 1 (1961), 144.
228. How Old Is Song (vln, pno): *Notes* 8 (1950-1951), 141; *Violin* 11 (Sep-Oct 1950), 274; *MA* 71 (Mar 1951), 40; *Repertoire* 1 (Jan 1952), 172-173; *MQ* 45 (1959), 494.
     Hymn and Fuguing Tunes: *MA* 75 (Oct 1955), 13; *ACABul* 12, No. 1 (1964), 18.
 32. Hymn and Fuguing Tune No. 2: *BSPB* (Mar 29, 1946), 1294; *EweCB*, 72.
 35. Hymn and Fuguing Tune No. 3: *MC* 150 (Nov 1, 1954), 24; *ACABul* 4, No. 4 (1955), 15; *CiSPN* (Oct 31, 1958); *POPN* (Nov 6, 1959); *ACABul* 10, No. 1 (1961), 20.
122. Hymn and Fuguing Tune No. 7: *Notes* 11 (1953-1954), 274.
 52. Hymn and Fuguing Tune No. 10: *ACABul* 5, No. 3 (1956), 17.
189. Hymn and Fuguing Tune No. 14: *Diap* 54 (Feb 1963), 23; *MA* 83 (Feb 1963), 23; *Am Org* 46 (Feb 1963), 14; *Mus J* 21 (Feb 1963), 98.
139. Hymn and Fuguing Tune No. 16: *NYPPN* (Oct 6, 1966), D; *NYT* (Oct 7, 1966), 34:1; *Mus J* 24 (Nov 1966), 70; *BMI* (Nov 1966), 17.

207. . . . if He please (Cantata): *MA* 76 (Mar 1956), 18; *Diap* 47 (Apr 1, 1956), 2.
190. Iridescent Rondo: *NYT* (Nov 22, 1959), 85:4.
217. The Lily's Lament: *Musicology* 2 (Apr 1949), 315.
 57. Music for Orchestra, 1957: *NW* 50 (Sep 23, 1957), 96; *MSPN* (Nov 1, 1957), 21.
 58. Ongaku: *MA* 79 (Jun 1959), 13.
 56. Persian Set: *NYHT* (Dec 4, 1958); *Nation* (Dec 27, 1958); *Notes* 17 (1959-1960), 656; *MA* 80 (Jul 1960), 85.
158. Piano Works: *Notes* 19 (1961-1962), 158; *Am Rec G* 30 (Feb 1964), 480; *Listen* 1 (Mar-Apr 1964), 22; *Cont Kybd* 3 (Jun 1977), 49.
 11. Polyphonica: *NYT* (Nov 5, 1932), 12:2; (Dec 8, 1963), 31:1.
101. Quartet Euphometric: *NYHT* (Feb 13, 1964).
100. Quartet Romantic: *NYHT* (Feb 13, 1964); *New Yorker* 54 (Jun 5, 1978), 104.
198. The Road Leads into Tomorrow: *Musicology* 2 (Apr 1949), 315.
136. Rondo (brass): *Notes* 17 (1959-1960), 650.
128. Sailor's Hornpipe (4 sax): *Notes* 10 (1952-1953), 143.
104. Seven Paragraphs: *Notes* 24 (1967-1968), 150.
 38. Short Symphony: (see "Symphony No. 4").
127. Set of Five: *ACABul* 2, No. 4 (1952-1953), 21; 3, No. 1 (1953), 23; *MC* 147 (Jan 1, 1953), 19.
  6. Sinfonietta: *MQ* 37 (1951), 579; 45 (1959), 491; *PNM* 4, No. 2 (1966), 25.
169. Sinister Resonance: *HitMU*, 187.
121. Sonata No. 1 for Violin and Piano: *Notes* 5 (1947-1948), 255; *ACABul* 4, No. 2 (1954), 17; *MQ* 40 (1954), 472, 475; *Strad* 66 (Sep 1955), 172.
203. Spring at Summer's End: *Notes* 10 (Jun 1953), 493.
232. Spring Comes Singing: *Notes* 16 (1958-1959), 621.
110. String Quartet No. 3 (Mosaic): *NYT* (Mar 8, 1964).
112. String Quartet No. 4 (United): *MQ* 45 (1959), 492.
132. String Quartet No. 5: *NYT* (Oct 6, 1956), 19:1; *MQ* 43 (1957), 98; *New Yorker* 39 (Jun 1963), 163.
107. Suite for Woodwind Quintet: *ACABul* 4, No. 2 (1954), 21.
219. Supplication: *Pan Pipes* 55, No. 1 (1962), 31.
 20. Symphony No. 2: *MA* 69 (Jan 1949), 8; (Feb 1949), 5.
 38. Symphony No. 4 (Short Symphony): *NYT* (Oct 24, 1947), 20:1; *BSPN* (Oct 24, 1947); *Notes* 6 (1949), 323; *ACABul* 3, No. 1 (1953), 23; No. 3 (1953), 18; *NYT* (May 9, 1953), 12:7; *MA* 74 (Feb 1, 1954), 15; *ACABul* 4, No. 2 (1954), 20; *EweCB*, 72.
 40. Symphony No. 5: *MA* 69 (Apr 15, 1949), 28; *MQ* 36 (1950), 446.
 45. Symphony No. 8: *NYT* (Dec 2, 1952), 39:7.
 48. Symphony No. 10: *NYT* (Feb 25, 1957), 21:1; *MC* 155 (Mar 1, 1957), 4.
 50. Symphony No. 11: *MQ* 41 (1955), 551-552; *ACABul* 5, No. 3 (1956), 15; *POPN* (Nov 19, 1957); *NYHT* (Nov 20, 1957); *NYT* (Nov 20, 1957), 42:1; *New Yorker* 33 (Nov 23, 1957), 186; (Nov 30, 1957), 201; *Nation* 185 (Dec 7, 1957), 443; *MA* 77 (Dec 15, 1957), 20; *MC* 156 (Dec 15, 1957), 12; *ACABul* 7, No. 3 (1958), 19; *MQ* 45 (1959), 496.
 55. Symphony No. 12: *MQ* 45 (1959), 497; *SFSPN* (Dec 20, 1961), 17; *Notes* 19 (1961-1962), 143.
 59. Symphony No. 13 (Madras): *Time* 72 (Apr 20, 1959); *MC* 159 (Apr 1959), 35; *World of Mus* 1 (May 1959), 11; *MC* 159 (Jun 1959), 8; *MA* 79 (Jun 1959), 13; *NYT* (Oct 20, 1959), 43:3; *MA* 79 (Nov 1, 1959), 23; *MC* 160 (Nov 1959), 17.
 62. Symphony No. 14: *MQ* 47 (1961), 533; *Intam Mus B* 23 (May 1961), 10; *MC* 163 (Jun 1961), 62.
 64. Symphony No. 15: *NYHT* (Nov 6, 1962); *Notes* 22 (1965-1966), 824.
 67. Symphony No. 16: *Am Rec G* 30 (Feb 1964), 481; *NYT* (Apr 26, 1964); *ACABul* 12, No. 1 (1964), 18.

71. Symphony No. 19: *BMI* (Dec 1965), 12.
8. Synchrony: *MQ* 45 (1959), 492; *PNM* 4, No. 2 (1966), 28.
28. Tales of Our Countryside: *EweCB*, 81.
125. Tall Tale: *Notes* 6 (1948-1949), 331; *Mus Ed J* 35 (Feb-Mar 1949), 42.
208. A Thanksgiving Psalm: *NYT* (Jul 9, 1956), 26:4; *MC* 154 (Aug 1956), 9; *HiFi/MA* 17 (Mar 1967), MA16.
155. The Tides of Manaunaun: *HitMU*, 186.
158. Tiger: *PNM* 4, No. 1 (1965), 4.
114. Three Ostinati with Chorales: *Notes* 4 (1946-1947), 101.
227. Toccanta: *MQ* 41 (1955), 551.
124. Tom Binkley's Tune: *Notes* 5 (1947-1948), 419.
Trio for Flute, Violin, Harp: *ACABul* 12, No. 1 (1964), 18.
Triple Rondo: *Harp N* 3, No. 6 (1962), 31.
137. Twenty-six Simultaneous Mosaics: *Mus J* 23 (Jan 1965), 100; *BMI* (Mar 1965), 8.
213. Ultima Actio: *Mus J* 23 (Nov 1965), 78; *BMI* (Dec 1965), 12.
53. Variations for Orchestra: *ASPN* (Nov 23, 1956), 203; *CiSPN* (Nov 23, 1956), 203-208; *MC* 154 (Dec 15, 1956), 20; *NYHT* (Apr 15, 1959); *Houston SPN* (Nov 2, 1959).

Dissertations about Henry Cowell and His Works

1. Godwin, Joscelyn. *The Music of Henry Cowell*. Cornell University, 1969.
2. Mead, Rita Hursh. *Henry Cowell's New Music, 1925-1936: The Society, the Music Editions and the Recordings*. City University of New York, 1978.
3. Van Norman, Clarendon E., Jr. *The French Horn—Its Use and Development in Musical Literature*. Columbia University, 1965.

OUTLINE VI

HOWARD (HAROLD) HANSON (b. 1896)

I. Life

1896   Born in Wahoo, Nebraska, October 28, of Swedish parents.

1903   Began his musical education with A. O. Petersen, Luther Junior College, Wahoo, continuing through high school.

1912   Studied at the University of Nebraska School of Music, Lincoln, Nebraska (1912-1913).

1914   Studied at the Institute of Musical Art, New York (1914-1915); James Friskin (piano), Percy Goetschius (theory and composition).

1915   Entered Northwestern University. Studied composition with Peter Christian Lutkin and Arne Oldberg; graduated in 1916 with a Bachelor of Music degree.

1916   Appointed to the theory and composition faculty of the College of the Pacific, San José, California; Dean of the Conservatory of Fine Arts (1919-1921).

1921   Awarded the American Prix de Rome (1921-1924). Composed *Symphony No. 1* and *North and West* (1923).

1924   Appointed Director of the Eastman School of Music of the University of Rochester, New York. Awarded honorary Doctor of Music degree from Northwestern University, the first of many honorary degrees (27 by 1955).

1925   Founded the American Composers Concerts.

1929   *Symphony No. 2* commissioned by the Boston Symphony Orchestra.

1930   President of the Music Teachers National Association (1930-1931).

1935   Elected a member of the National Institute of Arts and Letters.

1936   President of the National Association of Schools of Music (1936-1944).

1938   Elected a fellow of the Royal Academy of Music of Sweden.

1944   President of the National Music Council. Awarded the Pulitzer Prize for Music (*Symphony No. 4*).

1946   Married Margaret E. Nelson.

1960   Member of the Music Educators National Conference Board of Directors (1960-1964).

1964   Retired as Director of the Eastman School of Music.

1979   Elected to the American Academy of the National Institute of Arts and Letters.
Howard Hanson has been the recipient of many honors, awards and commissions in addition to those listed above.

Note: Biographies of varying lengths and importance will be found in many of the books listed in the Bibliography at the end of this *Outline* under "References to Howard Hanson."

II. Compositions

A. Orchestra	Date	Publisher
1. Symphonic Prelude, Op. 6	1916	
2. Symphonic Legend, Op. 8	1917	
3. Symphonic Rhapsody, Op. 14	1919	
4. Symphonic Poem, "Before the Dawn," Op. 17	1920	
5. Symphonic Poem, "Exaltation," Op. 20 (orch with pno obbl)	1920	
6. Symphony No. 1 (Nordic), Op. 21	1922	CF
7. Symphonic Poem, "Lux aeterna," Op. 24 (with vla obbl)	1923	CF

8.	Symphonic Poem, "North and West," Op. 22 (with choral obbl)	1923	Ms
9.	Symphonic Poem, "Pan and the Priest," Op. 26 (with pno obbl)	1926	S-B
10.	Heroic Elegy, Op. 28 (with wordless chorus)	1927	
11.	Symphony No. 2 (Romantic), Op. 30	1930	CF
12.	Suite from Merry Mount	1937	Harms
13.	Symphony No. 3, Op. 33	1937	CF
14.	Symphony No. 4 (Requiem), Op. 34	1943	CF
15.	Serenade for Flute, Harp and Strings, Op. 35	1945	CF
16.	Pastorale for Oboe, Harp and Strings, Op. 38	1949	CF
17.	Fantasy Variations on a Theme of Youth, Op. 40 (pno, str orch)	1951	CF
18.	Symphony No. 5 (Sinfonia Sacra), Op. 43	1955	CF
19.	Elegy in Memory of Serge Koussevitsky, Op. 44	1955	CF
20.	Mosaics	1957	CF
21.	Summer Seascape No. 1 (in Bold Island Suite)	1958	CF
22.	Bold Island Suite, Op. 46	1961	CF
23.	For the First Time	1963	CF
24.	Symphony No. 6	1966	CF
25.	Summer Seascape No. 2 for Viola and Strings (arr. from Summer Seascape No. 1)	1966	CF
26.	Die Natalis	1967	
27.	Symphony No. 7 (A Sea Symphony) (with chorus)	1977	

B.   Concerto

28.	Concerto for Organ, Op. 22 (based on North and West)	1926	
	(arr. for Organ, Harp and Strings)	1943	CF
29.	Concerto for Piano, Op. 36	1948	CF

C.   Band

30.	March-Carillon, Op. 19 (arr. from pno)	1920	Pres
31.	Symphony No. 1 (second movement arr. for band)	1922	CF
32.	Romantic Theme (arr. from Symphony No. 2)	1930	CF
33.	Symphony No. 2 (second movement arr. for band)	1930	CF
34.	Merry Mount Suite (arr. from Opera)	1933	Harms
35.	Chorale and Alleluia, Op. 42 (full and symphonic band)	1954	CF
36.	Fanfare for the Signal Corps (brass, perc)	1965	BH
37.	Laude (Chorale, Variations and Metamorphoses)		CF

D.   Chamber

38.	Piano Quintet in F minor, Op. 5	1916	
39.	Concerto da camera, Op. 7 (str qrt, pno)	1917	
40.	String Quartet, Op. 23	1923	AME
41.	Serenade, Op. 35 (arr. for fl, pno)	1945	CF
42.	Pastorale, Op. 38 (arr. for ob, pno)	1949	CF

E.   Piano

43.	Prelude and Double Concert Fugue, Op. 1 (2 pno)	1915	
44.	Four Poems, Op. 9	1917-1918	

    a. Peace   c. Yearning
    b. Joy   d. Desire

45.	Sonata for Piano, Op. 11	1918	
46.	Three Miniatures, Op. 12	1918	CF

    a. Reminiscence   b. Lullaby   c. Longing

47.	Scandinavian Suite, Op. 13	1918-1919	CF

    a. Vermeland   b. Elegy   c. Clog Dance

48.	Three Studies, Op. 18	1920	

    a. Rhythmic Etude   b. Melodic Etude   c. Idyllic Etude

E.   Piano (cont.)   1920   Pres
   49.   Two Yule-Tide Pieces, Op. 19
      a.   Impromptu   b.   March-Carillon
   50.   Dance of the Warriors   1936   CF
   51.   Enchantment   1936   CF
   52.   The Bell, Op. 13   1942   CF
   53.   For the First Time (arr. for pno)   1963   CF
   54.   Concerto, Op. 22 (arr. for org, pno)   1941   CF
   55.   Concerto, Op. 36 (arr. for 2 pno)   1948   CF
   56.   Fantasy, Op. 40 (arr. for 2 pno)   1951   CF

F.   Choral
   57.   The Lament for Beowulf, Op. 25   1925   CCB
   58.   Merry Mount Choruses (Richard H. Stokes) (SATB, orch or   1933   Harms
      pno or band)
   59.   Children's Dance (from "Merry Mount") (SSAA, pno 4 hands)   1933   Harms
   60.   Three Songs from "Drum Taps," Op. 32 (Walt Whitman)   1935   JF
      (Bar., SATB, orch)
   61.   Beat! Beat! Drums! (from "Drum Taps") (SATB, orch or pno)   1935   JF
   62.   Hymn for the Pioneers (TTBB)   1938   JF
   63.   Cherubic Hymn, Op. 37 (St. John Chrysostom)   1950   CF
      (SATB, orch or pno)
   64.   How Excellent Thy Name, Op. 41 (Psalm 8) (SATB,   1952   CF
      org; also SSAA, pno)
   65.   Song of Democracy, Op. 44 (Walt Whitman) (SATB or   1957   CF
      TTBB, pno or orch or band)
   66.   Sail, Sail Thy Best (from "Song of Democracy") (unison SATB) 1958   CF
   67.   Song of Human Rights, Op. 43 (orch or pno)   1963   CF
   68.   Four Psalms (Bar., str orch; also with str sextet or org or pno) 1964   CF
   69.   New Land, New Covenant (Isaac Watts, T. S. Eliot,   1976   CF
      John Newton, the Bible, Declaration of Independence) (SATB,
      S., Bar., Narr., org, small orch)
   70.   Streams in the Desert (chorus and orch)   1969

G.   Solo Vocal
   71.   Three Songs, Op. 2   1915
      a.   To Music   b.   Remembering   c.   Dawn
   72.   Schäfers Sonntagslied, Op. 4a (Uhland)   1916
   73.   Two Songs from the Rubaiyát of Omar Khayyám, Op. 4b   1916
      a.   The Worldly Hope   b.   Wake
   74.   Exaltation, Op. 10   1917-1918
   75.   Three Swedish Folksongs, Op. 15   1919
   76.   Three Songs for Children, Op. 29   1930
   77.   Three Songs from Walt Whitman (with orch)   1915
      a.   The Untold Want b.   Portals   c.   Joy! Shipmate, Joy!

H.   Opera
   78.   Merry Mount, Op. 31 (Richard H. Stokes)   1933   Harms

I.   Ballet
   79.   Nymph and Satyr   1979

J.   Incidental Music
   80.   California Forest Play of 1920, Op. 16   1919

Note: The complete collection, with minor exceptions, of the manuscript scores of Howard Hanson's music was presented by the composer to the Sibley Music Library of the Eastman School of Music, Rochester, New York.

Note: The following abbreviations are used in Section III of this *Outline*. The number indicates the number of the composition as listed in Section II.

57. *Beowulf*: The Lament for Beowulf
29. *Concerto*: Concerto for Piano
63. *Hymn*: Cherubic Hymn

6. *Sym*: Symphony No. 1
60. *Taps (III)*:   Three Songs from Drum Taps (third movement)

III. Style (techniques and devices)

[*Symphony No. 2* (Romantic)] "represents my escape from the rather bitter type of modern musical realism which occupies so large a place in contemporary thought. Much contemporary music seems to me to be showing a tendency to become entirely too cerebral. I do not believe that music is primarily a matter of the intellect, but rather a manifestation of the emotions. I have therefore aimed in this symphony to create a work that was young in spirit, lyrical and romantic in temperament, and simple and direct in expression.   Howard Hanson

A. General characteristics
 1.   Strong influence of Sibelius, Vaughan Williams, Ravel, MacDowell and others. Full orchestrations, sonorous harmonies, ostinato figures, pedal points, vigorous syncopated rhythms. Basically homophonic with some use of contrapuntal devices. "Trend in later works towards greater economy of material and more compact form."

SYMPHONIC WORKS

B. Melodic line
 1.   Built up of short characteristic motives: *Sym 1* (pp. 11-13).
 2.   Broadly lyrical: *Sym 2* (pp. 19-24).
 3.   Modal melodies:
   a.   Lydian: *Sym 1* (p. 11).
   b.   Dorian: *Sym 1* (pp. 1-6); *Sym 3* (pp. 61-69; pp. 152-154).
   c.   Aeolian: *Sym 3* (p. 68).
   d.   Mixolydian: *Sym 2* (p. 103).
 4.   Changing modes within course of melody: *Sym 3* (pp. 8-14: D - Dorian, D - Aeolian, D - major).
 5.   Disjunct line in parallel thirds: *Sym 1* (p. 51); *Sym 3* (second movement).
 6.   Quartal melody: *Sym 2* (pp. 7, 94).
 7.   Metamorphosis of themes: *Sym 1* (first movement, pp. 14-26); *Sym 2* (first movement, pp. 25-39); *Sym 3* (last movement, p. 125).
 8.   Chromatic: *Sym 2* (p. 2).
 9.   Artificial scales: *Concerto*.
C. Harmony
 1.   Characteristic harmony is the major seventh, surrounded by triads and ninths, elevenths, thirteenths in quartal-quintal voicing; added notes, chiefly in the framework of these intervals. Free chromatic technique, especially in early works.
 2.   Augmented eleventh chord on dominant: *Sym 2* (p. 47).
 3.   Quartal harmony with quartal melody: *Sym 2* (pp. 7, 11, 96; pp. 28-29).
 4.   Complex sonority with tritone predominating: *Sym 2* (pp. 1-5 uses sonority G, B-natural, D-flat, F, A-flat; later used melodically as principal theme of first movement).
 5.   Sharply dissonant sonorities used to heighten tension: *Sym 4* (pp. 6-7).
 6.   Chromatic: *Sym 2* (p. 2).
 7.   Pedal point: *Sym 1* (pp. 44-45); *Sym 2* (pp. 116-124); *Sym 3* (pp. 22-24).
D. Counterpoint
 1.   Combination of themes: *Sym 1* (p. 15); *Sym 2* (p. 40); *Sym 3* (pp. 125-127).

    2.   Broad theme with striking counter-theme: *Sym 2* (pp. 19-24).

    3.   Imitation: *Sym 3* (pp. 50-53); *Sym 2* (pp. 49, 123).

    4.   Augmentation: *Sym 3* (p. 158).

    5.   Diminution: *Sym 1* (pp. 15, 25); *Sym 2* (pp. 24, 66).

E.   Rhythm

    1.   Marked rhythms: *Sym 1* (p. 77); *Sym 2* (pp. 4, 103).

    2.   Syncopation: *Sym 2* (pp. 15, 129); *Sym 4* (p. 75); *Concerto*.

    3.   Metric changes (based on mathematical relation of a common time unit): *Sym 3* (fourth movement).

    4.   Alteration of rhythmic motives: *Sym 1* (pp. 11-13); *Sym 2* (p. 15).

    5.   Ostinato (tonal as well as rhythmic): *Sym 1* (p. 77); *Sym 2* (p. 103); *Sym 3* (pp. 1-8; pp. 127, 132).

    6.   Jazz rhythms: *Concerto*.

F.   Form

    1.   Cyclic form characteristic; used in many orchestral works.

    2.   Works in four movements: *Sym 3*; *Sym 4*. Works in three movements: *Sym 1*; *Sym 2* (Adagio introduction). Works in one movement: *Sym 5*.

    3.   Recurrence of earlier themes in last movement: all symphonies.

    4.   Sonata-allegro form (with modifications): *Sym 1* (first movement); *Sym 2* (first movement).

    5.   Use of Ternary form: *Sym 1* (second movement); *Sym 2* (second movement).

    6.   Rondo form (modified): *Sym 1* (third movement).

    7.   Scherzo form: *Sym 3 (third movement)*; *Sym 4* (third movement); *Concerto* (second movement).

    8.   One principal theme: *Sym 3* (second movement).

G.   Orchestration

    1.   Always colorful, sonorous and practical.

    2.   Full sonority of orchestra exploited: *Sym 1* (pp. 83, 86); *Sym 3* (p. 42).

    3.   Full orchestra in unison and octaves: *Sym 3* (pp. 164-165).

    4.   Use of solo instruments: *Sym 2* (p. 25); *Sym 3* (pp. 42-50; pp. 72-79); *Serenade*; *Pastorale*.

    5.   Contrast of various orchestral choirs: *Sym 3* (pp. 24-38).

    6.   "Lean" orchestration—individual lines made to stand out: *Sym 4* (first movement).

CHORAL WORKS

A.   Melodic line

    1.   Themes generally broad, flowing, diatonic. Frequent use of modal or quasi-modal melodies: *Beowulf* (p. 15).

    2.   Diatonic, with occasional chromaticism and false relations: *Beowulf* (p. 8, meas. 5-6; p. 10, meas. 2-3); *Taps* (III).

    3.   Diatonic within a scale system including chromatic steps: *Hymn* (p. 17, meas. 4-6, voice parts).

    4.   Angular: *Taps* (first movement).

    5.   Chromaticism and false relations: *Beowulf* (pp. 8, 10, 27); *Taps* (III).

    6.   Artificial scales: *Hymn* (meas. 1-24).

    7.   Modal: *Beowulf* (p. 15).

B.   Harmony

    1.   Tertian: *Beowulf* (p. 32, meas. 3-4; p. 33, meas. 1, 8, 9); *Taps* (second movement, p. 27, meas. 5, 6; third movement, p. 49, meas. 4); *Hymn* (p. 1, meas. 3, 7, 8; p. 12, meas. 4).

    2.   Quartal: *Beowulf* (almost entirely); *Taps* (I, p. 1, meas. 9 *et seq*; none in II; III, p. 52, meas. 2); *Hymn* (p. 14, meas. 3-9).

3. Text painting: *Beowulf* (pp. 15, 16, 17).
4. Ostinato figures: *Beowulf* (pp. 19, 25).
5. Pedal points: *Beowulf*.
6. Chords with added notes: *Beowulf* (pp. 4, 44).
7. Pandiatonic: *Beowulf* (pp. 16-19).
C. Counterpoint
  1. Fugal writing: *Taps* (III); *Hymn* (pp. 4-5; pp. 9, 11, 16, 17).
D. Rhythm
  1. Derived from the prosody: *Hymn* (p. 4, meas. 5-6); *Beowulf* (p. 10, second and third scores).
  2. Changes in meter: *Hymn* (p. 3, meas. 16, 18, 19).
E. Form
  1. *Beowulf* corresponds roughly to a large Sonata-allegro form with the following plan:
    a. Introduction (pp. 1-5).
    b. Exposition (orchestral and choral)
      1) First theme, melodic (p. 6, first score); second theme, rhythmic (p. 10).
    c. Development (pp. 14-25, first score).
    d. Recapitulation (p. 25, second score to end).
      1) The plan of the choral parts in the recapitulation is the same as in the exposition, with a short coda.
  2. Sectional: *Hymn*.

BIBLIOGRAPHY

Books by Howard Hanson

Harmonic Materials of Modern Music. New York: Appleton-Century-Crofts, 1960.
  MC 161 (Apr 1960), 46; *J Mus Theory* 4, No. 2 (1960), 236-243; *Mus Ed J* 46, No. 5 (1960), 87; *J Res Mus Ed* 8, No. 2 (1960), 128-130; *Notes* 18, No. 3 (1961), 415; *Can Mus J* 5, No. 4 (1961), 63; *PNM* 1, No. 2 (1963), 142-147; *JAMS* 17, No. 3 (1964), 408.

Articles by Howard Hanson

1. "Forward Look in American Composition," *Musician* 31 (Feb 1926), 14.
2. "Critics, Publishers and Patrons," *MM* 4, No. 2 (1926-1927), 28.
3. "What Shall I Do With My Music? " *Etude* 45 (Sep 1927), 641.
4. "Is Our Musical Progress a Mirage? " *Mus Dgt* 13 (May 1928), 13.
5. "Machine Music a Challenge to the Profession," *Musician* 35 (Mar 1930), 20.
6. "Training Course for School Music Supervisors," *MTNAPro* (1930), 87-96.
7. "Italy Awakens to Our Music Culture," *Musician* 36 (Feb 1931), 8.
8. "Conditions Affecting the Development of an American Music," *Etude* 50 (Apr 1932), 247.
9. "Music in Adult Education," *Music Supervisors' National Conference Yearbook* (1932), 65-69.
10. "Some Suggestions Concerning Graduate Study in Music in the United States," *MTNAPro* (1933), 99-104.
11. "Music's Place in the New Deal," *Musician* 38 (Jul 1933), 7.
12. "Music Camps in America," *Education* 54 (Oct 1933), 99.
13. "Music as a Recreation," *Mus Club Mag* 13 (Nov-Dec 1933), 7.
14. "All American," *Scholastic* 24 (Mar 3, 1934), 35.
15. "Present State of American Music; Report of the Committee on American Music," *MTNA-Pro* (1933), 198-200; *Sch Mus* 34 (Mar 1934), 5.

16. "Creative Attitude," *MTNAPro* (1934), 120-126.
17. "Music and American Youth," *Mus Ed J* 20 (Oct 1934), 13.
18. "Developing an American School of Music," *Musician* 39 (Dec 1934), 4.
19. "Music Everywhere," *Etude* 53 (Feb 1935), 84.
20. "What Do You Mean, American Music? " *Musician* 40 (Apr 1935), 8; (May 1935), 10.
21. "Music In Its Highest Fulfillment," *Mus Ed J* 21 (May 1935), 13.
22. "American Procession at Rochester," *MM* 13, No. 3 (1935-1936), 22.
23. "Report of the Committee on American Music," *MTNAPro* (1936), 336-342.
24. "Music Invades the Public School Curriculum," *American Association of School Administrators Official Report* (1936), 205-213; *Nat Ed Assn Pro* (1936), 496-504.
25. "Hanson Announces a Public Symposium," *MA* 56, No. 16 (1936), 4.
26. "The Supervisor and His Mission," *Musician* 42 (Aug 1937), 139-140.
27. "American Music for American Youth," *Mus Ed J* 24 (Dec 1937), 27.
28. "Dial Goes 'Round'," *Musician* 43 (Feb 1938), 36.
29. "Report of the Committee on American Music," *MTNAPro* (1938), 329-336.
30. "Status of Contemporary Music," *MENC Yearbook* (1938), 29-37.
31. "Music in American Life," *MENC Yearbook* (1939-1940), 9-12; excerpts in *NEA Pro* (1940), 505-506.
32. "Address at the American Conservatory, Chicago," *Mus Leader* 25 (1939), 23.
33. "Music Made in America, Past and Future," *Musician* 45 (Aug 1940), 138.
34. "Music in American Life Today," *Mus Club Mag* 20 (Nov 1940), 5.
35. "Major Problem in American Music," *MTNAPro* (1940), 20-27.
36. "Place of Music in the Culture of the World," *Nat Ed Assn Pro* (1940), 57-60.
37. "Democratization of Music," *Mus Ed J* 27 (Mar 1941), 14.
38. "The Past, Present and Future of the American Public School Orchestra," *Mus Leader* 28 (May 23, 1942), 16.
39. "Twenty Years Growth in America," *MM* 20, No. 2 (1942-1943), 95.
40. "On Musicians," *Mus Ed J* 29 (Apr 1943), 52-53.
41. "Bernard Rogers," *MM* 22, No. 3 (1944-1945), 170.
42. "Serge Koussevitsky," *Atlantic Monthly* 175 (May 1945), 47-51.
43. "National Music Council," *Ed Mus Mag* 25 (Jan 1946), 13.
44. "Report, 1946," *MTNAPro* (1946), 427.
45. "Cultivating a Climate for Creativity," *Mus Ed J* 46 (Jun 1960), 28-30.
46. "American Music Forum; Introductory Remarks," *MTNAPro* (1946), 70-72.
47. "Music in the Liberal Arts College," *J Gen Ed* 1 (Jan 1947), 156-159.
48. "Why American Music Needs Pioneers," *SR* 30 (Sep 27, 1947), 39.
49. "Challenge of Responsibility," *Musician* 53 (Jan 1948), 5.
50. "Scope of the Music Education Program," *Mus Ed J* 34 (Jun 1948), 7-8.
51. "Music, the Universal Langugage," *Etude* 67 (Aug 1949), 470.
52. "Flowering of American Music," *SR* 32 (Aug 6, 1949), 157.
53. "UNESCO and World Peace," *Ed Mus Mag* 29 (Jan-Feb 1950), 8-9.
54. "Artist's Role Today," *Nat Ed Assn J* 50 (Jan 1961), 13.
55. "1950 Fall Convocation Address at the Eastman School of Music," *Mus J* 9 (Jan 1951), 13;
56. "What is Happening to Music in America," *Etude* 69 (Jan 1951), 12-13.
57. "John Alden Carpenter," *SR* 34 (Feb 24, 1951), 50.
58. "Participation Values Surpass Observation," *Instrument* 6 (Mar-Apr 1952), 17.
59. "Curriculum Enrichment or Inflation," *Education* 74 (Sep 1953), 17-22.
60. "The Challenge of Music Therapy," *Mus Therapy* 4 (1954), 8-14.
61. "You Can't Boss a Conductor! " *Mus J* 12 (Nov 1954), 13.
62. "The Fulfillment of Your Capabilities," *Am Mus Tcr* 4 (May-Jun 1955), 2.
63. "The Arts in an Age of Science," *Mus Ed J* 44 (Sep 1957), 23-26.
64. "Farewell to Orchestras," *Good Housekeeping* 145 (Oct 1957), 96.
65. "Sail, Sail Thy Best Ship, Excerpt from 'Song of Democracy'," *Nat Ed Assn J* 46 (Mar

1957), 192.

66. "Arts In An Age of Science," *Nat Ed Assn J* 47 (Feb 1958), 73.

67. "Music Looks Forward," *Mus Ed J* 44 (Jun 1958), 28.

68. "The Arts in an Age of Science," (reprinted from *Mus Ed Assn J*) *Int Musician* 56 (Mar 1958), 9; *Pan Pipes* 50 (May 1958), 7; *NMC Bul* 19 (Spring 1959), 7.

69. "Education Must Give High Priorities to the Humanities," *MA* 79 (Feb 1959), 22.

70. "Music Education Faces the Scientific Age," *Mus Ed J* 45 (Jun 1959), 17-19.

71. "With His Baton He Ruled Finland," *SR* 42 (Jul 25, 1959), 17.

72. "Painting the Sound," *Am Assn Sch Adm Official Report* (1959), 88-97.

73. "Contemporary Music in Music Education," *NMC* 20, No. 1 (1960), 9.

74. "The American Experience," *NMC* 20, No. 2 (1960), 15.

75. "Science, Art, and the Good Life," *NMC* 20, No. 3 (1960), 4.

76. "Cultivating a Climate for Creativity," *Mus Ed J* 46, No. 6 (1960), 28-30.

77. "A Composer's Credo," *Mus J* 18 (Sep 1960), 26.

78. "Cultural Challenge," *Mus J* 19 (Jan 1961), 4.

79. "Artist's Role Today," *Nat Ed Assn J* 50 (Jan 1961), 12.

80. H. H. and A. J. Treanor. "Two Challenges to Our Schools and Universities," *MA* 81 (Feb 1961), 14.

81. "Mechanics or Music," *Int Mus* 59 (Feb 1961), 9.

82. "Are the Creative Arts in Danger? " *NMC* 21, No. 3 (1961), 19.

83. "The Place of Music in an Age of Science," *Int Mus* 59 (Mar 1961), 10.

84. "The Unwritten Note," *Mus J* 19 (Oct 1961), 58.

85. "MacDowell: American Romantic Supreme," *Mus J* 19 (Nov-Dec 1961), 30.

86. "Hope for the Future of Music," *Clavier* 1, No. 1 (1962), 30.

87. "Comments on Music Education by Howard Hanson," *Int Mus* 60 (Feb 1962), 26.

88. "Urgently Needed; More Musical Careers," *Mus J* 20 (May 1962), 22.

89. "American Youth on Tour," *Instrument* 16 (May 1962), 35.

90. "Are the Creative Arts in Danger? " *Am Org* 45 (Sep 1962), 9.

91. "Enlightened Leadership; Address, Sept. 16, 1962," *Vital Speeches* 29 (Oct 15, 1962), 28-30.

92. "Performing Artists from Eastman," *Mus J* 20 (Nov-Dec 1962), 53.

93. "The Message of the Arts," *Mus J* 21 (Jan 1963), 26.

94. "A Plea for the Arts," *Mus J* 21 (Nov 1963), 25.

95. "Place of Creative Arts," *Vital Speeches* 30 (Nov 15, 1963), 87-90.

96. "C Major Chord: A Dialogue With Howard Hanson," *Opera N* 28, No. 3 (Nov 16, 1963), 9.

97. "Everyone Must Have An Island," *Recreation* 56 (Dec 1963), 449.

98. "The Professional Doctorate in Music," *Int Mus* 62 (Mar 1964), 9 (reprinted in *NMC* 24, No. 3 (1964), 13.

99. "What Price Human Values? " *Mus J* 22 (Sep 1964), 30.

100. "Review of Books," *MQ* 50 (1964), 535-537.

101. "The New Eastman Institute of American Music," *Pan Pipes* 57, No. 2 (1965), 20.

102. "In Praise of Edward Alexander MacDowell," *Mus Club Mag* 44, No. 3 (1965), 19.

103. "Strange Gods for Young Composers," *Mus J Annual* 25 (1966), 39.

104. "Music 1967," *Mus Club Mag* 47, No. 1 (1967), 14.

105. "Case for Conservatism," *Time* 91 (Mar 8, 1968), 80.

106. "Wanted: A Music Survival Kit–The Arts Crisis Courts Disaster in the Seventies," *Mus Ed J* 57 (Apr 1971), 28-31.

107. "The Dilemma of American Music," *Pan Pipes* 64, No. 2 (1972), 2-4.

References to Howard Hanson

Books
(See the General Bibliography)

ASC-BD; ASC-SC; AusMT; Baker; BauTC; BIM; BloYA; BluPC; BroOH; Bull; CatPC; ChaAM; ClaEA; CobCS; CohCT; ComA; CowAC; CurB (1966); DalTT; DemMT; DerETM; DowO; DukLH; Edm-II; EdMUS; EweAC; EweCB; EweCS; EweDE; EweMC; EweNB; EweYA; GosMM; GroSH; Grove; HanIT; HinCP; HitMU; HowMM; HowOA; HowOC; HowSH; JabCAC; JohOA; JohSH; KinAI; MacAC; MueAS; MyeTC; NorLC; PavMH; PerTH; PeyNM; PleSM; PorM3S; ReiCA; ReiCC; SalMO; SalzTM; SanWM; SelMO; SloMS; SteveP; ThoAJ; ThoAM; ThoMR; ThompIC; ThoRL; UlrCM; WWM; WhiWW; YatTC; YouCT.

Articles

Brief mention: *MQ* 18 (1932), 13; *Musician* 42 (Apr 1937), 61; *MQ* 24 (1938), 25; 26 (1940), 102, 298; *NW* 15 (May 6, 1940), 44; *Musician* 47 (May 1941), 79; *MA* 62, No. 1 (Jan 10, 1942), 3; *MM* 20, No. 2 (1942-1943), 101; *MQ* 30 (1944), 315; *MQ* 31 (1945), 102, 105; *Musician* 50 (Sep 1945), 180; 51 (Dec 1946), 167; *MQ* 33 (1947), 18, 210; 35 (1949), 126; *MA* 69 (Dec 1, 1949), 10; *MQ* 38 (1952), 438; *MA* 74 (Feb 1, 1954), 27; 76 (Jun 19, 1956), 15.

1. "Howard Hanson: A Biographical Sketch and Portrait," *Mus Opin* 51 (Mar 1928), 34.
2. *NYT* (Jan 14, 1930), 24:7.
3. "Sails for Rome," *NYT* (Nov 30, 1930), 28:7.
4. "Returns to U. S." *NYT* (Dec 31, 1930), 10:8.
5. "Elected Member to National Institute of Arts and Letters," *NYT* (Jan 17, 1935), 21:8.
6. *NYT* (Apr 2, 1935), 23:6; (Aug 11, 1935), sec. 9, p. 4:7.
7. "Rochester's Decade of Achievement," *MA* 4, No. 14 (1935), 16.
8. Tuthill, Burnet C. "Howard Hanson, with List of Compositions," *MQ* 22 (1936), 140.
9. "Encyclopedia of Contemporary Musicians," *Musician* 41 (Jan 1936), 17.
10. *NYT* (Oct 13, 1936), 25:6; (Oct 18, 1936), sec. 10, p. 10:8; (Jun 10, 1937), 27:5; (Apr 27, 1938), 19:1.
11. "Elected Member of the Royal Swedish Academy of Music," *NYT* (Jul 3, 1938), sec. 9, p. 6:8.
12. Scherchen, Herman. "Are There American Composers? " *MA* 58, No. 16 (Oct 25, 1938), 8.
13. *Etude* 56 (Nov 1938), 706; *Time* 33 (May 8, 1938), 34.
14. *NYT* (Apr 25, 1939), 19:4; (Apr 29, 1939), 12:4; (Oct 8, 1939), 48:6.
15. "Rochester Holds 9th Annual American Music Festival," *MA* 59 (May 1939), 37.
16. "Orchestras," *MA* 59, No. 19 (Dec 10, 1939), 12, 37.
17. *NYT* (Dec 29, 1940), 24:2.
18. Alter, Martha. "Howard Hanson," *MM* 18, No. 2 (1940-1941), 84.
19. "Biography," *Current Biography* (Oct 1941); *Current Biography Yearbook*, 363-364.
20. *NYT* (Jan 19, 1941), sec. 9, p. 7:1; (Jan 26, 1941), sec. 9, 7:1; (Aug 9, 1941), 9:5; (Dec 18, 1941), 38:2.
21. "American Music in Rochester," *MA* 62, No. 9 (May 1942), 3.
22. *NYT* (Sep 15, 1942), 25:3; (Sep 19, 1942), 30:1.
23. "Composing Quartet," *NW* 23 (Jan 17, 1944), 72.
24. "Wins Pulitzer Prize," *NYT* (May 2, 1944), 1:2; 16:3; 18:2.
25. "Symphony No. 4, Op. 34 Wins Putlizer Prize," *Etude* 62 (Jun 1944), 313.
26. Slonimsky, Nicolas. "American Sibelius," *Chr Sc Mon Mag* (Oct 14, 1944), 4.
27. Sabin, Robert. "Meet the Composer," *MA* 64, No. 8 (1944), 7.
28. "American Sibelius," *NW* 25 (May 7, 1945), 95-96.

29. "Honorary Degree, Columbia University," *NYT* (Jun 5, 1946), 16:1.
30. *NYT* (Jan 18, 1946), 14:8; (Oct 15, 1946), 27:8; (Oct 20, 1946), sec. 2, p. 7:1.
31. "Becomes Secretary of National Association of Schools of Music," *NYT* (Dec 31, 1947), 11:3.
32. *NYT* (May 9, 1947), 29:3; (Apr 20, 1948), 32:2.
33. "The Fraternity Certificate of Merit Presented to Howard Hanson," *Pan Pipes* 41 (Apr 1949), 252-254.
34. "Eastman School of Music to Mark Dr. Hanson's 25th Year as Head," *MC* 140 (Nov 15, 1949), 25.
35. "Twenty-Fifth Anniversary," *MA* 69 (Nov 15, 1949), 14.
36. "Takes Executive Committee Post on International Music Council," *NYT* (Nov 23, 1949), 20:4.
37. Watanabe, Ruth. "Howard Hanson's Autographs in the Sibley Music Library," *Notes* 7 (Mar 1950), 240-242.
38. Rosenwald, Hans. "Eastman School of Music," *Mus News* 42 (Jan 1950), 12.
39. Wykes, Robert. "Howard Hanson: 25 Years of Progress," *MA* 70, No. 5 (Apr 1950), 37.
40. Taubman, Howard. "25-Year View: Thoughts on Composers of Quarter Century," *NYT* (Sep 17, 1950), sec. 2, p. 7:1.
41. "Let's Look at Their Minds and Hearts," *Mus J* 9 (Feb 1951), 8-9.
42. Rosenwald, Hans. "Contemporary Music," *Mus News* 43 (Feb 1951), 10.
43. "Hanson Announces New Musical Theory," *MA* 71 (Dec 15, 1951), 23.
44. "Howard Hanson Discusses Nationalism in Music," *News Let* 4 (Jul 1952), 3.
45. *NYT* (Oct 5, 1952), sec. 2, p. 11:6; (May 7, 1953), 37:2; (May 9, 1953), 12:7; (Oct 25, 1953), sec. 2, p. 7:8; (Nov 1, 1953), sec. 2, p. 9:6; (Nov 8, 1953), sec. 2, p. 7:4.
46. Kyle, Marguerite K. "AmerAllegro," *Pan Pipes* 46 (Jan 1954), 42.
47. Berger, Arthur. "Debt to Hanson," *SR* 37 (Jan 30, 1954), 56.
48. "Hanson Discusses Educational Inflation," *MA* 74 (Feb 1, 1954), 27.
49. "Dr. Hanson Elected to Hall of Fame," *SWMusician* 20 (Feb 1954), 5.
50. Keats, Sheila. "Reference Articles on American Composers: An Index," *Juilliard Rev* 1 (Fall 1954), 27.
51. "Dr. Hanson's 30th Anniversary at Eastman," *MC* 150 (Nov 1, 1954), 38.
52. "Howard Hanson," *Pan Pipes* 47 (Jan 1955), 49.
53. "Hanson Conducts Symphony of the Air," *MA* 75, No. 5 (Mar 1955), 17.
54. *NYT* (May 7, 1955), 9:8; (May 9, 1955), 28:3.
55. "National Education Association Commissions Hanson to Write Centennial Composition for Chorus and Orchestra," *Mus Ed J* 42 (Nov-Dec 1955), 58.
56. *NYT* (Nov 2, 1955), 31:7; (Feb 12, 1956), 82:4; (May 3. 1956), 35:2; (May 5, 1956), 12:8; (May 9, 1956), 36:5; (May 15, 1956), 26:5; (Oct 7, 1956), sec. 4, p. 10:7.
57. Ellsworth, Ray. "Americans on Microgroove," *HiFi* 6 (Aug 1956), 61.
58. Kyle, Marguerite K. "AmerAllegro," *Pan Pipes* 49 (Jan 1957), 51.
59. "Appointed to US National Commission of ENESCO," *NYT* (Mar 13, 1957), 23:1.
60. "Hanson is Guest with Oratorio Society," *MA* 77 (Apr 1957), 19.
61. "American Composers Alliance Laurel Leaf Award," *NYT* (May 24, 1957), 30:1.
62. "Honorary Degree Kentucky University," *NYT* (Sep 25, 1957), 21:1.
63. Conly, John M. "American Music Played Here," *HiFi* 8 (Feb 1958), 32.
64. *NYT* (Jan 31, 1958); (Feb 2, 1958); (Mar 14, 1958), 51:1; (May 1, 1958), 35:1; (May 3, 1958), 10:5; (May 5, 1959), 24:2; (May 12, 1958); (Aug 8, 1958); (Dec 5, 1958).
65. "We Salute Howard Hanson," *Mus Club Mag* 38 (Sep 1958), 8.
66. "Eastman Fetes Director's 35th Year," *MC* 158 (Nov 1958), 33.
67. Kyle, Marguerite K. "AmerAllegro," *Pan Pipes* 51 (Jan 1959), 66.
68. *NYT* (Feb 19, 1959), 28:5.
69. "American Composers—Howard Hanson," *MC* 159 (Apr 1959), 41.
70. "National Music Council Honor," *NYT* (May 2, 1959), 13:2.
71. "Eastman Fete Marks Hanson Anniversary," *MA* 79 (Jun 1959), 16.

72. "Howard Hanson," *Composers of the Americas* 5 (1959), 36-45.
73. Riker, C. C. "Howard Hanson: Outdoors Man," *MC* 161 (Mar 1960), 9.
74. "In the News," *Mus Ed J* 48, No. 1 (1961), 18.
75. Gates, Crawford. "A Sacred Choral Pageant," *Mus J* 19 (Feb 1961), 68-70.
76. *NYT* (Aug 27, 1961), sec. 2, p. 9:3.
77. Fennell, Frederick. "Hanson at 65," *NYT* (Oct 29, 1961), sec. 2, 11:8.
78. "Hanson Appraises Arts in U. S." *Instrument* 16 (Jan 1962), 33.
79. " 'Accent on Youth' Tour," *Showcase* 42, No. 1 (1962), 12.
80. "National Arts Club Gold Medal," *NYT* (Mar 9, 1962), 23:1.
81. *NYT* (Feb 27, 1962), 30:3; (Mar 5, 1962), 27:3.
82. "Plans to Leave Eastman," *NYT* (May 4, 1962), 28:2.
83. Fennell, Frederick. "Hanson at 65," *Pan Pipes* 54, No. 2 (1962), 15.
84. "Another Honor for Dr. Howard Hanson," *Mus Leader* 94 (May 1962), 5.
85. "MENC Award to Howard Hanson," *Mus Ed J* 48 (Jun 1962), 35.
86. "Hanson to Retire," *Instrument* 16 (Jun 1962), 37.
87. "Dr. Howard Hanson to Retire as Director of Eastman School July 1, 1964," *Mus Leader* 94 (Jun 1962), 9.
88. "Moore, Hanson Announce Retirements," *Mus Mag* 164 (Jul 1962), 62.
89. Helm, Everett. "To Talk of Many Things," *MA* 82 (Jul 1962), 46.
90. "Howard Hanson to Retire as Eastman School Director," *NMC* 22, No. 3 (1962), 9.
91. "Honorary Degree, NY State, Board of Regents," *NYT* (Oct 27, 1962), 52:4.
92. "Dr. Howard Hanson Blasts 'Rock and Roll'," *School Mus* 34 (Nov 1962), 39.
93. "Dr. Howard Hanson Named to Executive Committee of the International Music Council of UNESCO," *Mus Leader* 94 (Nov 1962), 14.
94. Brozen, Michael. "Orchestra in New York," *MA* 83 (Jan 1963), 109.
95. "Hanson Named to IMC of UNESCO," *Pan Pipes* 55, No. 3 (1963), 3.
96. "Salute to Howard Hanson," *Mus Leader* 95 (Oct 1963), 6.
97. Freeman, John W., ed. "C Major Chord: A Dialogue with H. Hanson," *Opera N* 28 (Nov 16, 1963), 8-12.
98. "Eastman School of Music Dr. Howard Hanson Honored," *Mus Leader* 95 (Dec 1963), 5.
99. Kyle, Marguerite K. "AmerAllegro," *Pan Pipes* 55, No. 2 (1963), 53; 56, No. 2 (1964), 60.
100. *NYT* (Nov 30 (1963), 19:2.
101. "Education: Eastman Eulogies," *MA* 84 (Jan 1964), 74.
102. "Howard Hanson Salutes Howard Mitchell," *Instrument* 18 (Mar 1964), 44.
103. *NYT* (May 7, 1964), 30:2.
104. "Dr. Howard Hanson," *Wood World* 5, No. 5 (1964), 13.
105. Southgate, Harry W. "New York," *MA* 84 (Jul 1964), 24.
106. "Retires as President of Eastman School of Music," *NYT* (May 5, 1964), 53:2; (Jun 9, 1964), 31:4.
107. Ashford, Gerald. "Other Puritans," *Opera N* 29 (Jan 23, 1965), 31.
108. Goldberg, A. "What Dr. Howard Hanson Said To Me," *School Mus* 36 (Mar 1965), 60.
109. Sheppard, W. "Music in Our Age (An Interview with Howard Hanson)," *Mus J Annual* 23 (1965), 50.
110. "Howard Hanson Week Scheduled at Eastman," *NMC* 27, No. 1 (1966), 5.
111. Kyle, Marguerite K. "AmerAllegro," *Pan Pipes* 58, No. 2 (1966), 66.
112. "The Scribner Music Library; Howard Hanson, ed.," *Notes* 22, No. 3 (1966), 1120.
113. "Howard Hanson's View on the Present State of Music," *Int Mus* 64 (Jul 1966), 6.
114. "Biography," *Current Biography* (Sep 1966); *Current Biography Yearbook* (1966), 152-154.
115. Waters, Edward N. "Harvest of the Year; Selected Acquisitions of the Music Division," *Q J Library Congress* 24, No. 1 (1967), 58.
116. "Presentation of Retirement Gift to Dr. Howard Hanson by Harold Spivacke," *NMC* 27,

No. 3 (1967), 9.

117. "A Salute to Howard Hanson," *School Mus* 39 (Dec 1967), 3.
118. "Dr. Howard Hanson to be Guest Speaker and Guest Conductor at Mid-West Clinic," *School Mus* 39 (Dec 1967), 76.
119. "Dr. Howard Hanson Honored at 21st Annual Mid-West National Band Clinic at Chicago," *School Mus* 39 (Jan 1968), 78.
120. "6th Symphony Premiered," *FoF* 28 (Feb 29, 1968), 597E1.
121. "Dr. Howard Hanson and Harold Bachman Honored," *School Mus* 39 (Mar 1968), 77.
122. *NYT* (Mar 1, 1968), 21:1; (Apr 14, 1968), sec. 4, p. 17:3.
123. Ashley, Patricia. "The Great American Composers: Howard Hanson," *HiFi R* 20 (Jun 1968), 47-55.
124. Kyle, Marguerite K. "AmerAllegro," *Pan Pipes* 61, No. 2 (1969), 56.
125. "Howard Hanson Praises Participants in USF Choral Symposium," *Choral J* 9, No. 5 (1969), 2.
126. Montgomery, Merle. "Howard Hanson—the Gentleman from Wahoo," *ASCAP* 5, No. 1 (1971), 14-16.
127. "Alice Tully Hall," *Mus J* 30 (Jun 1972), 38.
128. "Music Journal's 1972 Gallery of Living Composers," *Mus J Annual* 30 (1972), 44.
129. Heglund, Gerald. "The Wizard of Wahoo," *Mus J* 32 (Jan 1974), 16-17.
130. "University of Rochester Awarded President's Award," *NYT* (Feb 4, 1975), 29:1.
131. "Howard Hanson Honored (Eastman School of Music President's Medal)," *Clavier* 14, No. 6 (1975), 59.
132. Merkling, Frank. "Yankee Doodle Opera—How an Immigrant Art Took to the Rich Soil of the New World," *Opera N* 40 (Jun 1976), 10-13; 41 (Jul 1976), 8-12.
133. Nichols, Randolph. "From Our Readers (Performance Doctorates in Music)," *Mus J* 34 (July 1976), 74.
134. "People (80th Birthday Celebration)," *Sym News* 27, No. 5 (1976), 34.
135. "Howard Hanson Honored on His 80th Birthday," *School Mus* 48 (Jan 1977), 16.
136. "Howard Hanson: Eightieth Birthday Tributes," *HiFi/MA* 27 (Feb 1977), MA36.
137. "Howard Hanson Conducts His Music at Interlochen," *School Mus* 49 (Oct 1977), 52.
138. "Howard Hanson Elected to AWAPA," *Instrument* 32 (Nov 1977), 105.
139. "Notes From Our Schools," *Pan Pipes* 69, No. 4 (1977), 5-10.
140. "AWAPA's Awarded," *Mus Ed J* 64 (Sep 1977), 114.
141. Nelhybel, Vaclav. "Time In Your Hands (Chorale and Alleluia)," *Instrument* 32 (Sep 1977), 47-49.
142. Kyle, Marguerite K. "AmerAllegro," *Pan Pipes* 70, No. 2 (1978), 43.

References to Works by Howard Hanson

22. Bold Island Suite: *ClSPN* (Jan 25, 1962), 477; *NYT* (Feb 13, 1962); *New Yorker* 38 (Feb 24, 1962), 112; *MA* 82 (Mar 1962), 16; *Mus Mag* 164 (Apr 1962), 31.
63. Cherubic Hymn: *MC* 142 (Jun 1950), 6; *Notes* 7 (Jun 1950), 442-444; *MA* 70 (Aug 1950), 28; *Mus Club Mag* 30 (Oct 1950), 24; *Pan Pipes* 44 (Jan 1952), 12.
35. Chorale and Alleluia: *MA* 41 (1955), 407.
28. Concerto for Organ: *Notes* 5 (1947-1948), 259.
29. Concerto for Piano: *BSPN* (Dec 31, 1948), 52; *MC* 139 (Jan 15, 1949), 8; *MQ* 35 (1949), 287; *MC* 146 (Dec 1, 1952), 34; *Notes* 10 (1952-1953), 485-486; *MA* 73 (Jan 15, 1953), 26; *ML* 34 (Oct 1953), 352-353.
26. Die Natalis: *Strad* 78 (Feb 1968), 403; *Q J Library Congress* 27, No. 1 (1970), 60.
60. Drum Taps: *MA* 55, No. 11 (1935), 24; *MQ* 22 (1936), 146.
19. Elegy in Memory of Serge Koussevitsky: *BSPN* (Jan 20, 1956); *MA* 76 (Feb 1, 1956), 5; *NYT* (Feb 12, 1956), 82:3; *MA* 76 (Mar 1956), 16; *MC* 153 (Mar 1, 1956), 17; *How-OA*, 432.

Fanfare and Chorale: *Sym News* 27, No. 2 (1976), 30.

23. For the First Time: *NYT* (May 17, 1963), 67:5; *MA* 83 (Jun 1963), 34; *Am Mus Tcr* 12 No. 6 (1963), 30; *Mus Leader* 95 (Oct 1963), 14; *MA* 84 (May 1964), 53.

68. Four Psalms: *MA* 84 (Dec 1964), 64; *MQ* 51 (1965), 410.

64. How Excellent Thy Name: *Pan Pipes* 47 (Jan 1955), 76.

57. Lament for Beowulf: *EweCB*, 162; *HitMU*, 178.

7. Lux aeterna: *LAPPN* (Mar 27, 1925); *MQ* 22 (1936), 142, 147.

78. Merry Mount: *NYT* (Apr 8, 1930), 26:5; *Outlook* 154 (Apr 23, 1930), 653-654; *NYT* (Dec 15, 1930), 28:2; *NYT* (Feb 12, 1931), 24:2; (Feb 15, 1931), sec. 8, p. 7; (Mar 28, 1931), 15:2; (Jan 9, 1933), 22:3; (Jan 11, 1933), 5:6; (Mar 16, 1933), 21:3; (May 5, 1933), 13:5; (May 21, 1933), sec. 2, p. 3:8; (Dec 28, 1933), 1:4; (Dec 30, 1933), 12:4; (Jan 29, 1934), 11:4; (Feb 4, 1934), sec. 2, p. 3:1; sec. 9, p. 6:1; (Feb 10, 1934, 13:3; *NYHT* (Feb 11, 1934); *NYT* (Feb 11, 1934), 1:1; sec. 2, p. 3:1, 3; *NW* 3 (Feb 10, 1934), 36; *MA* 54 (Feb 1934), 3, 12; *Mus Rec* 1 (1934), 3, 12; *NW* 3 (Feb 17, 1934), 37; *NYT* (Feb 18, 1934), sec. 9, p. 6:8; sec. 9, p. 8:1, 3; *NYT* (Feb 20, 1934), 26:5; (Feb 25, 1934), sec. 9, p. 7:5; (Feb 26, 1934), 21:4; *Nation* 138 (Feb 28, 1934), 256; *New Republic* 78 (Feb 28, 1934), 75; *NYT* (Mar 1, 1934), 22:3; *Commonweal* 19 (Mar 2, 1934), 498; *Lit Dgt* 117 (Mar 3, 1934), 22; *NYT* (Mar 9, 1934), 22:3; (Mar 18, 1934), sec. 9, p. 7:5; (Mar 24, 1934), 9:4; (Apr 1, 1934), sec. 2, p. 6:5; (Mar 13, 1934), 24:3; *American Mag of Art* 27 (Apr 1934), 212; *NYT* (May 4, 1934), 25:1; *MQ* 22 (1936), 143, 147; *MQ* 28 (1942), 74; 31 (1945), 109; *ClSPN* (Oct 21, 1948), 79; *NYT* (May 17, 1955), 33:2; (May 18, 1955), 36:7; *MC* 151 (Jun 1955), 60; *Pan Pipes* 48 (Jan 1956), 5; *NYT* (May 6, 1962), 95:4; *Opera N* 28, No. 3 (Nov 16, 1963), 9; *Variety* 237 (Dec 16, 1964), 66; *Opera N* 29 (Jan 23, 1965), 31; 39 (Oct 1974), 50; *Hi-Fi/MA*   24 (Dec 1974), MA25;   26 (Oct 1976), MA22-23; *BroOH*, 480; *ChaAM*, 635; *EweCB*, 164; *GroSH*, 504; *HitMU*, 178; *HowOA*, 431; *HowOC*, 77; *HowSH*, 276; *KolMO*, 377; *SelMO*, 575.

12. Merry Mount Suite: *ClSPN* (Oct 21, 1948), 79.

20. Mosaics: *NYT* (Feb 12, 1958), 33:1; *MA* 78 (Mar 1958), 33; *MC* 157 (May 1958), 24; *MT* 99 (Oct 1958), 559; *Pan Pipes* 53, No. 4 (1961), 6; *CinSPN* (Oct 28, 1966), 99-106. The Mystic Trumpeter: *ASCAP* 4, No. 2 (1970), 31; *Pan Pipes* 63, No. 2 (1971), 34-35.

69. New Land, New Covenant: *ASCAP* 8, No. 1 (1976), 34-39; *HiFi/MA* 26 (Aug 1976), MA28; *Choral J* 16, No. 8 (1976), 36.

9. Pan and the Priest: *NYPPN* (Oct 14, 1926); *MC* 143 (Jun 1951), 16-17.

42. Pastorale: *POPN* (Oct 20, 1950), 60-61; *MC* 142 (Nov 1, 1950), 9; *ClSPN* (Oct 18, 1951), 62; *MC* 147 (Apr 15, 1953), 34; *Notes* 11 (Dec 1953), 157.

41. Serenade: *BSPN* (Oct 25, 1946); *MQ* 35 (1948), 287; *NYPPN* (Mar 26, 1949); *CinSPN* (Nov 16, 1962), 202-208; *ChiSPN* (Jan 14, 1967), 32.

67. Song of Human Rights: *NYT* (Dec 11, 1963), 41:2; *Notes* 21 (1963-1964), 619; *Mus Leader* 96 (Jan 1964), 5; *Choral G* 17 (Mar 1964), 6; *MA* 84 (Jun 1964), 66; *Showcase* 43, No. 3 (1964), 12.

65. Song of Democracy: *NYT* (Apr 10, 1957), 37:2; *Violins* 18 (Jul-Aug 1957), 164; *MQ* 44 (1958), 405.

40. String Quartet: *MQ* 22 (1936), 142.

70. Streams in the Desert: *Variety* 255 (May 21, 1969), 57.

25. Summer Seascape No. 2: *Mus Leader* 98 (May 1966), 14; *Mus J* 24 (Jun 1966), 54.

6. Symphony No. 1: *BSPN* (Apr 5, 1929); *NYT* (Nov 30, 1930), 28:7; *MQ* 22 (1936), 142, 144; *MC* 139 (Apr 15, 1949), 23.

11. Symphony No. 2: *BSPN* (Nov 28, 1930); *MQ* 22 (1936), 144, 148; *NYPPN* (Jan 17, 1946); *MQ* 33 (1947), 185; *MC* 139 (Apr 15, 1949), 23; *Detroit SPN* (Nov 23, 1969), 219-221; *ChaAM*, 550; *EweCB*, 163; *HanTC*, 330; *HitMU*, 178; *MacCM*, 546.

13. Symphony No. 3: *NYT* (Sep 19, 1937), sec. 11, p. 7:3; (Mar 27, 1938), sec. 2, p. 2:5; *BSPN* (Nov 3, 1939); *MA* 59 (Dec 10, 1939), 37; *MQ* 33 (1947), 186; *EweCB*, 165;

HowOC, 76; *SalMO*, 324.
14. Symphony No. 4: *BSPN* (Dec 3, 1943); *MQ* 63 (1943), 21; *NYT* (Oct 28, 1943), 28:3; (Jan 3, 1944), 16:3; *Etude* 62 (Jun 1944), 313; *ChiSPN* (Nov 24, 1950), 178-182; *Roch Phil* (Oct 21, 1971), 20; *EweCB*, 165; *MelMN*, 33.
18. Symphony No. 5: *POPN* (Feb 18, 1955); *MA* 75 (Mar 1955), 31; *MC* 151 (Apr 1955), 15; *MC* 151 (Jun 1955), 60; *Natl SPN* (Nov 30, 1965), 15.
24. Symphony No. 6: *NYPPN* (Feb 29, 1968), D-F; *NYT* (Mar 1, 1968), 31:1; *Int Mus* 66 (Apr 1968), 32; *Mus J* 26 (May 1968), 58; *MT* 109 (Jun 1968), 562; *Mus & Artists* 1, No. 2 (1968), 47; *Roch Phil* (Dec 19, 1968), 92; *HiFi/MA* 19 (Aug 1969), MA22.
27. Symphony No. 7 (Sea Symphony): *NMC* 37, No. 1 (1977), 33; *Mus Ed J* 64 (Nov 1977), 75.

Dissertations about Howard Hanson and His Works

1. Carnine, Albert Junior. *The Choral Music of Howard Hanson*. University of Texas, 1977.
2. Hanson, John R. *Macroform in Selected Twentieth-Century Piano Concertos*. Eastman School of Music, University of Rochester, 1969.
3. Mize, Lou Stem. *A Study of Selected Choral Settings of Walt Whitman's Poems*. Florida State University, 1967.
4. Monroe, Robert C. *Howard Hanson: American Music Educator*. Florida State University, 1970.
5. Prindl, Frank J. *A Study of Ten Original Compositions for Band Published in America Since 1946*. Florida State University, 1956.

OUTLINE VII

ROY (LEROY ELLSWORTH) HARRIS (1898-1979)

I. **Life**

1898 Born on Lincoln's birthday, February 12, in a log cabin in Lincoln County, Oklahoma. Parents of Scotch-Irish descent.

1903 Family moved to southern California; worked on his parents' farm; during the years he had a few piano, clarinet and organ lessons. Attended the Covina public schools. For many years he was largely a self-taught musician with many other interests.

1917 Enlisted in the heavy artillery in World War I (1917-1918).

1920 Worked as a truck driver for a dairy company (1920-1924). Attended the University of Southern California at Los Angeles. Studied economics, philosophy and music. Later studied privately with Arthur Farwell (theory) and Modest Altschuler (orchestration). Began to compose. Taught harmony at the Hollywood Conservatory; music critic for the *Los Angeles Illustrated Daily News*.

1926 First orchestral work, *Andante*, conducted by Willem van Hoogstraaten at the Hollywood Bowl. Studied with Nadia Boulanger in Paris (1926-1928). Awarded two Guggenheim Fellowships (1927-1928).

1929 Returned to the United States following a serious back injury.

1930 Awarded a creative fellowship from the Pasadena Music and Arts Association (1930-1931).

1934 First Symphony performed in Boston. Taught theory and composition at the Westminster Choir School, Princeton, New Jersey (1934-1938).

1936 Married the pianist Beula Duffy (his second wife), whom Harris "rechristened" Johana, after Johann Sebastian Bach.

1937 *Symphony No. 3.* Harris became known as a leading composer of music with "American" characteristics.

1941 Composer-in-residence at Cornell University, Ithaca, New York (1941-1943).

1942 Received the Elizabeth Sprague Coolidge Medal "for eminent services to chamber music."

1943 Honorary Doctor of Music degrees from Rutgers University and the University of Rochester. Composer-in-residence at Colorado College, Colorado Springs (1943-1948).

1948 Composer-in-residence at the State Agricultural College, Logan, Utah (1948-1949).

1949 Composer-in-residence at George Peabody College, Nashville, Tennessee (1949-1951).

1951 Composer-in-residence at the Pennsylvania College for Women (1951-1956). Organized the Pittsburgh Festivals of Contemporary Music (1952).

1956 Composer-in-residence at the University of Southern Illinois (1956-1957).

1957 Composer-in-residence at the Indiana University School of Music, Bloomington (1957-1960).

1958 Sent to U. S. S. R. by the State Department as a cultural ambassador of the United States.

1961 Composer-in-residence at the University of California at Los Angeles (1961-1973). From 1969 was guest lecturer in the Department of Music, California State University, Los Angeles.

1973 Composer-in-residence at California State University, Los Angeles.

1979 Died, October 1, in Santa Monica, California.

Roy Harris has been the recipient of many honors, awards and commissions in addition to those listed above.

Note: Biographies of varying lengths and importance will be found in many of the books listed in the Bibliography at the end of this *Outline* under "References to Roy Harris."

II. Compositions (selected)

A. Orchestra

		Date	Publisher
1.	Andante for Strings	1926	GS
2.	Chorale for Strings	1932	Shaw
3.	Symphony No. 1 (Symphony 1933)	1933	GS
4.	Symphony No. 2	1934	GS
5.	When Johnny Comes Marching Home Again (American Overture)	1935	GS
6.	Farewell to Pioneers (Symphonic Elegy)	1935	GS
7.	Prelude and Fugue for Strings	1936	GS
8.	Time Suite	1936	GS
9.	Three Symphonic Essays	1937	GS
10.	Symphony No. 3	1938	GS
11.	Symphony No. 4 (Folk Song Symphony) (SATB, orch)	1940	GS
12.	American Creed	1940	Bel-Mills

　　a.   Free to Dream - Prelude 　　　　b.   Free to Build - Fugue

		Date	Publisher
13.	Ode to Truth	1941	Bel-Mills
14.	Evening Piece (cham orch)	1941	Bel-Mills
15.	Acceleration	1941	Bel-Mills
16.	Children's Hour	1942	Bel-Mills
17.	Symphony No. 5, Op. 55	1942	Bel-Mills
18.	Folk Rhythms of Today (also band)	1942	Bel-Mills
19.	Fanfare	1942	Bel-Mills
20.	March in Time of War (Concert March)	1943	Bel-Mills
21.	Chorale for Orchestra	1943	Bel-Mills
22.	Symphony No. 6, Op. 60 (Gettysburg Address Symphony) (second movement arr. for band)	1944	Bel-Mills
23.	Ode to Friendship	1944	Bel-Mills
24.	Memories of a Child's Sunday	1945	CF
25.	Children at Play	1945	CF
26.	Melody	1946	CF
27.	Celebration: Variations on a Timpani Theme from Howard Hanson's Third Symphony	1946	CF
28.	Radio Piece (pno obbl)	1946	CF
29.	Theme and Variations for Accordion and Orchestra	1946	CF
30.	Mood	1947	Bel-Mills
31.	Mirage (cham orch)	1947	Bel-Mills
32.	Work	1947	Bel-Mills
33.	The Quest, a Concert March Passacaglia	1947	CF
34.	Elegy and Paean (vla, orch)	1948	AMP
35.	Kentucky Spring (Overture)	1949	CF
36.	Symphony No. 7	1951	AMP
37.	Symphonic Epigram	1954	AMP
38.	Ode to Consonance	1956	AMP
39.	Elegy and Dance (Elegy for Orchestra)	1958	AMP
40.	Reverie and Dance	1958	AMP
41.	Symphony No. 8 (St. Francis)	1962	AMP

42.	Symphony No. 9	1962	AMP
43.	These Times (orch, pno)	1962	AMP
44.	Epilogue to Profiles in Courage: J. F. K.	1962	AMP
45.	Horn of Plenty	1964	AMP
46.	Symphony No. 10 (Abraham Lincoln Symphony) (SATB, 2 amplified pno, orch)	1965	AMP
47.	Symphony No. 11	1967	AMP
48.	Symphony No. 12 (Pere Marquette)	1969	AMP
49.	Symphony No. 13	1969	
50.	Symphony No. 14	1974	
51.	Symphony No. 15	1978	

B.   Concerto (with orchestra unless otherwise indicated)

52.	Concerto for Piano, Clarinet, String Quartet (also listed under Chamber Music)	1927	AMP
53.	Concerto for String Sextet	1932	Shaw
54.	Concerto for Piano and Band	1942	Bel-Mills
55.	Concerto for Piano and Strings	1945	GS
56.	Concerto for Accordion	1945	CF
57.	Concerto for Two Pianos	1946	CF
58.	Concerto for Violin	1950	CF
59.	Concerto No. 2 for Piano	1953	Bel-Mills
60.	Fantasy for Piano and Orchestra	1954	AMP
61.	Concerto for Amplified Piano, Wind Instruments and Percussion	1967	AMP

C.   Band

62.	Cimarron (Overture)	1941	Bel-Mills
63.	Folk Rhythms of Today (also orch)	1942	Bel-Mills
64.	Fantasy for Piano and Band (also orch)	1942	Bel-Mills
65.	Conflict	1944	Bel-Mills
66.	Prairie Sunset	1944	AMP
67.	Fruit of Gold	1949	Bel-Mills
68.	Dark Devotion	1950	Bel-Mills
69.	Symphony for Band	1952	

D.   Chamber

70.	Concerto for Piano, Clarinet, String Quartet	1927	AMP
71.	String Quartet No. 1	1930	Bel-Mills
72.	String Quartet No. 2 (Three Variations on the Theme ESC)	1930	GS
73.	Fantasy (Sextet for Flute, Oboe, Clarinet, Bassoon, Horn, Piano)	1932	
74.	String Sextet (Concerto for String Sextet)	1932	Shaw
75.	Quintet (pno, fl, ob, hn, bsn)	1932	
76.	Trio for Violin, Cello, Piano (Piano Trio)	1934	AMP
77.	Four Minutes and Twenty Seconds (fl, str qrt)	1934	Bel-Mills
78.	Poem for Violin and Piano	1935	Bel-Mills
79.	Piano Quintet (pno, str qrt)	1936	GS
80.	String Quartet No. 3 (Four Preludes and Fugues)	1937	Bel-Mills
81.	Soliloquy and Dance (vla, pno)	1939	GS
82.	String Quintet (2 vln, 2 vla, cel)	1940	Bel-Mills
83.	Sonata for Violin and Piano	1941	Bel-Mills

a.   Fantasy   b.   Dance of Spring   c.   Melody

84.	Four Charming Little Pieces for Violin and Piano	1944	Bel-Mills

a.   Mood   c.   Summer Fields
b.   Afternoon Slumber Song   d.   There's a Charm About You

85.	Duo for Violoncello and Piano	1964	AMP
86.	Suite on American Folk Songs (hp, wdwd, perc)	1974	AMP

E.   Piano

87. Sonata for Piano, Op. 1	1928	AMP

    a.   Bells   c.   Children at Play
    b.   Sad News   d.   Slumber

88. Variations on an Irish Theme	1938	Bel-Mills
89. Little Suite	1939	GS
90. Children at Play	1942	Bel-Mills
91. American Ballads	1942	CF

    a.   Streets of Loredo   d.   Black is the Color of My
    b.   Wayfaring Stranger   True Love's Hair
    c.   The Bird   e.   Cod Liver Ile

92. Piano Suite	1944	Bel-Mills
93. Toccata	1950	CF
94. Five Etudes for Two Pianos	1973	AMP

F.   Organ

95. Chorale for Organ and Brass (hn, 3 trpt, 3 trb)	1943	Bel-Mills
96. Toccata for Organ and Brass (2 hn, 3 trpt, 3 trb)	1944	Bel-Mills
97. Etude for Pedals	1964	AMP
98. Fantasy for Organ, Brass and Timpani	1964	AMP

G.   Choral (a cappella unless otherwise indicated)

99. A Song for Occupations (Walt Whitman) (SSAATTBB)	1934	GS
100. The Story of Noah (John Jacob Niles) (SSAATTBB)	1934	GS
101. Sanctus (SATB)	1934	GS
102. When Johnny Comes Marching Home (SATB)	1935	GS
103. Symphony for Voices (Walt Whitman) (SSAATTBB)	1935	GS
104. Railroad Man's Ballad (TTBB, orch)	1938	Bel-Mills
105. He's Gone Away (S., B., SATB)	1939	GS
106. Folk Song Symphony (Symphony No. 4) (SATB, orch)	1939	GS
107. Rock of Ages (SATB, orch)	1939	Bel-Mills
108. Challenge (Bar., SATB, orch)	1940	GS
109. A Red Bird in a Green Tree (SATB)	1940	Bel-Mills
110. American Creed (Walt Whitman) (with orch)	1940	Bel-Mills
111. Walt Whitman Triptych (SSSA, pno)	1940	GS
112. Freedom's Land (SATB, orch)	1941	Bel-Mills
113. Songs of Democracy (SATB)	1941	Bel-Mills
114. Freedom, Toleration (SATB)	1941	Bel-Mills
115. To Thee, Old Cause (SATB)	1941	Bel-Mills
116. Year That Trembled (SATB)	1941	Bel-Mills
117. Black is the Color of My True Love's Hair (SATB)	1942	Bel-Mills
118. Sons of Uncle Sam (SATB, orch)	1942	Bel-Mills
119. Work Song (TTBB)	1942	Bel-Mills
120. Li'l Boy Named David (SATB)	1942	Bel-Mills
121. Bird's Courting Song (Roy Harris) (SATB)	1942	Bel-Mills
122. Easter Motet (SATB, brasses, org)	1944	Golden
123. Walt Whitman Suite (SATB, str, 2 pno)	1944	Bel-Mills
124. Alleluia (SATB, brass, org)	1945	Bel-Mills
125. Blow the Man Down (A., B., SATB, orch or pno or band or strs)	1946	CF
126. Mi Chomocho (Who is Mighty), an Israel motet (Bar., SATB, org)	1946	GS
127. Sammy's Fighting Sons (SATB, band)	1946	Bel-Mills
128. They Say That Susan Has No Heart For Learning (SSA, pno)	1947	AMP
129. Mass in C (TTBB, org)	1948	CF
130. Madrigal (S., SSA, pno)	1949	AMP

131. If I Had a Ribbon Bow (SATB)	1949	CF
132. Cindy (SATB)	1949	CF
133. Red Cross Hymn (SATB, band)	1951	AMP
134. Folk Fantasy for Festivals (S., T., Bar., Sp., SSAATTBB, pno)	1955	AMP
135. Fun and Nonsense Parody (SSATBB, pno)		AMP
136. Psalm 150 (SATB)	1957	Golden
137. My Praise Shall Never End (SSAATTBB, pno)		AMP
138. The Weeping Willow (S., SSAA)		AMP
139. Jubilation (SATB, brass, pno)	1964	
140. The Working Man's Pride (B., Sp., TTBB)		AMP
141. Peace and Good Will to All (Cantata: SATB, perc, org)	1970	AMP
142. Whether This Nation (SATB, sym band)	1971	AMP

H.   Solo Vocal (with piano unless otherwise indicated)

143. Waitin'	1939	Bel-Mills
144. Lullaby	1940	Bel-Mills
145. Evening Song (from "The Princess" by Alfred Lord Tennyson)	1941	Bel-Mills
146. Freedom's Land	1941	Bel-Mills
147. Take the Sun and Keep the Stars (Unison chorus)	1942	Bel-Mills
148. Sons of Uncle Sam	1942	Bel-Mills
149. Fog (Carl Sandburg)	1946	CF
150. Abraham Lincoln Walks at Midnight, "A Cantata of Lamentation" (Vachel Lindsay) (m-S., vln, vlc, pno)	1953	AMP
151. Give Me the Splendid Silent Sun (Walt Whitman) (Cantata: Bar., orch)	1955	AMP
152. Canticle of the Sun (Cantata: S., cham orch)	1961	AMP
153. Three Songs for Soprano (Kahlil Gibran) (S., wdwd, perc)	1972	AMP

I.   Film

154. One-Tenth of a Nation	1940	Bel-Mills

J.   Ballet

155. Western Landscape	1940	Bel-Mills
156. From This Earth	1941	Bel-Mills
157. What So Proudly We Hail	1942	Bel-Mills
158. Ballet on the Subject of War	1944	Bel-Mills

Note: The following abbreviations are used in Section III of this *Outline*. The number indicates the number of the composition as listed in Section II.

52. *Concerto*: Concerto for Piano, Clarinet, String Quartet
11. *Folk S*: Folk Song Symphony
83. *Melody*: Third movement of Sonata for Violin and Piano
79. *Pno Qnt*: Piano Quintet
87. *Son Pno*: Sonata for Piano, Op. 1

7. *P & F*: Prelude and Fugue for Strings
81. *Soliloquy*: Soliloquy and Dance
80. *Str Qrt 3*: String Quartet No. 3
89. *Suite*: Little Suite
10. *Sym 3*: Symphony No. 3
103. *Sym V*: Symphony for Voices
76. *Trio*: Trio for Violin, Cello, Piano

III.   Style

"Musical literature never has been and never will be valuable to society as a whole until it is created as an authentic and characteristic culture of and from the people it expresses." "We are possessed of a fierce driving power—optimistic, young, rough and ready,"   Roy Harris

A.   General characteristics
1.   "Romanticized neoclassicism." Stylistically consistent and rooted in the indigenous

folk culture of America. Believes in melody, the use of polyphonic forms and devices, and seeks to avoid the obvious. Music tonal, with frequent use of modes. Prefers large-scale works; modest use of instruments; uncluttered textures. Use of germ motifs, motif expansion.

B. Melodic line
1. Striking melodic gifts. Melodies generally long and asymmetrical, or motivistic; literal repetition and sequence avoided; secular folk idiom characteristic. Melodies often follow chord outline with skips of thirds, fourths (frequent) and fifths; rarely scalewise.
2. Long melody without repetition: *Sym 3* (beginning).
3. Based on motives: *Son Pno* (beginning).
4. Major or minor triad outlined: *Sym V* (movement I, beginning; movement III, beginning).
5. Chromatic changes infrequent: *Sym V* (movement II, meas. 7, 8, 13); *Sym 3* (p. 28, meas 243; p. 56, meas. 409); *Sym 7.*
6. Modal: *Sym 7* (third movement, meas. 39); *Str Qrt 3* (p. 10); *American Ballads* (p. 6).
7. Folk tunes: *Folk S* (The Girl I Left Behind Me, Western Cowboy, Mountaineer Love Song, Jump Up My Lady, Negro Fantasy, When Johnny Comes Marching Home); *Reverie and Dance.*
8. Twelve tones used in melodic material, but not in a row: *Sym 7.*

C. Harmony
1. Usually linear, basically simple with superimposed triads, and rarely fourths or fifths. Polytonality results from use of two or more tonal centers (often modal) simultaneously. Atonality and twelve-tone writing avoided. Some use of the seventh chords, but never augmented and rarely diminished. Definite cadences avoided; some use of plagal cadences (see Evett, *MM* 23, No. 2 [1946], 103).
2. Organum style: *Sym 3* (sec. I, V); *Son Pno 1.*
3. Triads in series, or with seventh chords: *Suite* (*Slumber*).
4. Polytonality (polychords): *Sym 3* (sec. III, p. 25, wdwd, str); *Sym 3* (sec IV, meas. 59, violins in Phrygian, lower strings in Lydian); *Soliloquy* (p. 7).
5. Chords built on fourths and fifths: *Concerto* (pp. 24-25).
6. Unison writing: *Piano Suite* (p. 4).
7. Parallel minor 6/3 chords: *Melody* (p. 4).
8. Parallel writing altered: *Sym 7* (p. 89).
9. Chromatic harmony, diatonic melody: *Suite* (p. 5).
10. Seventh and ninth chords: *Soliloquy* (p. 9).
11. With imitation: *Sym 3* (pp. 85-91).

D. Counterpoint
1. Frequent use of polyphonic devices, especially canon and fugue; generally based on harmonic sequences (harmonic counterpoint). Parallel fourths and fifths (organum style) used contrapuntally.
2. Voices divided into groups with consonant counterpoint, but with dissonance resulting from the combination of the group: *Sym 3* (p. 70).
3. Fugal and canonic development: *Sym 3* (sec. IV, p. 57).
4. Canon: *Sym 3* (sec. V, str and wdwd); *P & F* (*Prelude*, beginning).
5. Fugal style: *P & F* (double fugue with separate expositions); *Pno Qrt* (third movement, extended fugue subject; triple fugue); *Trio* (last movement); *Soliloquy* (*Dance*, double fugue); *Sym V* (Pt. III, triple fugue); *American Creed* (Pt. II, double fugue).

E. Rhythm
"Our rhythmic sense is less symmetrical than the European rhythmic sense. European musicians are trained to think of rhythm in its largest common denominator, while we are born for a feeling for its smallest units." Roy Harris
1. Rhythms vary from simple to complex. Cross-rhythms, frequent change of time

signatures, superimposed meters, mixed meters, irregular division of the beat, are characteristic ("American rhythms"). Regular rhythmic pulse usually avoided; occasional use of powerful driving rhythms.

    2.   Asymmetrical rhythmic figures: *Concerto*; *Pno Qnt* (pp. 5-6).

    3.   Changing time signatures: *Son Pno* (*Andante*).

    4.   Change of accent without change of meter: *Sym 3* (pp. 78-79).

    5.   Two-note rhythm: *Soliloquy* (p. 22).

    6.   Rhythmic figure altered in length to avoid a regular pulse: *Piano Suite* (*Recreation*).

F.   Form

    1.   Traditional sonata-allegro form avoided. Programmatic pieces rare. Polyphonic forms of early Baroque are freely interpreted. Balance between expressive content and formal means. Unity often achieved by transferring themes from one movement to another.

    2.   Growth from a germinal motif: *Sym 3*.

    3.   One movement symphony: *Sym 3* (five sections, unique form); *Sym 7*.

    4.   Passacaglia: *Pno Qnt* (first movement; theme stated by all instruments); *Sym 7*.

    5.   Prelude and Fugue: *Str Qrt 3*; *P & F*.

    6.   Free double fugue: *Concerto* (2 pno, last movement).

    7.   Free variation: *Son Pno*; *Concerto* (2 pno, second movement).

    8.   Programmatic: *Sym 6*.

G.   Orchestration

    1.   Restrained and functional; instrumental groups used in unison and integrated harmonically and contrapuntally. "Color" instruments (harp, celesta) avoided in symphonic scores. Some use of special effects (*Sym 8*, amplified piano).

BIBLIOGRAPHY

Articles by Roy Harris

1.   "Does Music Have to be European? " *Scribner's Mag* 91 (Apr 1932), 204-209.

2.   "Problems of American Composers," *CowAC*, 149.

3.   "Will We Produce a Second Rhythmic Ars Nova? " *MA* 54 (Apr 1934), 14.

4.   "The Growth of a Composer," *MQ* 20 (1934), 188.

5.   "American Music Enters a New Phase," *Scribner's Mag* 96 (Oct 1934), 218-221.

6.   "The Art of Fugue," *MQ* 21 (1935), 166.

7.   "Modern Melody: Its Resources," *MTNA Pro* 32 (1937), 41.

8.   "Aspects of the Modern Art-Song," *MQ* 24 (1938), 24.

9.   "Let's Make Music," *Composers Forum Laboratory*, New York: 1939.

10.   "Perspective at Forty," *Magazine of Art* 32 (Nov 1939), 638, 667.

11.   "Folksong—American Big Business," *MM* 18, No. 1 (1940-1941), 8 (reprinted in *SchCC*, 161).

12.   "Essays by Anderson, Carpenter, Harris, in *The Basis of Artistic Creation*. New Brunswick: Rutgers University Press, 1942.

13.   "The Creative Musician and the New Era," *MTNA Pro* 38 (1944), 38.

14.   "What Should the Academy Accord the Accordion? " *Music News* 41 (Oct 1949), 10.

15.   "Composing—An Art and a Living," *Mus J* 11 (Jan 1953), 31.

16.   "For Young Composers Only," *Mus J* 14 (Jan 1956), 13.

17.   "Music Education in the U. S. S. R.," *Int Mus* 57 (Nov 1958), 11, 37.

18.   "The Life of Professional Musicians in the U. S. S. R.," *Int Mus* 57 (Dec 1958), 11, 42.

19.   "Current Attitudes in the Musical Life of the U. S. S. R.," *Int Mus* 57 (Jan 1959), 10.

20.   "Contrasting Attitudes Toward Musical Life in the U. S. and the U. S. S. R.," *Int Mus* 57 (Mar 1959), 11, 48.

21. "How Can Our Gifted Youth of Music Serve the Total Culture? " *Int Mus* 57 (Apr 1959), 9, 38.
22. "International String Congress," *Int Mus* 58 (Sep 1959), 10.
23. "Comments," *Showcase* 40 No. 4 (1961), 14.
24. "Roy Harris Salutes Serge Prokofieff," *MA* 81 (May 1961), 12-14.
25. "The Basis of Artistic Creation in Music," in *The Bases of Artistic Creation*. New York: Octagon Books, 1942, 1969.

References to Roy Harris

Books
(See the General Bibliography)

AbrHY; ASC-SC; AusMT; Baker; BakSL; BauTC; BIM; BloYA; BluPC; BMI-C; BMI-MW; BMI-OP; BMI-P; BMI-SC; Bull; CatPC; ChaAC; ChaAM; ClaEA; CobCS; CohCT; ColHM; CopCM; Cop-MI; CopON; CopTN; CowAC; CurB (1940); DalTT; DemMT; DerETM; DowO; Edm-I; EdMUS; EweAC; EweCB; EweCS; EweDE; EweMC; EweNB; EweTC; EweYA; GosMM; Grove; HanIT; HitMU; HodSD; HowMM; HowOA; HowOC; HowSH; JabCAC; JohSH; KinAI; LeiMW; LeiSK; MacAC; MacIC; MelMN; MelMS; MelRT; MorrCA; MueAS; MyeTC; NorLC; PavMH; PersTH; PeyNM; PorM3S; ReiCA; ReiCC; RobCM; RosAH; RosDM; RowFC; SalMO; SalzTM; SamMO; SanWM; SchCC; SesRM; SloMS; SpaMH; SteiAS; StevePC; ThoAJ; ThoAM; ThoMR; ThoMS; ThompGM; ThompIC; ThoRL; WhiWW; WilTM; WWM; YatTC; YouCD; YouCT.

Articles

Brief mention: *MQ* 26 (1940), 102, 103, 106; *MM* 20, No. 2 (1942-1943), 100; *MQ* 31 (1945), 25; *Musician* 50 (Nov 1945), 234; *MQ* 33 (1947), 321; 34 (1948), 10; *SR* 32 (Aug 6, 1949), 162; *Etude* 69 (Jan 1951), 13; *Time* 60 (Dec 8, 1952), 76; *MQ* 41 (1955), 77; 42 (1956), 47; *PNM* 2, No. 1 (1963), 152, 160; 2, No. 2 (1964), 181; 3, No. 1 (1964), 107; 4, No. 1 (1965), 158, 179; 4, No. 2 (1966), 126.

1. "New York Première of Harris' Andante," *Mus Dgt* 10 (Jul 20, 1926), 2.
2. Weil, Irving. "The American Scene Changes," *MM* 6, No. 4 (1928-1929), 31.
3. Rosenfeld, Paul. "New American Music," *Scribner's Mag* 89 (Jun 1931), 624-632.
4. *NYT* (Oct 1, 1931), 23:2.
5. Mendel, Arthur. "A Change in Structure," *Nation* 134 (Jan 6, 1932), 26.
6. Farwell, Arthur. "Roy Harris," *MQ* 18 (1932), 18.
7. Cowell, Henry. "Roy Harris, an American Composer," *Sackbut* 12 (Apr 1932), 133.
8. Goldberg, Isaac. "Roy Harris," *Mus Rec* 1 (1933), 253.
9. Slonimsky, Nicolas. "The Gaiety and Sadness of Harris," *MM* 10, No. 3 (1933), 162.
10. Piston, Walter. "Roy Harris," *MM* 11, No. 2 (1933-1934), 73.
11. "Forecasts and Review," *MM* 11, No. 3 (1933-1934), 142.
12. Rosenfeld, Paul. "Harris before the World," *New Republic* 77 (Feb 7, 1934), 364-365.
13. *NYT* (Mar 12, 1934), 21:8; (Mar 26, 1934), 18:3.
14. "Roy Harris, Contrapuntist," *Lit Dgt* 117 (May 19, 1934), 24.
15. Rosenfeld, Paul. "Tragic and American," *New Republic* 81 (Nov 21, 1934), 47.
16. Burke, Kenneth. "Most Useful Composition: Song for Occupations," *Nation* 139 (Dec 19, 1934), 719-720.
17. Copland, Aaron. "America's Composer Gets a Break," *Amer Merc* 34 (Apr 1935), 490.
18. "Composers Get a Chance to Exhibit in One-Man Show," *NW* 6 (Nov 2, 1935), 41.
19. *NYT* (Nov 10, 1935), sec. 9, p. 6:1.
20. Copland, Aaron. "Our Younger Generation," *MM* 13, No. 4 (1935-1936), 4.
21. "Boston Symphony Program," *MA* 56, No. 5 (1936).
22. "Jansson Conducts in Philly," *MA* 56, No. 6 (1936), 49.

23. *NYT* (Aug 29, 1937), sec. 10, p. 5:5; (Sep 5, 1937), 6:8; (Sep 19, 1937), sec. 11, p. 8:3;
      (Oct 7, 1937), 30:1; (Oct 30, 1937), 22:4.
24. "Venice Holds Biennial Music Festival," *MA* 57 (Oct 1937), 8.
25. Rosenfeld, Paul. "The Newest American Composers," *MM* 15, No. 3 (1937-1938), 153.
26. *NYT* (Jan 30, 1938), sec. 10, p. 7:1; (May 5, 1938), 26:2; (Nov 27, 1938), sec. 9, p. 6:3.
27. Scherchen, Hermann. "Are There American Composers? " *MA* 58, No. 16 (Oct 25, 1938),
      8.
28. Carter, Elliott. "Season of Hindemith and Americans," *MM* 16, No. 4 (1938-1939), 250.
29. *NYT* (Jan 1, 1939), sec. 9, p. 7:1; (May 8, 1939), 20:4.
30. Rosenfeld, Paul. "Current Chronicle (Copland, Harris)," *MQ* 25 (1939), 376.
31. Mendel, Arthur. "Roy Harris Quintet," *MM* 17, No. 1 (1939-1940), 25.
32. Carter, Elliott. "American Music in the New York Scene," *MM* 17, No. 2 (1939-1940), 94.
33. "New Works at the Coolidge Festival," *MM* 17, No. 4 (1939-1940), 252.
34. Cohn, Arthur. "Americans at Rochester," *MM* 17, No. 4 (1939-1940), 257.
35. "Orchestras," *MA* 59 (Dec 1939), 12.
36. *NYT* (Dec 31, 1939), sec. 9, p. 8:5; (Jan 14, 1940), sec. 9, p. 8:5.
37. Mendel, Arthur. *Vic Rec Rev* (Apr 1940).
38. "Home-Grown Composer," *Time* 35 (Apr 8, 1940), 45.
39. "Biography," *Current Biography* (Aug 1940); *Current Biography Yearbook* (1940), 367.
40. "Gets National Commission for Music Appreciation Award (Folk Song Symphony)," *NYT*
      (May 4, 1940), 13:5.
41. "Milhaud, Carpenter, Harris in Chicago," *MM* 18, No. 1 (1940-1941).
42. "Appointed Cornell University Composer-in-Residence," *NYT* (May 4, 1941), sec. 2, p. 5:2.
43. Copland, Aaron. "From the '20's to the '40's and Beyond," *MM* 20, No. 2 (1942-1943),
      80.
44. "Re: Harris, from London," *Musician* 47 (August 1942), 122.
45. "Harris and Kroll Get Coolidge Award," *MA* 62, No. 15 (Nov 10, 1942), 25.
46. "League of Composers Mark Anniversary," *MA* 63, No. 1 (Jan 10, 1943), 23.
47. "Folk Rhythms of Today," *NYT* (Feb 7, 1943), sec. 2, p. 6:4.
48. Slonimsky, Nicolas. "Roy Harris, America's Composer No. 1," *Chr Sc Mon* (Feb 27,
      1943).
49. "Composer Born in a Log Cabin, Produces an American Fifth Symphony Honoring Soviet,"
      NW 21 (Mar 8, 1943), 64.
50. "Composes Song for USAAF," *NYT* (Jan 23, 1944), sec, 2, p. 5:8.
51. "Meet the Composer," *MA* 64, No. 5 (1944), 7.
52. Young, Percy M. "Roy Harris," *Mus Opin* 67 (1944), 314.
53. McGlinchee, Claire. "American Literature in American Music," *MQ* 31 (1945), 108.
54. *NYT* (Jun 23, 1945), 10:1.
55. Evett, Robert. "The Harmonic Idiom of Roy Harris," *MM* 23, No. 2 (1946), 100-107.
56. Slonimsky, Nicolas. "Roy Harris; with List of Works," *MQ* 33 (1947), 17.
57. *NYT* (Feb 15, 1948), sec. 2, p. 7:8; (Apr 18, 1948), sec. 2, p. 7:8.
58. "For Everybody Except Composers," *Time* 51 (May 24, 1948), 46.
59. "Roy Harris and Johana Harris," *Mus News* 41 (Aug 1949), 16.
60. "Festival at Sewanee, Tenn: Cumberland Forest Festival," *NW* 36 (Jul 10, 1950), 78.
61. "Roy Harris," *Pan Pipes* 43 (Dec 1950), 122.
62. "Contemporary Music," *Mus News* 43 (Feb 1951), 10-11.
63. Marx, Henry. "Cultural Colony of Europe," *Mus News* 43 (Apr 1951), 8.
64. "Mellon Grant Brings the Harrises to Pittsburgh," *Mus News* 43 (Sep 1951), 12.
65. Rosenwald, Hans. "Speaking of Music," *Mus News* 43 (Sep 1951), 8.
66. Lawrence, Valerie. "Great Southwest Composer," *SWMusician* 18 (Oct 1951), 14, 39.
67. "Roy Harris," *Pan Pipes* 44 (Jan 1952), 33.
68. "Festival Faculty Resigns at Sewanee," *MA* 72 (Jul 1952), 23.
69. "Receives Heinz Foundation Grant," *NYT* (Aug 24, 1952), sec. 2, p. 7:3.
70. Rosenwald, Hans. "Hindemith–Honegger–Harris," *Int Mus News* 1 (Nov 1952), 9-10.

71. Shaffer, Edward H. "Guilt by Dedication: International Contemporary Music Festival, Pittsburgh," *Nation* 175 (Dec 13, 1952), 548.

72. Lissfelt, J. F. "Report of the Pittsburgh International Contemporary Music Festival," *Mus Club Mag* 32 (Jan 1953), 12-13.

73. Maxwell, M. "Contemporary Festival in Pittsburgh," *Mus J* 11 (Jan 1953), 10-11.

74. RePass, R. "American Composers of Today," *London Mus* 9 (Dec 1953), 25.

75. Stoddard, H. "Music in Oklahoma," *Int Mus* 52 (May 1954), 12-13.

76. Glanville-Hicks, Peggy; "Rochester Hears American Music," *MA* 74 (Jun 1954), 3.

77. Keats, Sheila. "Reference Articles on American Composers: An Index," *Juilliard Rev* 1 (Fall 1954), 27.

78. "W. W. Naumburg Foundation Award for Symphony No. 7," *NYT* (Jan 20, 1955), 34:6.

79. Carter, Elliott. "The Rhythmic Basis of American Music," *Score* 12 (Jun 1955), 28.

80. Evett, Robert. "How Right is Right? " *Score* 12 (Jun 1955), 33.

81. "Roy Harris Hurt in Automobile Accident," *MA* 75 (Nov 1, 1955), 27.

82. Sargeant, Winthrop. "Musical Events," *New Yorker* 31 (Nov 12, 1955), 142.

83. Kyle, Marguerite K. "AmerAllegro," *Pan Pipes* 48 (Jan 1956), 53.

84. "Leaves Chatham College to Join Southern Illinois University," *NYT* (May 29, 1956), 31:1.

85. Ellsworth, Roy E. "Americans on Microgroove," *HiFi* 6, No. 8 (Aug 1956), 64.

86. Slonimsky, Nicolas. "The Story of Roy Harris—American Composer (Pt. I)," *Etude* 74 (Dec 1956), 11, 62; (Pt. II): 75 (Jan 1957), 12.

87. Kyle, Marguerite K. "AmerAllegro," *Pan Pipes* 49 (Jan 1957), 51.

88. Sabin, Robert. "Roy Harris—Still Buoyant as Composer and Teacher," *MA* 77, No. 2 (Jan 15, 1957), 17.

89. Sargeant, Winthrop. "Mr. Harris and Mr. Copland," *New Yorker* 32 (Feb 2, 1957), 72.

90. Schonberg, Howard C. "Exchange Composers; Harris, Sessions and Kay Discuss Their Forthcoming Trip to Soviet Union," *NYT* (Sep 21, 1958), sec. 2, p. 11.

91. "Visits U.S.S.R.," *NYT* (Sep 18, 1958), 37:4; (Sep 21, 1958), 62:8; (Oct 16, 1958), 46: 4; (Oct 18, 1958), 17:5; (Nov 2, 1958), 124:3.

92. "Roy Harris," *Int Mus* 57 (Jan 1959), 9.

93. Kyle, Marguerite K. "AmerAllegro," *Pan Pipes* 51 (Jan 1959), 67.

94. "The State of Music in the Soviet Union; Herman Neuman interviews Roy Harris," *Am Rec G* 25 (May 1959), 576-579.

95. "Founded Group to Interest Youth in Symphony Orchestra Careers," *NYT* (Jul 26 , 1959), sec. 2, p. 7:1.

96. Treanor, Aline J. "One Hundred Strings on the Reservation," *NYT* (Jul 26, 1959), sec. 2, p. 7.

97. *NYT* (Oct 25, 1959), 13:1.

98. "Airborne," *NYT* (Oct 2, 1960), sec. 2, p. 11.

99. Harman, Carter. "Harris as Head," *NYT* (Apr 2, 1961), sec. 2, p. 11.

100. "Director of International Music Institute of Inter-American University, San German, Puerto Rico," *NYT* (Apr 2, 1961), sec. 2, p. 11:8.

101. Eysler, G. "Otkliki iz-za rubensa," *Sovet Muz* 25 (Apr 1961), 32-36.

102. "Roy Harris Muffs Honor," *Variety* 222 (Apr 19, 1961), 59.

103. "Roy Harris Salutes Serge Prokofieff," *MA* 81 (May 1961), 13.

104. "Give Me the Splendid Silent Sun." *Intam Mus B* 23 (May 1961), 10.

105. Diether, Jack. "What the Real Roy Harris Sounds Like," *Am Rec G* 27 (July 1961), 866-867.

106. "Harris No. 8," *Time* 79 (Jan 26, 1962), 45.

107. "News Nuggets," *Int Mus* 61 (Jul 1962), 43.

108. "Roy Harris," *BMI Brochure* (1963).

109. Ardoin, John. "Orchestra," *MA* 83 (Apr 1963), 35.

110. "These Times," *NYT* (Jul 30, 1963), 19:2.

111. "Rhythms and Spaces," *Mus J* 23 (May 1965), 78; *BMI* (Jun 1965), 9.
112. Waters, J. Kevin. "Fine Arts," *America* 113 (Dec 18, 1965), 787.
113. "Views on Modern Music," *NYT* (Feb 4, 1968), sec. 3, p. 21:3.
114. "11th Symphony Premièred," *FoF* 28 (Feb 8, 1968), 597D1.
115. "Unwound Spring," *Time* 91 (Feb 16, 1968), 77.
116. Saal, Hubert. "American Rhythm," *NW* 71 (Feb 19, 1968), 102.
117. Chapin, Louis. "Roy Harris," *BMI* (Mar 1968), 19.
118. "In the Press," *BMI* (Jan 1969), 8.
119. "Composer Briefs," *Pan Pipes* 61, No. 2 (1969), 84.
120. Dexter, Dave. "Dexter's Scrapbook (Biography)," *BB* (Jun 21, 1969), 60.
121. Evett, Robert. "Music," *Atlantic* 224 (Dec 1969), 160-162.
122. "The Heroic View," *BMI* (Dec 1969), 22.
123. "Music Journal's 1972 Gallery of Living Composers," *Mus J Annual* 30 (1972), 45.
124. "17th Annual Creative Arts Award, Brandeis University," *NYT* (Apr 25, 1973), 39:1.
125. "Harris to Cal State," *Instrument* (Nov 1973), 33.
126. "Roy Harris 'Composer in Residence' at Cal State," *School Mus* 45 (Dec 1973), 9.
127. "Roy Harris Honored on 75th Birthday," *Pan Pipes* 66, No. 2 (1974), 14.
128. "Composers in Focus," *BMI* (Winter 1975), 21.
129. Smith, Rollin. "American Organ Composers," *MusicAGO* 10 (Aug 1976), 18.
130. Wright, D. "Roy Harris, at 80, Comes Home," *HiFi/MA* 28 (Jun 1978), MA32.
131. Cowell, Henry. "Roy Harris," *CowAC*, 64.

References to Works by Roy Harris

The number preceding the title indicates the number of the composition as listed in Section II.

150. Abraham Lincoln Walks at Midnight: *MC* 150 (Aug 1954), 39; *HiFi/MA* 24 (Jan 1974), MA22-23; *CohCT*, 118.
110. American Creed: *MQ* 31 (1945), 108; *Int Mus* 57 (Feb 1959), 9.
  1. Andante for Strings: *Mus Dgt* 10 (Jul 1959), 9.
125. Blow the Man Down: *Notes* 5 (1948), 264.
152. Canticle of the Sun: *Pan Pipes* 54, No. 2 (1962), 4.
  27. Celebration: *BSPN* (Oct 25, 1946); *MQ* 35 (1949), 287.
  2. Chorale for String Orchestra: *NYT* (Nov 11, 1934), sec. 9, p. 6:5.
132. Cindy: *Notes* 9 (Jun 1952), 493.
  55. Concerto No. 1 for Piano: *MA* 74 (Jan 15, 1954), 39; *MC* 149 (Jan 15, 1954), 9.
  52. Concerto for Piano, Clarinet, String Quartet: *MQ* 33 (1947), 18.
  57. Concerto for Two Pianos: *NYT* (Jun 8, 1947), 62:6; (Jan 22, 1947), 29:6.
       Cumberland Concerto: *School Mus* 23 (Oct 1951), 27; *ChiSPN* (Oct 19, 1951), 53-57; *MC* 144 (Nov 1, 1951), 5; *NYT* (Nov 12, 1951), 21:4; *MA* 71 (Dec 1, 1951), 17.
  85. Duo for Violoncello and Piano: *Mus J* 23 (Feb 1965), 106; *HiFi/MA* 15 (Mar 1965), 86J.
  44. Epilogue to Profiles in Courage: J. F. K.: *MM* 13 (Jan 1965), 38; *Am Rec G* 34 (Feb 1968), 460.
  39. Elegy for Orchestra: *Notes* 21 (1963-1964), 253.
  60. Fantasy for Piano and Orchestra: *MC* 151 (Jan 15, 1955), 32; *CohCT*, 116.
134. Festival Folk Fantasy: *NYT* (Feb 23, 1956), 33:1; *MA* 76 (Mar 1956), 37; *Notes* 17 (1959-1960), 477.
106. Folk Songs: *House & Garden* 106 (Dec 1954), 112.
  77. Four Minutes and Twenty Seconds: *MQ* 33 (1947), 26.
146. Freedom's Land: *MA* 61, No. 19 (Dec 10, 1941), 32.
  67. The Fruit of Gold: *MQ* 35 (1949), 611.
151. Give Me the Splendid Silent Sun: *MQ* 47 (1961), 533; *MC* 163 (Jun 1961), 62.

131. If I Had a Ribbon Bow: *Notes* 9 (1951-1952), 493.
 35. Kentucky Spring: *BSCBul* 12 (Jan 7, 1949), 617; 22 (Apr 14, 1950), 1188; *MQ* 41 (1955), 77.
 24. Memories of a Child's Sunday: *NYT* (Feb 22, 1946), 20:5.
 38. Ode to Consonance: *NYT* (Nov 11, 1957), 34:4; *MA* 77 (Dec 1, 1957), 30.
 23. Ode to Friendship: *NYT* (Nov 17, 1944), 6:4.
 79. Piano Quintet: *NYT* (Feb 13, 1936), 8:3; *MQ* 25 (1939), 378; *MM* 17, No. 1 (1939-1940), 25; *HitMU*, 205.
109. A Redbird in a Green Tree: *MQ* 33 (1947), 27.
 40. Reverie and Dance: *MQ* 44 (1958), 513-514.
 81. Soliloquy and Dance: *MQ* 25 (1939), 379; *MA* 62, No. 3 (Feb 1942), 236.
 87. Sonata for Piano: *MQ* 25 (1939), 378; *Juilliard Rev* 3 (Fall 1956), 12; *HitMU*, 205.
 83. Sonata for Violin and Piano: *Arts and Architecture* 61, No. 7 (Jul 1944), 15; *ACA-Bul* 4, No. 2 (1954), 17; *MQ* 40 (1954), 472; *CohCT*, 117.
 99. A Song for Occupations: *MM* 12, No. 2 (1934-1935), 90; *Nation* 139 (Dec 19, 1934), 719-720; *MQ* 31 (1945), 108.
 91. Streets of Loredo: *Clavier* 10, No. 6 (1971), 24-27.
 80. String Quartet No. 3: *MQ* 33 (1947), 27; *EweCB*, 167; *CobCS*, vol. 3, p. 156.
 74. String Sextet: *MQ* 25 (1939), 378.
      Symphonies: *NYT* (Feb 3, 1934), 9:1; (Feb 11, 1934), sec. 9, p. 8:3; *Mus Opin* 95 (Jan 1972), 180-181.
103. Symphony for Voices: *MA* 59 (Oct 1939), 36; *ChaAM*, 509; *HowOC*, 140.
  3. Symphony No. 1: *BSPN* (Jan 26, 1934); *Mus Rec* 1 (1934), 354; *CohCT*, 115; *ChaAM*, 507; *HowOA*, 436; *HowOC*, 137.
  4. Symphony No. 2: *BSPN* (Feb 28, 1936).
 10. Symphony No. 3: *BSPN* (Feb 24, 1939), 618; *MQ* 35 (1939), 378; *NYT* (Mar 12, 1939), sec. 3, p. 6:1; (Mar 19, 1939), sec. 9, p. 8:5; sec. 11, p. 6:5; *NYHT* (Mar 18, 1940); *MM* 21, No. 3 (1943-1944), 169; *BSCBul* 12 (Jan 7, 1949), 618-619; *CinSPN* (Mar 23, 1956), 599; *New Yorker* 32 (Feb 2, 1967), 90; *Gramophone* (Jun 1960), 13; *Int Mus* 59 (Mar 1961), 30; *Natl SPN* (Feb 21, 1967), 27; *Mus J* 25 (Dec 1967), 89; *Mus Opin* 92 (Nov 1968), 63; *Mus & Mus* 17 (Dec 1968), 50; *EweCB*, 168; *CohCT*, 115; *ChaAM*, 507; *DowOD*, 282; *HanIT*, 316; *HitMU*, 205-206; *HowOC*, 144; *MacIC*, 474; *MelMN*, 74.
 11. Symphony No. 4 (Folk Symphony): *NW* 15 (May 6, 1940), 44; *MM* 18, No. 2 (1940-1941), 113; *Time* 37 (Jan 6, 1941), 34; *BSPN* (Feb 21, 1941); *NYT* (Jan 31, 1943), sec. 2, p. 5:6; *MQ* 33 (1947), 25; *Am Rec G* 27 (Jul 1961), 866; *HiFi/AM* 26 (Jun 1976), 70-72; *Opera Can* 17, No. 2, (1976), 39; *MacAC*, 96; *YouCT*, 316.
 17. Symphony No. 5: *BSPN* (Feb 26, 1943); *NYT* (Feb 27, 1943), 11:2; *Time* 41 (Mar 9, 1943), 32; *NYT* (Mar 12, 1943), 12: 4; (Mar 21, 1943), sec. 2, p. 5:8; (Mar 28, 1943), sec. 2, p. 7:7; *MQ* 33 (1947), 21; *ChiSPN* (Oct 18, 1951), 23; *SFSPN* (Feb 20, 1963), 30; *EweCB*, 169; *ChaAM*, 509.
 22. Symphony No. 6: *NYT* (May 18, 1943), 18:6; (May 30, 1943), sec. 2, p. 6:8; *BSPN* (Apr 14, 1944); *MA* 64, No. 7 (1944), 18; *MT* 112 (Feb 1971), 151; *EweCB*, 169; *ChaAM*, 509; *HitMU*, 205.
 36. Symphony No. 7: *MC* 146 (Dec 1, 1952), 24-25; *Int Mus* 51 (Dec 1952), 13; *MA* 73 (Mar 1953), 28; *MC* 149 (Jun 1954), 36; *Pan Pipes* 47 (Jan 1955), 2; *POPN* (Oct 21, 1955), 91; *Time* 66 (Oct 31, 1955), 40; *Int Mus* 54 (Oct 1955), 15; *MA* 75 (Nov 15, 1955), 26; *Mus Denmark* No. 8 (Jan 1956), 3-4; *MA* 77 (Feb 1957), 232; *Notes* 15 (Dec 1957), 146; *MA* 81 (Jul 1961), 11; (Dec 1961), 59; *CohCT*, 116; *ChaAM*, 509; *MelMN*, 77.
 41. Symphony No. 8: *SFSPN* (Jan 17, 1962), 25; *NYT* (Jan 19, 1962), 28:2; *Mus West* 17 (Feb 1962), 12; *Int Mus* 60 (Mar 1962), 51; *Mus Mag* 164 (Apr 1962), 63.
 42. Symphony No. 9: *POPN* (Jan 18, 1963), 23; *NYT* (Jan 31, 1963), 5:7; *New Yorker* 38

(Feb 9, 1963), 77-78; *Int Mus* 61 (Feb 1963), 23; *Musica* 19, No. 4 (1965), 208.

46. Symphony No. 10: *BMI* (Jul 1965), 18; *Melos* 32 (Jul-Aug 1965), 269.

47. Symphony No. 11: *NYPPN* (Feb 8, 1968), 8-D; *NYT* (Feb 9, 1968), 51:1; *Time* (Feb 16, 1968), 77; *Strad* 78 (Apr 1968), 487; *Intam Mus B* No. 64-65 (Mar-May 1968), 80; *Int Mus* 66 (Apr 1968), 32; *Melos* 35 (Apr 1968), 165; *Mus J* 26 (May 1968), 58; *HiFi/MA* 18 (May 1968), MA26.

48. Symphony No. 12 (Pere Marquette): *NYT* (Feb 26, 1968), 43:2; *BMI* (May 1968), 19; *Int Mus* 68 (Mar 1970), 32.

50. Symphony No. 14: *Int Mus* 73 (Apr 1975), 14; *Sym News* 27, No. 2 (1976), 29; *NMC* 35, No. 2 (1976), 17.

8. Time Suite: *MQ* 23 (1947), 26; *HowOC*, 141.

93. Toccata for Piano: *MC* 141 (Mar 1, 1950), 28; *MA* 70 (Mar 1950), 44; *Notes* 7 (Jun 1950), 449; *Mus Club Mag* 30 (Oct 1950), 24.

76. Trio for Violin, Cello, Piano: *MQ* 25 (1939), 378; *CohCT*, 117; *MelMN*, 72; *HiFi/MA* 24 (Jan 1974), MA22-23.

5. When Johnny Comes Marching Home (American Overture): *MQ* 33 (1947), 25; *HitMU*, 205; *HowOA*, 436; *HowOC*, 138.

Dissertations about Roy Harris and His Works

1. Brookhart, Charles E. *The Choral Music of Aaron Copland, Roy Harris and Randall Thompson.* George Peabody College for Teachers, 1960.

2. Halen, Walter H. *An Analysis and Comparison of Compositional Practices Used by Five Contemporary Composers in Works Titled "Symphony."* Ohio State University, 1969.

3. James, Woodrow C. *The Use of Harmonic Tritone in Selected Passages from the Music of Representative Contemporary Composers.* Michigan State University, 1966.

4. King, Irvin J. *Neoclassical Tendencies in Seven American Piano Sonatas (1925-1945).* Washington University, 1971.

5. Mize, Lou Stem. *A Study of Selected Choral Settings of Walt Whitman's Poems.* Florida State University, 1967.

6. Pisciotta, Louis V. *Texture in the Choral Works of Selected Contemporary American Composers.* Indiana University, 1967.

7. Plinkiewisch, Helen E. *A Contribution to the Understanding of the Music of Charles Ives, Roy Harris, and Aaron Copland.* Columbia University, 1955.

8. Service, Alfred Roy, Jr. *A Study of the Cadence as a Factor in Musical Intelligence in Selected Piano Sonatas by American Composers.* State University of Iowa, 1958.

9. Tortolano, William. *The Mass and the Twentieth Century Composers.* University of Montreal, 1964.

10. Wolf, Henry S. *The Twentieth Century Piano Sonata.* Boston University, 1957.

OUTLINE VIII

CHARLES EDWARD IVES (1874-1954)

I. Life

1874   Born in Danbury, Connecticut, October 20. Encouraged to study music by his father, a Civil War bandmaster who experimented in unusual combinations of sounds, dissonances and quarter tones; began to compose at an early age.

1887   Organist of the West Street Congregational Church, Danbury. First Baptist Church, Danbury (1888). Composed his *Variations on "America"* for organ (1891).

1894   Entered Yale University; received Bachelor of Arts degree, 1898. Studied with Horatio Parker (composition) and Dudley Buck (organ). Organist of St. Thomas Church (1893-1894) and Centre Church, New Haven.

1898   Organist of the First Presbyterian Church, Bloomfield, New Jersey (1898-1899). Organist of the Central Presbyterian Church, New York (1899-1902). Creative life largely independent of outside influence. Decided against a career in music and went into the insurance business (1898) "because he wished to express himself musically in his own way and free from the trammels of expediency."

1904   *Symphony No. 3* completed, the first in a series of his most important works.

1906   Established the insurance firm of Ives and Company; Ives & (Julian) Myrick (1907). Married Harmony Twichell (1908). Continued composing evenings and weekends; most productive years (1907-1918).

1917   First performance of his music at a public concert in New York (*Sonata for Violin and Piano*).

1918   Following a serious heart attack he composed very little, principally songs. Compiled, edited and rewrote many works (1916-1936). *Sonata No. 2 (Concord)*, *Essays*, and *114 Songs* prepared for publication and distributed free of charge (1919-1922).

1927   Eugene Goossens conducted the first New York performance of an orchestral work by Ives (*Symphony No. 4*, prelude and second movement).

1930   Retired from the insurance business, due to continued ill health. Settled in West Reading, Connecticut. Performances of his works in Europe and America, beginning in 1930, gradually broke down public resistance from the 1940's on.

1939   John Kirkpatrick played the *"Concord" Sonata* in Town Hall, New York.

1946   Elected to the National Institute of Arts and Letters. First complete performance of *Symphony No. 3* (1901-1904).

1947   Awarded the Pulitzer Prize for Music (*Symphony No. 3*).

1951   Leonard Bernstein conducted the *Symphony No. 2*, but the composer could not bring himself to attend the concert.

1954   Died May 19, in New York.

1974   The centennial of Ives' birth was celebrated by a series of conferences at his alma mater, and in many other American and European cities.

Charles Ives has been the recipient of many honors in addition to those listed above.

Note: Biographies of varying lengths and importance may be found in many of the books listed in the Bibliography at the end of this *Outline* under "References to Charles Ives."

II.   Compositions (selected)

		Date	Publisher
A.	**Orchestra**		
1.	Holiday Quickstep (theatre orch)	1887	
2.	Fugue in Four Keys, on "The Shining Shore" (str orch; also str orch, trpt, fl, org)	1896	Meri
3.	Symphony No. 1	1896-1898	Peer
4.	Symphony No. 2	1897-1902	Peer
5.	Symphony No. 3 (The Campmeeting)	1901-1904; revised 1911	AMP
6.	Hymn: Largo Cantabile (str orch)	1904	Peer
7.	Calcium Light Night (cham orch; rescored for full orch by Henry Cowell)	1898-1907	NME
8.	The Unanswered Question (cham orch)	1908	Peer
9.	Three Outdoor Scenes	1898-1911	B-B

     a. Central Park in the Dark (cham orch) (1898-1907)
     b. The Pond (see No. 48 b.) (1906)
     c. Hallowe'en (see No. 48c.) (1911)

		Date	Publisher
10.	A Set of Pieces for Theatre or Chamber Orchestra	1904-1911	NME

     a. In the Cage (1906)   c. In the Night (1906)
     b. In the Inn (1904-1911)

		Date	Publisher
11.	Tone Roads No. 1 (cham orch)	1911	Peer
12.	Robert Browning Overture	1911	Peer
13.	The Gong on the Hook and Ladder, or Firemen's Parade on Main Street (cham orch)	1911	Peer
14.	Over the Pavements: Scherzo (cham orch)	1906-1913	Peer
15.	Holidays: A Symphony	1904-1913	

     a. Washington's Birthday (cham orch) (1909-1913)   AMP
     b. Decoration Day (1912)   Peer
     c. The Fourth of July (1912-1913)   AMP
     d. Thanksgiving and/or Forefathers' Day (orch; SATB ad lib) (1904)   Peer

		Date	Publisher
16.	Three Places in New England (Orchestral Set No. 1)	1903-1914	Merc

     a. The "St. Gaudens" in Boston Common   b. Putnam's Camp, Redding, Connecticut
          (Col. Shaw and His Colored Regiment)   c. The Housatonic at Stockbridge

		Date	Publisher
17.	The Rainbow (after the poem by William Wordsworth) (cham orch)	1914	Peer
18.	Tone Roads No. 3 (cham orch)	1915	Peer
19.	Orchestral Suite No. 2	1912-1915	Peer

     a. An Elegy to Our Forefathers   c. From Hanover Square North
     b. The Rockstrewn Hills

		Date	Publisher
20.	Symphony No. 4	1910-1916	AMP
21.	Chromâtimelôdtune (reconstructed and completed by Gunther Schuller)		MJQ
22.	Variations on "America" (arr. for orch by William Schuman)	(1891)	Meri
23.	Universe Symphony (incomplete fragments)	1911-1916	
24.	Orchestral Suite No. 3	1919-1927	
B.	**Band** (arrangements)		
25.	March Intercollegiate (arr. Keith Brion) (1973)		Boonin
26.	Finale from "Symphony No. 2" (arr. Jonathan Elkus)		Peer
27.	March: Omega Lambda Chi (arr. Keith Brion) (1974)		AMP
28.	Variations on "Jerusalem the Golden" (arr. Keith Brion) (1974)		AMP
29.	March III, with the air "Old Kentucky Home" (arr. Kenneth Singleton) (1975)		Meri
30.	Overture and March "1776" (arr. James Sinclair) (1975)		Meri

C. Chamber

31. String Quartet No. 1 (A Revival Service)	1896	Peer
32. Prelude from the "Pre-First Sonata" (vln, pno)	1900	
33. From the Steeples and the Mountains: Allegro (trpt, trb, bells/2 pno)	1901	Peer
34. Trio: Largo (vln, clar, pno) (also vln, pno)	1902	Peer
35. Scherzo (str qrt)	1903	Peer
36. Hymn: Largo Cantabile (str qrt, d-b)	1904	Peer
37. "Pre-Second String Quartet"	1905	
38. Space and Duration (mechanical pno, str qrt)	1907	Peer
39. Sonata No. 1 (vln, pno)	1903-1908	Peer
40. Scherzo: All the Way Around and Back (2 pno, vln/fl, clar/fl, trpt, hn, bells)	1907	Peer
41. The Innate: Adagio Cantabile (str qrt, pno)	1908	Peer
42. Largo Risoluto No. 1 (str qrt, pno)	1908	Peer
43. Largo Risoluto No. 2 (str qrt, pno)	1908	Peer
44. In Re Con Moto, et al (str qrt, pno)	1913	Peer
45. Allegretto Sombreoso (from Byron's "The Incantation") (3 vln, fl, E-hn/trpt, pno)	1910	Peer
46. Sonata No. 2 (vln, pno)	1903-1910	GS
47. Adagio Sostenuto (E-hn/fl, str qrt, pno/hp, celesta)	1910	Peer
48. Trio (vln, vlc, pno)	1904-1911	Peer
49. Three Outdoor Scenes	1898-1911	AMP
a. Central Park in the Dark (cham orch) (1898-1907)		
b. The Pond (fl, 2 hp, pno, celesta/bells) (1906-1911)		
c. Hallowe'en (str qrt, pno) (1911)		
50. The Indians (trpt, ob, str, pno)	1912	Peer
51. String Quartet No. 2	1907-1913	Peer
52. Sonata No. 3 (vln, pno)	1902-1914	NME
53. Set (str qrt, pno, d-b)	1903-1914	Peer
54. Sonata No. 4: Children's Day at the Campmeeting (vln, pno)	1914-1915	AMP

D. Piano

55. Three-page Sonata	1905	Merc
56. Some South-Paw Pitching!	1908	Merc
57. The Anti-Abolitionist Riots in the 1830's and 1840's	1908	Merc
58. Sonata for Piano No. 1	1902-1909	Peer
59. Twenty-Two	1912	NME
60. Three Protests	1900-1914	NME
a. March time or faster		
b. Adagio or Allegro or varied or/and variations, very nice		
c. A canon		
61. Eight Studies and Five Takeoffs	1900-1914	NME
62. Sonata for Piano No. 2 (Concord 1840-1860)	1909-1915	AMP
a. Emerson c. The Alcotts		
b. Hawthorne d. Thoreau		
63. Three Quarter-tone Pieces	1903-1924	Peer

E. Organ

64. Prelude on "Adeste Fideles"	1891	Merc
65. Variations on "America" (arr. for orch by William Schuman; arr. for band by William Rhoads)	1891	Meri

F. Choral (a cappella unless otherwise indicated)

66. Turn Ye, Turn Ye (Josiah Hopkins) (SATB, pno or org)	1889	Merc
67. The Circus Band: Parade (Charles Ives) (SSATTBB, cham orch)	1894	Peer

F.   Choral (cont.)

68. Psalm 67 (SATB)	1898	AMP
69. The Celestial Country (Tenebris vitae in lucem coeli) (Alford from St. Bernard) (SATB, soli, str, brass, org)	1898-1899	Peer
70. Processional: Let There be Light (John Ellerton) (SATB or TTBB, pno)	1901	Peer
71. Three Harvest Home Chorales (SATB, pno, org or orch)	1898-1912	Merc

    a. Harvest Home (George Burgess)   c. Come Ye Thankful People (Henry Alford)
    b. Lord of the Harvest (John Hampton Gurney)

72. Lincoln the Great Commoner (Edwin Markham) (SATB or SSAA or TTBB, orch)	1912	NME
73. The New River (Charles Ives) (SATB, cham orch)	1912	Peer
74. Vote for Names (voice or voices, 3 pno)	1912	Peer
75. December (unison TTBB, ww, brass)	1913	Peer
76. General William Booth Enters Into Heaven (Vachel Lindsay) (unison TTBB, orch)	1914	NME
77. Easter Carol (SATB, soli; SATB, org)		AMP
78. They are There: A War Song March (Charles Ives) (unison SATB, orch or pno)	1917	Peer
79. Serenity (John Greenleaf Whittier) (unison chant)	1919	AMP
80. Psalm 24 (SATB)		Merc
81. Psalm 90; Psalm 100; Psalm 150 (SATB)		Merc

G.   **Solo Vocal** (with piano unless otherwise indicated)

82. 114 Songs	1884-1921	PP, AMP, Meri, Peer

    Note: The following collections are for the most part taken from *114 Songs*.

    a. Four Songs
        1) Duty (Ralph Waldo Emerson) — 1921
        2) Luck and Work (Robert Underwood Johnson) — 1920
        3) 1, 2, 3 (Charles E. Ives)
        4) Vita (Manilius) — 1921

    b. Fourteen Songs
        1) The Cage (Charles E. Ives) — 1906
        2) De la drama: Rosamunde (Belanger) — 1898
        3) In Flanders Field (John McCrae) — 1919
        4) Marie (R. von Gottschall) — 1896
        5) Nature's Way (Charles E. Ives) — 1908
        6) Naught that Country Needeth (Henry Alford) — 1899
        7) On the Counter (Charles E. Ives) — 1920
        8) Romanzo di Central Park (Leigh Hunt) — 1900
        9) A Song—for Anything (Charles E Ives) — 1892
       10) Songs My Mother Taught Me (Heyduk) — 1895
       11) The Things Our Fathers Loved (Charles E. Ives) — 1917
            and the Greatest of These was Liberty
       12) Those Evening Bells (Thomas Moore) — 1907
       13) Watchman! (John Bowring) — 1913
       14) Weil' auf mir (Eyes so dark) (Charles E. Ives) — 1902

    c. Nine Songs
        1) Autumn (Harmony T. Ives) — 1908
        2) Dreams (Porteous) — 1897
        3) Elégie (Gallet) — 1901
        4) Evidence (Charles E. Ives) — 1910
        5) Grantchester (Rupert Brooke) — 1920
            (with a quotation from Debussy)
        6) His Exaltation (Robert Robinson) — 1913
        7) A Son of a Gambolier (anonymous) — 1895
        8) There is a Lane (Harmony T. Ives) — 1902
        9) They are There (fighting for the People's New Free World)
            (Charles E. Ives) — May 30, 1917

d. Nineteen Songs
    1) Aeschylus and Sophocles (Walter Savage Landor)   1922
    2) Canon (Thomas Moore)   1894
    3) A Christmas Carol (traditional)
    4) Cradle Song (A. L. Ives)   1919
    5) An Election (Charles E. Ives)   1920
    6) A Farewell to Land (Lord Byron)   1925
    7) From "Night of Frost in May" (George Meredith)   1899
    8) From "Paracelsus" (Robert Browning)   1912-1921
    9) General William Booth enters into Heaven (Vachel Linday)   1914
    10) In Summer Fields (Almers; tr. Chapman)   1898
    11) The Innate (Charles E. Ives) (str qrt, pno, 1908)   1916
    12) La fède (Lodovico Ariosto)   1920
    13) Majority (Charles E. Ives) (chorus, orch, 1915)   1921
    14) On the Antipodes (Charles E. Ives)   1915-1923
    15) Requiem (Robert Louis Stevenson)   November 1911
    16) Resolution (Charles E. Ives)   1921
    17) Slugging a Vampire (Charles E. Ives)   1902
    18) Tom Sails Away (Charles E. Ives)   1917
    19) Two Little Flowers (Charles E. Ives)   1921

e. Seven Songs
    1) Charlie Rutlage (cowboy song)
    2) Evening (John Milton, from "Paradise Lost")   1921
    3) The Indians (Charles Sprague)   1921
    4) Maple Leaves (Thomas Bailey Aldrich)   1920
    5) The See'r (Charles E. Ives)   1920
    6) Serenity (John Greenleaf Whittier)   1919
    7) Walking (Charles E. Ives)   1902

f. Ten Songs
    1) From "Amphion" (Alfred Tennyson)   1896
    2) The Circus Band (Harmony T. Ives)   1894
    3) Forward into Light, from "The Celestial
        Country" (Henry Alford)   1898
    4) I Travelled among Unknown Men (William Wordsworth)   1901
    5) Memories (a. Very Pleasant; b. Rather Sad)   1897
        (Harmony T. Ives)
    6) Mirage (Christina G. Rossetti)   1902
    7) Omens and Oracles (anonymous)   1900
    8) Slow March (Harmony T. Ives)   1888
    9) To Edith (Harmony T. Ives)   1892
    10) The World's Wanderers (Percy B. Shelley)   1895

g. Thirteen Songs
    1) Abide with Me (Rev. Henry Francis Lyte)   1890
    2) Allegro (Harmony T. Ives)   1900
    3) Berceuse (Charles E. Ives)   1900
    4) The Campmeeting, from Symphony No. 3 (Charlotte Elliott)   1912
    5) The Collection, Stanzas from Old Hymns   1920
    6) Down East (Charles E. Ives)   1919
    7) In the Alley (Charles E. Ives)   1896
    8) Old Home Day (Charles E. Ives)   1920
    9) An Old Flame (Charles E. Ives)   1896
    10) The Old Mother (Vinje; tr. Corder)   1900
    11) Tarrant Moss (Rudyard Kipling)   1902
    12) Where the Eagle (M. P. Turnbull)   1900
    13) The World's Highway (Harmony T. Ives)   1893

h. Thirty-four Songs
    1) Afterglow (J. Fenimore Cooper)   1919
    2) Ann Street (Maurice Morris)   1921
    3) At Parting (Frederick Peterson)   1889
    4) At the River (Robert Lowry)   1916
    5) At Sea (Robert Underwood Johnson)   1921
    6) The Children's Hour (Henry Wadsworth Longfellow)   1901
    7) December (Folgore da San Geminiano)   1920
    8) Duty (Ralph Waldo Emerson) and Vita (Manilius)   1921

h. Thirty-four Songs (cont.)

9)	From the "Incantation" (Lord Byron)	1921
10)	From "The Swimmers" (Louis Untermeyer)	1915-1921
11)	The Greatest Man (Anne Collins)	1921
12)	Harpalus, from Percy's Reliques (Thomas Percy)	1902
13)	Hymn (Charles Wesley)	1921
14)	Ich grolle nicht (I'll Not Complain) (Heinrich Heine)	1899
15)	Immortality (Charles E. Ives)	1921
16)	The Last Reader (Oliver Wendell Holmes)	1921
17)	Like a Sick Eagle (John Keats)	1920
18)	Luck and Work (Robert Underwood Johnson)	1920
19)	Mists (Harmony T. Ives) (also for theatre orch)	1910
20)	The New River (Charles E. Ives)	1921
21)	A Night Thought (Thomas Moore)	1895
22)	Premonitions (Robert Underwood Johnson)	1921
23)	The Rainbow (William Wordsworth)	1921
24)	Rough Wind (Percy B. Shelley)	1902
25)	September (Folgore da San Geminiano)	1920
26)	Soliloquy or a Study in 7ths and Other Things (Charles E. Ives)	1907
27)	Song for Harvest Season (Old Hymn)	1894
28)	The South Wind (Charles E. Ives)	1899
29)	Thoreau (Charles E. Ives)	1915
30)	Tolerance (Arthur T. Hadley)	1909
31)	Walt Whitman (Walt Whitman)	1921
32)	West London (Matthew Arnold)	1921
33)	When Stars in the Quiet Skies (Edward Bulwer-Lytton)	1891
34)	The White Gulls (Maurice Morris)	1921

i. Twelve Songs

1)	August (Folgore da San Geminiano)	1920
2)	Disclosure (Charles E. Ives)	1921
3)	The Housatonic at Stockbridge (Robert Underwood Johnson)	1921
4)	Kären (anonymous)	1894
5)	My Native Land (anonymous)	1897
6)	Qu'il m'irait bien (anonymous)	1901
7)	Religion (James T. Bixby)	1920
8)	Remembrance (Charles E. Ives)	1921
9)	The Side Show (Charles E. Ives)	1921
10)	Spring Song (Harmony T. Ives)	1904
11)	Waltz (Charles E. Ives)	1895
12)	The Waiting Soul (William Cowper)	1908

j. Twelve Sacred Songs (included in the previous collections)

1) Abide with Me (Rev. Henry Francis Lyte); 2) The Campmeeting (Charlotte Elliott); 3) The Collection (Stanzas from Old Hymns); 4) Disclosure (Charles E. Ives); 5) Down East (Charles E. Ives); 6) Foward into Light (Henry Alford); 7) His Exaltation (Robert Robinson); 8) Naught that Country Needeth (Henry Alford); 9) Religion (James T. Bixby); 10) The Waiting Soul (William Cowper); 11) Watchman! (John Bowring); 12) Where the Eagle (M. P. Turnbull).

83.	A Night Song (Thomas Moore)	1895	Peer
84.	Flag Song	1898	Peer
85.	Where the Eagle (M. P. Turnbull) (from Thirteen Songs)	1900	Peer
86.	Chanson de Florian (Charles E. Ives)	1901	Merc
87.	Walking (Charles E. Ives) (from Seven Songs)	1902	AMP
88.	The All-Enduring	1902	Merc
89.	Ilmenau: Over the Tree Tops (Johann Goethe)	1902	Peer
90.	The Light that is Felt (John Greenleaf Whittier)	1904	Merc
91.	Vote for Names (Charles E. Ives)	1912	Peer
92.	General William Booth Enters into Heaven (Vachel Lindsay)	1914	NME
93.	Evening (John Milton) (from Seven Songs)	1921	AMP
94.	The Greatest Man (Anne Collins) (from Thirty-four Songs)	1921	AMP
95.	It Strikes Me That (Charles E. Ives)	1921	NME
96.	"Lincoln the Great Commoner" (Edwin Markham) (SSAA, orch)	1921	Peer

Note: The following abbreviations are used in Section III of this *Outline*. The number indicates the number of the composition as listed in Section II.

15. *Birthday*: Washington's Birthday (Holidays)
62. *Concord*: Sonata for Piano No. 2 (Concord)
15. *4 July*: Fourth of July (Holidays)
16. *Housatonic*: The Housatonic at Stockbridge (Three Places)
14. *Pavements*: Over the Pavements: Scherzo
58. *Son Pno 1*: Sonata for Piano No. 1

54. *Son Vln Pno 4*: Sonata for Violin and Piano No. 4
5. *Sym 3*: Symphony No. 3
63. *3 Pieces*: Three Quartertone Pieces
16. *3 Places*: Three Places in New England
31. *Str Qrt 1*: String Quartet No. 1

III. Style

"The future of music may not be entirely with music itself—but rather in the way it makes itself a part with—in the way it encourages and extends, rather than limits, the aspirations and ideals of the people—the finer things that humanity does and dreams of; and perhaps the time is coming, but not in our time, when it will develop possibilities inconceivable now—a language so transcendent that its heights and depths will be common to all mankind."

Charles Ives in *Essays before a Sonata* (**Prologue**, *c*. 1919)

A. General characteristics
  1. Largely self-taught, Ives broke with tradition in the 1890's. Experimented years before Cowell, Schoenberg, Stravinsky and others with tone clusters, atonality, polytonality, poly-meters, poly-tempos, extreme dissonance, quarter tones, complicated rhythms and other devices. Musical style ranges from simplicity to extreme complexity. Music rooted in American life.
B. Melodic line
  1. Melodies often begin with a version of a well-known tune. Motifs developed into a theme in various ways.
  2. Jagged, covering three or four octaves: *Concord* (p. 8).
  3. Chromatic line: *Concord* (p. 6, score 3; p. 18, score 3; p. 41, score 5; p. 19, scores 1-2).
  4. Lyrical: *Concord* (p. 53).
  5. Whole tone: *Concord* (p. 57, score 1); *Mists* (*Thirty-four Songs*, p. 46).
  6. Quarter tones: *3 Pieces*; *Sym 4*.
  7. Twelve-tone scale: *Concord* (p. 13, score 4).
  8. Parallel seconds: *Concord* (first movement).
  9. Notes a half-step apart placed in different octaves: *Birthday* (last variation).
  10. Borrowed melodies frequent: *Concord* (pp. 3, 18, 19, 23, 33, 54, 55, 64, 67; *Son Vln Pno 1* (third movement); *Son Vln Pno 2 & 4* (movements 1, 3); *4 July* (p. 3); *Sym 3* (end of movements 1, 2); *Sym 4* (movement 1); *Str Qrt 1, 2* (all movements); *Decoration Day*; *General Booth* (*Nineteen Songs*).
  11. Diatonic: *Son Vln Pno 4* (p. 19).
C. Harmony
  1. All styles from classical to the most advanced modernism with every possible type of chord. Dissonances are rarely resolved; complex harmonies often mixed with simple. Imitation of the playing of familiar tunes by amateurs often results in atonal and polytonal writing.
  2. Classical or conventional harmonies: *Concord* (p. 43); *Sym 3* (all three movements).
  3. Polychords: *Concord* (p. 6, score 2; p. 57, score 4; p. 65, score 2).
  4. Added notes: *Son Vln Pno 4* (p. 4).
  5. Chromatic: *Son Vln Pno 4* (p. 19).
  6. Atonal: *Aeschylus* (*Nineteen Songs*) (p. 46, meas. 3; p. 47, meas. 1).

7. Polytonal: *Concord* (p. 5, score 5; pp. 37, 53); *Variations on "America"* (earliest use).

8. Tone clusters: *Concord* (p. 25; use of a strip of wood 14¾ inches long called for on page 42, scores, 1, 2; use of five consecutive notes: *4 July* (p. 17); *Majority* (*Nineteen Songs*).

9. Harmony with perfect fifths: *Son Pno 1* (p. 21).

10. Combination of mixed intervals: *Concord* (p. 42).

11. Pedal tone: *Concord* (pp. 30, 31, 66).

12. Major ninth: *Concord* (p. 49, score 3); seventh and ninth chords: *Walking* (*Seven Songs*).

13. Twelve-note chords: *Majority* (*Nineteen Songs*, p. 42).

14. Use of twelve-tone technique: Tone Roads No. 3.

15. Fifteenth and seventeenth chords: *On the Antipodes* (*Nineteen Songs*, p. 44).

16. Quarter tones: *Sym 4* (pno, str); *3 Pieces*.

17. Bi-tonal: *Psalm 67* (sections 1, 2).

18. Typical cadence: *3 Places* (p. 81, meas. 1-3).

D. Counterpoint

1. Contrapuntal writing infrequent and free; emphasis on harmony and rhythm. Canonic imitation rare.

2. Use of imitation: *4 July* (p. 3, meas. 1-4); *Sym 3* (p. 5, meas. 4; p. 10, meas. 2, 3).

3. Fugal style: *Sym 4* (third movement).

4. Combination of popular tunes: *In the Inn* (end).

5. Free use of ground bass: *Concord* (*Emerson*); *Sym 4* (p. 153).

6. Non-functional, free counterpoint: *3 Places* (p. 61, meas. 1).

E. Rhythm

1. All types of rhythmic devices from simple to the most complex. Irregular meters, syncopation, off-beat accents are common. Individual players sometimes instructed to use their own rhythms in a passage. Sometimes a player will continue a tempo while the orchestra changes tempo.

2. Complex rhythm, no barlines, no time signatures, little or no feeling of pulse: *Concord* (p. 1).

3. Jazz-like rhythms: *Concord* (p. 37, score 4).

4. Cross-rhythms: *Concord* (p. 48, score 2); *4 July* (pp. 5-10, 12-16).

5. Regular beat and pulse: *Sym 3* (entire work uses key and time signatures).

6. Accented off-beat "Stravinsky" rhythms: *Putnam's Camp* (No. 16b).

7. Complex subdivisions: *3 Places* (p. 84, meas. 1).

8. Rhythmic counterpoint: *Birthday*; *Housatonic*.

9. Polyrhythms: *Sym 3* (p. 26); *Pavements* (p. 59).

F. Form

1. Form varies from a pre-classical form to an unorthodox, organic form in which musical ideas grow in various directions, and often lack coherence.

2. Sectional: *3 Places* (contrasts of dynamics and texture); *Pavements*.

3. Cyclic idea: *Concord* (Beethoven's "Fate" theme and a short chromatic motif recur).

4. Sonata-allegro: *Sym 1* (first movement).

5. A - B - A: *Sym 3* (second movement).

6. A - B - C - B - A: *Psalm 67*.

7. Unique form using consonance in one group and dissonance in the other: *The Unanswered Question*.

8. Free, rhapsodic: *Sym 3* (third movement).

G. Orchestration

1. Varies from ordinary (*Sym 3*) to extraordinary (*Holidays*).

2. Sometimes writes passages for an "ideal" instrument which does not exist.

3. Instrumentation often at the discretion of the conductor or player (*Set of Pieces for*

Theatre or Chamber Orchestra).

4.   Has written for two or three orchestras or bands playing at the same time, each with different harmony, melody and meter (*Central Park in the Dark*).

5.   Use of unusual instruments: *Holidays* (Jew's harp, first movement, p. 11).

BIBLIOGRAPHY

Writings by Charles Ives

1.   *Epilogue from "Essays Before a Sonata,"* ed. Howard Boatwright. New Haven, CT: Paul Boatwright, 1956.

2.   *Essays Before a Sonata.* New York: Privately printed, 1920. Reprint: New York: Dover, 1962, in *Three Classics in the Aesthetic of Music.*

3.   *Essays Before a Sonata and Other Writings*, ed. Howard Boatwright. New York: W. W. Norton, 1962. *Mus News* 42 (Feb 1950), 22-23; *Mus J* 20 (Mar 1962), 104; *Clavier* 2, No. 1 (1963), 7; *Instrument* 17 (Feb 1963), 32; *MA* 83 (Feb 1963), 52; *Pan Pipes* 55, No. 2 (1963), 29; *JAMS* 17, No. 2 (1964), 229-231; *MQ* 50 (1964), 101-103; *J Res Mus Ed* 13, No. 1 (1965), 61-63; *ML* 50, No. 4 (1969), 526-527; *MT* 110 (Jul 1969), 744-745; *Tempo* 89 (summer 1969), 34; *Mus in Ed* 34, No. 341 (1970), 36; *Mus Tcr* 52 (Oct 1973), 31; *Mus & Mus* 21 (Apr 1973), 48-49; *MT* 115 (Nov 1974), 947-948.

4.   *Preface to 114 Songs.* Redding, CT: Privately printed, 1922.

5.   "Some Quarter-tone Impressions," *France-American Music Society Quarterly Bulletin* (March 1925).

6.   *Charles E. Ives Memos*, ed. John Kirkpatrick. New York: W. W. Norton, 1972. *HiFi/MA* 21 (Oct 1971), MA66-MA72; *Pan Pipes* 64, No. 2 (1972), 30; *Mus J* 30 (Dec 1972), 49; *Mus Ed J* 55 (Jan 1973), 86; *Pan Pipes* 65, No. 2 (1973), 32; *HiFi/MA* 23 (Mar 1973), MA29-31; *Mus & Mus* 21 (Apr 1973), 48-49; *Notes* 29, No. 4 (1973), 825-826; *Mus Tcr* 52 (Oct 1973), 31; *MQ* 60 (1974), 284-290; *ML* 55, No. 1 (1974), 112-113; *MT* 115 (Nov 1974), 947-948; *Mus Tcr* 54 (Jun 1975), 27.

References to Charles Ives

Books
(See the General Bibliography)

ACA-Bul IV/3; ASC-SC; AusMT; Baker; BakSL; BauTC; BIM; BloYA; BluPC; BMI-OP; BMI-SC; Bull; CatPC; ChaAC; ChaAM; ClaEA; CobCS; CohCT; ColHM; ComA; CopMI; CopON; CopTN; CowAC; CurB (1954); DalTT; DavPM; DemMT; DerETM; DowO; DukLH; Edm-I; EdMUS; EweAC; EweCB; EweCS; EweCT; EweDE; EweMC; EweNB; EweWT; EweYA; FraMG; GolTP; GonSS; GosMM; Grove; HanIT; HigTG; HitMU; HodSD; HowCC; HowMM; HowOA; HowSH; JohSH; KinAI; KreMH; LanOH; LeiMW; LeiSK; MacAC; MacIC; MelMN; MelMS; MelRT; MitLM; MorgCM; MorrCA; MueAS; MyeTC; NorLC; NymEM; PAC; PanMC; PavMH; PersTH; PeyNM; PorM3S; ReiCA; ReiCC; RobCM; RosDM; RosMI; RowFC; SalMO; SalzTM; SamLM; SamMO; SanWM; SchWC; SesRM; SloMS; StevHS; StevePC; ThoAJ; ThoAM; ThompIC; ThoMR; ThoMS; ThoRL; WhiWW; WooWM; WWA (1946-1947); YatTC; YouCD.

1.   *The National Cyclopedia of American Biography*, vol. 42, p. 12.

2.   *American Contemporary Composers: Charles Ives.* American Music. American Embassy, Cultural Affairs Office, USIA. London: October, 1959.

3.   Bernlef, Door J., and Reinbert de Leeuw. *Charles Ives.* Amsterdam: De Bezige Bij, 1969 (paper). Reviews: *Mens en Mel* 24 (Nov 1969), 349; *Melos* 37 (Sep 1970), 347.

4.   *Charles Ives Centennial Festival-Conference, New York, New Haven.* New York: G. Schirmer, 1974.

5. Cowell, Henry and Sidney. *Charles Ives and His Music*. New York: Oxford University Press, 1955, 1969. *SR* 37 (Jan 15, 1955), 29; *NW* 45 (Jan 17, 1955), 90; *Notes* 12 (1955), 217; *Perspectives USA* No. 13 (1955), 38-56; *SR* 52 (Jun 21, 1969), 62; *Instrument* 24 (Aug 1969), 16; *MT* 110 (Nov 1969), 1144; *Mus Opin* 93 (Apr 1970), 369; *NATS* 26, No. 3 (1970), 41-42.

6. de Lerma, Dominique-René. *Charles Edward Ives, 1874-1954: A Bibliography of His Music*. Kent, OH: Kent State University Press, 1970.

7. Elkus, Jonathan. *Charles Ives and the American Band Tradition: A Centennial Tribute*. Exeter: Exeter University Press, 1974. *Mus & Mus* 23 (Mar 1975), 27; *Notes* 32, No. 2 (1975), 273-275; *Tempo* 114 (Sep 1975), 28-30.

8. Furnas, T. Chalmers. "Charles E. Ives, An Essay," in *The Mills of God*. Amesbury, MA: The Whittier Press, 1937.

9. *A Garland for Charles Ives*. New York: Parnassus, 1975.

10. Hitchcock, H. Wiley. *Charles Ives*. London: 1977. *Mus in Ed* 41, No. 387 (1977), 241; *Composer* 62 (winter 1977-1978), 49; *MT* 119 (Mar 1978), 239; *Cont Kybd* 4 (Apr 1978), 6; *Musica* 32, No. 1 (1978), 63.

11. Hitchcock, H. Wiley, and Vivian Perlis. *An Ives Celebration: Papers and Panels of the Charles Ives Centennial Festival-Conference*. Urbana, IL: University of Illinois Press, 1977.

12. Kirkpatrick, John. *A Temporary Mimeographed Catalogue of the Music Manuscripts and Related Materials of Charles Edward Ives, 1874-1954, given by Mrs. Ives to the Library of the Yale School of Music, September 1955*. New Haven, CT: Yale University Library, 1960.

13. Maske, Ulrich. *Charles Ives in seiner Kammermusik für drei bis sechs Instruments*. Regensburg: G. Bosse, 1971.

14. McClendon, James W. *Biography as Theology: How Life's Stories Can Remake Today's Theology*. Nashville, TN: Abingdon Press, 1974. *Response* 15, No. 1 (1976), 38.

15. Perlis, Vivian. *Charles Ives Remembered, An Oral History*. New Haven, CT: Yale University Press, 1974; New York: W. W. Norton, 1976. *Sym News* 25, No. 5 (1974), 25.

16. Perry, Rosalie Sandra. *Charles Ives and the American Mind*. Kent, OH: Kent State University Press, 1974. *MusicAGO* 9 (Feb 1975), 52.

17. Rossiter, Frank R. *Charles Ives and His America*. New York: Liveright, 1975.

18. Rukeyser, Muriel. "Ives, a Poem," in *A Turning Wind*. New York: Viking Press, 1939.

19. Sive, Helen R. *Music's Connecticut Yankee: An Introduction to the Life and Music of Charles Ives*. New York: Atheneum, 1977.

20. *Three Classics in the Aesthetic of Music, by Debussy, Busoni and Ives*. New York: Dover, 1962; London: Constable, 1962. *Mus in Ed* 27, No. 303 (1963), 149; *Mus J* 21 (May 1963), 62; *Mus Tcr* 42 (Jul 1963), 291; *ZVUK* No. 89 (1968), 598.

21. Vinay, Gianfranco. *L'american musicale di Charles Ives*. Turin: G. Einaudi, 1974.

22. Warren, Richard. *Charles E. Ives Discography*. New Haven, CT: Yale University Library, 1972; Yale University Press, 1978. *Rec Coll* 21, Nos. 5-6 (1973), 143; *MR* 34, No. 2 (1973), 175-176; *MT* 115 (Nov 1974), 947-948; *Notes* 31, No. 1 (1974), 63-64.

23. Wooldridge, David. *Charles Ives: A Portrait*. London: Faber, 1975. *Mus & Mus* 23 (Aug 1975), 37; *Tempo* 114 (Sep 1975), 28-30; *ML* 57, No. 2 (1976), 173-175.

24. ——————*From the Steeples and Mountains, A Study of Charles Ives*. New York: Alfred A. Knopf, 1974. *HiFi/MA* 24 (Sep 1974), MA33-36; *Sym News* 25, No. 3 (1974), 21; *Notes* 31, No. 2 (1974), 291-293.

25. Timreck, Theodor W., director and producer. A movie for television: "A Good Dissonance Like a Man." Under the supervision of Vivian Perlis, 1977.

Articles

Brief mention: *MQ* 10 (1924), 623; *MQ* 19 (1933), 351; *Etude* 66 (Sep 1948), 526; *MQ* 36

(1950), 584; *MQ* 40 (1954), 400; *PNM* 1, No. 2 (1963), 98, 148, 203; *PNM* 2, No. 2 (1964), 16, 17, 160; *PNM* 4, No. 1 (1965), 3, 7, 10, 157; *PNM* 4, No. 2 (1966), 25, 135, 182.

1. Bellamann, Henry. "Concord, Mass., 1840-1860," *Double Dealer* 2, No. 10 (Oct 1921), 166-169.
2. "Ives and Myrick to Move in May," *National Business Rev* (Apr 1926).
3. Downes, Olin. "Music: Pro-Musica Society," *NYT* (Jan 30, 1927), 28:3.
4. Gilman, Lawrence. "Music: a New Symphony (Ives)," *NYHT* (Jan 31, 1927), 11.
5. Bellamann, Henry. "The Music of Charles Ives," *Pro-Musica* 5, No. 1 (Mar-Apr 1927), 16-22.
6. Cowell, Henry. "Four Little-Known Modern Composers: Chávez, Ives, Slonimsky, Weiss," *Aesthete* 1, No. 3 (Aug 1928), 1, 19.
7. Slonimsky, Nicolas. "Composers in New England," *MM* 7, No. 2 (1929-1930), 24-27.
8. Cowell, Henry. "Three Native Composers: Ives, Ruggles, Harris," *The New Freeman* 1 (May 3, 1930), 184-186.
9. Myrick, Julian S. "What the Business Owes to Charles Ives," *The Eastern Underwriter* (Sep 19, 1930), 18.
10. Cowell, Henry. "Charles Ives," *MM* 10, No. 1 (1932-1933), 24.
11. Citkowitz, Israel. "Experiment and Necessity," *MM* 10, No. 2 (1932-1933), 112.
12. Rosenfeld, Paul. "Remonstrances and Arrears," *New Republic* 71 (Jul 13, 1932), 236.
13. —————"Charles Ives, Pioneer Atonalist," *New Republic* 71 (Jul 20, 1932), 262-264.
14. Cowell, Henry. "Charles E. Ives," *Disques* 3, No. 9 (Nov 1932), 374.
15. Herrmann, Bernard. "Charles Ives," *Trend* 1, No. 3 (Sep-Nov 1932), 99-101.
16. Bellamann, Henry. "Charles Ives: The Man and His Music," *MQ* 19 (1933), 45.
17. Copland, Aaron. "One Hundred and Fourteen Songs," *MM* 11, No. 2 (Jan 1934), 59-64.
18. Slonimsky, Nicolas. "Composer Who Has Clung to His Own Way," *Boston Evening Transcript* (Feb 3, 1934), sec. 3, pp. 4-5.
19. Darrell, Robert D. "Living American Composers," in *Music Lover's Guide*. New York: 1934, p. 173.
20. Gilman, Lawrence. "A Masterpiece of American Music: The Concord Sonata," *NYHT* (Jan 21, 1939), 9.
21. Downes, Olin. "A Lonely American Composer," *NYT* (Jan 29, 1939), sec. 9, p. 7:1.
22. "Insurance Man: Individual and Authentically American U. S. Composer," *Time* 34 (Jan 30, 1939), 44.
23. *NYT* (Feb 25, 1939), 18:4.
24. Lieberson, Goddard. "An American Innovator: Charles Ives," *MA* 49 (Feb 10, 1939), 22, 322.
25. Mellers, Wilfrid H. "Music in the Melting Pot; Charles Ives and the Music of the Americas," *Scrutiny* 7, No. 4 (Mar 1939), 390-403.
26. Carter, Elliott. "The Case of Mr. Ives," *MM* 16, No. 3 (Mar 1939), 172-176.
27. Rosenfeld, Paul. "The Advance of American Music," *Kenyon Rev* 2 (Spring 1939), 187.
28. Seeger, Charles. "Charles Ives and Carl Ruggles," *Magazine of Art* 32 (Jul 1939), 396-399, 435-437.
29. —————"Grass Roots for American Composers," *MM* 16, No. 3 (Mar 1939), 144-149.
30. Rosenfeld, Paul. "The Advent of American Music," *Kenyon Rev* 1, No. 1 (winter, 1939), 50.
31. Carter, Elliott. "Stravinsky and Other Moderns in 1940," *MM* 17, No. 3 (1939-1940), 164.
32. Cohn, Arthur. "Americans at Rochester," *MM* 17, No. 4 (1939-1940), 256.
33. Rosenfeld, Paul. "A Plea for Improvisation," *MM* 19, No. 1 (1941-1942), 15.
34. Mellers, Wilfrd, H. "American Music, an English Perspective," *Kenyon Rev* 5, No. 3 (summer 1943), 365.
35. Morton, Lawrence. "Western Evenings with Ives," *MM* 22, No. 3 (1944-1945), 186.
36. Herrmann, Bernard. "Four Symphonies by Charles Ives," *MM* 22, No. 4 (1944-1945), 215.
37. Carter, Elliott. "Ives Today: His Vision and Challenge," *MM* 21, No. 4 (1944), 199-202.

38. Harrison, Lou. "The Music of Charles Ives," *Listen* 9, No. 1 (Nov 1946), 7.
39. *NYT* (Apr 14, 1946), sec. 2, p. 5:1.
40. Harrison, Lou. "On Quotation; New Attitude Towards Quoted Material Taken from Life," *MM* 23, No. 3 (summer 1946), 166.
41. Lang, Paul Henry. "Hearing Things," *SR* 29 (Jun 1, 1946), 43-44.
42. Carter, Elliott. "An American Destiny," *Listen* 9, No. 1 (Nov 1946), 4.
43. "Thoreau and Music," *The Thoreau Society Bulletin* 18 (Jan 1947).
44. Lederman, Minna. "Some American Composers," *Vogue* 137 (Feb 1, 1947), 184.
45. "Wins Pulitzer Prize," *NYT* (May 6, 1947), 1:6; 26:3.
46. "Biography," *Current Biography* (Jun 1947); *Current Biography Yearbook* (1947), 330-332.
47. Girson, Rochelle. "Biographical Sketch," *SR* 31 (Aug 28, 1948), 45.
48. Slonimsky, Nicolas. "Bringing Ives Alive," *SR* 31 (Aug 28, 1948), 45.
49. Moor, Paul. "On Horseback to Heaven, Charles Ives," *Harper's* 197 (Sep 1948), 65-73.
50. Perkins, Francis D. "On Horseback to Heaven—A Reply," *Harper's* 197 (Dec 1948), 14.
51. Slonimsky, Nicolas. "Unique American Composer," *Etude* 67 (Mar 1949), 138.
52. "Choral and Piano Works by Charles Ives Issued," *MA* 69 (Jun 1949), 28.
53. Cowell, Henry. "Chronological Relationship of Only Three Works for Piano by Charles Ives," *MQ* 35 (1949), 459-462.
54. ––––––"Charles Ives," *MQ* 35 (1949), 458.
55. Kelley, J. "American Music Comes of Age," *Mus J* 7 (Sep 1949), 11, 48.
56. Taubman, Howard. "Forget Posterity," *NYT* (Oct 23, 1949), sec. 2, p. 11.
57. ––––––"Posterity Catches up with Charles Ives—An Interview," *NYT* (Oct 23, 1949), sec. 6, p. 15.
58. Smith, W. Eugene. "Charles Ives, a Photograph," *Life* 27 (Oct 31, 1949), 45.
59. "Ives Honored on 75th Birthday," *MC* 140 (Nov 1, 1949), 20.
60. "Seventy-fifth Birthday," *Int Mus* 48 (Nov 1949), 19.
61. Moor, Paul. "Two Titans, Schoenberg and Ives," *Theatre Arts* 34 (Feb 1950), 49.
62. Morton, Lawrence. "American Culture and the Serious Composer," *Score* 4 (May 1950), 8.
63. "Charles Ives," *Pan Pipes* 43 (Dec 1950), 123.
64. "Gets N Y Newspaper Guild Award," *NYT* (Apr 14, 1951), 5:2.
65. "Concert Records," *New Yorker* 27 (Feb 17, 1951), 97-99.
66. Rosenwald, Hans. "Speaking of Music," *Mus News* 43 (Feb 1951), 11; (Mar 1951), 8.
67. Sear, H. G. "Charles Ives: Song-Writer," *Monthly Music Record* 81 (Feb 1951), 34-42.
68. "The Light that is Felt," *Mus Club Mag* 30 (Feb 1951), 19.
69. "Yankee Music," *Time* 57 (Mar 5, 1951), 72.
70. Stoddard, Harry. "Music in Connecticut," *Int Mus* 49 (Mar 1951), 12-13.
71. van Zanten, G. "Charles Ives, Amerikaans Componist," *Mens en Mel* 6 (May 1951), 145-148.
72. Sear, H. G. "Background to American Music," *Mus Parade* 2, No. 7 (1951), 12-13.
73. "Charles E. Ives," *Pan Pipes* 44 (Jan 1952), 34-35; 45 (Jan 1953), 56.
74. "Charles Ives, American Composer," *Vogue* 121 (May 1, 1953), 120.
75. "Chronological Catalog of the Works of the American Composer Charles Ives," *Boletin de musica y artes visuales* 65 (Jul-Aug 1953), 35.
76. Slonimsky, Nicolas. "Charles Ives, Musical Rebel," *Américas* 5 (Sep 1953), 6, 41.
77. Repass, R. "American Composers of Today," *London Mus* 8 (Dec 1953), 24.
78. "Unanswered Question," *MA* 74 (Jan 1, 1954), 26.
79. Kyle, Marguerite K. "AmerAllegro," *Pan Pipes* 46 (Jan 1954), 47.
80. Slonimsky, Nicolas. "Charles Ives—America's Musical Prophet," *MA* 74 (Feb 15, 1954), 18-19.
81. "Charles Ives Dies," *NYT* (May 19, 1954), 31:1.
82. "Obituary," *Time* 63 (May 31, 1954), 71; *MA* 74 (Jun 1954), 28.
83. "Charles Ives, 79, Pulitzer Winner, Dies in New York," *BB* 66 (May 29, 1954), 33.

84. Downes, Olin. "American Original," *NYT* (May 30, 1954), sec. 2, p. 7:1.
85. "Musical Whitman," *NW* 43 (May 31, 1954), 78.
86. "Cronologia," *Mus Y Artes*, 51-52 (May-Jun 1954), 7-8.
87. Lyons, James. "A Prophet Passes," *Am Rec G* 20 (Jun 1954), 313-315.
88. "Obituary," *Variety* 194 (May 26, 1954), 91; *Am Org* 37 (Jun 1954), 189; *MC* 150 (Jul 1954), 29.
89. "Charles Ives Dead," *Symphony* 8 (Jun 1954), 2.
90. Downes, Olin. "Composer's Need," *NYT* (Jun 6, 1954), sec. 2, p. 7:1.
91. "Great Innovator," *MA* 74 (Jun 1954), 78.
92. "Charles Ives, Organist and Noted Composer, Dies," *Diap* 45 (Jul 1, 1954), 20.
93. Berger, Arthur. "Ives in Retrospect (recordings)," *SR* 37 (Jul 31, 1954), 62.
94. Helm, Everett. "Charles Ives, American Composer," *MT* 95 (Jul 1954), 356-361.
95. "Obituary," *Current Biography* (Jul 1954); *Current Biography Yearbook* (1954), 361.
96. Evett, Robert. "Music Letter: A Post-Mortem for Mr Ives," *Kenyon Rev* 16, No. 4 (1954), 628-636.
97. Cowell, Henry. "The Music and Motives of Charles Ives," *Center* 1 (Aug-Sep 1954), 2-5.
98. Chase, Gilbert. "Reply to Robert Evett's 'Music Letter: A Post-Mortem for Mr Ives'," *Kenyon Rev* 17 (summer 1955), 504-506.
99. Downes, Olin. "Charles Ives," *ACA-Bul* 4, No. 1 (1954), 17.
100. Balanchine, George. "Ivesiana," *Center* 1 (Aug-Sep 1954), 5.
101. Keats, Sheila. "Reference Articles on American Composers: An Index," *Juilliard Rev* 1 (fall, 1954), 28-29.
102. Denby, E. "Balanchine's American Ballets," *Center* 1 (Oct 1954), 14-18.
103. Grunfeld, Fred. "Charles Ives, Yankee Rebel," *HiFi* 4 (Nov 1954), 34; *ACA-Bul* 4, No. 3 (1955), 2-5.
104. Frankenstein, Alfred. "Charles Ives and His Music," *MQ* 41 (1955), 253.
105. Slonimsky, Nicolas. "Charles Ives—America's Musical Prophet," *Pan Pipes* 47 (Jan 1955), 20.
106. Cowell, Henry. "Current Chronicle (Ivesiana)," *MQ* 41 (1955), 85-89.
107. "Yale University Gets Complete Ives Manuscripts," *MA* 75 (Feb 1, 1955), 27.
108. "Ives Collection Goes to Yale," *MC* 151 (Feb 15, 1955), 39.
109. Daniel, Oliver. "The New Festival," *ACA-Bul* 5, No. 1 (1955), 15.
110. "World of Music: Complete Set of Manuscript Works Given to Yale University," *Etude* 73 (Mar 1955), 7.
111. *NYT* (Jan 9, 1955), sec. 7, p. 3:1; (Jan 18, 1955); (Mar 13, 1955), sec. 6, p. 15.
112. Krenek, Ernst. "Charles Ives," *School Mus* 27 (Apr 1955), 141.
113. Downes, Olin. "Ives Memorial: His Scores and Papers Given to Yale," *NYT* (Jun 5, 1955), sec. 2, p. 9:1.
114. Schrade, Leo. "Charles E. Ives," *Yale Rev* 44, No. 4 (Jun 1955), 535-545.
115. Carter, Elliott. "The Rhythmic Basis of American Music," *Score* 12 (Jun 1955), 29-31.
116. "Chronological List of the Compositions of Charles Edward Ives," *ACA-Bul* 4, No. 3 (1955), 6-9.
117. "Chronological Catalog of the Works of the American Composer Charles E. Ives," *Mus Y Artes* 65-66 (Jul-Aug 1955), 35-43.
118. "Notes of the Day (Value of Technical Skill in Composing Music)," *Monthly Music Record* 85 (Jul-Aug 1955), 141-144.
119. Frankenstein, Alfred. "American Music at Home," *Juilliard Rev* 2 (winter 1955), 5.
120. Stambler, Bernard. "Four American Composers," *Juilliard Rev* 2 (winter 1955), 7-16.
121. "Yale University, Room in Jackson Library Dedicated," *NYT* (Feb 23, 1956), 33:8.
122. "Ives Collection to Yale," *MC* 153 (Mar 15, 1956), 35.
123. "Complete Works of Ives Go to Yale Music Library," *Diap* 47 (Apr 1, 1956), 6.
124. "Becker, John J. "Charles Ives, Composer With Something to Say," *Etude* 74 (May 1956), 11; (Jul 1956), 14.

125. Ellsworth, Ray. "Americans on Microgroove," *HiFi* 6, No. 8 (Aug 1956), 62.
126. "Charles Ives," *Composer of the Americas* 2 (1956), 90-100.
127. McClure, John. "Charles Ives, Lonely American Giant," *Gramophone* 35 (Apr 1957), 516.
128. *NYT* (Feb 9, 1958), 88:1.
129. Helm, Everett. "Charles Ives—Pionier der modernen Musik," *Melos* 25 (Apr 1958), 119-123.
130. Sargeant, Winthrop. "Musical Events, Opening Concert," *New Yorker* 34 (Oct 11, 1958), 168-171.
131. Taubman, Howard. "Forget Posterity," *NYT* (Nov 23, 1958), sec. 2, p. 11.
132. Trimble, Lester. "Music: Opening Program of New York Philharmonic," *Nation* 187 (Oct 25, 1958), 229.
133. Schonberg, Harold. "America's Greatest Composer," *Esquire* 50, No. 6 (Dec 1958), 229.
134. "Charles E. Ives on What to Listen for in New Music," *HiFi R* 2 (May 1959), 6.
135. Mitchell, Donald. "A Great American Composer," *Gramophone* 37 (Jul 1959), 651.
136. *NYT* (Aug 26, 1959), 25:1; (Oct 19, 1959), 37:8.
137. Neuburg, Betsy. "Charles Ives, Yankee Rebel," *Mus Club Mag* 39 (Nov 1959), 8.
138. Warrack, John. "A Quarterly Retrospect," *Gramophone* 37 (Nov 1959), 217.
139. "Lincoln, the Great Commoner," *MA* 80 (Mar 1960), 24.
140. "Radical from Connecticut," *Time* 76 (Aug 22, 1960), 36.
141. Carter, Elliott. "Shop Talk by an American Composer," *MQ* 46 (1960), 198-201.
142. Copland, Aaron. "A Businessman Who Wrote Music on Sunday," *MM* 9 (Nov 1960), 18.
143. *NYT* (Mar 5, 1961), sec. 2, p. 9:1; (Jun 25, 1961), sec. 2, p. 11; (Sep 8, 1961), 36:4.
144. Schonberg, Harold. "Stubborn Yankee," *NYT* (Mar 5, 1961), sec. 2, p. 9:1.
145. Mellers, Wilfrid H. "Charles Ives and the Sonata," *Listener* (Nov 30, 1961), 950.
146. Cohn, Arthur. "Bravo, Mr. Bernstein! Bravo, Columbia!" *Am Rec G* 28 (Dec 1961), 302-304.
147. Martynov, Ivan. "Forum muzykovedov," *Sovet Muz* 26 (Jan 1962), 126.
148. Kolodin, Irving. "Music to My Ears; Ives in Central Park," *SR* 45 (May 19, 1962), 26.
149. Hanuszewska, Mieczyslawa. "Geniusz na pustyni—Charles Ives," *Ruch Muz* 6, No. 2 (1962), 7-9.
150. Chávez, Carlos. "Ives y Copland," *Clave* 49 (Aug-Sep 1962), 19-23.
151. Carter, Elliott. "An American Destiny," *BSPN* (Nov 2, 1962), 355.
152. Burk, John N. "Composer from Connecticut," *BSPN* (Nov 2, 1962), 344.
153. *NYT* (Dec 1, 1962), 17:4.
154. Pollikoff, Max. "Music in Our Time," *Mus J* 21 (May 1963), 27.
155. "The Legacy of Charles Ives," *Pan Pipes* 55, No. 2 (1963), 13.
156. "Ives Revived," *NW* 62 (Oct 14, 1963), 65.
157. Kirkpatrick, John. "What Music Meant to Charles Ives," *Cornell University Music Rev* (1963), 13.
158. "A Treasure Trove of Ives," *MA* 83 (Dec 1963), 278.
159. Clarke, Henry Leland, and Kurt Stone. "Reviews of Records," *MQ* 50 (1964), 114-118.
160. Carter, Elliott. "The Case of Mr. Ives," *PNM* 2, No. 2 (1964), 27-29.
161. Cohn, Arthur. "On Cambridge, CRI, and Vox, That Supremely Individual Creative Genius, Chas. E. Ives," *Am Rec G* 30 (May 1964), 760-762.
162. Dickinson, Peter. "Charles Ives, 1874-1954," *MT* 105 (May 1964), 347-349.
163. "American Giant," *MA* 84 (May 1964), 63.
164. Helms, Hans G. "Der Komponist Charles Ives; Leben, Werk und Einfluss auf die heutige Generation," *Neue ZFM* 125, No. 10 (1964), 425-433.
165. Dwinell, Paul. "The Resurrection of Charles Edward Ives," *Listen* 1 (Sep-Oct 1964), 15.
166. Hall, David. "Charles Ives: An American Original," *Stereo R* 13 (Sep 1964), 41-58.
167. ———— "Charles Ives: A Discography," *HiFi R* 13 (Oct 1964), 142-146; (Dec 1964), 92.
168. Jacobson, Bernard. "American Trail-Blazer," *Records & Recording* (Dec 1964), 82.

169. Boatwright, Howard. "Ives' Quarter-Tone Impressions," *PNM* 3, No. 2 (1965), 22-31.

170. Cox, David. "Charles Ives, 'The First Truly American Composer'," *Listener* (Mar 11, 1965), 384.

171. "Fourth Symphony Première," *FoF* 25 (Apr 26, 1965), 486E1.

172. "Cantankerous Yankee; World Première of Fourth Symphony," *Time* 85 (May 7, 1965), 56.

173. "Transcendentalist," *NW* 65 (May 10, 1965), 101-102.

174. Kolodin, Irving. "Stokowski's Performance with the American Symphony Orchestra of C. Ives's Fourth Symphony," *SR* 48 (May 15, 1965), 32.

175. Cohn, Arthur. "On Five Labels Simultaneously, More Music by Chas. E. Ives," *Am Rec G* 31 (Jun 1965), 958-961.

176. "Years Add Luster to Ives Legacy," *Pan Pipes* 57, No. 3 (1965), 35.

177. Crump, Peter. "Ives, Then and Now: A Note on Originality and the Establishment," *Composer* 17 (Oct 1965), 12-13.

178. "Time Cycle," *ClSPN* (Oct 28, 1965), 175.

179. Cohn, Arthur. "Divine Document, the Ives Fourth," *Am Rec G* 32 (Nov 1965), 220-222.

180. Frankenstein, Alfred. "Ives's Fourth Symphony or Unplayable Work Gets Played," *HiFi* 15 (Nov 1965), 83-84.

181. Franceschini, Romulus. "Postscript on Ives's Fourth," *Am Rec G* 32 (Nov 1965), 223.

182. Newlin, Thomas J. "Letters: The Ives Homestead," *HiFi/MA* 15, No. 12 (Dec 1965), 6.

183. Brown, P. "Ives on a Birthday," *Mus & Mus* 14 (Dec 1965), 49.

184. "Charles Ives," *SFSPN* (Mar 1, 1966), 31.

185. Helm, Hans G. "Über statistisches Komponieren bei Charles Ives," *Neue ZFM* 127 (Mar 1966), 90-93.

186. Weerts, Richard K. "His Name Is Ives," *Mus J* 24 (Mar 1966), 46-47.

187. "Concert Music (Danbury, Conn., Birthplace to be Restored)," *BMI* (May 1966), 7.

188. Salzman, Eric. "New Record Discs for a Further Look at Ivesian Questions and Answers," *HiFi* 16 (Jun 1966), 70-71.

189. Goodfriend, John. "Charles Ives: Making Up for Lost Time," *HiFi R* 17 (Jul 1966), 72.

190. Cohn, Arthur. "From RCA Victor: After Sixty-Eight Years, the First Symphony of Chas. E. Ives," *Am Rec G* 32 (Jul 1966), 1032-1033.

191. Malloch, William. "More Stravinsky by Stravinsky—and Ivesian Explorations," *HiFi/MA* 16 (Aug 1966), 12.

192. *NYT* (Sep 20, 1966), 74:5.

193. Mayer, Martin. "Recordings," *Esquire* 66 (Oct 1966), 54.

194. Cooper, Paul. "Charles Ives i njegova muzika," *ZVUK* 68 (1966), 363-374.

195. "Records: Songs," *Opera N* 31 (Nov 19, 1966), 30.

196. Holland-Axelsen, Doris. "Omkring Charles Ives," *Dansk Mus* 41, No. 2 (1966), 52.

197. Butterworth, Neil. "American Composers," *Music (SMA)* 2, No. 1 (1967), 38.

198. Kirby, Frank. "Ives' Boom Boon to Peer-South'n," *BB* 79 (Apr 22, 1967), 32.

199. Salzman, Eric. "Charles Ives: Music Big as Life—Columbia and RCA Victor Contribute Welcome Additions to a Swelling Discography," *HiFi R* 19 (Aug 1967), 65-67.

200. Shirley, Wayne. "Ives's Holidays: A Glorious Fourth and No Anticlimax," *HiFi* 17 (Sep 1967), 79-80.

201. *NYT* (Nov 4, 1967), 37:1.

202. Cohn, Arthur. "Ten Records: Keeping Up with Charles Ives," *Am Rec G* 34 (Jan 1968), 376-381.

203. Price, Jonathan. "The Rough Way Up the Mountain (Typographical Tribute to the Spirit of Charles Ives)," *Mus Ed J* 55 (Oct 1968), 38-45; reprinted from *Yale Alumni Mag* (Apr 1968).

204. Rich, Alan. "The Ives Canon," *SR* 51 (Apr 27, 1968), 75.

205. Marshall, Dennis. "Charles Ives' Quotations: Manner or Substance," *PNM* 6, No. 2 (1968), 45.

206. Drew, James. "Information, Space, and a New Time-Dialectic," *J Mus Theory* 12, No. 1 (1968), 95.
207. Daniel, Oliver. "Ives Is a Four-Letter Word," *SR* 51 (May 25, 1968), 59.
208. Shirley, Wayne. "Challenge of Ives Brings a New Round of Challengers," *HiFi* 18 (Jun 1968), 80-81.
209. Barlow, Jon. "The Music of Charles Ives," *Mus Opin* 91 (Jun 1968), 487.
210. "Five Takeoffs," *Mus J* 26 (May 1968), 44; *HiFi/MA* 18 (Jun 1968), MA17.
211. Paap, Wouter. "Charles Ives, een herontdekt Componist," *Mens en Mel* 23 (Jul 1968), 197-200.
212. "Charles Ives Society Founded in Holland," *Sonorum Speculum*, Donemus, Amsterdam, No. 35 (Summer 1968), 13-16.
213. Salzman, Eric. "Charles Ives, American," *Commentary* 46 (Aug 1968), 37-43.
214. Eger, Joseph. "1967-1968: Ives and Beatles!" *Mus J* 26 (Sep 1968), 46.
215. Goodman, John. "An Urbanized Thoreau," *New Leader* 51 (Sep 23, 1968), 23.
216. Dickinson, Peter. "Charles Ives," *Mus in Ed* 32, No. 331 (1968), 138-140.
217. "Peer," *MH* 19, No. 4 (1968), 194.
218. Miller, Philip L. "Songs by Charles Ives, and Others," *Am Rec G* 35 (Dec 1968), 305.
219. *NYT* (Mar 30, 1969), sec. 2, p. 19:1; (Jun 8, 1969), sec. 2, p. 19:4.
220. Moore, David W. "John Kirkpatrick: Concord Revisited," *Am Rec G* 35 (Mar 1969), 546-547.
221. Cohn, Arthur. "Alan Mandel Plays All Twenty-Seven of the Piano Works of Ives," *Am Rec G* 35 (Mar 1969), 548-549.
222. Romano, Jacobo. "Retratos de musicos americanos: Charles Edward Ives," *Buenos Aires Mus* 24, No. 398 (1969), 3.
223. Jensen, Joergen I. "Charles Ives—en musikalsk modernist," *Dansk Mus* 44, No. 1 (1969), 13-19.
224. Evett, Ronald. "Shadow and Substance in Ives," *Atlantic* 223 (May 1969), 110-111.
225. Bach, Eleanor, and Robert Offergeld. "An Experiment in Astromusicology," *Stereo R* 23 (Jul 1969), 73.
226. Jacobson, Bernard. "The 'In' Composers: Mahler, Ives, Nielsen, Sibelius, Vivaldi, Berlioz—Are They Permanent Classics or Just Temporary Fads?" *HiFi/MA* 19 (Jul 1969), 54-57.
227. Vermeulen, Ernest. "Compositions by Louis Andriessen and Peter Schat," *Son Spec* 35 (Summer 1969), 1-12.
228. Tippett, Michael K. "The American Tradition," *Am Mus Dgt* 1 (Oct 1969), 21.
229. Burk, James M. "The Wind Music of Charles Ives," *Instrument* 24 (Oct 1969), 36-40.
230. Frankenstein, Alfred. "New Ivesian Discoveries," *HiFi/MA* 20, sec. 1 (Mar 1970), 92.
231. Tipton, Julius R. "Some Observations on the Choral Style of Charles Ives," *Am Choral R* 12, No. 3 (1970), 99-105.
232. Davidson, Colleen. "Winston Churchill and Charles Ives: The Professive Experience in Literature and Music," *Student Musicology* 3 (1968-1869), 168-194; 4 (1970-1971), 154-180.
233. Voss, Egon. "Bemerkungen zur Musik von Charles E. Ives (1874-1954)," *Schallplatte U. Kir* 2 (1970), 145-148.
234. Davidson, Audrey. "Transcendental Unity in the Works of Charles Ives," *Amer Q* 22 (Sep 1970), 35-44.
235. Johnston, Benjamin, and Edward G. Kobrin. "Phase la," *Source* 4, No. 1 (1970), 27-45.
236. Cohn, Arthur. "Playing and Conducting That Simply Could Not Be Bettered," *Am Rec G* 37 (Nov 1970), 148-151.
237. Kay, Norman. "Aspects of Copland's Development," *Tempo* 95 (Winter 1970-1971), 26.
238. Mellers, Wilfrid. "Homage to Aaron Copland," *Tempo* 95 (Winter 1970-1971), 2-4.
239. Rakhmanova, M. "Charl'z Ayvs," *Sovet Muz* 35 (Jan 1971), 97-108.
240. Miller, Philip L. "Gunther Schuller, A Very Right Man to Interpret Ives," *Am Rec G* 37 (Feb 1971), 353.

241. "The Yale-Princeton Football Game," *BMI* (Feb 1971), 13.

242. "Instrumental Works," *Am Rec G* 37 (Feb 1971), 353.

243. Dujmic, Dunja. "The Musical Transcendentalism of Charles Ives," *Int R Aesthetics & Soc Mus* 2, No. 1 (1971), 89-95.

244. Boody, Charles G., and Margaret Snell. "Report from Minneapolis: The Charles Ives Festival, Spring 1970," *Current Musicology* 11 (1971), 57-58.

245. Miller, Philip Lieson. "House of Many Mansions: The Songs of Charles Ives and the American Experience," *Am Rec G* 37 (May 1971), 563.

246. Rosa, Alfred F. "Charles Ives: Music, Transcendentalism, and Politics," *New England Q* 44 (Sep 1971), 433-443.

247. Goudie, Andrea. "Exploring the Broad Margins: Charles Ives's Interpretation of Thoreau," *Midwest Q* 13 (Apr 1972), 309-317.

248. Greenfield, Edward. "Ives from England; Second Symphony, Conducted by Bernard Herrmann," *HiFi* 22 (Apr 1972), 20.

249. Konold, Wulf. "Schallplatten: Werke von Charles Ives," *Musica* 26, No. 3 (1972), 296.

250. ———"Neue Musik in der Neuen Welt; der Komponist Charles Ives," *Musica* 26, No. 3 (1972), 239-244.

251. Kolter, Horst. "Zur Kompositionstechnik von Charles Edward Ives," *NZ* 133 (Oct 1972), 559-567.

252. Bader, Yvette. "The Chamber Music of Charles Edward Ives," *MR* 33, No. 4 (1972), 292-299.

253. Perlis, Vivian. "Ives and Oral History," *Notes* 28, No. 4 (1972), 629-642.

254. *NYT* (Jan 28, 1973), 49:4; (Jun 3, 1973), sec. 2, p. 15:5; (Aug 26, 1973), sec. 2, p. 13:1.

255. Ringger, Rolf Urs. "Charles Ives—zwischen Folksong und Utopie," *Schweiz Mus* 113, No. 1 (1973), 1-7.

256. Gilbert, Steven Edward. "The Ultra-Modern 'Idiom': A Survey of New Music," *PNM* 12, Nos. 1-2 (1973-1974), 282-284.

257. Morgan, Robert Porter. "Rewriting Music History; Second Thoughts on Ives and Varèse," *Mus News* 3, No. 1 (1973), 3-12; No. 2 (1973), 15-23.

258. Wuellner, Guy Snyder. "The Smaller Piano Works of Charles Ives," *Am Mus Tcr* 22, No. 5 (1973), 14-16.

259. Koch, Gerhard R. "Charles Ives, Musik als reale Utopie," *HiFi Stereophonie* 12 (Jul 1973), 689-692.

260. Dujmic, Dunja. "Glaxbeni transcendentalizam Charles Ivesa," *ZVUK* 2 (Summer 1973), 125-129.

261. Battisti, Frank L., and Donald R. Hunsberger. "The Wind Music of Charles Ives," *Instrument* 28 (Aug 1973), 32-34.

262. Small, Christopher. "Words on Music—Ives and Varèse," *Mus in Ed* 37, No. 362 (1973), 187-188.

263. Isham, Howard. "The Musical Thinking of Charles Ives," *J Aesthetics* 31, No. 3 (1973), 395-404.

264. *NYT* (Mar 6, 1974), 25:2; "Career and Music," *NYT* (Apr 21, 1974), sec. 6, p. 12.

265. Wooldridge, David. "A Cultural Heritage Is Any Nation's Defense," *Sym News* 25, No. 2 (1974), 13-14.

266. Ziegler, Sister Mirelda. "Ives: First American Vanguardist," *Mus J* 32 (Apr 1974), 20.

267. "Charles E. Ives Centennial—20th Century American Music Pioneer," *Pan Pipes* 66, No. 2 (1974), 28-29.

268. Clark, Sondra Rae. "Element of Choice in Ives's Concord Sonata," *MQ* 60 (1974), 167-186.

269. *NYT* (Apr 1, 1974), 38:1; (Apr 13, 1974), 17:2; (Jun 18, 1974), 32:3; (Jul 5, 1974), 12:1; (Jul 6, 1974), 14:2; (Sep 5, 1974), 45:2; (Oct 21, 1974), 50:1; (Nov 19, 1974), 52:1.

270. Schonberg, Howard C. "Natural American, Natural Rebel, Natural Avant-Gardist," *NYT Mag* (Apr 21, 1974), 12-13.

271.   Hamilton, David. "Centenary Concert in Danbury, Conn.," *New Yorker* 50 (Jul 22, 1974), 73-74.

272.   "Band Music," *Instrument* 29, No. 2 (1974), 60-62.

273.   Daniel, Oliver. "The Charles Ives Centennial—A Personal Memoir Celebrates the Man and His Music," *BMI* 3 (1974), 32-35.

274.   Bolcom, William E. "The Old Curmudgeon's Corner," *Mus News* 4, No. 4 (1974), 20-21.

275.   Wells, William B. "Sacred Choral Octavos," *Notes* 30, No. 3 (1974), 634-640.

276.   Deutsch, Nina. "Ives of the World: Seen and Unseen," *Mus J* 32 (Sep 1974), 10.

277.   Serebrier, José. "Ives: The Most Difficult Ever," *Mus J* 32 (Sep 1974), 14-15.

278.   Middleton, Richard. "Ives and Schoenberg: An English View," *SR/World* 2 (Sep 21, 1974), 39-41.

279.   Bunke, Jerome S. "The Fabric of Existence Weaves Itself Whole," *Mus J* 32 (Sep 1974), 12-13.

280.   Chase, Gilbert. "Charles Ives and American Culture," *HiFi/MA* 24 (Oct 1974), MA17-19.

281.   *NYT* (Oct 20, 1974), sec. 2, p. 21:3; sec. 7, p. 3.

282.   Cowell, Stanley. "More Than Something Just Usual," *HiFi/MA* 24 (Oct 1974), MA14-16.

283.   Norris, Christopher. "American Pioneer," *Mus & Mus* 23 (Oct 1974), 36-38.

284.   Morgan, Robert Porter. "Recordings of Charles Ives's Music; with Discography," *HiFi* 24 (Oct 1974), 70-76.

285.   "Orchestral Music," *Mus Ed J* 61 (Oct 1974), 29-41; 64-70.

286.   Morgan, Robert Porter. "Let's Hear It from Ives," *HiFi* 24 (Oct 1974), 79-81.

287.   "Mini-Festivals," *NYT* (Oct 6, 1974), sec. 2, p. 17:1; (Oct 10, 1974), 62:1; (Oct 11, 1974), 23:1; (Oct 12, 1974), 19:1; (Oct 13, 1974), 78:5; (Oct 14, 1974), 43:1; (Oct 20, 1974), sec. 2, p. 21:1.

288.   Dickinson, Peter. "A New Perspective for Ives," *MT* 115 (Oct 1974), 836-838.

289.   "Charles Ives: Notes in Stone," *Christianity Today* 19 (Oct 11, 1974), 31.

290.   "Charles Ives: October 20, 1874-May 19, 1954: A Symposium," *Mus Ed J* 61 (Oct 1974), 22-71.

291.   Stover, Harold. "Charles Ives and Us, A Guest Essay," *Diap* 65 (Oct 1974), 2.

292.   "Charles Ives Published (Vivian Perlis)," *FoF* 34 (Nov 2, 1974), 906B2.

293.   "Connecticut Yankee," *NW* 84 (Nov 4, 1974), 71.

294.   "Ives the Innovator," *Time* 104 (Nov 4, 1974), 35.

295.   Porter, Andrew. "Songs His Father Taught Him," *New Yorker* 50 (Nov 4, 1974), 187-190.

296.   Hamilton, David. "Music," *Nation* 219 (Nov 16, 1974), 507-508.

297.   McCord, Phyllis. "Land of Ives," *Holiday* 55 (Nov 1974), 28-29.

298.   Wooldridge, David. "Reply with Rejoinder," *HiFi/MA* 24 (Dec 1974), MA18-20.

299.   Wooldridge, David, and John Kirkpatrick. "The New Ives Biography: A Disagreement," *HiFi/MA* 24 (Dec 1974), MA18-20.

300.   Serebrier, José. "Unplayable Fourth Symphony of Ives," *Am Mus Tcr* 24 (Jan 1975), 8-10.

301.   ——————"Ives for Orchestra," *Instrument* 29 (Feb 1975), 40-41.

302.   "Concert," *NYT* (Feb 17, 1975), 31:1.

303.   Fleming, Shirley. "Of Ives, Elephants, and Polish Independence: Centennial Festival-Conference in New York and New Haven," *HiFi/MA* 25 (Feb 1975), MA26-29.

304.   Palmer, Bob. "Perspectives; What is American Music?" *Down Bt* 42 (Feb 27, 1975), 11.

305.   Mayer, Martin. "Recordings," *Esquire* 83 (Mar 1975), 48.

306.   Yellin, Victor F. "Charles Ives Festival-Conference," *MQ* 61 (1975), 295-299.

307.   Muser, Frani. "Charles Ives Remembered, by Vivian Perlis; a Review," *MQ* 61 (Jul 1975), 485-488.

308.   —————— "Charles Ives and the American Mind by R. S. Perry; a Review," *MQ* 61 (1975), 488-490.

309.   "To Make Film Biography on Life of Ives," *NYT* (Sep 4, 1975), 32:2.

310. Ward, Charles W. "Charles Ives' Concept of Music," *Current Musicology* 18 (1974), 114-119.

311. Crunden, Robert M. "Charles Ives' Innovative Nostalgia," *Choral J* 15, No. 4 (1974), 5-12.

312. Koprowski, Richard. "In Tribute to Charles Edward Ives on the 100th Anniversary of His Birth," *Current Musicology* 18 (1974), 69-119; 133-134.

313. Perison, Harry. "The Quarter-Tone System of Charles Ives," *Current Musicology* 18 (1974), 96-104.

314. Tick, Judith. "Ragtime and the Music of Charles Ives," *Current Musicology* 18 (1974), 103-113.

315. Archabal, Nina. "Report from Minneapolis: Ives Festivals in Minneapolis, Spring 1971 and Spring 1972," *Current Musicology* 18 (1974), 43-45.

316. Gratovich, Eugene. "The Violin Sonatas of Charles Ives," *Strad* 85 (Dec 1974), 471.

317. Hinson, G. Maurice. "The Solo Piano Works of Charles Ives (1874-1954," *Piano Q* 23, No. 88 (1974-1975), 32-35.

318. Childs, R. Barney. "Some Anniversaries (Ives and Schoenberg)," *ASUC* 9-10 (1974-1975), 13-27.

319. Babcock, Michael J. "Ives' 'Thoreau': A Point of Order," *ASUC* 9-10 (1974-1975), 89-102.

320. Jack, A. "Ives (Centennial Celebration)," *Mus & Mus* 23 (Jan 1975), 52.

321. "Spotlight Review: The 100th Anniversary," *Down Bt* 42 (Jan 16, 1975), 32.

322. "Yale-Princeton Bands Revived Ives at Halftime," *School Mus* 46 (Jan 1975), 37.

323. Schwarz, E. "Directions in American Music Since the Second World War, Part I—1945-1960," *Mus Ed J* 61 (Feb 1975), 29-39.

324. Anderson, William. "Composer Charles Ives Enters History," *Stereo R* 34 (Mar 1975), 4.

325. Daniel, Oliver. "An Appreciation," *Mus Club Mag* 54, No. 3 (1975), 28.

326. Slonimsky, Nicolas. "Charles Ives as I Remember Him," *Choral J* 15, No. 5 (1975), 15.

327. "Ives Festivals-Conferences," *Pan Pipes* 62, No. 2 (1975), 28.

328. "Charles Edward Ives—Ideal American or Social Critic? " *Current Musicology* 19 (1975), 37-44.

329. Wallach, Laurence D. "The Ives Conference: A Word from the Floor," *Current Musicology* 19 (1975), 32-36.

330. Kerr, Hugh H. "Report from Miami: Ives Centennial Festival," *Current Musicology* 19 (1975), 41.

331. Lamb, Gordon H. "Interview with Robert Shaw (or the Music of Charles Ives)," *Choral J* 15, No. 8 (1975), 5-7.

332. "Can You Play Over 100 Songs by Ives on One Program? " *Triangle* 69, No. 4 (1975), 9.

333. Palisca, Claude V. "Report on the Musicological Year 1974 in the United States," *Acta Mus* 47, No. 2 (1975), 283-289.

334. Saylor, Bruce. "Looking Backwards: Reflections on Nostalgia in the Musical Avant-Garde," *Centerpoint* 1, No. 3 (1975), 4.

335. Smith, M. "Music Tells the Story about Life in Minnesota: Minnesota Centennial Ives Festival," *School Mus* 47 (Oct 1975), 44-45.

336. "Lenox Arts Center: 'Ives' ('Meeting Mr. Ives')," *HiFi/MA* 25 (Dec 1975), MA26.

337. "Prophets, Seers and Sages: An M M Guide to the Major Movements in Avant Garde Music," *Mel Maker* 51 (Apr 24, 1976), 26.

338. Gillespie, Don C. "John Becker, Musical Crusader of Saint Paul: Address, June 22, 1974," *MQ* 62 (1976), 195-217.

339. von Buchau, Stephanie. "San Francisco ('Meeting Mr. Ives')," *Opera N* 40 (May 1976), 39.

340. Vermeulen, Ernest. "Holland Festival presenteert Amerikaanse musiek," *Mens en Mel* 31 (Jun 1976), 161-167.

341. Lyles, Jean Caffey. "Charles Ives's America," *Christian Century* 93 (Jun 23, 1976), 589-591.

342. Serebrier, José. "Charles Ives—A Composer for All Directions," *Stereo R* 35 (Jul 1975), 48-51.

343. Engen, David P. "The Choral Psalms of Charles Ives: A Performer's Analysis of Psalm 90 (Includes List of Church and Organ Music)," *Church Mus* 1 (1976), 2-27.

344. Carter, Elliott. "Documents of a Friendship with Ives," *Tempo* 117 (Jun 1976), 2-10.

345. Morgan, Robert Porter. "De Gaetani's Ives: Up to All Expectations," *HiFi/MA* 26 (Aug 1976), 84.

346. Freed, R. "Songs of Charles Ives: A Listening Experience One is as Eager to Share as to Repeat," *Stereo R* 37 (Sep 1976), 86.

347. "Film Biography of Charles Ives," *Instrument* 31 (Oct 1976), 82.

348. "Composer in Focus," *BMI* (Winter 1976), 24.

349. Bloomingdale, Wayne. "Must a Song Always be a Song? " *Am Mus Tcr* 26, No. 5 (1977), 14.

350. Starr, Lawrence. "Charles Ives: the Next Hundred Years—Towards a Method of Analyzing Music," *MR* 38, No. 2 (1977), 101-111.

351. Blum, Robert Stephen. "Ives' Position in Social and Musical History," *MQ* 63 (1977), 459-482.

352. "Charles Ives Film Biography," *NATS* 34, No. 3 (1978), 54.

353. Morgan, Robert Porter. "Ives and Mahler: Mutual Responses at the End of an Era," *Nine Cen Mus* 2, No. 1 (1978), 72-81.

354. Elson, James. "The Songs of Charles Ives (1874-1954)," *NATS* 35, No. 1 (1978), 9-11.

355. Yates, Peter. "Charles Ives," *Arts and Architecture* (Sep 1944), 20, 40; (Feb 1950), 13; (May 1950), 8; (Oct 1954), 6, 32.

References to Works by Charles Ives

The number preceding the title indicates the number of the composition as listed in Section II.

57. The Anti-Abolitionist Riots: *Notes* 6 (1948-1949), 486-487; *MC* 139 (Apr 1949), 23; *Mus News* 41 (Aug 1949), 19.

7. Calcium Light Night: *Notes* 11 (Sep 1954), 607; *HiFi/MA* 18 (Dec 1968), MA14.

69. Celestial Country: *Mus J* 30 (May 1972), 50; *MQ* 60 (1974), 500-508.

20. Celestial Railroad (arr. from Symphony No. 4, second movement): *MC* 143 (Feb 15, 1951), 67.

9. Central Park: *MQ* 41 (1955), 88; *CohCT*, 136; *HitMU*, 165; *MelMN*, 46.

86. Chanson de Florian: *Notes* 7 (1949-1950), 636-637; *MA* 70 (Sep 1950), 26; *Mus Club Mag* 30 (Feb 1951), 19.

82. h 6) The Children's Hour: *MQ* 19 (1933), 53.
    Choral Works: *HiFi R* 18 (Jan 1967), 74; *Choral J* 15, No. 2 (1974), 12-13; *Mus Ed J* 61 (Oct 1974), 48-52.

21. Chromâtimelôdtune: *NYT* (Dec 8, 1962), 31:1.

15. b. Decoration Day: *MA* 81 (Apr 1961), 65; *MM* 16 (Dec 1967), 46.

61. Eight Studies: *Mus J* 26 (May 1968), 44; *HiFi/MA* 18 (Jun 1968), MA17.

81. Psalms: *BMI* (Jul 1966), 7.

15. c. Fourth of July: *PNM* 4, No. 1 (1965), 53; *MR* 27, No. 4 (1966), 331; *MM* 15 (Oct 1966), 42.

33. From the Steeples and the Mountains: *NYT* (Jul 31, 1965), 11:2; *Down Bt* 32 (Sep 9, 1965), 38; *Mus J* 23 (Sep 1965), 88; *BuffaloPPN* (Feb 20, 1966), 8; *SFSPN* (Feb 1968), 22a; *HiFi/MA* 24 (Sep 1974), MA33-36.

2. Fugue in Four Keys on "The Shining Shore": *New Haven SPN* (Oct 1973), 7; *Mus J* 32 (Mar 1974), 8; *Mus Ed J* 60 (Apr 1974), 125.

13. The Gong on the Hook and Ladder: *NYPPN* (Jan 21, 1967), A.

49. c. Hallowe'en: *MA* 69 (Dec 1, 1949), 28; *Notes* 7 (Jun 1950), 432.

71. Three Harvest Home Chorales: *Notes* 6 (Jun 1949), 486-487; *HitMU*, 163.
15. Holidays: *Symphony* 8 (May 1954), 7; *MC* 150 (Nov 1, 1954), 42; *HiFi/MA* 17 (Sep 1967), 79; *Melos* 37 (Feb 1970), 53; *Am Mus Dgt* 1, No. 6 (1970), 23; *NYT* (Dec 13, 1971), 54:1; *HitMU*, 153.
10. In the Cage: *MQ* 19 (1933), 53.
95. It Strikes Me That: *Mus Club Mag* 30 (Feb 1951), 19.
34. Largo (vln, clar, pno): *Notes* 11 (1953-1954), 157; *CohCT*, 141.
19. Orchestral Suite No. 2: *Melos* 33 (Apr 1966), 122; *Mus U Ges* 16 (May 1966), 338; *ChiSPN* (Feb 11, 1967), 34; *BMI* (Apr 1967), 14; *Buffalo PPN* (Apr 20, 1969), 21-23; *HiFi/MA* 19 (Aug 1969), MA12; *ZVUK* 101 (1970), 50; *Mus & Mus* 20 (Nov 1971), 58.
24. Orchestral Suite No. 3: *NYT* (Dec 8, 1962), 31:1.
    Organ Music: *Clavier* 13, No. 7 (1974), 29-30; *Mus Ed J* 61 (Oct 1974), 64-70.
    Piano Music: *HiFi/MA* 18 (Jun 1968), 81; *BMI* (Jun 1968), 19; *HiFi R* 21 (Aug 1968), 72; *Clavier* 13, No. 7 (1974), 14-25, 31-32; *Mus Ed J* 61 (Oct 1974), 53-57, 58-63.
9. b. The Pond: *RochPPN* (Feb 12, 1970), 108-111.
70. Processional: Let There be Light: *Notes* 13 (1955-1956), 349.
80. Psalm 24: *Notes* 14 (Sep 1957), 618.
12. Robert Browning Overture: *NYT* (Oct 15, 1956), 28:1; *MA* 76 (Nov 1, 1956), 23; *MQ* 43 (1957), 90-93; *ACA-Bul* 6, No. 2 (1957), 21; *Notes* 17 (1959-1960), 857; *NYHT* (Oct 3, 1963); *MA* 83 (Nov 1963), 24; *HiFi R* 16 (May 1966), 69; *ChiSPN* (Jan 14, 1967), 34; *HiFi/MA* 17 (Mar 1967), MA16; *HitMU*, 154.
14. Over the Pavements: *Notes* 12 (1954-1955), 326; *MQ* 41 (1955), 87; *ClSPN* (Oct 28, 1965), 34; *CohCT*, 137; *HitMU*, 154.
10. Set of Pieces for Theatre Orchestra: *Mus & Mus* 20 (Mar 1972), 66; *Mus Opin* 95 (Mar 1972), 295-296.
56. Some South-Paw Pitching!: *Notes* 6 (1948-1949), 486; *MC* 139 (Apr 15, 1949), 23; *Mus News* 41 (Aug 1949), 19; *HitMU*, 164.
58. Sonata for Piano No. 1: *MQ* 35 (1949), 458, 461; *MQ* 39 (1953), 323-325; *MQ* 40 (1954), 471, 473; *Notes* 12 (1954-1955), 331; *PNM* 1, No. 2 (1963), 148; *PNM* 4, No. 1 (1965), 10, 158; *HitMU*, 152; *MelMN*, 57.
62. Sonata for Piano No. 2 (Concord): *MQ* 19 (1933), 51; *MM* 16, No. 2 (1938-1939), 109; *MM* 16, No. 3 (1938-1939), 172; *MQ* 31 (1945), 109; *MQ* 34 (1948), 3; *MQ* 35 (1949), 458; *MA* 82 (Jun 1962), 27; *ACA-Bul* 10, No. 2 (1962), 17; *HiFi* 12 (Apr 1962), 62; *Am Rec G* 28 (Jun 1962), 802; *NYT* (May 27, 1962), sec. 2, p. 18; *Am Mus Dgt* 1 (Oct 1969), 5-6; *MQ* 60 (1974), 167-186; *ChaAM*, 418; *CohCT*, 138; *EweCB*, 195; *HanIT*, 78; *HitMU*, 148, 168.
    Sonatas for Violin and Piano: *HiFi/MA* 16 (Apr 1966), 152; *MM* 16 (Jun 1968), 45.
39. Sonata No. 1 (vln, pno): *MQ* 39 (1953), 323; *MC* 148 (Sep 1953), 33; *Notes* 11 (1953-1954), 156; *HitMU*, 169.
46. Sonata No. 2 (vln, pno): *MA* 71 (Oct 1951), 31; *Repertoire* 1 (Nov 1951), 112; *Notes* 9 (1951-1952), 329-330; *Mus Club Mag* 32 (Jan 1953), 32; *CohCT*, 139; *MelMN*, 59.
52. Sonata No. 3 (vln, pno): *MA* 71 (Oct 1951), 31; *ML* 33 (Jan 1952), 91-92; *MQ* 39 (1953), 324; *CohCT*, 139.
54. Sonata No. 4 (vln, pno): *MM* 19, No. 2 (1941-1942), 115; *MQ* 34 (1948), 11; *MelMN*, 60.
82. Songs (114): *MM* 11, No. 2 (1933-1934), 50; *MQ* 19 (1933), 55; *Am Rec G* 35 (Dec 1968), 305; *Mus Ed J* 56 (Mar 1970), 116; *MelMN*, 40; *StevHS*, 431.
82. b. Fourteen Songs: *Notes* 13 (Mar 1956), 354.
82. f. Ten Songs: *MC* 148 (Nov 15, 1953), 26; *Notes* 11 (1953-1954), 449-450; *MA* 74 (Nov. 1, 1954), 26; *Am Rec G* 35 (Dec 1968), 305.
82. i. Twelve Songs: *Notes* 13 (1955-1956), 354; *HitMU*, 148, 151, 155, 162.
82. i. 1) August: *MQ* 19 (1933), 55.
38. Space and Duration: *PNM* 2, No. 1 (1963), 7.
35. Scherzo: *Notes* 16 (1958-1959), 314.

31. String Quartet No. 1: *NYT* (Apr 25, 1957), 35:4; *ACA-Bul* 6, No. 4 (1957), 23; *Notes* 21 (1963-1964), 453; *MA* 84 (Feb 1964), 40; *ACA-Bul* 13, No. 1 (1965), 27; *HitMU*, 169.
51. String Quartet No. 2: *Notes* 12 (1954-1955), 489; *CohCT*, 141; *HitMU*, 151; *MelMN*, 57.
    Symphonies: *MM* 22, No. 4 (1944-1945), 215; *HiFi/MA* 18 (Jun 1968), 80; *Audio* 52 (Jul 1968), 47; *MT* 125 (Dec 1968), 1126; *HitMU*, 170-173.
 3. Symphony No. 1: *MM* 22, No. 4 (1944-1945), 215; *Washington Post* (Apr 27, 1953); *MC* 147 (Jul 1953), 29; *Am Rec G* 32 (Jul 1966), 1032; *POPN* (Feb 10, 1967), 17-21; *Houston SPN* (Jan 27, 1969), 15-17.
 4. Symphony No. 2: *MM* 22, No. 4 (1944-1945), 215; *MA* 71 (Mar 1951), 32; *MQ* 37 (1951), 399-402; *NYPPN* (Feb 22, 1951); *NYT* (Feb 23, 1951), 33:4; *Time* 57 (Mar 5, 1951), 72; *NYT* (Mar 11, 1951), sec. 2, p. 6:3; *MC* 143 (Mar 15, 1951), 12; *MA* 71 (Mar 1951), 32-33; *Int Mus* 49 (Mar 1951), 10; *MC* 143 (May 1, 1951), 29; *MA* 71 (Aug 1951), 30; *Notes* 9 (1951-1952), 499-500; *Pan Pipes* 44 (Jan 1952), 8; *SFSPN* (Feb 24, 1955), 437; *NYPPN* (Oct 2, 1958); *NYT* (Sep 25, 1960), sec. 2, p. 21; *HiFi* 10 (Nov 1960), 75; *Am Rec G* 28 (Dec 1961), 302; *NatlSPN* (Oct 23, 1962), 18; *BSPN* (Nov 2, 1962), 334; *PNM* 2, No. 2 (1964), 160; *ClSPN* (Nov 10, 1966), 282; *MR* 28, No. 2 (1967), 102-111; *Dallas SPN* (Sep 28, 1968), 11-23; *ML* 52, No. 1 (1971), 39-45; *HiFi/MA* 22 (Apr 1972), 20; *SR* 55, No. 37 (1972), 57-58; *Stereo R* 33 (Nov 1974), 134-135; *CohCT*, 134.
 5. Symphony No. 3: *MM* 22, No. 4 (1944-1945), 215; *NYT* (Apr 6, 1946), 10:4; *SFSPN* (Feb 7, 1952), 333; *ACA-Bul* 5, No. 2 (1955), 22; *MQ* 42 (1956), 122; *SFSPN* (Jan 25, 1961), 11; *NYPPN* (Nov 25, 1965), B-C; *ChiSPN* (Apr 17, 1969), 13-19; *CohCT*, 135; *EweCB*, 193; *MelMN*, 58.
20. Symphony No. 4: *MQ* 19 (1933), 51, 57; *MM* 22, No. 4 (1944-1945), 215; *NYT* (Apr 13, 1965), 33:3; (Apr 25, 1965), sec. 2, p. 13:1; (Apr 26, 1965), 33:3; (Apr 27, 1965), 29:1; (May 2, 1965), sec. 2, p. 11:1; (Jun 14, 1965), 44:2; *Time* (May 7, 1965); *New Yorker* 41 (May 8, 1965), 169; *SR* 48 (May 15, 1965), 32; *Stereo R* 24 (Jul 1965); *HiFi R* 15 (Jul 1965), 55-58; *MM* 13 (Jul 1965), 43; *HiFi/MA* 15 (Jul 1965), 96-97; *Melos* 32 (Jul-Aug 1965), 271; *HiFi/MA* 15 (Nov 1965), 83; *Ruch Muz* 9, No. 10 (1965), 14; *Mus J Annual* 23 (1965), 93; *BMI* (Jul 1965), 17; *HiFi R* 15 (Nov 1965), 81; *Am Rec G* 32 (Nov 1965), 220-223; *Melos* 33 (Feb 1966), 60; *MQ* 52 (1966), 1-16; *ChiSPN* (Mar 31, 1966), 15; *MM* 14 (Aug 1966), 28; *New Statesman* 72 (Sep 30, 1966), 489-490; *MM* 15 (Nov 1966), 44; *RochSPN* (Jan 12, 1967), 77; *POPN* (Feb 24, 1967), 17-22; *Mus & Mus* 19 (Sep 1970), 56; *Mus Opin* 93 (Sep 1970), 631; *PNM* 10, No. 1 (1971), 291-303; *Mus J* 32 (Sep 1974), 14-15; *NYT* (Oct 14, 1974), 43:1; *Mus Ed J* 61 (Oct 1974); *Sym News* 25, No. 5 (1974), 11-12; *Clavier* 13, No. 7 (1974); *Stereo R* 33 (Nov 1974), 134-135; *MelMN*, 58.
15. d. Thanksgiving: *NYT* (Apr 25, 1963), 39:5; *Down Bt* 31 (Jun 18, 1964); *MT* 125 (Jun 1968), 562.
78. They are There: *Notes* 20 (1962-1963), 565.
55. Three-page Sonata: *Notes* 6 (1948-1949), 486; *MQ* 35 (1949), 459; *R Mus de Suisse Romonde* 22, No. 3 (1969), 3; *Melos* 39, No. 5 (1972), 277-279; *HitMU*, 164.
16. Three Places in New England: *BSPN* (Feb 13, 1948); *MQ* 34 (1948), 251; *MQ* 35 (1949), 287; *ACA-Bul* 3, No. 1 (1953), 17; *Rassegna Musicale* 26 (Jan 1956), 51; *Musica* 12 (Jun 1958), 340; *PNM* 2, No. 2 (1964), 160; *Detroit SPN* (Dec 8, 1966), 235; *Chi-SPN* (Mar 18, 1967), 32; *Melos* 34 (Sep 1967), 313; *RochSPN* (Feb 12, 1970), 108-111; *Am Rec G* 37 (Nov 1970), 148-151; *NYT* (Dec 24, 1973), 20:1; *CohCT*, 135; *EweCB*, 194; *HitMU*, 153, 155.
60. Three Protests: *HitMU*, 164.
63. Three Quarter-tone Pieces: *MA* 83 (Nov 1963), 37; *Am Rec G* 34 (Aug 1968), 1086-1088.
11. Tone Roads No. 1: *Notes* 7 (1949-1950), 432; *MC* 141 (Jan 1, 1950), 44; *HitMU*, 167.
18. Tone Roads No. 3: *MC* 146 (Dec 1, 1952), 34; *MA* 73 (Jan 1, 1953), 24.
48. Trio for Violin, Cello, Piano: *MA* 75 (Jul 1955), 25; *Notes* 13 (Jun 1956), 527; *MA* 80 (Feb 1960), 264; *Am Rec G* 33 (Oct 1966), 142.

8. The Unanswered Question: *Notes* 11 (1953-1954), 607; *MQ* 41 (1955), 87; *NYT* (Aug 26, 1959), 25:1; (Sep 13, 1959), sec. 2, p. 11:1; *PNM* 1, No. 2 (1963), 184; *Am Mus Dgt* 1 (Oct 1969), 21; *CohCT*, 137; *HitMU*, 165; *MelMN*, 46.

23. Universe Symphony (unfinished): *MQ* 41 (1955), 254.

64. 65. Variations on "America" and Prelude on "Adeste Fideles" (organ): *Notes* 7 (1949-1950), 446.

22. Variations on "America": *MC* 144 (Nov 15, 1951), 30; *NatlSPN* (Oct 11, 1966), 21; *Notes* 23 (1966-1967), 157; *MA* 84 (Jul 1964), 36.

Dissertations about Charles Ives and His Works

1. Albert, Thomas R. *The Harmonic Language of Charles Ives' "Concord Sonata."* University of Illinois, 1974.

2. Arlton, Dean L. *American Piano Sonatas of the Twentieth Century: Selective Analyses and Annotated Index.* Columbia University, 1958.

3. Ausubel, Hillel. *The Effect of Chromaticism on Tonality: as Found in Selected Compositions from the Period between 1890 and 1910.* Columbia University, 1953.

4. Badolato, James V. *The Four Symphonies of Charles Ives: A Critical, Analytical Study of the Musical Style of Charles Ives.* Catholic University of America, 1978.

5. Brooks, William F. *Sources and Errata List for Charles Ives' Symphony No. 4, Movement II.* University of Illinois, 1976.

6. Bruderer, Conrad. *A Study of the Etudes of Charles Ives.* Indiana University, 1969.

7. Call, William A. *A Study of the Transcendental Aesthetic Theories of John S. Dwight and Charles E. Ives and the Relationship of These Theories to Their Respective Work as Music Critic and Composer.* University of Illinois, 1971.

8. Carlson, Paul B. *An Historical Background and Stylistic Analysis of Three Twentieth Century Compositions for Violin and Piano.* University of Missouri, 1965.

9. Clark, Sondra Rae S. *The Evolving "Concord Sonata": A Study of Choices and Variants in the Music of Charles Ives.* Stanford University, 1972.

10. Cordes, Joan Kunselman. *A New American Development in Music: Some Characteristic Features Extending from the Legacy of Charles Ives.* Louisiana State University, 1976.

11. Easter, Stanley E. *A Study Guide for the Performance of Twentieth Century Music from Selected Ballet Repertoires for Trombones and Tuba.* Columbia University, 1969.

12. Eiseman, David. *Charles Ives and the European Symphonic Tradition: A Historical Reappraisal.* University of Illinois, 1972.

13. Frank, Alan Robert. *The Music of Charles Ives: For Presentation in the Listening Program of the Secondary School.* Columbia University, 1969.

14. Frantz, Donald H., Jr. *Search for Significant Form, 1905-1915: An Evaluation of the Symbols of Tradition and Revolt in American Literature, Painting, and Music.* University of Southern California, 1960.

15. Gaburo, Kenneth L. *Studies in Pitch Symmetry in Twentieth Century Music.* University of Illinois, 1962.

16. Gratovich, Eugene. *The Sonatas for Violin and Piano by Charles E. Ives: A Critical Commentary and Concordance of the Printed Editions and the Autographs and Manuscripts of the Yale Ives Collection.* Boston University, 1968.

17. Greenfield, Ruth Wolkowsky. *Charles Edward Ives and the Stylistic Aspects of His First Piano Sonata.* University of Miami, 1976.

18. Henderson, Clayton W. *Quotation as a Style Element in the Music of Charles Ives.* Washington University, 1969.

19. Hurst, Rolland W. *A Study, Analysis, and Performance of Selected Songs by Charles Ives.* Columbia University, 1971.

20. Joyce, Sister Mary Ann, C. S. J. *"The Three Page Sonata" of Charles E. Ives: An Analysis and a Corrected Version.* Washington University, 1970.

21. Kumlien, Wendell C. *The Sacred Choral Music of Charles Ives: A Study in Style Development*. University of Illinois, 1969.

22. Layton, Bentley. *An Introduction to the "114 Songs" of Charles Ives*. Bachelor's Thesis, Harvard University, 1963.

23. Magers, Roy V. *Aspects of Form in the Symphonies of Charles E. Ives*. Indiana University, 1975.

24. Milligan, Terry G. *Charles Ives: A Study of the Works for Chamber Ensemble Written between 1898 and 1908 Which Utilize Wind Instruments*. University of Texas, 1978.

25. Newman, Philip E. *The Songs of Charles Ives*. University of Iowa, 1967.

26. Perry, Rosalie S. *Charles Ives and American Culture*. University of Texas, 1971.

27. Plinkiewisch, Helen E. *A Contribution to the Understanding of the Music of Charles Ives, Roy Harris, and Aaron Copland*. Columbia University, 1955.

28. Rinehart, John McLain. *Ives' Compositional Idioms: An Investigation of Selected Short Compositions as Microcosms of His Musical Language*. Ohio State University, 1970.

29. Robison, Richard W. *Reading Contemporary Choral Literature: An Analytical Study of Selected Contemporary Choral Compositions with Recommendations for the Improvement of Choral Reading Skills*. Brigham Young University, 1969.

30. Rossiter, Frank R. *Charles Ives and American Culture: The Process of Development, 1874-1921*. Princeton University, 1970.

31. Sahr, Hadassah Gallup. *Performance and Analytic Study of Selected Piano Music by American Composers*. Columbia University, 1969.

32. Service, Alfred R., Jr. *A Study of the Cadence as a Factor in Music Intelligibility in Selected Piano Sonatas by American Composers*. State University of Iowa, 1958.

33. Sole, Kenneth G. *A Study and Performance of Five Psalm Settings and "The Celestial Country" by Charles Edward Ives*. University of Southern California, 1976.

34. Stein, Alan. *The Musical Language of Charles Ives' "Three Places in New England."* University of Illinois, 1975.

35. Ward, Charles W. *Charles Ives: The Relationship between Aesthetic Theories and Compositional Processes*. University of Texas, 1974.

36. Wolf, Henry Samuel. *The Twentieth Century Piano Sonata*. Boston University, 1957.

Addendum

References to Works by Charles Ives

82. h. 2) Ann Street: *PNM* 15, No. 2 (1977), 23-33.

69. The Celestial Country: *Choral J* 15, No. 7 (1975), 16-20.

9a. Central Park in the Dark: *BSPN* (Oct 17-19, 1974), 19-21.

15. Holidays: *BSPN* (Feb 6-18, 1975), 21; *HiFi/MA* 26 (Jun 1976), 70-72.
    Organ Music: *Diap* 67 (Jan 1976), 9.

30. Overture and March "1776": *Instrument* 32 (Sep 1977), 52.
    Piano Music: *Am Rec G* 40 (Aug 1977), 16-19.

10. A Set of Pieces for Theatre Orchestra: *R Mus Ital* 10, No. 1 (1976), 149-151.

62. Sonata for Piano No. 2 (Concord): *ASUC* 9-10 (1974-1975), 89-102; *HiFi/MA* 26 (Jun 1976), 70-72; *Stereo R* 39 (Aug 1977), 124; *Cont Kybd* 3 (Sep 1977), 59.

54. Sonata No. 4 (vln, pno): *NYT* (Feb 22, 1942), sec. 8, p. 7:4.
    Symphonies: *Opernwelt* 18, No. 6 (1977), 48.

 4. Symphony No. 2: *PitSPN* (Oct 25-27, 1974), 201; *LAPPN* (Mar 1975), 32.

20. Symphony No. 4: *Harmonie* 13, No. 125 (1977), 54.

55. Three-page Sonata: *Am Rec G* 40 (Nov 1976), 22.

63. Three Quarter-tone Pieces: *New Yorker* 51 (Jun 2, 1975), 86-89.

22. Variations on "America": *New Haven SPN* (Oct 15, 1974).

OUTLINE IX

DOUGLAS (STUART) MOORE (1893-1969)

I.   Life

1893   Born in Cutchogue, Long Island, New York, August 10. Parents were descendants of early New Englanders; father was the publisher of the *Ladies' World*; his mother the editor.

1908   Student at the Hotchkiss School, Lakeville, Connecticut; graduated in 1911.

1911   Entered Yale University; studied music with Horatio Parker and D. S. Smith. Bachelor of Arts degree in music and philosophy (1915); Bachelor of Music degree (1917).

1917   Lieutenant in the Navy during World War I (1917-1919).

1919   Studied composition at the Schola Cantorum, Paris, with Vincent d'Indy.

1920   Married Emily Bailey.

1921   Assistant Curator of Music at the Cleveland Museum of Art (1921); Curator (1922-1925). Studied with Ernest Bloch (1921-1922).

1923   Organist at Western Reserve University, Cleveland, Ohio (1923-1925).

1925   Awarded a Pulitzer Traveling Fellowship (*Four Museum Pieces*); studied composition in Paris with Nadia Boulanger and organ with Charles Tournemire (1925-1926).

1926   Appointed to the Department of Music, Columbia University; associate professor (1928); full professor (1940).

1927   Lecturer at the Metropolitan Museum of Art (1927-1929).

1934   Awarded a Guggenheim Fellowship.

1940   Succeeded Daniel Gregory Mason as chairman of the Department of Music, Columbia University. Appointed MacDowell Professor of Music (1943).

1941   Elected to membership in the National Institute of Arts and Letters.

1945   Inaugurated an annual Festival of American Music.

1946   Awarded honorary Doctor of Music degrees at the Cincinnati Conservatory (1946); University of Rochester (1947); Yale University (1955). President of the National Institute of Arts and Letters (1946-1952).

1951   Awarded the Pulitzer Prize in Music (*Giants in the Earth*).

1958   New York Music Critics Circle Award (*The Ballad of Baby Doe*).

1959   President of the American Academy of Arts and Letters (1960-1962).

1960   Honorary L. H. D. (Doctor of Humanities) degree, Adelphi College; Great Teacher Award, Columbia Society of Older Graduates.

1962   Retired from Columbia University as MacDowell Professor of Music, emeritus.

1969   Died, July 25, 1969, in Greenport, Long Island, New York.

Douglas Moore has been the recipient of many honors, awards and commissions in addition to those listed above.

Note: Biographies of varying lengths and importance will be found in many of the books listed in the Bibliography at the end of this *Outline* under "References to Douglas Moore."

II.   Compositions

		Date	Publisher
A.	**Orchestra**		
1.	Four Museum Pieces (originally for organ)	1922	CF
2.	Pageant of P. T. Barnum	1924	CF

        a. Boyhood at Bethel   d. Jenny Lind
        b. Joice Heth   e. Circus Parade
        c. General and Mrs. Tom Thumb

		Date	Publisher
3.	Moby Dick (after Herman Melville)	1927	
4.	A Symphony of Autumn	1930	GS
5.	Overture on an American Tune (after Sinclair Lewis' "Babbitt")	1931	CF
6.	Village Music (cham orch)	1941	Pres

        a. Square Dance   c. Nocturne
        b. Procession   d. Jig

		Date	Publisher
7.	In Memoriam	1943	E-V
8.	Down East Suite (vln, orch; also vln, pno)	1944	CF
9.	Symphony No. 2 in A major	1945	GS
10.	Farm Journal (cham orch)	1947	CF

        a. Up Early   c. Lamplight
        b. Sunday Clothes   d. Harvest Song

		Date	Publisher
11.	Cotillion Suite (str orch)	1952	CF

        a. Grand March   d. Galop
        b. Polka   e. Cake-Walk
        c. Waltz   f. Quickstep

		Date	Publisher
B.	**Band**		
12.	The People's Choice		Gal
13.	Three Contemporaries (arr. from pno)	1935	CF
C.	**Chamber**		
14.	Sonata for Violin and Piano	1929	Ms
15.	String Quartet No. 1	1933	GS
16.	Ballade of William Sycamore (Bar., fl, trb, pno)	1937	
17.	Quintet for Winds (fl, ob, clar, bsn, hn)	1942	GS
18.	Down East Suite (vln, pno)	1944	CF
19.	Quintet for Clarinet, String Quartet	1946	CF
20.	Trio (vln, vlc, pno)	1953	Gal
21.	String Quartet No. 2	1959	CF
D.	**Piano**		
22.	Careful Etta	1935	CF
23.	Fiddlin' Joe	1935	CF
24.	Grievin' Annie	1935	CF
25.	Suite for Piano	1948	CF

        a. Prelude   d. Barn Dance
        b. Reel   e. Air
        c. Dancing School f. Procession

		Date	Publisher
E.	**Organ**		
26.	Passacaglia (Dirge)	1939	HWG
F.	**Choral** (a cappella unless otherwise indicated)		
27.	God Rest You Merry, Gentlemen (SSAATTBB)	1932	CF
28.	Simon Legree (Vachel Lindsay) (TTBB, pno)	1937	CF
29.	Perhaps to Dream (Stephen Vincent Benét) (SSA)	1937	CF
30.	Now May There be a Blessing (from "The Devil and Daniel Webster") (SSA)	1938	BH
31.	Dedication (Archibald MacLeish) (SSATBB)	1938	BH
32.	Prayer for England (Stephen Vincent Benét) ((TTBB, pno)	1941	BH

33. Prayer for the United Nations (Stephen Vincent Benét) (A., SATB, orch or pno)	1943	HWG
34. The Mysterious Cat (Vachel Lindsay) (SSA)	1960	S-B

G. Solo Vocal (with piano unless otherwise indicated)

35. Sigh No More, Ladies (William Shakespeare)	1927	BH
36. Fingers and Toes (Guiterman)	1928	BH
37. The Cupboard (Walter de la Mare)	1929	BH
38. Adam Was My Grandfather (Stephen Vincent Benét)	1937	Gal
39. I've Got a Ram (from "The Devil and Daniel Webster")	1938	BH
40. Mary's Prayer (from "The Devil and Daniel Webster")	1938	BH
41. Now May There Be a Blessing (from "The Devil and Daniel Webster")	1938	BH
42. Three Divine Sonnets (John Donne)	1942	GS

    a. Thou Hast Made Me   c. Death, Be Not Proud
    b. Batter My Heart

43. The Token (John Donne)	1942	GS
44. Not This Alone (Pierson Underwood)	1943	BH
45. Old Song (Theodore Roethke)	1949	CF
46. Under the Greenwood Tree (William Shakespeare)	1949	CF
47. Silver Song (from "The Ballad of Baby Doe")	1958	Chap
48. The Dove Song (from "The Wings of the Dove")	1962	GS
49. Come Away Death (William Shakespeare) (unacc.)	1964	Bel-Mills
50. Dear Dark Head (Irish, tr. Sir Samuel Ferguson)	1964	Gal

H. Opera

51. White Wings (Philip Barry)	1935	
52. The Headless Horseman (Stephen Vincent Benét, after Washington Irving's "Legend of Sleepy Hollow")	1936	ECS
53. The Devil and Daniel Webster (Stephen Vincent Benét)	1937	BH
54. Puss in Boots (Raymond Abrashkin, based on a fable by Charles Perrault) (children's opera)	1949	CF
55. The Emperor's New Clothes (Raymond Abrashkin from Hans Christian Andersen) (children's opera)	1949	CF
56. Giants in the Earth (Arnold Sundgaard, from Ole Edvart Rölvaag)	1950; revised 1963	CF
57. The Ballad of Baby Doe (John Latouche)	1955	Chap
58. Gallantry: A Soap Opera (Arnold Sundgaard)	1958	GS
59. The Wings of the Dove (Ethan Ayer, from Henry James)	1961	GS
60. The Greenfield Christmas Tree (Arnold Sundgaard)	1962	GS
61. Carry Nation (William North Jayme)	1965	Gal

I. Film Music

62. Power and the Land (music used in "Farm Journal")	1940	Ms
63. Youth Gets a Break	1940	Ms
64. Bip Goes to Town	1941	Ms

Note: The following abbreviations are used in Section III of this *Outline*. The number indicates the number of the composition as listed in Section II.

38. *Adam*: Adam Was My Grandfather
57. *Baby Doe*: The Ballad of Baby Doe
2. *Barnum*: The Pageant of P. T. Barnum
42. *Batter*: Batter My Heart
53. *The Devil*: The Devil and Daniel Webster
18. *Down East*: Down East Suite
52. *Horseman*: The Headless Horseman

19. *Qnt Clar Str*: Quintet for Clarinet, String Quartet
42. *Sonnets*: Three Divine Sonnets
15. *Str Qrt 1*: String Quartet No. 1
4. *Sym Autumn*: A Symphony of Autumn
9. *Sym 2*: Symphony No. 2

III. Style (techniques and devices)

"Above all I think that American composers should avoid being selfconsciously nationalistic but keep their ears and eyes open for the flavor of American life which is going on around us. If the American composer is drawn today toward American material, it may very well be because it is a part of his background and he understands it." Douglas Moore

A. General characteristics
1. "The particular ideal which I have been striving to attain is to write music that will reflect the exciting quality of life, traditions, and country which I feel all about me."
   Douglas Moore
2. Style generally conservative and varied. A master of music for the lyric theatre; resourceful in the use of musical materials; writes with clarity and simplicity. Strong influence of American folklore, humor, literature and poetry ("American flavor").
3. 1923-1935: program music, folk element prominent. After 1935: emphasis on opera, songs, absolute music.
B. Melodic line
1. Unusual gift for melody: lyric themes and movements characteristic. Melodic line in songs follows the rhythms and inflections of American speech. Perfect intervals prominent, horizontally and vertically. Falling fourth, upward leap to a dissonant note is typical.
2. Diatonic: *Batter* (p. 3).
3. Modal: *Adam* (p. 7).
4. Whole tone scale: *Down East*.
5. Spoken dialogue: *The Devil*.
6. Melodic sequence: *Down East* (pp. 4, 6, 7).
7. Lyric: *Sym 2* (Introduction; second movement); *Farm Journal* (third movement).
C. Harmony
1. Basically homophonic and generally romantic in spirit. French influence in early works; some use of German chromaticism.
2. Individual and expressive use of diatonic materials: *Qnt Clar Str*.
3. Simple triadic harmony: *Horseman* (p. 34).
4. Fauxbourdon: *Horseman* (p. 35).
5. Profuse use of all types of seventh and ninth chords: *Sonnets* (p. 5).
6. Polymodal style: *Str Qrt 1* (p. 3).
7. Juxtaposition of tonally unrelated seconds and fourths: *Sym Autumn*.
8. Triads moving by second relationship: *Baby Doe* (p. 155).
D. Counterpoint
1. Moderate use of polyphonic forms and devices.
2. Free polyphonic writing: *Sym 2* (third movement).
3. Imitation: *Str Qrt 1* (p. 3).
4. Madrigal and motet style with free imitation: *Horseman* (p. 36).
5. Canonic: *Sym 2* (third movement).
E. Rhythm
1. Generally simple, but strong. Frequent use of dotted rhythms.
2. Intricate and difficult patterns: *Sym Autumn* (fourth movement).
3. Frequent meter changes: *Sym 2* (pp. 1-7).
4. Shifting rhythm in two and three beat groups: *Sym 2* (pp. 87-89).
5. Frequent syncopated figures: *Down East* (p. 3).
6. Use of one rhythmic pattern throughout a movement: *Sym 2* (fourth movement, p. 87); *Qnt Clar Str*.
7. Ragtime: *Quintet* (winds) (first movement).
F. Form
1. Forms often modified classic, without strong thematic contrast within the movement.

Forms not rigid; serve as a point of departure.
2. Use of classical sonata-allegro form: *Sym 2* (first and fourth movements).
3. Rondo-like form with recurring refrain: *Qnt Clar Str* (first movement).
4. Slow introduction: *Sym 2*.
5. Passacaglia with interludes between the repetitions of the theme: *Barnum* (second movement); *Passacaglia* (org).

BIBLIOGRAPHY

Books by Douglas Moore

1. *Listening to Music*. New York: W. W. Norton, 1933; rev. ed., 1963. *Mus Leader* 95 (Aug 1963), 23; *Response* 5, No. 2 (1963), 95; *Mus J* 21 (Nov 1963), 64.
2. *From Madrigal to Modern Music: A Guide to Musical Styles*. New York: W. W. Norton, 1942; rev. ed., 1963.

Articles by Douglas Moore

1. "Music in Cleveland," *Art and Archeology* 16 (Oct 1923), 181-185.
2. "Inhospitable Theatre," *Theatre Arts Monthly* 12 (Aug 1928), 559-565.
3. D. Moore and Daniel Gregory Mason. "Recent Developments in Music at Columbia and Barnard," *Assn Am Col B* 17 (Nov 1931), 355-358.
4. "College Music Study," *Assn Am Col B* 19 (1933), 99-102.
5. "Music and the Movies," *Harper's* 171 (Jul 1935), 181.
6. "General Music Course for College Students," *MENC Yearbook* (1936), 124-149.
7. "The Importance of Music in Wartime," *SR* 26 (Jan 30, 1943), 12.
8. "Strictly Personal," *SR* 28 (Jan 20, 1945), 15.
9. "Gregarious Art," *SR* 28 (Jan 20, 1945), 22.
10. "Homage to Béla Bartók," *MM* 23, No. 1 (Winter 1946), 13.
11. "Concerning Program Notes," *SR* 29 (Jan 26, 1946), 18-19.
12. "The Cause of Native Music," *SR* 30 (Jan 25, 1947), 24.
13. "True Tale of the West," *NYT* (Jul 1, 1956), sec. 2, p. 9.
14. "Opera as Theatre," *NYT* (Apr 12, 1959), sec. 2, p. 9.
15. "Something About Librettos," *Opera N* 26 (Sep 30, 1961), 8-13.
16. "Opera and Symphony Orchestras," *ASOL* 13, Nos. 5-6 (1962), 12.
17. "Opera by American Composers of Today," *Pan Pipes* 59, No. 2 (1967), 12-14.

References to Douglas Moore

Books
(See the General Bibliography)

ASC-BD; ASC-SC; AusMT; Baker; BauTC; BIM; BloYA; BMI-OP; Bull; CatPC; ChaAC; ChaAM; ClaEA; CobCS; ColHM; CopTN; CurB (1947); DukLH; Edm-II; EdMUS; EweAC; EweCB; EweCS; EweDE; EweMC; EweNB; EweWT; EweYA; GosMM; GroSH; Grove; HitMU; HowMM; HowOA; HowOC; HowSH; JohOA; KinAI; KolMO; LanOH; LeiMW; MacAC; MacIC; MelMN; MorrCA; MueAS; MyeTC; NorLC; PavMH; PersTH; PorM3S; ReiCA; ReiCC; RosAH; SalMO; SalzTM; SamLM; SamMO; SanWM; SchWC; StevePC; ThoAM; ThompIC; ThoMR; ThoRL; WWA (1946-1947); WWM.

Articles

Brief mention: *MQ* 21 (1935), 112; *MM* 20, No. 2 (1942-1943), 97; *MQ* 33 (1947), 325; 34 (1948), 297; 36 (1950), 584; *Showcase* 42, No. 1 (1962), 7.

1. Copland, Aaron. "America's Young Men of Promise," *MM* 3, No. 3 (1925-1926), 13.
2. *NYT* (Dec 18, 1932), sec. 10, p. 9:5.
3. Copland, Aaron. "Our Younger Generation–Ten Years Late," *MM* 13, No. 4 (1935-1936), 3.
4. Upton, William T. "Aspects of the Modern Art Song," *MQ* 24 (1938), 13.
5. Rhodes, Willard. "Douglas Moore's Music," *Columbia University Quarterly* 32 (1940), 223.
6. "Named Columbia University Music Department Head," *NYT* (Apr 25, 1940), 26:4.
7. Luening, Otto. "Douglas Moore," *MM* 20, No. 4 (1942-1943), 248.
8. Frankenstein, Alfred. "The Plight of the American Composer," *American Scholar* (Autumn 1943).
9. "Named President of National Institute of Arts and Letters," *NYT* (Jan 14, 1946), 17:5.
10. "Newly Appointed President of National Institute of Arts and Letters," *Musician* 51 (Feb 1946), 29-30.
11. *NYT* (Oct 15, 1946), 27:6; (Oct 20, 1946), sec. 2, p. 7:1.
12. "Composers vs. the Assembly Line," *NW* 29 (Jan 27, 1947), 86.
13. "Biography," *Current Biography* (Nov 1947); *Current Biography Yearbook* (1947), 449-451.
14. *NYT* (Feb 2, 1947), sec. 2, p. 9:1; (Feb 23, 1947), sec. 2, p. 9:1; (May 23, 1947), 18:5.
15. *NYT* (Feb 7, 1948), 1:6; (Feb 8, 1948), 9:2.
16. "Re-elected President of National Institute of Arts and Letters," *NYT* (Jan 18, 1950), 23:2.
17. "Douglas Moore," *Pan Pipes* 43 (Dec 1950), 126.
18. *NYT* (Feb 5, 1951), 18:5.
19. Slater, M. "Music on the Peninsula," *Opera* 16 (Apr 1951), 31.
20. "Wins Pulitzer Prize," *NYT* (May 8, 1951), 1:2.
21. "Douglas Moore Wins Pulitzer Prize," *MC* 71 (Jul 1951), 23.
22. "Elected to the American Academy of Arts and Letters," *NYT* (Dec 1, 1951), 11:4.
23. "Douglas Moore," *Pan Pipes* 44 (Jan 1952), 39.
24. "Elected Director of the National Institute of Arts and Letters," *NYT* (Dec 12, 1952), 31:7.
25. "Douglas Moore Wins American Academy Honor," *MA* 73 (Jan 1, 1953), 22.
26. "Douglas Stuart Moore," *Mus Club Mag* 32 (Mar 1953), 42.
27. *NYT* (Jun 27, 1953), 13:7.
28. "Head of Columbia University Music Department Commissioned by Koussevitsky Music Foundation," *NYT* (Dec 15, 1953), 53:2.
29. "Academy Secretary of National Institute of Arts and Letters," *NYT* (Dec 16, 1953), 46:4.
30. Parmenter, Ross. "Story of 'Baby Doe' Tabor, Wife of Silver Miner, to be Made into Opera," *NYT* (Dec 20, 1953), sec. 2, p. 9.
31. Kyle, Marguerite K. "AmerAllegro," *Pan Pipes* 46 (Jan 1954), 53.
32. *NYT* (Feb 15, 1954), 20:4.
33. Keats, Sheila. "Reference Articles on American Composers: An Index," *Juilliard Rev* 1 (Fall 1954), 30.
34. "Re-elected Secretary of American Academy of Arts and Letters," *NYT* (Dec 17, 1954), 28:5.
35. "Yale University Honorary Degree," *NYT* (Jun 14, 1955), 27:1.
36. Kyle, Marguerite K. "AmerAllegro," *Pan Pipes* 49 (Jan 1957), 60.
37. "Elected One of Four Directors of ASCAP," *NYT* (Mar 27, 1957), 28:5.
38. Kyle, Marguerite K. "AmerAllegro," *Pan Pipes* 50 (Jan 1958), 64.

39. *NYT* (Sep 22, 1957), 11:1.
40. "Contemporary American Composers," *Instrument* 12 (Aug 1958), 37.
41. Kyle, Marguerite K. "AmerAllegro," *Pan Pipes* 51 (Jan 1959), 76.
42. *NYT* (Apr 12, 1959), sec. 2, p. 9:3; (Jun 13, 1959), 13:6.
43. "We Salute–Douglas Moore," *Mus Club Mag* 39 (Nov 1959), 7.
44. "Named President of National Institute of Arts and Letters," *NYT* (Dec 5, 1959), 8:4.
45. "Columbia University Great Teacher Award," *NYT* (Jan 14, 1960), 18:5.
46. Kyle, Marguerite K. "AmerAllegro," *Pan Pipes* 52, No. 2 (1960), 62.
47. "American Composers and Conductors Association Hadley Medal," *NYT* (May 20, 1960), 27:5.
48. "Re-elected American Arts and Letters Academy President," *FoF* 20 (Dec 2, 1960), 488E1.
49. "National Institute of Arts and Letters, President," *NYT* (Dec 3, 1960), 25:2.
50. "H. Hartford Foundation Award," *NYT* (Dec 10, 1960), 21:2.
51. "U. S. Opera Composers Produce and Talk," *Mus Mag* 163 (Oct 1961), 7.
52. *NYT* (Dec 7, 1961), 53:1.
53. Kyle, Marguerite K. "AmerAllegro," *Pan Pipes* 54, No. 2 (1962), 63.
54. "Retires from Columbia University Faculty," *NYT* (May 6, 1962), 134:3.
55. *NYT* (Jun 23, 1962), 14:5.
56. Rich, Alan. "Busily Inactive," *NYT* (Jul 1, 1962), sec. 2, p. 7.
57. "Moore, Hanson Announce Retirements," *Mus Mag* 164 (Jul 1962), 62.
58. "Dates and Places," *Opera N* 27 (Oct 20, 1962), 7.
59. "Operas," *NYT* (Nov 18, 1962), sec. 2, p. 9: 1, 4.
60. Kyle, Marguerite K. "AmerAllegro," *Pan Pipes* 55, No. 2 (1963), 62.
61. "Previously Unpublished Composers' Letters as Written to Claire R. Reis," *MA* 83 (Jan 1963), 16.
62. "The Greenfield Christmas Tree," *Int Mus* 61 (Feb 1963), 23.
63. "Columbia University Honorary Degree," *NYT* (Jun 5, 1963), 27:1.
64. *NYT* (Aug 10, 1963), 9:5.
65. Brozen, Michael. "Douglas Moore, The Good Life," *MA* 83 (Aug 1963), 26.
66. Kyle, Marguerite K. "AmerAllegro," *Pan Pipes* 56, No. 2 (1964), 72; 58, No. 2 (1966), 77; 59, No. 2 (1967), 88; 60, No. 2 (1968), 85.
67. "Douglas Moore Birthday in 1968," *Mus Club Mag* 47, No. 5 (1968), 7.
68. Miller, Philip L. "New York City Opera Performance of Douglas Moore's 'Carry Nation'," *Am Rec G* 35 (Feb 1969), 452-454.
69. Kyle, Marguerite K. "AmerAllegro," *Pan Pipes* 61, No. 2 (1969), 68-69.
70. Nissim, Rudolf. "Homage to Douglas Moore," *ASCAP* 3, No. 2 (1969), 19.
71. Lackey Lionel. "The Battle of Baby Doe," *Opera N* 33 (Mar 8, 1969), 9.
72. "Dies," *FoF* 29 (July 25, 1969), 800F3.
73. "Dies," *NYT* (Jul 28, 1969), 31:3.
74. "Obituary," *Current Biography* (Oct 1969); *Current Biography Yearbook* (1969), 471.
75. Scherman, Thomas. "Douglas Moore: the Optimistic Conservative," *Mus J* 27 (Oct 1969), 24-25.
76. Beeson, Jack. "In Memoriam: Douglas Moore (1893-1969)–An Appreciation, Written in a Country Churchyard," *PNM* 8, No. 1 (1969), 158-160.
77. Rudel, Julius. "Douglas Moore," *Opera N* 34 (Oct 11, 1969), 21.
78. "Obituary," *Variety* 255 (Aug 6, 1969), 63; *MT* 110 (Sep 1969), 975; (Nov 1969), 1173; *Mus Ed J* 56 (Oct 1969), 95; *Mus & Artists* 2, No. 3 (1969), 47; *HiFi/MA* 19 (Oct 1969), MA8; *Opera* 20 (Oct 1969), 884-885; *Pan Pipes* 62, No. 2 (1970), 16; *Central Opera* 12 (May-Jun 1970), 21.
79. "A Tribute to Douglas Stuart Moore," *Mus Club Mag* 49, No. 2 (1969-1970), 28.
80. Waters, Edward N. "Variations on a Theme; Recent Acquisitions of the Music Division," *Q J Library Congress* 27, No. 1 (1970), 56.
81. Hardee, Lewis J. "The Published Songs and Arias," *Notes* 29, No. 4 (1973), 28-31.

References to Works by Douglas Moore

57. The Ballad of Baby Doe: *NYT* (Dec 20, 1953), sec. 2, p. 9; (Feb 11, 1956), 13:1; (Jul 1, 1956), sec. 2, p. 9:5; (Jul 9, 1956), 26:5; *Variety* 203 (Jul 11, 1956), 60; *Time* 68 (Jul 16, 1956), 40; *Theatre Arts* 40 (Jul 1956), 80; *Life* 41 (Aug 6, 1956), 109; *MA* 76 (Aug 1956), 3; *MQ* 42 (1956), 527-529; *NYT* (Aug 28, 1956), 55:3; *Dance Mag* 30 (Sep 1956), 33; *Opera N* 21 (Nov 5, 1956), 12; *Opera* 7 (Nov 1956), 676-678; *Etude* 74 (Nov 1956), 12; *Canon* 10 (Dec 1956), 187; *NYT* (Feb 11, 1957), 53:2; *SR* 40 (Feb 23, 1957), 59; *New Republic* 136 (Feb 25, 1957), 22; *MC* 155 (Mar 1957), 10; *NYHT* (Apr 4, 1958); *NYT* (Apr 4, 1958), 19:1; (Apr 12, 1958), 13:6; *New Yorker* 34 (Apr 12, 1958), 70; *SR* 41 (Apr 19, 1958), 35; *NYT* (Apr 27, 1958), 79:2; *MC* 157 (May 1958), 14; *Nation* 186 (May 3, 1958), 399; *Opera* 9 (Jul 1958), 415; *NYT* (Oct 10, 1958), 35:2; (Oct 27, 1958), 32:4; *MA* 78 (Nov 1, 1958), 14; *NYT* (Jan 21, 1959), 25:3; (Apr 4, 1959), 13:6; *MA* 79 (May 1959), 7; (Aug 1959), 35; *NYT* (Nov 8, 1959), sec. 2, p. 12; *Am Rec G* 26 (Feb 1960), 443; *MA* 80 (May 1960), 16; *Can Mus J* 4, No. 2 (1960), 44; *Mus & Dance* 51 (Oct 1960), 20; *Mus West* 16 (Jan 1961), 13; *Zvuk* 51 (1961), 115; *MC* 163 (Aug 1961), 63; *MA* 82 (May 1962), 24; *New Yorker* 39 (May 11, 1963), 150-152; *HiFi/MA* 15 (Jun 1965), 116; *Opera N* 30 (Jan 29, 1966), 30; (Jun 4, 1966), 24; *Opera N* 33 (Mar 8, 1969), 8-11; *Opera* 20 (Jun 1969), 496-497; *HiFi/MA* 19 (Jun 1969), MA12-13; *NYT* (Oct 4, 1969), 35:4; (Oct 6, 1969), 57:3; *Opera N* 35 (Jan 30, 1971), 33; 39 (Nov 1974), 50; *New Yorker* 52 (May 10, 1976), 128; *Opera N* 40 (May 1976), 40; (Jun 1976), 38; *Mus & Mus* 24 (Jul 1976), 42; *Opera* 27 (Jul 1976), 650; *Stereo R* 37 (Jul 1976), 50; *Opera N* 41 (Jul 1976), 43; *HiFi/MA* 26 (Oct 1976), MA17; *Opera N* 41 (Dec 18, 1976), 62-65; *EweCB*, 489; *HitMU*, 209; *MacIC*, 467.

61. Carry Nation: *HiFi/MA* 16 (Feb 1966), 129; *NW* 67 (May 16, 1966), 115; *Opera N* 30 (Jun 4, 1966), 24; *HiFi/MA* 16 (Jul 1966), MA27; *Opera* 17 (Jul 1966), 566; (Sep 1966), 737); *Opera N* 32 (Mar 30, 1968), 26-27; *NYT* (Mar 29, 1968), 35:1; *Opera J* 1, No. 3 (1968), 24; *New Yorker* 44 (Apr 6, 1968), 143-144; *SR* 51 (Apr 13, 1968), 58; *Commonweal* 88 (May 10, 1968), 237; *Opera N* 32 (May 18, 1968), 24; *Mus J* 26 (May 1968), 59; *HiFi/MA* 18 (Jun 1968), MA29; *Mus & Artists* 1, No. 2 (1968), 59; *Opera N* 33 (Feb 1, 1969), 35.

11. Cotillion Suite: *NYT* (Feb 15, 1954), 20:4.

53. The Devil and Daniel Webster: *NYT* (Jun 5, 1938), sec. 9, p. 5:8; *NYT* (Apr 16, 1939), sec. 10, p. 7:1; (Apr 30, 1939), sec. 11, p. 8:5; (May 14, 1939), sec. 11, p. 1:6; (May 19, 1939), 26:1; *SR* 20 (May 20, 1939), 10; *NYT* (May 21, 1939), sec. 10, p. 1:1; *SR* 20 (May 27, 1939), 8; *Commonweal* 30 (Jun 2, 1939), 160; *NYT* (Feb 12, 1940), 15:2; *NYT* (Jan 5, 1941), 44:2; (Jan 14, 1945), (Mar 2, 1945); *MQ* 31 (1945), 103; *NYT* (Jan 19, 1946), 18:3; *MQ* 34 (1948), 8; *NYT* (Jul 24, 1952), 31:5; (Jul 20, 1953), 14:7; *MA* 73 (Aug 1953), 4; *NYT* (Apr 6, 1959), 33:1; *Variety* 214 (Apr 8, 1959), 72; *SR* 42 (Apr 18, 1959), 43; *MA* 79 (May 1959), 7; *EweCB*, 264.

18. Down East Suite: *Notes* 4 (1946-1947), 106; *HitMU*, 209.

10. Farm Journal: *LOSPN* (Jan 19, 1948), 46; *MC* 142 (Dec 1, 1950), 42; *Notes* 8 (1950-1951), 573; *MA* 71 (Apr 1, 1951), 28.

58. Gallantry: *NYT* (Mar 20, 1958), 34:3; *Time* 71 (Mar 31, 1958), 44; *New Yorker* 34 (Mar 29, 1959), 107; *OeMZ* 24 (May-Jun 1969), 336.

56. Giants in the Earth: *NYT* (Mar 25, 1951), sec. 2, p. 7:8; (Mar 29, 1951), 25:1; *MA* 71 (Apr 1, 1951), 8; *Time* 57 (Apr 9, 1951), 66; *MQ* 37 (1951), 402; *MC* 143 (Apr 15, 1951), 18; *Opera* 2 (Sep 1951), 526; *Pan Pipes* 44 (Jan 1952), 12; *Opera J* 7, No. 2 (1974), 34-37.

52. The Headless Horseman: *NYT* (Mar 6, 1937), 10:4; *MA* 57 (Mar 25, 1937), 29; 58 (Feb 10, 1938), 235; *HitMU*, 209.

7. In Memoriam: *NYPPN* (Jan 11, 1945); *Notes* 3 (1945-1946), 381.

3. Moby Dick: *MQ* 31 (1945), 112.

45. Old Song: *MC* 142 (Nov 1, 1950), 28; *Notes* 8 (1950-1951), 405; *ML* 32 (1951), 187.

2. The Pageant of P. T. Barnum: *RPPN* (Dec 6, 1929); *MQ* 18 (1932), 11; 33 (1947), 318; *EweCB*, 263.
29. Perhaps to Dream: *MA* 58 (Aug 1938), 24.
54. Puss in Boots: *NYPPN* (Nov 18, 1951).
19. Quintet for Clarinet, String Quartet: *MQ* 40 (1954), 472; *Am Rec G* 32 (Apr 1966), 686.
28. Simon Legree: *MA* 58 (Aug 1938), 24.
15. String Quartet No. 1: *NYT* (Jun 18, 1938), 18:1; *EweCB*, 264.
21. String Quartet No. 2: *NYHT* (Mar 30, 1959).
25. Suite for Piano: *MA* 69 (Jan 1, 1949), 30; *Notes* 8 (Sep 1951), 749-750.
 9. Symphony No. 2: *NYT* (Apr 16, 1946), 33:3; (Nov 3, 1946), sec. 2, p. 7:5; (Jan 12, 1947), sec. 2, p. 7:4; *RPPN* (Nov 6, 1947); *NYPPN* (Feb 19, 1948); *MQ* 34 (1948), 410; *EweCB*, 265.
20. Trio (vln, vlc, pno): *NYT* (Jan 22, 1958), 23:3; *MQ* 48 (1962), 392.
46. Under the Greenwood Tree: *MC* 142 (Nov 1, 1950), 28; *Notes* 8 (Mar 1951), 405; *ML* 32 (Apr 1951), 187.
 6. Village Music: *MA* 62 (May 1942), 38.
59. The Wings of the Dove: *NYT* (Mar 13, 1960), sec. 2, p. 11:4; (Oct 13, 1961), 31:1; *Variety* 224 (Oct 18, 1961), 65; *Time* 78 (Oct 20, 1961), 93; *New Yorker* 37 (Oct 21, 1961), 166-168; *NW* 58 (Oct 23, 1961), 64; *SR* 44 (Oct 28, 1961), 39-41; *Nation* 193 (Nov 11, 1961), 384; *Opera N* 26 (Nov 18, 1961), 34; *Int Mus* 60 (Nov 1961), 35; *Mus Mag* 163 (Nov 1961), 29; *MA* 81 (Dec 1961), 26; *Opera* 12 (Dec 1961), 786; *Mus West* 17 (Dec 1961), 17; *Hudson R* 14 (Winter 1961-1962), 595-596; *Schweiz Mus* 102, No. 1 (1962), 40; *Show* 2 (Jan 1962), 4; *MQ* 48 (1962), 99-104; *Pan Pipes* 54, No. 2 (1962), 7; *PNM* 3, No. 1 (1964), 157.
51. White Wings: *MC* 139 (Mar 15, 1949), 20; *MA* 69 (Mar 1949), 7; *MQ* 35 (1949), 448-451; *Mus J* 7 (Jul-Aug 1949), 14.

Dissertations About Douglas Moore and His Works

1. Bethea, Sara Kathryn. *Opera for Children: An Analysis of Selected Works*. University of Kansas, 1971.
2. Cavendish, Thomas H. *Folk Music in Selected Twentieth Century American Opera*. Florida State University, 1966.
3. Reagan, Donald J. *Douglas Moore and His Orchestral Works*. Catholic University, 1972.
4. Weitzel, Jay Harold. *A Melodic Analysis of Selected Vocal Solos in the Operas of Douglas Moore*. New York University, 1971.

OUTLINE X

WALTER (HAYMOR) PISTON, JR. (1894-1976)

I. Life

1894   Born in Rockland, Maine, January 20. Ancestors were Maine Yankees, except for his paternal grandfather, Italian-born Antonio Pistone.

1905   Moved to Boston; attended the Mechanic Arts High School (1908-1912); began to take violin lessons.

1912   Studied drawing and painting at the Massachusetts Normal Art School; graduated in 1916. Studied piano (with Harris Shaw) and violin (with Theodorowicz Fiumara and Felix Winternitz) privately and worked as an artist.

1918   "Second class musician" during World War I; played saxophone in a band stationed at Massachusetts Institute of Technology.

1919   Entered Harvard University Department of Music; special student for one year. Studied with Archibald T. Davison (counterpoint) and Edward Burlingame Hill (composition). Conducted concerts of the University orchestra.

1920   Married Kathryn Nason, an artist.

1924   Graduated from Harvard with highest honors (summa cum laude), Bachelor of Arts degree. Received the John Knowles Paine Traveling Fellowship. For a time was a draftsman with the Boston Elevated Railway.

1924   Studied with Nadia Boulanger and Paul Dukas at the École Normale de Musique, Paris (1924-1926).

1926   Appointed to the music faculty at Harvard; chairman of the department (1944); Naumberg Professor (1948). Has had great influence as a teacher; among his pupils were Elliott Carter, Harold Shapero, Leonard Bernstein.

1928   First performance of an orchestral work (Boston Symphony, *Symphonic Piece*).

1935   Awarded a Guggenheim Fellowship.

1938   Elected to the National Institute of Arts and Letters.

1940   Elected a member of the American Academy of Arts and Sciences.

1944   Received the New York Music Critics Circle Award (*Symphony No. 2*).

1948   Awarded the Pulitzer Prize for Music (*Symphony No. 3*).

1952   Awarded an honorary Doctor of Music degree from Harvard University. Others from the New York College of Music and Bowdoin College.

1956   First performance of *Symphony No. 5*, commissioned by the Juilliard School of Music for its fiftieth anniversary.

1960   Retired from Harvard as Emeritus Professor of Music.

1961   Awarded a second Pulitzer Prize for Music (*Symphony No. 7*).

1976   Died on November 12 in Belmont, Massachusetts.

Walter Piston has been the recipient of many honors, awards and commissions in addition to those listed above.

Note: Biographies of varying lengths and importance will be found in many of the books listed in the Bibliography at the end of this *Outline* under "References to Walter Piston."

II.   Compositions

A.   Orchestra

1.	Symphonic Piece	1927	Ms
2.	Suite for Orchestra, No. 1	1929	AMP
3.	Prelude and Fugue	1934	AMP
4.	Symphony No. 1	1937	GS
5.	The Incredible Flutist (Ballet Suite)	1938	AMP
6.	Sinfonietta (cham orch)	1941	BH
7.	Symphony No. 2	1943	AMP
8.	Prelude and Allegro (org, str)	1943	AMP
9.	Fanfare for the Fighting French (brass, timp, perc)	1943	BH
10.	Fugue on a Victory Tune	1944	
11.	Symphony No. 3	1947	BH
12.	Toccata	1948	BH
13.	Suite for Orchestra, No. 2	1948	AMP

    a. Prelude   d. Passacaglia
    b. Sarabande   e. Fugue
    c. Intermezzo

14.	Symphony No. 4	1950	AMP
15.	Fantasy for English Horn, Harp, Strings	1952	AMP
16.	Symphony No. 5	1954	AMP
17.	Symphony No. 6 (commissioned by Boston Symphony)	1955	AMP
18.	Serenata	1956	AMP
19.	Three New England Sketches	1959	AMP

    a. Seaside   b. Summer Evening   c. Mountains

20.	Symphony No. 7	1960	AMP
21.	Symphonic Prelude	1961	AMP
22.	Lincoln Center Festival Overture	1962	AMP
23.	Variations on a Theme by Edward Burlingame Hill	1963	AMP
24.	Capriccio for Harp, Strings	1963	AMP
25.	Variations for Cello, Orchestra	1964	AMP
26.	Symphony No. 8	1965	AMP
27.	Pine Tree Fantasy	1965	AMP
28.	Ricercare	1967	AMP

B.   Concerto (with orchestra unless otherwise indicated)

29.	Concerto for Orchestra	1933	AMP
30.	Concertino for Piano (cham orch)	1937	AMP
31.	Concerto for Violin, No. 1 (also vln, pno)	1939	BH
32.	Concerto for Viola	1957	AMP
33.	Concerto for Two Pianos	1959	AMP
34.	Concerto for Violin, No. 2	1960	AMP
35.	Concerto for Clarinet	1966	AMP
36.	Concerto for Flute	1971	
37.	Fantasia for Violin, Orchestra	1975	
38.	Concerto for String Quartet, Wind Instruments and Percussion	1976	

C.   Band

39.	Tunbridge Fair (Intermezzo for Symphonic Band)	1950	BH

D.   Chamber

40.	Three Pieces for Flute, Clarinet, Bassoon	1926	AMP
41.	Sonata for Flute, Piano	1930	AMP
42.	Suite for Oboe, Piano	1931	ECS

    a. Prelude   d. Nocturne
    b. Sarabande   e. Gigue
    c. Minuet

D.   Chamber (cont.)

43. String Quartet No. 1	1933	AMP
44. String Quartet No. 2	1935	GS
45. Trio for Violin, Cello, Piano	1935	AMP
46. Sonata for Violin, Piano	1939	AMP
47. Interlude for Viola, Piano	1942	BH
48. Quintet for Flute, String Quartet	1942	AMP
49. Partita for Violin, Viola, Organ	1944	AMP

      a.   Prelude   c.   Variations
      b.   Sarabande   d.   Burlesca

50. Sonatina for Violin, Harpsichord	1945	BH
51. Divertimento for Nine Instruments (fl, ob, clar, bsn, str qrt, c-b)	1946	BMI
52. String Quartet No. 3	1947	BH
53. Quintet for Piano, String Quartet (Piano Quintet)	1949	AMP
54. Duo for Viola, Cello	1949	AMP
55. String Quartet No. 4	1951	AMP
56. Quintet for Wind Instruments (fl, ob, clar, bsn, hn)	1956	AMP
57. String Quartet No. 5	1962	AMP
58. String Sextet (2 vln, 2 vla, 2 vlc)	1964	AMP
59. Piano Quartet (pno, vln, vla, vlc)	1964	AMP
60. Ceremonial Fanfare (brass, perc)	1971	AMP
61. Trio No. 2 (vln, vlc, pno)	1974	AMP
62. Counterpoint (vln, vla, vlc)	1975	AMP

E.   Keyboard

63. Sonata (pno)	1926	
64. Passacaglia (pno)	1943	Merc
65. Prelude and Allegro (org, str orch) (No. 8 above)	1943	AMP
66. Improvisation (pno)	1946	Delk
67. Chromatic Study on the Name B A C H (org)	1940	HWG
68. Partita (vln, vla, org) (No. 49 above)	1944	AMP

F.   Choral

69. Carnival Song (Lorenzo de' Medici) (TTBB, 11 brass inst)	1938	AMP
70. Psalm and Prayer of David (SATB, fl, clar, bsn, str)	1958	AMP

G.   Solo Vocal

71. Four Songs	1933

     a.   The Lover in Winter Plaineth for the Spring (16th c. anonymous) (with vla)
     b.   Comfort to a Youth Who has Lost His Love (Robert Herrick) (with vln, vla)
     c.   She Weeps Over Rahoon (James Joyce) (with str qrt)
     d.   Tilly (James Joyce) (with 2 vln, vlc)

Note: The following abbreviations are used in Section III of this *Outline*. The number indicates the number of the composition as listed in Section II.

67. *BACH*: Chromatic Study on BACH
69. *Carnival*: Carnival Song
30. *Concertino*: Concertino for Piano
29. *Concerto Orch*: Concerto for Orchestra
 5. *Flutist*: The Incredible Flutist
 3. *P & F*: Prelude and Fugue for Orchestra
48. *Qnt Fl*: Quintet for Flute, String Quartet
53. *Qnt Pno*: Quintet for Piano, String Quartet
41. *Son Fl Pno*: Sonata for Flute, Piano

46. *Son Vln Pno*: Sonata for Violin, Piano
43. *Str Qrt 1*: String Quartet No. 1
42. *Suite Ob Pno*: Suite for Oboe, Piano
 2. *Suite Orch 1*: Suite for Orchestra No. 1
 7. *Sym 2*: Symphony No. 2
40. *3 Pieces*: Three Pieces for Flute, Clarinet, Bassoon
19. *3 Sketches*: Three New England Sketches
45. *Trio*: Trio for Viola, Cello, Piano

III. Style (techniques and devices)

"The self-conscious striving for nationalism gets in the way of the establishment of a strong school of composition and even of significant individual expression. The composer cannot afford the wild-goose chase of trying to be more American than he is."   Walter Piston

A. General characteristics
1. "An American classicist." Works written before 1938 show some experimentation with modern dissonant techniques and complexities. After 1938 there is a tendency toward directness and simplicity, but the harmonic idiom is not radically different.
2. Texture generally contrapuntal; forms clear; three-movement works and classical forms preferred. Economy of material; rare use of dynamic extremes; expert craftsmanship. Works of uniformly high quality; almost all are instrumental and absolute music. An exception is *The Incredible Flutist* (1938) which is programmatic and in a more popular style.

B. Melodic line
1. Strong melodic gifts. Frequent use of chromatic lines; large leaps (diminished or augmented octaves); scale lines broken by leaping down a ninth, up a seventh, down a ninth.
2. Chromatic: *3 Pieces* (No. 2; No. 3).
3. Diatonic: *Carnival* (p. 18, meas. 4 to p. 19, meas. 10).
4. Diatonic and chromatic: *Son Fl Pno* (p. 3, meas. 1-4).
5. Angular: *Sinfonietta* (second movement, oboe).
6. Legato and flowing: *Sym 2* (first movement, first theme).
7. Vigorous and rhythmic: *Sym 2* (Finale, first theme).
8. Melodic sequences: *3 Pieces* (No. 1); *Str Qrt 1* (first movement).
9. Interval of fourth: *Str Qrt 1* (p. 5, meas. 17-28, first violin).
10. Whole-tone scale (experimental): *Concertino* (meas. 37, 38).

C. Harmony
1. Basically tonal and often dissonant; freely chromatic. All types of chord structures are used. Chords built on seconds and fourths frequent, on thirds less frequent; some use of diminished and augmented triads. Major and minor triads and complete seventh and ninth chords avoided.
2. Modal: *Suite Ob Pno* (*Sarabande*: Phrygian, p. 6, meas. 1; meas. 3-9).
3. Chords built on fourths: *Son Vln Pno* (third movement, p. 25, meas. 18-19); *Suite Ob Pno* (*Gigue*: p. 13, meas. 20, 21); *Qnt Pno* (first movement, middle section).
4. Tonal (triadic): *Sym 2* (p. 76, meas. 1).
5. Triads with added tones, homophonic style: *Suite Ob Pno* (*Sarabande*). Added tones usually a second or fourth, or a diminished or augmented octave.
6. Impressionistic harmonies (rare): *Sym 1* (*Adagio*, pp. 50, 56); *Flutist*.
7. Parallel major and minor ninths: *Str Qrt 5* (second movement).
8. Twelve-tone idea (rare): *Son Fl Pno*; *Sym 1* (beginning); *Partita* (org, vln, vla) (third movement); *Suite Orch 2* (*Passacaglia*).
9. Polytonal (rare): *Concertino* (meas. 37); *Son Vln Pno* (first movement, p. 1, meas. 191-192); *Concerto Orch*.
10. Sharp dissonances (major sevenths) in combination with consonances: *Suite Ob Pno* (*Prelude*, p. 4, meas. 9; *Gigue*, p. 12, meas. 1); *Str Qrt 1* (first movement, p. 25, meas. 5; p. 30, meas. 1).
11. Eleventh and thirteenth chords: *Carnival* (p. 26).
12. Atonality (rare): *Suite Orch 1*.

D. Counterpoint
1. Contrapuntal devices used frequently.
2. Dissonant counterpoint usual: *Str Qrt 1* (p. 6, meas. 2-6); *Sym 1*.
3. Fugal writing in Sonata form: *Son Vln Pno* (third movement, p. 24).

4. Fugal: *Sym 1*; *3 Sketches* (*Mountains*).
5. Retrograde motion: *Concerto Orch* (second movement, recapitulation).
6. Invertible: *3 Pieces* (No. 2, p. 7, meas. 2); *Son Vln* (last movement); *Sym 1* (third movement); *P & F* (subject and countersubject); *Str Qrt 2*; *Concerto Orch*.
7. Canonic: *Suite Ob Pno* (*Gigue*, p. 13, meas. 13); *Concertino* (end of slow section); *Trio* (fourth movement); *Sym 2* (first movement, end); *Sym 1* (third movement, second theme); *Sym 2* (pp. 14, 106).
8. Mirror Canon: *Trio* (first movement, p. 18, meas. 1-4; last movement).
9. Cancrizans: *Concertino* (meas. 111-112, between clar and bsn); *Concerto Orch* (third movement); *BACH*.
10. Stimmtausch: *Trio* (p. 15, meas. 1-2 with p. 18, meas. 26-27).

E. Rhythm
1. Meters generally conventional with some use of changing time signatures. Frequent use of syncopation.
2. Changing time signatures: *Str Qrt 1* (third movement, p. 22).
3. Ostinato: *3 Pieces* (first movement); *Sym 1* (first movement).
4. Syncopated rhythms; irregular meters: *Str Qrt 1* (*Finale*); *Sinfonietta* (first movement); *Sym 2* (first movement).
5. Cross meters: *3 Pieces* (No. 1: bsn in 4/8, upper parts in 3/8; No. 2: two against three).
6. Jazz or popular rhythms: *Sym 2* (first movement, pp. 12, 42; second movement, p. 22); *Suite Orch 1*; *Flutist* (second movement).
7. Asymmetrical rhythms: *Str Qrt 3*.

F. Form
1. Extensive use of classical forms.
2. Sonata-Allegro: *Sym 1* (first movement); *Son Fl Pno* (first movement); *Qnt Fl* (first movement); *Sym 2* (first movement).
3. Rondo Types: *Str Qrt 1* (first movement, A - B - A - B - A - Coda); *3 Pieces* (No. 3, A - B - A - C - A); *Sym 2* (third movement).
4. Fugue: *Suite Orch 1* (third movement); *P & F* (fugue answer a third higher); *Qnt Fl* (third movement).
5. Fugato: *Sinfonietta* (third movement, conclusion; intervals of subject altered); *Sym 1*; *3 Sketches* (*Mountains*).
6. Continuous (non-sectional): *Sym 2* (second movement).
7. Tutti alternating with solo groups: *Concerto Orch*.
8. Three-part, usually da capo: *3 Pieces* (Nos. 1, 2: A - B - A); *Suite Ob Pno* (*Minuetto*: A - B - A).
9. One movement: *Concertino* (three sections, A - B - A).
10. Passacaglia: *Concerto Orch* (third movement, 4/4 meter); *Passacaglia*.
11. Four movements: *Sym 3* (second movement a Scherzo).

BIBLIOGRAPHY

Books by Walter Piston

1. *Principles of Harmonic Analysis*. Boston: E. C. Schirmer, 1933.
2. *Harmony*. New York: W. W. Norton, 1941; 3rd ed., 1962. *Mus Ed J* 49, No. 2 (1962), 126; *Mus J* 21 (Jan 1963), 104; *PNM* 2, No. 2 (1964), 150-158.
3. *Counterpoint*. New York: W. W. Norton, 1947.
4. *Orchestration*. New York: W. W. Norton, 1955. *Notes* 12 (1954-1955), 437; *MQ* 42 (1956), 103; *MR* 18 (Feb 1957), 56.

Articles by Walter Piston

1. "Stravinsky as Psalmist–1931," *MM* 8, No. 2 (1930-1931), 43.
2. "Roy Harris," *MM* 11, No. 2 (1933-1934), 73.
3. "The Music Criticism Racket," *MM* 22, No. 4 (1944-1945), 282.
4. "Teaching as a Composer's Craft," *Composers News-Record* 9 (Spring 1949), 1.
5. "Review: *Harmonic Practice* by Roger Sessions," *MQ* 38 (1952), 457.
6. "More Views on Serialism," *Score* 23 (Jul 1958), 46-49.
7. "Problems of Intonation in the Performance of Contemporary Music," in *Instrumental Music*, ed. by D. G. Hughes. Cambridge: Harvard University Press, 1959, p. 70.
8. "Review: *Traité de l'Orchestration* by Charles Kœchlin," *MQ* 41 (1955), 247.
9. "Can Music be Nationalistic? " *Mus J* 19 (Oct 1961), 25.

References to Walter Piston

Books
(See the General Bibliography)

AbrMM; ASC-SC; AusMT; Baker; BauTC; BakSL; BIM; BloYA; BMI-C; BMI-MW; BMI-OP; BMI-P; BMI-SC; Bull; CatPC; ChaAC; ChaAM; ClaEA; CobCS; CohCT; ColHM; ComA (4); CopON; Cop-TN; CopWL; CowAC; CurB (1948, 1961); DalTT; DerETM; DowO; DukLH; Edm-II; EscCF; Ewe-AC; EweCB; EweCS; EweDE; EweWT; EweYA; FraMG; GosMM; Grove; HanIT; HitMU; HodSD; HowOA; HowOC; HowSH; JohSH; KinAI; LanOH; LeiMW; LeiSK; MacAC; MacIC; MasTA; MelMN; MueAS; MyeTC; NorLC; PAC; PavMH; PersTH; PeyNM; PleSM; ReiCC; RobCM; RowFC; SalMO; SalzTM; SamLM; SanWM; SchWC; SloMS; SpaMH; ThoAJ; ThoAM; ThoLR; ThompIC; ThoMR; ThomsMS; WilTM; WhiWW; WooWM; Who's Who (1968-1969); WWA; WWM; YatTC; YouCD.

Articles

Brief mention: *NW* 6 (Nov 2, 1935), 41; *NYT* (Dec 7, 1935), 22:6; *MM* 20, No. 2 (1942-1943), 100; *MQ* 33 (1947), 19, 314, 315, 317, 321; *PNM* 1, No. 2 (1963), 190; 2, No. 2 (1964), 16, 150; 4, No. 2 (1966), 35; *BMI-MW* (May 1967), 14.

1. Copland, Aaron. "American Composer Gets a Break," *Amer Merc* 34 (Apr 1935), 491.
2. Citkowitz, Israel. "Walter Piston–Classicist," *MM* 13, No. 2 (1935-1936), 3.
3. Slonimsky, Nicolas. "The Six of American Music," *Chr Sc Mon Mag* (Mar 17, 1937), 8-9.
4. "New Symphonies," *Time* 31 (Apr 18, 1938), 36.
5. Stutsman, Grace M. "Boston Symphony Plays Piston Novelty: Composer Conducts His First Symphony," *MA* 58, No. 8 (1938), 12.
6. *NYT* (May 8, 1939), 20:4.
7. Smith, George Henry Lovett. "Walter Piston: American Composer," *Mag of Art* 33 (Feb 1940), 98.
8. "Music Critics Award for Symphony," *NYT* (Jun 3, 1945), sec. 2, p. 4:3.
9. Carter, Elliott. "Walter Piston," *MQ* 32 (1946), 354.
10. "Wins Pulitzer Music Award," *NYT* (May 4, 1948), 1:6; 22:5.
11. "Competition for a Well-Digger," *Time* 51 (Jan 19, 1948), 48.
12. "Biography," *Current Biography* (Jun 1948); *Current Biography Yearbook* (1948), 496-499.
13. *SR* 32 (Aug 6, 1949), 162.
14. "Piston Symphony for the One-Hundredth Anniversary of University of Minnesota," *Chr Sc Mon Mag* (May 27, 1950), 17.
15. "Noted American Composer, Walter Piston," *Violins* 11 (Jul-Aug 1950), 211.
16. Boosey and Hawkes, *Brochure* (1950).

17. Rosenwald, Hans. "Contemporary Music," *Mus News* 43 (Feb 1951), 10.
18. "Honorary Degree Harvard University," *NYT* (Jun 20, 1952), 18:1, 4, 5.
19. "Piston May Follow Schuman in BMI," *BB* 64 (Dec 6, 1952), 14.
20. "Gets N. Y. Music College Honorary Degree," *NYT* (Jun 19, 1953), 17:5.
21. "Recipient of Honorary Degree," *Etude* 71 (Aug 1953), 56.
22. RePass, R. "American Composer of Today," *London Mus* 8 (Dec 1953), 25.
23. *Canon* 6 (Dec 1953), 219.
24. Taubman, Howard. "Piston at 60," *NYT* (Jan 31, 1954), sec. 2, p. 7:8.
25. "H. Hartford Foundation Award," *NYT* (Jul 10, 1954), 6:5.
26. Keats, Sheila. "Reference Articles on American Composers: An Index," *Juilliard Rev* 1 (Fall 1954), 30-31.
27. Berger, Arthur. "Stravinsky and His Firmament," *SR* 37 (Nov 27, 1954), 58.
28. "Walter Piston," *Pan Pipes* 47 (Jan 1955), 61.
29. Austin, William. "Piston's Fourth Symphony; An Analysis," *MR* 16 (May 1955), 120-137.
30. Evett, Robert. "How Right is Right? " *Score* 12 (Jun 1955), 33.
31. "Inducted into American Academy of Arts and Letters," *NYT* (May 24, 1956), 25:1.
32. Ellsworth, Roy. "Americans on Microgroove," *HiFi* 6 (Aug 1956), 65.
33. Kyle, Marguerite K. "AmerAllegro," *Pan Pipes* 49 (Jan 1957), 64.
34. Epstein, David M. "Orchestra and Chamber Works by Piston," *MA* 77 (Dec 1, 1957), 26.
35. "We Salute Walter Piston," *Mus Club Mag* 37 (Jan 1958), 9.
36. "Walter Piston," *Composers of the Americas* 4 (1958), 16-24.
37. "Classified Chronological Catalog of Works by the United States Composer Walter Piston," *InterAmer Mus Bul* 9-10 (Jan-Mar 1959), 59-65.
38. *NYT* (Mar 23, 1960), 31:6; (Apr 25, 1960), 34:2.
39. "Retires from Harvard University," *NYT* (May 15, 1960), 124:4.
40. "Piston Retires after 30 Years on Harvard Staff," *Diap* 51 (Jul 1, 1960), 18.
41. Salzman, Eric. "Piston; Ex-Teacher," *NYT* (Mar 26, 1961), sec. 2, p. 13:7.
42. Parmenter, Ross. "A Program of Chamber Music by Walter Piston," *NYT* (Mar 31, 1961), 23:3.
43. "Wins Pulitzer," *FoF* 21 (May 1, 1961), 160A1.
44. "Wins Pulitzer Prize for Symphony No. 7," *NYT* (May 2, 1961), 40:2, 6; *NYHT* (May 2, 1961).
45. Kerr, Russell. "Piston Pulitzer–The Winner Speaks," *MC* 163 (Jun 1961), 5-7.
46. Rich, Alan. "Composer's Showcase," *MA* 81 (Jun 1961), 48.
47. "Biography," *Current Biography* (Dec 1961); *Current Biography Yearbook* (1961), 366-368.
48. *NYT* (Feb 4, 1962), sec. 4, p. 24; (May 19, 1962), 19:2; (Jul 22, 1962), 68:1; (Sep 26, 1962).
49. "Creative Arts Award, Brandeis University," *NYT* (May 1, 1963), 32:4.
50. Chapin, Louis. "Walter Piston at Seventy," *MA* 83 (Dec 1963), 34.
51. Novack, Saul. "Recent Approaches to the Study of Harmony," *PNM* 2, No. 2 (1964), 150.
52. "Works by Walter Piston," *MA* 84 (Jul 1964), 47.
53. "Letters: Brickbats and a Bouquet for Sir John (Sir John Barbirolli and Contemporary Music," *MA* 84 (Sep 1964), 4.
54. Taylor, Clifford. "Walter Piston: For His 70th Birthday," *PNM* 3, No. 1 (1964), 102-114.
55. Daniel, Oliver. "Walter Piston," New York: *BMI Brochure* (1964).
56. Westergaard, Peter. "Conversation with Walter Piston," *PNM* 7, No. 1 (1968), 3–17.
57. "Die Information," *NZ* 130 (Jan 1969), 16.
58. *NYT* (Feb 5, 1969), 38:1.
59. Roy, Klaus G. "Walter Piston," *Stereo R* 24 (Apr 1970), 57-67.
60. Haieff, Alexei. "Stravinsky: A Composers' Memorial," *PNM* 9, No. 2 (1971), 6-7.
61. Archibald, Bruce. "Current Chronicle: Fantasia for Violin and Orchestra and the Concerto for Flute and Orchestra by Boston Symphony," *MQ* 59 (Jan 1973), 121-125.

62. "The Pulitzer Prizes (Some Winners in Music)," *BMI* No. 2 (1974), 22.
63. "Awarded Edward MacDowell Medal," *NYT* (Aug 19, 1974), 32:1.
64. Pfeifer, Ellen. "Walter Piston: Musician of the Month," *HiFi/MA* 24 (Aug 1974), MA4-5.
65. "Composers in Focus," *BMI* (Winter 1976), 26.
66. Smith, Rollin. "American Organ Composers," *MusicAGO* 10 (Aug 1976), 18.
67. "Obituary," *FoF* 29 (Jul 25, 1976), 800F3; *Variety* 285 (Nov 17, 1976), 78; *Clavier* 16, No. 1 (1977), 9; *Down Bt* 44 (Jan 13, 1977), 10; *Instrument* 31 (Jan 1977), 95; *MT* 118 (Jan 1977), 64; *Sym News* 27, No. 6 (1977), 28; *Mus Ed J* 63 (Feb 1977), 106; *HiFi/MA* 27 (Mar 1977), MA7; *Melos/NZ* 3, No. 1 (1977), 59; *MusicAGO* 11 (Mar 1977), 29; *Tempo* 120 (Mar 1977), 23; *Gramophone* 55 (Jun 1977), 31; *Hud Roz* 30, No. 3 (1977), 128; *Central Opera* 20, No. 1 (1977-1978), 22; *R Mus Ital* 11, No. 1 (1977), 154; *Pan Pipes* 69, No. 3 (1977), 32; *Current Biography* (Jan 1977); *Current Biography Yearbook* (1977), 471.
68. Curtis, William D. "A Fitting Memorial (The Incredible Flutist) (Including Discography)," *Am Rec G* 40 (Jun 1977), 36-40.
69. de Voto, M. "In Memoriam: Walter Piston (1894-1976)," *PNM* 15, No. 2 (1977), 243.

References to Works by Walter Piston

The number preceding the title indicates the number of the composition as listed in Section II.

24. Capriccio for Harp, Strings: *Int Am Mus B* 45 (Jan 1965), 2.
69. Carnival Song: *MA* 59 (Oct 10, 1939), 26; *MM* 17, No. 4 (1939-1940), 237; *MQ* 32 (1946), 363, 369.
30. Concertino for Piano: *MA* 59 (Oct 10, 1939), 26; *BSPN* (Nov 10, 1939); *MA* 59 (Nov 25, 1939); *DowO*, 281.
35. Concerto for Clarinet: *BMI* (Oct 1967), 24.
36. Concerto for Flute: *MQ* 59 (1973), 121-125; *Sym News* 24, No. 1 (1973), 21.
29. Concerto for Orchestra: *BSPN* (Mar 8, 1934); *NYT* (Feb 15, 1936), 19:4; *MQ* 32 (1946), 365; *CinSPN* (Apr 11, 1958), 754; *Roch Phil* (Oct 25, 1962), 8; *PNM* 3, No. 1 (1964), 109; *HiFi/MA* 16 (Jul 1966), MA17.
33. Concerto for Two Pianos: *MT* 110 (Jan 1969), 55.
38. Concerto for Strings, Wind Instruments, Percussion: *Sym News* 27, No. 6 (1975), 30.
32. Concerto for Viola: *Boston Herald* (Mar 8, 1958); *Time* 71 (Mar 17, 1958), 68; *NYT* (Mar 20, 1958), 34:3; *SR* 41 (Apr 5, 1958), 22; *MC* 157 (Apr 1958), 36; *MA* 78 (Apr 1958), 16; *MC* 157 (May 1958), 18; *NYHT* (Feb 13, 1959); *Notes* 18 (1960-1961), 315; *SFSPN* (Mar 25, 1964), 26.
31. Concerto for Violin, No. 1: *MM* 17, No. 4 (1939-1940), 237; *MQ* 32 (1946), 369; *PitSPN* (Dec 5, 1947), 204.
34. Concerto for Violin, No. 2: *MA* 80 (Dec 1960), 21; *MC* 162 (Dec 1960), 27; *MA* 81 (Mar 1961), 22; *MC* 163 (Jun 1961), 62; (Jul 1961), 54; *MA* 81 (Jul 1961), 10; *SR* 45 (Jun 2, 1962), 19; *MA* 82 (Jul 1962), 24; *Mus Mag* 164 (Jul 1962), 22; *Notes* 21 (1963-1964), 254; *PNM* 3, No. 1 (1964), 105; *Houston Sym* (Oct 31, 1966), 19-23.
51. Divertimento for Nine Instruments: *MQ* 32 (1946), 372.
54. Duo for Viola, Cello: *MC* 141 (Mar 15, 1950), 10; *MA* 77 (Dec 1, 1957), 26.
Duo for Cello, Piano (1972): *NYT* (Feb 9, 1975), 47:3.
15. Fantasy for English Horn, Harp, Strings: *BSNBul* 11 (Jan 1, 1954), 498; *MC* 149 (Jan 15, 1954), 7.
37. Fantasia for Violin, Orchestra: *HiFi/MA* 23 (Aug 1973), MA10-11.
5. The Incredible Flutist: *NYPPN* (Jan 17, 1946); *MQ* 32 (1946), 363, 368; *CohCT*, 164; *EweCB*, 270; *MacAC*, 61.
47. Interlude for Viola, Piano: *ML* 34 (Apr 1953), 174-175.
22. Lincoln Center Festival Overture: *NYT* (Sep 26, 1962), 32:2; *MA* 82 (Nov 1962), 19; *Notes* 21 (1963-1964), 254; *POPN* (Nov 9, 1972), 13-16.

19. Three New England Sketches: *MA* 79 (Nov 15, 1959), 5; *MC* 160 (Dec 1960), 6; *MA* 80 (Dec 1960), 16.

49. Partita for Violin, Viola, Organ: *NYT* (Oct 30, 1944), 15:6; *PNM* 3, No. 1 (1964), 103.

27. Pine Tree Fantasy: *BMI* (Feb 1966), 7.

 8. Prelude and Allegro: *Clev Orch* (Oct 6, 1967), 59-65; *Roch Phil* (Oct 31, 1968), 33.

 3. Prelude and Fugue: *MQ* 34 (1948), 10; *CinSPN* (Feb 20, 1953), 467-469.

53. Quintet for Piano, String Quartet: *Opera* 16 (Jan 1951), 30; *MQ* 39 (1953), 657-659; *Notes* 13 (1955-1956), 145.

48. Quintet for Flute, String Quartet: *MQ* 32 (1946), 371; *MM* 23, No. 4 (1946), 307; *Canon* 7 (Mar 1954), 332.

56. Quintet for Wind Instruments: *MQ* 44 (1958), 551; *Notes* 17 (1959-1960), 469; *PNM* 3, No. 1 (1964), 108, 110.

28. Ricercare: *NYT* (Mar 8, 1968), 49:1; *Mus J* 26 (May 1968), 58; *BMI* (May 1968), 20; *MT* 109 (Jun 1968), 562; *HiFi/MA* 18 (Jun 1968), MA20; *Mus & Artists* 1, No. 2 (1968), 48.

18. Serenata: *MC* 154 (Nov 15, 1956), 21; *Notes* 17 (1959-1960), 318; *CohCT*, 164.

 6. Sinfonietta: *BSPN* (Nov 24, 1942); *StLSPN* (Nov 24, 1951), 165.

41. Sonata for Flute, Piano: *MQ* 32 (1946), 316.

46. Sonata for Violin, Piano: *MA* 59 (May 10, 1939), 34; *MM* 17, No. 4 (1939-1940), 168; *MQ* 32 (1946), 369; *CohCT*, 168; *HanIT*, 320.

50. Sonatina for Violin, Harpsichord: *MQ* 32 (1946), 361; 40 (1954), 474.

43. String Quartet No. 1: *Musica* 10 (Feb 1956), 144; *PNM* 3, No. 1 (1964), 113; *CobCS*, 159.

44. String Quartet No. 2: *MA* 56 (May 10, 1936), 11; *MQ* 32 (1946), 367; *Notes* 4 (1946-1947), 356; *CobSC*, 159.

52. String Quartet No. 3: *Notes* 7 (1949-1950), 131; *EweCB*, 271; *CobSC*, 159.

55. String Quartet No. 4: *MA* 72 (Jun 1952), 10; *Notes* 11 (1953-1954), 435; *MA* 74 (Mar 1954), 36; *MC* 149 (May 15, 1954), 41; *CobSC*, 159.

57. String Quartet No. 5: *MA* 82 (Nov 1962), 42; (Dec 1962), 20; *Musica* 17, No. 1 (1963), 27; *Notes* 21 (1963-1964), 453; *NYT* (Feb 11, 1964), 43:4; *PNM* 3, No. 1 (1964), 113.

58. String Sextet: *MQ* 51 (1965), 410.

42. Suite for Oboe, Piano: *MQ* 32 (1946), 365.

 2. Suite for Orchestra, No. 1: *NYT* (Feb 9, 1934), 22:4; *MQ* 32 (1946), 363.

13. Suite for Orchestra, No. 2: *BSPN* (Oct 14, 1949); *MQ* 36 (1950), 594; *BSCBul* No. 2 (Oct 14, 1951), 65; *Notes* 12 (1954-1955), 326; *MC* 152 (Jul 1955), 45; *MA* 77 (Dec 1, 1957), 26.

 1. Symphonic Piece: *BSPN* (Mar 23, 1928).

21. Symphonic Prelude: *MC* 163 (Jun 1, 1961), 56; *MA* 81 (Jun 1961), 23; *StLSPN* (Mar 9, 1962), 511; *Seattle SPN* (Feb 11, 1963), 508.

 4. Symphony No. 1: *MA* 58, No. 8 (1938), 12; *BSPN* (Apr 8, 1938); *MQ* 32 (1946), 364; *Notes* 4 (1946-1947), 107.

 7. Symphony No. 2: *MM* 21, No. 3 (1943-1944), 179; *BSPN* (Apr 6, 1944); *Notes* 2 (1944-1945), 117; *MQ* 32 (1946), 363; *BSCBul* No. 24 (Apr 29, 1955), 1164-1166; *PNM* 3, No. 1 (1964), 109, 113; *Am Rec G* 32 (Apr 1966), 685; *EweCB*, 271.

11. Symphony No. 3: *BSPN* (Jan 9, 1948); *MQ* 34 (1948), 249; 35 (1949), 287; *MC* 149 (Jun 1954), 36; *SFSPN* (Feb 17, 1955), 409; *MA* 79 (Mar 1959), 24; *CohCT*, 165; *FraMG*.

14. Symphony No. 4: *Pan Pipes* 43 (Dec 1950), 93; *MC* 143 (May 15, 1951), 28; *MA* 72 (Nov 1, 1952), 27; *NYT* (Nov 13, 1952), 34:1; *MA* 72 (Dec 1, 1952), 22; *MC* 148 (Sep 1953), 33; *MA* 73 (Nov 1, 1953), 26; *Notes* 11 (1953-1954), 146-147; *POPN* (Apr 2, 1954), 367; *MQ* 41 (1955), 551-555; *MR* 16 (1955), 120; *MC* 153 (Feb 1, 1956), 98; *PNM* 3, No. 1 (1964), 109; *CohCT*, 166; *HanIT*, 322; *MacIC*, 509.

16. Symphony No. 5: *MA* 76 (Mar 1956), 37; (Dec 1, 1956), 18; *MQ* 42 (1956); *Notes* 14 (1956-1957), 449.
17. Symphony No. 6: *NYT* (Dec 8, 1955), 47:4; *MA* 75 (Dec 15, 1955), 26, 33; *SR* 38 (Dec 24, 1955), 28; *Melos* 23 (Mar 1956), 87; *NYT* (Aug 27, 1956), 16:5; *Notes* 15 (1957-1958), 146; *PitSPN* (Apr 26, 1968), 785-787; *CohCT*, 166.
20. Symphony No. 7: *POPN* (Feb 10, 1961); *MA* 81 (Mar 1961), 41; *MC* 163 (Mar 1961), 23; *NYT* (May 2, 1961), 36:2; *Pan Pipes* 54, No. 2 (1962), 10; *BSPN* (Sep 21, 1962), 22-24; *Notes* 20 (1962-1963), 121; *Canon* 6 (Dec 1962-Jan 1963), 219-220; *ChiSPN* (Jan 17, 1963), 7-15; *PNM* 3, No. 1 (1964), 111.
26. Symphony No. 8: *NYT* (Apr 1, 1965), 29:1; *HiFi/MA* 15 (Jun 1965), 122.
40. Three Pieces for Flute, Clarinet, Bassoon: *MQ* 32 (1946), 354, 359; *ACA-Bul* 4, No. 2 (1954), 21; *MQ* 43 (1957), 421; *CohCT*, 169.
12. Toccata for Orchestra: *ChiSPN* (Mar 10, 1949), 7; *BSCBul* 24 (Apr 25, 1952), 1148; *SFSPN* (Nov 19, 1953), 49; *Notes* 11 (1953-1954), 276; *POPN* (Dec 2, 1955), 215; (Jan 28, 1966), 15.
45. Trio for Violin, Cello, Piano: *MA* 59 (Oct 10, 1939), 26.
39. Tunbridge Fair: *MQ* 36, (1950), 594; *Symphony* 6 (Feb 1952), 14; *CohCT*, 167.
25. Variations for Cello, Orchestra: *NYT* (Mar 3, 1967), 27:4; *Time* 89 (Mar 10, 1967), 74-75; *BMI* (Apr 1967), 14; *Natl Sym* (May 12, 1967), 24; *Mus J* 25 (May 1967), 63; *HiFi/MA* 17 (May 1967), MA9.
23. Variations on a Theme by Edward Burlingame Hill: *Mus J* 21 (May 1963), 14.

Dissertations about Walter Piston and His Works

1. Burke, James R. *A Study of Theories of Non-Chord Tones Pertaining to the Music of the Period c. 1650 and c. 1875.* Indiana University, 1963. (Includes discussion of theories by Walter Piston and Roger Sessions)
2. Colucci, Matthew J. *A Comparative Study of Contemporary Musical Theories in Selected Writings of Piston, Krenek and Hindemith.* University of Pennsylvania, 1957.
3. Donahue, Robert L. *A Comparative Analysis of Phrase Structure in Selected Movements of the String Quartets of Béla Bartók and Walter Piston.* Cornell University, 1964.
4. Gaburo, Kenneth L. *Studies in Pitch Symmetry in Twentieth Century Music.* University of Illinois, 1962.
5. Halen, Walter J. *An Analysis and Comparison of Compositional Practices Used by Five Contemporary Composers in Works Titled "Symphony."* Ohio State University, 1969.

WALLINGFORD RIEGGER (1885-1961)

I. Life

1885   Born in Albany, Georgia, April 29. Father a lumber mill owner, and violinist and choir director; mother a pianist.

1900   Family moved to New York.

1904   Attended Cornell University (1904-1905). After one year he decided to become a musician.

1905   Studied at the Institute of Musical Art, New York, with Percy Goetchius (theory, composition), Alwin Schroeder (cello); graduated 1907.

1907   Studied cello at the Hochschule für Musik in Berlin with Robert Hausman and later with Anton Hekking. Also studied with Max Bruch and Edgar Stillman Kelley (composition).

1911   Returned to America; married Rose Schramm. Engaged as a cellist by the St. Paul Symphony (1911-1914).

1915   Decided to become a conductor; returned to Germany; conducted opera in Würzburg and Königsburg (1915-1916); Blüthner Orchestra of Berlin (1916-1917).

1918   Returned to America; taught theory and cello at Drake University in Des Moines (1918-1922). Began to compose (*c.* 1920); received the Paderewski Prize in 1922 (*Trio, Op. 1*).

1924   Taught at the Institute of Musical Art, New York (1924-1925). Awarded an honorary Doctor of Music degree from the Cincinnati Conservatory of Music (1925). Awarded the Ethel Sprague Coolidge Prize for his setting of *La Belle Dame sans Merci.*

1926   Taught at the Ithaca Conservatory of Music (1926-1928). First atonal work, *Study in Sonority*, Op. 7 (1927).

1928   Settled in New York; active as a composer and in societies promoting contemporary music. Taught for a short time at Teachers College of Columbia University, New School for Social Research, Metropolitan Music School.

1933   Composed many works for the modern dance (1933-1941).

1948   Elected president of the United States section of the International Society of Contemporary Music (I. S. C. M.). Works began to receive increased public recognition. Received the New York Music Critics Circle Award (*Symphony No. 3*).

1951   Visiting professor, Northwestern University (1951-1952).

1956   Began one of his most important and productive periods.

1959   Conducted his works during the 1959-1960 season of the Kansas City Philharmonic Orchestra.

1961   Received a Brandeis Creative Arts Award.

1961   Died in an accident in New York, April 2.

Wallingford Riegger has been the recipient of many honors and commissions in addition to those listed above. He used numerous pseudonyms: William Richards, Walter Scotson, Gerald Wilfring Gore, John H. McCurdy, George Northrup, Robert Sedgwick, Leonard Gregg, Edwin Farell, Edgar Long.

Note: Biographies of varying lengths and importance will be found in many of the books listed in the Bibliography at the end of this *Outline* under "References to Wallingford Riegger."

II.   Compositions

A.   Orchestra

		Date	Publisher
1.	American Polonaise: Triple Jazz, Op. 3 (withdrawn)	1922	
2.	Rhapsody, Op. 5	1926	ACA
3.	Study in Sonority, Op. 7 (10 violins or any multiple of 10)	1927	AMP
4.	Fantasy and Fugue, Op. 10 (org with 2 players, orch)	1931	ACA
5.	Dichotomy, Op. 12	1932	AMP
6.	Scherzo, Op. 13 (cham orch)	1932	Peer
7.	Evocation, Op. 17a (from No. 62)	1933	Peer
8.	New Dance, Op. 18b (from No. 63)	1935	AMP
9.	The Cry, Op. 22	1935	Peer
10.	Consummation, Op. 31	1939	
11.	Canon and Fugue, Op. 33 (str orch; also full orch, Op. 33a)	1941	Flam
12.	Passacaglia and Fugue, Op. 34a (From No. 36)	1942	Mm
13.	Funeral March (Processional), Op. 36a (From No. 37)	1943	Duch
14.	Symphony No. 1, Op. 37 (withdrawn)	1944	
15.	Little Black Sambo, Op. 40 (small orch)	1946	
16.	Symphony No. 2, Op. 41 (withdrawn)	1946	
17.	Symphony No. 3, Op. 42	1947; revised 1957	AMP
18.	Music for Brass Choir, Op. 45 (10 trpt, 4 hn, 10 trb, 2 tba, timp, cym)	1949	Mm
19.	Canon on a Ground Bass by Henry Purcell (str orch; also str qrt)	1951	AMP
20.	Music for Orchestra, Op. 50	1951	AMP
21.	Variations for Piano, Orchestra, Op. 54 (also for 2 pno and orch, Op. 54a)	1953	AMP
22.	Suite for Younger Orchestras, Op. 56	1954	AMP
23.	Romanza, Op. 56a (str orch) (from Suite, Op. 56)	1954	AMP
24.	Dance Rhythms, Op. 58	1955	AMP
25.	Overture, Op. 60	1955	AMP
26.	Preamble and Fugue, Op. 61	1955	AMP
27.	Variations for Violins, Violas, Op. 57 (also for vln, vla)	1956	AMP
28.	Symphony No. 4, Op. 63	1957	AMP
29.	Festival Overture, Op. 68	1957	AMP
30.	Variations for Violin, Orchestra, Op. 71	1958	AMP
31.	Quintuple Jazz, Op. 72	1958	AMP
32.	Sinfonietta, Op. 73	1959	AMP
33.	Introduction and Fugue, Op. 74	1959	AMP
34.	Duo for Piano, Orchestra, Op. 75	1960	AMP

B.   Band

		Date	Publisher
35.	New Dance, Op. 18c (from No. 63)	1935	AMP
36.	Passacaglia and Fugue, Op. 34	1942	Mm
37.	Funeral March (Processional), Op. 36 (concert band)	1943	Duch
38.	Dance Rhythms, Op. 58a (concert band) (from No. 24)	1957	AMP
39.	Introduction and Fugue, Op. 74 (vlc, symphonic winds, timp)	1960	AMP

C.   Chamber

		Date	Publisher
40.	Trio in B minor, Op. 1 (vln, pno, vlc)	1920	AMP
41.	Whimsy, Op. 2 (vlc, pno)	1920	AMP
42.	Suite for Flute Solo, Op. 8	1929	NME
43.	Three Canons for Woodwinds, Op. 9 (fl, ob, clar, bsn)	1931	NME
44.	Divertissement, Op. 15 (fl, hp, vlc)	1933	ACA
45.	Frenetic Rhythms, Op. 16 (pno, fl, clar, perc)	1933	ACA
46.	New Dance, Op. 18e (vln, pno) (from No. 63)	1935	ACA

47.	String Quartet No. 1, Op. 30	1939	AMP
48.	Duos for Three Woodwinds, Op. 35 (fl, ob, clar)	1943	NME
49.	Sonatina for Violin, Piano, Op. 39	1947	EBM
50.	String Quartet No. 2, Op. 43	1948	AMP
51.	Quintet for Piano, String Quartet, Op. 47	1950	AMP
52.	Nonet for Brass, Op. 49 (3 trpt, 2 hn, 3 trb, tba)	1951	AMP
53.	Quintet for Winds, Op. 51 (fl, ob, clar, bsn, hn)	1952	AMP
54.	Concerto for Piano, Wind Quintet, Op. 53	1952	AMP
	(pno, fl, ob, bsn, clar, hn)		
55.	Romanza, Op. 56a (str qrt) (from Suite Op. 56)	1954	AMP
56.	Variations for Violin, Viola, Op. 57 (also for violins, violas)	1956	AMP
57.	Movement, Op. 66 (2 trpt, trb, pno)	1957	Peer
58.	Introduction and Fugue, Op. 69 (4 vlc or vlc orch)	1957	AMP

D.   Keyboard (for solo piano unless otherwise indicated)

59.	Blue Voyage, Op. 6	1927	AMP
60.	Scherzo, Op. 13 (pno; 2 pno; pno 4 hands)	1932	Peer
61.	Four Tone Pictures, Op. 14	1932	AMP

    a.   Prelude   c.   Wishful Thinking
    b.   Angles and Curves   d.   Grotesque

62.	Evocation, Op. 17 (pno 4 hands; 2 pno)	1933	Peer
63.	New Dance, Op. 18 (pno; pno 4 hands; 2 pno; 3 pno)	1935	AMP
64.	Finale from New Dance, Op. 18	1935	AMP
65.	The Cry, Op. 22 (pno 4 hands; 2 pno)	1935	Peer
66.	New and Old, Op. 38 (12 study pieces)	1944	BH

    a. The Augmented Triad e. Shifted Rhythms i. Dissonant Counterpoint
    b. The Major Second   f. Twelve Upside Down j. Tone Cluster
    c. The Tritone   g. Seven Times Seven k. Polytonality
    d. The Twelve Tones   h. Chromatics   l. Fourths and Fifths

67.	Toccata (No. 12 from No. 66) 1944; revised 1957		
68.	Canon and Fugue, Op. 33b (org) (from No. 11)	1954	Flam
69.	Canon and Fugue, Op. 33c (2 pno) (from No. 11)	1954	Flam
70.	Variations, Op. 54a (from No. 21) (2 pno)	1954	AMP
71.	Petite Etude, Op. 62 (pno or harpsichord)	1956	Pres
72.	Cooper Square, Op. 70 (accordion)	1958	Deiro

E.   Choral

73.	La Belle Dame sans Merci, Op. 4 (John Keats) (S., m-S., A., T.,	1923	Peer
	fl, ob, bsn, hn, 2 vln, vlc, c-b. SSA, augmented str optional)		
74.	Eternity, Op. 32a (Emily Dickinson) (SSA, fl, 2 hn, c-b)	1942	Flam
75.	From Some Far Shore, Op. 32b (Walt Whitman) (SATB, pno)	1946	Flam
76.	Easter Passacaglia, Op. 32c (SATB, org or pno; also SSA; SAB)	1946	Flam
77.	Who Can Revoke, Op. 44 (Catherine Harris) (SATB, pno)	1948	EBM
78.	In Certainty of Song, Op. 46 (Catherine Harris) (Cantata:	1950	Peer
	Soli, SATB, pno or cham orch)		
79.	Non Vincit Malitia, Op. 48 (Liber Sapientiae) (double	1951	BCS
	chorus: SSA-SSA, or SSA-TBB, or TBB-TBB)		
80.	A Shakespeare Sonnet (No. 138), Op. 65 (Bar., SSAB, pno or	1956	AMP
	cham orch)		

F.   Solo Vocal (with piano unless otherwise indicated)

81.	The Somber Pine (Egmont Arens)	1902	AMP
82.	Ye Banks and Braes (Robert Burns)	1910	Peer
83.	Two Bergerettes (anon)	1920	Peer

    a. Charmant bocage   b. Toi, dont les yeux

84.	La Belle Dame sans Merci, Op. 4 (John Keats)	1923	Peer
	(S., m-S., A., T., cham orch)		

85.	Music for Voice, Flute, Op. 23 (also for 2 fl)	1936	Bom
86.	The Dying of the Light, Op. 59 (Dylan Thomas) (also with orch, Op. 59a)	1956	AMP

G.   **Dance and Ballet** (commissioned works)

87.	Bacchanale, Op. 11 (Martha Graham) (pno 4 hands)	1930	
88.	Frenetic Rhythms, Op. 16 (Martha Graham) (pno, fl, clar, drums)	1933	ACA
89.	Evocation, Op. 17 (Martha Graham) (pno 4 hands)	1933	Peer
90.	Trilogy (Doris Humphrey)		AMP

    a. New Dance, Op. 18 (pno 4 hands, perc) (1935)
    b. Theatre Piece, Op. 19 (pno, cham orch) (1935)
    c. With My Red Fires, Op. 20 (pno, cham orch) (1936)

91.	Chronicle, Op. 21 (Martha Graham) (pno, cham orch)	1936	
92.	The Cry, Op. 22 (Hanya Holm) (pno 4 hands)	1935	Peer
93.	Candide (Charles Weidman) (pno, perc)	1937	
94.	Trend, Op. 25 (Hanya Holm) (one section by Riegger, remainder by Varèse) (pno, perc)	1937	
95.	Trojan Incident, Op. 26 (Helen Tamiris) (pno, perc)	1938	
96.	Case History No. . . , Op. 27 (Anna Sokolow) (pno, perc)	1937	
97.	Machine Ballet, Op. 28 (Saida Gerrard) (pno, orch)	1938	
98.	Pilgrim's Progress, Op. 29 (Eric Hawkins) (pno)	1941	

H.   **Anthems and Folk Song Arrangements**

    99.   The Riegger Anthem Book (SAB)

Note: The following abbreviations are used in Section III of this *Outline*. The number indicates the number of the composition as listed in Section II.

18. *Brass*: Music for Brass Choir
11. *Canon*: Canon and Fugue for Strings
78. *Cantata*: In Certainty of Song
54. *Concerto*: Concerto for Piano, Wind Instruments
48. *Duos*: Duos for Three Woodwinds
52. *Nonet*: Nonet for Brass
61. *Pictures*: Four Tone Pictures

19. *Purcell*: Canon on a Ground Bass by Henry Purcell
51. *Qnt Pno Str*: Quintet for Piano, String Quartet
3. *Sonority*: Study in Sonority
50. *Str Qrt 2*: String Quartet No. 2
17. *Sym 3*: Symphony No. 3
27. *Variations*: Variations for Violins, Violas

III.   Style (techniques and devices)

"What intrigues the composer about twelve-tone techniques is their severe restrictions. To keep within them is a challenge, as it is to a poet to stick to the rhyming scheme, once decided upon, of a sonnet." "The abandonment of keys does not necessarily mean the complete negation of 'music,' . . ., but rather its potential enrichment in the discovery of new tonalities, with new possibilities of texture, both harmonic and polyphonic, of melody (albeit in a new disguise) and of form . . ., all truly expressive of the age in which we live, while losing nothing of the universally human."

Wallingford Riegger

A.   General characteristics
    1.   Early works (1919-1923) are in the traditional style of German romanticism (*Trio*, Op. 1). Some use of whole tone and impressionistic techniques (*Blue Voyage*); changing time signatures; conventional classic forms.
    2.   Trend toward atonality and twelve-tone techniques (1926-1931). Music written for the modern dance (1933-1941) uses polytonality, but is not atonal.
    3.   From 1942 twelve-tone techniques are used in a highly personal and original way,

rarely strict. Complete integrity, unusual expressiveness, vitality, freshness, and clarity. Expert craftsmanship in relating the twelve-tone techniques to traditional forms and concepts.

B.   Melodic line
  1.   Motives developed from parts of a row: *Duo* (*Lento*).
  2.   Statement of twelve-tone row: *Sym 3* (first movement, meas. 3, ob).
  3.   Two tone rows, one eleven tones, one ten tones: *Dichotomy*.
  4.   Thirteen-tone row: *Dichotomy*.
  5.   Thirty-six tone row: *Suite for Flute Solo*.
  6.   Tone row with many semitones: *Nonet*.
  7.   Minor seconds: *Brass* (throughout).
  8.   Tritones: *Brass* (p. 8, meas. 4); *Sonority* (beginning).
  9.   Unison melody alternating with dissonant chords: *Sonority* (beginning).
  10.   Quarter tones: *Sonority* (No. 24).
  11.   Chromatic and modal lines: *Concerto* (*Andante*).
  12.   Lyric theme: *Sym 3* (second movement).

C.   Harmony
  1.   All possible tone combinations used and applied to the principles of conventional harmony.
  2.   Atonality: *Sonority*; *Str Qrt 2*; *Sym 3*; *Petite Etude* (middle section).
  3.   Polytonality, use of seconds: *Sonority*; *New and Old* (p. 31); *Toccata*.
  4.   Free twelve-tone techniques: *Dichotomy*; *Sym 3*; *Nonet*.
  5.   Strict twelve-tone techniques: *Str Qrt 1*.
  6.   Chromaticism without a tonic: *The Dying of the Light*.
  7.   Parallel motion of chords by half steps or scale tones: *Sym 3*; *Brass* (p. 12, meas. 3).
  8.   Tone clusters: *Pictures* (No. 4); *Brass* (pp. 1, 5, 23; p. 12, meas. 3); *Qnt Pno Str* (*Finale*, second theme, str, pno); *Cantata*.
  9.   "Lyric atonalism": *Concerto*.
  10.   Characteristic use of an original six-tone chord leading to a chord with the other six tones in a dominant (active)-tonic (quiet) relationship: *Sonority*.

D.   Counterpoint
  1.   Extensive use of contrapuntal devices in all possible ways.
  2.   Imitation in mirror: *Brass* (p. 26, meas. 3, trb).
  3.   Augmentation in stretto: *Brass* (p. 37, second theme).
  4.   Double counterpoint: *Brass* (p. 7, meas. 6; p. 8, meas. 4).
  5.   Retrograde: *Brass* (p. 1, first theme; p. 5, meas. 4, trpt).
  6.   Fugato: *Nonet*; *Sym 3* (second movement) (see *Form*: Fugue).
  7.   Canon: *Qnt Pno Str* (second movement); *Purcell*; *Three Canons for Woodwinds*; *Canon*.

E.   Rhythm
  1.   Strong, rugged rhythms; syncopation, changes in meter, and irregular groupings, contrasted with regular meter. Rhythm less complex than with many composers using tone rows.
  2.   Changing time signatures: *Str Qrt 1*.
  3.   Rhythmic episodes: *Variations*.
  4.   Parts of a tone row used to form a rhythmic pattern: *Str Qrt 1* (*Vivo*); *Sym 3*.
  5.   Ostinato: *Toccata*.

F.   Form
  1.   Development from classical forms to free, quasi-variation types and Baroque forms.
  2.   Sonata-allegro: *Brass* (first theme, meas. 2, hn; second theme, p. 7, meas. 2, trpt); *Sym 3* (first movement modified sonata-allegro); *Qnt Pno Str* (second movement).
  3.   Fugue: *Sym 3* (fugal passages in all four movements); *Passacaglia and Fugue*; *Qnt Pno Str* (first movement, canon and fugue); *Canon and Fugue*; *Cantata* (third move-

ment); *Sym 3* (fourth movement).

4. Triple fugue: *Preamble and Fugue*.
5. Ground bass: *New Dance (Finale)*.
6. Passacaglia and Fugue: *Cantata* (third movement); *Sym 3* (fourth movement).

G. Orchestration

1. Orchestration grows out of the musical idea; color effects rarely used. Comparatively few works for large orchestra. Wide variety of instrumentation in all orchestral music. Emphasis on percussion.

BIBLIOGRAPHY

Articles by Wallingford Riegger

1. "Wallingford Riegger, Autobiography," *Magazine of Art* 32 (Aug 1939).
2. "State of Dissonance," *ACA-Bul* 2, No. 3 (Oct 1953), 13.
3. "Discovering the Orchestra Conductor; A New Basis of Selection," *ACA-Bul* 6, No. 2 (1957), 15.
4. "The Music of Vivian Fine," *ACA-Bul* 8, No. 1 (1958), 2-6.
5. "For a Department of Fine Arts," *ACA-Bul* 9, No. 3 (1960), 12.

References to Wallingford Riegger

Books
(See the General Bibliography)

ACA-Bul II/1, IV/3; ASC-AC; AusMT; Baker; BarMA; BauTC; BIM; BloYA; BMI-P; BMI-SC; Bull; CatPC; ChaAM; CobCS; CohCT; ComA; CopTN; CowAC; DerETM; DukLH; Edm-I; Ed-MUS; EscCF; EweAC; EweCS; EweCT; EweDE; EweWT; EweYA; FraMG; GosMM; Grove; Hit-MU; HowMM; HowOA; HowOC; HowSH; KinAI; LanOH; LeiMW; MacIC; MelMN; MueAS; Mye-TC; PavMH; PersTH; PeyNM; PorM3S; ReiCA; RobCM; RosDM; SalMO; SalzTM; SamLM; San-WM; SchWC; SloMS; StevHS; ThoAJ; ThoAM; ThompIC; YatTC.
Armitage, Merle, ed. *Martha Graham*. Los Angeles, 1937.

Articles

1. *NYT* (Mar 12, 1936), 19:8.
2. Upton, William Treat. "Aspects of Modern Art-Song," *MQ* 24 (1938), 23.
3. "To the New Through the Old," *Magazine of Art* 32 (Aug 1939), 472-473.
4. "Awarded A. M. Ditson Fund Commission to Write Symphony," *NYT* (Jan 5, 1947), sec. 2, p. 7:4.
5. Slepian, Dorothy. "Polyphonic Forms and Devices in Modern American Music," *MQ* 33 (1947), 313, 314, 315, 316, 318.
6. "Wins N. Y. Music Critics Circle Orchestral Award (Third Symphony)," *NYT* (Jun 8, 1948).
7. *NYT* (Jun 13, 1948), sec. 2, p. 7:7.
8. Goldman, Richard F. "Current Chronicle: Third Symphony," *MQ* 34 (1948), 594-599.
9. Cowell, Henry. "Wallingford Riegger," *MA* 68 (Dec 1, 1948), 9.
10. Goldman, Richard F. "The Music of Wallingford Riegger; with List of Works," *MQ* 36 (1950), 39-61.
11. "Wallingford Riegger (includes works)," *Pan Pipes* 43 (Dec 1950), 128.
12. "Riegger Symphony Wins Naumburg Award," *MA* 71 (Jan 15, 1951), 17.
13. Rosenwald, Hans. "Contemporary Music," *Mus News* 43 (Mar 1951), 8.
14. "In Certainty of Song," *MC* 144)Dec 1, 1951), 34.

15. Carter, Elliott. "Wallingford Riegger (Includes Record of Performances of Works)," *ACA-Bul* 2, No. 1 (1952), 3-5.

16. "The Concert Hall," *ACA-Bul* 2, No. 3 (1952), 18.

17. Goldman, Richard F. "Current Chronicle," *MQ* 38 (1952), 437-440.

18. "Wallingford Riegger," *Pan Pipes* 44 (Jan 1952), 43; 45 (Jan 1953), 65.

19. "Elected Member of National Institute of Arts and Letters," *NYT* (Feb 19, 1953), 25:2.

20. *MA* 73 (Aug 1953), 20.

21. Kyle, Marguerite K. "AmerAllegro," *Pan Pipes* 46 (Jan 1954), 57-58.

22. Keats, Shiela. "Reference Articles on American Composers, An Index," *Juilliard Rev* 1, No. 3 (Fall 1954), 31.

23. "Wallingford Riegger," *Pan Pipes* 47 (Jan 1955), 63.

24. "Wallingford Riegger," *MC* 151 (Feb 15, 1955), 25.

25. Berger, Arthur. "Silent Composers," *SR* 38 (Feb 26, 1955), 58.

26. Cowell, Henry. "A Note on Wallingford Riegger," *Juilliard Rev* 2, No. 2 (Spring 1955), 53-55.

27. Taubman, Howard. "If One Only Had Time," *NYT* (Apr 17, 1955), sec. 2, p. 9.

28. Schmoll, Joseph B. "Dedicated Contemporary (Includes Discussion of His Compositional Devices)," *MA* 75 (May 1955), 8.

29. Yates, Peter. "Tributes and Temper (Includes Discussion of Works)," *Arts and Architecture* 72 (Jul 1955), 7-9.

30. Daniel, Oliver. "The New Festival (Includes List of Recordings)," *ACA-Bul* 5, No. 1 (1955), 20.

31. *NYT* (Jan 24, 1955), 19:3; (Apr 17, 1955), sec. 2, p. 9:7.

32. Kyle, Marguerite K. "AmerAllegro," *Pan Pipes* 48 (Jan 1956), 69.

33. "Riegger is Guest at Oberlin Festival," *MA* 76 (Feb 15, 1956), 208.

34. "Reigger, Blacher, Cowell," *Instrument* 10 (Apr 1956), 23.

35. Elwell, Herbert. *Cleveland Plain Dealer* (Apr 1, 1956).

36. Ellsworth, Ray. "Americans on Microgroove," *HiFi* 6 (Aug 1956), 64.

37. Elwell, Herbert. "Riegger's Modesty Fails to Conceal His Greatness," *ACA-Bul* 5, No. 3 (1956), 23.

38. Goldman, Richard F. "Wallingford Riegger, Composer and Pedagog," *Etude* 74 (Oct 1956), 11.

39. Kyle, Marguerite K. "AmerAllegro," *Pan Pipes* 49 (Jan 1957), 66.

40. Trimble, Lester. "Current Chronicle: New York," *MQ* 43 (1957), 236-238.

41. "Identified as Communist Party Branch Organizer," *NYT* (Apr 10, 1957), 18:5; (Jun 30, 1957), 19:1.

42. Kyle, Marguerite K. "AmerAllegro," *Pan Pipes* 50 (Jan 1958), 70.

43. "Honored by N. Y. Philharmonic," *NYT* (Oct 17, 1958), 33:1; (Oct 18, 1958), 17:2.

44. "Lennie's Grand Old Men," *Time* 72 (Oct 27, 1958), 54.

45. Kyle, Marguerite K. "AmerAllegro," *Pan Pipes* 51 (Jan 1959), 80.

46. Becker, John J. "W. Riegger," *ACA-Bul* 9, No. 1 (1959), 2-7.

47. "Wallingford Riegger," *Juilliard Rev* 7, No. 1 (1959-1960), 15.

48. Kyle, Marguerite K. "AmerAllegro," *Pan Pipes* 52, No. 2 (1960), 68.

49. *NYT* (Feb 15, 1960), 22:2; (Apr 20, 1960), 45:1; (Apr 28, 1960), 31:6; (Apr 29, 1960), 27:1; (Nov 17, 1960), 45:4.

50. Lewis, Robert. "Contemporary Baroque Ensemble Honors Riegger," *MA* 80 (May 1960), 36.

51. Ardoin, John. "Riegger Honored on 75th Birthday," *MA* 80 (May 1960), 36.

52. Becker, John J. "Wallingford Riegger," *ACA-Bul* 9, No. 3 (1960), 13.

53. "The Newest 'New Festival'," *ACA-Bul* 9, No. 3 (1960), 22.

54. Cowell, Henry. "A Note on Wallingford Riegger," *ACA-Bul* 9, No. 3 (1960), 14.

55. "Riegger: List of Works [and] Discography," *ACA-Bul* 9, No. 3 (1960), 16-19.

56. Goldman, Richard F. "The Music of Wallingford Riegger," *ACA-Bul* 9, No. 3 (1960), 15.

57. "Pioneer from Georgia," *Time* 75 (May 9, 1960), 61.
58. Daniels, Oliver. "Wallingford Riegger," *Mus Club Mag* 39, No. 4 (1960), 18.
59. Kolodin, Irving. "Music To My Ears," *SR* 43 (Oct 22, 1960), 24.
60. Kyle, Marguerite K. "AmerAllegro," *Pan Pipes* 53, No. 2 (1961), 72.
61. "Wins Creative Arts Award; Brandeis University," *NYT* (Mar 30, 1961), 21:2.
62. *NYT* (Apr 1, 1961), 36:4; (Apr 2, 1961), 1:1; (Apr 3, 1961), 30:2; (Apr 4, 1961), 37:1; (Apr 5, 1961), 37:3.
63. Luening, Otto. "Wallingford Riegger, 1885-1961," *NYT* (Apr 9, 1961), sec. 2, p. 13:4.
64. Daniel, Oliver. "Cohn on Riegger, and Others," *SR* 44 (Apr 29, 1961), 44-45.
65. Cohn, Arthur. "Unexpectedly Posthumous Tribute to a Man of the Greatest Honesty," *Am Rec G* 27 (May 1961), 713.
66. Dumm, Robert. "Wallingford Riegger," *MC* 163 (May 1961), 13.
67. Haverlin, Carl. "Wallingford Riegger—A Tribute," *Juilliard Rev* 8, No. 2 (1961), 26.
68. Ardoin, John. "Wallingford Riegger Dies at 75," *MA* 81 (May 1961), 65.
69. Salzman, Eric. "The Size of Reigger's Universe," *NYT* (May 28, 1961), sec. 2, p. 16.
70. "Wallingford Riegger," *Composers of the Americas* 7 (1961), 73-82.
71. "Obituary," *MA* 81 (May 1961), 65-66; *MT* 102 (May 1961), 309; *Int Mus* 40 (May 1961); *Mus d'Oggi* 4 (May-Jun 1961), 131; *FoF* 21 (Appendix to the Index, 1961), 163; *MQ* 47 (1961), 398-400.
72. Goldman, Richard F. "Current Chronicle," *MQ* 47 (1961), 398.
73. *NYT* (Jun 11, 1961), 63:1; (Dec 1, 1961), 25:1.
74. "Classified Chronological Catalog of Works by the United States Composer Wallingford Riegger," *Intam Mus B* 31 (Sep 1962), 22-29.
75. *PNM* 1, No. 2 (1962), 203.
76. "Previously Unpublished Composers' Letters as Written to Claire R. Reis," *MA* 83 (Jan 1963), 15.
77. *PNM* 2, No. 2 (1964), 16; 4, No. 1 (1965), 3; 4, No. 2 (1966), 25.
78. Limon, José. "Dancers Are Musicians Are Dancers," *Juilliard Rev Annual* (1966-1967), 6.
79. Goldman, Richard F. "The Great American Composers: Wallingford Riegger," *HiFi R* 20 (Apr 1968), 57-67.
80. Goodfriend, James. "Riegger Recorded," *HiFi R* 20 (Apr 1968), 66.
81. Ober, William B. "De mortibus musicorum—Some Cases Drawn from a Pathologist's Notebook," *Stereo R* 25 (Nov 1970), 81.
82. Daniel, Oliver. "Wallingford Riegger," *BMI* (Nov 1971), 11.
83. Swift, Frederic F. "Assessing the Innovative," *WoodWorld* 13, No. 1 (1974), 4.
84. "Study in Sonority," *Mus & Mus* 23 (Oct 1974), 56-58.
85. Brown, Royal Scott. "Essential American-Music Document—from England," *HiFi* 24 (Nov 1974), 97.
86. "Composers in Focus," *BMI* (Winter 1976), 27.
87. Salzman, Eric. "Has the Avant Garde Become the Establishment?" *Stereo R* 37 (Aug 1976), 100.

References to Works by Wallingford Riegger

The number preceding the title indicates the number of the composition as listed in Section II.

1. American Polonaise: *MQ* 36 (1950), 43.
84. La Belle Dame sans Merci: *MQ* 36 (1950), 43; *Notes* 8 (Mar 1951), 404-405.
59. Blue Voyage: *MQ* 36 (1950), 44.
11. Canon and Fugue: *CinSPN* (Apr 1, 1955), 587-591; *Notes* 12 (Sep 1955), 650; *POPN* (Oct 7, 1955), 39; *EweWT*.
54. Concerto for Piano, Wind Quintet: *ACA-Bul* 4, No. 1 (1954), 24; *MT* 97 (Nov 1956), 599; *MQ* 43 (1957), 236; *Mus & Mus* 17 (Feb 1969), 55; *Mus Events* 24 (Feb 1969), 32; *SR* 53 (Nov 21, 1970), 58.

72. Cooper Square: *NYT* (Nov 22, 1959), 85:4; *School Mus* 32 (Feb 1961), 45.
65. The Cry: *Notes* 10 (1952-1953), 684.
24. Dance Rhythms: *NYT* (Mar 6, 1955), 87:5; *CinSPN* (Apr 1, 1955), 587-591; *MA* 75 (Oct 1955), 26; *NYT* (Feb 19, 1956), 79:4; *MA* 76 (Mar 1956), 16; *MQ* 44 (Apr 1958), 267.
 5. Dichotomy: *MQ* 33 (1947), 318; *MA* 68 (Dec 1, 1948), 9; *MQ* 36 (1950), 47; *NYT* (May 16, 1960); *MA* 82 (Jan 1962), 254; *ChiSPN* (Oct 28, 1965), 17; *PNM* 4, No. 1 (1965), 4; *HiFi/MA* 24 (Nov 1974), 97; *BloYA*, 21; *HitMU*, 223.
 7. Evocation: *MQ* 36 (1950), 51; *Notes* 10 (1952-1953), 684.
 4. Fantasy and Fugue: *MQ* 36 (1950), 46.
29. Festival Overture: *MC* 155 (Jun 1957), 28; *MA* 80 (May 1960), 34.
45. Frenetic Rhythms: *MQ* 36 (1950), 50.
78. In Certainty of Song: *MQ* 38 (1952), 438; *Notes* 9 (1951-1952), 325.
58. Introduction and Fugue: *MA* 81 (Jan 1961), 184; *Notes* 21 (1963-1964), 249; *BMI* (Apr 1965), 10.
57. Movement: *Notes* 21 (1963-1964), 249.
    Music for Band: *Wood Mag* 5 (Jun 1953), 12-13.
18. Music for Brass Choir: *Int Musician* 47 (May 1949), 10; *Mus News* 41 (Jun 1949), 8; *MQ* 35 (1949), 462-463; *Notes* 7 (1949-1950), 437; *MQ* 36 (1950), 54; 38 (1952), 439; *Notes* 9 (1952), 325; *HitMU*, 223.
20. Music for Orchestra: *Notes* 12 (1954-1955), 327; *MA* 75 (Apr 1955), 26; *MC* 151 (Jun 1955), 62; *MQ* 44 (1958), 267.
 8. New Dance: *MQ* 36 (1950), 50; *ACA-Bul* 3, No. 3 (1953), 18; *MQ* 40 (1954), 312.
79. Non Vincit Malitia: *MQ* 38 (1952), 439.
52. Nonet for Brass: *Notes* 9 (1951-1952), 661; *MQ* 38 (1952), 439.
25. Overture: *CinSPN* (Oct 26, 1956), 83.
36. Passacaglia and Fugue: *MQ* 36 (1950), 51, 594; *Am Mus Dgt* 1 (Dec 1969), 45-46.
51. Quintet for Piano, String Quartet: *MQ* 38 (1952), 438; *MA* 73 (Mar 1953), 35.
53. Quintet for Winds: *NYT* (Jan 19, 1953), 20:5; *ACA-Bul* 3, No. 1 (1953), 26; *Notes* 11 (1953-1954), 158; *ACA-Bul* 4, No. 2 (1954), 21.
 2. Rhapsody: *MQ* 36 (1950), 44.
23. Romanza: *MQ* 44 (1958), 267.
60. Scherzo: *Notes* 12 (1954-1955), 649; *MA* 76 (Apr 1956), 20.
32. Sinfonietta: *MA* 81 (Jan 1961), 240.
49. Sonatina for Violin, Piano: *MQ* 36 (1950), 52; *MA* 76 (Mar 1956), 21.
47. String Quartet No. 1: *MM* 23 (Winter 1946), 54; *MQ* 36 (1950), 52.
50. String Quartet No. 2: *Mus News* 41 (Apr 1949), 28; (May 1949), 8; *Notes* 7 (1949-1950), 132; *MQ* 36 (1950), 52; *ACA-Bul* 3, No. 1 (1953), 15; *MQ* 40 (1954), 472; *Am Rec G* 27 (May 1961), 713.
 3. Study in Sonority: *MQ* 33 (1947), 313; *MA* 68 (Dec 1, 1948), 9; *MQ* 36 (1950), 42, 44; *MA* 78 (Nov 15, 1958), 9; *NYHT* (Mar 31, 1962); *Notes* 20 (1962-1963), 574; *MA* 84 (Feb 1964), 19; *Houston SPN* (Apr 21-22, 1975), 15; *EweWT*.
42. Suite for Flute Solo: *MQ* 36 (1950), 46.
17. Symphony No. 3: *MQ* 34 (1948), 594-599; *MA* 68 (Dec 1, 1948); *Notes* 6 (1948-1949), 637; *MQ* 36 (1950), 40, 55; *MA* 71 (Jan 15, 1951), 17; *NYT* (May 29, 1951), 20:6; *MQ* 41 (1955), 558; *ACA-Bul* 4, No. 4 (1955), 19; *SFSPN* (Jan 22, 1958), 247; *N. Y. World Telegram* (Dec 7, 1964); *ACA-Bul* 13 No. 1 (1965), 30; *EweWT*; *HitMU*, 223.
28. Symphony No. 4: *NYT* (Apr 21, 1957), sec. 2, p. 11:7; *MA* 77 (Jun 1957), 10; *Am Rec G* 25 (Dec 1958), 271-273; *NYT* (Jan 18, 1959), 84:1; *SR* 42 (Jan 31, 1959), 28; *MA* 79 (Feb 1959), 264; *Kansas City Star* (Feb 14, 1960); *MA* 81 (Feb 1961), 15; *Notes* 19 (1961-1962), 143; *EweWT*.
43. Three Canons for Woodwinds: *MQ* 36 (1950), 46; 43 (1957), 236.
67. Toccata: *Notes* 15 (1957-1958), 661.
40. Trio in B minor: *NYT* (Mar 27, 1933), 13:3; *MQ* 36 (1950), 40, 43; *Am Rec G* 27 (May 1961), 713.

83. Two Bergerettes: *MA* 70 (Nov 15, 1950), 32; *MC* 143 (Feb 15, 1951), 66.
21. Variations for Piano, Orchestra: *MC* 149 (Mar 1, 1954), 34; *MQ* 41 (1955), 78; *N. Y. Journal-American* (Oct 8, 1960); *SR* 43 (Oct 22, 1960), 24.
30. Variations for Violin, Orchestra: *Notes* 20 (1962-1963), 124.
56. Variations for Violin, Viola: *Notes* 20 (1962-1963), 309.
41. Whimsy: *MQ* 36 (1950), 43.

Dissertations about Wallingford Riegger and His Works

1. Freeman, Paul D. *The Compositional Technique of Wallingford Riegger as Seen in Seven Major Twelve-Tone Works*. Eastman School of Music, University of Rochester, 1963.
2. Gatwood, Dwight D., Jr. *Wallingford Riegger: A Biography and Analysis of Selected Works*. George Peabody College for Teachers, 1970.
3. Ott, Leonard W. *An Analysis of the Later Orchestral Style of Wallingford Riegger*. Michigan State University, 1970.
4. Savage, Newell G. *Structure and Cadence in the Music of Wallingford Riegger*. Stanford University, 1972.
5. Schmoll, Joseph B. *An Analytical Study of the Principal Instrumental Compositions of Wallingford Riegger*. Northwestern University, 1954.

OUTLINE XII

BERNARD ROGERS (1893-1968)

I. Life

1893 Born in New York City, February 4. Father a jeweler of English-Irish ancestry; mother Czech-Jewish.

1900 Early education in New York City and New Rochelle (1906).

1906 Developed an early interest in art and later in music after hearing his first orchestral concert in New York. Began composing in 1909.

1912 Worked in an architect's office in New York for two years at his father's request. Studied music at night.

1915 Became associated with *Musical America*. Studied with Arthur Farwell and later met Ernest Bloch.

1918 Awarded a Pulitzer Traveling Fellowship (*To the Fallen*); went to Paris.

1919 Returned to New York. Attended the Institute of Musical Art, working with Percy Goetschius.

1920 Studied composition with Ernest Bloch in Cleveland (1920-1922).

1923 Married Lillian Soskin; divorced in 1933.

1925 Went to England to compose.

1927 Awarded Guggenheim Fellowships (1927-1929). Studied with Frank Bridge in London for several months (*Fuji in the Sunset Glow*). Worked with Nadia Boulanger in Paris during the summer (*The Raising of Lazarus*).

1929 Appointed to the faculty of the Eastman School of Music, Rochester, New York, teaching composition and orchestration (1929-1967). Among his pupils were Wayne Barlow, David Diamond, Peter Mennin, Burrill Phillips, Robert Ward.

1934 Married Ann Thacher who died in 1935.

1938 Married Elizabeth Clarke.

1942 Completed one of his greatest works, *The Passion*.

1946 Elected a member of the National Institute of Art and Letters. Won the Alice M. Ditson Fund Award (*The Warrior*; produced at the Metropolitan Opera House, January 11, 1947).

1951 *The Art of Orchestration* published.

1953 Received a Fulbright Grant.

1959 Awarded an honorary Doctor of Music degree from Valparaiso University, Indiana.

1962 Awarded an honorary Doctor of Humane Letters degree from Wayne State University, Detroit, Michigan. Received the Lillian B. Fairchild Award (1963).

1967 Retired as chairman of the department of composition at the Eastman School of Music.

1968 Died May 24, in Rochester, New York.

Bernard Rogers has been the recipient of many honors and commissions in addition to those listed above.

Note: Biographies of varying lengths and importance will be found in many of the books listed in the Bibliography at the end of this *Outline* under "References to Bernard Rogers."

II.   Compositions

A.   Orchestra

	Date	Publisher
1. To the Fallen: Dirge	1918	FLP
2. The Faithful: Overture	1922	FLP
3. Soliloquy for Flute, Strings	1922	CF
4. Symphony No. 1: Adonais	1925	E-V
5. Prelude to Hamlet	1926	FLP
6. Fuji in the Sunset Glow: Tone Poem (inspired by Japanese prints)	1927	FLP
7. Rhapsody: Nocturne (cham orch)	1927	FLP
8. Symphony No. 2 in A-flat	1928	FLP
9. Three Japanese Dances (orch, m-S., ad lib; also wind sym)	1928	Pres
10. Two American Frescoes	1931	E-V
11. Once Upon a Time: Five Fairy Tales (drawn from Andrew Lang) (cham orch)	1935	Pres
12. Symphony No. 3 in C (on a Thanksgiving song)	1936	FLP
13. Elegy (from Symphony No. 3) (cham orch)	1936	E-V
14. Fantasy for Flute, Viola, Orchestra	1937	E-V
15. The Supper at Emmäus (after Rembrandt)	1937	E-V
16. The Dance of Salomé	1938	E-V
17. Soliloquy No. 2 for Bassoon, String	1938	E-V
18. The Colours of War	1939	E-V
19. The Song of the Nightingale: Suite (after Hans Christian Andersen)	1939	E-V
20. The Plains: Three Landscapes (small orch)	1940	E-V
21. The Sailors of Toulon	1942	E-V
22. Invasion	1943	E-V
23. Characters from Hans Christian Andersen: Four Drawings for Small Orchestra	1944	E-V
24. In Memory of Franklin Delano Roosevelt (cham orch)	1945	E-V
25. Symphony No. 4	1945	Peer
26. Suite from "The Warrior"	1945	FLP
27. Amphitryon: Overture	1946	GS
28. Leaves from "The Tale of Pinocchio" (Narr., cham orch or pno)	1950	Peer
29. The Silver World (fl, ob, strings)	1950	Peer
30. Three Dance Scenes (inspired by Japanese art)	1952	Peer
31. Fantasia (hn, str, timp)	1954	Pres
32. Portrait (vln, orch)	1956	Pres
33. The Musicians of Bremen: A Folk Tale After Grimm (Narr., cham orch)	1957	Pres
34. Africa: Symphony in Two Movements	1958	Pres
35. Variations on a Song by Mussorgsky (Child Song)	1960	Pres
36. Pictures from the "Tale of Aladdin"	1961	CFP
37. New Japanese Dances	1962	Pres
38. Allegory (2 fl, mar, str)	1962	Pres
39. Anzacs	1963	E-V
40. Apparitions: Scenes from the "Temptation of St. Anthony"	1966	E-V

B.   Chamber

	Date	Publisher
41. Pastorale (11 instruments)	1924	FLP
42. String Quartet	1928	
43. Trio (vln, vla, vlc)	1952	Peer
44. Sonata for Violin, Piano	1954	Pres

B.	Chamber (cont.)		
	45. Mirage (solo marimba)	1958	Peer
	46. Ballade (pno, vla, bsn)	1965	Peer
C.	**Organ**		
	47. Miniature Suite		Pres
	48. Second Suite		Pres
D.	**Choral**		
	49. The Raising of Lazarus (cantata: 2 S., T., SATB, orch)	1927	CCB
	50. The Exodus (cantata: T., A., Bar., SATB)	1933	CCB
	51. The Passion (Charles Rodda) (oratorio: S., A., T., B., SATB, orch)	1942	E-V
	52. Response to Silent Prayers	1945	
	53. Psalm 99 (SATB, org)	1947	GS
	54. A Letter from Pete (Walt Whitman) (cantata: S., T., SATB, orch or cham orch)	1948	Peer
	55. Psalm 68 (Bar., orch or pno)	1952	Peer
	56. Hear My Prayer, O God (S., A., SATB, org)	1955	Pres
	57. The Prophet Isaiah (SATB., orch)	1960	Peer
	58. Psalm 89: Lord God of Hosts (Bar., SATB, pno)	1962	Pres
	59. Psalm 18 (TTBB, pno)	1963	Pres
	60. The Light of Man (oratorio: S., A., Bar., SATB, org or pno)	1964	Pres
E.	**Opera**		
	61. The Marriage of Aude (Charles Rodda, based on the "Chanson de Roland") (a lyric drama in three scenes)	1931	
	62. The Warrior (Norman Corwin, based on the story of Samson and Delilah)	1944	
	63. The Veil (Robert Lawrence) (opera in one act)	1949	Peer
	64. The Nightingale (Bernard Rogers, after Hans Christian Andersen	1955	Peer

Note: The following abbreviations are used in Section III of this *Outline*. The number indicates the number of the composition as listed in Section II.

33. *Bremen*: The Musicians of Bremen
23. *Characters*: Characters from Hans Christian Andersen
49. *Lazarus*: The Raising of Lazarus
19. *Nightingale*: The Song of the Nightingale

16. *Salomé*: The Dance of Salomé
 3. *Soliloquy*: Soliloquy for Flute, Strings
11. *Tales*: Five Fairy Tales
35. *Variations*: Variations on a Song by Mussorgsky

III.   Style (techniques and devices)

"Music is a spiritual art, and a work of art should serve a moral value (and beauty, too, is a moral value),"
                                                                                   Bernard Rogers

A.   General characteristics
   1.   Style highly personal and individual. Strongly influence by Ernest Bloch, French impressionism and the Orient.
   2.   Style varies from the fanciful to the epic. Interest in the analogies between poetry, music and painting results in the frequent use of pictorial realism with programmatic or poetic titles. One of the few American composers to use Biblical texts extensively.
   3.   Music characterized by expert workmanship, subtlety, simplicity of means, transparent texture and extraordinary use of orchestral color.
   4.   Powerful dramatic impact and intense personal expression, particulary in the choral and large orchestral works.

B. Melodic line
   1.   Often broken down into small, significant figures or motives which are varied and developed in various ways: *Tales* (pp. 25, 50); *Characters* (beginning).
   2.   Pointillistic technique: *Salomé*; *Nightingale*; *Passion*.
   3.   Folk-like: *Tales* (p. 2); *Bremen*.
   4.   Parlando style: *Passion*.
   5.   Diatonic: *Passion* (p. 68); Chromatic: *Passion* (p. 96).
   6.   Flowing: *Soliloquy*; *Lazarus* (beginning; pp. 24-25); *Sym 3* (*Elegy*).
   7.   Based on harmonic materials: *Lazarus* (p. 36).
   8.   Modal: *Variations* (theme).
C. Harmony
   1.   Ranges from diatonic structures to elaborate mixtures. Economical and varied use of material with a strong sense of tonal balance. Triads rarely used.
   2.   Open fifths: *Exodus* (p. 2); *Passion* (pp. 26, 98, 104-105).
   3.   Ostinato bass under changing harmony: *Exodus* (pp. 8-9); *Passion* (p. 38).
   4.   Harsh dissonance in bass: *Exodus* (p. 12).
   5.   Use of superimposed fourths; perfect and augmented: *Tales* (pp. 1-8).
   6.   Twelve-note chords: *Passion* (p. 98).
   7.   Modal: *Passion* (p. 25); *Characters* (pp. 4-5).
   8.   Major and minor triads superimposed: *Passion* (p. 52).
   9.   Impressionistic: *Fuji*; *Characters* (p. 9).
D. Counterpoint
   1.   Moderate use of polyphonic forms and devices.
   2.   Fugal: *Lazarus* (p. 36); *Passion* (p. 115); *Sym 4* (*Epilogue*).
   3.   Contrapuntal treatment: *Lazarus* (p. 2); *Soliloquy*.
   4.   Canon: *Exodus* (p. 40); *Sym 4* (*Epilogue*).
E. Rhythm
   1.   Rhythm always important; rhythmic life often dependent on the percussion.
   2.   Dramatic rhythmic effects: *Passion* (pp. 32, 60).
F. Form
   1.   Traditional forms rarely used, except in larger works. Simple forms preferred; structure clear.
   2.   Three-part: *Soliloquy*.
   3.   Rhapsody: *In Memory of Franklin Delano Roosevelt*.
   4.   Arch (A - B - B - A): *Passion*.
   5.   Tonality as a unifying device: *Passion* (the tonality of D major is used for the crowd, people, scenes; the tonality of B-flat major is used for the words of Jesus).
G. Orchestration
   1.   Music characterized by the unusual use of instruments and orchestral color. Leanness of scoring in many works.
   2.   Piano and xylophone; unusual harp effects: *Characters* (No. III); *Passion*.
   3.   Flutter tonguing: *Tales* (p. 14, trpt; p. 31, pic; p. 40, fl).
   4.   Extreme registers: *Tales* (p. 9, meas 3, fl; p. 14, meas. 3, clar; p. 47, meas. 1, clar; p. 18, meas. 2, bsn).
   5.   Percussive and coloristic effects used to emphasize and intensify the dramatic elements: *Passion*.

BIBLIOGRAPHY

Books by Bernard Rogers

The Art of Orchestration. New York: Appleton-Century-Crofts, 1951. Review in *Notes* 9 (1951-1952), 404.

Articles by Bernard Rogers

1. "If You Would Compose–," *Musician* 21 (Aug 1927), 9.
2. "Fifteen New Works in Rochester Debut," *MM* 22, No. 1 (1944-1945), 45.
3. "Rochester Twenty Years After," *MM* 22, No. 4 (1944-1945), 262.
4. "Intentions of *The Warrior*," *Opera N* 12 (Jan 6, 1947), 5.
5. "Afterthoughts on *The Warrior*," *Mus Dgt* 3 (Apr 1948).
6. "Religious Music (Answer to W. R. Weagly's Article on American Composer and Protestant Church Music)," *NYT* (Feb 26, 1956), sec. 2, p. 7.
7. "Teaching to Compose: An Inflamed Art," *Mus J Annual* 21 (1963), 25.

References to Bernard Rogers

Books
(See the General Bibliography)

ASC-BD; ASC-SC; AusMT; Baker; BauTC; BIM; BloYA; Bull; CatPC; ChaAC; ChaAM; CobCS; CopTN; CowAC; DerETM; DukLH; EdMUS; EweAC; EweNB; EweYA; GosMM; Grove; HinCP; HipAO; HitMU; HowOA; HowOC; HowSH; KinAI; KolMO; LeiMW; MacIC; MelMN; MueAS; PavMH; PersTH; ReisCA; SalMO; SamLM; SamMO; SanWM; SchWC; SelMO; ThoAJ; ThoAM; ThompIC; ThoMR; ThoRL; WWA; WWM.

Articles

1. Thompson, Oscar. "Heard in New York," *MM* 6, No. 4 (1928-1929), 24.
2. *NYT* (Jun 11, 1933), sec, 9, p. 5:1.
3. "Premier in Rochester," *MM* 13, No. 2 (1935-1936), 42.
4. "New Native Works Performed," *MA* 56, No. 2 (1936), 3.
5. "Composers Forum-Laboratory–Bernard Rogers," *Forum Discussion* (Mar 21, 1937).
6. "Marriage to Ann Thacher," *NYT* (Jun 1, 1934), 26:2; (Jun 11, 1934), 21:4.
7. *NYT* (Apr 1, 1937), 19:2.
8. Scherchen, Hermann. "Are There American Composers? " *MA* 58 (Oct 25, 1938), 8.
9. Cohn, Arthur. "Americans at Rochester," *MM* 17, No. 4 (1939-1940), 255.
10. Hanson, Howard. "Bernard Rogers," *MM* 22, No. 3 (1944-1945), 170.
11. "Wins A. M. Ditson Fund Award For Opera 'Warrior'," *NYT* (Feb 18, 1946), 16:5; (Mar 3, 1946), 44:4.
12. "Elected Member of the National Institute of Arts and Letters," *NYT* (Jan 3, 1947), 23:5.
13. "Elected to National Institute of Arts and Letters," *Etude* 65 (Feb 1947), 61.
14. Diamond, David. "Bernard Rogers with List of Works," *MQ* 33 (1947), 207-227.
15. Bruno, A. "Rogers' Passion at Juilliard," *MA* 69 (Mar 1949), 7.
16. Heinsheimer, Hans W. "Opera in America Today," *MQ* 37 (1951), 328.
17. Keats, Sheila. "Reference Articles on American Composers: An Index," *Juilliard Rev* 1 (Fall 1954), 31.
18. "News Nuggets (Winner of Choral Contest)," *Int Mus* 53 (Mar 1955), 39.
19. "Recent Prize Winners," *MC* 151 (May 1955), 37.
20. "In the News," *Mus Ed J* 42 (Sep-Oct 1955), 70.
21. Kyle, Marguerite K. "AmerAllegro," *Pan Pipes* 48 (Jan 1956), 70.
22. "Contemporary American Composers," *Instrument* 12 (Aug 1958), 39.
23. "Meet the Author," *Mus J Annual* 21 (1963), 3.
24. Kyle, Marguerite K. "AmerAllegro," *Pan Pipes* 56, No. 2 (1964), 78.
25. "Bernard Rogers," *Composers of the Americas* 10 (1964), 91-97.
26. "Bernard Rogers to Retire from Eastman Faculty," *Mus Leader* 99 (May 1967), 11.
27. "Dies," *NYT* (May 25, 1968), 35:1.

28. "Bernard Roger [*sic*] Is Dead at 75," *BB* 80 (Jun 8, 1968), 40.
29. "Obituary," *Variety* 251 (May 29, 1968), 63; *Opera* 19 (Jul 1968), 581; *HiFi/MA* 18 (Aug 1968), MA16; *Instrument* 23 (Sep 1968), 12; *Mus Ed J* 55 (Sep 1968), 4.
30. "Memorial Established Honoring Late Composer," *Triangle* 64, No. 4 (1970), 35.
31. "Bernard Rogers Memorial Award Established," *Mus Club Mag* 49, No. 3 (1970), 33.
32. Koch, Frederick. "Bernard Rogers—A Teacher of Composers, 1893-1968)," *Am Mus Tcr* 26, No. 6 (1977), 26.

References to Works by Bernard Rogers

The number preceding the title indicates the number of the composition as listed in Section II.

34. Africa: *MC* 159 (Apr 1959), 32.
38. Allegory: *Notes* 22 (1964-1965), 822.
40. Apparitions: *CinSPN* (Dec 15, 1967), 315-318; *ASCAP* 2, No. 2 (1968), 39.
23. Characters from Hans Christian Andersen: *Notes* 4 (1946-1947), 359; *MQ* 33 (1947), 212, 217.
16. The Dance of Salomé: *MQ* 33 (1947), 219.
13. Elegy: *MQ* 33 (1947), 215.
31. Fantasia: *Notes* 14 (1956-1957), 448.
 6. Fuji in the Sunset Glow: *MQ* 33 (1947), 210.
56. Hear My Prayer, O God: *Notes* 13 (1955-1956), 348.
24. In Memory of Franklin Delano Roosevelt: *MQ* 33 (1947), 215; *Notes* 5 (1947-1948), 725.
22. Invasion: *MQ* 33 (1947), 215.
28. Leaves from "The Tale of Pinocchio": *MC* 143 (Jun 1951), 16-17; *MC* 153 (Apr 1956), 44.
54. A Letter from Pete: *Notes* 10 (1952-1953), 680; *MC* 148 (Nov 1, 1953), 31; *MA* 73 (Dec 15, 1953), 24.
61. The Marriage of Aude: *MQ* 33 (1947), 220.
45. Mirage: *Notes* 16 (1958-1959), 317.
33. The Musicians of Bremen: *Notes* 23 (1966-1967), 156.
11. Once Upon a Time: *NYT* (Jun 11, 1936), 31:4; *MQ* 33 (1947), 212; 44 (Apr 1958), 269.
51. The Passion: *MA* 64 (Mar 25, 1944), 32; *MQ* 33 (1947), 222; *MA* 69 (Mar 1949), 7.
32. Portrait: *MA* 76 (Nov 1, 1956), 7.
57. The Prophet Isaiah: *MA* 82 (Jul 1962), 31.
55. Psalm 68: *NYT* (May 9, 1955), 28:3; *Notes* 14 (1956-1957), 205.
49. The Raising of Lazarus: *MQ* 18 (1932), 13; 33 (1947), 210, 212, 214, 216, 217.
29. The Silver World: *MA* 73 (Dec 15, 1953), 24; *Notes* 11 (1953-1954), 276.
 3. Soliloquy for Flute, Strings: *MQ* 33 (1947), 210, 212, 214.
19. The Song of the Nightingale: *MQ* 33 (1947), 215, 218.
64. The Nightingale: *NYT* (May 11, 1955), 34:1; *Time* 65 (May 23, 1955), 62; *MA* 75 (Jun 1955), 32; *MC* 151 (Jun 1955), 50; *NYT* (May 7, 1957), 40:1.
15. The Supper at Emmäus: *MA* 57 (May 1937), 3; *MQ* 33 (1947), 210, 212.
25. Symphony No. 4: *MQ* 33 (1947), 221; 34 (1948), 415-417.
30. Three Dance Scenes: *MC* 148 (Dec 1, 1953), 3; *MA* 74 (Jan 15, 1954), 14; *MQ* 41 (1955), 77.
 9. Three Japanese Dances: *MQ* 33 (1947), 210; *Notes* 13 (1955-1956), 704; *MA* 76 (Jan 15, 1956), 24; *Notes* 16 (1958-1959), 163; *Detroit Sym* (Feb 8, 1968), 419-421.
 1. To the Fallen: *MQ* 8 (1922), 551; 33 (1947), 209.
43. Trio: *Notes* 15 (1957-1958), 151.

35. Variations on a Song of Mussorgsky: *MC* 163 (Jan 1961), 35; *MA* 81 (Feb 1961), 61; (May 1961), 28; *MQ* 49 (1963), 6, 123; *MelMN*, 219.
63. The Veil: *MA* 70 (Jun 1950), 11; *Mus News* 42 (Jul 1950), 19; *MC* 142 (Jul 1950), 8; *MQ* 37 (1951), 328; *NYT* (Oct 27, 1954), 35:1; *New Yorker* 30 (Nov 6, 1954), 163; *MA* 74 (Dec 15, 1954), 31.
62. The Warrior: *NYT* (Dec 30, 1946), 16:5; (Jan 5, 1947), sec. 2, p. 7:1; *MA* 67 (Jan 10, 1947), 3; *NYT* (Jan 12, 1947), 53:3; *New Yorker* 22 (Jan 18, 1947), 80; *NYT* (Jan 19, 1947), sec. 2, p. 9:1; *NW* 29 (Jan 20, 1947), 86; *Time* 49 (Jan 20, 1947), 74; *Chr Sc Mon* (Jan 25, 1947); *New Republic* 116 (Jan 27, 1947), 43-44; *Theatre Arts* 31 (Mar 1947), 22; *MQ* 33 (1947), 215, 218, 220; *KolMO*, 464.

Dissertation about Bernard Rogers and His Works

Intili, Dominic Joseph. *Text-Music Relationships in the Large Choral Works of Bernard Rogers.* Case-Western Reserve University, 1977.

OUTLINE XIII

CARL (CHARLES SPRAGUE) RUGGLES (1876-1971)

I. Life

1876   Born in Marion (Cape Cod), Massachusetts, March 11; parents of New England heritage. Received lessons on the violin at an early age.

1890   Moved to East Boston following the death of his mother. Attended high school in Lexington.

1900   Studied theory and composition with Josef Clauss, a Central European teacher at the Boston Conservatory of Music, and violin with Felix Winternitz.

1903   Studied with John Knowles Paine of Harvard University as a special student.

1907   Appointed to teach violin at the Mar d'Mar Music School in Winona, Minnesota (1907-1917).

1908   Married Charlotte Snell, a singer. Organized and conducted the Winona Symphony Orchestra (1908-1912). Coached in conducting by his concertmaster, Christian Timner, also concertmaster of the St. Paul Symphony and formerly concertmaster of the Concertgebouw Orchestra of Amsterdam under Willem Mengelberg.

1917   Returned to New York; conducted a chorus and orchestra at the Rand School.

1920   *Angels* marks the beginning of his most productive period (1920-1932). Only eight works remain, lasting about 90 minutes.

1922   Began a long association with the International Composers Guild and the Pan-American Association of Composers. First performance of *Toys* and *Angels* at Guild concerts, New York.

1924   Moved to Arlington, Vermont. Received an annuity for life from Harriette Miller of New York.

1932   Première of *Sun Treader* in Paris with Nicolas Slonimsky conducting.

1935   During a vacation in Jamaica he took up painting, which he continued throughout his life. His paintings hang in many galleries, among them the Brooklyn and Whitney museums.

1936   Composer-in-residence at the University of Miami, Coral Gables, Florida (1936-1944). Worked on his last compositions (*Evocations*; *Organum*).

1945   Retired to Arlington, Vermont, and began to revise some of his works.

1949   First performance of *Organum* (New York Philharmonic, November 24).

1954   Elected a member of the National Insitute of Arts and Letters.

1957   Charlotte died, October 2.

1960   Awarded an honorary Doctor of Music degree from the University of Vermont.

1964   Awarded the Creative Arts Medal by Brandeis University.

1966   Carl Ruggles Festival held at Bowdoin College. First American performance of *Sun Treader* on January 24 in Portland, Maine, by the Boston Symphony Orchestra. Moved to Bennington, Vermont.

1968   Complete works performed at Bennington, Vermont, in honor of the composer.

1971   Died at Bennington, Vermont, October 24.

Carl Ruggles has been the recipient of many honors and awards in addition to those listed above. Most of his compositions have been recorded.

Note: Biographies of varying lengths and importance will be found in many of the books listed in the Bibliography at the end of this *Outline* under "References to Carl Ruggles."

II.   Compositions

		Date	Publisher
1.	Toys (Carl Ruggles) (voice, pno; also orch)	1919	HWG
2.	Angels (6 muted trpt) (revised from "Men and Angels")	1921	Curwen
	2a. Angels (arr. for 4 trpt, 3 trb, muted, or str)	1938	NME
3.	Symphonia Dialecta (unfinished)	1923	
4.	Vox clamans in deserto (Walt Whitman) (solo voice, cham orch)	1923	NME

4a.   This work was withdrawn in the early 1930's. It was later revised as a song cycle and performed in Bennington, Vermont (1968).

		Date	Publisher
5.	Men and Mountains (after William Blake)	1924	NME

       a.   Men: Rhapsodic Proclamation (orch)
       b.   Lilacs (str orch in seven parts)
       c.   Marching Mountains (orch)

		Date	Publisher
6.	Portals (after Walt Whitman) (str orch)	1926	AME
7.	Sun Treader (after Robert Browning) (orch)	1931	NME
8.	Evocations: Four Chants for Piano (ed. John Kirkpatrick, 1954)	1937-1943; revised 1954	NME

       a.   Largo (1937)
       b.   Andante con Fantasia (1941)
       c.   Moderato Appassionato (1943)
       d.   Adagio Sostenuto (1940)

   8a.   Evocations (arr. for orch, 1971)

		Date	Publisher
9.	Polyphonic Composition (3 pno)	1940	
10.	Organum (orch)	1947	NME

  10a.   Organum (arr. for pno by John Kirkpatrick; also for 2 pno)

		Date	Publisher
11.	Exaltation for "Congregation in Unison" and organ	1958	
12.	The Sunken Bell (opera) (after Gerhart Hauptmann)		

III.   Style (techniques and devices)

"Creation is soul-searching. There's nothing easy about it. It is bringing into being that tremendous deep emotion, that feeling of the sublime, that comes only from the heart." "My whole conception is based on the rhythms and movement of line. It's the same with painting. There shouldn't be any straight lines. It's against nature."   Carl Ruggles

A.   General characteristics
   1.   Early works in late-romantic style, except *Toys*, were destroyed (including the opera, *The Sunken Bell*).
   2.   Mature and highly original style began with *Angels* (1920). Atonal and basically contrapuntal, fluctuating rhythms, generally thick textures. Extreme dissonance alternating with less dissonant passages.
   3.   Repetition of a tone generally avoided until eight or more tones have intervened. Octave leaps avoided. Strict serial techniques not used. Usually a balance between rise and fall of melodic lines and disjunct and conjunct motion.

B.   Melodic line
   1.   Non-repetition of a tone (see letter A3 above): *Evocation* II (meas. 1-6); *Angels*; *Men and Mountains*; *Sun Treader* (12 notes used before a repetition).
   2.   Repetition of a tone: *Portals* (meas. 6-7; 9-10); *Evocation* III (meas. 6); *Sun Treader* (meas. 125, 144); *Angels* (meas. 9-10, first trumpet).
   3.   Long melodic line: *Evocation* II (meas. 19-32); *Angels*.
   4.   Conjunct: *Angels*; *Sun Treader* (chromatic).
   5.   Disjunct: *Men and Mountains*; *Sun Treader* (beginning).
   6.   Wide range: *Lilacs*; *Sun Treader*.

7. Tritones: *Portals*; *Lilacs*.
8. Exchange of notes between two instruments: *Angels* (Nos. 2, 6); *Lilacs* (meas. 3-5, cellos).

C. Harmony
1. Dissonant and atonal: Chords usually include a minor second, major seventh, or minor ninth. Tendency toward a thinner texture in *Organum*.
2. Chords in seconds: *Men and Mountains* (p. 12).
3. Chromatic harmony and melody: *Men and Mountains* (p. 15); *Evocation* I.
4. Parallel motion: *Organum* (meas. 29); *Portals* (meas. 10, 14, 57); *Angels* (meas. 6, 11, 20); *Sun Treader* (meas. 24).
5. Consonant harmony: *Evocation* III; *Portals* (meas. 19);
6. Sequence: *Sun Treader* (meas. 25-28); *Men and Mountains* III (meas. 9, 41).
7. Two- and three-part writing: *Organum*; *Portals* (meas. 14).
8. Double pedal point: *Men and Mountains* (third movement, end).

D. Counterpoint
1. Generally chromatic and dissonant; exact imitation avoided. Secundal counterpoint characteristic.
2. Free imitation with varied rhythms: *Sun Treader* (meas. 20, 35, 38); *Organum* (meas. 5, 50); *Evocation* II (meas. 19).
3. Canon: *Sun Treader* (meas. 52, 124, 139).
4. Cancrizan: *Organum* (meas 5 = meas. 42); *Sun Treader* (meas. 52 = meas. 124).
5. Free twelve-tone techniques: *Evocation* II.

E. Rhythm
1. Basically free and flexible. Frequent changes in meter; use of fermatas and pauses; variations of rhythmic pattern and tempo are found in all works.
2. Complex rhythms: *Organum* (meas. 11, 57); *Sun Treader*; *Lilacs* (polyrhythms).
3. Ritards and accelerandos indicated by metronome speeds: *Evocation* II (meas. 13-19).

F. Form
1. Form grows out of the music. Free with subtle underlying formal elements; including the repetition, often fragmentary, of material.
2. Free A - B - A: *Angels*; *Lilacs*; *Organum*.
3. Free rondo with A section varied: *Portals*.
4. Free sonata-allegro: *Sun Treader*.
5. Form developed from an expanding melodic motive (minor second).

G. Orchestration
1. Emphasis on strength, fullness, blend of tone colors contrasting with individual choirs (strings, brass, woodwinds).
2. Strings divisi: *Portals* (3 first vln, 2 second vln, 3 vla, 3 vlc, 2 c-b).
3. Large orchestra: *Sun Treader*.
4. Antiphonal choirs: *Organum* (meas. 19-28).
5. Unusual pianistic effects: *Evocation* II (meas. 30-31, 42-47).

BIBLIOGRAPHY

References to Carl Ruggles

Books
(See the General Bibliography)

ASC-SC; AusMT; Baker; BauTC; BIM; BloYA; BMI-OP; Bull; CatPC; ChaAM; ClaEA; CopTN; CowAC; DemMT; DerETM; DukLH; Edm-I; EdMUS; EweAC; EweCS; EweMC; EweWT; GosMM; Grove; HipAO; HitMU; HowOA; HowOC; HowSH; KinAI; LanOH (31); LeiMW; LeiSK; MacIC;

MelMN; MelRT; MorrCA; MueAS; MyeTC; PanMC; PersTH; PeyNM; PorM3S; ReiCA; ReiCC; RosAH; RosMI; SalMO; SalzTM; SamLM; SamMO; SanWM; SchWC; SloMS; ThoAM; ThompIC; ThoMR; ThoRL; UptAS; YatTC; YouCD.

Harrison, Lou. *About Carl Ruggles*. A pamphlet: Yonkers, NY: Alicat Bookshop, 1946.

Burt, Warren. *Aardvarks: II: Mr. Natural Encounters Flakey Foont!* Piano solo in memoriam, Carl Ruggles. Lingua Press, 1977.

Articles

Brief mention: *MQ* 24 (1938), 12, 21, 22; *PNM* 1, No. 2 (1963), 203; *PNM* 2, No. 2 (1964), 16; *PNM* 4, No. 1 (1965), 3, 4, 8, 10, 159; *PNM* 4, No. 2 (1966), 25.

1. Sanborn, Pitts. "A Glance Toward the Left," *MM* 4, No. 2 (1927).
2. Cowell, Henry. "Three Native Composers: Ives, Ruggles, Harris," *New Freeman* 1 (May 3, 1930), 184-186.
3. ─────"Carl Ruggles," *Carmelite* 3 (Aug 1930).
4. Lopatnikoff, Nikolai. "Christophe Colomb," *MM* 7, No. 4 (1930).
5. Rosenfeld, Paul. "New American Music," *Scribner's Mag* 89 (Jun 1931), 624-632.
6. Seeger, Charles. "Carl Ruggles," *MQ* 18 (1932), 578; *NYHT* (Feb 10, 1935).
7. *NYT* (Sep 1, 1935), sec. 9, p. 9:4.
8. Seeger, Charles. "Charles Ives and Carl Ruggles," *Magazine of Art* 32 (Jul 1939), 396-399, 435.
9. King, A. H. "Mountains, Music and Musicians," *MQ* 31 (1945), 417.
10. Harrison, Lou. "Ruggles, Ives, Varèse," *View* 5, No. 4 (Nov 1945), 11.
11. Rosenwald, Hans. "Contemporary Music," *Mus News* 43 (Mar 1951), 8.
12. Reed, Frances. "Carl Ruggles," *Vermont Life* (Fall 1951), 7.
13. RePass, R. "American Composers of Today," *London Mus* 8 (Dec 1953), 24.
14. "Elected into American Institute of Arts and Letters," *NYT* (Feb 10, 1954), 36:1.
15. Keats, Sheila. "Reference Articles on American Composers: An Index," *Juilliard Rev* 1 (Fall 1954), 32.
16. "Inducted into American Institute of Arts and Letters," *NYT* (May 27, 1954), 25:5.
17. Harrison, Lou. "Carl Ruggles," *Score* 12 (Jun 1955), 15-26.
18. Ellsworth, Roy. "Americans on Microgroove," *HiFi* 6 (Aug 1956), 63.
19. "Honored by N. Y. Public Library Exhibit," *NYT* (Oct 13, 1957), 66:3.
20. "Honored by N. Y. Philharmonic," *NYT* (Oct 17, 1958), 33:1; (Oct 18, 1958), 17:2.
21. Briggs, J. "Crusty Composer," *NYT* (Oct 12, 1958), sec. 2, p. 11:8.
22. "Lennie's Grand Old Men," *Time* 72 (Oct 27, 1958), 54.
23. Perle, George. "Atonality and the Twelve-Note System in the United States," *Score* 27 (Jul 1960), 55-58.
24. *NYT* (Mar 3, 1961), 16:3.
25. Diether, Jack. "Composer's Showcase," *MA* 81 (May 1961), 52.
26. "Brandeis University Award," *NYT* (May 27, 1964), 12:7.
27. *NYT* (Jan 24, 1966), 27:1.
28. "Carl Ruggles' Season in the Sun," *NW* 67 (Feb 7, 1966), 80.
29. Boretz, Benjamin. "Music," *Nation* 202 (Mar 7, 1966), 278-280.
30. Cohn, Arthur. "Now That Other American Giant: Carl Ruggles," *Am Rec G* 32 (Mar 1966), 588-590.
31. Yates, Peter. "Sun Treader, the Work of an American Radical, in Its First American Hearing," *HiFi* 16 (Apr 1966), 85-86.
32. Fleming, Shirley. "Carl Ruggles Festival; Brunswick Report," *HiFi* 16 (Apr 1966), 158.
33. Kupferberg, Herbert. "Music Of Our Time," *Atlantic* 217 (May 1966), 118-120.
34. Salzman, Eric. "Carl Ruggles: A Lifetime Is Not Too Long To Search For The Sublime," *HiFi R* 17 (Sep 1966), 53-63.

35. Kirkpatrick, John. "The Evolution of Carl Ruggles (A Chronicle Largely in His Own Words)," *PNM* 6, No. 2 (1968), 146-166.
36. "Old Salt," *Time* 92 (Oct 11, 1968), 88.
37. Marcus, Leonard. "Ruggles All at Once," *HiFi/MA* 18 (Dec 1968), MA20.
38. Cohn, Arthur. "Playing and Conducting That Simply Could Not Be Bettered," *Am Rec G* 37 (Nov 1970), 148-151.
39. "Dies (Age 95)," *FoF* 31 (Oct 24, 1971), 1039C2; *NYT* (Oct 26, 1971), 45:2.
40. "Obituary," *Variety* 264 (Oct 27, 1971), 79; *Time* 95 (Nov 8, 1971), 98; *MT* 112 (Dec 1971), 1205; *R Mus Ital* 5, No. 6 (1971), 1121-1122; *Mus Artists* 4, No. 5 (1971-1972), 45; *Mus Ed J* 58 (Jan 1972), 14; *HiFi/MA* 22 (Feb 1972), MA2; *Central Opera* 14 (Summer 1972), 18.
41. "Carl Ruggles (1876-1971)," *Sym News* 22, No. 6 (1971), 16.
42. Gilbert, Steven E. "Carl Ruggles (1876-1971): An Appreciation," *PNM* 11, No. 1 (1972), 224-232.
43. –––––––" 'The Ultra-Modern Idiom': A Survey of New Music," *PNM* 12, Nos. 1-2 (1973-1974), 282-284.
44. Harvey, J. H. "Minneapolis: Ruggles Festival," *HiFi/MA* 24 (Aug 1974), MA30-31.
45. "Notes For Notes (Manuscripts and Papers to Yale)," *Notes* 31, No. 2 (1974), 281-285.
46. Mandel, Alan R. and Nancy. "Composers to Re-Emphasize: Six Americans Who Should Not Be Forgotten," *Clavier* 14, No. 4 (1975), 17.
47. Fisher, Fred. "Contemporary American Style: Show Three Representative Composers Use the 'Row'," *Clavier* 14, No. 4 (1975), 34-37.
48. "Mood," *Mus J* 34 (Feb 1976), 49.
49. Harman, Dave R. "The Musical Language of Carl Ruggles (1876-1971)," *Am Mus Tcr* 25, No. 5 (1976), 25-27.
50. Tenney, James C. "The Chronological Development of Carl Ruggles' Melodic Style," *PNM* 16 (1977), 36-69.

References to Works by Carl Ruggles

2. Angels: *MQ* 18 (1932), 578, 584; *MR* 29, No. 3 (1968), 184-196; *Mus & Mus* 19 (Mar 1971), 68.
8. Evocations: *Score* 12 (Jun 1955), 19-24; *MQ* 41 (1955), 551; *PNM* 4, No. 1 (1965), 10; *Mus & Artists* 4, No. 1 (1971), 44.
8a. Evocations (arr. for orch): *Buffalo Phil* (Nov 21, 1971), 11-14.
5b. Lilacs: *MQ* 37 (1951), 578-579; 41 (1955), 551-552; *MA* 78 (Nov 1, 1958), 78; *Mus & Mus* 19 (Mar 1971), 68.
5. Men and Mountains: *NYPPN* (Mar 19, 1936); *MQ* 31 (1945), 417; *NYPPN* (Oct 16, 1958); *MA* 78 (Nov 1, 1958), 78; *PNM* 4, No. 1 (1965), 9; *Natl Sym* (Feb 21, 1967), 23; *ChiSPN* (Oct 18-20, 1973), 11; *EweWT*; *HitMU*, 187.
10 Organum: *NYPPN* (Nov 24, 1949); *MQ* 36 (1950), 272-274; *Mus News* 42 (Jan 1950), 21; *EweWT*.
6. Portals: *MQ* 18 (1932), 578, 585; 41 (1955), 551; *Mus & Mus* 19 (Mar 1971), 68; *EweWT*.
7. Sun Treader: *NYT* (Jan 25, 1966), 46:3; *HiFi/MA* 16 (Apr 1966), 85; *ChiSPN* (Jan 26, 1967), 19; *HiFi/MA* 18 (Feb 1969), MA8; *BSPN* (Apr 4, 1970); *HiFi/MA* 20 (Jun 1970), 17; *Am Rec G* 37 (Nov 1970), 148-151; *Mus Opin* 94 (Sep 1971), 606; *MT* 112 (Sep 1971), 875; *Strad* 82 (Sep 1971), 233; *Mus & Mus* 20 (Nov 1971), 57-58; *Intam Mus Res Yearbook* 7 (1971), 43-50; *EweWT*.
1. Toys: *MQ* 18 (1932), 578; 24 (1938), 12, 21-22.
4. Vox clamans in deserto: *HiFi/MA* 18 (Jul 1968), MA20; 24 (Aug 1974), MA32.

Dissertation about Carl Ruggles and His Works

Peterson, Thomas E. *The Music of Carl Ruggles.* University of Washington, 1967.

OUTLINE XIV

WILLIAM (HOWARD) SCHUMAN (b. 1910)

I. Life

1910   Born in New York City, August 4. Parents of German-Jewish descent; father a business man.

1921   Began the study of the violin and piano. Primary interest was in sports; later in popular music.

1924   Entered George Washington High School. Organized a jazz band, playing piano, banjo, saxophone, clarinet.

1928   Graduated from high school. Wrote successful popular music, played in night clubs.

1930   Attended first symphony concert (New York Philharmonic) and decided to study music seriously. Studied with Max Persin (harmony), Charles Haubiel (counterpoint).

1933   Entered Teachers College of Columbia University; graduated in 1935 with a Bachelor of Science degree. Composed first serious music (*Four Canonic Choruses*, 1933).

1935   Received a scholarship in conducting at the Mozarteum in Salzburg (summer 1935). Became a member of the faculty of Sarah Lawrence College, Bronxville, teaching harmony, music appreciation, choral singing (1935-1941).

1936   Married Frances Prince. Taught at Columbia University (summer, 1936); studied with Roy Harris at the Juilliard School (summer 1936) and privately during two years (1936-1938).

1937   Awarded a Master of Arts degree in music by Columbia University.

1939   Awarded two Guggenheim Fellowships (1939-1941).

1943   Awarded the first Pulitzer Prize ever given for music (*A Free Song*); *Symphony No. 3* commissioned by the Koussevitzky Music Foundation.

1944   Succeeded Carl Engel as director of publications for G. Schirmer. Elected a member of the National Institute of Arts and Letters.

1945   Appointed president of the Juilliard School of Music (1945-1962); instituted many important reforms in music education. Continued with G. Schirmer as a consultant (1945-1951).

1946   Awarded honorary Doctor of Music degrees from the Chicago Musical College (1946), University of Wisconsin (1949), Columbia University (1954), Brandeis University (1962), and many other institutions.

1950   Received the New York Music Critics Circle Award (1950-1951). Received the first Brandeis University Creative Arts Award.

1962   Appointed president of the Lincoln Center for the Performing Arts (1962-1969).

1967   Received the Concert Artists Guild Award.

1968   Awarded the John H. Finley Medal by City College for significant service to the City of New York.

1969   Resigned as president of Lincoln Center in order to devote himself to composition.

1970   Elected Chairman of the Videorecord Corporation of America.

1973   Elected to the American Academy of the National Institute of Arts and Letters. Became board chairman of the MacDowell Colony (1974).

William Schuman has been the recipient of many honors, awards and commissions in addition to those listed above.

Note: Biographies of varying lengths and importance will be found in many of the books listed in the Bibliography at the end of this *Outline* under "References to William Schuman."

II. Compositions

A. Orchestra

		Date	Publisher
1.	Symphony No. 1 (for 18 instruments)	1935	Ms
2.	Prelude and Fugue	1937	Ms
3.	Symphony No. 2 (in one movement)	1937	
4.	American Festival Overture	1939	GS
5.	Symphony No. 3	1941	GS

    a. Passacaglia and Fugue   b. Chorale and Toccata

		Date	Publisher
6.	Symphony No. 4	1941	GS
7.	Newsreel in Five Shots	1941	GS

    a. Horse Race   d. Monkeys at the Zoo
    b. Fashion Show   e. Parade
    c. Tribal Dance

		Date	Publisher
8.	Concerto for Piano (cham orch)	1942	GS
9.	Prayer in Time of War	1943	GS
10.	Symphony No. 5 (Symphony for Strings)	1943	GS
11.	William Billings Overture	1943	GS
12.	Variations on a Theme by Eugene Goossens	1944	Ms
13.	Circus Overture: Side Show	1944	GS
14.	Undertow: Choreographic Episodes	1945	GS
15.	Concerto for Violin and Orchestra	1947; revised 1954, 1958	GS
16.	Symphony No. 6	1948	GS
17.	Judith: Choreographic Poem	1949	GS
18.	Credendum	1955	Meri

    a. Articles of Faith Declaration   b. Chorale   c. Finale

		Date	Publisher
19.	New England Triptych: Three Pieces After William Billings	1956	Meri

    a. Be Glad Then, America   c. Chester
    b. When Jesus Wept

		Date	Publisher
20.	Symphony No. 7	1960	Meri
21.	Song of Orpheus: Fantasy for Cello and Orchestra (inspired by William Shakespeare)	1961	Meri
22.	Symphony No. 8	1962	Meri
23.	Variations on America (based on the organ piece by Charles Ives)	1963	Meri
24.	The Orchestra Song	1963	Meri
25.	Dynamic IV	1965	Meri
26.	To Thee Old Cause: An Evocation (ob, brass, timp, pno, str)	1966	Meri
27.	Symphony No. 9: Le fosse Ardeatine	1968	Meri
28.	In Praise of Shahn (canticle for orchestra)	1969	Meri
29.	Voyage for Orchestra	1971	
30.	Symphony No. 10 (American Muse)	1976	Meri

B. Band

		Date	Publisher
31.	Newsreel in Five Shots (arr. from orch, No. 7 above)	1941	GS
32.	George Washington Bridge; an Impression for Band	1950	GS
33.	Chester Overture	1956	Meri
34.	When Jesus Wept (from No. 19 above)	1958	Meri
35.	Be Glad Then, America (from No. 19 above)	1975	Meri

C. Chamber

		Date	Publisher
36.	Canon and Fugue (vln, vlc, pno)	1934	Ms
37.	Choreographic Poem for seven instruments	1934	Ms
38.	String Quartet No. 1	1936	
39.	String Quartet No. 2	1937	BH

    a. Sinfonia   b. Passacaglia   c. Fugue

C.   **Chamber** (cont.)

40.	String Quartet No. 3	1939	GS
	a. Introduction and Fugue b. Intermezzo c. Rondo Variations		
41.	Quartettino for Four Bassoons (also for 4 clar or 4 sax)	1939	Peer
42.	String Quartet No. 4	1950	GS
43.	Amaryllis: Variations for String Trio	1964	Meri
44.	Prelude for a Great Occasion (brass, perc)	1975	Meri

D.   **Piano**

45.	Three-Score Set	1943	GS
46.	Voyage: A Cycle of Five Pieces	1953	Meri

     a. Anticipation   d. Decision
     b. Caprice   e. Retrospection
     c. Realization

47.	Three Piano Moods	1960	Meri

     a. Lyrical   b. Pensive   c. Dynamic

E.   **Choral** (a cappella unless otherwise indicated)

48.	Four Canonic Choruses (SATB)	1933	GS

     a. Epitaph (Edna St. Vincent Millay)   c. Night Stuff (Carl Sandburg)
     b. Epitaph for Joseph Conrad   d. Come Not (Alfred Tennyson)
       (Countee Cullen)

49.	Pioneers (Walt Whitman) (SSAATTBB)	1937	GS
50.	Choral Etude (vocalise; SATB)	1937	CF
51.	Prologue (Genevieve Taggard) (SATB, orch or pno)	1939	GS
52.	Prelude for Voices (Thomas Wolfe) (S., SATB or SSA)	1939	GS
53.	This is Our Time (Genevieve Taggard) (orch or pno)	1940	BH
	(Secular Cantata No. 1)		

     a. Celebration (SATB)   d. Questions (SSAA)
     b. Work (TTBB)   e. Fanfare (SATB)
     c. Foundation (SATB)

54.	Requiescat (vocalise; SATB or SSAA, pno)	1942	GS
55.	Holiday Song (Genevieve Taggard) (SATB; SSA; TTBB, pno)	1942	GS
56.	A Free Song (Walt Whitman) (SATB, orch or pno)	1942	GS
	(Secular Cantata No. 2)		
57.	Te Deum (SATB)	1944	GS
	(Coronation Scene: William Shakespeare's "Henry VIII")		
58.	Truth Shall Deliver (Geoffrey Chaucer;	1946	GS
	adapted by Marion Farquhar) (TBB)		
59.	Carols of Death (Walt Whitman) (SATB)		Meri

     a. The Last Invocation   c. To All, To Each
     b. The Unknown Region

60.	Four Rounds on Famous Words (aphorisms)	1957	Meri

     a. Health (SATB; SSAA)   c. Thrift (SATB; SSAA)
     b. Beauty (SATB; SSAA)   d. Caution (SSA; SAB)

61.	Choruses from "The Mighty Casey"	1953	GS
62.	The Lord Has A Child (Langston Hughes)	1957	Meri
	(SATB or SSA, pno or org)		
63.	Deo Ac Veritati (SATB or TTB)	1960	Meri
64.	Concerto on Old English Rounds (vla, women's chorus, orch)	1975	Meri

     a. Amaryllis   d. Come, Follow Me
     b. Great Tom is Cast   e. Combinations
     c. Who'll Buy Mi Roses?   f. Amaryllis

F.   **Solo Vocal**

65.	Orpheus With His Lute (William Shakespeare) (S., pno)	1944	GS
66.	The Lord Has A Child (Langston Hughes)	1957	Meri

67. The Young Dead Soldiers (Archibald MacLeish) (S., hn, ww, str) 1976

G.   Opera

68. The Mighty Casey: A Baseball Opera in Three Scenes (Jeremy   1953   GS
    Gury) (revised as a cantata, retitled "Casey at the Bat," 1975)

H.   Ballet

69. Night Journey   1947   GS
70. Judith   1949   GS
71. Undertow   1945   GS
72. The Witch of Endor   1961   GS

I.   Film

73. Steel Town   1944   Ms
74. The Earth is Born   1957

The following abbreviations are used in Section III of this *Outline*. The number indicates the number of the composition as listed in Section II.

11. *Billings*: William Billings Overture	40. *Str Qrt 3*: String Quartet No. 3
15. *Con Vln*: Concerto for Violin	45. *Set*: Three-Score Set
4. *Festival*: American Festival Overture	10. *Sym Str*: Symphony No. 5
56. *Free*: A Free Song	5. *Sym 3*: Symphony No. 3
55. *Holiday*: Holiday Song	19. *Triptych*: New England Triptych
65. *Orpheus*: Orpheus With His Lute	58. *Truth*: Truth Shall Deliver

III.   Style (techniques and devices)

"If a composer assumes a cloak that doesn't fit, he's in the fashion business, not the composing business. No real work of art ever failed because its vocabulary was out of vogue." "An important consideration for the American composer is that he can have abundant performances and a vitally interested audience if he is willing to create music that is serviceable to other than strictly professional groups."   William Schuman

A.   General characteristics
  1.   Compositions before 1937 are mostly in manuscript and have been withdrawn. Early style somewhat reserved; much use of interval of the fourth (harmonically) and jazz rhythms.
  2.   Highly individual style developed quickly after 1939. Characterized by economy of means, dramatic intensity, linear writing based on vocal concepts, complex rhythmic structure, lyricism and expressiveness, and a sure technique. Movements often grow out of the principal subject.
  3.   New harmonic developments, particularly in the direction of chromaticism, began about 1948. Even greater clarity, more interest in contrapuntal lines, continued growth in formal concepts. Less use of chords in fourths.
  4.   Increasingly vigorous, rhythmically complex and dissonant; less emphasis on lyrical elements. First programmatic symphony (No. 9).

B.   Melodic line
  1.   Long, singing melodic lines often broken up into thematic ideas which generate rhythmic, harmonic and formal structure. Melodies may be angular with skips (fourths, fifths, octaves); diatonic within tonalities which may include from seven to twelve tones; in many different scale patterns; sometimes folk-like.
  2.   Long, flowing lines (usually slow): *Festival* (p. 19, fl); *Sym 3* (p. 46, vla; p. 58, meas. 10); *Sym Str* (p. 8, vln).
  3.   Short, terse lines (often fast): *Sym 3* (p. 16, fugue subject); *Str Qrt 3* (p. 12, meas. 150, vlc); *Festival* (p. 13, meas. 84).

4. Angular, emphasis on leaps: *Festival* (p. 9); *Sym 3* (p. 1, meas. 1; p. 10, meas. 5; p. 16, fugue); *Con Vln* (first movement); *Sym 4* (ostinato beginning); *Str Qrt 3* (p. 47).

5. Empasis of fourths: *Festival* (p. 27, meas. 282); *Str Qrt 2* (p. 15, meas. 2); *Str Qrt 3* (p. 4, meas. 54); *Sym 3* (p. 1, meas. 2, 6); *Sym Str* (p. 8, meas. 5); *Set* (p. 3, cadence).

C. Harmony
1. Principally tertian and quartal. Expressive dissonance an essential part of style. Frequent use of superimposed triads (polychords or polyharmony); some polytonal writing. Resolution of nonharmonic tones often delayed. Little use of conventional harmonic progressions, sevenths, ninths, diminished sevenths, cadential and 6/4 chords. Works for voices generally less involved harmonically and contrapuntally, but not rhythmically, than instrumental music.

2. Triadic: *Con Vln* (*Finale*); *Sym 3* (p. 5, meas. 3; p. 7, meas. 1; p. 46, meas. 22; *Undertow* (*Hymn*); *Judith* (beginning).

3. Triads with added tones: *Set* (No. 1).

4. Third relationship: *Sym 4* (p. 34).

5. Major-minor alternation: *Str Qrt 3* (p. 2, meas. 34); *Sym 7*; *Con Vln*.

6. Chords of fourths (quartal): *Festival* (meas. 17, final section); *Sym 3* (p. 77, meas. 1-3); *Set* (beginning).

7. Polychords: *Sym 3* (p. 8, meas. 1; p. 13, meas. 3; p. 77, meas. 4); *Sym Str* (second movement, p. 8); *Set* (No. 2, meas. 1-4); *Sym 6* (beginning); *Judith* (beginning); *Str Qrt 3* (p. 41, meas. 187); *Festival* (final chord).

8. Polytonal: *Undertow* (drunk scene).

9. Combination of mixed intervals: *Sym 6* (pp. 1, 49).

10. Overtones: *Undertow* (p. 40).

11. Contrapuntal harmony, essentially triadic, often bitonal: *Sym Str* (p. 11); *Str Qrt 2* (p. 18); *Sym 3* (p. 175); *Str Qrt 3* (p. 11); *Con Vln* (slow movement).

12. Parallel chord progressions: *Free*; *Truth*; *Set*.

13. Open fifths: *Sym 3* (p. 70).

14. Pedal point: *Triptych* (p. 2).

15. Cadences: movements often end with a consonant chord or unison, preceded by a dissonant chord: *Sym 3* (end); *Sym Str* (first movement, end).

D. Counterpoint
1. Principles of polyphonic devices and forms, extended and used with great skill and originality, are an essential part of style. Harmonic basis generally strong. Canons and fugal writing are characteristic.

2. Alternation between free and contrapuntal textures: *Sym 3*.

3. Two-part imitation: *Sym 3* (pp. 59-60); *Sym 4* (p. 1); *Sym Str* (p. 6); *Set* (No. 2); *Requiescat*; *Str Qrt 2* (p. 1); *Str Qrt 3* (p. 12, meas. 150; p. 17; pp. 46-47).

4. Three- and four-part: *Sym 3* (p. 17, meas. 15; p. 19; p. 23, meas. 3); *Sym Str* (p. 10); *Str Qrt 2* (pp. 5, 18); *Str Qrt 3* (p. 11).

5. Fugal writing: *Festival* (p. 13, meas. 83); *Free* (introduction to Part 2); *Str Qrt 2* (third movement); *Str Qrt 3* (p. 4, meas. 57); *Con Pno* (third movement, piano cadenza).

6. Triple fugue: *Sym 3* (p. 16, meas. 5; countersubject used consistently; first and second sections separated by a trumpet fanfare; second subject in augmentation; three subjects never combined).

E. Rhythm
1. Strong: often jazz-like in earlier works. In later works rhythms became increasingly individual and unpredictable. Regular meter with shifting accents characteristic.

2. Short, agitated patterns (jazz influence): *Festival* (pp. 4-5); *Sym Str* (pp. 1, 12); *Sym 3* (p. 29, meas. 273; pp. 34-35); *Str Qrt 3* (p. 27).

3. Longer patterns: *Str Qrt 3* (p. 1); *Festival* (pp. 20-23, vln).

4. Cross-rhythms with short, shifting rhythmic patterns over a fundamental beat: *Sym 3* (p. 7, meas. 4; pp. 16-17).
5. Contrapuntal rhythm (cross-accents): *Sym 3*.
6. Syncopation: *Sym 3* (p. 5, meas. 3; p. 13, meas. 4; p. 9, meas. 2); *Con Vln* (first and last movements).
7. Characteristic use of dynamics and rests: *Judith* (p. 60).

F. Form
1. Form grows out of musical ideas and is logical; sometimes sectional, especially in early works. Baroque and classical forms frequently used, but with great freedom. Literal recapitulations and introductions (except in vocal works) are avoided. Descriptive titles and program music rare (*Newsreel*; *Sym 9*).
2. Passacaglia: *Str Qrt 2* (second movement); *Sym 3* (p. 1).
3. Sinfonia: *Str Qrt 2* (first movement).
4. One-movement work: *Sym 6* (6 sections).
5. Ostinato: *Con Pno* (*Finale*); *Sym 4* (beginning); *Sym Str* (Coda).
6. Chorale and Toccata: *Sym 3* (second movement, pp. 46, 54).
7. Rondo (with variation techniques): *Str Qrt 3* (*Finale*); *Sym Str* (*Finale*).

G. Orchestration
1. Clear, clean texture; generally bright; orchestral "effects" avoided; lean, with little doubling; possibilities of all instruments exploited. Use of chorale style in sonorous passages; wide leaps and strong attacks in writing for strings.
2. Muted strings: *Sym 3*.
3. Use of orchestral choirs characteristic: *Festival* (pp. 4-5); *Sym 3* (pp. 23-25; 54-62).
4. Chorale style: *Triptych*; *Credendum*; *Sym 3*.
5. Brass used percussively, melodically and for background: *Festival* (pp. 1, 7, 23); *Sym 3* (p. 16); *Undertow*.
6. Timpani solo: *Sym 6*.
7. Piano: *Sym 3*; *Undertow*.

BIBLIOGRAPHY

Book about William Schuman

Schreiber, Flora R., and Vincent Persichetti. *William Schuman*. New York: G. Schirmer, 1954. Reviews: *Notes* 11 (1954), 560; *Mus Club Mag* 34 (Jan 1955), 39; *Pan Pipes* 47 (Jan 1955), 80; *MQ* 41 (1955), 105; *ML* 36 (Jan 1955), 76; *Mus Ed J* 41 (Feb-Mar 1955), 75; *Mus Opin* 78 (Apr 1955), 413; *J Research* 3 (Spring 1955), 65; *MR* 16 (Aug 1955), 246; *HiFi* 5 (Sep 1955), 13; *MA* 75 (Dec 15, 1955), 24.

Articles by William Schuman

1. Review: *Music Since 1900*, Nicolas Slonimsky. *MM* 15, No. 2 (1937-1938), 128-130.
2. "Unconventional Case History," *MM* 15, No. 4 (1937-1938), 222-227.
3. Review: "Layman's Guide and Student Opera," *MM* 16, No. 2 (1938-1939), 135-137.
4. Review: "Taylor-Made Topics," *MM* 17, No. 3 (1939-1940), 197-199.
5. "Writing for Amateurs and Pros," *NYT* (Jun 30, 1940), 5.
6. "A Brief Study of Music Organizations Founded in the Interest of the Living Composer," *Twice a Year* 5-6 (1940-1941), 361-367.
7. "Songs America Has Sung," *NYT* (Jun 13, 1943), book reviews, p. 8.
8. "Music Master," *NYT* (Jun 27, 1943), 4.
9. "A Symphonic Composer on Some Current Problems," *Mus Pub J* (Sep 1943), 5, 39.
10. "Opportunities for Music Workers," *Etude* 64 (Sep 1946), 500.

11. "On Teaching the Literature and Materials of Music," *MQ* 34 (1948), 155-168.
12. "The Final Triumph," in *Stravinsky in the Theatre*, ed. Minna Lederman.   New York (1948), 134.
13. "A Composer Looks at Critics," *MA* 68 (Nov 15, 1948), 8, 31.
14. "Virtuosity in Discernment" in *Paul Rosenfeld, Voyager in the Arts*, ed. Jerome Mellquist and Lucie Wiese. New York (1948), 105-108.
15. "On Freedom in Music," in *The Arts in Renewal*, ed. Bradley. Philadelphia (1951), 67.
16. "The Side of the Angels," *Etude* 69 (Jun 1951), 9, 50.
17. "The Place of Composer Copland," *NYT* (Nov 8, 1953), book reviews, pp. 3, 49.
18. Introduction to *Juilliard Report on Teaching the Literature and Materials of Music*. New York: W. W. Norton, 1953, pp. 7-24. Review in *MQ* 40 (1954), 249.
19. Review: *Thesaurus of Orchestral Devices* by Gardner Read. *MQ* 40 (1954), 419.
20. "The Juilliard Festival of American Music," *Juilliard Rev* (Winter 1955-1956), 28.
21. Review: *Orchestration* by Walter Piston. *MQ* 42 (1956), 103.
22. "Responsibility of Music Education to Music," *Mus Ed J* 42 (Jun 1956), 17-19; also in *Etude* 74 (Sep 1956), 11-12.
23. "Music as Usual," *Mus J* 17 (Apr 1959), 12; *Am Mus Tcr* 8 (May-Jun 1959), 6; *Juilliard Rev* 6 (Spring 1959), 3.
24. "Teaching Our Youth," *NYT* (Mar 15, 1959), sec. 2, p. 9.
25. "From the Mail Pouch: Aim of Naumburg Competition," *NYT* (Nov 13, 1960), sec. 2, p. 11.
26. "A Birthday Salute to Aaron Copland," *Juilliard Rev* 8, No. 1 (1960-1961), 6.
27. "William Schuman Summarizes Juilliard Objectives," *MA* 81 (Feb 1961), 18-19.
28. "Complete Musician: Vincent Persichetti and Twentieth-Century Harmony," *MQ* 47 (1961), 379-385.
29. "Civic Values in the Arts," *Mus J* 20 (Mar 1962), 37.
30. "The Responsibility of Lincoln Center to Education," *Mus Ed J* 49, No. 1 (1962), 35-38.
31. "Idea; A Creative, Dynamic Force," *NYT Mag* (Sep 23, 1962), part 2, p. 11.
32. "An American Partnership," *ClSPN* (Oct 11, 1962), 60-62.
33. "The Arts in Our Colleges," *MA* 83 (Jun 1963), 5.
34. "Have We Culture? Yes, and No," *NYT Mag* (Sep 22, 1963), 21.
35. "Fritz Reiner (Eulogy Delivered by William Schuman at the Funeral)," *MA* 83 (Dec 1963), 283.
36. "Case for a Center; Questions from Opera News Answered," *Opera N* 29 (Sep 26, 1964), 6-11.
37. "The Prejudice of Conformity," *Mus J* 23 (Sep 1965), 44.
38. "The Heart of an Arts Center," *Mus Ed J* 53, No. 3 (1966), 34-36.
39. "The Arts in America," *Mus J Annual* 25 (1967), 23.
40. "A korusmu mar nem keszult el . . .," *Magyar Zene* 8, No. 2 (1967), 170.
41. "Arts; Address January 17, 1968," *Vital Speeches* 34 (Feb 15, 1968), 281-283.
42. "A Special Editorial," *Mus & Artists* 1, No. 2 (1968), 1.
43. "The Malady Lingers On," *Mus J Annual* 26 (1968), 30-32; *Musart* 21, No. 1 (1968), 10.
44. "Cultivating Student Taste; Excerpts from Address," *Todays Ed* 57 (Nov 1968), 10-13.
45. "The Arts: A New Priority," *Composer US* 1, No. 1 (1969), 8-13.
46. "Semper fidelis: Address on the Occasion of the Enshrinement of John Philip Sousa into the Hall of Fame for Great Americans," *School Mus* 48 (Oct 1976), 42-44.

References to William Schuman

Books
(See the General Bibliography)

AbrHY; AbrMM; ASC-SC; AusMT; BacMM; Baker; BakSL; BauTC; BloYA; BluPC; BMI-C; BMI-

MW; BMI-OP; BMI-P; BMI-SC; Bull; CatPC; ChaAC; ChaAM; ClaEA; CobCS; CohCT; ColHM; ComA; CopCM; CopTN; CopWL; CurB (1962); DalTT; DavPM; DemMT; DerETM; DowO; Duk-LM; Edm-II; EdMUS; EweAC; EweCB; EweCS; EweCT; EweDE; EweMC; EweNB; EweWT; EweYA; GolMM; GosMM; Grove; HanIT; HitMU; HowMM; HowOA; HowOC; HowSH; JabCAC; JohOA; JohSH; KinAI; LanOH (32); LeiMW; LeiSK; MacAC; MacIC; MelMN; MelMS; MueAS; MyeTC; NorLC; PavMH; PersTH; PeyNM; PorM3S; ReiCA; ReiCC; RobCM; SalMO; SalzTM; SamLM; SanWM; SmiWM; StevePC; ThoAJ; ThoAM; ThompIC; ThoMR; ThoRL; ThomsMS; WooWM; WWA; WWM; YatYC; YouCD; YouCT.

Articles

Brief mention: *MQ* 25 (1939), 379; *MA* 60 (Mar 25, 1940), 31; *MM* 20, No. 2 (1942-1943); *MQ* 26 (1940), 109; 31(1945), 103; *Etude* 63 (May 1945), 259; *MQ* 33 (1947), 33, 315, 316, 317, 321, 315; 34 (1948), 6, 10; 37 (1951), 317; *MQ* 42 (1956), 143; *MA* 76 (Feb 15, 1956), 30; *Americas* 9 (Sep 1957), 9; *PNM* 2, No. 2 (1964), 18, 125; 4, No. 1 (1965), 180; *BMI-MW* (Mar 1967), 6; (May 1967), 14; (Feb 1968), 17; (Oct 1968), 23; (Mar 1969), 12.

1. Copland, Aaron. "Scores and Records," *MM* 15, No. 4 (1937-1938), 244.
2. "Wins Musicians Committee to Aid Spanish Democracy Contest," *NYT* (Apr 17, 1938), sec. 10, p. 6:5.
3. Lieberson, Goddard. "Over the Air," *MM* 16, No. 1 (1938-1939), 65.
4. Bernstein, Leonard. "The Latest from Boston," *MM* 16, No. 3 (1938-1939), 183.
5. *NYT* (Mar 19, 1939), sec. 11, p. 6:5.
6. "Wins Guggenheim Fellowship," *NYT* (Mar 27, 1939), 21:6.
7. Rosenfeld, Paul. "Copland, Harris, Schuman," *MQ* 25 (1939), 379.
8. "Composers Win Guggenheim Awards," *MA* 59 (Apr 10, 1939), 4.
9. *NYT* (May 8, 1939), 20:4.
10. "Wins Town Hall-Composers League Music Composition Award," *NYT* (Nov 5, 1939), sec. 9, p. 7:7.
11. "William Schuman Wins New Composer's Award," *MA* 59 (Nov 10, 1939), 11.
12. "Events in the New York Stadium," *MA* 60, No. 12 (Jul 1940), 27.
13. Carter, Elliott. "American Music in the New York Scene," *MM* 17, No. 2 (1939-1940), 96.
14. Pettis, Ashley. "The WPA and the American Composer," *MQ* 26 (1940), 109.
15. "Rodzinski Offers New Schuman Work," *MA* 62 (Feb 25, 1942), 21.
16. Bernstein, Leonard. "Young American—William Schuman," *MM* 19, No. 2 (1941-1942), 97.
17. *NYT* (Apr 5, 1942), sec. 8, p. 6:5; (Apr 12, 1942), sec. 8, p. 6:5; (Apr 19, 1942), sec. 8, p. 6:5; (Aug 9, 1942), sec. 8, p. 5:8.
18. "Schuman, No Kin," *Time* 39 (Apr 20, 1942), 60.
19. "Wins NY Music Critics Circle Award," *NYT* (May 15, 1942), 24:4; (May 31, 1942), sec. 8, p. 6:2.
20. "Biography," *Current Biography* (June 1942); *Current Biography Yearbook* (1942), 746-748.
21. Eyer, Ronald F. "William Schuman is First Subject of Music Forum," *MA* 63 (Jan 25, 1943), 19.
22. Copland, Aaron. "From the '20's to the '40's and Beyond," *MM* 20, No. 2 (1942-1943), 80.
23. "Wins Pulitzer Prize," *NYT* (May 2, 1943), 12:8; (May 4, 1943), 12:3.
24. Frankenstein, Alfred. "William Schuman," *MM* 22, No. 1 (1944-1945), 23.
25. Eyer, Ronald F. "William Schuman," *MA* 64 (Jan 25, 1944), 8, 25.
26. Garoutte, Nancy. "Bill Schuman," *Sarah Lawrence Alumni Mag* (Fall 1944), 14, 22.
27. "Appointed G. Schirmer, Inc., Director," *NYT* (Sep 30, 1944), 16:3.
28. "Elected President of Juilliard School of Music," *NYT* (Aug 1, 1945), 15:4.
29. "Maestro in Play Clothes," *NW* 26 (Aug 13, 1945), 100.

30. "New Juilliard President," *Musician* 50 (Aug 1945), 161.
31. Broder, Nathan. "The Music of William Schuman, with List of Works," *MQ* 31 (1945), 17-28.
32. Glock, William. "Schuman's Music," *The Observer*, London (Sep 2, 1945), 2.
33. *NYT* (Oct 10, 1945), 23:1.
34. "Ventilation for Juilliard," *Time* 46 (Oct 23, 1945), 57.
35. *NYT* (Jan 16, 1946), 19:1; (May 6, 1946), 17:3; (May 13, 1947), 30:2.
36. Canby, Edward T. "Schuman Syntheses," *SR* 30 (Nov 1, 1947), 46.
37. *NYT* (May 14, 1948), 28:4.
38. "Receives $1000 Commission for New Symphonic Work–Dallas Symphony Society," *NYT* (Jun 6, 1948), sec. 2, p. 7:3.
39. "Dushkin Premiers U. S. Works," *MC* 139 (Jan 15, 1949), 18.
40. "Honorary Degree Wisconsin University," *NYT* (May 15, 1949), 79:5.
41. Cowell, Henry. "Given for the First Time in New York (Symphony No. 2)," *MQ* 36 (1950), 268-270.
42. *NYT* (Oct 12, 1950), 42:6; (Dec 24, 1950), sec. 2, p. 9:6.
43. "William Schuman," *Pan Pipes* 43 (Dec 1950), 129.
44. Marx, H. "Music Has a Stake in the Ideological Struggle," *Mus News* 42 (Dec 1950), 4.
45. "Sigma Alpha Iota Award," *Mus of the West* 6 (Jan 1951), 6.
46. Rosenwald, Hans. "Contemporary Music," *Mus News* 43 (Apr 1951), 11.
47. *NYT* (Jun 2, 1951), 13:2; (Oct 4, 1951), 37:8.
48. Berger, Arthur. "Spotlight on the Moderns," *SR* 34 (Sep 29, 1951), 60.
49. "Resigns as Publication Director, G. Schirmer, Inc.," *NYT* (Sep 30, 1951), 61:3.
50. "G. Schirmer Announces Schuman Resignation," *Mus Dealer* 5 (Nov 1951), 27.
51. "Wins WQXR-NY Times Student Auditions," *NYT* (Jan 8, 1952), 22:1.
52. "William Schuman," *Pan Pipes* 44 (Jan 1952), 44.
53. Marx, H. "UNESCO, U. S. Government and Music," *Mus News* 44 (Mar 1952), 3-4.
54. "On the Cover," *Mus News* 44 (Mar 1952), 3.
55. "Piston May Follow Schuman in BMI," *BB* 64 (Dec 6, 1952), 14.
56. "William Schuman," *Pan Pipes* 45 (Jan 1953), 66.
57. *NYT* (Apr 28, 1953), 31:2.
58. RePass, R. "American Composers of Today," *London Mus* 8 (Dec 1953), 25.
59. "Columbia University Honorary Degree," *NYT* (Jan 12, 1954), 16:2, 3, 7.
60. Kyle, Marguerite K. "AmerAllegro," *Pan Pipes* 46 (Jan 1954), 59.
61. Heinsheimer, Hans W. "Bugles and Bells (Generation of American Composers of Importance Without Interest in Musical Theatre," *MC* 149 (Mar 1, 1954), 6.
62. "Juilliard President Asks Government Aid to Music," *Down Beat* 21 (Jul 14, 1954), 1.
63. Schreiber, Flora R., and Vincent Persichetti. "William Schuman," *Notes* 11 (Sep 1954), 560-561.
64. Keats, Sheila. "Reference Articles on American Composers: An Index," *Juilliard Rev* 1 (Fall 1954), 32.
65. *NYT* (Oct 25, 1954), 30:7.
66. "William Schuman," *Pan Pipes* 47 (Jan 1955), 64.
67. Evett, Robert. "How Right is Right?" *Score* 12 (Jun 1955), 34.
68. Schreiber, Flora R. "A Model for Music Teachers," *Mus J* 13 (Oct 1955), 28.
69. Stambler, Bernard. "Four American Composers (Schuman, Barber, Copland, Ives)," *Juilliard Rev* 2 (Winter 1955), 7-16.
70. *NYT* (Jan 14, 1956), 21:2.
71. Kyle, Marguerite K. "AmerAllegro," *Pan Pipes* 47 (Jan 1956), 71.
72. Milburn, Frank. "The Juilliard School of Music–Its First 50 Years," *MA* 76 (Feb 15, 1956), 30.
73. "Schuman Signs Exclusive Contract," *Etude* 74 (Mar 1956), 9.
74. Ellsworth, Ray. "Americans on Microgroove," *HiFi* 6 (Aug 1956), 65.

75. Downes, Edward. "Twenty-One Years of Composers Forums," *NYT* (Oct 7, 1956), sec. 2, p. 9:1.
76. "Brandeis University Creative Arts Award (first winners)," *NYT* (Dec 27, 1956), 6:5.
77. Kyle, Marguerite K. "AmerAllegro," *Pan Pipes* 49 (Jan 1957), 68.
78. *NYT* (Feb 7, 1957), 1:5.
79. "Brandeis University Creative Arts Award," *NYT* (Mar 6, 1957), 25:3.
80. "William Schuman," *Mus Club Mag* 37 (Sep 1957), 12.
81. Sabin, Robert. "William Schuman Pays Tribute to Billings," *MA* 78 (Feb 1958), 212.
82. *NYT* (May 31, 1958), 6:8; (Dec 12, 1958), 2:3.
83. "American Composers," *MC* 159 (Jan 1959), 41.
84. Marguerite K. Kyle. "AmerAllegro," *Pan Pipes* 51 (Jan 1959), 82.
85. *NYT* (Jan 9, 1959), 12:5; (Mar 15, 1959), sec. 2, p. 9:8.
86. "Named to Advisory Commission on Cultural Information," *NYT* (Feb 11, 1959), 32:6.
87. "Classified Chronological Catalog of Works by the United States Composer William Schuman," *Intam Mus B* 12 (Jul 1959), 34-41.
88. "William Schuman," *Composers of the Americas* 5 (1959), 69-77.
89. "Schuman to Head Naumburg Board," *MC* 160 (Dec 1959), 5.
90. *NYT* (Feb 19, 1960), 20:4.
91. "Composers Showcase," *MA* 80 (Mar 1960), 33.
92. "Colgate University Honorary Degree," *NYT* (Jun 14, 1960), 34:4.
93. *NYT* (Nov 13, 1960), sec. 2, p. 11:6.
94. Salzman, Eric. "He Marks Milestones," *NYT* (Nov 27, 1960), sec. 2, p. 9.
95. "William Schuman Summarizes Juilliard Objectives," *MA* 81 (Feb 1961), 18.
96. Sabin, Robert. "Dangers of Being a Destructive Reactionary," *MA* 81 (Feb 1961), 8.
97. Stoddard, H. "William Schuman Discusses Problems in the Field of Music Education," *Int Mus* 59 (Mar 1961), 22.
98. "William Schuman, Juilliard's President," *Juilliard Rev* 8, No. 3 (1961), 6.
99. "Named President of Lincoln Center for Performing Arts Effective January 1, 1962," *NYT* (Sep 13, 1961), 1:2; 44:2; 51:2.
100. "Inside Stuff—Music," *Variety* 224 (Sep 20, 1961), 50.
101. "Casey at the Baton," *Time* 78 (Sep 22, 1961), 67-68.
102. "Named President Emeritus of Juilliard School of Music," *NYT* (Sep 23, 1961), 17:2.
103. "Faculty Honors Schuman," *Juilliard Rev* 9, No. 1 (1961), 3.
104. "William Schuman Elected President of Lincoln Center," *Juilliard Rev* 9, No. 3 (1961), 3.
105. "Schuman Named Lincoln Center President," *Mus Mag* 163 (Oct 1961), 2.
106. "Schuman to Head Lincoln Center," *MA* 81 (Oct 1961), 16.
107. "Appointment," *FoF* 21 (1961, Appendix to the Index), 144.
108. "Resigned as President of W. W. Naumburg Foundation," *NYT* (Oct 25, 1961), 30:1.
109. "Artistic Standards; Schuman Stresses Orchestra Role in Maintaining High Artistic Standards," *ASOL* 12, Nos. 5-6 (1961), 10.
110. *NYT* (Nov 14, 1961), 1:7; (Dec 14, 1961), 52:2; (Dec 20, 1961), 37:3; (Dec 31, 1961), sec. 6, p. 8.
111. Schonberg, Howard C. "Man to Orchestrate Lincoln Center," *NYT Mag* (Dec 31, 1961), p. 8.
112. *NYT* (Jan 14, 1962), sec. 6, p. 4; (Jan 25, 1962), 24:4; (Feb 20, 1962), 31:1.
113. Sabin, Robert. "Lincoln Center Challenge," *MA* 82 (Feb 1962), 6.
114. *NYT* (Mar 18, 1962), 85:1; (Mar 28, 1962), 34:1; (May 4, 1962), 25:4; (May 7, 1962), 1:2.
115. "Honored by Winchester Orchestral Society," *NYT* (Apr 26, 1962), 24:5.
116. "Appointed to Music Advisory Commission, Hopkins Center, Dartmouth College," *NYT* (May 27, 1962), 96:2.
117. *NYT* (May 15, 1962), 47:5; (Jun 14, 1962), 25:2; (Jul 25, 1962), 30:3; (Sep 23, 1962), sec. 6, part 2, p. 11; (Nov 3, 1962), 16:5; (Dec 4, 1962), 46:1.

118. "Brandeis University Honorary Degree," *NYT* (May 31, 1962), 13:4.

119. "William Schuman Testimonial Dinner," *Juilliard Rev* 9, No. 2 (1962), 4.

120. Kyle, Marguerite K. "AmerAllegro," *Pan Pipes* 54, No. 2 (1962), 70.

121. "New York University Alumni Award," *NYT* (Jun 7, 1962), 27:1.

122. Eyer, Ronald. "William Schuman; Profile," *MA* 82 (Sep 1962), 26.

123. Jacobi, P. "Schuman of the Center; An Interview with William Schuman," *Mus Mag* 164 (Sep 1962), 8-11.

124. "Two Schumans," *Time* 80 (Oct 12, 1962), 54.

125. Schonberg, Howard C. "Need For Critics (Informed Opinion)," *NYT* (Nov 11, 1962), sec. 2, p. 9.

126. "Dartmouth College Honorary Degree," *NYT* (Nov 19, 1962), 39:8.

127. "Biography," *Current Biography* (Dec 1962); *Current Biography Yearbook* (1962), 377-379.

128. "Previously Unpublished Composer's Letters as Written to Claire R. Reis," *MA* 83 (Jan 1963), 15.

129. *NYT* (Apr 14, 1963), 77:3; (May 1, 1963), 35:4; (Sep 22, 1963), sec. 6, p. 21; (Oct 13, 1963), sec. 6, p. 102.

130. Palatsky, Eugene. "Lincoln Center Situation," *Dance Mag* 37 (May 1963), 36-38.

131. Kyle, Marguerite K. "AmerAllegro," *Pan Pipes* 55, No. 2 (1963), 68.

132. "Adelphi University Honorary Degree," *NYT* (Jun 13, 1963), 22:2; (Jul 26, 1963), 16:1.

133. "Mixing Business and Art," *Business Week* (Aug 3, 1963), 42-45.

134. Harrison, Jay S. "The New York Music Scene (Orchestration of Charles Ives' 'Variations on America'," *MA* 84 (Jul 1964), 36

135. "The Case for a Center; William Schuman Answers Questions from Opera News," *Opera N* 29 (Sep 26, 1964), 6-11.

136. *NYT* (Oct 2, 1964), 1:3; (Oct 10, 1964), 19:1; (Oct 23, 1964), 35:1; (Dec 5, 1964), 1:5; (Dec 6, 1964), 88:4; (Dec 8, 1964), 1:1; (Dec 14, 1964), 49:2.

137. "Inside Job," *NW* 64 (Dec 21, 1964), 74-75.

138. *NYT* (Jan 12, 1965), 32:2; (Apr 1, 1965), 31:1; (May 13, 1965), 39:5; (Jun 14, 1965), 44:1; (Jun 20, 1965), sec. 2, p. 13:6; (Nov 16, 1965), 59:1; (Dec 1, 1965), 55:2.

139. "Shiny New Image," *NW* 65 (Jan 25, 1965), 84-85.

140. Kyle, Marguerite K. "AmerAllegro," *Pan Pipes* 57, No. 2 (1965), 78.

141. "Philharmonic Fanfare," *Variety* 239 (Aug 18, 1965), 56; *BB* 77 (Aug 21, 1965), 40.

142. Kay, Norman. "William Schuman," *MM* 14 (May 1966), 38-41.

143. *NYT* (Nov 2, 1966), 35:2; (Dec 6, 1966), 1:2; (Jan 10, 1967), 34:3; (Jan 13, 1967), 22:4; (Mar 17, 1967), 36:4; (Apr 1, 1967), 18:4; (May 2, 1967), 54:1; (May 20, 1967), 39:1; (Jun 27, 1967), 34:4.

144. "Receives Concert Artists Guild Award," *NYT* (Jan 20, 1967).

145. "Receives New York City Handel Medallion," *NYT* (Mar 13, 1967).

146. Chapin, Louis. "William Schuman," *BMI-MW* (May 1967), 14.

147. "Fordham University Honorary Degree," *NYT* (Jun 11, 1967), 21:1.

148. *NYT* (Jul 14, 1967), 18:1.

149. Chapin, Louis. "William Schuman," *BMI* (Jul 1967), 14.

150. Rees, C. B. "Impressions—Dr. William Schuman of the Lincoln Centre," *Mus Events* 22 (Jul 1967), 8.

151. *NYT* (Feb 27, 1968), 35:1; (Jul 23, 1968), sec. 2, p. 17:1; (Jan 19, 1969), sec. 2, p. 13:2; (Oct 26, 1969), sec. 2, p. 29:2.

152. "Certificate of Merit to William Schuman," *Pan Pipes* 60, No. 2 (1968), 42.

153. "Activities of Member Organizations," *NMC* 28, No. 2 (1968), 31.

154. "Resigns Lincoln Center President," *NYT* (Dec 5, 1968), 1:4.

155. "Replaced at Lincoln Center," *FoF* 29 (Jan 14, 1969), 857C3.

156. "Here and There," *HiFi/MA* 19 (Feb 1969), MA16.

157. Kyle, Marguerite K. "AmerAllegro," *Pan Pipes* 61, No. 2 (1969), 74.

158. "New York," *NZ* 130 (Mar 1969), 131-133; *Opera* 20 (Feb 1969), 113.
159. "Concert Music," *BMI* (Mar 1969), 12.
160. *NYT* (Jan 28, 1970), 48:2.
161. "Canticle of Shahn Premiered," *FoF* 30 (Jan 29, 1970), 213G1.
162. Waters, Edward N. "Variations on a Theme; Recent Acquisitions of the Music Division," *Q J Library Congress* 27, No. 1 (1970), 64.
163. "Elected Chairman Videorecord Corporation of America," *NYT* (Mar 3, 1970), 83:4.
164. "Named Director of Videorecord Corporation of America," *NYT* (Apr 5, 1970), sec. 3, p. 12:7.
165. *NYT* (Oct 1, 1970), 83:4.
166. "Concert by N Y Philharmonic Played in Honor of 60th Birthday," *NYT* (Dec 19, 1970), 18:2.
167. Kyle, Marguerite K. "AmerAllegro," *Pan Pipes* 63, No. 2 (1971), 76.
168. "Schuman Receives MacDowell Medal," *Triangle* 66, No. 1 (1971), 27.
169. "Awarded MacDowell Colony Medal for Exceptional Contributions to American Arts," *NYT* (Aug 9, 1971), 21:2.
170. *NYT* (Sep 10, 1971), 40:1.
171. "In the News," *BMI* (Oct 1971), 7.
172. "MacDowell Medal to Schuman, Edward MacDowell Day, August 8, 1971," *Pan Pipes* 64, No. 2 (1972), 20-21.
173. "Music Journal's 1972 Gallery of Living Composers," *Mus J* 30 (Annual 1972), 57.
174. Pooler, F., and Others. "In Quest of Answers: An Interview with William Schuman," *Choral J* 13, No. 6 (1973), 5-15.
175. *NYT* (Nov 21, 1973), 26:1.
176. "Elected as New Member to American Academy of Arts and Letters," *NYT* (Dec 10, 1973), 58:4.
177. "Lincoln Center Head Becomes MacDowell Colony Board Chairman," *NYT* (Jan 24, 1974), 44:3.
178. "The Pulitzer Prizes (Some Winners in Music)," *BMI* No. 2 (1974), 21.
179. "William Howard Schuman Elected to American Academy of Arts and Letters," *Diap* 65 (Mar 1974), 1.
180. *NYT* (Apr 24, 1974), 49:6; (Aug 19, 1974), 32:1; (Sep 27, 1974), 52:1.
181. Keats, Sheila. "William Schuman," *Stereo R* 32 (Jun 1974), 68-77.
182. "Symphonic Highlights," *Int Mus* 73 (Dec 1974), 15.
183. *NYT* (Apr 18, 1975), 22:1; (Nov 28, 1975), 44:1.
184. Freedman, Guy. "Schuman at the Bat; Interview," *Mus J* 34 (Jul 1976), 14-16.
185. "National Symphony: Schuman Prems:," *HiFi/MA* 26 (Aug 1976), MA30.
186. "Composers in Focus," *BMI* (Winter 1976), 29.
187. "1977 ACDA National Convention (Profiles of Resource People)," *Choral J* 17, No. 4 (1976), 18-21.
188. Weber, J. F. "A William Schuman Discography," *ARSC* 8, Nos. 2-3 (1976), 74-82.
189. Griffin, Malcolm J. "William Schuman's 'Carols of Death'—An Analysis," *Choral J* 17, No. 6 (1977), 17.
190. "Winter Meeting: January 12, 1977," *NMC* 36, No. 2 (1977), 6.

References to Works by William Schuman

The number preceding the title indicates the number of the composition as listed in Section II.

43. Amaryllis: *MA* 84 (Dec 1964), 64; *MQ* 51 (1965), 408; *Mus J* 23 (Sep 1965), 88; *HiFi/MA* 21 (Apr 1971), MA21; *EweWT*.
 4. American Festival Overture: *BSPN* (Oct 6, 1939); *MA* 59 (Dec 10, 1939), 27; *NYPPN* (Nov 5, 1942); *MQ* 31 (1945), 18; 33 (1947), 312, 315; *SFSPN* (Mar 4, 1949), 453;

LAPPN (Apr 12. 1951), 17; *NOPPN* (Jan 9, 1962), 3; *Detroit Sym* (Nov 21, 1968), 213; *EweCB*, 356; *EweWT*; *HitMU*, 212; *NorLC*, 411.

59. Carols of Death: *Mus J* 24 (Jun 1966), 63.
33. Chester Overture: *NYT* (Jun 20, 1957), 24:2; *School Mus* 28 (Jun 1957), 10.
13. Circus Overture: Side Show: *MQ* 31 (1945), 22, 25; *ISPN* (Dec 1, 1945), 15; *NYPPN* (Feb 26, 1949).
 8. Concerto for Piano: *MQ* 33 (1947), 319.
15. Concerto for Violin: *BSPN* (Feb 10, 1950), 802; *Time* 55 (Feb 20, 1950), 46; *MC* 141 (Mar 1, 1950), 22; *Int Mus* 48 (Mar 1950), 16; *MA* 70 (Mar 1950), 12; *MQ* 36 (1950), 279-282; 42 (1956), 390; *MA* 76 (Mar 1956), 37; 80 (May 1960), 26; (Aug 1960), 33; *Mus Mag* 163 (Nov 1961), 61; *Notes* 20 (1962-1963), 125; *EweCB*, 359; *EweWT*.
64. Concerto on Old English Rounds: *Sym News* 25, No. 6 (1974), 27; *BSPN* (Nov 29-Dec 3, 1974), 19-23; *New Yorker* 52 (May 3, 1976), 117; *SR* 3 (May 29, 1976), 49.
18. Credendum: *Juilliard Rev* (Winter 1955-1956), 52; *POPN* (Mar 9, 1956), 567; *New Yorker* 32 (Mar 24, 1956), 137; *MC* 153 (Apr 1956), 19; *MA* 76 (Apr 1956), 15; *MT* 97 (May 1956), 268; *MQ* 42 (1956), 386-389; *SFSPN* (Feb 19, 1958), 393; *MA* 84 (Nov 1964), 31; *SFSPN* (Jan 20, 1965), 43; *EweWT*; *MacIC*, 519.
67. Young Dead Soldiers: *BMI* (Spring 1976), 32-35; *Mus Trades* 124 (May 1976), 126; *Mus J* 34 (May 1976), 38; *HiFi/MA* 26 (Aug 1976), MA30; *Mus Ed J* 63 (Dec 1976), 14; *Village Voice* 22 (Nov 7, 1977), 69.
56. A Free Song: *BSPN* (Mar 26, 1943), 873; *MA* 63 (May 1943), 25; *MQ* 31 (1945), 108; *Natl Sym* (Dec 10, 1962), 17; *EweCB*, 357; *EweWT*; *HitMU*, 212.
32. George Washington Bridge: *Symphony* 5 (Dec 1951), 15; *HitMU*, 212.
28. In Praise of Shahn: *NYPPN* (Jan 29, 1970), F-H; *NYT* (Jan 30, 1970), 29:1; *World Mus* 12, No. 2 (1970), 80; *SR* 53 (Feb 14, 1970), 58; *Int Mus* 68 (Mar 1970), 32; *Am Mus Dgt* 1, No. 5 (1970), 23, 26; *HiFi/MA* 20, sec. 2 (Apr 1970), 20; *BMI* (Apr 1970), 10-11; *Intam Mus B* No. 78 (Jul-Oct 1970), 99; *HiFi/MA* 21 (Mar 1971), 82; *MT* 114 (Nov 1973), 1149; *PitSPN* (Jan 4-6, 1974), 479-487.
17. Judith: *MA* 70 (Jan 15, 1950), 67; *MC* 141 (Feb 15, 1950), 35; *Notes* 8 (1950-1951), 564; *Mus Opin* 74 (Feb 1951), 217; *MQ* 37 (1951), 255-260, 317; *MR* 12 (Aug 1951), 241; *LAPPN* (Feb 14, 1952), 23-25; *MQ* 41 (1955), 77; *EweWT*.
66. The Lord Has a Child: *Notes* 17 (1960), 474.
68. The Mighty Casey: *NYT* (May 13, 1951), sec. 2, p. 7:3; (May 5, 1953), 34:5; *Time* 61 (May 18, 1953), 60; *MC* 147 (Jun 1953), 12; *MA* 73 (Jun 1953), 7; *MR* 14 (Aug 1953), 227; *Pan Pipes* 46 (Jan 1954), 44; *Notes* 12 (1954-1955), 485; *NYT* (Mar 7, 1955); *SR* 38 (Mar 19, 1955), 26; *Mus Opin* 78 (Apr 1955), 415; *MQ* 41 (1955), 106; *NYT* (Aug 16, 1967), 35:1; (Aug 31, 1967), 28:2; *BMI* (Spring 1976), 32-35; *Mus Trades* 124 (May 1976), 126; *Mus J* 34 (May 1976), 38; *HiFi/MA* 26 (Aug 1976), MA30; (Sep 1976), MA20; *Mus Ed J* 63 (Dec 1976), 14; *Sym News* 28, No. 3 (1977), 47.
19. New England Triptych: *NYT* (Nov 5, 1956), 41:4; *MA* 76 (Nov 15, 1956), 18; *MC* 155 (May 1957), 29; *MA* 78 (Feb 1958), 212; *SFSPN* (Jan 10, 1959), 13; (May 2, 1962), 21; *HoustonSPN* (Jan 7, 1963), 11; *Natl Sym* (Nov 2, 1965), 13; *POPN* (Feb 18, 1966), 24; *Mus Leader* 98 (Aug 1966), 9.
 7. Newsreel: *MA* 64 (Apr 10, 1944), 28; *HitMU*, 212.
69. Night Journey: *BloYA*, 286.
24. The Orchestra Song: *NYT* (May 30, 1964), 9:2; *Notes* 23 (1966-1967), 157.
65. Orpheus With His Lute: *MQ* 31 (1945), 18.
49. Pioneers: *MQ* 31 (1945), 108.
 9. Prayer in Time of War: *BSPN* (Oct 6, 1944), 38; *MA* 64 (Oct 1944), 5; *MQ* 35 (1949), 286; *Notes* 8 (1950-1951), 129-130; *MC* 142 (Dec 1, 1950), 42; *MA* 71 (Feb 1951), 232.
51. Prologue: *MQ* 25 (1939), 381.
41. Quartettino for Four Bassoons: *MA* 77 (Oct 1957), 26; *Notes* 15 (1957-1958), 649.

21. Song of Orpheus: *MA* 82 (Apr 1962), 29; *Mus Mag* 164 (May 1962), 27; *NYT* (Sep 29, 1962), 14:2; *Mus Leader* 96 (Mar 1964), 10; *MA* 83 (Dec 1963), 288; 84 (Dec 1964), 48; *Am Rec G* 31 (Jan 1965), 392; *EweWT*.

39. String Quartet No. 2: *MQ* 25 (1939), 380.

40. String Quartet No. 3: *NYT* (Feb 28, 1940), 16:1; *MQ* 31 (1945), 17, 20; *EweCB*, 357.

42. String Quartet No. 4: *MC* 142 (Nov 15, 1950), 3; *MA* 70 (Nov 15, 1950), 6; *MQ* 37 (1951), 394; *Notes* 12 (1954-1955), 324; *MQ* 40 (1954), 472, 474; *EweWT*.

 3. Symphony No. 2 (withdrawn): *BSPN* (Feb 17, 1939), 729; *MQ* 25 (1939), 380.

 5. Symphony No. 3: *BSPN* (Oct 17, 1941); *NYHT* (Nov 23, 1941); *MM* 19, No. 2 (1941-1942), 97; *MQ* 31 (1945), 17, 19, 21; 33 (1947), 313, 320; *POPN* (Mar 9, 1951), 495; *BSCBul* 23 (Apr 18, 1952), 1099-1102; *CinSPN* (Feb 6, 1953), 398-400; *Hudebni Rozhledy* 12, No. 4 (1959), 162; *ChiSPN* (Feb 9, 1963), 5-15; *SFSPN* (Dec 11, 1963), 29-34; *Sovet Muz* 29 (Jan 1965), 94; *Neue ZFM* 129 (Nov 1968), 462; *MT* 110 (Apr 1969), 394; *Mus & Mus* 17 (May 1969), 63; *EweCB*, 357; *EweWT*.

 6. Symphony No. 4: *MA* 62 (Feb 25, 1942), 21; *POPN* (Apr 4, 1942), 608; *MQ* 31 (1945), 19, 23; *MC* 142 (Dec 1, 1950), 42; *Notes* 8 (1950-1951), 129-130; *MA* 71 (Feb 1951), 232.

10. Symphony No. 5 (Symphony for Strings): *BSPN* (Nov 12, 1943); *NYT* (Nov 13, 1943), 19:3; *MQ* 31 (1945), 17, 20, 23; *ClSPN* (Mar 3, 1949), 529; *SLSPN* (Jan 23, 1953), 337; *Mus & Mus* 23 (Oct 1974), 56-58; *EweCB*, 358; *HitMU*, 212.

16. Symphony No. 6: *MA* 69 (Apr 15, 1949), 27; *POPN* (Nov 9, 1951), 113; *Int Mus* 50 (Dec 1951), 15; *MQ* 38 (1952), 298-301; *Mus Opin* 75 (Sep 1952), 737; *MC* 146 (Nov 1, 1952), 29; *MA* 72 (Dec 1, 1952), 28; *Notes* 10 (1952-1953), 482; *POPN* (Nov 6, 1953), 125-126; *MQ* 41 (1955), 551, 553; *NYHT* (Apr 28, 1958); *POPN* (Jan 11, 1963), 20-23; *EweCB*, 359; *EweWT*.

20. Symphony No. 7: *MA* 80 (Dec 1960), 16; *MC* 162 (Dec 1960), 27; *New Yorker* 36 (Dec 10, 1960), 231-233; *MC* 163 (Jan 1961), 22; *MA* 81 (Jan 1961), 244; *MT* 103 (Nov 1962), 783; *Pan Pipes* 54, No. 2 (1962), 3; *Notes* 20 (1962-1963), 407; *POPN* (Feb 2, 1968), 17-19.

22. Symphony No. 8: *NYPPN* (Oct 4, 1962); *NYT* (Oct 5, 1962), 29:3; *NYPPN* (Oct 11, 1962), 38-40; *New Yorker* 38 (Oct 13, 1962), 219; *MA* 82 (Dec 1962), 27; *MQ* 49 (1963), 91; *MA* 84 (Apr 1964), 61; *Am Rec G* 31 (Jan 1965), 393; *SFSPN* (Jan 12, 1966), 11; *ChiSPN* (Nov 30, 1967), 13-19.

27. Symphony No. 9: *NYT* (Apr 9, 1968), 57:1; *POPN* (Jan 10, 1969), 15-20; *NYT* (Jan 15, 1969), 37:1; *World Mus* 11, No. 1 (1969), 72; *BMI* (Mar 1969), 14; *HiFi/MA* 19 (Apr 1969), MA22; *Stereo R* 28 (Apr 1972), 70-71.

30. Symphony No. 10: *BMI* (Spring 1976), 32-35; *Mus Trades* 124 (May 1976), 126; *HiFi/MA* 26 (Aug 1976), MA30; *Mus Ed J* 63 (Dec 1976), 14.

47. Three Piano Moods: *Notes* 18 (1960-1961), 489.

45. Three-Score Set: *HitMU*, 212.

53. This Is Our Time: *NYT* (Jun 30, 1940), sec. 9, p. 5:5; *MA* 60 (Jul 1940), 27.

26. To Thee Old Cause: *NYT* (Oct 4, 1968), 35:1; *Variety* 252 (Oct 9, 1968), 54; *SR* 51 (Oct 19, 1968), 56; *Mus & Artists* 1, No. 5 (1968), 42; *HiFi/MA* 18 (Dec 1968), MA16; *Mus J* 26 (Dec 1968), 105; *Melos* 35 (Dec 1968), 488; *BMI* (Nov-Dec 1968), 40; *NYPPN* (Oct 3, 1969), B-E; *Intam Mus B* Nos. 69-70 (Jan-Mar 1969), 72; *NZ* 130 (Jan 1969), 11.

14. Undertow: *NYPPN* (Oct 3, 1946); *Notes* 4 (1946-1947), 362; *MQ* 40 (1954), 623-624; *EweCB*, 358; *EweWT*.

23. Variations on America (Charles Ives): *NY Post* (May 22, 1964); *Notes* 23 (1966-1967), 157.

29. Voyage: *Pan Pipes* 46 (Nov 1953), 3; 46 (Jan 1954), 44; *MA* 75 (Mar 1955), 34; *Notes* 12 (1954-1955), 329; *MQ* 41 (1955), 551, 553; *Mus Opin* 79 (Sep 1956), 703.

11. William Billings Overture: *NYPPN* (Feb 17, 1943); *MA* 64 (Mar 10, 1944), 8; *CinSPN* (Nov 12, 1954), 151.
72. The Witch of Endor: *HiFi/MA* 16 (Jan 1966), 142.

Dissertations about William Schuman and His Works

1. Armstrong, Donald J. *A Study of Some Important Twentieth Century Secular Compositions for Women's Chorus with a Preliminary Discussion of Secular Choral Music from a Historical and Philosophical Viewpoint.* University of Texas, 1968.
2. Griffin, Malcolm J. *Style and Dimension in the Choral Works of William Schuman.* University of Illinois, 1972.
3. Johnson, Charles E. *Common Musical Idioms in Selected Contemporary Wind-Band Music.* Florida State University, 1969.
4. Laney, Maurice I. *Thematic Material and Developmental Techniques in Selected Contemporary Compositions.* Indiana University, 1964.
5. Mize, Lou Stem. *A Study of Selected Choral Settings of Walt Whitman's Poems.* Florida State University, 1967.
6. Pisciotta, Louis V. *Texture in the Choral Works of Selected Contemporary American Composers.* Indiana University, 1967.
7. Prindl, Frank Joseph. *A Study of Ten Original Compositions for Band Published in America Since 1946.* Florida State University, 1956.
8. Robison, Richard W. *Reading Contemporary Choral Literature: An Analytical Study of Selected Contemporary Choral Compositions with Recommendations for the Improvement of Choral Reading Skills.* Brigham Young University, 1969.

OUTLINE XV

ROGER (HUNTINGTON) SESSIONS (b. 1896)

I. Life

1896   Born in Brooklyn, New York, December 28. Early years in Massachusetts; studied piano with his mother.

1907   Attended the Kent School, Connecticut (graduated 1911).

1911   Entered Harvard University at the age of 14; studied music with Edward Burlingame Hill; Bachelor of Arts degree in music (1915).

1915   Studied at Yale University with Horatio Parker (composition); Bachelor of Music degree (1917).

1917   Engaged as an assistant instructor in music at Smith College (1917-1921). Studied with Ernest Bloch in New York.

1921   Continued studying with Bloch at the Cleveland Institute of Music; became his assistant and head of the theory department (1921-1925).

1923   First major composition, incidental music for *The Black Maskers*, performed at Smith College.

1926   Awarded two Guggenheim Fellowships (Italy, 1926-1928); Damrosch Fellowship at the American Academy (Rome, 1928-1931); Carnegie Grant (Berlin, 1931-1933). Made occasional visits to the United States during 1926-1933.

1927   *Symphony No. 1* performed by the Boston Symphony Orchestra.

1928   Collaborated with Aaron Copland in organizing the Copland-Sessions Concerts (1928-1931).

1933   Returned to the United States; associated as a lecturer with the New School for Social Research, New York (1933-1934); Boston Conservatory (1933-1935). Teacher at the Malkin Conservatory, Boston (1933-1934); Dalcroze School of Music, New York (1933-1935); New Music School, New York (1934-1935).

1934   Elected president of the International Society for Contemporary Music (1934-1942).

1935   Married Elizabeth Franck. Appointed to the music department at Princeton University (1935-1945).

1945   Appointed Professor of Composition at the University of California, Berkeley (1945-1954).

1949   First New York performance of *Symphony No. 1* (composed in 1927). Awarded the Naumburg Foundation Prize (1949).

1950   Received the New York Music Critics Circle Award (*Symphony No. 2*); Lectured at the University of Southern California.

1951   Awarded a Fulbright Fellowship (Florence, 1951-1952).

1953   Appointed Professor of Music at Princeton University (1953-1965). Pupils, during his years of teaching, include Milton Babbitt, Paul Bowles, Edward T. Cone, David Diamond, Ross Lee Finney, Andrew Imbrie, Leon Kirchner, Hugo Weisgall.

1955   Guest teacher of composition at the Berkshire Music Center summer school, Tanglewood.

1958   *The Black Maskers Suite* performed in Moscow.

1959   Appointed a co-director of the Electronic Music Center at Columbia and Princeton Universities.

1961   Sessions Festival at Northwestern University. Received the Gold Medal for Music from the National Institute of Arts and Letters.

1964   World première of the opera, *Montezuma*, in West Berlin. Awarded an honorary Doctor of Music degree by Harvard University.

I. Life (cont.)

1965   Appointed to the Juilliard School of Music faculty.

1966   Returned to teach at the University of California, Berkeley (1966-1967).

1968   Appointed to the Advisory Board of the Alban Berg Society. Concert of music by Roger Sessions (Carnegie Recital Hall, March 31, 1968). Returned to teach at Harvard University (1968-1969).

1969   Sessions Festival, Occidental College, Los Angeles (March 3, 4, 5).

1974   Elected to the American Academy of the National Institute of Arts and Letters; received special Pulitzer citation for his distinguished work.

Sessions has been the recipient of many honors, awards and commissions in addition to those listed above.

Note: Biographies of varying length and importance will be found in many of the books listed in the Bibliography at the end of this *Outline* under "References to Roger Sessions."

II. **Compositions**

A. **Orchestra**	Date	Publisher
1. The Black Maskers	1923; (arr. 1928)	EBM
2. Symphony No. 1	1927	EBM
3. Concerto for Violin	1935	EBM
4. Symphony No. 2	1946	GS
5. Idyll of Theocritus (Virgil) (S., orch)	1956	EBM
6. Concerto for Piano	1956	EBM
7. Symphony No. 3	1957	EBM
8. Symphony No. 4	1958	EBM
a. Burlesque b. Elegy c. Pastorale		
9. Divertimento	1959	EBM
10. Psalm 140 (S., orch)	1963	EBM
11. Symphony No. 5	1964	EBM
12. Symphony No. 6	1965	EBM
13. Symphony No. 7	1966	EBM
14. Symphony No. 8	1967	EBM
15. Rhapsody for Orchestra	1970	
16. Concerto for Violin, Viola, Violoncello, Orchestra	1970-1971	
17. Concertino for Chamber Orchestra	1971-1972	EBM
B. **Band**		
18. Finale from "The Black Maskers"	1923; (arr. 1928)	EBM
C. **Chamber**		
19. Pastorale for Solo Flute	1929	Ms
20. String Quartet No. 1	1936	EBM
21. Duo for Violin, Piano	1942	EBM
22. String Quartet No. 2	1951	EBM
23. Sonata for Solo Violin	1953	EBM
24. String Quintet (2 vln, 2vla, vlc)	1958	EBM
25. Sonata for Violin, Piano	1961	EBM
26. Six Pieces for Solo Violoncello	1966	EBM
27. Canons (to the memory of Igor Stravinsky) (str qrt)	1972	
D. **Piano**		
28. Sonata for Piano, No. 1	1930	AMP

II. Compositions (cont.)
    29. Four Pieces for Children   CF
        a. Scherzino (1935)   c. Waltz for Brenda (1935)
        b. March (1935)   d. Little Piece (for John, age 1) (1939)
    30. From My Diary (four pieces)   1939   EBM
    31. Sonata for Piano, No. 2   1946   EBM
    32. Sonata for Piano, No. 3   1965   EBM
    33. Five Pieces   1975
E. Organ
    34. Three Chorale Preludes   1925   EBM
    35. Chorale   1938   HWG
F. Choral
    36. Turn, O Libertad (Walt Whitman) (SATB, pno 4 hands or 2 pno) 1943 EBM
    37. Mass (unison SATB, org)   1956   EBM
    38. How Long, O Lord   1960   EBM
    39. When Lilacs Last in Dooryard Bloom'd (cantata)   1965   EBM
    40. Three Choruses on Biblical Texts (SATB, cham orch)   1971   Meri
        1. Out of the Depths, from Psalm 130
        2. Ah, Sinful Nation, from Isaiah 1 and 2
        3. Praise Ye the Lord, from Psalms 148, 149, 150
G. Solo Vocal
    41. On the Beach at Fontana (James Joyce) (pno)   1930   EBM
    42. Idyll of Theocritus (Virgil) (S., orch)   1954   EBM
    43. Psalm 140 (S., org; also with orch)   1963   EBM
H. Opera
    44. Lancelot and Elaine   1910
    45. Montezuma (G. A. Borgese)   1941; revised 1962   EBM
    46. The Trial of Lucullus (Bertolt Brecht)   1947   EBM
I. Incidental Music
    47. The Black Maskers (Leonid Andreyev)   1923   EBM
    48. Turandot (Volkmüller)   1925

The following abbreviations are used in Section III of this *Outline*. The number indicates the number of the composition as listed in Section II.

 6. *Con Pno*: Concerto for Piano   31. *Son Pno 2*: Sonata for Piano No. 2
30. *Diary*: From My Diary   24. *Str Qnt*: String Quintet
21. *Duo*: Duo for Violin, Piano   20. *Str Qrt 1*: String Quartet No. 1
47. *Maskers*: The Black Maskers Suite   4. *Sym 2*: Symphony No. 2

III. **Style (techniques and devices)**

"For a composer musical ideas have infinitely more substance, more reality, more specific meaning, and more vital connection with experience than any words that could be found to describe them." "I am not trying to write 'modern,' 'American,' or 'neo-classic' music; I am seeking always and only the coherent and living expression of my musical ideas." "Immediate response is not what one is preoccupied with. The job of the composer is to write music he loves best. I think that's true of anything anyone does seriously."   Roger Sessions

A. General characteristics
    1. Early impressionistic and neo-classic tendencies develop toward the dissonant. Expressionism and a completely personal and distinctive "atonal" style, with free use of twelve-tone techniques.

    2.   Highly developed technical equipment, extraordinary craftsmanship, intensity of expression. Continuity of musical flow of primary importance.

B.   Melodic line
    1.   Long, smooth lines: *Str Qrt 1* (second movement, beginning); *Duo*; *Sym 2* (p. 17, solo vln); *Con Pno* (third movement).
    2.   Development of rhythmic motive: *Maskers* (second movement, beginning).
    3.   Use of nine, ten or eleven different tones: *Str Qrt 1* (first movement, meas. 1-6); *Duo* (meas. 1-7).
    4.   Strong, rhythmic: *Sym 2* (pp. 4, 5, hn, trpt).
    5.   Somber, dark: *Sym 2* (pp. 82, 86).
    6.   Dance-like: *Sym 2* (p. 67).
    7.   Chromatic: *Con Pno* (p. 34).

C.   Harmony
    1.   Harmony often complex. Texture basically contrapuntal. Dissonance often created by contrapuntal lines.
    2.   Use of specific intervals: *Maskers* (p. 10).
    3.   Polytonality: *Diary* (first section, beginning).
    4.   Overtones: *Son Pno 2* (p. 16).
    5.   Juxtaposition of triads: *Str Qrt 1* (movement 1, last chord).
    6.   Chromatic: *Con Pno* (p. 34); *Idyll*; *Son Pno 2*; *Sym 2*.
    7.   Quartal: *Sym 2* (pp. 67, 72).
    8.   Free serial techniques: *Str Qnt*; *Sym 2*; many works.
    9.   Interval of a seventh: *Sym 2* (p. 65, hn). Perfect fifths: *Son Pno 2* (p. 8).
  10.   Parallel: *Sym 2* (p. 99).
  11.   Harmonization at interval of second: *Sym 2* (pp. 29, 47).

D.   Counterpoint
    1.   Much use of counterpoint, but moderate use of canon and fugue.
    2.   Contrapuntal devices: *Sym 2* (throughout); many works.

E.   Rhythm
    1.   Generally complex and intricate.
    2.   Meter changes: *Sym 1* (p. 7); *Sym 2* (throughout); *Diary* (p. 4).
    3.   Dislocation of accent: *Sym 1* (first movement).
    4.   Syncopations, accents, irregular groupings: *Sym 2*.
    5.   Polyrhythms: *Duo* (p. 12); *Son Pno 1*.
    6.   Rhythmic modulation: (see Elliott Carter, *Outline III*); *Duo*.

F.   Form
    1.   Orthodox feeling for form with freedom and individual concepts. "A product of the composer's feeling and imagination."
    2.   A - B - A: *Sym 1* (second movement).
    3.   Rondo: *Str Qnt* (last movement); *Sym 2* (last movement).
    4.   Modified sonata-allegro: *Con Pno* (first movement); *Sym 4* (first movement).
    5.   Rhapsody: *Sym 4* (second movement).

G. Orchestration
    1.   A master of orchestration; varies from colorful scoring for full orchestra (*Maskers*) to soloistic treatment (*Sym 1*, second movement) and use of unusual instruments.

BIBLIOGRAPHY

Books by Roger Sessions

1.   *The Musical Experience of Composer, Performer, Listener*. Princeton: Princeton University Press, 1950, 1971; New York: Atheneum, 1962. Reviews: *Notes* 8 (1950-1951), 168;

Mus & Mus 21 (Jan 1973), 44; *Strad* 83 (Jan 1973), 429; *MQ* 97 (1973), 73.

2. *Harmonic Practice.* New York: Harcourt, Brace, 1951. Reviews: *Notes* 9 (1951-1952), 409; *Mus Ed J* 38 (Jan 1952), 51; *Etude* 70 (Jan 1952), 57; (Aug 1952), 7; *Mus Club Mag* 31 (May 1952), 20; *MQ* 38 (1952), 457-468; *JAMS* 5 (1952), 265-268; *MA* 72 (Aug 1952), 22.

3. *Reflections on the Music Life in the United States.* New York: Merlin Press, 1956.

4. *Questions About Music.* Cambridge, MA: Harvard University Press, 1970; New York: W. W. Norton, 1971. Reviews: *Mus J* 28 (Jul 1970), 96; *MT* 111 (Nov 1970), 1113; *Instrument* 25 (Dec 1970), 14; *Int Mus* 69 (Dec 1970), 30; *Mus Club Mag* 50, No. 2 (1970-1971), 41; *Brit J Aesthetics* 11, No. 4 (1971), 412-415; *J Aesthetics* 29, No. 4 (1971), 551-552; *ML* 52, No. 1 (1971), 71-72; *Mus Ed J* 58 (Sep 1971), 72-73; *MR* 32, No. 1 (1971), 73-74; *Notes* 27, No. 4 (1971), 705-707; *Intam Mus Res Yrbk* 7 (1971) 184-185; *PNM* 10, No. 2 (1972), 164-170; *Am Mus Tcr* 22, No. 2 (1972), 43; *Int R Aesthetics & Soc Mus* 3, No. 1 (1972), 139-140; *Am Recorder* 13, No. 4 (1972), 138; *Pan Pipes* 64, No. 2 (1972), 87; No. 4 (1972), 32.

5. *Roger Sessions on Music: Collected Essays*, ed. Edward T. Cone. Princeton: Princeton University Press, 1979.

Articles by Roger Sessions

1. "An American Evening Abroad," *MM* 4 (Nov 1926), 33-36.
2. "Ernest Bloch," *MM* 5 (Nov 1927), 3-11.
3. "On *Oedipus Rex*," *MM* 5 (Mar 1928), 9-15.
4. "Music in Crisis: Some Notes on Recent Music History," *MM* 10, No. 2 (1932-1933), 63-78.
5. "Music and Nationalism," *MM* 11, No. 1 (1933-1934), 3-12.
6. "New Vistas in Musical Education," *MM* 11, No. 3 (1933-1934), 115-120.
7. "Heinrich Schenker's Contribution," *MM* 12, No. 4 (1934-1935), 170-178.
8. "America Moves to the Avant-Scene," *AMS Papers* (Washington 1937), 108-119.
9. "The New Musical Horizon," *MM* 14, No. 2 (1936-1937), 59-66.
10. Review: "Hindemith's *Mathis der Maler*," *MM* 15, No. 1 (1937-1938), 13-17.
11. Review: "Hindemith on Theory," *MM* 15, No. 1 (1937-1938), 57-63.
12. Review: "Exposition by Krenek," *MM* 15, No. 2 (1937-1938), 123-128.
13. Review: "To Revitalize Opera," *MM* 15, No. 3 (1937-1938), 145-152.
14. Review: "Escape by Theory," *MM* 15, No. 3 (1937-1938), 192-197.
15. Review: "The Function of Theory," *MM* 15, No. 4 (1937-1938), 257-262.
16. "Vienna-Vale, Ave," *MM* 15, No. 5 (1937-1938), 203-208.
17. Review: "A Lesson from Mozart," *MM* 16, No. 2 (1938-1939), 137.
18. "On the American Future," *MM* 17, No. 2 (1939-1940), 71-75.
19. "American Music and the Crisis," *MM* 18, No. 4 (1940-1941), 211-217.
20. "Musicology and the Composer," *Bul AMS* 5 (Aug 1941), 5-7.
21. "The Composer and His Message," in *The Intent of the Artist* by Augusto Centeno. Princeton: Princeton University Press, 1941, 101-134.
22. "No More Business-as-Usual," *MM* 19, No. 3 (1941-1942), 156-162.
23. "Artists and This War," *MM* 20, No. 1 (1942-1943), 3-7.
24. "How Far Will We Go With Popularization?" *SR* 27 (Jan 22, 1944), 25-26.
25. Review: "Sir Donald Tovey: Musical Articles and Essays," *Ken Rev* 7 (Summer 1945), 504-507.
26. Roger Sessions translated volume II: Alfred Einstein. *The Italian Madrigal*, 3 vols. Princeton: Princeton University Press, 1949.
27. "How a 'Difficult' Composer Gets That Way," *NYT* (Jan 8, 1950), sec. 2, p. 9.
28. "Some Notes on Schoenberg and the 'Method of Composing with 12 Tones'," *Score* 6 (May 1952), 7-10.

29. "Composer and the Public Today," *Perspectives USA* 9 (1954), 112-117.
30. "Song and Pattern in Music Today," *Score* 17 (Sep 1956), 73-84.
31. "Thoughts on Stravinsky," *Score* 20 (Jun 1957), 32-37.
32. "Contemporary Music in Our Concert Halls," *Newsletter* (Charleston, WV) 8, No. 6 (1957), 15; *MC* 158 (Sep 1958), 26.
33. "Art, Freedom and the Individual," *Sewanee Rev* 66 (1958), 382-396.
34. "To the Editor," *Score* 23 (Jul 1958), 58-64.
35. "Music and the Crisis of the Arts," *Frontiers of Knowledge* (1958), 32-39.
36. "Problems and Issues Facing the Composer Today," *MQ* 46 (1960), 159-171 (also in *ChaAC*).
37. "To the Editor," *PNM* 5, No. 2 (1967), 81-97.
38. "Schoenberg in the United States," *Tempo* No. 103 (1972), 8-17.
39. "In Memoriam: Luigi Dallapiccola (1904-1975)," *PNM* 13, No. 1 (1974), 240-245.

References to Roger Sessions

Books
(See the General Bibliography)

ASC-SC; AusMT; Baker; BarMA; BasSM; BauTC; BloYA; BluPC; BMI-MW (1965); BMI-OP; BMI-P; BMI-SC; CatPC; ChaAC; ChaAM; ClaEA; CobCS; CohCT; ColHM; CopON; CopTN; CopWL; CowAC; DavPM; DemMT; DerETM; DukLH; Edm-I; EdMUS; EweAC; EweCB; EweCS; EweDE; EweMC; EweNB; EweWT; GosMM; Grove; HanIT; HitMU; HodSD; HowMM; HowOA; HowOC; HowSH; JohOA; JohSH; KinAI; LanOH; LanPM; LeiMW; LeiSK; MacAC; MacIC; MasTA; Mel-MN; MelRT; MorgCM; MorrCA; MueAS (277); MyeTC; PanMC; PAC; PavMH; PersTH; PleSM; PorM3S; ReiCA; ReiCC; RobCM; RosAH; RosMI; RowFC; SalMO; SalzTM; SamLM; SamMO; SanWM; SchCC; SchWC; SloMS; SpaMH; SteiAS; StevePC; ThoAJ; ThoAM; ThompIC; ThoMR; ThoRL; UptAM; WhiWW; WilTM; WooWM; YatTC; YouCD.

Rosenfeld, Paul. *Port of New York*. New York: Harcourt, Brace, 1924, p. 145.
Schoenberg, ed. Merle Armitage. New York: G. Schirmer, 1937, p. 9.

Articles

Brief mention: *NW* 6 (Nov 2, 1935), 41; *MQ* 26 (1940), 102; *MM* 20, No. 2 (1942-1943), 100; *MM* 23, No. 1 (Winter 1946), 8; *MQ* 36 (1950), 584; *SR* 34 (Jul 28, 1951), 18; *Holiday* 8 (Dec 1950), 51; *MQ* 39 (1953), 28; *PNM* 1, No. 1 (1962), 110, 117, 126, 142, 144; *PNM* 1, No. 2 (1963), 151, 203; *PNM* 2, No. 1 (1963), 4, 152; *PNM* 2, No. 2 (1964), 14-17, 19, 125, 127; *PNM* 3, No. 1 (1964), 139, 146, 158; *PNM* 4, No. 1 (1965), 158; *BMI-MW* (Feb 1967), 4; (Apr 1967), 15; (May 1967), 14; (Dec 1967), 6; *BMI-MW* (Mar 1968), 8; *BMI-MW* (May 1969), 8.
1. Welch, R. D. "A Symphony Introduces Roger Sessions," *MM* 4, No. 4 (1926-1927), 27.
2. *NYT* (Feb 10, 1930), 21:1; (Mar 17, 1930), 20:4; (Apr 14, 1930), 24:7.
3. *NYT* (Mar 16, 1931), 24:3.
4. "New American Music," *Scribner's Mag* 89 (Jun 1931), 624-632.
5. Brunswick, Mark. "Roger Huntington Sessions," *MM* 10, No. 4 (1932-1933), 182.
6. "Returns from Germany," *NYT* (Jun 12, 1933), 20:5.
7. *NYT* (Jun 25, 1933), sec. 9, p. 4:1.
8. *NYT* (Jan 30, 1934), 16:5; (Mar 11, 1934), sec. 10, p. 6:7; (Oct 28, 1934), sec. 10, p. 8:3.
9. Thompson, Randall. "Jacobi's Quartet and Sessions' Sonata," *MM* 12, No. 3 (1934-1935), 135.
10. "American Composer Gets a Break," *American Mercury* 34 (Apr 1935), 491.
11. "Appointed to New Jersey College for Women Faculty," *NYT* (Sep 15, 1935), sec. 2, p. 5:8.

12. *NYT* (Nov 23, 1935), 22:6.
13. "Musician's Encyclopedia," *Musician* 40 (Dec 1935), 3.
14. Saminsky, Lazare. "The Work of Roger Sessions," *MM* 13, No. 2 (1935-1936), 40.
15. Copland, Aaron. "The Younger Generation," *MM* 13, No. 4 (1935-1936), 5.
16. Rosenfeld, Paul. "The Newest American Composers," *MM* 15, No. 3 (1937-1938), 153.
17. Slonimsky, Nicolas. The Six of American Music," *Chr Sc Mon Mag* (Mar 17, 1937), 8-9.
18. *NYT* (Apr 12, 1937), 14:3; (Nov 30, 1939), 18:2.
19. Carter, Elliott. "American Music in the New York Scene," *MM* 17, No. 2 (1939-1940), 95.
20. Cone, Edward T. "Roger Sessions' String Quartet," *MM* 18, No. 3 (1940-1941), 159.
21. *NYT* (Sep 24, 1944), sec. 2, p. 4:5.
22. "Appointed Music Professor, University of California," *NYT* (Jul 15, 1945), sec. 2, p. 4:4.
23. Schubart, M. A. "Roger Sessions: A Portrait of an American Composer," *MQ* 32 (1946), 196-214.
24. "Wins First W. W. Naumburg Foundation Recording Award," *NYT* (May 17, 1949).
25. *NYT* (Jan 8, 1950), sec. 2, p. 9:5; (Jan 10, 1950), 39:2.
26. Cowell, Henry. "Current Chronicle," *MQ* 36 (1950), 94, 268.
27. "Gets Serge Koussevitzky Music Foundation Commission," *NYT* (Aug 21, 1950), 15:6.
28. Berger, Arthur. "Enduring Sessions," *SR* 33 (Aug 26, 1950), 53.
29. Rosenman, L. "KPFA and Contemporary Music," *Opera* 15 (Oct 1950), 11-14.
30. "Roger Sessions," *Pan Pipes* 43 (Dec 1950), 129.
31. Rosenwald, Hans. "Contemporary Music," *Mus News* 43 (Jan 1951), 7.
32. Levenson, R. "Music for Today," *Opera* 16 (Mar 1951), 15-16.
33. "Contributors to This Issue," *Score* 6 (May 1952), 65.
34. "Sessions for Princeton Faculty," *MC* 145 (May 15, 1952), 31.
35. "The Musical Experience," *ML* 33 (Oct 1952), 360-361.
36. "First One Named to Conant Music Chair," *NYT* (Sep 20, 1953), 77:3.
37. "Elected to American Academy of Arts and Letters," *NYT* (Dec 13, 1953), 90:1.
38. RePass, R. "American Composers of Today," *London Mus* 8 (Dec 1953), 25.
39. "Sessions is Elected to American Academy," *MA* 74 (Jan 1, 1954), 27.
40. "Sessions Heads Schnabel Memorial," *MC* 149 (May 15, 1954), 33.
41. "Inducted into American Academy of Arts and Letters," *NYT* (May 27, 1954), 25:5.
42. Cook, J. Douglas. "The Composer Tells How," *SR* 37 (Jun 26, 1954), 51.
43. Keats, Sheila. "Reference Articles on American Composers: An Index," *Juilliard Rev* 1 (Fall 1954), 32-33.
44. "Board Chairman, League of Composers International Society for Contemporary Music," *NYT* (Dec 2, 1954), 38:1.
45. "Roger Sessions," *Pan Pipes* 47 (Jan 1955), 65.
46. "Sessions Completes Four Commissioned Works," *MC* 151 (Mar 1955), 45.
47. Taubman, Howard. "Summer Teacher: Roger Sessions Discusses Center's Importance," *NYT* (Aug 21, 1955), sec. 2, p. 7:1.
48. "Masterpieces in Louisville? " *Time* 67 (Jan 30, 1956), 58.
49. "Moderns on Parade," *Time* 67 (Feb 20, 1956), 64.
50. "U. S. Composers in a Bright Era," *Life* 40 (May 21, 1956), 145.
51. Kerman, Joseph. *Perspectives* 16 (Summer 1956).
52. Ellsworth, Ray E. "Americans on Microgroove," *HiFi* 6 (Aug 1956), 64.
53. "Contributors to This Issue," *Score* 17 (Sep 1956), 93.
54. Trimble, Lester. "Current Chronicle: New York," *MQ* 43 (1957), 238-240.
55. Ellsworth, Ray E. "Classic Modern," *Down Beat* 24 (Jul 25, 1957), 39.
56. Epstein, D. M. "Sessions at 60—an Appraisal of His Work," *MA* 77 (Sep 1957), 28.
57. Sargeant, Winthrop. "Musical Events," *New Yorker* 33 (Dec 21, 1957), 91.
58. "Brandeis University Creative Arts Award," *NYT* (Mar 6, 1958), 32:6.
59. Maren, Roger. "A Musician's Musician Within Everyone's Reach," *Reporter* 18 (May 1, 1958), 35.

60. "Receives Wesleyan University Honorary Degree," *NYT* (Jun 9, 1958), 1:7.
61. *NYT* (May 12, 1958), 25:1; (Sep 18, 1958), 37:4; (Sep 21, 1958), 62:8; (Oct 16, 1958), 46:4; (Oct 18, 1958), 17:5.
62. Schonberg, Howard C. "Exchange Composers; Harris, Sessions and Kay Discuss Their Forthcoming Trip to Soviet Union," *NYT* (Sep 21, 1958), sec. 2, p. 11.
63. "Roger Sessions," *Mus Club Mag* 38 (Nov 1958), 9.
64. "Music Exchanges with Reds Urged," *NYT* (Nov 2, 1958), sec. 1, p. 124:3.
65. "Composers Describe Training, Goals and Pressures of USSR Composers," *NYT* (Nov 13, 1958), 38:3.
66. Carter, Elliott. "Current Chronicle," *MQ* 45 (1959), 375.
67. "Shoptalk: Princeton Seminar in Advanced Musical Studies," *NW* 54 (Aug 31, 1959), 76.
68. *NYT* (Apr 12, 1960), 39:2.
69. Cone, Edward T. "Analysis Today," *MQ* 46 (1960), 178.
70. Parmenter, Ross. "A Sessions Festival at Northwestern Will Honor the American Composer," *NYT* (Oct 23, 1960), sec. 2, p. 11.
71. "Honored by National Institute of Arts and Letters," *NYT* (Jan 14, 1961), 15:4.
72. "Composer for Titans," *Time* 77 (Feb 3, 1961), 46.
73. Janson, D. "Sessions on Campus," *NYT* (Feb 5, 1961), sec. 2, p. 11:3.
74. Boretz, Benjamin. "Sessions Festival," *MA* 81 (Mar 1961), 25.
75. "Symphony No. 1," *Metro* 78 (May 1961), 38.
76. Boretz, Benjamin. "Current Chronicle (Three-Day Festival of Session's Music, Evanston, Illinois)," *MQ* 47 (1961), 389-396.
77. *NYT* (Sep 28, 1961), 50:5.
78. "Rutgers University Honorary Degree," *NYT* (Jun 7, 1962), 26:6.
79. Imbrie, Andrew. "Roger Sessions, in Honor of His 65th Birthday," *PNM* 1, No. 1 (1962), 117-147.
80. Cogan, R., and P. Escot. "Roger Sessions," *Intam Mus B* 33 (Jan 1963), 3-10.
81. Joachum, Heinz. "Montezuma and the Messiah; West Berlin Première," *MA* 84 (May 1964), 20.
82. "Bland Giant," *Time* 83 (May 8, 1964), 50.
83. "Harvard University Honorary Degree," *NYT* (Jun 12, 1964), 40:1.
84. "Letters: Brickbats and a Bouquet for Sir John (Sir John Barbirolli and Contemporary Music)," *MA* 84 (Sep 1964), 4.
85. "Appointed to Faculty of Juilliard School of Music," *NYT* (Mar 1, 1965), 20:5.
86. "Los Conciertos," *Buenos Aires Mus* 20, No. 331 (1965), 2.
87. Romano, Jacobo. "Musicos de hoy; Roger Sessions," *Buenos Aires Mus* 20, No. 332 (1965), 5.
88. "Entrevista All Compositor Norteamericano Roger Sessions," *R Mus Chile* 19, No. 94 (1965), 94.
89. "Roger Sessions," *SFSPN* (Mar 1, 1966), 21.
90. Cone, Edward T. "Conversation with Roger Sessions," *PNM* 4, No. 2 (1966), 29-46.
91. " 'Best' Piano Teaching Pieces 1965," *Piano Q* 55 (Spring 1966), 2.
92. "Potpourri," *Instrument* 21 (Jan 1967), 4.
93. Kastendieck, Miles. "Roger Sessions," *BMI-MW* (Feb 1968), 9.
94. "Named C. E. Norton Poetry Professor for 1968-1969," *NYT* (Apr 15, 1968), 50:1.
95. *NYT* (Apr 1, 1968), 56:5; (Apr 14, 1968), sec. 2, p. 17:1; (May 3, 1968), 41:2.
96. "His Own Thing," *Time* 91 (May 10, 1968), 85.
97. Sargeant, Winthrop. "Musical Events," *New Yorker* 44 (May 11, 1968), 140.
98. Saal, Hubert. "Symphonic Sessions," *NW* 71 (May 13, 1968), 112.
99. Hamilton, David. "New Craft of the Contemporary Concerto: Carter and Sessions," *HiFi* 18 (May 1968), 67-68.
100. Cohn, Arthur. "After Thirty-Three Years, a First Recording of the Violin Concerto by Roger Sessions," *Am Rec G* 35 (Nov 1968), 200-201.

101. Sutcliffe, James H. "New Hall for Montezuma," *Opera N* 33 (May 17, 1969), 6-7.
102. "In the News," *BMI-MW* (May 1969), 8.
103. "International Music Congress: Forum (The Sound of Things to Come)," *Mus & Artists* 2, No. 1 (1969), 28.
104. Romano, Jacobo. "Retratos de Musicos Americanos: Roger Sessions," *Buenos Aires Mus* 24, No. 400 (1969), 3.
105. Evett, Robert. "Lucky One," *Atlantic* 224 (Jul 1969), 107.
106. Heyworth, Peter. "Three American Summer Schools," *Am Mus Dgt* 1 (Nov 1969), 26-27.
107. "First Recordings: Sessions and Lees," *Am Rec G* 36 (Dec 1969), 298.
108. Evett, Robert. "Questions About Sessions," *New Republic* 162 (May 9, 1970), 40-42.
109. Weinberg, H., and P. Petrobelli. "Roger Sessions e la Musica Americana," *R Mus Ital* 5 (Mar-Apr 1971), 249-263.
110. Haieff, Alexei. "Stravinsky: a Composers' Memorial," *PNM* 9, No. 2 (1971), 12.
111. Powers, Harold S. "Current Chronicle," *MQ* 58 (1972), 297-307.
112. Cone, Edward T. "In Honor of Roger Sessions," *PNM* 10, No. 2 (1972), 130-141.
113. Imbrie, Andrew. "The Symphonies of Roger Sessions," *Tempo* No. 103 (1972), 24-32.
114. *NYT* (Feb 9, 1973), 32:1.
115. DeRhen, Andrew. "Galimir Quartet: Sessions," *HiFi/MA* 23 (Jun 1973), MA20.
116. Wright, L. A., and A. Bagnall. "Roger Huntington Sessions: A Selective Bibliography and a Listing of His Compositions," *Current Mus* 15 (1973), 107-125.
117. "Elected to American Academy," *MA* 24 (Jan 1, 1974), 27.
118. "Wins Special Pulitzer," *FoF* 34 (May 7, 1974), 448F2.
119. "Sessions Gets Special Pulitzer," *BB* 86 (Jan 8, 1974), 32.
120. "Receives Pulitzer Special Citation for Life's Work as Distinguished Composer," *NYT* (May 7, 1974), 40:5.
121. "Biographical Sketch," *NYT* (May 7, 1974), 40:1.
122. Smith, F. J. "Traditional Harmony? A Radical Question," *MR* 35, No. 1 (1974), 63-64.
123. Kastendieck, Miles. "Roger Sessions," *BMI* No. 2 (1974), 30-31.
124. Brown, Royal S. "Essential American-Music Document—from England," *HiFi* 24 (Nov 1974), 97.
125. "Biography," *Current Biography* (Jan 1975); *Current Biography Yearbook* (1975), 380-383.
126. Wilder, K. "Sessions on the Drums," *Mus J* 33 (Feb 1975), 44-45.
127. Hamilton, David. "Music," *Nation* 220 (Apr 18, 1975), 478.
128. "Amherst College: Sessions Prem: Three Choruses on Biblical Texts," *HiFi/MA* 25 (Jun 1975), MA27.
129. Eckert, Thor. " 'Montezuma'—Sarah Caldwell's Personal Triumph," *Chr Sc Mon* 68 (Apr 5, 1976), 31.
130. Soria, Dorle J. "Artist Life, Interview," *HiFi/MA* 26 (Jul 1976), MA5.
131. Smith, Rollin. "American Organ Composers," *MusAGO* 10 (Aug 1976), 18.
132. Kerner, Leighton. "Music: A Sessions Memorial Score," *Village Voice* 22 (Nov 7, 1977), 69.

References to Works by Roger Sessions

The number preceding the title indicates the number of the composition as listed in Section II.

1. The Black Maskers Suite: *MQ* 32 (1956), 209; *PitSPN* (Jan 5, 1962), 19-21; *Notes* 22 (1964-1965), 821; 23 (1965-1966), 1102; *CohCT*, 195; *GosMM*, 255.
27. Canons (to the memory of Igor Stravinsky): *Tempo* No. 98 (1972), 22-23.
6. Concerto for Piano: *MQ* 42 (1956), 390; *NYT* (Feb 11, 1956), 13:2; *MA* 76 (Feb 15, 1956), 232; *Time* 67 (Feb 20, 1956), 64; *MC* 153 (Mar 1, 1956), 24; *Melos* 23 (May 1956), 150; *Musica* 11 (Jun 1957), 344; *MQ* 45 (1959), 375; 47 (1961), 388-391; *Notes* 20 (1962-1963), 124.

3. Concerto for Violin: *NYPPN* (Feb 19, 1959); *NYT* (Feb 20, 1959), 18:5; (Feb 21, 1959), 24:2; *SR* 42 (Mar 7, 1959), 30; *Variety* 214 (Mar 11, 1959), 83; *MQ* 45 (1959), 375-381; *MA* 79 (Mar 1959), 25; *MC* 159 (Apr 1959), 17; *PNM* 1, No. 1 (1962), 126, 127, 142, 144; *MQ* 54 (1968), 385; *HiFi/MA* 18 (May 1968), 67; *SFSPN* (May 1968), 18e-f; *Am Rec G* 35 (Nov 1968), 200; *EweCB*, 365; *EweWT*; *HitMU*, 209.

16. Concerto for Violin, Viola, Violoncello, Orchestra: *Nation* 188 (Mar 7, 1959), 216; *SR* 42 (Mar 7, 1959), 30; *NYT* (Nov 7, 1971), 83:2; *Intam Mus B* No. 82 (Nov-Feb 1971-1972), 11; *Mus J* 29 (Dec 1971), 76-77; 30 (Jan 1972), 74-75; *BMI* (Jan 1972), 14-15; *HiFi/MA* 22 (Feb 1972), MA19-20; *Tempo* 118 (Sep 1976), 46.

9. Divertimento: *BMI* (Apr 1965), 10.

21. Duo for Violin, Piano: *MQ* 32 (1946), 201; *Notes* 5 (1947-1948), 417; *Int Mus* 49 (Sep 1950), 14.

30. From My Diary: *Notes* 5 (1947-1948), 417; *MQ* 38 (1952), 481; *Mus News* 2 (Apr 1971), 13; *CohCT*, 197.

5. The Idyll of Theocritus: *Time* 67 (Jan 30, 1956), 58; *MC* 153 (Feb 1956), 89; *Etude* 74 (Mar 1956), 10; *MT* 98 (Mar 1957), 157; *Rassegna Musicale* 26 (Apr 1956), 141; *MR* 17 (Aug 1956), 248; *Notes* 15 (1957-1958), 656; *CohCT*, 199; *MacIC*, 586.

39. When Lilacs Last in the Dooryard Bloom'd: *BMI* (Oct 1971), 12; *MQ* 58 (1972), 297-307; *PNM* 10, No. 2 (1972), 175; *World Mus* 14, No. 2 (1972), 79; *ChiSPN* (Jan 29, 1976), 5; *SR* 3 (May 15, 1976), 42; *HiFi/MA* 26 (Jun 1976), MA22; *New Yorker* 53 (May 16, 1977), 133-136; *HiFi/MA* 28 (Feb 1978), 70; *Tempo* 125 (Jun 1978), 35-37.

37. Mass: *MT* 97 (May 1956), 268; *Notes* 16 (1958-1959), 151; *MT* 102 (Nov 1961), 696; *Diap* 60 (Apr 1969), 18-19.

45. Montezuma: *NYT* (Dec 15, 1963), sec. 2, p. 13; (Apr 20, 1964), 32:2; (Apr 21, 1964), 43:1; (May 3, 1964), sec. 2, p. 11:3; *MA* 84 (May 1964), 20; *Opera* 15 (Jun 1964), 401; *Melos* 31 (Jun 1964), 192-194; *Neue ZFM* 125, No. 6 (1964), 265; *Musica* 18, No. 4 (1964), 206; *Mus U Ges* 14 (Oct 1964), 623; *PNM* 4, No. 1 (1965), 95-108; *BMI* (Nov 1966), 18; *Opera N* 40 (Apr 3, 1976), 10-14; *Time* 107 (Apr 12, 1976), 84; *New Yorker* 52 (Apr 19, 1976), 115-120; *Nation* 222 (Apr 24, 1976), 510; *SR* 3 (May 15, 1976), 42-43; *Opera N* 40 (Jun 1976), 32-33; *Opernwelt* 6 (Jun 1976), 41; *HiFi/MA* 26 (Jul 1976), MA5, MA23; *Opera Can* 17, No. 4 (1976), 36; *Heterofonia* 9, No. 48 (1976), 16; *Opera* 27 (Sep 1976), 846; *Tempo* 121 (Jun 1977), 25; *ChaAM*, 656; *EweWT*.

41. On the Beach of Fontana: *PNM* 8, No. 1 (1969), 79.

43. Psalm 140: *BSPN* (Feb 11, 1966), 982.

15. Rhapsody for Orchestra: *HiFi/MA* 20 (Jun 1970), MA17; *Mus & Mus* 20 (Nov 1971), 58; *HiFi/MA* 24 (Nov 1974), 97.

28. Sonata for Piano, No. 1: *MQ* 32 (1946), 200; *Am Rec G* 32 (Mar 1966), 600; *MelMN*, 131; *HitMU*, 209.

31. Sonata for Piano, No. 2: *Musicology* 2 (Jul 1949), 429; *Notes* 7 (1949-1950), 312; *MC* 139 (Feb 1, 1949), 23; *BloYA*, 237; *CohCT*, 197; *HitMU*, 209.

32. Sonata for Piano, No. 3: *World Mus* 11, No. 3 (1969), 66; *SR* 53 (Dec 26, 1970), 47; *Mus J* 29 (Jul 1971), 88.

23. Sonata for Solo Violin: *NYT* (Feb 22, 1954), 15:1; *MT* 97 (Dec 1956), 656; *MQ* 43 (1957), 236, 238-240; *Am Str Tcr* 12, No. 3 (1962), 7.

26. Six Pieces for Violoncello: *NYT* (Apr 1, 1968), 56:5; *BMI-MW* (Jun 1968), 20.

24. String Quintet: *MQ* 41 (1955), 94; 44 (1958), 370-371; *NYT* (Nov 24, 1959), 46:1; (Dec 6, 1959), 13; *MA* 79 (Dec 15, 1959), 27; *MQ* 46 (1960), 71-73; *PNM* 1, No. 1 (1962), 136.

20. String Quartet No. 1: *MM* 18, No. 3 (1940-1941), 159; *MQ* 32 (1946), 203; *HitMU*, 209.

22. String Quartet No. 2: *Opera* 16 (Jul 1951), 26-28; *MQ* 41 (1955), 94; *MC* 152 (Dec 1, 1955), 42; *Notes* 13 (1955-1956), 523; *Perspectives USA* No. 16 (1956), 78-89; *MQ* 43 (1957), 140; *SFSPN* (Mar 1, 1966); *Mus & Mus* 25 (Dec 1976), 51; *CohCT*, 198; *CobSC*, 160; *MelMN*, 135.

2. Symphony No. 1: *MM* 4, No. 4 (1926-1927), 27; *BSPN* (Apr 22, 1927); *NYT* (Dec 21, 1935), 10:8; *MQ* 36 (1950), 94-98; *Score* 12 (Jun 1955), 29; *MQ* 42 (1956), 244; *HitMU*, 209; *MacIC*, 585.

4. Symphony No. 2: *Time* 49 (Jan 20, 1947), 72; *MA* 67 (Jan 24, 1947), 4; *Notes* 7 (1949-1950), 438; *NYPPN* (Jan 12, 1950); *MA* 70 (Jan 15, 1950), 57; *Time* 55 (Jan 23, 1950), 37; *MQ* 36 (1950), 268-270; *MC* 141 (May 1, 1950), 28; *Chr Sc Mon Mag* (Jul 15, 1950), 8; *Mus News* 42 (Sep 1950), 5; *Mus Club Mag* 30 (Oct 1950), 24; *SFSPN* (Jan 1967), 34; *BloYA*, 147; *CohCT*, 195; *EweCB*, 366; *EweWT*; *GosMM*, 259; *HanIT*, 326; *MelMN*, 132.

7. Symphony No. 3: *BSPN* (Dec 6, 1957), 476; *NYT* (Dec 8, 1957), sec. 2, p. 13:8; (Dec 12, 1957), sec. 2, p. 13:8; *New Yorker* 33 (Dec 21, 1957), 84; *MC* 157 (Jan 1, 1958), 15; *MA* 78 (Jan 1, 1958), 35; (Jan 15, 1958), 3; *MQ* 44 (1958), 228-230; *Notes* 20 (1962-1963), 121; *ChiSPN* (Nov 25, 1965), 5; *Mus Events* 23 (Apr 1968), 23; *MT* 109 (Apr 1968), 351; *MM* 16 (May 1968), 48; *Mus Opin* 91 (May 1968), 424; *Orchester* 22 (Mar 1974), 161-162; *Oper U Konzert* 12, No. 3 (1974), 33.

8. Symphony No. 4: *MC* 161 (Mar 1960), 17; *MQ* 47 (1961), 391-393; *PitSPN* (Feb 18, 1966), 19; *MM* 17 (Oct 1968), 47; *MelMN*, 138.

11. Symphony No. 5: *NYT* (Feb 19, 1964), 35:1; *MA* 84 (Mar 1964), 35; *Listen* 1 (Mar-Apr 1964), 20; *MQ* 50 (1964), 381-382.

12. Symphony No. 6: *NYT* (Jan 20, 1966), 28:6; *BMI* (Mar 1966), 6; *NJOPN* (Nov 19, 1966); *BMI* (Feb 1967), 6; *Tempo* 121 (Jun 1977), 49.

13. Symphony No. 7: *ChiSPN* (Oct 5, 1967), 13-21; *BMI* (Dec 1967), 8.

14. Symphony No. 8: *NYPPN* (May 2, 1968), B-D; *NYT* (May 3, 1968), 41:1; *Time* (May 10, 1968), 85; *New Yorker* 44 (May 11, 1968), 140; *Mus & Artists* 1, No. 3 (1968), 40; *Int Mus* 66 (Jun 1968), 32; *BMI* (Jul 1968), 26; *HiFi/MA* 18 (Jul 1968), MA21; *Intam Mus B* 69-70 (Jan-Mar 1969), 72; *HiFi/MA* 24 (Nov 1974), 97.

40. Three Choruses on Biblical Texts: *Sym News* 26, No. 2 (1975), 26; *Diap* 66 (May 1975), 8; *HiFi/MA* 25 (Jun 1975), MA27; *MusicAGO* 9 (Jun 1975), 24; *Mus Ed J* 62 (Sep 1975), 96.

46. Trial of Lucullus: *Time* 65 (May 9, 1955), 69; *MA* 75 (Jun 1955), 13; *MC* 151 (Jun 1955), 41; *Melos* 23 (Feb 1956), 54; 24 (May 1957), 137; *MQ* 47 (1961), 393-395; *SR* 49 (Jun 4, 1966), 38; *Mus Leader* 98 (Jun 1966), 4; *HiFi/MA* 16 (Aug 1966), MA7; *Opera N* 31 (Sep 10, 1966), 28; *BMI* (Oct 1966), 4.

36. Turn, O Libertad: *Notes* 10 (1952-1953), 494; *Pan Pipes* 46 (Mar 1954), 8; *MA* 75 (Jan 1, 1955), 32.

Dissertations about Roger Sessions and His Works

1. Burke, James R. *A Study of Theories of Non-Chord Tones Pertaining to the Music of the Period c. 1650 to c. 1875.* Indiana University, 1963. (Includes theories of Walter Piston and Roger Sessions)

2. King, Irvin Jean. *Neoclassical Tendencies in Seven American Piano Sonatas (1925-1945).* Washington University, 1971.

3. Schweitzer, Eugene W. *Generation in String Quartets of Carter, Sessions, Kirchner and Schuller: A Concept of Forward Thrust and Its Relationship to Structure in Aurally Complex Styles.* Eastman School of Music, University of Rochester, 1966.

4. Service, Alfred R., Jr. *A Study of Cadence as a Factor in Musical Intelligibility in Selected Piano Sonatas by American Composers.* State University of Iowa, 1958.

OUTLINE XVI

RANDALL THOMPSON (b. 1899)

I. Life

1899   Born in New York City, April 21, of New England heritage. Early years in Lawrence-
        ville, New Jersey.
1916   Entered Harvard University; graduated in 1920 with a Bachelor of Arts degree; 1922
        with a Master of Arts degree; studied with Edward Burlingame Hill, Walter R. Spalding,
        Archibald T. Davison. Studied with Ernest Bloch in New York (1920-1921).
1922   Awarded a Fellowship at the American Academy in Rome (1922-1925).
1927   Assistant Professor of Music, Wellesley College (1927-1929).
1929   Guggenheim Fellowships (1929, 1930).
1931   Conductor of Juilliard School Madrigal Choir and Dessoff Choir, New York.
1933   Honorary Doctor of Music degree from the University of Rochester.
1936   Assistant Professor of Music, Wellesley College (1936-1937). *The Peaceable Kingdom*
        commissioned by the League of Composers.
1937   Professor of Music and Director of the University Chorus, University of California,
        Berkeley (1937-1939).
1939   Director of the Curtis Institute of Music, Philadelphia (1939-1941).
1941   Head of the Music Division of the School of Fine Arts of the University of Virginia
        (1941-1946).
1946   Professor of Music at Princeton University (1946-1948).
1948   Professor of Music at Harvard University (1948-1965).
1959   Named "Cavaliere ufficiale al merito" by the Italian government.
1965   Retired from Harvard as Professor Emeritus.

Randall Thompson has been the recipient of many honors, awards and commissions in addition to those listed above.

Note: Biographies of varying length and importance will be found in many of the books listed in the Bibliography at the end of this *Outline* under "References to Randall Thompson."

II. Compositions

	Date	Publisher
A. Orchestra		
1. Pierrot and Cothurnus (Prelude to a play in one act by Edna St. Vincent Millay)	1922	Ms
2. The Piper at the Gates of Dawn (symphonic prelude)	1924	Ms
3. Jazz Poem (pno, orch)	1928	Ms
4. Symphony No. 1	1929	CF
5. Symphony No. 2	1931	CF
6. Symphony No. 3	1948	ECS
7. A Trip to Nahant	1955	ECS
B. Chamber		
8. The Wind in the Willows (after Kenneth Grahame) (str qrt)	1924	
9. Suite for Oboe, Clarinet, Viola	1940	ECS
10. String Quartet No. 1	1941	CF
11. Trio for Three Double Basses	1969	ECS
12. String Quartet No. 2	1969	ECS

C.   Piano

13.	Sonata in C minor	1923	
14.	Suite	1924	
15.	The Boats are Talking	1926	
16.	Little Prelude	1935	ECS
17.	Song After Sundown	1935	ECS

D.   Choral (a cappella unless otherwise indicated)

18.   Odes of Horace   1924   ECS
   a.   O Venus (SSATTBB, pno or orch)   d.   O fons Bandusiae (SSATBB)
   b.   Vitas hinnuleo (SATB)   e.   Felices ter (SATB)
   c.   Montium custos (SATB)   f.   Quis multa gracilis (TTBB)

19.   Pueri Hebraeorum (SSAA/SSAA)   1928   ECS

20.   Rosemary (Stephen Vincent Benét) (4 choruses, SSAA)   1929   ECS

21.   Americana (a sequence of five transcripts from the   1932   ECS
      American Mercury) (SATB, pno or orch)
   a.   May Every Tongue   d.   The Sublime Process of Law Enforcement
   b.   The Staff Necromancer   e.   Loveli-lines
   c.   God's Bottles (SSAA)

22.   The Peaceable Kingdom: A Sequence of Sacred Choruses (Isaiah) 1936   ECS
   a.   Say Ye to the Righteous (SATB)   e.   The Paper Reeds by the Brooks (SATB)
   b.   Woe Unto Them (SATB)   f.   But These are They (SATB/SATB)
   c.   The Noise of a Multitude (SATB)   g.   Have Ye Not Known (SATB)
   d.   Howl Ye (SATB/SATB)   h.   Ye Shall Have a Song (SATB/SATB)

23.   Tarantella (Hilaire Belloc) (TTBB, pno or orch)   1937   ECS

24.   The Lark in the Morn (Somersetshire folk song) (SATB) 1938   ECS

25.   Alleluia (SATB or SSAA or TTBB)   1940   ECS

26.   The Testament of Freedom (a setting of four passages from   1942   ECS
      the writings of Thomas Jefferson) (TTBB, pno or orch or band)
   a.   The God Who Gave Us Life   c.   We Fight Not For Glory
   b.   We Have Counted the Cost   d.   I Shall Not Die Without a Hope

27.   The Last Words of David (II Samuel 23:3-4) (TTBB or SATB;   1949   ECS
      pno or orch)

28.   Now I Lay Me Down to Sleep (Percy B. Shelley) (motet: SSA) 1954   ECS

29.   Mass of the Holy Spirit (Communion Service: SATB; Gloria,   1957   ECS
      SSAATTBB; Sanctus, SAATTBB)

30.   Ode to the Virginian Voyage (Michael Drayton)   1957   ECS
      (SATB, pno or orch)

31.   Velvet Shoes (arr. for SA, pno)   1958   ECS

32.   Requiem (a dramatic dialogue in five parts)   1958   ECS
      (SATB/SATB, optional str)

33.   Glory to God in the Highest (SATB)   1958   ECS

34.   Frostiana: Seven Country Songs (Robert Frost) (pno or orch) 1959   ECS
   a.   The Road Not Taken (SATB)   e.   A Girl's Garden (SSA)
   b.   The Pasture (TTB)   f.   Stopping by Woods (TBB)
   c.   Come In (SSA)   g.   Choose Something Like a Star (SATB)
   d.   The Telephone (SAA/TTBB)

35.   Mass for Solo Voice (or unison chorus)   1960   ECS

36.   The Gate of Heaven (TTBB or SSAA or SATB)   1961   ECS

37.   The Nativity According to St. Luke   1961   ECS
   a.   Nowell (SATB; SSAA; TTBB, pno)   c.   Lullaby (S., pno, 4-part ending ad lib)
   b.   And the Child Grew (SATB, pno)

38.   The Lord is My Shepherd (SATB or SSAA; org or pno)   1966   ECS

39.   The Best of Rooms (Robert Herrick) (SATB)   1963   ECS

40.   The Feast of Praise (cantata: SATB,   1963   ECS
      2 trpt, 2 hn, 2 trb, tba, hp or pno)

41.	The Passion According to Saint Luke (oratorio: soloists, SATB, org, cham orch)	1965	ECS
42.	A Psalm of Thanksgiving (cantata: two-part children's choir, pno or org or orch)	1967	ECS
43.	The Place of the Blest (Robert Herrick; Richard Wilbur) (cantata: SSAA boys voices, cham orch)	1968	

E.   Solo Vocal (with piano unless otherwise indicated)

44.	A Ship Starting (Walt Whitman)	1922	
45.	Tapestry (William Douglas)	1925	
46.	Five Songs (Merle St. Croixwright)	1925	
47.	Three Songs	1926	

    a.   Doubts (Eleanor Dougherty)   c.   Southwind (Elizabeth Anne Moses)
    b.   A Ballad (Elizabeth Anne Moses)

48.	Five Songs for "New Songs for New Voices"	1927	ECS

    a.   Some One (Walter de la Mare)   d.   My Master hath a Garden (anon.)
    b.   The Wild Home Pussy (Emma Rounds) e.   Velvet Shoes (Elinor Wylie)
    c.   Echo Child (May Ely Baker)

49.	The Passenger (M. A. De Wolfe Howe)	1961	ECS
50.	My Soul Doth Magnify the Lord (from "The Nativity According to Saint Luke")	1961	ECS
51.	Lullaby (from "The Nativity According to Saint Luke") (S., with optional four-part ending)	1961	ECS

F.   Opera

52.	Solomon and Balkis (radio opera in one act) (libretto by Randall Thompson based on Rudyard Kipling's "The Butterfly That Stamped," from the *Just-So Stories*)	1942	

G.   Incidental Music

53.	The Grand Street Follies	1926
54.	The Straw Hat	1926

The following abbreviations are used in Section III of this *Outline*. The number indicates the number of the composition as listed in Section II.

22.	*Peaceable*: The Peaceable Kingdom	5.	*Sym 2*: Symphony No. 2
10.	*Str Qrt 1*: String Quartet No. 1	26.	*Testament*: The Testament of Freedom
9.	*Suite*: Suite for Oboe, Clarinet, Viola		

III.   Style (techniques and devices)

"A composer's first responsibility is, and always will be, to write music that will reach and move the hearts of his listeners in his own day."   Randall Thompson

A.   General characteristics
   1.   Basically traditional, simple, unaffected, melodious and objective. Mature personal style (*Symphony No. 2*), inspired by "our own musical heritage," often makes use of folk-like material and traditional forms.
   2.   A master of choral technique; often utilizes the simplest possible resources "with the hope of reaching large masses." All works reveal superior craftsmanship.
B.   Melodic line
   1.   Melodies characterized by spontaneity and freshness; often modal and folk-like. Themes frequently derived from neighboring-tone figures.
   2.   Diatonic: *Peaceable* (p. 51); *Testament* (p. 17); *Sym 3* (first movement); *Str Qrt 1* (p. 5; last movement); *Alleluia* (throughout).

3. Broad: *Sym 2* (third movement).
4. Modal: *Peaceable* (Aeolian, pp. 18-19; p. 34); *Sym 2* (p. 117); *Suite* (Dorian, last movement, ob); *Str Qrt 1* (Phrygian, p. 12, meas. 10-14).
5. Gapped: *Suite* (first movement, p. 3, ob).
6. Pentatonic: *Peaceable* (pp. 55-56, tenor); *Str Qrt 1* (p. 3, meas. 1).
7. Melismatic: *Peaceable* (p. 12, meas. 6; p. 59, meas. 5).
8. Unison: *Peaceable* (p. 55); *Testament* (pp. 13-15).
9. Folk-like: *Sym 2* (second movement, p. 65); *Sym 3* (third and fourth movements); *Suite*.

C. Harmony
1. Basically diatonic and tertian; rarely very dissonant. Strong modal influence; style generally consistent in all works.
2. Tertian: *Sym 2* (last movement, p. 124); *Sym 3* (first movement); *Peaceable* (p. 1); *Testament* (pp. 3-5).
3. Quartal: *Sym 3* (second movement).
4. Quintal: *Peaceable* (p. 29, meas. 5-6).
5. Polytonal (very rare): *Str Qrt 1* (second movement).
6. Dissonant (rare): *Peaceable* (third chorus).
7. Modal: *Peaceable* (p. 34).
8. Sequence of fifths: *Sym 3* (first movement).
9. Pedal point: *Suite* (p. 3); *Sym 3* (first movement). Drone bass: *Str Qrt 1* (second movement).
10. Phrygian cadence: *Str Qrt 1* (p. 3, meas. 5, 10).
11. Final cadence, II 6/5 - I, characteristic: *Str Qrt 1* (end).
12. Final chords: *Sym 3* (end of third movement, added sixth); *Sym 2* (end of first movement, lowered seventh).

D. Counterpoint
1. Moderate use of polyphonic devices and forms. Choral music generally chordal in texture, but often conceived contrapuntally.
2. Imitation: *Peaceable* (pp. 47, 49); *Str Qrt 1* (p. 8, meas. 1-2).
3. Fugal devices: *Peaceable* (pp. 38-40); *Americana* (*Loveli-lines*).
4. Inversion: *Peaceable* (pp. 1, 3); *Testament* (p. 45); *Str Qrt 1* (first movement, second theme, p. 7, meas. 17).
5. Canon: *Testament* (fourth movement, pp. 42-44).
6. Mirror: *Testament* (p. 45).
7. Augmentation: *Peaceable* (p. 67); *Str Qrt 1* (first movement, first theme, p. 11, meas. 6).

E. Rhythm
1. Often shows the influence of native American rhythms. Particularly successful in setting the rhythm of the text in choral music (*Testament*, pp. 12-13).
2. Simple rhythmic schemes: *Testament* (p. 3).
3. Syncopation: *Peaceable* (p. 26, meas. 8).
4. Displaced accents: *Alleluia* (p. 11); *Peaceable* (p. 62, chorus I, bass); *Str Qrt 1* (p. 8, meas. 24).
5. Rhythmic motif: *Str Qrt 1* (first movement, beginning).
6. Rhythmic ostinato: *Sym 2* (p. 65); *Sym 3* (second movement).
7. Blues: *Sym 2* (second movement).
8. Meter changes: *Str Qrt 1* (p. 3, meas. 2, 5, 7, 10); *Sym 2* (pp. 106-107).

F. Form
1. A strong sense of form; use of four movements and classical forms in symphonies and quartets.
2. Sonata-allegro: *Str Qrt 1* (first movement); *Sym 2* (first movement); *Sym 3* (last movement).

3. Scherzo: *Str Qrt 1* (third movement); *Sym 2* (third movement).
4. Rondo (often modified): *Str Qrt 1* (fourth movement); *Sym 2* (fourth movement, Allegro); *Sym 3* (second movement); *A Trip to Nahant*.
5. A - B - A: *Str Qrt 1* (second movement).
6. A - B - C - A - B: *Peaceable* (first chorus).
7. Cyclic: *Testament* (fourth chorus uses material from the first chorus); *Peaceable* (eighth chorus).
    G. Orchestration
    1. Conventional use of instruments with effective scoring; sparing use of percussion.
    2. Full sonority: *Sym 2* (p. 176).
    3. Solo instruments: *Sym 2* (p. 67).

BIBLIOGRAPHY

Books by Randall Thompson

1. *Catalogue of the College Music Set.* New York: Carnegie Corporation, 1933 (with Howard Hinners, J. B. Munn, Jeffrey Mark).
2. *College Music: An Investigation for the Association of American Colleges.* New York: The Macmillan Co., 1935.

Articles by Randall Thompson

1. "George Antheil," *MM* 8, No. 4 (1930-1931), 17.
2. "The Bartered Cow," *MM* 9, No. 1 (1931-1932).
3. "The Contemporary Scene in American Music," *MQ* 18 (1932), 9.
4. "The Vivid Contemporary Scene in American Music," *MA* 52 (Apr 10, 1932), 8; (Apr 25, 1932), 12.
5. "The Emperor at the Opera," *MM* 10, No. 2 (1932-1933), 109.
6. "The Second Year at Yaddo," *MM* 11, No. 1 (1933-1934), 40.
7. "On Modern Art-Song," *MQ* 34 (1938), 24.
8. "Neglected Works: A Symposium," *MM* 23, No. 1 (Winter 1946), 3.
9. "A Letter to Douglas Moore" in *Letters of Composers*, ed. Gertrude Norman and Miriam Shrifte. New York: Alfred A. Knopf, 1946.
10. "College Music in the Post-War World," in *On General and Liberal Education*. Association for General and Liberal Education, 52-56.

References to Randall Thompson

Books
(See the General Bibliography)

ASC-BD; ASC-SC; AusMT; Baker; BarMA; BauTC; BIM; BloYA; BluPC; BMI-OP; Bull; CatPC; ChaAC; ChaAM; CopON; CopTN; CowAC; DemMT; DerETM; DowO; DukLH; Edm-II; EdMUS; EweAC; EweCB; EweCS; EweMC; EweNB; EweWT; GroSH; Grove; HitMU; HowMM; HowOA; HowOC; HowSH; JohSH; KinAI; LanOH; LeiMW; LeiSK; MacIC; MueAS; MyeTC; NorLC; PavMH; PersTH; PeyNM; ReiCA; ReiCC; SalMO; SamLM; SamMO; SanWM; SchWC; SloMS; SmiWM; StevePC; ThoAJ; ThoAM; ThompIC; ThoMR; ThoRL; UptAS; UlrCM; WooWM; WWA; YouCD; YouCT.

Articles

Brief mention: *MM* 20, No. 2 (1942-1943), 97; 22, No. 4 (1944-1945), 255; *MQ* 34 (1948), 10; 36 (1950), 91.

1. *NYT* (Dec 17, 1931), 26:3.
2. Copland, Aaron. "Our Younger Generation," *MM* 13, No. 4 (1935-1936), 5.
3. "Appointed Director of Curtis Institute of Music," *NYT* (Mar 22, 1939), 20:4.
4. Hussey, D. "American Symphony," *Spec* 166 (Jan 17, 1941), 60.
5. "Resigns as Director, Curtis Institute of Music," *NYT* (Feb 21, 1941), 16:4.
6. *NYT* (Jun 1, 1941), sec. 9, p. 10:3.
7. Porter, Quincy. "Randall Thompson," *MM* 19, No. 4 (1941-1942), 237.
8. Walz, Jay. "Meet the Composer: Randall Thompson," *MA* 64 (Nov 10, 1944), 8.
9. "Appointed Music Professor, Harvard University," *NYT* (May 16, 1948), 65:1.
10. Forbes, Elliot. "The Music of Randall Thompson, with List of Works," *MQ* 35 (1949), 1-25.
11. Lang, Paul Henry. "Current Chronicle," *MQ* 36 (1950), 91.
12. Rosenwald, Hans. "Contemporary Music," *Mus News* 43 (1951), 11.
13. Keats, Sheila. "Reference Articles on American Composers: An Index," *Juilliard Rev* 1 (Fall 1954), 33.
14. Ellsworth, Ray. "American on Microgroove," *HiFi* 6 (Aug 1956), 61.
15. Kyle, Marguerite K. "AmerAllegro," *Pan Pipes* 48 (Jun 1956), 74.
16. Sargeant, Winthrop. "Musical Events," *New Yorker* 36 (May 14, 1960), 191.
17. Banta, L. "Choral Works of Randall Thompson," *Am Org* 44 (Sep 1961), 24.
18. "Elected to National Institute of Arts and Letters," *FoF* 21 (1961 Appendix to the Index), 145.
19. Haar, James. "Randall Thompson and the Music of the Past," *Am Choral R* 16, No. 4 (1974), 7-15.
20. " 'Requiem'—Notes by the Composer," *Am Choral R* 16, No. 4 (1974), 16-32.
21. "Psalm and Gospel Settings Editorials," *Am Choral R* 16, No. 4 (1974), 33-39.
22. Forbes, Elliot. "Americana (Inspiration of His Choral Works)," *Am Choral R* 16, No. 4 (1974), 40-55.
23. ———————"List of Choral Works by Randall Thompson," *Am Choral R* 16, No. 4 (1974), 56-61.

References to Works by Randall Thompson

The number preceding the title indicates the number of the composition as listed in Section II.

25. Alleluia: *MQ* 35 (1949), 20; *CinSPN* (Dec 21, 1950), 267; (Nov 24, 1951), 141; *EweCB*, 433; *EweWT*.
21. Americana: *PitSPN* (Mar 7, 1941), 5; *MQ* 35 (1949), 12.
34. Frostiana: *Notes* 18, No. 4 (1960-1961), 659; *MA* 82 (May 1962), 11.
27. The Last Words of David: *Diap* 42 (Jun 1, 1951), 22.
37. The Nativity According to Saint Luke: *Mus Mag* 164 (Feb 1962), 26; *Am Choral R* 4, No. 2 (1962), 1.
18. Odes of Horace: *MQ* 35 (1949), 9.
30. Ode to the Virginian Voyage: *NYT* (Apr 7, 1957), sec. 2, p. 9:8; *MC* 155 (May 1957), 6; *MA* 77 (Jul 1957), 5; *MT* 99 (Apr 1958), 209; *MA* 80 (Jun 1960), 38.
41. The Passion According to Saint Luke: *NYT* (Mar 29, 1965), 44:5; *Am Choral R* 7, No. 4 (1965), 1.
22. The Peaceable Kingdom: *MQ* 35 (1949), 15; *HiFi* 11 (Feb 1961), 59; *EweCB*, 433; *Nor-LC*, 388.
2. The Piper at the Gates of Dawn: *BSPN* (Mar 28, 1929); *MQ* 35 (1949), 3.

43. The Place of the Blest: *Diap* 60 (Apr 1969), 1; *Am Org* 52 (1969), 27.
42. Psalm of Thanksgiving: *Mus J* 26 (Jan 1968), 14; *Am Choral R* 10, No. 2 (1968), 69-71.
19. Pueri Hebraeorum: *MQ* 35 (1949), 12.
32. Requiem: *MQ* 44 (1958), 370.
52. Solomon and Balkis: *Time* 39 (Apr 6, 1942), 59-60; *MA* 62, No. 7 (1942), 11; *MA* 64, No. 6 (1944), 29; *MQ* 35 (1949), 21.
10. String Quartet No. 1: *MQ* 35 (1949), 7; *Musicology* 2 (Jul 1949), 431.
9. Suite for Oboe, Clarinet, Viola: *MA* 61, (Jul 1941), 32; *MQ* 35 (1949), 6; 43 (1957), 422; *CobCS*, 169.
4. Symphony No. 1: *NYT* (Mar 11, 1934), sec. 10, p. 6:3; *MQ* 35 (1949), 3.
5. Symphony No. 2: *NYT* (Apr 17, 1932), sec. 8, p. 9:6; (Nov 3, 1933), 22:6; *NYHT* (Nov 3, 1933); *NYT* (Nov 12, 1933), sec. 9, p. 6:1; *BSPN* (Apr 13, 1934); *POPN* (Oct 20, 1939), 59; *NYPPN* (Nov 14, 1940); *ClSPN* (Dec 2, 1943), 155; *MQ* 35 (1949), 5; *BSPN* (Mar 25, 1955), 882; *HiFi* 6 (Aug 1956), 61; *EweCB*, 434; *EweWT*.
6. Symphony No. 3: *MQ* 35 (1949), 465; *NYHT* (May 15, 1949); *BSPN* (Mar 31, 1950), 1098; *CinSPN* (Nov 24, 1951), 141; *EweCB*, 434; *EweWT*.
26. Testament of Freedom: *MA* 64, No. 10 (1944), 30; *MM* 22, No. 4 (1944-1945), 255; *BSPN* (Apr 6, 1945), 1305; *NYT* (Apr 22, 1945), sec. 2, p. 4:1; *MQ* 35 (1949), 20, 286; *NYT* (May 3, 1952), 18:6; *HiFi* 6 (Aug 1956), 61; *Mus Ed J* 54 (Oct 1967), 52-54; *EweCB*, 433; *EweWT*; *MacIC*, 477.
7. A Trip to Nahant: *POPN* (Mar 18, 1955), 571; *NYT* (Apr 20, 1955), 39:1; *MA* 75 (May 1955), 23; *MC* 151 (Jun 1955), 44.

Dissertations about Randall Thompson and His Works

1. Armstrong, Donald J. *A Study of Some Important Twentieth Century Secular Compositions for Women's Chorus with a Preliminary Discussion of Secular Choral Music from a Historical and Philosophical Viewpoint.* University of Texas, 1968.
2. Brookhart, Charles E. *The Choral Music of Aaron Copland, Roy Harris and Randall Thompson.* George Peabody College for Teachers, 1960.
3. Pisciotta, Louis V. *Texture in the Choral Works of Selected Contemporary American Composers.* Indiana University, 1967.
4. Smedley, Bruce R. *Contemporary Sacred Chamber Opera: A Medieval Form in the Twentieth Century.* George Peabody College for Teachers, 1977.

OUTLINE XVII

VIRGIL (GARNETT) THOMSON (b. 1896)

I. Life

1896   Born in Kansas City, Missouri, November 25. Father a post-office clerk of Scottish descent; mother English-Welsh.

1901   Began his education in music with local teachers. A child prodigy at the age of twelve; began to perform professionally.

1908   Attended Central High School, Kansas City Polytechnic Institute, and Junior College in Kansas City.

1917   Left school to enlist in the Army; commissioned a second lieutenant in the Military Aviation Corps at Columbia University (1918).

1918   Entered Harvard University; studied philosophy, languages, English composition, and music with Archibald T. Davison, Edward Burlingame Hill, and privately with Wallace Goodrich (organ) and Heinrich Gebhard (piano). Studied in Paris with Nadia Boulanger for one year under a John Knowles Paine Traveling Fellowship (1921-1922). Returned to Harvard; appointed assistant instructor in music; organist at King's Chapel, Boston (1922-1923).

1923   Graduated from Harvard (Bachelor of Arts degree). Studied composition with Rosario Scalero at the Mannes School, New York, and conducting with Chalmers Clifton (1923-1924).

1924   Returned to Harvard as assistant instructor. Wrote articles for *Vanity Fair* and *American Mercury*; began the composition of over 100 "musical portraits" of his friends.

1925   Returned to Paris (1925-1940). Came under the influence of Erik Satie, Darius Milhaud, the Dadists, and Gertrude Stein (*Capital Capitals*, 1927; *Four Saints in Three Acts*, 1928). Made frequent visits to the United States and his reputation as a composer was established.

1940   Appointed music critic for the *New York Herald Tribune* (1940-1954). Composed a large amount of music of all types; guest conductor of symphony orchestras in North and South America and Europe.

1941   One of the founders of the Music Critics Circle of New York (1941-1965).

1947   Officer in the *Legion d'Honneur*.

1948   Elected a member of the National Institute of Arts and Letters.

1949   Honorary doctorates from Syracuse University (1949) and Rutgers University (1956). Awarded a Pulitzer Prize for Music (*Louisiana Story*, 1949).

1956   Composed incidental music for several Shakespeare plays produced at Stratford, Connecticut.

1961   Visited Japan for the World Festival of Music.

1965   Commissioned by the Koussevitzky and Ford Foundations for an opera based on the life of Lord Byron for the Metropolitan Opera.

1966   Appointed Andrew Mellon Professor of Music, Carnegie Institute of Technology, Pittsburgh. Awarded the Gold Medal of the National Institute of Arts and Letters.

Virgil Thomson has been the recipient of many honors, awards and commissions in addition to those listed above.

Note: Biographies of varying lengths and importance will be found in many of the books listed in the Bibliography at the end of this *Outline*.

II.   Compositions (selected)

		Date	Publisher
A.	**Orchestra**		
1.	Two Sentimental Tangos	1923	
2.	Symphony on a Hymn Tune	1928	Peer
3.	Symphony No. 2	1931; revised 1941	Leeds
4.	Suite from "The Plow that Broke the Plains"	1936	Merc
5.	Suite from "The River" (cham orch)	1937	Peer
6.	Suite from "Filling Station"	1937	BH
7.	The John Mosher Waltzes from "Filling Station"	1937	BH
8.	Canons for Dorothy Thompson	1942	Peer
9.	The Mayor La Guardia Waltzes	1942	Peer
10.	Portraits for Orchestra	arr. 1944	Merc

    a. The John Mosher Waltzes   f. Barcarolle for Woodwinds (Georges Hugnet)
    b. The Mayor La Guardia Waltzes   (fl, ob, E.hn, clar, bass clar, bsn)
    c. Canons for Dorothy Thompson   g. Fugue (Alexander Smallens)
    d. Fanfare for France (Max Kahn)   h. Tango Lullaby (Flavie Alvárez de Toledo)
        (3 hn, 3 trpt, 3 trb, drums)   i. Bugles and Birds (Pablo Picasso)
    e. Cantabile for Strings (Nicolas de Châtelain)

		Date	Publisher
11.	Election Day Suite from "Tuesday in November"	1945	Merc
12.	The Seine at Night	1947	GS
13.	Suite No. 1 from "Louisiana Story"	1948	GS

    a. Pastorale: The Bayou and the Marsh-Buggy   c. Passacaglia: Robbing the Alligator's Nest
    b. Chorale: The Derrick Arrives   d. Fugue: Boy Fights Alligator

		Date	Publisher
14.	Acadian Songs and Dances: Suite No. 2 from "Louisiana Story"	1948	GS

    a. Sadness   e. Super-Sadness
    b. Papa's Tune   f. Walking Song (also arr. 2 pno)
    c. A Narrative   g. The Squeeze-Box
    d. The Alligator and the Coon

		Date	Publisher
15.	Wheatfield at Noon	1948	GS
16.	Suite from "The Mother of Us All"	1949	Merc

    a. Prelude   c. Wedding Hymn and Finale
    b. Cold Weather   d. A Political Meeting

		Date	Publisher
17.	Concerto for Violoncello and Orchestra	1949	FC

    a. Rider on the Plains   c. Children's Games
    b. Variations on a Southern Hymn

		Date	Publisher
18.	Five Songs from William Blake (Bar., orch)	1951	FC

    a. The Divine Image   d. The Little Black Boy
    b. Tiger! Tiger!   e. "And did those feet"
    c. The Land of Dreams

		Date	Publisher
19.	Sea Piece with Birds	1952	GS
20.	Concerto for Flute, Harp, Strings, Percussion (also fl, pno)	1954	FC
21.	The Harvest According (from the ballet)	arr. 1954	FC
22.	Eleven Chorale Preludes by Brahms (transcribed by V. T.)	1956	BH
23.	A Solemn Music and A Joyful Fugue	1957	GS
24.	Autumn: Concertino for Harp, Strings, Percussion	1957	GS
25.	Fugues and Cantilenas (from the film "Power Among Men")	arr. 1958	GS
26.	Journey to America (Suite from the film)	arr. 1965	GS
27.	Fugue and Chorale on Yankee Doodle (from the film "Tuesday in November")	arr. 1966	GS
28.	Fantasy in Homage to an Earlier England	1967	GS
B.	**Band**		
29.	Fanfare for France (Portrait of Max Kahn) (brass, perc)	1944	BH
30.	A Solemn Music	1949	GS
31.	At the Beach: Concert Waltz (trpt, band; also trpt, pno)	1949	CF

B.   Band (cont.)

   32.   Ode to the Wonders of Nature (brass, perc)   1966   GS

C.   **Chamber**

   33.   Sonata da chiesa (clar, trpt, vla, hn, trb)   1926   NME

   34.   Seven Portraits for Solo Violin   1928   Ms

      a.   Señorita Juanita de Medina   e.   Mrs. C. W. L.
      b.   Madame Marthe-Marthine   f.   Georges Hugnet, Poet and Man of Letters
      c.   Miss Gertrude Stein as a Young Girl   g.   Sauguet, from Life
      d.   Cliquot-Pleyel in F

   35.   Five Portraits for Four Clarinets   1929   Ms

      a.   Portrait of Ladies   c.   Three Portraits of Christian Bérard
      b.   Portrait of a Young Man in Good Health   1.   Christian Bérard, Prisonier
            2.   Bébé Soldat
            3.   En Personne (chair et os)

   36.   Le Bains-Bar (vln, pno)   1929   Ms

   37.   Four Portraits for Violin and Piano

      a.   Alice Toklas (1930)   c.   Mary Reynolds (1930)
      b.   Ann Miracle (1930)   d.   Yvonne de Casa Fuerte (1940)

   38.   Sonata for Violin and Piano No. 1   1930   BH
   39.   String Quartet No. 1   1931   BH
   40.   Serenade for Flute, Violin   1931   Peer
   41.   String Quartet No. 2   1932   BH
   42.   Four Portraits (transcribed for vlc, pno by Luigi Silva)   1942   Merc

      a.   Fanfare for France (Max Kahn)   c.   In a Bird Cage (Lise Deharme)
      b.   Tango Lullaby (Mlle. Alvárez de Toledo)   d.   Bugles and Birds (Pablo Picasso)

   43.   Sonata for Flute Alone   1943   E-V
   44.   Barcarolle for Woodwinds (Portrait of Georges Hugnet)   arr. 1944   Merc
      (fl, ob, E-hn, clar, bass clar, bsn)
   45.   At the Beach (trpt, pno; also trpt, band)   1949   CF
   46.   Three Portraits (transcribed for vln, pno by Samuel Dushkin)   1947   Merc

      a.   Barcarolle (Georges Hugnet)   c.   Tango Lullaby (Mlle. Alvárez de Toledo)
      b.   In a Bird Cage (Lise Deharme)

   47.   Four Songs to Poems by Thomas Campion   1951   FC
      (m-S., vla, clar, hp)
   48.   Ondine (fl, hp, str qrt, perc)   1954   FC
   49.   The Feast of Love (cantata: Bar., cham orch)   1965   GS

D.   **Piano**

   50.   Prelude   1921   Ms
   51.   Two Sentimental Tangos   1923   Ms
   52.   Synthetic Waltzes (2 pno, 4 hands; also 1 pno, 4 hands)   1925   E-V
   53.   Five Inventions (also 2 pno)   1926   E-V

      a.   With Marked Rhythm   d.   Rhythmically
      b.   Freely   e.   Firmly
      c.   Flowing

   54.   Ten Easy Pieces with a Coda   1926   Ms
   55.   Sonata No. 1   1929   BH
   56.   Sonata No. 2   1929
   57.   Sonata No. 3 (on the white keys)   1930   Merc
   58.   A Day Dream (Portrait of Herbert Whiting)   1935   CF
   59.   Sonata No. 4 (Guggenheim Jeune)   1940   E-V
   60.   Eccentric Dance (Portrait of Madame Tonny)   1940   CF

61. Ten Etudes for Piano, Set I   1943-1944   CF
    a. Repeating Tremolo: Fanfare   f. For the Weaker Fingers: Music-Box Lullaby
    b. Tenor Lead: Madrigal   g. Oscillating Arm: Spinning Song
    c. Fingered Fifths: Canon   h. Five-Finger Exercise: Portrait of
    d. Fingered Glissando: Aeolian Harp   Briggs Buchanan
    e. Double Glissando: Waltz   i. Parallel Chords: Tango
                                                       j. Ragtime Bass (two versions, one simplified)

62. Portraits, for Piano Solo (5 Albums)   Merc
    Album 1
        a. Bugles and Birds (Pablo Picasso)   April 30, 1940
        b. With Fife and Drums (Mina Curtiss)   June 15, 1941
        c. An Old Song (Carrie Stettheimer)   May 5, 1935
        d. Tango Lullaby (Flavie Alvárez de Toledo)   April 24, 1940
        e. Solitude (Lou Harrison)   December 5, 1945
        f. Barcarolle (Georges Hugnet)   April 17, 1940
        g. Fugue (Alexander Smallens)   September 6, 1940
        h. Alternations (Maurice Grosser)   October 28, 1929
    Album 2
        a. Aria (Germaine Hugnet)   May 12, 1940
        b. A Portrait of R. Kirk Askew, Jr.   May 1, 1935
        c. In a Bird Cage (Lise Deharme)   April 8, 1940
        d. Catalan Waltz (Ramon Senabre)   November 2, 1929
        e. Five-Finger Exercise (Léon Kochnitzky)   May 4, 1940
        f. Sea Coast (Constance Askew)   April 30, 1935
        g. Meditation (Jere Abbott)   September 6, 1935
        h. Fanfare for France (Max Kahn)   April 15, 1940
    Album 3
        a. Cantabile (Nicolas de Châtelain)   May 29, 1940
        b. Toccata (Mary Widney)   May 13, 1940
        c. Pastoral (Jean Ozenne)   February 20, 1930
        d. Prelude and Fugue (Agnes Rindge)   September 2, 1935
        e. The Dream World of Peter Rose-Pulham   May 7, 1940
        f. The Bard (Sherry Mangan)   April 1, 1940
        g. Souvenir (Paul Bowles)   May 20, 1935
        h. Canons with Cadenza (André Ostier)   July 9, 1940
    Album 4
        a. Tennis (Henry McBride)   May 9, 1935
        b. Hymn (Josiah Marvel)   May 22, 1935
        c. Lullaby Which is Also a Spinning Song (Howard Putzel)   May 3, 1940
        d. Swiss Waltz (Sophie Tauber-Arp)   April 18, 1940
        e. Poltergeist (Hans Arp)   April 12, 1940
        f. Insistences (Louise Crane)   July 6, 1941
        g. The Hunt (A. Everett Austin, Jr.)   May 21, 1935
        h. Wedding Music (Jean Watts)   October 1, 1942
    Album 5
        a. Travelling in Spain (Alice Branlière)   October 24, 1929
        b. Scottish Memories (Peter Monro Jack)   July 29, 1942
        c. Duet (Clarita, Comtesse de Forceville)   July 2, 1940
        d. Russell Hitchcock, Reading   May 29, 1930
        e. Connecticut Waltz (Harold Lewis Cook)   September 16, 1935
        f. Polka (Ettie Stettheimer)   May 5, 1935
        g. Invention (Theodate Johnson)   April 29, 1940
        h. Parades (Florine Stettheimer)   October 5, 1941

63. Nine Etudes for Piano, Set II   CF
        a. With Trumpet and Horn (Louise Ardant)   April 11, 1940
        b. Pivoting on the Thumb   June 23, 1951
        c. Alternating Octaves   June 26, 1951
        d. Double Sevenths   July 7, 1951
        e. The Harp   June 22, 1951
        f. Chromatic Major Second (The Wind)   June 20, 1951
        g. Chromatic Double Harmonics (Sylvia Marlowe)   June 17, 1951
        h. Broken Arpeggios (The Waltzing Waters)   July 10, 1951
        i. Guitar and Mandolin   June 18, 1951

E.   Organ

64.	Pastorale on a Christmas Plainsong	1921	HWG
65.	Fanfare	1921	HWG
66.	Prelude	1922	Ms
67.	Passacaglia	1922; revised 1974	
68.	Variations and Fugues on Sunday School Tunes	1927	HWG

    a.   Come, Ye Disconsolate   c.   Will there be Any Stars in My Crown?
    b.   There's not a Friend like the Lowly Jesus   d.   Shall We Gather at the River?

69.	Wedding Music	1940	Ms

    a.   To Go In   b.   To Come Out

70.	Pange Lingua	1964	GS
71.	Prelude	1977	GS

F.   Choral (a cappella unless otherwise indicated)

72.	De Profundis (SATB)	1920; revised 1951	Wein
73.	Sanctus (TTBB)	1922	Ms
74.	Tribulationes Civitatum (SATB or TTBB)	1922	Wein
75.	Three Antiphonal Psalms (Psalms 123, 133, 136) (SA or TB)	1922-1924	Leeds
76.	Agnus Dei (canon for three equal voices)	1924	Merc
77.	Missa Brevis No. 1 (TTBB)	1925	Ms
78.	Capital, Capitals (Gertrude Stein) (four men's solo voices, TTBB, pno)	1927	NME
79.	Saints Procession (from "Four Saints in Three Acts") (m-S., B., SATB or TTBB, pno)	1928	Merc
80.	Missa Brevis No. 2 (SA, perc ad lib)	1934	Merc
81.	Seven Choruses from the "Medea of Euripides" (tr. Countee Cullen) (SSAA, perc ad lib)	1934	Leeds

    a.   O, Gentle Heart   e.   Go Down, O Sun
    b.   Love, Life a Leaf   f.   Behold, O Earth
    c.   O, Happy Were Our Fathers   g.   Immortal Zeus Controls the Fate of Man
    d.   Weep for the Little Lambs

82.	My Shepherd Will Supply My Need (Isaac Watts) (SATB or TTBB or SSAA)	1937	HWG
83.	Scenes from the Holy Infancy (SATB)	1937	Merc

    a.   Joseph and the Angels   c.   The Flight into Egypt
    b.   The Wise Men

84.	Psalm XXIII (SATB)	1938	
85.	Welcome to the New Year (Eleanor Farjean) (SATB)	1941	Ms
86.	Hymns from the Old South		HWG

    a.   My Shepherd Will Supply My Need   c.   Green Fields (John Milton) (1949)
       (Isaac Watts) (1938)   d.   Death, 'tis a Melancholy Day (Isaac Watts)
    b.   The Morning Star (anon.) (1949)   (1949)

87.	Four Songs to Poems of Thomas Campion	1951	FC

    a.   Follow Your Saint   c.   Rose-cheek'd Laura, Come
    b.   There is a Garden in Her Face   d.   Follow Thy Fair Sun

88.	Tiger! Tiger! (William Blake) (arr. from "Five Songs" by V. T. for SATB or TTBB, pno)	1951	FC
89.	Kyrie (SATB)	1953	Ms
90.	Song for the Stable (Amanda B. Hall) (SATB)	1955	UChiP
91.	Never Another (Mark Van Doren) (SATB)	1956	UChiP
92.	Crossing Brooklyn Ferry (Walt Whitman) (SSATB, pno)	1958	BH
93.	Missa pro defunctis (Requiem Mass) (SATB, orch)	1960	HWG
94.	Dance in Praise (SATB, orch)	1961	GS
95.	The Holly and the Ivy (SATB, pno)	1961	GS

96. My Master Hath a Garden (SAT or SAA)	1962	GS
97. The Nativity as Sung by the Shepherds	1970	
98. Cantata on Poems of Edward Lear (S., B., SATB, orch)		GS

G.   Solo Vocal (with piano unless otherwise indicated)

99. Vernal Equinox (Amy Lowell)	1920	Ms
100. The Sunflower (William Blake)	1920	Ms
101. Susie Asado (Gertrude Stein)	1926	BH
102. Five Phrases from "The Song of Solomon" (with perc)	1926	AME

    a. Thou that Dwellest in the Gardens   d. I am My Beloved's
    b. Return, O Shulamite   e. By Night
    c. O, My Dove

103. The Tiger (William Blake)	1926	GS
104. Presciosilla (Gertrude Stein)	1927	GS
105. La Valse grégorienne (four poems by Georges Hugnet)	1927	PP
106. Trois Poèmes de la Duchesse de Rohan	1928	Ms

    a. A son Altesse le Princesse Antoinette Murat
    b. Jour de chaleur aux bains de mer   BH
    c. La Seine

107. La Berceau de Gertrude Stein	1928	Ms
108. Commentaire sur Saint Jérôme (Marquis de Sade)	1928	Merc
109. Les Soirées bagnolaises	1928	Ms
110. Portrait of F. B. [Frances Blood] (Gertrude Stein)	1929	GS
111. Le Singe et le Léopard (La Fontaine)	1930	SMPC
112. Oraison Funèbre (Funeral oration) (Bossuet)	1930	Ms
113. Air de Phèdre (Jean Baptiste Racine)	1930	Ms
114. Chamber Music (Kreymbourg)	1931	Ms
115. La Belle en Dormant	1931	GS

    a. Pour cherchez sur la carte des mers (Georges Hugnet)
      (Scanning brooklets from ocean resorts) (Elaine de Sirçay)
    b. La première de toutes (Georges Hugnet)
      (My true love sang me no song) (Elaine de Sirçay)
    c. Mon amour est bon à dire (Georges Hugnet)
      (Yes, my love is good to tell of) (Elaine de Sirçay)
    d. Partis les vaisseaux (Georges Hugnet)
      (All gone are the ships) (Elaine de Sirçay)

116. Stabat Mater (Max Jacob) (S., str qrt or str orch)	1931	BH
117. Pigeons on the Grass Alas (from "Four Saints in Three Acts) (Bar., pno or orch)	1934	Merc
118. Two Lullabies	1937	

    a. Pare McTaggett Lorenz   b. Alexander Smallens, jun.

119. Dirge (John Webster)	1939	GS
120. The Bugle Song (Alfred Tennyson)	1941	Ms
121. Four Songs to Poems of Thomas Campion (m-S., vla, clar, hp; also with pno)	1951	FC

    a. Follow Your Saint   c. Rose-Cheek'd Laura, Come
    b. There is a Garden in Her Face   d. Follow Thy Fair Sun

122. Five Songs from William Blake (Bar., orch or pno)	1951	FC

    a. The Divine Image   d. The Little Black Boy
    b. Tiger! Tiger!   e. "And Did Those Feet"
    c. The Land of Dreams

123. Old English Songs for Soprano	1955	Ms

    a. Look, How the Floor of Heav'n   b. The Holly and the Ivy (anon.)
      (Shakespeare)   c. At the Spring (Jasper Fisher)

124. Old English Songs for Baritone	1955	Peer

    a. Consider, Lord (John Donne)   c. Remember Adam's Fall (anon.)
    b. The Bell doth Toll (Thomas Heywood)   d. John Peel (John Woodcock Graves)

G.   Solo Vocal (cont.)

125. If Thou for a Reason doth Desire to Know (Sir Francis Kynaston) 1955   Peer

126. Tres estampas de niñez (Reyna Rivas)   1957   Peer
    a. Todas las horas   c. Nadie lo oye comos ellos
    b. Son amigos de todos

127. Five Shakespeare Songs   1957   Peer
    a. Pardon, Goddess of the Night   d. Tell Me Where is Fancy Bred?
    b. Sigh No More, Ladies   e. Was This Fair Fore the Cause?
    c. Take, O Take, Those Lips Away

128. Selected Poems (Kenneth Koch) (S., Bar., orch)   1959

129. Mostly About Love   1960   GS
    a. Love Song   c. Let's Take a Walk
    b. Down at the Docks   d. A Prayer to Saint Catherine

130. Praises and Prayers   1962   GS
    a. From the Canticle of the Sun   c. Sung by the Shepherds (Richard Crashaw)
      (St. Francis of Assisi)   d. Before Sleeping (Anon.)
    b. My Master Hath a Garden (Anon.)   e. Jerusalem, My Happy Home (St. Augustine)

131. The Feast of Love (Bar., cham orch)   1964   GS
132. When I Survey the Bright Celestial Sphere (William Habbington)   HWG
133. English Usage (Marianne Moore)   GS
134. My Crow Pluto (Marianne Moore)   GS
135. The Courtship of the Yongly Bongly Bo   1977   GS

H. Opera

136. Four Saints in Three Acts (Gertrude Stein)   1928   Merc
137. The Mother of Us All (Gertrude Stein)   1947   Merc
138. Lord Byron (Jack Larson)   1972

I. Ballet

139. Filling Station (Lew Christensen)   1939   BH
140. Bayou (Acadian Songs and Dances from "Louisiana Story")   1952   GS
    (Georges Balanchine)
141. The Harvest According (Agnes de Mille)   1954   FC

J. Film

142. The Plow that Broke the Plains (Pare Lorentz)   1936
143. The Spanish Earth (Hemingway and Ivans with Marc Blitzstein)   1937
144. The River (Pare Lorentz)   1937
145. Life of a Careful Man   1941
146. Tuesday in November (John Houseman)   1945
147. Louisiana Story (Robert Flaherty)   1948
148. The Goddess (Paddy Chayevsky)   1957
149. Power Among Men (Thorold Dickinson)   1957
150. Journey to America (John Houseman)   1964

K. Incidental Music (music for 19 plays, the following among them)

151. Antony and Cleopatra (William Shakespeare)   1937
152. A Bride for the Unicorn (Denis Johnson)   1938
153. Injunction Granted (Living Newspaper)   1938
154. Hamlet (William Shakespeare)   1938
155. The Trojan Woman (Euripides, tr. Gilbert Murray)   1940
156. Oedipus Tyrannus (Sophocles)   1941
157. King Lear (William Shakespeare)   1952
158. The Grass Harp   1953
159. Ondine (Jean Giraudoux)   1954   FC
160. King John (William Shakespeare)   1956
161. Measure for Measure (William Shakespeare)   1956
162. Othello (William Shakespeare)   1957

K.   Incidental Music (cont.)
   163.   Much Ado About Nothing (William Shakespeare)   1957
   164.   Bertha (Kenneth Koch)   1959

The following abbreviations are used in Section III of this *Outline*. The number indicates the number of the composition as listed in Section II.

   8.   *Canons*: Canons for Dorothy Thompson
  17.   *Con Vlc*: Concerto for Violoncello
  53.   *Inventions*: Five Inventions
  13.   *Louisiana*: Louisiana Story
  81.   *Medea*: Seven Choruses from "Medea"
  16.   *Mother*: The Mother of Us All
   4.   *Plow*: The Plow that Broke the Plains
  62.   *Portraits*: Portraits (5 vols.)
136.   *Saints*: Four Saints in Three Acts

  12.   *Seine*: Seine at Night
  30.   *Solemn*: A Solemn Music
  55.   *Son Pno 1*: Sonata for Piano No. 1
  38.   *Son Vln Pno 1*: Sonata for Violin and Piano No. 1
   2.   *Sym Hymn*: Symphony on Hymn Tune
  68.   *Variations*: Variations and Fugues on Sunday School Tunes
  15.   *Wheat*: Wheatfield at Noon

III.   Style (techniques and devices)

"We are not out to impress, and we dislike inflated emotions." "The new romanticism strives neither to unify mass audiences nor to impress the specialists of intellectual objectivity [and] it is wary about the conventionalistic tendencies bound up with consistent and obligatory dissonance."
                                                       Virgil Thomson

A.   General characteristics
   1.   Early influence (1925-1932) of the music of Satie, the "French Six" and the Dada movement in art and literature (Gertrude Stein).
   2.   Old conventions dissolved; absorbed many ingredients without being imitative.
   3.   Economy of materials, understatement, deceptive simplicity, sudden changes of idiom, allusions to other styles, melody and lyricism, descriptive writing are all a part of his style.
B.   Melodic line
   1.   Diatonic chord line: *Mother* (p. 84).
   2.   Octave skips as a device: *Medea* (pp. 20, 25).
   3.   Sequences: *Inventions* (pp. 8, 10, 11).
   4.   Repeated notes, diatonic steps, and chord line: *Mother* (p. 56).
   5.   Chromaticism: *Str Qrt 1, 2*; *Son Vln Pno 1* (p. 1); *Louisiana* (*Fugue*).
   6.   Hymn and folk tunes: *Sym Hymn*; *Plow*; *River* (No. 5); *Louisiana* (*Pastorale*); *Filling Station*; *Variations*.
   7.   Twelve-tone experiments: *Wheat*; *Louisiana* (chorale); *Seine*.
   8.   Modal writing: *Saints* (p. 90, Aeolian); *Louisiana* (*Pastorale*); *Seine*.
   9.   Whole-tone scales: *Sea Piece with Birds*; *Canons*.
  10.   Artificial scales: *Seine* (sky rockets).
C.   Harmony
   1.   Basically simple and consonant with ultra-sophisticated content.
   2.   I - IV - V: *Saints* (p. 24); with parallel fifths (p. 29, No. 30, plagal and authentic cadences).
   3.   Third relation: *Mother* (p. 20, meas. 5-7); *Solemn* (p. 7).
   4.   Polytonality: *Mother* (p. 68); *Seine* (end of A section); *Portraits* (*Prelude and Fugue*, vol. 3).
   5.   Tone clusters: *Variations*.
   6.   Bitonality: *Seine*.
   7.   Leap modulations: *Saints*.

8. Organ sonorities: *Seine*; *Saints*.
9. Parallel harmony: *Saints* (p. 13).
D. Counterpoint
 1. Polyphonic forms and devices moderately used. Canonic imitation characteristic.
 2. Fugal devices: *Sonata da chiesa* (*Fugue*); *Plow* (*Devastation*).
 3. Two simple diatonic lines combined in non-stylistic counterpoint: *Son Pno 3* (first movement).
 4. Quintal and secundal counterpoint: *Missa Brevis*; *Inventions* (No. 1).
 5. Free canons: *Canons*; *Inventions* (No. 1).
 6. Superimposed diatonic line in bitonal polyphony: *Seine*.
E. Rhythm
 1. Rhythmic devices generally traditional.
 2. Frequent meter changes: *Saints* (p. 1).
 3. Tango: *Plow*; *Sonata da chiesa* (second movement).
 4. Waltz: *Son Vln Pno 1*; *Str Qrt 1*; *Str Qrt 2*.
F. Form
 1. Usually sectional, in unrelated blocks.
 2. Sonata: *Con Vlc* (Allegretto).
 3. Free: *Sea Piece with Birds*.
 4. No recapitulation, little development: *Son Pno 4* (second movement).
 5. A - B - A - Coda: *Solemn*.
 6. A - A - B - A: *Seine*; *Wheat*.
G. Orchestration
 1. Colorful and varied. Wide spacing gives impression of volume and richness. Changes in instrumentation often abrupt.
 2. Unusual scoring: *Plow* (sax, tom tom, banjo).

BIBLIOGRAPHY

Books by Virgil Thomson

1. *The State of Music*. New York: W. Morrow, 1939; 2nd rev. ed., New York: Random House, 1962. Review by Aaron Copland: *MM* 17, No. 1 (Nov 1939), 63.
2. *The Musical Scene*. New York: Alfred A. Knopf, 1945; New York: Greenwood Press, 1968.
3. *The Art of Judging Music*. New York: Alfred A. Knopf, 1948; New York: Greenwood Press, 1969. *Mus Ed J* 51, No. 2 (1964), 37-40.
4. *Music, Right and Left*. New York: Henry Holt, 1951.
5. *Virgil Thomson*. New York: Alfred A. Knopf, 1966. *HiFi/MA* 16 (Nov 1966), MA21; *Opera N* 31 (Dec 10, 1966), 32; *Mus J* 25 (Jan 1967), 89; *Am Rec G* 33 (Feb 1967), 460-463; *Tempo* 80 (Spring 1967), 36; *Mus Tcr* 46 (May 1967), 25; *MT* 108 (Aug 1967), 710; *MM* 15 (Aug 1967), 17; *ML* 48 (1967), 268-270; *Mus Opin* 91 (Jan 1968), 214; *MR* 29, No. 1 (1968), 53-56; *Pan Pipes* 60, No. 2 (1968), 49.
6. *Music Reviewed 1940-1954; a Collection of Criticisms*. New York: Vintage Books, 1967. *Am Rec G* 34 (Sep 1967), 65; *HiFi/MA* 19 (Apr 1969), MA29-MA30.
7. *American Music Since 1910*. New York: Holt, Rinehart and Winston, 1971. *NYT* (Mar 12, 1971), 35:2; *Intam Mus Res Yrbk* 7 (1971), 186; *Clavier* 10, No. 4 (1971), 8; *HiFi/MA* 21 (Jul 1971), MA31; *Mus Events* 26 (Aug 1971), 12-13; *MT* 112 (Sep 1971), 861-862; *Mus & Mus* 20 (Apr 1972), 50-51; *Composer* No. 44 (Summer 1972), 34-35; *Am Rec G* 38 (May 1972), 444; *Mus Ed J* 58 (May 1972), 61-62; *Mus J* 30 (Sep 1972), 48-49; *Sym News* 23, No. 1 (1972), 20-21; *Mus in Ed* 37, No. 363 (1973), 260.
8. *Parnassus: Poetry in Review*, ed. Herbert A. Leibowitz. New York: Poetry in Review Foundation, 1977.

Book about Virgil Thomson

Hoover, Kathleen, and John Cage. *Virgil Thomson: His Life and Music*. New York: Thomas Yoseloff, 1959; Freeport, NY: Books for Libraries Press, 1970. *SR* 42 (May 30, 1959), 54; *Am Rec G* 25 (Jul 1959), 769-771; *HiFi* 9 (Oct 1959), 41; *Mus Opin* 83 (Dec 1959), 171; *Opera N* 24 (Dec 5, 1959), 30; *Notes* 17, No. 1 (1959), 47; *MT* 101 (Jan 1960), 25; *Mus E Radio* 52 (Dec 1962), 403.

Articles by Virgil Thomson

1. "Jazz," *American Mercury* 2 (Aug 1924), 465-467.
2. "Aaron Copland," *MM* 9, No. 2 (1931-1932), 67-73.
3. "Igor Markevitch," *MM* 10, No. 1 (1932-1933), 19.
4. "Home Thoughts," *MM* 10, No. 2 (1932-1933), 107.
5. "Now in Paris," *MM* 10, No. 3 (1932-1933), 141.
6. "A Little About Movie Music," *MM* 10, No. 4 (1932-1933), 188.
7. "Most Melodious Tears," *MM* 11, No. 1 (1933-1934), 13.
8. "Paris News," *MM* 11, No. 1 (1933-1934), 42.
9. "George Gershwin," *MM* 13, No. 1 (1935-1936), 13-19.
10. "Swing Music," *MM* 13, No. 4 (1935-1936), 12-17.
11. "The Official Stravinsky," *MM* 13, No. 4 (1935-1936), 57.
12. "In the Theatre," *MM* 14, Nos. 2, 3, 4 (1936-1937), 101, 170, 233.
13. "Films Seen in New York," *MM* 14, No. 4 (1936-1937), 239.
14. "In the Theatre," *MM* 15, Nos. 2, 3 (1937-1938), 112, 183.
15. "Swing Again," *MM* 15, No. 3 (1937-1938), 160.
16. "French Landscape With Figures," *MM* 16, No. 1 (1938-1939).
17. "More from Paris," *MM* 16, No. 2 (1938-1939), 104.
18, "More and More from Paris," *MM* 16, No. 4 (1938-1939), 229.
19. "Paris, April 1940," *MM* 17, No. 4 (1939-1940), 203.
20. "Chaplin Scores," *MM* 18, No. 1 (1940-1941), 15.
21. "What Shall Band Music Be? " *Etude* 60 (Jul 1942), 453, 489.
22. "Looking Forward," *MQ* 31 (1945), 157-162.
23. "Les comptes d'Orphée," *Contrepoints* 5 (1946), 17-45.
24. "Putting Space into Opera Recordings," *SR* 30 (Aug 30, 1947), 5.
25. "Is Reviewing Fun? " *Harpers* 195 (Nov 1947), 406-409.
26. "Review," *Atlantic* 180 (Dec 1947), 73-75.
27. "Answers to Questions by Eight Composers," *Possibilities* (Winter 1947-1948), 21-24.
28. "Surréalisme et musique," *Contrepoints* 6 (1949), 74-78.
29. "Three Essays (1. Taste in Music; 2. Tempos; 3. The French Style)," *Score* 4 (Jan 1950), 3-9.
30. "Review: Milhaud's Sabbath Morning Service," *MQ* 36 (1950), 99.
31. "Three More Essays," *Score* 5 (1951), 19-25.
32. "Problem of Sincerity," with biographical note. *Etude* 69 (Mar 1951), 3.
33. "Too Many Languages," *Etude* 69 (Jun 1951), 17.
34. "Atonality Today," *Etude* 69 (Nov 1951), 18, 64.
35. "Reflections (reprinted from *The Art of Judging Music*)," *Score* 6 (May 1952), 11-14.
36. "Notes sur les perspectives du ballet et de l'opera en Amerique," *Rev Mus* 212 (1952), 39-40.
37. "La place de Satie dans la musique du XXe siecle," *Rev Mus* 214 (1952), 13-15.
38. "Forum of Critics," *Mag of Art* 46 (May 1953), 231.
39. "The Art of Improvisation," *Choral G* 6 (Nov 1953), 17-18.
40. "Review: Satie–Socrate," *MQ* 39 (1953), 147.
41. "Scientists Get Curious," *BSCBul* 12 (Jan 8, 1954), 563-567.

42. "The Relation of Critic to Performing Artist," *MA* 74 (Mar 1954), 14-15.
43. "Komponist und Kritiker," *Melos* 21 (Sep 1954), 245-247.
44. "The Music of Scandinavia—1954," *Amer-Scand Rev* 42, No. 4 (Dec 1954), 337-343.
45. "The Music Reviewer and His Assignment," *Amer Academy of Arts and Letters Proceedings* Ser. 2, No. 4 (1954), 36-46.
46. "Transplanted Traditions: Influence of European Teachers, Once Strong in American Composition, Now Probably on the Decline," *MA* 75 (Feb 15, 1955), 29.
47. "The Abstract Composers," *Score* 12 (Jun 1955), 62-64.
48. "House of Ricordi," *Mus J* 16 (Mar 1958), 16.
49. " 'Americanismes' dans la musique," *Rev Mus* 242 (1958), 93-95.
50. "Ending the Great Tradition; a Modest Proposal," *Encounter* 12 (Jan 1959), 64-67.
51. "Music Tradition of Constant Change," *Atlantic* 203 (Feb 1959), 84.
52. "From 'Regina' to 'Juno'," *SR* 42 (May 16, 1959), 82.
53. "Music for Much ado," *Theatre Arts* 43 (Jun 1959), 14-19.
54. "John Cage Late and Early," *SR* 43 (Jan 30, 1960), 38.
55. "Stravinsky—Gesualdo," *NYT* (Oct 2, 1960), sec. 2, p. 11.
56. "Music in the 1950's; a Decade Reviewed," *Harpers* 221 (Nov 1960), 59-63.
57. "Music in the 1950's," *Mus J* 19 (Jan 1961), 12.
58. "Virgil Thomson Survey's the State of Music in Europe Today," *MA* 81 (Jan 1961), 10.
59. "Music Now," *Opera N* 25 (Mar 11, 1961), 8-11.
60. "Twain Meet: East and West United in Tokyo Assembly," *NYT* (May 21, 1961), sec. 2, p. 9.
61. "Letters to the Editor: Thomson Answers Helm," *MA* 81 (Jun 1961), 4.
62. "Toward Improving the Musical Race," *MA* 81 (Jul 1961), 5.
63. "The Gallic Approach," *Juilliard Rev* 9, No. 1 (1961-1962), 9.
64. "The Philosophy of Style (included list of works)," *Showcase* 41, No. 2 (1961-1962), 10.
65. "America's Musical Maturity," *Yale R* 51 (Oct 1961), 66-74.
66. "Vanishing Intellectual," *Show* 1 (Oct 1961), 120-122.
67. "La critica musical," *Clave* 46 (Nov-Dec 1961), 22-25.
68. "Opera: 'The Crucible' and 'The Dove'," *Show* 2 (Jan 1962), 4.
69. " 'Greatest Music Teacher'—at 75," *NYT* (Feb 4, 1962), mag sec. p. 24; reprinted in *Mus Ed J* 49, No. 1 (1962), 42-44; *Piano Q* 39 (Jan-Mar 1962), 16-19.
70. "La filosofia del estilo," *Buenos Aires Mus* 17, No. 274 (1962), 1.
71. "Opera: It is Everywhere in America," *NYT* (Sep 23, 1962), mag sec., pt. 2, p. 16.
72. "Aaron Copland," *PNM* 2, No. 2 (1964), 21; reprinted from *MM* 9, No. 2 (1931-1932), 67.
73. "About Four Saints," *Am Rec G* 31 (Feb 1965), 520-521.
74. "The Art of Improvisation," *Choral G* 18 (May 1965), 24; reprinted from *NYHT*.
75. "Review: *Music in a New Found Land* by Wilfrid Mellers," *New York Review of Books* 4 (Jun 3, 1965), 3.
76. "Then and Now (American Creative Minds in France)," *Paris R* 9 (Winter 1965), 158-170.
77. "Burning Question," *Opera N* 30 (Mar 5, 1966), 8-11.
78. "Distaste for Music," *Vogue* 148 (Sep 1, 1966), 292-295.
79. "The Paper: a Critic's Tale," *HiFi R* 17 (Nov 1966), 53-58.
80. "Authenticity," *Am Mus Dgt* 1 (Oct 1969), 30.
81. "Where is Music Going? " *Vogue* 160 (Oct 1, 1972), 58.
82. "Stravinsky's Operas," *Mus News* 4, No. 4 (1974), 3-7.
83. "Creators vs. Consumers per Virgil Thomson," *Variety* 291 (Jun 7, 1978), 68.

References to Virgil Thomson

Books
(See the General Bibliography)

ASC-BD; ASC-SC; AusMT; Baker; BarMA; BasSM; BauTC; BIM; BloYA; BMI-OP; BroOH; Bull; CatPC; ChaAC; ChaAM; ClaEA; CobCS; CohCT; ColHM; ComA; CopCM; CopON; CopTN; Cop-WL; CowAC; CurB (1966); DavPM; DemMT; DerETM; DowO; DukLH; Edm-I; EdMUS; EweAC; EweCB; EweCS; EweCT; EweDE; EweMC; EweNB; EweWT; EweYA; FraMG; GolMM; GolTP; GosMM; GroSH; Grove; HanIT; HipAO; HitMU; HodSD; HowMM; HowOA; HowOC; HowSH; JohOA; KinAI; KolMO; LanOH; LeiMW; LeiSK; MacAC; MacIC; MelMN; MorgCM; MueAS; MyeTC; NorLC; PavMH; PersTH; PeyNM; PleSM; PorM3S; ReiCA; ReiCC; RosAH; RosDM; RowFC; SalMO; SalzTM; SamLM; SanWM; SchCC; SchWC; SloMS; SpaMH; StevHS; StevePC; ThoAJ; ThoAM; ThoLR; ThompIC; ThoMR; ThomsMS; UptAS; VinED; WooWM; WWA; WWM; YatTC; YouCD; YouCT.

Stein, Gertrude. *The Autobiography of Alice B. Toklas.* New York: Harcourt-Brace, 1933.
Twentieth-Century Authors (1942; supplement, 1955).

Articles

Brief mention: *MQ* 18 (1932), 14; *MQ* 24 (1938), 24, 25; *MQ* 26 (1940), 106; *MQ* 27 (1941), 54, 163; *Time* 39 (May 11, 1942), 53; *MQ* 28 (1942), 140; *MM* 20, No. 2 (1942-1943), 101; *MQ* 32 (1946), 357; *MQ* 33 (1947), 324; *MQ* 32 (1948), 6; *SR* 31 (Dec 25, 1948), 41; *MQ* 35 (1949), 115, 121; *MQ* 36 (1950), 55, 259, 584; *Time* 57 (Apr 2, 1951), 76; *SR* 34 (May 26, 1951), 20; *MQ* 37 (1951), 484; *PNM* 1, No. 2 (1963), 190n; *PNM* 2, No. 2 (1964), 14, 16, 18; *PNM* 4, No. 1 (1965), 124, 152, 160.
1. *NYT* (Dec 25, 1932), sec. 9, p. 10:3.
2. Thompson, Oscar. "Heard in New York," *MM* 11, No. 4 (1933-1934), 24.
3. Seldes, Gilbert. "Delight in the Theatre," *MM* 11, No. 3 (1933-1934), 139.
4. *NYT* (Mar 11, 1934), sec. 10, p. 6:7.
5. Copland, Aaron. "Our Younger Generation," *MM* 13, No. 4 (1935–1936), 5.
6. *NW* 6 (Nov 2, 1935), 41; *NYT* (Nov 9, 1935), 18:2; *NYT* (Feb 17, 1936), 20:7.
7. "Biography," *Current Biography* (Nov 1940); *Current Biography Yearbook* (1940), 802.
8. Barlow, Samuel L. M. "Virgil Thomson," *MM* 18, No. 4 (1940-1941), 242.
9. "Music Critic with a Punch," *NW* 16 (Dec 16, 1940), 60.
10. "Four Saints and Mr Thomson," *Time* 37 (Jun 9, 1941), 65-66.
11. Haggin, Bernard H. "Music," *Nation* 154 (Jan 3, 1942), 20; (Jan 17, 1942), 74.
12. Krenek, Ernst. "Opera Between the Wars," *MM* 20, No. 2 (1942-1943), 104.
13. *NYT* (Jul 24, 1942), 22:1; (Jan 6, 1943), 18:1.
14. "Composers in Chicago," *MM* 21, No. 4 (1943-1944), 244.
15. de Vore, N. "Ssh. Lilly Wears a Girdle," *Musician* 48 (Dec 1943), 147-148.
16. Haggin, Bernard H. "Music: Mr Thomson's Imagination," *Nation* 158 (Jan 22, 1944), 110.
17. Eyer, Ronald F. "Virgil Thomson," *MA* 64 (Apr 25, 1944), 7.
18. *NYT* (Feb 23, 1945), 20:5.
19. "Critic's Morning After," *Time* 45 (Mar 5, 1945), 73.
20. Haggin, Bernard H. "Musical Scene," *Nation* 160 (May 5, 1945), 527.
21. "Virgil Thomson: Gadfly of Musical Criticism," *Chr Sc Mon Mag* (May 19, 1945), 15.
22. *NYT* (Jun 9, 1946), sec. 2, p. 4:5.
23. Smith, Cecil. "Gertrude S., Virgil T., and Susan B.," *Theatre Arts* 31 (Jul 1947), 17.
24. "Louisville Raises a Crop," *Time* 52 (Dec 20, 1948), 63.
25. "Works of Virgil Thomson," *MQ* 35 (Jan 1949), 115-121.
26. "Recordings," *Mus Guide* (Jan 1949), 4.
27. "Virgil Thomson Wins 1949 Pulitzer Prize," *MA* 69 (May 1949), 37.
28. Glanville-Hicks, Peggy. "Virgil Thomson (with autobiographical sketch and list of works)," *MQ* 35 (1949), 209-225.

29. Sternfield, F. W. "Louisiana Story," *MTNA Studies in Music Education, History and Aesthetics* Ser 43 (1949), 40.

30. Kolodin, Irving. "Music to My Ears," *SR* 33 (Apr 15, 1950), 56.

31. Glanville-Hicks, Peggy. "Colorado College Presents Summer Festival Programs," *MA* 70 (Sep 1950), 12.

32. "Contributors to This Issue," *Score* 4 (Jan 1951), 65.

33. Rosenwald, Hans. "Contemporary Music," *Mus News* 43 (Feb 1951), 10.

34. "Authors in This Issue," *Etude* 69 (Mar 1951), 3.

35. "Made French Legion of Honor Officer," *NYT* (Apr 2, 1951), 27:6.

36. "Music for the Millions," *Time* 57 (Apr 2, 1951), 76.

37. Haggin, Bernard H. "Virgil Thomson as Critic," *Nation* 173 (Sep 22, 1951), 242.

38. Smith, Cecil. "Thomson's Four Saints Live Again on Broadway," *MA* 72 (May 1952), 7.

39. Berger, Arthur. "American Perspective," *SR* 35 (Sep 27, 1952), 58.

40. "The Harvest According," *MA* 72 (Nov 1, 1952), 6.

41. "N Y Music Crix Following Legiters' Lead, Rapping Concerts; Thomson's Blast," *Variety* 189 (Dec 10, 1952), 62.

42. "Virgil Thomson," *Pan Pipes* 45 (Jan 1953), 69.

43. *NYT* (Oct 21, 1953), 26:3; (Feb 3, 1954), 20:3; (Apr 11, 1954), 84:5; (Jul 27, 1954), 18:5; (Oct 25, 1954), 30:7.

44. Haggin, Bernard H. "Music," *Nation* 178 (Feb 20, 1954), 157.

45. "The Relation of Critic to Performing Artist," *MA* 74 (Mar 1954), 14-15.

46. Field, M. G. "Virgil Thomson and the Maturity of American Music," *Chesterian* 28 (Apr 1954), 111-114.

47. Helm, Everett. "Virgil Thomson's Four Saints in Three Acts," *MR* 15 (May 1954), 127-132.

48. "Thomson, 'Peck's Bad Boy' of Music Critics, Seen Leaving N. Y. Herald Tribune," *Variety* 194 (May 12, 1954), 43.

49. "Resigns from New York Herald Tribune," *NYT* (Jul 28, 1954), 28:5.

50. "Tired of Listening," *Time* 64 (Aug 2, 1954), 43.

51. "Virgil Thomson Leads Chamber Orchestra," *MA* 74 (Aug 1954), 4.

52. Haggin, Bernard H. "Resigns as Tribune Critic," *MA* 74 (Aug 1954), 4.

53. Weinstock, Herbert. "V. T. of the H. T." *SR* 37 (Aug 28, 1954), 48.

54. "Thomson Resigns from N. Y. Herald-Tribune," *MC* 150 (Sep 1954), 14.

55. Keats, Sheila. "Reference Articles on American Composers: an Index," *Juilliard Rev* 1 (Fall 1954), 34.

56. Haggin, Bernard H. "Music; Virgil Thomson as a Critic," *Nation* 179 (Dec 4, 1954), 499.

57. Garvin, H. R. "Sound and Sense in Four Saints in Three Acts," *Bucknell Rev* 5, No. 1 (Dec 1954), 1.

58. "Music is Apples," *Variety* 197 (Jan 19, 1955), 71.

59. "Virgil Thomson," *Pan Pipes* 47 (Jan 1955), 69.

60. Goldman, Richard F. "Music Criticism in the U. S.," *Score* 12 (Jun 1955), 86.

61. "Virgil Thomson," *Rev Mus Chilena* 10 (Jul 1955), 29.

62. Bronson, A. "Sharply-Changed Music Crix Scene in N. Y.: Taubman Up, New Downes In," *Variety* 200 (Sep 21, 1955), 73.

63. "Thumb Nail Notes on American Composers," *Mus Tcr* 35 (Mar 1956), 159.

64. Wolf, A. W. "Los Angeles Music Events," *Mus of the West* 11 (May 1956), 18.

65. Kolodin, Irving. "Thomson Novelties," *SR* 39 (May 5, 1956), 34.

66. "Rutgers University Honorary Degree," *NYT* (Jun 7, 1956), 24:7.

67. Ellsworth, Ray. "Americans on Microgroove," *HiFi* 6 (Aug 1956), 61.

68. "Virgil Thomson will Judge European Contests," *MC* 155 (May 1957), 5.

69. "Virgil Thomson," *Composers of the Americas* 3 (1957), 96-119.

70. *NYT* (Feb 16, 1958), 17:3.

71. "Virgil Thomson on the House of Ricordi," *Mus J* 16 (Mar 1958), 16.

72. "Entr'acte American of Ages," *BSCBul* 13 (Jan 21, 1959), 671-675.
73. "Treasurer of National Institute of Arts and Letters," *NYT* (Feb 3, 1959), 33:8.
74. "Power among Men," *MA* 79 (Apr 1959), 34.
75. Howes, Frank, and Peter Heyworth. "Ending the Musical Tradition? Two Comments on Virgil Thomson's 'Modest Proposal'," *Encounter* 12 (May 1959), 53-56.
76. Trimble, Lester. "Music: Composers' Showcase," *Nation* 188 (May 2, 1959), 415.
77. Weill, Irving. "The American Scene Changes," *MM* 6, No. 4 (May 1959), 31.
78. "Much ado about nothing," *Theatre Arts* 43 (Jun 1959), 14-19.
79. "Elected to American Academy of Arts and Letters," *NYT* (Dec 5, 1959), 8:4.
80. *NYT* (Jan 8, 1960), 1:1.
81. Stowe, George W. "Nostalgic Return," *MA* 80 (Jan 15, 1960), 29.
82. "Inducted into American Academy of Arts and Letters," *NYT* (May 26, 1960), 38:6.
83. "Songs for Alice Esty," *MA* 80 (May 1960), 41.
84. Gruen, John. "Thomson Conducts World Première of His Requiem Mass," *MA* 80 (Jun 1960), 17.
85. Bennett, Elsie M. "Virgil Thomson," *School Mus* 32 (Nov 1960), 36.
86. "Named Director of the American Academy, National Institute of Arts and Letters, Dec 3, 1960," *FoF* 21 (1961 Appendix to the Index), 145.
87. "Virgil Thomson Surveys the State of Music in Europe Today," *MA* 81 (Jan 1961), 11.
88. "Music Now," *Opera N* 25 (Mar 11, 1961), 9-11.
89. "Helm, Everett. "Corrections (to Errors of Fact in Article by Virgil Thomson on the State of Music in Europe Today)," *MA* 81 (May 1961), 4.
90. "U. S. Long Hair on Japanese Music," *Variety* 223 (Jun 14, 1961), 48.
91. "Jubilare," *Neue ZFM* 122 (Nov 1961), 477.
92. *NYT* (Dec 7, 1961), 53:1; (Dec 19, 1961), 37:4.
93. "Sophisticate from Missouri," *Time* 78 (Dec 15, 1961), 41.
94. "Collected Poems," *MA* 82 (Feb 1962), 43.
95. Harrison, Lou. "Virgil Thomson," *Mus Mag* 164 (Feb 1962), 22.
96. "Greatest Music Teacher, at Seventy-Five," *NYT* (Feb 4, 1962), sec. 6, p. 24.
97. Sabin, Robert. "Birthday Tribute to Virgil Thomson," *MA* 82 (Feb 1962), 44.
98. Dethier, Jack. "The River (orch suite)," *Am Rec G* 28 (May 1962), 704.
99. ––––––"Five Films and Three Composers," *Am Rec G* 28 (May 1962), 704-707.
100. *NYT* (Jun 4, 1962), 34:4; (Sep 23, 1962), sec. 4, pt. 2, p. 16.
101. Briggs, John. "The Role of the Critic," *Showcase* 41, No. 3 (1962), 7.
102. "Tokio: 1961 forum de la critica musical," *Buenos Aires Mus* 17, No. 276 (1962), 5.
103. "A Solemn Music and a Joyful Fugue," *MA* 83 (Apr 1963), 19.
104. *NYT* (Nov 5, 1963), 24:3.
105. Freeman, John W. "Return of Susan B. Presentation of Mother of Us All at Carnegie Hall," *Opera N* 28 (May 2, 1964), 27.
106. *NYT* (Nov 29, 1964), sec. 2, p. 14:4.
107. Rich, Alan. "Four Saints: Humanity is the Key Word," *HiFi* 15 (Feb 1965), 70-71.
108. Schonberg, Howard C. "Virgil Thomson: Parisian from Missouri," *HiFi R* 14 (May 1965), 43-56.
109. Cook, Eugene. "Virgil Thomson: the Composer in Person (interview)," *HiFi R* 14 (May 1965), 58-61.
110. Hall, David. "A Thomson Discography," *HiFi R* 14 (May 1965), 57.
111. "Virgil Thomson," *MM* 13 (Aug 1965), 15.
112. Flanner, J., ed. "Then and Now (American Creative Minds in Paris)," *Paris R* 9 (Winter 1965), 158-170.
113. "Receives National Institute of Arts and Letters Gold Medal," *NYT* (Feb 15, 1966), 34:2.
114. "Wins National Institute Medal," *FoF* 26 (Feb 15, 1966), 360F3.
115. "The Burning Question–Virgil Thomson Talks to Opera News," *Opera N* 30 (Mar 5, 1966), 8-11.

116. Luten, C. J. "After Thirty-Eight Years, a Landmark: the Thomson Symphony on a Hymn Tune," *Am Rec G* 32 (Mar 1966), 596-597.

117. "Named Andrew Mellon Professor of Music at Carnegie Institute of Technology," *NYT* (Apr 5, 1966), 43:4.

118. Fleming, Shirley. "Brunswick Report: a Carl Ruggles Festival," *HiFi/MA* 16 (Apr 1966), 158.

119. *NYT* (Apr 8, 1966), 26:2; (Oct 9, 1966), sec. 7, p. 5; (Oct 18, 1966), 43:1.

120. Soria, Dorle J. "Artist Life," *HiFi/MA* 16 (Jun 1966), 112.

121. "Biography," *Current Biography* (Oct 1966); *Current Biography Yearbook* (1966), 405-408.

122. Saal, Hubert. "Self-Portrait," *NW* 68 (Nov 7, 1966), 98.

123. McMullen, Roy. "Virgil Thomson's Self Portrait," *HiFi/MA* 16 (Nov 1966), MA21.

124. Evett, Ronald. "Portraitist Portrayed," *New Republic* 155 (Nov 26, 1966), 40-42.

125. Craft, Robert. "Selective Self-Portrait," *Harper* 233 (Dec 1966), 120.

126. "Composer's Components," *HiFi R* 18 (Jan 1967), 67.

127. Ringo, James. "Virgil," *Am Rec G* 33 (Feb 1967), 460-463.

128. Steinberg, Michael. "Musician as Writer," *Commentary* 43 (May 1967), 96-97.

129. Haggin, Bernard H. "Imagined World of Virgil Thomson," *Hudson R* 20 (Winter 1967-1968), 625-635.

130. *NYT* (Jun 30, 1967), 29:1; (Feb 5, 1969), 38:1; (Apr 30, 1969), 40:3; (Nov 2, 1969), sec. 2, p. 19:1; (Dec 12, 1969), 73:1.

131. "Brandeis University Creative Arts Award," *NYT* (Mar 7, 1968), 53:2; (Apr 11, 1968), 42:5.

132. "Shipwreck and Love Scene from Byron's Don Juan," *NYPPN* (Apr 11, 1968), F-1.

133. "Song Cycle Collected Poems (Kenneth Koch)," *NYT* (May 22, 1968), 55:1.

134. "Denies Opera is Dead," *NYT* (Jun 16, 1968), sec. 2, p. 13:1.

135. Clurman, Harold. "In the Air of Several Worlds." *Nation* 203 (Oct 24, 1968), 421-422.

136. *NYT* (Feb 5, 1969), 38:1.

137. "The Music Whirl," *HiFi/MA* 20 (May 1970), MA22-MA23.

138. Smith, Patrick J. *The Tenth Muse*, reviewed by Virgil Thomson, *NYT* (Oct 4, 1970), sec. 7, p. 6.

139. *NYT* (Mar 21, 1971), sec. 2, p. 15:1; (Oct 14, 1971), 54:1; (Oct 24, 1971), sec. 2, p. 13:5; (Nov 14, 1971), 79:4; (Nov 15, 1971), 52:5; (Nov 18, 1971), 57:3; 59:1, 3.

140. "Tribute to I. Stravinsky on His Death," *NYT* (Apr 7, 1971), 49:1.

141. Stevenson, Florence. "A Continuous Present," *Opera N* 35 (Apr 10, 1971), 8-13.

142. "Names, Dates, and Places," *Opera N* 35 (Apr 10, 1971), 4-5.

143. "An Interview with Virgil Thomson, Seventy-Five Years Sassy," *Sym News* 22, No. 6 (1971), 5-6.

144. Rossi, Nick. "Virgil Thomson at 75," *Mus J* 29 (Nov 1971), 11-12.

145. "New York University Honorary Degree," *NYT* (Nov 19, 1971), 51:3.

146. Sargeant, Winthrop. "Musical Events: Birthday Concert Performed by Clarion Music Society in Alice Tully Hall," *New Yorker* 47 (Nov 27, 1971), 97-98.

147. Smith, Patrick J. "Musician of the Month," *HiFi/MA* 21 (Nov 1971), MA8-MA9.

148. "Virgilian Knack," *Time* 98 (Dec 6, 1971), 84.

149. "Homage," *New Yorker* 47 (Dec 25, 1971), 39.

150. Heinsheimer, Hans. "New York: 'Phantasium in einem Rathskeller'," *NZ* 132 (Dec 1971), 661-663.

151. *NYT* (Jan 9, 1972), sec. 2, p. 15:1; (Apr 28, 1972), 34:1.

152. "People are Talking about . . .," *Vogue* 159 (Apr 15, 1972), 86-87.

153. Luten, C. J. "Thomson at Seventy-Five," *Opera N* 36 (Apr 15, 1972), 12-13.

154. Heinsheimer, Hans. "A Well-Tempered Composer: Birthday Greeting for Virgil Thomson," *ASCAP* 5, No. 3 (1972), 14-17.

155. "A Virgil Thomson Festival," *Mus Club Mag* 51, No. 3 (1972), 17.

156. "Sneden's Landing Variations," *HiFi/MA* 22 (Aug 1972), MA13.
157. "ACDA Salutes Virgil Thomson," *Choral J* 13, No. 7 (1973), 1.
158. "Church and Secular Music," *NYT* (Jun 4, 1972), sec. 7, p. 4; (Apr 14, 1973), 18:6.
159. Gold, Arthur, and Robert Fizdale. "Fond Surprises from Virgil Thomson," *Vogue* 162 (Aug 1973), 110-111.
160. Soria, Dorle J. "Artist Life," *HiFi/MA* 24 (Aug 1974), MA6-MA7.
161. *NYT* (Oct 27, 1974), sec. 2, p. 1:1; (Nov 17, 1974), sec. 2, p. 19:1.
162. Fisher, Fred. "Contemporary American Style: How Three Representative Composers Use the 'Row'," *Clavier* 14, No. 4 (1975), 34-37.
163. Tucker, Marilyn. "Forest Meadows: Some Honest Anwers; a New Summer Session Gives Teen-Age Musicians a Taste of the Profession," *HiFi/MA* 25 (Apr 1975), MA24-MA25.
164. "Toland, William M., and Barbara B. Lundeen. "Concord's Bicentennial Salute to the Performing Arts," *Mus Ed J* 62 (Apr 1976), 51-54.
165. "Film Music," *Stereo R* 37 (Jul 1976), 83.
166. Smith, Rollin. "American Organ Composers," *MusicAGO* 10 (Jul 1976), 42.
167. Dulman, Martin. "Independent Spirit," (an interview) *Opera N* 41 (Jul 1976), 16-18.
168. Potter, K. "York Festival (80th Birthday Celebration)," *Mus & Mus* 25 (Nov 1976), 64.
169. "Virgil Thomson, Richard Rodgers Receive National Music Awards," *Mus Trades* 125 (Jan 1977), 44.
170. Freedman, Guy. "Everbest, Virgil Thomson," *Mus J* 35 (Mar 1977), 8-10.
171. "Les comptes d'Orphée," *Rev Mus* 306-307 (1977), 87-106 (reprint from *Contrepoints* 5 (1946), 17-45.
172. Livingstone, W. "Classical Roto," *Stereo R* 41 (Nov 1978), 147.
173. "Yale Music Library Receives Thomson Papers," *Notes* 36, No. 1 (1979), 78.

References to Works by Virgil Thomson

The number preceding the title indicates the number of the composition as listed in Section II.

14. Acadian Songs and Dances: *MM* 14 (Sep 1965), 44; *CohCT*, 205; *EweWT*.
76. Agnus Dei: *Mus News* 43 (Apr 1951), 25.
31. At the Beach: *Notes* 22 (1965-1966), 1102.
123. At the Spring: *MA* 79 (Dec 15, 1959), 23.
24. Autumn: *Harp N* 3, No. 10 (1964), 2; *Intam Mus B* 45 (Jan 1965), 2.
44. Barcarolle for Woodwinds: *MC* 143 (May 15, 1951), 29; *Notes* 9 (Dec 1951), 166.
115. La Belle en Dormant: *Notes* 8 (Jun 1951), 580-581; *MA* 71 (Jul 1951), 30.
98. Cantata on Poems of Edward Lear: *NYT* (Apr 30, 1975), 24:1.
78. Capital, Capitals: *MQ* 40 (1954), 415, 471; *CohCT*, 210; *MelMN*, 208.
20. Concerto for Flute, Harp, Strings, Percussion: *POPN* (Feb 10, 1956), 471; *MQ* 42 (1956), 389; *SFSPN* (Feb 12, 1958), 363; *MC* 157 (Apr 1958), 45; *LsvlOPN* (Feb 1, 1966); *Am Rec G* 33 (Nov 1966), 221; *EweWT*.
17. Concerto for Violoncello and Orchestra: *MC* 141 (Apr 15, 1950), 3; *Chesterian* 25 (Oct 1950), 49; *MA* 73 (Jan 1, 1953), 24; *Notes* 10 (Jun 1953), 482-483; *Strad* 84 (Aug 1973), 225; *CohCT*, 206; *EweWT*.
94. Dance in Praise: *MA* 83 (Feb 1963), 16.
60. Eccentric Dance: *CohCT*, 209.
65. Fanfare: *CohCT*, 208.
28. Fantasy in Homage to an Earlier England: *Mus Leader* 98 (Jun 1966), 23; *MT* 107 (Jul 1966), 618; *HiFi/MA* 16 (Aug 1966), MA9; *PitSPN* (Sep 30, 1966), 67; *Mus Leader* 98 (Dec 1966), 22.
49. Feast of Love: *MA* 84 (Dec 1964), 64; *MQ* 51 (1965), 411; *POPN* (Dec 6, 1968), 19-25; *NYT* (Dec 11, 1968), 50:7; *HiFi/MA* 19 (Mar 1969), 30; *Mus & Artists* 2, No. 1 (1969), 36; *Intam Mus B* 72 (Jul 1969), 70.

6. Filling Station: *MQ* 34 (1948), 8; *CohCT*, 212; *EweWT*.

102. Five Phrases from "The Song of Solomon": *MQ* 38 (1952), 596; *Notes* 12 (Mar 1955, 333.

122. Five Songs from William Blake: *MC* 145 (Mar 15, 1952), 14; *POPN* (Oct 10, 1952), 50-53; *Notes* 12 (Dec 1954), 154; *MQ* 41 (1955), 77; *MA* 81 (Dec 1961), 44; *NATS* 23, No. 3 (1967), 16; *NYT* (Jan 15, 1968); *MelMN*, 212; *SteHS*, 442.

136. Four Saints in Three Acts: *NYT* (Dec 31, 1933), sec. 9, p. 8:3; (Jan 21, 1934), sec. 10, p. 6:8; (Feb 9, 1934), 22:1; (Feb 18, 1934), sec. 9, p. 2:1; (Feb 21, 1934), 22:3; (Feb 23, 1934), 22:6; (Feb 25, 1934), sec. 9, p. 6:1, p. 8:1; (Feb 27, 1934), 18:4; (Mar 1, 1934), 22:7; (Mar 4, 1934), sec. 9, p. 18:6; (Apr 3, 1934), 27:1; (Apr 11, 1934), 24:2; (Nov 9, 1934), 24:2; *Lit Dgt* 117 (Feb 3, 1934), 21; (Mar 10, 1934), 22; *NW* 3 (Feb 17, 1934), 37-38; *New Republic* 78 (Feb 21, 1934), 48; (Mar 7, 1934), 105; (Apr 11, 1934), 246; *Commonweal* 19 (Feb 23, 1934), 452; (Mar 9, 1934), 525; *Nation* 138 (Feb 28, 1934), 256-258; (Apr 4, 1934), 396; *MA* 54 (Feb 1934), 7, 17; (Aug 1934), 12; *SR* 10 (Mar 3, 1934), 519; (Mar 24, 1934), 572; *Amer Mag Art* 27 (Apr 1934), 211; *Catholic World* 139 (Apr 1934), 87-88; *Theatre Arts* 18 (Apr 1934), 246-248; *American Mercury* 32 (May 1934), 104-108; *NYT* (May 28, 1941), 32:3; *New Yorker* 17 (Jun 7, 1941), 67; *NYT* (May 25 (1947), sec. 2, p. 9:5; *Gramophone* 26 (Jan 1949), 125; *MC* 139 (Mar 1, 1949), 23; *Notes* 6 (Mar 1949), 328-330; *MA* 69 (May 1949), 36; *ML* 30 (Jul 1949), 290-291; *MQ* 35 (1949), 210, 217; *MR* 10 (Nov 1949), 314; *Time* 59 (Apr 28, 1952), 42; *New Yorker* 28 (Apr 26, 1952), 121-122; *NW* 39 (Apr 28, 1952), 52; *Nation* 174 (May 3, 1952), 437; *SR* 35 (May 3, 1952), 33; *New Leader* 35 (May 5, 1952), 27; *Int Mus* 50 (May 1952), 37; *Commonweal* 56 (May 9, 1952), 116; *MA* 72 (May 1952), 7; *NYT* (May 31, 1952); *Catholic World* 175 (Jun 1952), 228; *Theatre Arts* 36 (Jun 1952), 19; *Sch & Society* 75 (Jun 21, 1952), 393; *Opera* 3 (Jul 1952), 398; *MR* 15, No. 2 (May 1954), 127-132; *HiFi* 4 (Jul 1954), 50; *MA* 74 (Aug 1954), 14; *Bucknell Rev* 5, No. 1 (Dec 1954), 1; *Amer Rec G* 31 (Feb 1965), 518-519, 521-522; *HiFi/MA* 15 (Feb 1965), 70; *HiFi R* 14 (Mar 1965), 64-67; *Opera N* 29 (Apr 3, 1965), 34; *MM* 13 (Aug 1965), 29; *NYT* (Apr 26, 1970), 19:1; *Opera N* 35 (Oct 10, 1970), 23; *NYT* (Jan 16, 1972), 65:5; (Dec 15, 1972), 60:2; (Dec 22, 1972), 17:1; *Opera N* 36 (Feb 19, 1972), 32; *HiFi/MA* 22 (Apr 1972), MA31; (Jun 1972), MA20; *NYT* (Feb 15, 1973), 50:1; (Feb 18, 1973), sec. 2, p. 17:1; (Feb 24, 1973), 17:1; *Opera N* 37 (Feb 17, 1973), 10-13; *New Yorker* 49 (Mar 3, 1973), 102-103; *SR* 1 (Mar 24, 1973), 105; *Opera N* 37 (Apr 7, 1973), 22-23; *Mus J* 31 (Apr 1973), 55; *SR Sci* 1 (Apr 1973), 105; *Mus & Mus* 21 (May 1973), 56; *Opernwelt* 5 (May 1973), 24-26; *HiFi/MA* 23 (Jun 1973), MA12-MA13; 28 (Mar 1978), MA23; *EweCB*, 436; *HitMU*, 203; *HowOC*, 261; *MacIC*, 543; *MelMN*, 208.

121. Four Songs to Poems of Thomas Campion: *NYT* (Feb 12, 1952), 22:2; *Notes* 12 (Dec 1954), 154.

95. The Holly and the Ivy: *MA* 79 (Dec 15, 1959), 23.

138. Lord Byron: *NYT* (Nov 28, 1965), sec. 2, p. 13:4; (Oct 21, 1968), 59:5; *SR* 52 (Nov 22, 1969), 61; *HiFi/MA* 20 (Jan 1970), MA12; *Intam Mus B* 75-76 (Jan-Mar 1970), 64; *NYT* (Mar 14, 1972), 50:1; (Apr 9, 1972), sec. 2, p. 17:4; (Apr 16, 1972), sec. 8, p. 1:4; (Apr 22, 1972), 38:2; *New Yorker* 48 (Apr 29, 1972), 106; *Time* 99 (May 1, 1972), 67; *New Republic* 166 (May 6, 1972), 23-24; *Variety* 266 (May 10, 1972), 81; *SR* 55 (May 20, 1972), 21; *R Mus Ital* 6, No. 2 (1972), 256-258; *Opera* 23 (Jun 1972), 518-520; *Opera N* 36 (Jun 1972), 23-24; *HiFi/MA* 22 (Jul 1972), MA11; *Opernwelt* 7 (Jul 1972), 22; *MT* 113 (Jul 1972), 689; *ASCAP* 6, No. 1 (1972), 32; *Pan Pipes* 65, No. 2 (1973), 24-26; *NYT* (Dec 17, 1975), 67:3.

13. Louisiana Story: *MA* 68 (Dec 15, 1948), 28; *NYPPN* (Jan 29, 1949); *MQ* 35 (1949), 115-121, 220; *MTNA* Ser. 43 (1949), 40; *Variety* 174 (May 2, 1949), 2; *Mus Survey* 2 (Autumn 1949), 101-102; *Mus Club Mag* 29 (Dec 1949), 16; *BSCBul* 23 (Apr 21, 1950), 1260; *Mus Survey* 2 (Winter 1950), 188-189; *Notes* 8 (Dec 1950), 130-131;

13. Louisiana Story (cont.): *POPN* (Jan 11, 1952), 334-336; *EweCB*, 438; *MacIC*, 543; *Mel-MN*, 216; *EweWT*.

77. Missa Brevis No. 1: *MQ* 34 (1948), 10.

80. Missa Brevis No. 2: *MA* 80 (Nov 1960), 63; *MC* 162 (Dec 1960), 34; *MA* 71 (Aug 1951), 18.

93. Missa pro defunctis: *MA* 80 (Jun 1960), 17; *MQ* 47 (1961), 400-407; *New Yorker* 38 (May 19, 1962), 183-184; *SR* 45 (May 26, 1962), 39; *MA* 82 (Jul 1962), 24; *EweWT*; *MelMN*, 214; *YatTC*, 107.

72. De profundis: *Notes* 9 (Jun 1950), 494.

137. Mother of Us All: *NYT* (Apr 17, 1947), 34:4; (May 8, 1947), 30:1; *New Yorker* 23 (May 17, 1947), 103; *NW* 29 (May 19, 1947), 94; *Time* 49 (May 19, 1947), 47; *Commonweal* 46 (May 30, 1947), 167; *Nation* 164 (May 31, 1947), 667; *New Republic* 116 (Jun 2, 1947), 33; *Theatre Arts* 31 (Jul 1947), 17; *School & Society* 66 (Jul 26, 1947), 67; *MR* 10 (Feb 1949), 70-71; *MQ* 35 (1949), 210, 219; *NYPPN* (Apr 2, 1950); *NYT* (Apr 15, 1956), sec. 2, p. 7; (Apr 17, 1956); *Nation* 182 (May 19, 1956), 438; *MA* 76 (May 1956), 23; *MC* 153 (Jun 1956), 35; *Opera* 7 (Jul 1956), 423; *Commonweal* 64 (Sep 28, 1956), 634; *Opera* 14 (Jun 1963), 396; *NYT* (Apr 1, 1964), 42:1; *Opera N* 28 (May 2, 1964), 27; *MA* 84 (May 1964), 29; *NYT* (Jan 29, 1967), 67:2; *Opera N* 31 (Mar 25, 1967), 32; *NYT* (Aug 2, 1971), 12:1; *Opera N* 36 (Sep 1971), 23; *NYT* (Nov 28, 1971), 82:5; *HiFi/MA* 21 (Nov 1971), MA10-MA11; *NYT* (Jul 3, 1972), 7:5; (Nov 27, 1972), 43:1; *Opera N* 37 (Jan 20, 1973), 25; *HiFi/MA* 23 (Mar 1973), MA28; (Dec 1973), MA18; *Opera N* 38 (Jun 1974), 32; *NYT* (Dec 14, 1975), 73:4; *Opera N* 40 (May 1976), 41; *Wall St J* 56 (Aug 13, 1976), 6; *Time* 108 (Aug 23, 1976), 37; *HiFi/MA* 26 (Sep 1976), MA26; *Opera N* 41 (Sep 1976), 67; *Opera* 27 (Sep 1976), 848; *Opernwelt* 10 (Oct 1976), 37; *Opera N* 41 (Nov 1976), 88; *HiFi/MA* 26 (Dec 1976), MA21-MA23; *Opera* 27 (Dec 1976), 1137-1141; *Stereo R* 38 (Jun 1977), 89-90; *HiFi/MA* 27 (Jul 1977), 92-94; *Am Rec G* 40 (Aug 1977), 30; *Opera N* 42 (Apr 8, 1978), 72; *EweCB*, 437; *EweWT*; *MacIC*, 543; *MelMN*, 211; *YatTC*, 106.

134. My Crow Pluto: *MA* 84 (Feb 1964), 34.

82. My Shepherd Will Supply My Need: *Choir G* 2 (May-Jun 1949), 39; *Notes* 11 (Jun 1954), 439; *CohCT*, 211.

97. The Nativity as Sung by the Shepherds: *Am Choral R* 9, No. 4 (1967), 53.

63. Nine Etudes for Piano: *Notes* 12 (1954-1955), 329; *HiFi/MA* 17 (Feb 1967), MA11.

70. Pange lingua: *Diap* 54 (Feb 1963), 23; *MA* 83 (Feb 1963), 23; *Am Org* 46 (Feb 1963), 14; *Mus J* 21 (Feb 1963), 98.

64. Pastorale on a Christmas Plainsong: *CohCT*, 208.

4. The Plow that Broke the Plains: *MQ* 35 (1949), 115, 116, 210, 221; *MQ* 39 (1952), 308-310; *Am Rec G* 28 (May 1962), 704; *EweWT*; *HitMU*, 205; *MelMN*, 216.

46. Portraits (vln, pno): *MM* 23, No. 2 (Spring 1946), 124; *MC* 143 (Feb 15, 1951), 66.

62. Portraits (pno): *Mus Club Mag* 28 (Jan-Feb 1949), 15; *MA* 69 (Feb 1949), 291; *MC* 142 (Nov 1, 1950), 29; *MA* 70 (Nov 15, 1950), 30; *Notes* 8 (Dec 1950), 137; *Mus Club Mag* 30 (Feb 1951), 19; *Rev Mus* 212 (1952), 16; *MA* 73 (Dec 15, 1953), 24; *Canon* 7 (Dec 1953-Jan 1954), 220; *MR* 16 (Aug 1955), 269.

130. Praises and Prayers: *MA* 83 (Nov 1963), 98.

104. Presciosilla: *MC* 139 (Jan 1, 1949), 31.

124. Remember Adam's Fall: *MA* 79 (Dec 15, 1959), 23.

5. The River: *MQ* 35 (1949), 116, 210, 222; *MQ* 37 (1951), 161; *HitMU*, 205; *MelMN*, 216.

19. Sea Piece with Birds: *Buffalo Phil* (Mar 19, 1967), 12.

12. The Seine at Night: *MQ* 34 (1948), 413-415; *MQ* 35 (1949), 220; *MC* 141 (May 1, 1950), 28.

40. Serenade for Flute and Violin: *MA* 72 (Nov 15, 1952), 26; *MC* 146 (Nov 15, 1952), 31; *Notes* 10 (Dec 1952), 144; *HiFi/MA* 23 (Sep 1973), 96.

22. Six Chorale Preludes by Brahms: *NYT* (Oct 30, 1957), 25:1.
     Six Pieces for Birds: *Mus Opin* 78 (Mar 1955), 351; *Notes* 13 (Dec 1955), 130.
     Shipwreck and Love Scene: *NYT* (Apr 12, 1968), 42:1.
 30. A Solemn Music: *Int Mus* 48 (Jul 1949), 15; *MQ* 35 (1949), 619; *MQ* 36 (1950), 594;
     Notes 7 (Jun 1950), 440; *MQ* 41 (1955), 407; *CohCT*, 206; *EweWT*; *MelMN*, 213.
 33. Sonata da chiesa: *MQ* 35 (1949), 211; *HitMU*, 202; *MelMN*, 206.
 59. Sonata for Piano No. 4: *CohCT*, 207.
 38. Sonata for Violin and Piano No. 1: *MA* 75 (Dec 15, 1955), 27.
143. Spanish Earth: *MQ* 35 (1949), 116.
116. Stabat Mater: *MQ* 40 (1954), 471, 475; 41 (1955), 475; *CohCT*, 210.
 41. String Quartet No. 2: *MQ* 41 (1955), 551-555; *CohCT*, 209.
  2. Symphony on a Hymn Tune: *MQ* 18 (1932), 12; 35 (1949), 214; *Notes* 13 (Dec 1955),
     130; *MA* 76 (Nov 1, 1956), 24; *SFSPN* (Feb 12, 1958), 365; *Am Rec G* 32 (Mar
     1966), 596; *EweWT*; *HitMU*, 202, 207; *MelMN*, 215.
  3. Symphony No. 2: *MQ* 35 (1949), 215; *NYPPN* (Nov 30, 1950); *MA* 70 (Dec 15, 1950),
     32; *Notes* 13 (Dec 1955), 130.
 52. Synthetic Waltzes: *Mus Club Mag* 28 (Jan-Feb 1949), 15; *MA* 69 (Feb 1949), 293; *Musicology* 2 (Apr 1949), 317.
 61. Ten Etudes for Piano: *MQ* 40 (1954), 629.
 75. Three Antiphonal Psalms: *CohCT*, 211.
     Three Pictures for Orchestra: *CinSPN* (Jan 8, 1954), 329-335; *POPN* (Jan 22, 1954), 401;
     HiFi/MA 22 (Feb 1972), MA23.
 74. Tribulationes civitatum: *Notes* 9 (Jun 1952), 494.
 11. Tuesday in November: *MQ* 35 (1949), 116; *HitMU*, 205.
138. Two Songs from "Lord Byron": *NYT* (Nov 7, 1969).
 68. Variations and Fugues on Sunday School Tunes: *Diap* 45 (Nov 1, 1954), 34; *CohCT*, 208;
     HanIT, 334; *HitMU*, 202; *MelMN*, 208.
 14. Walking Song: *Mus Opin* 76 (Mar 1953), 353.
 15. Wheatfield at Noon: *MC* 139 (Jan 15, 1949), 16; *MA* 69 (Feb 1949), 367; *NYPPN* (Mar
     24, 1949); *MQ* 37 (1951), 255; *Mus Opin* 78 (Mar 1955), 351; *MQ* 41 (1955), 77;
     Notes 13 (Dec 1955), 130.

Dissertations about Virgil Thomson and His Works

1. Anagnost, Dean Z. *The Choral Music of Virgil Thomson*. Columbia University, 1977.
2. Arlton, Dean L. *American Piano Sonatas of the Twentieth Century: Selective Analyses and
    Annotated Index*. Columbia University, 1968.
3. Greer, Thomas H. *Music and Its Relation to Futurism, Cubism, Dadaism, and Surrealism,
    1905 to 1950*. North Texas State University, 1969.
4. Prindl, Frank J. *A Study of Ten Original Compositions for Band Published in America Since
    1946*. Florida State University, 1956.
5. Rickert, Lawrence G. *Selected American Song Cycles for Baritone Composed Since 1945*.
    University of Illinois, 1965.
6. Sahr, Hadassah Gallup. *Performance and Analytic Study of Selected Piano Music by American Composers*. Columbia University, 1969.
7. Service, Alfred R., Jr. *A Study of the Cadence as a Factor in Musical Intelligibility in Selected Piano Sonatas by American Composers*. State University of Iowa, 1958.

GENERAL BIBLIOGRAPHY

Books

General histories of music are not included in the following bibliography. Books devoted to one composer are listed in the bibliography at the end of each Outline.

1. AbrHY   Abraham, Gerald. **A Hundred Years of Music**, 3rd edition. Chicago: Aldine Publishing Co., 1964, 1967. (Barber, Copland, Harris, Schuman)

2. AbrMM   Abraham, Gerald. **This Modern Music**, 3rd edition. London: Gerald Duckworth, 1955. (Barber, Copland, Cowell, Piston, Schuman)

3. ACA-Bul   **American Composers Alliance Bulletin.** New York: American Composers Alliance, 1951. (Avshalomov, Vol. III, No. 3; Becker IX/1; Berger III/1; Berlinski VIII/3; Binkerd X/3; Carter III/2; Cazden VIII/2; Chou Wen-chung IX/4; Clarke IX/3; Cowell III/4, X/2; Donovan V/4; Fine VII/1; Flanagan IX/4; Franco VIII/3; Gerschefski X/1; Gideon VII/4; Glanville-Hicks IV/1; Goeb II/2; L. Harrison IX/2; Haufrecht VIII/4; Hovhaness II/3; Ives IV/3; Johnson VIII/4; Kahn IX/2; Kay VII/1; Kerr VIII/2; Kohs VI/1; Lockwood VI/4; Luening III/3; McBride VII/1; Overton X/4; Perle X/3; Pinkham X/1; Pisk IX/1; Porter VII/3; Riegger II/1, IX/3; Scott VI/2; Stevens IV/2; Verall VII/4; Ward IV/4; Weber V/2; Weisgall VII/2; Weiss VII/3)

4. ACAM   **American Composers on American Music**, 2nd edition. New York: Frederick Ungar, 1962.

5. AndCAC   Anderson, E. Ruth. **Contemporary American Composers: a Biographical Dictionary.** Boston: G. K. Hall, 1976. (Identifies over 6,000 American composers born since 1870, including a separate listing of women composers)

6. AntBB   Antheil, George. **Bad Boy of Music.** Garden City, NY: Doubleday, Doran, 1945. (Antheil, Brant, Copland, Gershwin, Harris, Sesssions, Thomson, Weill)

7. ASC-BD   **The ASCAP Biographical Dictionary of Composers, Authors and Publishers**, 3rd edition. New York: The American Society of Composers, Authors and Publishers, 1966.

8. ASC-SC   **ASCAP Symphonic Catalog**, 3rd edition. New York: R. R. Bowker Co., 1977. (Includes instrumentation, duration, publisher)

9. AusMT   Austin, William W. **Music in the 20th Century from Debussy through Stravinsky.** New York: W. W. Norton, 1966. (Antheil, Babbitt, Barber, Berger, Bernstein, Cage, Carpenter, Carter, Copland, Cowell, Creston, Dello Joio, Diamond, Gershwin, Hanson, Harris, Hovhaness, Ives, Kirchner, Mennin, Moore, Partch, Persichetti, Piston, Riegger, Rochberg, Rogers, Ruggles, Schuller, Schuman, Sessions, Sowerby, Still, Thompson, Thomson, Ussachevsky, Varèse, Ben Weber and many others)

10. BacMM   Bacharach, Alfred Louis, ed. **The Music Masters**, vol 4. Cassel: 1954. (Barber, Copland, Harris, Schuman)

11. BakSL   Bakeless, Katherine Little. **Story-Lives of American Composers.** New York: J. B. Lippincott, 1953. (Barber, Carpenter, Copland, Gershwin, Griffes, Harris, Ives, Piston, Schuman and others)

12. Baker   Baker, Theodore. **Biographical Dictionary of Musicians**, 6th edition, revised by Nicolas Slonimsky. New York: Schirmer Books, 1978.

13. BarMA   Barzun, Jacques. **Music in American Life.** Bloomington: Indiana University Press, 1965. (Cage, Cowell, Gershwin, Ives, McBride, Riegger, Sessions, Thompson, Thomson, Varèse)

14. BasSM   Basart, Ann Phillips. **Serial Music; a Classified Bibliography of Writings on Twelve-Tone and Electronic Music.** Berkeley: University of California Press, 1961.

15. BauTC   Bauer, Marion. **Twentieth Century Music.** New York: G. P. Putnam, 1947. (Antheil, Barber, Bauer, Bennett, Berezowsky, Bergsma, Bernstein, Blitzstein, Cage, Carpenter, Copland, Cowell, Dello Joio, Foss, Gershwin, Gruenberg, Hanson, Harris, Ives, Jacobi, Moore, Piston, Riegger, Rogers, Ruggles, Schuman, Sessions, Sowerby, Thompson, Thomson, Varèse and many others)

16.   BecMC   Beckwith, John, and Udo Karemets, eds. **The Modern Composer and His World.** Toronto: University of Toronto Press, 1961. (Luening, pp. 127, 129, 132; Rochberg, pp. 56, 74; Schuller, pp. 37, 45, 97; Varèse, pp. 126, 130)

17.   BIM   **Bio-Bibliographical Index of Musicians in the United States of America from Colonial Times**, 2nd edition. Washington, D. C.: Music Section, Pan-American Union, 1956.

18.   BloYA   Bloom, Julius, ed. **The Year in American Music: September 1946-May 1947.** Also 1947-1948, edited by David Ewen (EweYA).

19.   BluPC   Blume, Friedrich. **Protestant Church Music, A History.** New York: W. W. Norton, 1974. (Barber, Copland, Cowell, Hanson, Harris, Ives, Schuman, Sessions, Thompson)

20.   BMI-C   **BMI Composers Participating in the American Symphony Orchestra League** (1961 Convention; Philadelphia, Jun 21-24). New York: Broadcast Music Inc., 1961. (Carter, Wen-Chung, Cowell, Dello Joio, Etler, Evett, Goeb, Harris, Kay, Overton, Parris, Pinkham, Piston, Schuller, Schuman, Surinach, Trimble, Ward, Weber) (Includes brief biographies, selected lists of works, duration)

21.   BMI-MW   **BMI: The Many Worlds of Music.** New York: Broadcast Music Inc. (a bulletin prepared by BMI Public Relations Department)

22.   BMI-OP   **BMI Orchestral Program Survey**, 1967-1968 season. New York: Broadcast Music Inc. (Includes composers of all nationalities, list of composers and works most performed)

23.   BMI-P   **Broadcast Music, Inc.** New York. A series of pamphlets, each devoted to a single composer. (list of music includes publisher, instrumentation, duration)

24.   BMI-SC   **BMI Symphonic Catalogue.** New York: Broadcast Music Inc., 1963. (Includes BMI composers of all nationalities, lists of compositions, publishers, instrumentation, duration)

25.   BriNM   Brindle, Reginald Smith. **The New Music: the Avante-Garde Since 1945.** New York: Oxford University Press, 1975.

26.   BroOH   Brockway, Howard, and Herbert Weinstock. **The Opera: A History of its Creation and Performances, 1600-1941.** New York: Simon & Schuster, 1941. (Antheil, Blitzstein, Copland, Gershwin, Gruenberg, Hanson, Menotti, Taylor, Thomson)

27.   BrooCG   Brook, Donald. **Composers' Gallery.** London: Rockliff, 1946. (Copland, Harris)

28.   Bull   Bull, Storm. **Index to Biographies of Contemporary Composers.** New York: The Scarecrow Press, 1964. (Includes foreign sources and a summary of the contents of the reference books used)

29.   CatPC   **Catalog of Published Concert Music by American Composers**, 2nd edition, Angelo Eagon, ed. Metuchen, NJ: Scarecrow Press, 1969.

30.   ChaAC   Chase, Gilbert, ed. **The American Composer Speaks.** Baton Rouge: Louisiana State University Press, 1966. (Babbitt, Barber, Berger, E. Brown, Cage, Carpenter, Carter, Copland, Cowell, Flanagan, Gershwin, Hamm, Harris, Ives, Moore, Partch, Piston, Ruggles, Schuller, Schuman, Sessions, Thomson, Varèse and others)

31.   ChaAM   Chase, Gilbert. **America's Music**, 2nd edition. New York: McGraw-Hill, 1966. (Antheil, Babbitt, Barber, Becker, Berger, Bernstein, Blitzstein, Brant, Brown, Cage, Carpenter, Carter, Chou Wen-Chung, Copland, Cowell, Creston, Dello Joio, Diamond, Fine, Finney, Foss, Gershwin, Hadley, Haieff, Hanson, Harris, Harrison, Hill, Hovhaness, Imbrie, Ives, Kirchner, Luening, Menotti, Moore, Partch, Perle, Piston, Pinkham, Riegger, Rogers, Ruggles, Schuman, Sessions, Shapero, Shapey, Still, Swanson, Thompson, Thomson, Varèse, Ward, Weisgall, Weiss and many others)

32.   ClaBD   Claghorn, Charles E. **Biographical Dictionary of American Music.** West Nyack, NY: Parker Publishing Co., 1973.

33.   ClaEA   Clarke, Garry E. **Essays on American Music.** Westport, CT: Greenwood Press, 1977. (Cage, Carter, Copland, Cowell, Hanson, Harris, Hill, Ives, Luening, Moore, Piston, Ruggles, Schuman, Sessions, Thomson, Varèse, Webern)

34.   CobCS   Cobbett, Walter W., ed. **Cobbett's Cyclopedic Survey of Chamber Music**, 2nd edition. London: Oxford University Press, 1963. (Vol. III, pp. 152-191, "Chamber Music in America" by Nicolas Slonimsky: Antheil, Barber, Becker, Berger, Bergsma, Bernstein, Blackwood, Cage, Carter, Clarke, Copland, Cowell, Ruth Crawford, Creston, Dello Joio, Diamond, Feldman, Fine, Finney, Foss, Harris, Hovhaness, Imbrie, Ives, Jacobi, Kirchner, Kohs, Lees, Mennin, Moore, Palmer, Perle, Persichetti, Piston, Porter, Read, Riegger, Rochberg, Rogers, Schuller, Schuman, Sessions, Shapero, H. Stevens, Thompson, Thomson, Varèse, Verall, Weber, Weiss and others)

35.   CohCT   Cohn, Arthur. **The Collector's Twentieth-Century Music in the Western Hemisphere.** New York: J. B. Lippincott, 1961. (Selected records with comments: Barber, Carter, Copland, Cowell, Creston, Dello Joio, Fine, Foss, Hanson, Harris, Hovhaness, Ives, Kirchner, Menotti, Piston, Riegger, Schuman, Sessions, Shapero, Thomson, Varèse, Weber)

36.   ColHM   Collaer, Paul. **A History of Modern Music,** tr. from French by Sally Abeles. New York: Grosset & Dunlap, 1963. (Brief references to Antheil, Barber, Cage, Carter, Copland, Gershwin, Harris, Harrison, Ives, Menotti, Moore, Piston, Schuman, Sessions, Still, Thomson, Tansman, Varèse, Weill)

37.   ComA   **Composers of the Americas** (Compositores de América), 12 vols. to date. Washington, D. C.: Pan American Union, 1955– (Barber, vol. 5; Bergsma, 6; Bernstein, 6; Blitzstein, 5; Brant, 6; Cage, 8; Carter, 5; Copland, 1; Cowell, 2; Crawford-Seeger, 2; Creston, 4; Dello Joio, 9; Evett, 10; Fine, 6; Finney, 11; Fletcher, 7; Foss, 7; Gould, 6; Hanson, 5; Harrison, 8; Hovhaness, 11; Ives, 2; Kay, 7; Kirchner, 7; La Montaine, 9; Luening, 7; McBride, 9; Mennin, 5; Parris, 10; Partch, 5; Piston, 4; Porter, 4; Powell, 9; Read, 8; Riegger, 7; Rochberg, 10; Rogers, 10; Schuller, 10; Schuman, 5; Stevens, 11; Still, 5; Thomson, 3; Trimble, 10; Ussachevsky, 9; Vincent, 8; Waldrop, 6; Ward, 9; Weber, 9; Yardumian, 11) (Includes biographical data, lists of compositions with date, duration, publisher)

38.   CopCM   Copland, Aaron. **Copland on Music,** 2nd edition. New York: W. W. Norton, 1963. 1976. (pp. 141-178: brief mention of many composers from 1926-1959; pp. 228-241: Wolpe, Kirchner, Schuman, Thomson)

39.   CopMI   Copland, Aaron. **Music and Imagination.** Cambridge: Harvard University Press, 1961. (pp. 85-102; 111-113: Ives)

40.   CopON   Copland, Aaron. **Our New Music.** New York: McGraw-Hill, 1941. (Bauer, Blitzstein, Carpenter, Carter, Copland, Gershwin, Gould, Gruenberg, Harris, Ives, Jacobi, Piston, Sessions, Taylor, Thompson, Thomson, Varèse)

41.   CopTN   Copland, Aaron. **The New Music, 1900-1960.** New York: W. W. Norton, 1968 (revised and enlarged edition of **Our New Music).** (Antheil, Babbitt, Barber, Brant, Cage, Carpenter, Carter, Copland, Cowell, Foss, Gershwin, Gruenberg, Harris, Ives, Jacobi, Moore, Piston, Riegger, Rogers, Ruggles, Schuller, Schuman, Sessions, Still, Thompson, Thomson, Varèse, Weill and others)

42.   CopWL   Copland, Aaron. **What to Listen for in Music.** New York: McGraw-Hill, 1939, rev. ed. 1959, (Mentor), 1964. (Blitzstein, Copland, Gershwin, Harris, Ives, Menotti, Piston, Schuman, Sessions, Thomson, Varèse)

43.   CowAC   Cowell, Henry, ed. **American Composers on American Music: A Symposium.** Palo Alto: Stanford University Press, 1933; New York: Frederick Ungar, 1962 (with a new introduction by the editor). (Antheil, Becker, Brant, Chanler, Copland, Cowell, Crawford, Gershwin, Hanson, Harris, Ives, McPhee, Piston, Riegger, Rogers, Ruggles, Salzedo, Seeger, Sessions, Slonimsky, Still, Taylor, Thompson, Thomson, Varèse, Weiss)

44.   CurB   **Current Biography,** ed. A. Rothe. New York: H. W. Wilson, 1940–. (Barber, 1944, 1963; Carpenter, 1951; Carter, 1960; Copland, 1940, 1951; Hanson, 1966; Harris, 1940; Ives, 1947, 1954; Moore, 1947, 1969; Piston, 1948, 1961; Schuman, 1942, 1962; Sessions, 1975; Thomson, 1940, 1966)

45.   DalTT   Dallin, Leon. **Techniques of Twentieth Century Composition,** 3rd edition. Dubuque, Iowa: Wm C. Brown, 1974. (Barber, Cage, Carter, Copland, Cowell, Foss, Hanson, Harris, Hovhaness, Ives, Menotti, Piston, Schuman, Varèse)

46.   DavPM   Davies, Laurence. **Paths to Modern Music.** New York: Charles Scribner's Sons, 1971. (Babbitt, Cage, Carter, Copland, Cowell, Foss, Gershwin, Ives, Schuman, Sessions, Thomson, Varèse)

47.   DemMT   Demuth, Norman. **Musical Trends in the Twentieth Century.** London: Rockliff, 1952. (Antheil, Barber, Copland, Cowell, Gershwin, Hanson, Harris, Ives, Piston, Ruggles, Schuman, Sessions, Still, Taylor, Thompson, Thomson, Varèse)

48.   DerETM   Deri, Otto. **Exploring Twentieth-Century Music.** New York: Holst, Rinehart and Winston, 1968. (Babbitt, Barber, Berg, Bernstein, Blitzstein, Busoni, Cage, Carter, Casella, Copland, Cowell, Dallapiccola, Finney, Foss, Gershwin, Hanson, Harris, Ives, Krenek, Luening, Menotti, Persichetti, Piston, Riegger, Rogers, Ruggles, Schuller, Schuman, Sessions, Thompson, Thomson, Ussachevsky, Varèse, Ward, Webern, Weill, Weisgall and others)

49. DowO Downes, Irene, ed. **Olin Downes on Music**. New York: Simon & Schuster, 1957. (Barber, Bernstein, Blitzstein, Carpenter, Copland, Diamond, Dello Joio, Foss, Gershwin, Gruenberg, Harris, Hanson, Ives, Menotti, Piston, Schuman, Shapero, Still, Taylor, Thompson, Thomson, Weill)

50. DukLH Duke, Vernon. **Listen Here! A Critical Essay on Music Depreciation**. New York: Ivan Obolensky, Inc., 1963. (Antheil, Babbitt, Barber, Bernstein, Carpenter, Carter, Copland, Diamond, Elwell, Finney, Foss, Gershwin, Griffes, Hanson, Ives, Kay, Kubik, Moore, Piston, Riegger, Rogers, Ruggles, Schuman, Sessions, Siegmeister, Sowerby, Thompson, Thomson, Varèse)

51. EatMU Eaton, Quaintance, ed. **Musical U. S. A.** New York: Allen, Towne & Heath, 1949. (a history of music in thirteen American cities by various authors)

52. Edm-I Edmunds, John, and Gordon Boelzner, eds. **Some Twentieth Century American Composers. A Selective Bibliography**, 2 vols. New York: The New York Public Library.
Vol. I, 1959: Introductory Essay by Peter Yates. (Brant, Cage, Carter, Copland, Cowell, Harris, Harrison, Hovhaness, Ives, Partch, Riegger, Ruggles, Sessions, Thomson, Varèse)

53. Edm-II Vol. II: Introductory Essay by Nicolas Slonimsky. (Barber, Bernstein, Blitzstein, Creston, Dello Joio, Diamond, Foss, Glanville-Hicks, Hanson, Kirchner, Mennin, Moore, Piston, Porter, Schuman, Thompson, Weber)

54. EdMUS Edwards, Arthur C., and W. Thomas Marrocco. **Music in the United States**. Dubuque, Iowa: Wm C. Brown, 1968. (Barber, Carter, Carpenter, Cowell, Creston, Diamond, Ellington, Finney, Foss, Frederick Grant Gleason, Griffes, Hanson, Harris, Ives, Jacobi, Loeffler, Moore, Persichetti, Riegger, Rogers, Ruggles, Schuman, Sessions, Siegmeister, William Grant Still, Thompson, Thomson and others)

55. EscCF Eschman, Karl. **Changing Forms in Modern Music**, 2nd edition. Boston: E. C. Schirmer, 1968. (Copland, Cowell, Donovan, Gershwin, Piston, Riegger)

56. EweAC Ewen, David. **American Composers Today: A Biographical and Critical Guide**. New York: H. W. Wilson, 1949. (Includes a large number of composers)

57. EweCB Ewen, David. **The Complete Book of 20th Century Music**, rev. ed. New York: Prentice-Hall, 1961. (Antheil, Barber, Bernstein, Blitzstein, Carpenter, Copland, Cowell, Creston, Dello Joio, Diamond, Foss, Gershwin, Gould, Grofé, Gruenberg, Hanson, Harris, Ives, McDonald, Menotti, Moore, Piston, Porter, Schuman, Sessions, Siegmeister, Thompson, Thomson, Weill)

58. EweCT Ewen, David. **Composers of Tomorrows Music**. New York: Dodd, Mead & Co., 1971. (Babbitt, Barber, Bernstein, Cage, Dallapiccola, Foss, Ginastera, Ives, Luening, Menotti, Partch, Riegger, Schuman, Thomson, Ussachevsky, Varèse and others)

59. EweCS Ewen, David. **Composers Since 1900: A Biographical and Critical Guide**. New York: H. W. Wilson Co., 1969. (Barber, Cage, Carpenter, Carter, Copland, Cowell, Creston, Diamond, Finney, Floyd, Foss, Gershwin, Giannini, Hanson, Harris, Hovhaness, Ives, Moore, Persichetti, Piston, Porter, Read, Riegger, Rorem, Ruggles, Schuller, Schuman, Sessions, Sowerby, Still, Thompson, Thomson, Ward and many others)

60. EweDE Ewen, David. **David Ewen Introduces Modern Music**. Philadelphia: Chilton Book Co., 1962, rev. 1969. (Antheil, Barber, Bernstein, Bennett, Blitzstein, Brant, Cage, Carpenter, Casella, Copland, Cowell, Dahl, Dallapiccola, Dello Joio, Feldman, Gershwin, Gould, Grofé, Gruenberg, Hanson, Harris, Hill, Hovhaness, Ives, Luening, McDonald, McPhee, Menotti, Moore, Piston, Riegger, Schuman, Sessions, Siegmeister, Taylor, Thomson, Ussachevsky, Varèse, Weber)

61. EweMC Ewen, David. **Music Comes to America**. New York: Thomas Y. Crowell, 1942, 1947. (Barber, Bennett, Blitzstein, Copland, Diamond, Gershwin, Gruenberg, Hanson, Harris, Ives, Moore, Piston, Porter, Rogers, Ruggles, Schuman, Taylor, Thompson, Thomson and others)

62. EweNB Ewen, David. **The New Book of Modern Composers**, 3rd edition, revised and enlarged. New York: Alfred A. Knopf, 1969. (previously published under the title **The Book of Modern Composers**) Introduction by Nicolas Slonimsky. (Barber, Copland, Gershwin, Harris, Menotti, Schuman; brief reference to Antheil, Bernstein, Blitzstein, Brant, Cage, Carpenter, Carter, Cowell, Creston, Dello Joio, Diamond, Feldman, Giannini, Gould, Grofé, Gruenberg, Hanson, Ives, Moore, Persichetti, Piston, Riegger, Schuller,

Sessions, Siegmeister, Slonimsky, Thompson, Thomson, Varèse, Weill and others)

63.   EweTC   Ewen, David. **Twentieth Century Composers.** New York: Thomas Y. Crowell, 1937; Freeport, NY: Books for Libraries Press, 1968. (Gershwin, Harris)

64.   EweWT   Ewen, David. **The World of Twentieth-Century Music.** Englewood Cliffs, NJ: Prentice-Hall, 1969. (Antheil, Barber, Bernstein, Blitzstein, Copland, Blackwood, Cage, Carpenter, Carter, Copland, Cowell, Creston, Dello Joio, Diamond, Floyd, Foss, Gershwin, Gruenberg, Hanson, Harris, Hovhaness, Ives, Kirchner, Mennin, Menotti, Moore, Persichetti, Piston, Porter, Read, Rogers, Ruggles, Schuller, Schuman, Sessions, Sowerby, Taylor, Thompson, Thomson, Varèse, Ward, Weill and others)

65.   EweYA   Ewen, David, ed. **The Year in American Music.** (June 1947-May 1948 inclusive). New York: Allen, Towne & Heath, 1948. (Antheil, Bacon, Barber, Barlow, Becker, Bennett, Berger, Bergsma, Bernstein, Blitzstein, Bowles, Cage, Carter, Chanler, Chasins, Cowell, Creston, Dello Joio, Diamond, Donovan, Elwell, Finney, Hanson, Harris, Harrison, Hovhaness, Ives, Jacobi, Kay, Kohs, Lockwood, Luening, McKay, Mennin, Moore, Moross, Palmer, Persichetti, Piston, Porter, Riegger, Rogers, Schuman, Shapero, Sowerby, Stevens, Still, Thomson, Ward, Weber and others)

66.   FraMG   Frankenstein, Alfred. **A Modern Guide to Symphonic Music.** New York: Merideth Press, 1966. (Copland, Gershwin, Harris, Ives, Piston, Riegger, Thomson)

67.   GonSS   Godwin, Joscelyn. **Schirmer Scores: A Repertory of Western Music.** New York: Macmillan Publishing Co., 1975. (Cage, Cowell, George Crumb, Ives, Terry Riley, Leland Smith)

68.   GolTP   Goldberg, Isaac. **Tin Pan Alley.** New York: Frederick Ungar, 1961. (Antheil, Bernstein, Copland, Cowell, Gershwin, Ives, Shapero, Thomson, Weill)

69.   GolMM   Goldin, Milton. **The Music Merchants.** London: The Macmillan Co., 1969. (Barber, Copland, Schuman, Thomson)

70.   GosMM   Goss, Madeleine. **Modern Music-Makers: Contemporary American Composers.** New York: E. P. Dutton, 1952; Westport, CT: Greenwood Press, 1970. (Antheil, Barber, Bauer, Bennett, Bergsma, Bernstein, Blitzstein, Branscome, Britain, Carpenter, Copland, Cowell, Creston, Daniels, Dello Joio, Diamond, Foss, Gould, Gruenberg, Hanson, Harris, Howe, Ives, McDonald, Moore, Piston, Riegger, Rogers, Ruggles, Schuman, Sessions, Shapero, Sowerby, Still, Talma, Taylor, Thomson)

71.   GraMM   Graf, Max. **Modern Music; Composers and Music of Our Time,** tr. Beatrice R. Maier. New York: Philosophical Society, 1946. (Antheil, Carpenter, Copland, Gershwin, Weill)

72.   GroSH   Grout, Donald J. **A Short History of Opera,** 2nd edition. New York: Columbia University Press, 1969. (Antheil, Bacon, Bennett, Blitzstein, Copland, Gruenberg, Hanson, Lockwood, Menotti, Moore, Saminsky, Taylor, Thompson, Thomson)

73.   Grove   Sadie, Stanley, ed. **Grove's Dictionary of Music and Musicians,** 6th edition. New York: St. Martin's Press, 1979.

74.   HanIT   Hansen, Peter S. **An Introduction to Twentieth Century Music,** 3rd edition. Boston: Allyn and Bacon, 1971. (Barber, Cage, Copland, Carter, Hanson, Harris, Ives, Piston, Schuman, Sessions, Thomson)

75.   HayTV   Hays, William, ed. **Twentieth-Century Views of Music History.** New York: Charles Scribner's Sons, 1972. (Articles by Milton Babbitt, Elliott Carter, Anthony Cross, Sidney Finkelstein, Ernst Krenek, Eric Salzman and Kurt Stone)

76.   HigTG   Highet, Gilbert. **Talents and Geniuses.** New York: Oxford University Press, 1957. (pp. 48-55: Ives)

77.   HinCP   Hines, Robert Stephan. **The Composer's Point of View. Essays on Twentieth-Century Choral Music by Those Who Wrote It.** Norman: University of Oklahoma Press, 1963. (Articles by Lucas Foss, Howard Hanson, Ernst Krenek, Peter Mennin, Vincent Persichetti, Bernard Rogers and Leo Sowerby)

78.   HinOC   Hines, Robert S. **The Orchestral Composer's Point of View.** Norman: University of Oklahoma Press, 1970. (Babbitt, Carter, Finney, Fricker, Henze, Krenek, Lutoslawski, Martin, Persichetti, Schuller, Tippett, Vogel)

79.   HipAO   Hipscher, Edward Ellsworth. **American Opera and Its Composers, 1871-1948.** New York: Presser, 1954; Da Capo Press, 1978. (Antheil, Carpenter, Converse, Gruenberg, Hanson, Luening, Rogers, Ruggles, Taylor, Thomson)

80.   HitMU   Hitchcock, H. Wiley. **Music in the United States: A Historical Introduction.** Englewood

Cliffs, NJ: Prentice-Hall, 1969; rev. ed., 1974. (Babbitt, Bergsma, Cage, Carpenter, Carter, Copland, Cowell, Diamond, Gershwin, Hanson, Harris, Ives, Moore, Piston, Riegger, Rogers, Ruggles, Schuman, Sessions, Sowerby, Thompson, Thomson and others)

81. HodSD Hodeir, André. **Since Debussy: A View of Contemporary Music**, tr. Noel Burch. New York: Grove Press, 1961. (Babbitt, Barber, Cage, Carpenter, Copland, Harris, Ives, Menotti, Piston, Schuller, Sessions, Thomson, Weber)

82. HowMM Howard, John Tasker, and James Lyons. **Modern Music**. New York: Thomas Y. Crowell, rev. ed., 1957. (Antheil, Barber, Becker, Bennett, Blitzstein, Cage, Carpenter, Carter, Copland, Cowell, Creston, Gershwin, Hanson, Harris, Ives, Kirchner, Luening, Moore, Partch, Piston, Riegger, Schuman, Sessions, Still, Thompson, Thomson, Ussachevsky, Varèse, Weiss and others)

83. HowOA Howard, John Tasker. **Our American Music**, 4th edition. New York: Thomas Y. Crowell, 1966. (Antheil, Babbitt, Bacon, Barber, Barlow, Bauer, Beeson, Bennett, Berezowsky, Berger, Bergsma, Berlinski, Bernstein, Blackwood, Bowles, Brant, Brecht, Cage, Carpenter, Carter, Copland, Cowell, Creston, Dahl, Dello Joio, Diamond, Donovan, Elwell, Fine, Foss, Gershwin, Gillis, Goeb, Gould, Grofé, Gruenberg, Haieff, Hanson, Harris, J. Harrison, Hill, Hovhaness, Imbrie, Ives, Jacobi, Kay, Kirchner, Kohs, Luening, McPhee, Mennin, Menotti, Moore, Nordoff, Palmer, Phillips, Pinkham, Piston, Riegger, Rogers, Ruggles, Schuman, Sessions, Still, Sowerby, Taylor, Thompson, Thomson, Ussachevsky, Varèse, Wagenaar, Ward, Weisgall, Weiss and others)

84. HowOC Howard, John Tasker. **Our Contemporary Composers**. New York: Thomas Y. Crowell, 1941. (Antheil, Bacon, Barber, Barlow, Bauer, Becker, Bennett, Berezowsky, Bergsma, Bingham, Blitzstein, Bloch, Bowles, Branscombe, Brant, Carpenter, Chanler, Converse, Copland, Cowell, Creston, Diamond, Donovan, Finney, Gershwin, Giannini, Gould, Grofé, Gruenberg, Hadley, Hanson, Harris, Ives, Jacobi, Lockwood, Luening, McDonald, Menotti, Moore, Morris, Palmer, Phillips, Piston, Porter, Riegger, Rogers, Ruggles, Schuman, Sessions, Shepherd, Sowerby, Still, Thompson, Thomson, Wagenaar, Weiss and others)

85. HowSH Howard, John T., and George Kent Bellows. **A Short History of Music in America**. New York: Thomas Y. Crowell, 1967. (Antheil, Bacon, Barber, Bauer, Berger, Bergsma, Bernstein, Blitzstein, Bowles, Brant, Cage, Carpenter, Converse, Copland, Cowell, Creston, Dello Joio, Diamond, Elwell, Foss, Gershwin, Giannini, Gould, Gruenberg, Haieff, Hanson, Harris, Hovhaness, Hill, Howe, Ives, James, Kay, Kelly, Luening, Mennin, Menotti, Moore, Nordoff, Palmer, Persichetti, Phillips, Piston, Porter, Read, Riegger, Rogers, Ruggles, Schuman, Sessions, Shapero, Shepherd, Smith, Sowerby, Still, Swanson, Taylor, Thompson, Thomson, Varèse, Wagenaar, Ward, Weber, Weisgall and others)

86. IMB **Inter-American Music Bulletin**. Washington, D. C.: Pan American Union, 1957.

87. JacUSB Jackson, Richard. **U. S. Bicentennial Music I**. Institute for Studies in American Music Special Publications: No. 1. New York: Brooklyn College, 1977.

88. JacUSM Jackson, Richard. **United States Music**. Sources of Bibliography and Collective Biography. Institute for Studies in American Music, Monograph No. 1. New York: Brooklyn College, 1973.

89. JabCAC Jacobi, Hugh William. **Contemporary American Composers Based at American Colleges and Universities**. Paradise, CA: Paradise Arts Publishers, 1975. (Carter, Hanson, Harris, Schuman and many others. 240 pages)

90. JohOA Johnson, H. Earle. **Operas on American Subjects**. New York: Coleman-Ross, 1964. (Antheil, Bacon, Beeson, Bennett, Bernstein, Blitzstein, Converse, Copland, Dello Joio, Floyd, Foss, Gershwin, Giannini, Gruenberg, Hadley, Hanson, Haufrecht, Lockwood, Luening, Menotti, Moore, Schuman, Sessions, D. S. Smith, Still, Thomson, Ward, Weill and others)

91. JohSH Johnson, H. Earle. **Symphony Hall, Boston**. Boston: Little, Brown, 1956. (Barber, Bernstein, Bingham, Carpenter, Copland, Cowell, Dello Joio, Diamond, Foss, Gershwin, Gould, Gruenberg, Hanson, Harris, Ives, Jacobi, Menotti, Piston, Schuman, Sessions, Shapero, Sowerby, Still, Taylor, Thompson and others)

92. KinAI Kinsella, Hazel G. **American Index to the Musical Quarterly**. Washington, D. C., 1958. Reprint from the "Journal of Research in Music Education," 6, No. 2 (1958).

93.   KolMO   Kolodin, Irving. **The Metropolitan Opera, 1883-1966**, 4th edition. New York: Alfred A. Knopf, 1968. (Barber, Beeson, Bernstein, Blitzstein, Copland, Carpenter, Converse, Dello Joio, Floyd, Giannini, Gilbert, Gruenberg, Hanson, J. Harrison, Menotti, Moore, Rogers, Rorem, Taylor, Thomson, Ward, Weisgall)

94.   KreMH   Krenek, Ernst. **Music Here and Now**, tr. Barthold Fles. New York: Russell and Russell, 1967. (Gershwin, Ives, Weill)

95.   LanOH   Lang, Paul Henry, ed. **One Hundred Years of Music in America**. New York: G. Schirmer, 1961. (pp. 30-35: "The Evolution of the American Composer," by Nathan Broder; brief mention of many composers)

96.   LanPM   Lang, Paul Henry, ed. **Problems of Modern Music**. New York: W. W. Norton, 1962. (Introduction by P. H. Lang; articles by Babbitt, Carter, Cone, Forte, Fromm, Krenek, Sessions, Ussachevsky)

97.   LeiMW   Leichtentritt, Hugo. **Music of the Western Nations**. Cambridge: Harvard University Press, 1956. (pp. 277-310: "The United States," by Nicolas Slonimsky: Antheil, Bacon, Barber, Bauer, Berezowsky, Bergsma, Bernstein, Blitzstein, Bowles, Carpenter, Carter, Chanler, Copland, Cowell, Crawford, Creston, Dello Joio, Diamond, Elwell, Fine, Foss, Freed, Gershwin, Giannini, Gould, Harris, Ives, James, Kay, Kubik, Luening, Mennin, Menotti, Moore, Morris, Palmer, Phillips, Pisk, Piston, Porter, Read, Riegger, Rogers, Ruggles, Saminsky, Schuman, Sessions, Shapero, Sowerby, Still, Swanson, Talma, Taylor, Thompson, Thomson, Varèse, Wagenaar, Wolpe and others)

98.   LeiSK   Leichtentritt, Hugo. **Serge Koussevitsky. The Boston Symphony Orchestra and the New American Music**. Cambridge: Harvard University Press, 1946. (Barber, Bennett, Berezowsky, Bernstein, Carpenter, Converse, Copland, Cowell, Creston, Diamond, Foss, Gershwin, Gould, Gruenberg, Hadley, Hanson, Harris, Hill, Ives, Jacobi, James, Menotti, Piston, Read, Ruggles, Schuman, Sessions, Sowerby, Still, Thompson, Thomson, Whithorne and others)

99.   LevSI   Levant, Oscar. **A Smattering of Ignorance**. Garden City, NY: Doubleday, Doran, 1940 (pp. 147-248); Doubleday, 1959 (pp. 111-179).

100.   MacAC   Machlis, Joseph. **American Composers of Our Time**. New York: Thomas Y. Crowell, 1963. (Barber, Bernstein, Carter, Copland, Dello Joio, Foss, Gershwin, Hanson, Harris, Ives, Menotti, Moore, Piston, Schuman, Sessions, Thomson)

101.   MacIC   Machlis, Joseph. **Introduction to Contemporary Music**, 2nd edition. New York: W. W. Norton, 1979. (Antheil, Babbitt, Bacon, Barber, Barlow, Berger, Bernstein, Blitzstein, Brant, Cage, Carpenter, Carter, Chanler, Copland, Cowell, Creston, Dello Joio, Diamond, Foss, Gershwin, Hanson, Harris, Ives, Jacobi, Kirchner, Mennin, Menotti, Moore, Piston, Porter, Powell, Riegger, Rogers, Ruggles, Schuman, Sessions, Still, Thompson, Thomson, Varèse, Weisgall and others)

102.   MasDA   Mason, Daniel Gregory. **The Dilemma of American Music**. New York: MacMillan, 1928; Greenwood Press, 1969.

103.   MasMM   Mason, Daniel Gregory. **Music in My Time**. New York: MacMillan, 1938. (pp. 387-402)

104.   MasTA   Mason, Daniel Gregory. **Tune in, America**. New York: Alfred A. Knopf, 1931; Freeport, NY: Books for Libraries Press, 1969. (Includes performances of American music, 1925-1930)

105.   MelMN   Mellers, Wilfrid. **Music in a New Found Land: Themes and Developments in the History of American Music**, 2nd edition; New York: Hillstone, 1975. (Antheil, Babbitt, Barber, Bernstein, Blitzstein, Brown, Brant, Cage, Carter, Copland, Chanler, Cowell, Feldman, Fine, Finney, Floyd, Foss, Gershwin, Haieff, Hanson, Harris, Harrison, Hovhaness, Imbrie, Ives, Kirchner, Mennin, Menotti, Moore, Overton, Palmer, Partch, Persichetti, Pinkham, Piston, Porter, Mel Powell, Riegger, Rochberg, Rogers, Ruggles, Schuller, Schuman, Sessions, Shapero, Shapey, Shifrin, Sydeman, Thomson, Varèse, Weber, Weisgall, Wuorinen and others)

106.   MelMS   Mellers, Wilfrid. **Music and Society**, 2nd edition. London: Dennis Dobson, 1950. (pp. 89-224: Blitzstein, Carpenter, Copland, Cowell, Harris, Ives, Schuman, Varèse)

107.   MelRT   Mellers, Wilfrid. **Romanticism and the Twentieth Century**. New York: Shocken, 1969. (Barber, Bernstein, Blitzstein, Busoni, Carter, Copland, Gershwin, Harris, Ives, Rubbra, Ruggles, Sessions, Varèse, Webern, Weill and others)

108.   MeyMA   Meyers, Leonard B. **Music, the Arts, and Ideas**. Chicago: University of Chicago Press, 1967.

109. MitLM Mitchell, Donald. **The Language of Modern Music**, 3rd edition. New York: St. Martin's Press, 1970. (Cage, Carter, Ives, Krenek, Pfitzner, Varèse, Webern)

110. MorgCM Morgenstern, Sam, ed. **Composers on Music**. New York: Pantheon Books, 1956. (Antheil, Copland, Gershwin, Ives, Sessions, Thomson)

111. MorCA Morris, Harold. **Contemporary American Music**. Houston, Texas: Rice Institute Pamphlets, 1934. (Vol. 21, pp. 83-169: Bauer, Carpenter, Copland, Cowell, Gershwin, Gruenberg, Hanson, Harris, Ives, Jacobi, Moore, Ruggles, Sessions, Taylor, Whithorne and others)

112. MueAS Mueller, John Henry. **The American Symphony Orchestra. A Social History of Musical Taste**. Bloomington: Indiana University Press, 1951. (Antheil, Barber, Brant, Carpenter, Copland, Cowell, Creston, Delamarter, Dello Joio, Diamond, Foss, Fuleihan, Gershwin, Gillis, Gould, Gruenberg, Hanson, Harris, Hill, Ives, Jacobi, Mennin, Menotti, Moore, Persichetti, Piston, Powell, Rogers, Schuman, Sessions, Shapero, Sowerby, Still, Taylor, Thompson, Thomson, Varèse, Wagenaar, Ward)

113. MyeTC Myers, Rollo H., ed. **Twentieth Century Music: A Symposium**. London: Calder and Boyars, 1968. (pp. 197-205: "Music in the United States," by Robert Layton: Antheil, Barber, Bernstein, Blitzstein, Bowles, Cage, Carter, Copland, Cowell, Creston, Dello Joio, Diamond, Floyd, Foss, Gershwin, Hanson, Harris, Ives, Kohs, Mennin, Menotti, Moore, Persichetti, Piston, Riegger, Ruggles, Schuman, Sessions, Shapero, Swanson, Thompson, Thomson, Varèse)

114. NarCM Nardone, Thomas R., James H. Nye and Mark Resnick, eds. **Choral Music in Print**. Vol. I: Sacred Choral Music; Vol. II: Secular Choral Music; Vol. III: Supplement. Philadelphia: Musicdata, Inc., I: 1974; II: 1974; III: 1976.

115. NarVM Nardone, Thomas R., ed. **Classical Vocal Music in Print**. Philadelphia: Musicdata, 1976.

116. NarOM Nardone, Thomas R., ed. **Organ Music in Print**. Philadelphia: Musicdata, 1975.

117. NOH-X Cooper, Martin, ed. **New Oxford History of Music**, Vol. X. **The Modern Age, 1890-1960**. London: Oxford University Press, 1974. (Antheil, Blitzstein, Cage, Carter, Copland, Cowell, Dello Joio, Gershwin, Gruenberg, Hanson, Harris, Ives, Luening, Menotti, Moore, Piston, Riegger, Rogers, Ruggles, Schuman, Sessions, Sowerby, Thomson, Varèse)

118. NorLC Norman, Gertrude, and Miriam L. Shrifte. **Letters of Composers: An Anthology; 1603-1945**. New York: Grosset & Dunlap, 1970. (Antheil, Bennett, Copland, Cowell, Creston, Diamond, Gruenberg, Hanson, Harris, Ives, Moore, Piston, Schuman, Thompson, Thomson, Varèse)

119. NymEM Nyman, Michael. **Experimental Music, Cage and Beyond**. New York: Schirmer Books, 1974. (Cage, Cowell, Ives and others)

120. OveFA Overmyer, Grace. **Famous American Composers**. New York: Thomas Y. Crowell, 1944. (Copland, Gershwin)

121. PanMC Pannain, Guido. **Modern Composers**, tr. Michael R. Bonavia. Freeport, NY: Books for Libraries Press, 1970. (pp. 239-252: Carpenter, Copland, Hill, Ives, Jacobi, Ruggles, Sessions, Shepherd, Taylor, Varèse, Wagenaar, Weiss, Whithorne)

122. ParGM Partch, Harry. **Genesis of a Music**, 2nd edition. New York: Da Capo Press, 1974.

123. PavMH Pavlakis, Christopher. **The American Music Handbook**. New York: The Free Press, 1974. (Barber, Carpenter, Carter, Copland, Cowell, Diamond, Elwell, Finney, Foss, Hanson, Harris, Ives, La Montaine, Moore, Ron Nelson, Piston, Read, Riegger, Rogers, Schuman, Sessions, Siegmeister, Thompson, Thomson and many others, including various aspects of American music and its production)

124. PerlSC Perle, George. **Serial Composition and Atonality**, 4th edition. Berkeley: University of California Press, 1977. (Babbitt)

125. PersTH Persichetti, Vincent. **Twentieth-Century Harmony**. New York: W. W. Norton, 1961.

126. PAC Boretz, Benjamin, and Edward T. Cone, eds. **Perspectives on American Composers**. New York: W. W. Norton, 1971. (Howard Boatwright, "Ives' Quarter-Tone Impressions," pp. 3-12; Dennis Marshall, "Charles Ives' Quotations: Manner or Substance," pp. 13-24; Andrew Imbrie, "Roger Sessions: In Honor of His Sixty-Fifth Birthday," pp. 59-89; Edward T. Cone, "Conversation with Roger Sessions," pp. 90-107; Roger Sessions, "To the Editor," pp. 108-124; Edward T. Cone, "Conversation with Aaron Copland," pp. 131-146; Peter Evans, "Copland on the Serial Road: An Analysis of

Perspectives on American Composers (cont.) 'Connotations'," pp. 147-155; Peter Westergaard, "Conversation with Walter Piston," pp. 156-170; Clifford Taylor, "Walter Piston: For His Seventieth Birthday," pp. 171-182; Martin Boykan, "Elliott Carter and the Postwar Composers," pp. 213-216; Elliott Carter, "Expressionism and American Music," pp. 217-229)

127. PeyNM Peyser, Joan. **The New Music. The Sense Behind the Sound.** New York: Delacorte Press, 1971. (Babbitt, Barber, Bernstein, Cage, Carter, Copland, Cowell, Diamond, Foss, Hanson, Harris, Ives, Piston, Riegger, Ruggles, Schuman, Sessions, Thompson, Thomson, Varèse)

128. PleSM Pleasants, Henry. **Serious Music—and All That Jazz!** New York: Simon and Schuster, 1969. (Barber, Cage, Copland, Gershwin, Hanson, Piston, Sessions, Thomson)

129. PorM3S Porter, Andrew. **Music of Three Seasons: 1974-1977.** New York: Farrar Strauss Giroux, 1978. (Barber, Blitzstein, Cage, Carter, Casella, Chou Wen-Chung, Copland, Cowell, Dallapiccola, Diamond, Hanson, Harris, Ives, Krenek, Menotti, Moore, Riegger, Rorem, Ruggles, Schuman, Sessions, Stockhausen, Thomson, Ussachevsky, Varèse and others.

130. ReiCA Reis, Claire R. **Composers in America.** New York: MacMillan, 1947; Da Capo Press, 1977. (Includes a brief biography, list of works, date, publisher, duration)

131. ReiCC Reis, Claire R. **Composers, Conductors and Critics.** New York: Oxford University Press, 1955. (Antheil, Bacon, Barber, Bauer, Berger, Bergsma, Bennett, Berezowsky, Bernstein, Blitzstein, Bowles, Cage, Carpenter, Carter, Copland, Cowell, Dello Joio, Fine, Foss, Gershwin, Gruenberg, Hadley, Hanson, Harris, Hill, Ives, Jacobi, Kay, Kirchner, Kubik, Luening, Menotti, Moore, Morris, Nordoff, Partch, Piston, Rogers, Ruggles, Schuman, Sessions, Shepherd, Siegmeister, Still, Taylor, Thompson, Thomson, Ussachevsky, Varèse, Wagenaar and others)

132. RobCM Robertson, Alec, ed. **Chamber Music.** New York: Penguin Books, 1960. (Chapter on "American Chamber Music," by David Drew, pp. 322-328: Babbitt, Barber, Berger, Carpenter, Carter, Copland, Fine, Harris, Ives, Kirchner, Kohs, Piston, Riegger, Schuman, Sessions, Shapero and others)

133. RosAH Rosenfeld, Paul. **An Hour with American Music.** Philadelphia: J. B. Lippincott, 1929; reprint: Westport, CT: Hyperion Press, 1979. (Copland, Cowell, Gershwin, Harris, Moore, Ruggles, Sessions, Taylor, Thomson, Varèse, Weiss and others)

134. RosDM Rosenfeld, Paul. **Discoveries of a Music Critic.** New York: Harcourt, Brace, 1936. (Antheil, Copland, Cowell, Gershwin, Gruenberg, Hanson, Harris, Ives, Riegger, Taylor, Thomson)

135. RosMI Rosenfeld, Paul. **Musical Impressions: Selections from Paul Rosenfeld's Criticisms.** New York: Hill & Wang, 1969. (Copland, Gershwin, Ives, Ruggles, Sessions, Varèse)

136. RowFC Rowland-Entwistle, Theodore, and Jean Cooke. **Famous Composers.** London: David & Charles, n. d. (Barber, Cage, Copland, Gershwin, Harris, Ives, Menotti, Piston, Sessions, Thomson, Weill)

137. SalMO Salazar, Adolfo. **Music in Our Time.** New York: W. W. Norton, 1946. (Antheil, Bauer, Blitzstein, Bowles, Cage, Carpenter, Copland, Cowell, Creston, Diamond, Gershwin, Gruenberg, Hanson, Harris, Ives, Jacobi, McBride, McPhee, Moore, Piston, Porter, Riegger, Rogers, Schuman, Sessions, Slonimsky, Still, Thompson, Thomson, Varèse, Weiss, Whithorne)

138. SalzTM Salzman, Eric. **Twentieth-Century Music: An Introduction,** 2nd edition. New York: Prentice-Hall, 1974. (Antheil, Babbitt, Barber, Berger, Bernstein, Blitzstein, Bowles, Brant, Brown, Cage, Carter, Chou Wen-Chung, Copland, Cowell, Diamond, Feldman, Fine, Flanagan, Foss, Gershwin, Gruenberg, Hanson, Harris, Hovhaness, Ives, Kirchner, Luening, McPhee, Mennin, Menotti, Moore, Partch, Powell, Riegger, Ruggles, Schuller, Schuman, Sessions, Shapey, Shifrin, Thomson, Ussachevsky, Varèse, Weber, Weill, Wuorinen and others)

139. SamLM Saminsky, Lazare. **Living Music of the Americas.** New York: Howell, Soskin and Crown, 1949. (Antheil, Bacon, Barber, Berger, Bergsma, Bernstein, Blitzstein, Brant, Carter, Chanler, Copland, Cowell, Creston, Diamond, Dello Joio, Elwell, Etler, Fine, Finney, Foss, Freed, Gershwin, Gould, Gruenberg, Hanson, Harris, Ives, Jacobi, Lockwood, Luening, Mennin, Moore, Palmer, Persichetti, Piston, Porter, Riegger, Rogers, Ruggles, Schuman, Sessions, Shepherd, Sowerby, Taylor, Thompson, Thomson, Ward, Weber and others)

140.   SamMO   Saminsky, Lazare. **Music of Our Day; Essentials and Prophecies.** New York: Thomas Y. Crowell, 1932; reprint: Freeport, NY: Books for Libraries Press, 1970. (Blitzstein, Carpenter, Copland, Cowell, Gershwin, Gruenberg, Hanson, Harris, Ives, Jacobi, Moore, Rogers, Ruggles, Sessions, Shepherd, Slonimsky, Thompson)

141.   SanWM   Sandried, K. B., ed. **The World of Music: An Illustrated Encyclopedia**, 4 volumes. New York: Abradale Press, 1963. (Antheil, Barber, Bernstein, Blitzstein, Carpenter, Carter, Copland, Cowell, Creston, Hanson, Harris, Harrison, Ives, Kennen, Moore, Partch, Piston, Porter, Riegger, Rogers, Ruggles, Schuman, Sessions, Shapero, Shapey, Sowerby, Thompson, Thomson)

142.   SayWC   Saylor, Bruce, ed. **The Writings of Henry Cowell.** Institute for Study of American Music Monograph No. 7. New York: Brooklyn College, 1977.

143.   SchCOD   Scholes, Percy A. **Concise Oxford Dictionary of Music**, 2nd edition edited by John Owen Ward. New York: Oxford University Press, 1964.

144.   SchCC   Schwartz, Elliott, and Barney Childs, eds. **Contemporary Composers on Contemporary Music.** New York: Holt, Rinehart and Winston, 1967. (Babbitt, Barber, Beeson, Brant, Cage, Carter, Chou Wen-Chung, Copland, Cowell, Feldman, Foss, Harris, Luening, Maxfield, Partch, Sessions, Thomson, Varèse, Wolpe, Wuorinen)

145.   SchWC   Schickel, Richard. **The World of Carnegie Hall.** New York: Julian Messner, 1960; Westport, CT: Greenwood Press, 1973. (Barber, Bennett, Bernstein, Blitzstein, Cage, Carpenter, Converse, Copland, Cowell, Creston, Dello Joio, Diamond, Foss, Gershwin, Gould, Grofé, Hanson, Harris, Harrison, Hovhaness, Ives, Mennin, Menotti, Moore, Persichetti, Piston, Riegger, Rogers, Ruggles, Sessions, Still, Taylor, Thompson, Thomson, Varèse and others)

146.   SelMO   Seltsam, William H. **Metropolitan Opera Annals.** New York: H. W. Wilson, 1947. Supplement I, 1957; Supplement II, 1966. (Gruenberg, Hadley, Hanson, Menotti, Rogers, Taylor)

147.   SesME   Sessions, Roger. **The Musical Experience of Composer, Performer and Listener.** Princeton: Princeton University Press, 1950, 1971; New York: Athenaeum, 1962.

148.   SesRM   Sessions, Roger. **Reflections on the Music Life in the United States.** New York: Merlin Press, 1956. (pp. 140-184: Copland, Gershwin, Harris, Ives and others)

149.   ShiMM   Shirley, Wayne D., and William and Carolyn Lichtenwanger, eds. **Modern Music: An Analytic Index.** New York: AMS Press, 1976.

150.   SloMS   Slonimsky, Nicolas. **Music Since 1900**, 4th edition. New York: Charles Scribner's Sons, 1971.

151.   SmiWM   Smith, Cecil Michener. **Worlds of Music.** New York: Lippincott, 1952. (Barber, Copland, Cowell, Gershwin, Harris, Ives, Rogers, Ruggles, Schuman, Thompson, Thomson)

152.   SpaMH   Spalding, Walter Raymond. **Music at Harvard.** New York: Coward-McCann, 1935; Da Capo Press, 1977.

153.   SteiAS   Stein, Erwin, ed. **Arnold Schoenberg Letters.** New York: St. Martin's Press, 1965. (Cowell, Harris, Sessions, Varèse)

154.   StevHS   Stevens, Denis, ed. **A History of Song.** New York: W. W. Norton, 1970. (pp. 426-460 by Hans Nathan: Babbitt, Bacon, Barab, Barber, Carpenter, Carter, Chanler, Copland, Diamond, Gershwin, Gideon, Homer, Ives, Nordoff, Riegger, Thomson, Wagenaar, Weber and others)

155.   StevePC   Stevenson, Robert Murrell. **Protestant Church Music in America.** New York: W. W. Norton, 1970. (Barber, Copland, Cowell, Dello Joio, Finney, Foss, Gershwin, Hanson, Harris, Ives, Moore, Pinkham, Schuman, Sessions, Sowerby, Thompson, Thomson)

156.   StuTC   Stuckenschmidt, Hans Heinz. **Twentieth Century Music.** New York: McGraw-Hill, 1969.

157.   TpsDCC   Thompson, Kenneth. **A Dictionary of 20th Century Composers (1911-1971).** New York: St. Martin's Press, 1973. (Ives, pp. 251-263)

158.   ThompGM   Thompson, Oscar. **Great Modern Composers.** New York: World Publishing Co., 1943. (Copland, Harris)

159.   ThompIC   Thompson, Oscar, ed. **The International Cyclopedia of Music and Musicians**, 10th edition edited by Bruce Bohle. New York: Dodd, Mead, 1975.

160.   ThoAM   Thomson, Virgil. **American Music Since 1910.** New York: Holt, Rinehart and Winston, 1971. (Babbitt, Barber, Beeson, Bennett, Bergsma, Bernstein, Cage, Carpenter, Carter, Copland, Cowell, Creston, Dello Joio, Diamond, Finney, Floyd, Foss, Gershwin, Hadley, Hanson, Harris, Hill, Ives, Jacobi, Kay, Kirchner, Kubik, Luening, Menotti, Moore,

American Music Since 1910 (cont.) Piston, Riegger, Rogers, Rorem, Ruggles, Schuller, Schuman, Sessions, Thompson, Thomson, Ussachevsky, Varèse, Wagenaar, Ward, Weber, and others)

161. ThoAJ Thomson, Virgil. **The Art of Judging Music.** New York: Alfred A. Knopf, 1948; Greenwood Press, 1969. (Antheil, Bacon, Bergsma, Bernstein, Blitzstein, Bowles, Cage, Carter, Chanler, Copland, Creston, Dello Joio, Diamond, Foss, Gershwin, Haieff, Hanson, Harris, Ives, Menotti, Piston Riegger, Rogers, Schuman, Sessions, Still, Thompson, Thomson and others)

162. ThoMR Thomson, Virgil. **Music Reviewed 1940-1954.** New York: Vintage Books, 1967. (Antheil, Barber, Bernstein, Cage, Carpenter, Carter, Copland, Cowell, Creston, Dello Joio, Foss, Hanson, Harris, Hill, Ives, Moore, Piston, Rogers, Ruggles, Schuman, Sessions, Thompson, Thomson, Varèse, Weber, Wolpe and others)

163. ThoRL Thomson, Virgil. **Music Right and Left.** New York: Henry Holt, 1951. (Antheil, Barber, Berger, Blitzstein, Cage, Carter, Copland, Cowell, Diamond, Hanson, Harris, Ives, Menotti, Moore, Persichetti, Piston, Rogers, Ruggles, Schuman, Sessions, Shepherd, Swanson, Thompson, Thomson, Varèse and others)

164. ThoMS Thomson, Virgil. **The Musical Scene.** New York: Alfred A. Knopf, 1945; Greenwood Press, 1968. (Antheil, Barber, Bennett, Bernstein, Blitzstein, Chanler, Copland, Cowell, Creston, Gershwin, Gould, Grofé, Harris, Ives, Palmer, Piston, Schuman, Thomson, Wagenaar)

165. ThoSM Thomson, Virgil. **The State of Music.** New York: Alfred A. Knopf, rev. ed., 1962.

166. UlrCM Ulrich, Homer. **A Survey of Choral Music.** New York: Harcourt, Brace, Jovanovich, 1973. (Barber, Bernstein, Dello Joio, Foss, Hanson, Persichetti, Pinkham, Thompson)

167. UptAS Upton, William Treat. **Art Song in America.** New York: Oliver Ditson, 1930; Johnson Reprint, 1969. (Carpenter, Gruenberg, Jacobi, Shepherd, Whithorne and others) Supplement, 1930-1938. Oliver Ditson, 1938. (Antheil, Barber, Carpenter, Chanler, Citkowitz, Copland, Cowell, Crawford, Fine, Giannini, Gruenberg, Harris, Ives, Jacobi, Ruggles, Saminsky, Sessions, Shepherd, Sowerby, Thompson, Thomson, Wagenaar, Whithorne and others)

168. VinDCM Vinton, John, ed. **Dictionary of Contemporary Music.** New York: E. P. Dutton, 1974.

169. VinED Vinton, John. **Essays after a Dictionary.** Canbury, NJ: Associated Universities Presses, 1977. (Includes essays by Virgil Thomson, pp. 30-75)

170. WhiWW Whitall, Arnold. **Music Since the First World War.** London: J. M. Dent, 1977. (Babbitt, Bernstein, Cage, Carter, Copland, Cowell, Dallapiccola, Hanson, Harris, Ives, Piston, Sessions, Varèse)

171. WWA **Who's Who in America.** A. N. Marquis.

172. WWM **Who's Who in Music,** ed. Peter Townsend and David Simmons. New York: Haffner Publishing Co. Also Addenda.

173. WilTM Wilder, Robert D. **Twentieth-Century Music.** Dubuque, Iowa: Wm C. Brown, 1969. (Babbitt, Carter, Copland, Foss, Harris, Piston, Sessions)

174. WooWM Woodworth, George Wallace. **The World of Music.** Cambridge: Harvard University Press, 1964. (Babbitt, Brant, Carter, Copland, Harris, Ives, Kirchner, Luening, Piston, Schuman, Thompson, Thomson)

175. YatTC Yates, Peter. **Twentieth Century Music.** New York: Pantheon Books, 1967. (Antheil, Babbitt, Bernstein, Blitzstein, Brant, Brown, Cage, Carpenter, Carter, Copland, Cowell, Dahl, Feldman, Foss, Gershwin, Hanson, Harris, Harrison, Hovhaness, Ives, Krenek, Luening, Menotti, Partch, Perle, Piston, Powell, Riegger, Ruggles, Schuller, Schuman, Seeger, Sessions, Shapero, Stevens, Strang, Taylor, Thomson, Tremblay, Ussachevsky, Varèse, Weiss)

176. YouCD Young, Percy M. **A Critical Dictionary of Composers and Their Music.** London: Dennis Dobson, 1954. (Antheil, Barber, Blitzstein, Bowles, Carpenter, Copland, Cowell, Gershwin, Harris, Ives, Piston, Ruggles, Schuman, Sessions, Sowerby, Still, Taylor, Thompson, Thomson, Varèse, Wagenaar)

177. YouCT Young, Percy M. **The Choral Tradition.** New York: W. W. Norton, 1971. (Barber, Carpenter, Converse, Copland, Delamarter, Dello Joio, Hadley, Hanson, Harris, Lockwood, Schuman, Still, Thompson, Thomson)